The Scholastic Analysis of Usury

The Scholastic Analysis of Usury

JOHN T. NOONAN, JR.

CL Reprints

CL Press | Fraser Institute

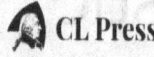 **CL Press**

Published by CL PRESS

A Project of the Fraser Institute 1770

Burrard Street, 4th Floor Vancouver,

BC V6J 3G7 Canada

www.clpress.net

The Scholastic Analysis of Usury

By John T. Noonan Jr.

The Scholastic Analysis of Usury

was originally published in 1957 by the President and Fellows of Harvard College.

Republished (print and online) with permission from the estate of John T. Noonan JR.

First printed: September 2025

Cover image: Cover illustration titled "Gutenberg's Press" by Dave

Grey, licensed under a Creative Commons Attribution-NoDerivs

2.0 Generic license.

ISBN: 978-1-957698-17-5

To My Parents

Acknowledgments

I am much indebted to Raymond de Roover, Professor of Economics at Boston College and Member of the Royal Flemish Academy of Letters, for the criticism and comment he has generously given and for his kindness in making available his excellent collection of authors on the subject. I am also grateful for the encouragement afforded by Reverend Edmund O. Bernard, Professor of Theology, and Right Reverend John K. Ryan, Professor of Philosophy, at The Catholic University of America, both of whom were wise and stimulating guides in the early stages of this work.

I am also indebted to the editorial staff of the Harvard University Press and, in particular, to the painstaking work of Mrs. Carl A. Pitha.

J. T. N., Jr.

May 1957

Contents

PART THREE

THE USURY THEORY FROM THREE PERSPECTIVES

The Scholastic Analysis of Usury

'Ancora un poco indietro ti involvi'
diss'io, 'là dove di'che usura offende
la divina bontade, e il groppo svolvi.'

Inferno, XI: 94–96

INTRODUCTION

Usury today strikes most of us as a rare and inconsequential vice, one moral fault which is not the concern of any large portion of humanity. To be sure, we may be aware that usurious exactions still effect social disaster in many agricultural communities in Asia, and we may believe that not all the pawnbrokers and small loan companies of our own great cities and agricultural communities offer the most equitable of terms. Nonetheless, the opportunities for committing usury, as compared with those for committing other sins, must seem confined; we cannot believe that more than a small, specialized class have even a chance to be guilty of it; and living in a prosperous commercial civilization, where credit provides the lifeblood of the economy, and where payment of a premium for credit is the normal condition of its extension, we find it impossible to imagine that usury could once have been defined as "profit on a loan," that the vice of usury could have implicated every part of Western society, and that concern with his culpability of it could have plagued every European businessman and land-owner.

How, then, can we appreciate the intensity of the intellectual interest in usury in the sixteenth and seventeenth centuries, when its nature and extent were as lively an issue, and as voluminously discussed by reflective observers of commerce, as the nature and cure of business cycles are debated in similar circles today? How much less can we grasp the spirit of a yet earlier age whose most perspicacious moralists described usury as the great vice which corrupted cities and Church alike and held all men of property in bondage? Usury today is a dead issue, and except by a plainly equivocal use of the term, or save in the mouths of a few inveterate haters of the present order, it is not likely to stir to life.

Yet if usury is not a central problem of the present, it still may be rewarding to attempt to grasp the spirit and record the doctrine of this earlier age. What was the intellectual concern of our European ancestors cannot be wholly alien to us, and the simple history of a concept once apparently embedded in Western culture is actively instructive. Why a certain theory affecting all of economic life was once embraced, and how it was gradually modified till it became the notion of usury generally current today, are questions whose answers are not without relevance in an age fascinated by economic problems. How such a theory, rigid, abstract, yet possessed of immense practical importance, could gradually be modified from its medieval to its modern shape is a question whose answer reveals much about the relation of religion, reason, and economic facts in the West; and the very variety of the question's aspects — at once theological, legal and economic — offers a multiplicity of perspectives from which this fundamental triangular relation may be observed. At the same time, economics, law, theology, and ethics are all, in measure, illuminated by the history of a theory that involves them all.

Most obviously, the scholastic theory of usury is an embryonic theory of economics. Indeed it is the first attempt at a science of economics known to the West. Of the ancient philosophers, such universal geniuses as Plato and Aristotle touch briefly and disdainfully on certain economic topics, but there is no proper economic analysis to be found in them save a crude outline of a theory of money. Nor in any other writers of antiquity is there to be found a coherent and extended body of economic thought. To classify economic activities, to determine the nature of money and the factors affecting its price, to essay a theory of economic value, and to develop a theory of interest are original scholastic achievements. In this way, the scholastic analysis of usury is the midwife of modern economics.

Yet if most obviously usury analysis treats of economics, economics to the scholastics is always secondary to law; and a legalistic concern with types of contracts both distinguishes and obscures their economic analysis proper. The scholastics are disciples of the Roman law, and from the earliest revival of medieval culture, canon law and moral theology are impregnated with the concepts of Roman jurisprudence. The scholastics do not accept this jurisprudence unmodified, but they do accept it in substance, and well before the Renaissance regal jurists appealed to it, they established its basic concepts in a realm which concerned practical life most closely. At the same time, the scholastic authors on their own initiative developed the contracts of irregular deposit, insurance, annuity, and bills of exchange. These are all essentially medieval discoveries, and they are directly nurtured, if not fathered, by the necessities of the usury theory. The law on contracts and on credit, both on the continent and in England, thus received a double impetus from scholastic usury analysis.

Neither economics nor law, however, are at the origin of the scholastic theory. Originally and primarily it is a theological creation. That usury is a sin was and is a dogma of the Catholic Church; it is as part of the content of Christian revelation that the prohibition of usury became the object of detailed, rational exploration. In this way usury, like many other problems of natural philosophy, was first made a subject for intensive investigation in the West by Christian theology; and throughout the scholastic treatment of the subject, the decisions of ecclesiastical authority play a dominant role. It is the effort of scholastic writers to explain, to expand, and to apply the positive teaching of the Church which results in the natural-law analysis of usury.

Yet far more important than its theological origin and direction is the fact that the theory does issue in this natural-law analysis. The scholastics do not depend on authority or revelation or Roman law alone. Increasingly, they make a determined effort to rest their case against usury on the nature of man and on the nature of things in themselves; similarly they try to determine what forms of credit are naturally lawful and just. Attempting to appeal to reason alone, they build the structure of the usury theory.

This effort to build a moral code on rational grounds is peculiarly characteristic of Catholic theology, in which no moral command, save some concerning the sacraments, stands only on the basis of a divine fiat or divine revelation. The Catholic moral theologians have appealed to the natural law, as well as to the divine law, and in scholastic theology there has been an immense interest in showing the rational basis for the duty commanded by God. The nineteenth-century rationalists' notion of religious dogma operating without reference to reason, or in defiance of it, is a myth; and consideration of the conditions of moral life shows how false such a notion must be. Moral rules do not exist in a vacuum: they must be applied; and to apply a rule to human conduct means first that its rational foundation and purpose must be discovered in order that the type of acts it prescribes or prohibits may successfully be determined. At the same time it means that distinctions between different related acts will be found, exceptions recognized, logical extensions made, and deductions drawn. This is the task of human reason, and it is indispensable to the life of morals.

With such legal refinement, of course, may also go artificial distinctions that are devices for evasion of a law. The reader may observe these occasionally in the scholastic discussions, as he may in the history of any judicial development of a precept. More critically, it may be also observed that the scholastics had a fondness for preserving legal fictions as analytical aids in cases where modern American jurists would brush aside the obsolescent forms and deal directly with the substantive issues. Sometimes these forms obscured the issues; sometimes they were valuable vehicles for an advance in theory. They would seem almost unavoidable in any discipline where appeal to past authority and precedent is part of the intellectual process.

The American lawyer will be less apt to criticize another main attribute of the scholastics' approach, their casuistry. This kind of examination of moral principles on a case-by-case basis may, indeed, seem to consist in hairsplitting and useless subtlety to the simple-minded zealot, but such nice and detailed differentiation by examples is the price law must pay if it is to be applied at all to the varied and complex activity of men. If any criticism is to be made of the scholastics here, it is only that they did not put enough cases and tended too often to reëxamine the classic situations.

Of course, it may be objected that in the rational development of the scholastic theory of usury, theology dominates reason still: for part of the work of reason here consists in the application and extension of ready-made theological rules, while the effort to show the natural basis of the usury prohibition is to some extent an academic exercise conducted to a conclusion set in advance by the Church. Do not the principles drawn from reason alone, it may well be asked, become merely slaves to theological exigencies? Does not the Church decide a priori what the scholastics must then prove a posteriori? Undeniably, the scholastics are all either theologians or canonists; undeniably they start their investigation with an awareness of the teaching of the Church; and undeniably their opinions will not run counter to her positive determinations. Indeed, it cannot be denied that in the medieval period many flimsy and fatuous arguments were seized on to support "rationally" what the author knew he was bound by authority to believe. Nor can it be overlooked that many medieval theologians, anxious to preserve the effectiveness and range of the dogmatic rule, arbitrarily rejected interest titles and contracts which later scholastics were to find lawful. Yet along with the foolish arguments there developed a sound analysis of usury and a valid, if narrow and technical, case against it; the later scholastics did correct their predecessors' zeal; and it is in the medieval period itself that the theory of legitimate interest and alternative methods of credit originates. The rules of the Church were more often the result than the cause of the scholastics' reasoning; and usury analysis developed not only from a study of the sources of revelation, as would a purely theological analysis, but also from a consideration of the demands of natural justice in concrete economic circumstances. At no time was the usury theory in scholastic hands wholly removed from rational investigation and development; after 1500, this rational approach was dominant.

The present study centers on the history of this rational analysis of usury.

The formation of a natural-law theory of usury, the rational development of exceptions to the usury prohibition, the alternative methods of capitalistic finance permitted are the topics it will explore. The purely economic, legal, and theological aspects of the subject are thus subordinated here, as they were eventually in the scholastic treatment, to the problem of natural ethics. Such an approach is not only most faithful to the authors investigated; it also provides the most central way of surveying the large amount of material pertaining to the usury theory which also belongs to economics, law, or theology.

Focusing directly on the heart of the usury analysis, this study has not explored very fully such collateral problems as the restitution of usury, the detection and punishment of usurers, or the exegesis of biblical texts relating to the usury rule. Such problems, although not without interest for their own sake, have not been considered, except where they were directly related to the main question of the nature of usury. So, for example, the doctrine on the restitution of usury has been treated as it throws light on the concept of money's unfruitfulness; but nothing has been said on the practical means of enforcing restitution. Again, this is not primarily a history of legislation or commercial practice or the effect of usury analysis on daily life. Ecclesiastical legislation will be noted as it affects, or issues from, scholastic opinion. Commercial practice will be presented briefly when it forms a necessary background to the scholastic analysis. Because of a modern effort to link usury theory and the creation of bank credit, medieval banking practices in particular will be described in detail. The relation of usury analysis and daily life will be observed to the extent that common customs challenge the analysis. But this is not a study of economic life as such, and although the danger of describing the history of thought as if it developed in an abstract void is obvious, it has been necessary to keep to a relevant minimum references to actual economic practice.

This is a history of thought, and the facts in this case consist precisely in opinions — the opinions of the Catholic theologians and canonists writing between 1150 and the present, using the traditional terminology and methods of the medieval schools. This is the body of writers that I take the term scholastic to designate. It includes the men who were the acknowledged intellectual and moral leaders of all of Europe for several hundred years and the men who were the acknowledged leaders of part of Europe for the later centuries. The writers chosen for examination have been chosen for their representativeness, influence, originality, or astuteness. Obviously, no account of scholastic thought can be exhaustive in the sense of being a record of the opinion of every scholastic writer, just as it would not be possible or profitable to make a history recording the opinion of every economic theorist today. But the scholastic field, in which the authors work within a common tradition and constantly refer to each other's work, is a particularly easy one in which to determine what authors were representative, influential, original, or astute. The subjects investigated themselves provide a continuous cross-check; by consulting this multitude of witnesses one may reasonably be sure of the origin of an opinion or the commonness of a concept.

A chronological method of approach has been stressed, because nothing is more evident than that the scholastic theory developed, and no error is more widespread than treatment of the theory as if it had been immutable. Reputable economic historians will see no incongruity in citing thirteenth- and seventeenth-century writers together for a proposition, although the analytical context in which the later writer speaks may have substantially altered the significance of any language he shares with the earlier authority. To be sure, the vocabulary, precedents, method of analysis remain the same; these similarities should not obscure the mutation and growth. To turn to an analogous field, Chief Justice Marshall and Chief Justice Warren expound the same constitution; but it would be a naïve, or very distant, interpreter who considered American constitutional law from Marshall to Warren to be an undifferentiated mass of doctrine. In the scholastic theory there is a conspicuous difference between the theory as it stood in 1450 and as it stood in 1550; to the extent that discontinuities can be recognized in history, the 100 years between those dates are the decisive ones. But there are also lesser yet important differences between 1250 and 1450 and between 1550 and 1700. If I have resisted the temptation of the expository lucidity afforded by a purely synthetic, timeless view of scholastic doctrine, it is in an effort to catch these differences and developments which the comprehensive term "scholastic" often hides.

A simple history, this study acquires its interest only from the interest of the ideas it investigates and its value only from the value that inheres in the intellectual life of the past. At least I find no single lesson, nor any simple thesis. The study does not attempt to demonstrate either the futility and inconsistency or the wisdom and logic of the scholastic position. If the reader finds this position inadequate, he will do so from the texts presented; if he finds it essentially coherent and basically sensible, he will do so on a full presentation of the evidence. The study does not try to condemn the present by extolling the morality of the past, nor to slur the past by praising the economic insights of the present. Nor do I have a favorite theory to establish on the connection of religion and capitalism. What the study suggests is the interaction of the intellectual and the economic, of religious demands and business pressures. Similarly, the presentation of the evidence may insinuate that sometimes the scholastics were inane formalists, sometimes astute economists and wise moralists. But the reader who wants a single point of view, an all-explaining formula, or a demonstration of a theorem, must consult other treatments of their efforts. Here attention is directed at the intrinsic interest of this intellectual enterprise of the scholastics, the only detailed and comprehensive philosophical effort in history to explore the requirements of justice in the credit operations central to commercial life.

Part One

THE SCHOLASTIC THEORY, 1150–1450

CHAPTER I

THE ROOTS OF THE THEORY

1. *The Teaching of the Church*

It will be well to know where the scholastics start and what guides them in their rational discussion of usury. There can be no question but that here the initiating force and illuminating rule for them were the positive teaching authority of the Church. Usury analysis would not have begun if the Church had not prohibited usury, and no other intellectual or economic force exerted so strong a pressure on the formation of the early theory. It is the Christian tradition as transmitted, taught, and interpreted by the living ecclesiastical institution which is at the origin of the scholastic discussion of usury.

If we take A.D. 750 as the beginning of the specifically medieval developments on usury and ask what particular sources of Christian doctrine determined medieval thought upon it, we shall not find any single source dominant. It is sometimes asserted that the Bible by itself was the chief influence.[1] But in the early development of the teaching on usury, only one Old Testament text was cited with any frequency, and it was only about 1050 that a specific New Testament text was decisively used. The Bible helped to form opinion against usury but its influence was not predominant. Of as much initial influence on the Middle Ages as the Bible were the writings of the Fathers against usury and the numerous condemnations of clerical usurers by earlier Councils. Taken together, the Bible, the patristic writings, and the Councils witnessed that the Christian tradition itself condemned usury, and it was the combined weight of these authorities, and no single authority by itself, that was responsible for the medieval position.

Moreover, the force of these sources lay not in their character of literary documents of a past age, as some historians tend often to regard them. Their force lay in the living teaching of the Church. What texts and documents the contemporary Church selected, and how ecclesiastical authority interpreted them were what was important for the medieval mind. Only in the context of the Christian tradition, to which these documents testified, but

---

[1] E.g., Wilhelm Endemann, *Studien in der romanisch-kanonistischen Wirthschafts- und Rechtslehre bis gegen Ende des siebenzehnten Jahrhunderts* (Berlin, 1874–1883), II, 359.

which they did not constitute, did the texts acquire full power. The Church stated what the tradition was and authoritatively declared what the documents meant. In particular, as far as the scholastic writers are concerned, since they began their analyses 400 years after the first medieval developments on usury, it is abundantly clear that what mattered for them was the biblical, patristic, and early conciliar texts which had been taken as decisive by medieval pontiffs and councils. Their concern was solely with these texts as understood and taught by ecclesiastical authority.

Appreciating the dominance of the theological teaching on usury, we may at once reject three hypotheses sometimes put forward to account for the medieval stand on usury. One gross hypothesis sees it founded on the doctrine of Aristotle.[2] But the medieval position was well established long before Aristotle was known in Western Europe. The Aristotelian teaching on money, when it belatedly came to the attention of the scholastics, was a simple auxiliary instrument of the usury prohibition.[3]

A more reasonable, but still erroneous, hypothesis suggests a direct causal connection between the scholastic usury theory and the economic conditions of the time.[4] The fact that later, in the sixteenth century, economic pressure to modify the usury theory clearly triumphed over logic and past opinion suggests that at every point the usury theory was equally responsive to economic needs, and that when we find the usury rule generally accepted, this acceptance must be understood as testimony to the economic wisdom of the law. But it is dangerous to generalize about one historical epoch on the basis of another, and it seems clear that what might be true of a period of Renaissance culture would not necessarily be true of a more religious period. The sixteenth century was a commercial, humanistic age, in which economic rationalism was already of importance. The early Middle Ages, on the contrary, were neither commercial nor humanistic; people were inclined to accept a bare theological rule simply because it was a theological rule and to apply that rule in all its bleakness. That the usury prohibition was accepted by the secular power and ratified by civil legislation is therefore no evidence that the mundane interests of medieval Europe led to the adoption of the prohibition. The hope of living by an ideal standard may much more

[2] Ernst Troeltsch, *The Social Teachings of the Christian Churches*, trans. Olive Wyon (New York, 1931), I, 320. Edmund Schreiber also at least overemphasizes Aristotle's place: *Die volkswirtschaftlichen Anschauungen der Scholastik seit Thomas v. Aquin* (Jena, 1913), p. 93.

[3] This point is well developed by G. Lefèvre in his introduction to *Le traité "De usura" de Robert de Courçon* (Lille, 1902), pp. iii–viii.

[4] F. X. Funk, *Zins und Wucher* (Tübingen, 1869), p. 48.

readily have brought about acceptance of the rule. Undeniably, the condition of the European economy in the ninth century was strikingly similar to that of the Judaic economy, in which the Mosaic law on usury was first applied,[5] and certainly the facts that the economy was almost completely agrarian and that borrowing was nearly always for consumption[6] were largely responsible for the emphasis upon the doctrine in the ninth century. The sudden zeal with which usury legislation is welcomed in this period may be partially understood as a last effort to save the small free farmers from absorption by the landholders who were the usual lenders. But it was in the twelfth century in Italy, as trade revived,[7] that the papal efforts to suppress usury became most strenuous; and it was in the thirteenth century, when the Italian city-states were already in an early capitalistic stage,[8] that the scholastic analysis of usury began. Even at this point of economic development there was probably a real need to prevent a choking of commerce by too high demands from the few possessors of liquid funds; and the bulk of the European economy remained agrarian. Conditions were still receptive to a usury rule. It is safe to say that there would not have been a rule in the shape it took, with the dominance it achieved, if economic conditions were not such as partially to justify it. But at the level of conscious motivation the theological decisions were more important to most scholastic authorities than the economic facts; and when one speaks of the origin of "the scholastic analysis," it is fair to say that the chief source was the prior ecclesiastical teaching.

We may more readily dismiss the suggestion that the usury prohibition was related to the Church's own interests.[9] It is true that one reason for papal concern over twelfth-century usury was the need to protect noble borrowers going on the Crusades.[10] Also, the papacy, like most governments, frequently resorted to deficit financing, while individual bishops and monasteries often had to seek credit from the cameral banking firms.[11] It is pos-

[5] Franz Schaub, *Der Kampf gegen den Zinswucher, ungerechten Preis und unlautern Handel in Mittelalter: Von Karl dem Grossen bis papst Alexander III* (Freiburg in Br., 1905), p. 66.

[6] Henri Pirenne, *Medieval Cities*, trans. F. D. Halsey (Princeton, 1925), pp. 46, 76; cf. Schaub, pp. 41 and 73–74.

[7] Pirenne, p. 113; Schaub, p. 147.

[8] Fedor Schneider, *Das kirchliche Zinsverbot und die kuriale Praxis im 13 Jahrhunderts*, in *Festgabe enthaltend vornehalich vorresformationsgeschichtliche Forschungen*

Heinrich Finke (Munster, 1904), p. 146; cf. Henri Sée, *Modern Capitalism*, trans. Homer B. Vanderbleu, Georges Doriot (New York, 1928), pp. 7, 25.

[9] James Westfall Thompson, *Economic and Social History of Europe of the Middle Ages* (New York, 1931), p. 410.

[10] Robert of Courçon, *De usura*, p. 77.

[11] Edouard Jordan, *De mercatoribus apostolicae camerae in XIII saeculo* (Paris, 1909), pp. 117, 53. See also *infra*, Chapter VIII, section 2.

sible that the usury prohibition played a part in keeping the charges made by these firms moderate and the cost of papal finance low. At the same time, many churches and monasteries were heavily endowed and under a constant pressure to find suitable investments for their funds. The monasteries were, indeed, the chief lenders to the nobles departing on the Crusades.[12] The purchase of annuities by churches and pious institutions was on a very large scale.[13] The higher clergy, too, were generally men of wealth with money to invest or loan.[14] The papacy itself often had large idle sums on deposit in banks. Moreover, the cameral banking firms were so closely associated with the Holy See that their welfare was almost identical with the papacy's.[15] There was, throughout the Middle Ages, therefore, ample temptation to change the usury prohibition for a rule more favorable to investors, bankers, and creditors. But instead of yielding to this temptation, the Church insisted on a law which convicted of sin its most trusted emissaries and many of its highest dignitaries. At the beginning of the Middle Ages the evidence that the usury prohibition ran counter to ecclesiastical economic interests is even stronger: the usury law was first applied and told most heavily against the monasteries.[16]

No biblical or ancient Christian text by itself, nor Aristotle, nor economic conditions or interests, but the vital present authority of the teaching Church stands at the head of all later developments on usury.

2. *Development of the Positive Prohibition*

As a condition for understanding the scholastic analysis, we must now survey briefly the process by which the positive Christian law on usury was clarified and made explicit in the early Middle Ages. We shall be concerned to note the past and present authorities the medieval men found definitive on usury; the increasingly clearer notion of the essence of usury; the immensely important shift from treating usury as a sin of uncharitableness or avarice to treating it as a sin of injustice; and the extension of the usury prohibition so that it applied unmistakably not only to clerics, but to all

---

[12] Thompson, p. 394.

[13] On the Church's interest in the *census* contract, see the evidence offered by medieval contemporaries such as Henry of Hesse, *Tractatus de contractibus*, IV, Dub. 10ff., in John Gerson, *Opera omnia* (Cologne, 1484-1485), Vol. IV; and St. Antoninus, *Summa sacrae theologiae* (Venice, 1581-1582), Part 2, Title 1, c.8.

[14] William of Auxerre, *Summa aurea*

(Paris, 1500), III:21:13, f.225v:a; also Matthew of Paris, *Chronica majora*, ed. H. R. Luard (London, 1874), V, 245.

[15] Jordan, pp. 119-127.

[16] R. Génestal, *Le rôle des monastères comme établissements de credit étudié en Normandie du 11ᵉ à la fin de 13ᵉ siècle* (Paris, 1901), p. 85; Schaub, p. 154; see also Schneider, p. 132.

men. We shall cite only the documents which bear significantly on these matters. Although there is never any real discontinuity in history, and any starting-point is to some degree arbitrary, we may begin with the commencement of Charlemagne's empire, for this period forms the immediate background of the medieval treatment of usury.[17]

The First Period, 750–1050

The *Hadriana*, a collection of canons, was to be the most influential body of ecclesiastical legislation for Charlemagne's empire. In it is contained the single most important document of the early Church on usury: the epistle *Nec hoc quoque* of Pope Leo the Great, a papal decree that categorically forbids clerics to take usury and declares that laymen who take it are guilty of seeking *turpe lucrum* (shameful gain). It is the most formal general prohibition of usury enunciated by supreme ecclesiastical authority before 1179. It forms the cornerstone of later usury legislation.

A number of early conciliar prohibitions of usury are also contained in the *Hadriana*, but all of them apply only to clerics. One, however, is of exceptional importance. It is a canon passed by the first general council, Nicea, and although it is aimed specifically at clerics, it includes a reference to Psalm 14 wherein the unrestricted and absolute rejection of usury is implied. The Psalm asks, "Lord, who shall dwell in thy tabernacle?" and answering by an enumeration of the crimes the just man avoids, it says, "He that hath not put out his money to usury." Both because it admits no exceptions and because of its use by the first ecumenical council, Psalm 14 becomes the favorite early medieval biblical text against usury.

At the same time that the *Hadriana* appeared, the Christian teaching found expression, for the first time in history, in the secular legislation of the State. Citing Nicea, *Nec hoc quoque*, the "Apostolic Canons," and the "law of the folk," the capitularies of Charlemagne forbade usury to everyone. That the State should ban usury, and ban it for laity as well as clergy, is an important event. Here in the formative age of medieval civilization, the usury rule is acknowledged by the secular power as obligatory on all Christians.

From this time on, State and Church both press the fight against usury. The Empire several times renews the basic prohibition; and the Nynweger capitulary of 806 gives the first medieval definition of usury. Usury, it declares, is "where more is asked than is given." The Church continues the

---

[17] For this summary of early legislation, Schaub has been closely followed: see espe- cially pp. 19, 26, 28, 29, 30, 37–39, 58, 59, 61, 66, 121–122, 178.

battle by means of episcopal capitularies and by local and national synods, although the synods devote their attention chiefly to clerical usurers. The Paris synod of 829 shows a wider use of biblical authorities, citing, in addition to Psalm 14:5, Exodus 22:25, Leviticus 25:35–37, Deuteronomy 15:7–10, Amos 8:4–6, and Ezekiel 18:8, and, obliquely, the New Testament without specific reference.[18] The synod also uses St. Jerome's commentary upon Ezekiel where he declares that usury may occur in commodity loans of goods such as wheat, as well as in money. This commentary is of particular interest in that it rejects the natural commercial argument that the loan is the source of gain to the borrower, in which the lender is entitled to share. The contention is dismissed simply on the ground that usury is against God's command.

The Synod of Pavia in 850 excommunicates lay usurers and prescribes full restitution to their victims if living, or, if they are dead, at least half the usury taken to their heirs. The obligation of restitution is apparently intended as a penalty, rather than considered as a requisite of commutative justice which demands the restoration of stolen goods. The censures of this synod are the sharpest measures yet taken against lay usury. In 889 an episcopal capitulary contains the first legislation referring to usury taken by means of a contract. The tenth century, in which European economy and culture both reach their nadir, shows no development and less interest in the usury prohibition than the eighth or ninth.

To sum up, the first period, from 750 to 1050, sees the enactment of the usury prohibition into the law of the land in the Holy Roman Empire and much local legislation by bishops against usury, the collection of some biblical texts against usury, the rejection of the defense that the usurer is entitled to a reward for helping the borrower productively, and the recognition, in one influential collection of canons, of a papal condemnation of usury which is applicable to laymen. Nonetheless, the period's thought on usury is primitive. Strong sanctions are laid only against clerical usurers. The papacy sponsors no general legislation on the subject. Usury itself is barely defined, and

[18] The relevant texts, besides Psalm 14:5, read as follows:

"If thou lend money to any of my people that is poor, that dwelleth with thee, thou shalt not be hard upon them as an extortioner, nor oppress them with usuries." Exodus 22:25.

"If thy brother be impoverished and weak of hand, and thou receive him as a stranger and sojourner, and he live with thee: Take not usury of him, nor more than thou gavest. Fear thy God, that thy brother may live with thee. Thou shalt not give him thy money upon usury: nor exact of him any increase of fruits." Leviticus 25:35–37.

"And if a man be just and do judgment . . . [and] Hath not lent upon usury, nor taken any increase . . . he is just, he shall surely live, saith the Lord God." Ezekiel 18:5–9.

Amos 8:4–6 and Deuteronomy 15:7–10 have nothing specifically on usury, but urge the rich not to exploit the poor.

although it presumably occurs in loans, no attempt is made to define what a loan is. At no time is it said that usury is a sin against justice, nor is restitution of usuries prescribed as an obligation of justice. The generic category of usury remains *turpe lucrum*; and while the taking of usury is treated as a serious sin, it is denounced as a form of avarice or uncharitableness.

The Second Period, 1050–1175

The Christian teaching upon the subject enters a second stage of development around 1050. Its growth may be ascribed in part to a general development in learning, entailing a more detailed knowledge of the Fathers and a clearer realization of the nature of usury, and in part to the revival of trade. As commerce grew, it soon became clear that usury on business loans through which borrower-merchants made themselves profits could not very easily be condemned as greed or lack of charity.

St. Anselm of Canterbury (1033–1109), an Italian familiar with the commercial revival, is the first medieval author to suggest the similarity of usury and robbery.[19] This is one of the earliest indications that usury is to be considered a sin against justice. His still undeveloped comparison is then given real force by his disciple Anselm of Lucca, another Italian and the native of a city where the textile industry was just beginning to develop. In his collection of canons, made about 1066, Anselm of Lucca is the first medieval author to treat usury as specifically a sin against the Seventh Commandment, and the first to demand restitution of usuries as stolen goods. Anselm's classification of usury under theft is an influential precedent; it is followed by Hugh of St. Victor (1096–1141),[20] Peter Comestor (d. 1178),[21] and, above all, by Peter Lombard (d. 1160),[22] whose *Sentences* are of such importance in directing later medieval thought. Anselm is also the first to use a quotation from one of the Fathers as a canon upon usury; he cites St. Augustine's condemnation of usury and demand for restitution to reinforce his own position.

---

[19] St. Anselm of Canterbury, *Homiliae et exhortationes*, in J. P. Migne, *Patrologiae cursus completus, Series latina* (Paris, 1844–1861), CLVIII, col. 659 (hereafter cited as *P.l.*).

[20] Hugh of St. Victor, *Summa sententiarum*, Tract. IV, c.4, in Migne, *P.l.*, CLXXVI, col. 122.

[21] Schaub, p. 148–149.

[22] Peter Lombard, *Sententiarum libri quatuor*, Book III, Dist. 37, c.3, in Migne, *P.l.*, CXCII. Although the *Sentences* are the

basis for so many later treatments of usury, there is nothing in them, except this determination that usury is against justice, which concerns the rational analysis of usury.

Even at this date what was to become the standard analysis of usury was not universal. In the work of Bartholomew of Exeter (c. 1150–1170), usury is simply treated as *turpe lucrum* and there is no attempt to define it in relation to a loan; see Bartholomew of Exeter, *Penitential*, ed. A. Morey (Cambridge, 1937), c.92, *De usuris*.

Ivo of Chartres (d. 1097) in his collection of canons, the *Collectio trium partium*, uses quotations from St. Augustine, St. Jerome, and St. Ambrose as canons against usury. One citation from St. Augustine points out that usuries, as stolen goods, may not be given as charity — a restriction which emphasizes the unjust character of their acquisition. Another citation from St. Augustine declares that usury occurs when you "expect to receive something more than you have given." Ivo does not emphasize the possibility of mental sin implicit in the reference to expectation but takes the text in a general sense as simply saying paraphrastically that usury is anything taken beyond the principal. The seeds of legal analysis are also apparent. Ivo's citation from St. Augustine specifically mentions a loan as the contract in which usury occurs, and Ivo distinguishes the loan from the lawful partnership contract, *societas*.[23]

In 1139, the Second Lateran Council prohibits usury to all men and declares that usurers shall be held infamous.[24] This is the first explicit decree of universal prohibition passed by a body of bishops having the absolute authority of an infallible ecumenical council. The Council is also the first general council to declare that usury is reprobated both by the Old and New Testaments. It does not, however, give specific references, nor does it say explicitly that usury is a sin against justice. Nine years later the central authority of the Church supplemented the conciliar decree with action aimed at a favorite practice of the monasteries.[25] Pope Eugene III decreed that mortgages, in which the lender enjoyed the fruits of a pledge without counting them towards the principal, were usurious.[26]

In 1159 the legal form of the usury prohibition received another stiffening and began to approach definitive shape with Gratian. His *Concordia discordantium canonum* is a collection of canons which, however modified and revised, form a part of the law of the Church until the complete revision of canon law in the new Code in 1917. It is an authority directly governing the scholastic writers throughout the medieval period. In it usury is for the first time treated as a special topic — a probable proof of the growing importance of the subject with the growing influence of commerce. St. Augustine, St. Jerome, and St. Ambrose, as well as the Nynweger statute under the errone-

---

[23] Schaub, pp. 134, 160.
[24] Second Lateran Council, Canon 13, *Porro detestabilem*, in Karl Joseph von Hefele, *Histoire des conciles*, trans. H. Leclerq (Paris, 1907–1938), V, Part 1, 729. Local councils in the eleventh century had previously forbidden usury to all: for example, the council of Reims in 1049 under Leo IX (Schaub, p. 126), and synods at Gerona in Spain, 1068 and 1078 (Schaub, p. 128).
[25] Schaub, p. 155; cf. Génestal, p. 78.
[26] Eugene III, *Epistolae*, in Migne, *P.l.*, CLXXX, col. 1567.

ous title of the Council of Agde, are all used to prove that usury is "whatever is demanded beyond the principal." *Nec hoc quoque* of Leo the Great is still the most general ecclesiastical condemnation of usury which Gratian can cite, and Psalm 14 is his only biblical reference. The inadmissibility of usuries as charitable offerings is reaffirmed. Gratian particularly insists on the obligation of restitution as in theft.[27]

The climax of the early medieval campaign against usury is reached with the vigorous actions of two twelfth-century popes, Alexander III and Urban III. Alexander (1159–1181) began by closing a loophole as important as the earlier one of mortgages. He declared that credit sales at a price higher than the cash price should be considered usury. Significantly, this is the first extension of the usury prohibition to cases where the explicit form of the transaction is not that of a loan. The Pope asserts that God will judge beyond the form of the contract.[28] Alexander III also determines that the Church cannot dispense from the prohibition against usury, even to raise money for such a worthy cause as the ransoming of Christian captives from the Saracens. His reason is that usury is "a crime detested by the pages of both Testaments."[29] It is thus made clear that usury is not merely a matter of a simple ecclesiastical rule. It is not yet, however, said to be against the natural law.

The Third Council of the Lateran, an ecumenical council presided over by Alexander in 1179, declares usury condemned by both Testaments, excommunicates and denies Christian burial to manifest usurers, and prohibits the reception of offerings made by them.[30] The Council notes that usury is waxing strong "in almost all places, so that many, leaving other businesses, exercise usury as if it were licit." The Pope later supports the Council by declaring that usurers who had taken usury before the decrees of the Council are not exempt from the obligation of restitution enjoined by it, except by reason of poverty.[31]

These strong measures are confirmed by Urban III (1185–1187). In a letter which becomes the decretal *Consuluit*, he cites the words of Christ,

[27] Gratian, *Decretum Gratiani*, Part II, Causa 14, Q.4, in *Corpus juris canonici*, ed. E. Friedberg (Leipzig, 1879–1881); and cf. Part I, Dist. 46, c.9 and 10.

[28] Gregory IX, *Decretales*, V: 19:6, *In civitate*, in *Corpus juris canonici*.

[29] *Decretales*, V:19:4, *Super eo*. It is curious that in his own writings as a canonist before he was elected to the papacy, Alexander III makes no reference to credit sales or to the intrinsically evil character of usury. His commentary on the subject is instead a trite repetition of earlier authorities. See Roland Bandinelli, *Die summa magistri Rolandi, nachmals papstes Alexander III*, ed. Freidrich Thaner (Innsbruck, 1874), C.14, Q.3.

[30] Third Lateran Council, Canon 25, *Quia in omnibus*, in Hefele, V, Part 2, 1105.

[31] *Decretales*, V:19:5, *Quam tu*.

"Lend freely, hoping nothing thereby" (Luke 6:35).[32] The immense importance of this citation can hardly be exaggerated. Here, for the first time in the entire tradition, a specific command of Christ is authoritatively interpreted by a pope as prohibiting usury. Henceforth, effectively unquestioned till Dominic Soto in the sixteenth century, Luke 6:35 will stand as an absolute divine prohibition of gain from a loan. Moreover, not only is the papal reference of the highest interest in itself, but the use made of it by Urban is of equal importance. He has been called on to decide two cases in which it is questioned whether usury is present. In one no contractual stipulation for usury has been made, but the lender would not lend without hope of gain; the other is the old case of sales at a higher price on credit. Urban decides both by the criterion of intention. The lender in each case intends to receive gain from a loan; this is prohibited by Luke 6:35; the lenders are therefore guilty of mortal usury. Again and again, scholastic writers will recur to this biblical text and to the Pope's application of it to show that intention to gain will alone constitute usury.

Conclusion

The development from 1050 is evident. Usury has now become a sharply defined notion. It is treated without hesitation as a sin specifically against justice. It has been localized in the loan contract, but some credit contracts taking usury in some other way than by a simple payment on a loan have been detected as evasions of the law. General papal and conciliar legislation with heavy sanctions has been enacted against the widespread sin. Biblical and patristic authority has been marshaled to condemn it, and "Lend freely, hoping nothing thereby" has been made a central text. By 1187, the date of *Consuluit*, the essential bases of the medieval position on usury have been laid: (1) Usury is whatever is demanded in return in a loan beyond the loaned good itself; (2) the taking of usury is a sin prohibited by the Old and New Testaments; (3) the very hope of a return beyond the good itself is sinful; (4) usuries must be restored in full to their true owner; (5) higher prices for credit sales are implicit usury. These five basic theses, which come not from the Bible alone, nor from Aristotle, nor result simply from economic conditions, nor are scientifically defended on a rational level, must be ascribed to the vital, active authority of the Church herself. They form the foundation of all later scholastic thought upon usury.

[32] *Decretales*, V:19:10, *Consuluit*.

CHAPTER II

THE PHILOSOPHICAL FRAMEWORK

Before examining the scholastic analysis of the injustice of usury in historical detail, we should investigate certain assumptions which are shared by all the scholastics and which are essential to their analyses of usury. These common elements of all the usury treatments concern the nature of law; the rightness of private property; the character of justice; the nature of profit; the place of intention in human acts; and the difference between public and private sinners.

1. *The Nature of Law*

Since the usury prohibition is first of all a matter of law, the scholastic concept of law underlies the scholastic analysis of usury. A firm belief in the rationality, immutability, and universality of law is at the heart of the scholastic approach to all moral problems; it is in this larger context that their discussion of any special moral question must be understood.

As is so frequently the case, the origins of a scholastic theory lie in a combination of Christian tradition, Roman law, and Aristotle. The Christian teaching on law begins with the Bible itself, and it is most succinctly stated in St. Paul's Epistle to the Romans. According to St. Paul's doctrine, there are three major kinds of law: the Law of the Old Testament, a divine revelation to the Jews; the New Law of the Gospel, also a divine revelation, which replaces the Old Law for Christians; and a law which is written in the hearts of all men, Christians, Jews, or pagans, and which binds them, even in the absence of revelation, to certain natural moral duties. The specifically Christian tradition on law is nothing but a commentary on these words of St. Paul.[1]

Even earlier, Aristotle had sharply distinguished between the merely local,

---

[1] Romans 5:20; 8:2; 2:14, 15. The influential *Glossa ordinaria* on the Bible gives the classic Christian interpretation of the Pauline text when it declares that by the last kind of law, St. Paul means "the natural law, by which man knows and is conscious of what is good and what is evil." Walafrid Strabo (d. 849), *Glossa ordinaria*, in Migne, *P.l.*, CXIV, col. 476.

changeable civil law and the natural law, which depended on no positive institution. The natural law, he said, bound all men, and although not completely immutable, was clearly different from purely conventional agreement.[2] But he did not develop this concept.

The Roman law similarly made a clear distinction between positive and natural law. The natural law, says Ulpian, closely following Aristotle, is "what nature has taught all animals."[3] The *ius gentium*, add the *Institutes*, is specifically human law, but it is the work of natural reason and rules all men; it is assimilated to the natural law in opposition to purely local, positive ordinances.[4] The natural law, the *Digest* notes, is as old as man himself, and there is no dispensation from its precepts.[5]

The Epistle to the Romans and the Roman law, which includes the Aristotelian notions,[6] furnish all the essential elements of the scholastic concept of law. Beginning with Gratian, we find unanimous acceptance of the major teachings of both Christian and pagan antiquity: there is a positive, local, mutable law, and there is an unwritten, universal, unchangeable law, which is rooted in human nature and undistinguishable from it.[7] The natural law may not be dispensed from by any human authority.[8] It binds all men. Its first principles are innate, though experience is necessary for their application or development.[9] Sometimes the natural law is considered in its subjective

---

[2] Aristotle, *Ethica Nichomachea*, Bk. V:7, in *Works of Aristotle*, trans. and ed. W. D. Ross (Oxford, 1928), Vol. IX.

[3] *Digesta Justiniani Augusti, Corpus juris civilis*, ed. T. Mommsen, W. Kroll, P. Krueger, and R. Schoell (Berlin, 1928–1929), I:1:1.

[4] *Justiniani Institutiones, Corpus juris civilis*, II:1:11. Cf. Gaius, who identifies the *ius gentium* and the law of reason, *Digesta*, I:1:9.

[5] *Digesta*, IV:5:8; VII:5:2.

[6] There is no evidence that Aristotle influenced the early scholastic writers on law, but it is abundantly clear that the Roman law, containing Aristotelian concepts, was of great influence, so that it seems best to include all initial Aristotelian influence under the Roman law.

[7] Gratian, *Decretum Gratiani*, D.5, D.6, D.13; cf. Rufinus, *Die Summa Decretorum des Magister Rufinus*, ed. Heinrich Singer (Paderborn, 1902), p. 6; William of Auxerre, *Summa aurea*, III:7:1; Alexander of Hales, *Summa theologica* (Quarrachi, 1924–1948), Bk. III, Part 2:2:4:1:1 and 2; St. Bonaventure, *In IV libros sententiarum*, IV:33:1:1, in *Opera*

omnia (Quarrachi, 1882–1902), Vol. IV; St. Albert, *Summa theologica*, II:16:99:3:2, in *Opera omnia*, ed. A. Borgnet (Paris, 1890–1899), Vol. XXXIII. See also the opinions of Simon of Bisiamo, Huguccio, John Teutonicus, and William of Auvergne reported in P. Odon Lottin, "Le droit naturel chez S. Thomas et ses predecesseurs," *Ephemerides Theologicae Lovaniensis* (1924), I, 384ff. and II, 32ff. Lottin's series of articles are excellent on this whole subject.

[8] Gratian, D.13; Rufinus, p. 31; Huguccio, in Lottin, I, 385.

[9] The Platonic Augustinians hold that the natural law is known prior to experience and is an intuition of God. So William of Auxerre, III:7:1:4, and Alexander of Hales, III:2:2:1:2. The normally Platonic St. Bonaventure, however, as well as Aristotelians like St. Albert, hold that experience is necessary before the terms of the judgments of the natural law can be known, although the judgments will be self-evident on experience (St. Bonaventure, II:39:1:1; St. Albert, *Summa de creaturis*, unpublished MS. cited in Lottin, II, 47). All would probably agree that the natural law

principles, and then it is identified with reason itself;[10] sometimes it is considered in its objective content and then it is identified with what is taught by reason.[11] More broadly, it is considered by some authors to reside in the intrinsic tendencies of all beings or of all animals.[12] But, fundamentally, as it applies to men, these tendencies are considered natural only as they are governed by reason.[13] The natural law is usually said to teach such acts of animal necessity or common equity as the rightness of the union of the sexes, the procreation and education of children, the return of property held as a deposit, and the wrongness of adultery and theft.[14] Gratian sums up the natural law in the Golden Rule; other authors say it consists essentially in two precepts: Love God; do no evil to your neighbor.[15]

The early canonists generally fail to distinguish clearly between the natural and divine law. Ignoring the teaching of St. Paul, Gratian declares that "the natural law is what is contained in the Law and the Gospel,"[16] thus confusing the Old Testament, the New Testament, and natural law. This error, entrenched in the canon law itself, is not corrected by the early canonists.[17] But it is rectified by the theologians. Before Gratian, Hugh of St. Victor had contrasted the law of nature and the law of grace, although without defining them.[18] Later, William of Auxerre, Alexander of Hales, and St. Bonaventure consider the law of reason as the most proper signification of natural law, while the canonists' usage is ignored.[19] St. Albert says decisively that the law of grace is natural only in an improper sense. The natural law is essentially the law which human reason finds that man as man must obey.[20]

What emerges as the common scholastic doctrine after a hundred years'

does depend on experience for application and even development.

[10] Rufinus, p. 9; William of Auxerre, III:7, ante c.1. So also Huguccio and Simon of Bisiamo, in Lottin, II, 379–380.

[11] St. Bonaventure, II:39:2:1; Huguccio, in Lottin, I, 383; *Glossa ordinaria* on Gratian, *Corpus juris canonici* (Venice, 1605), D.1, c.7. The *Gloss* on Gratian is by John Teutonicus, completed in 1215 and revised about 1240 by Bartholomew of Brescia.

[12] *Glossa ordinaria*, D.1, c.7; Rufinus, p. 6; Huguccio, in Lottin, I, 383; Simon of Bisiamo, in Lottin, I, 379; William of Auxerre, III:7:1, ante c.1.

[13] *Glossa ordinaria*, D.1, c.7; Huguccio, in Lottin, I, 300; Simon of Bisiamo, in Lottin, I, 379; St. Albert the Great, MS. cited in

Lottin, II, p. 45; William of Auxerre, III:7, ante c.1, c.1:1 and 4.

[14] Gratian, D.1; *Glossa ordinaria*, D.1, c.7; William of Auxerre, III:7:1:5; Alexander of Hales, III:2:3:2:1:2:6 and 7; Stephen of Tournai, *Summa des Stephanus Tornacensis über das Decretum Gratiani*, ed. J. F. von Schulte (Giessen, 1891), p. 7.

[15] Gratian, D.1; Huguccio, in Lottin, I, 385; Rufinus, p. 6; William of Auxerre, III: 7:1:3.

[16] Gratian, D.1.   [17] Cf. Lottin, I, 387.

[18] Hugh of St. Victor, *De sacramentis*, in Migne, *P.l.*, CLXXVI, cols. 343 and 347.

[19] William of Auxerre, III:7, ante c.1; Alexander of Hales, III:2:2:4:1; St. Bonaventure, IV:33:1:1.

[20] St. Albert the Great, MS. cited in Lottin, II, 48.

discussion is best summed up by St. Thomas Aquinas, and his synthesis will
be generally accepted throughout the Middle Ages. His opinions will therefore be presented a little more fully. According to St. Thomas, law is a dic-
tate of reason ordering acts to an end, and the most fundamental kind of
law is the eternal law, which is identical with God's intelligence directing
all beings to their proper ends.[21] All created beings participate in the eternal
law by deriving from it their inclination to their proper acts and ends.[22]
The good is being, considered as an end, and as every being seeks its end
or good, it tends naturally to the maximum of being attainable by its capacities.[23] Thus, every being as being tends to preserve its substance. Every
animal being tends to preserve its species by copulation and the rearing of its
offspring. Every rational being, because he can know being in general, seeks
the good in general.[24]

On this metaphysical foundation of the innate dynamism of all creatures
towards the good, St. Thomas finds the natural law is built. Man not only
has certain natural innate tendencies: he is conscious of them, and his
rational apprehension of what are his natural ends or goods constitutes
the natural law in him. Man knows, first of all, that the good is what all
seek, and he knows, then, that the first precept of the natural law is, Seek
the good.[25] Then he apprehends that as a substance, he must preserve his
being; that as an animal, some of his species must have sexual intercourse
and rear children; that as a rational being, he must seek the good which
can satisfy his spiritual will and consequently that he must seek to know
God.[26] Inasmuch as man is essentially rational, the entitative and animal
tendencies will be directed to their ends, subordinate to reason.[27]

Further, as the natural tendencies to certain ends are innate to man, so
is his awareness of them, and consequently he has in principle and potency
an innate knowledge of the primary precepts of the natural law. These precepts consist in certain judgments of the practical reason which like any
judgment will not be formed prior to sense experience.[28] But once experience
has made known the terms of the propositions to a man, he will appre-
hend them as naturally and necessarily binding. Like the first principles of
the speculative reason, the first principles of the practical reason are self-
evident and nondemonstrable.[29] Most strictly considered, they will consist

[21] St. Thomas Aquinas, *Summa theologica*,
I–II, Q.93, art. 1, in *Opera omnia*, ed. P.
Maré and S. E. Fretté (Paris: Vivès edition,
1871–1880). Hereafter cited as *S.T.*

[22] *S.T.*, I–II:94:2.

[23] *Summa contra gentiles*, III:24; cf. *S.T.*,
I:5:1; I:6:1.

[24] *S.T.*, I–II:94:2.
[25] *S.T.*, I–II:94:2.
[26] *S.T.*, I–II:74:2.
[27] *S.T.*, I–II:84:6.
[28] *S.T.*, I–II:24:2.
[29] *S.T.*, I–II:94:2.

in "what nature has taught all animals."[30] But the most fundamental precepts of the natural law are those specifically proper to man: Love God and love your neighbor.[31] These primary principles can never be abolished from the heart of man, although they may be ignored in particular sinful actions.[32]

There are also secondary precepts of the natural law, which are not immediately self-evident but which follow rationally from the primary principles. The union of the sexes, for example, is dictated by a primary natural law, whereas polygamy, which hinders but does not prevent the natural objective of the education of offspring, is dictated by only a secondary natural law.[33] The secondary precepts of the natural law can be erroneously deduced from the primary ones or corrupted by custom, so that whole societies may exist in ignorance of them.[34] Nonetheless, they are as binding on man as the primary precepts if they are known. The natural law is, then, universal in its general principles for all, and obligatory for all as to the conclusions from these principles if the conclusions are known.[35] Similarly, the natural law is unchangeable in its primary principles, though in its secondary principles it may be changed by being ignored or, on the other hand, by being developed.[36]

The *ius gentium* is part of the secondary teaching of the natural law.[37]

---

[30] S.T., I–II:95:4; *Commentum in IV libros sententiarum*, IV:33:1:1 ad 4, in *Opera omnia*, Vol. X. Hereafter cited as *In IV lib. sent.*

[31] S.T., I–II:100:3. By "God" in this context St. Thomas may not necessarily mean the one true God, but simply the good in general; for he has granted that the knowledge of God's existence is not innate (S.T., I–I:2:1); therefore he can hardly mean to say that one innately loves God. Also he restates the other primary precept as "Do not harm your neighbor" (S.T., I–II:100:5 ad 4 and 95:2) so that neither of the primary laws are as rigorous as they may seem at first glance.

There is a little inconsistency in St. Thomas' language here, since, on the one hand, he makes the fundamental natural laws consist in specifically rational inclinations, while on the other hand, he calls the natural law in the strictest sense the law common to animals and man. I think the latter usage is to be explained by a wish to save the authority of Aristotle and Isidore, who speak in this sense. Cf. Lottin, I. 349–350.

[32] S.T., I–II:94:6.

[33] *In IV lib. sent.*, IV:33:1:2.

[34] S.T., I–II:94:6. It is noteworthy that St. Thomas here asserts that even unnatural sexual vice can be generally practiced in a society as if it were not sinful. This opinion seems to indicate that not even all acts against the animal tendency towards union of the sexes and procreation can be considered against the primary precepts of the natural law; for the primary precepts can never be so generally ignored. This confirms the interpretation given above that for St. Thomas personally the natural law consists primarily in certain specifically human duties.

[35] S.T., I–II:94:4.

[36] S.T., I–II:94:5.

[37] St. Thomas himself never directly identifies the *ius gentium* and the secondary precepts of the natural law; but since the characteristics of the *ius gentium* as conceived by St. Thomas surely fit the description of the secondary natural law, it seems correct to say that it forms part of this law. Moreover, in commenting on Aristotle, he says the *ius gentium* is part of the natural law in Aristotle's sense of the term, *In X libros ethicorum*

As man is naturally made to seek God and develop his rational nature in society, so reason teaches him certain acts necessary to social life, such as the observance of justice in buying and selling, and the institution of government. These rational deductions from a natural premise compose the *ius gentium*.[38] Reason here naturally selects the means essential to attain the ends set by nature, and the observance of these means becomes as obligatory a part of the natural law as the obligation to attain the ends themselves.[39] Indeed, since man is essentially rational, every act in accordance with reason is natural to him and prescribed in a general way by the natural law. To be virtuous for man is to be rational, and the natural law thus prescribes every virtue, as it prescribes in general, "Be rational."[40]

Clearly distinct from natural law and the broad dictates of reason is human positive law. Human positive law is mutable, dispensable, different with different times and places.[41] Human law is not innate or universal. It is made by particular governments, secular or ecclesiastical, or by local customs.[42] It neither forbids all natural vices nor prescribes all natural virtues; for it is made to direct the majority who find virtue difficult.[43] It is essentially, however, only the detailed application of the natural law. So it is naturally just to punish a criminal; the particular punishment is a matter of positive institution. Or human law may prescribe particular acts of virtue which the natural law in a general way indicates are good.[44] Always the natural law is the norm and measure of positive law;[45] and positive laws contrary to it are *ipso facto* unjust, while positive law made by competent authority in accordance with it has the sanction and obligatory force of the natural law itself.[46]

Besides natural and human law, there is also the divine law. The divine law is contained in the revelation made by God directing man to a supernatural end beyond that which he might naturally attain.[47] It was imperfectly set forth in the Old Law of the Jews and is now perfectly set out in the New Law of the Gospel.[48] The New Law is instilled in man by grace,

---

ad Nichomachum, V:12, in *Opera*, Vol. XXV (hereafter cited as *In X lib. eth.*).

[38] *S.T.*, I–II:95:4.
[39] *S.T.*, II–II:57:3.
[40] *S.T.*, I–II:94:3.
[41] *S.T.*, I–II:91:3; 97:2 and 4.
[42] *S.T.*, I–II:97:1 and 3.
[43] *S.T.*, I–II:96:2.
[44] *S.T.*, I–II:95:2 and 96:3.
[45] *S.T.*, I–II:91:3.
[46] This sanction is either direct, as when

human law draws a conclusion from a primary precept of nature, or it is indirect, as when the law is purely a positive determination. In the latter case the natural obligation to seek the common good entails the obligation of following the law of a ruler directing the community to the common good. *S.T.*, I–II:95:2; I–II:96:4.

[47] *S.T.*, I–II:91:4.
[48] *S.T.*, I–II:107:1 ad 2.

and as the natural law is innate in rational man, so the New Law is inscribed in the heart of the Christian, directing him as to what he should do and helping him to do it: indeed as the natural law consists in reason, so the New Law consists chiefly in grace.[49] In its secondary aspect, it consists in precepts concerning the reception of grace by the sacraments.[50] These precepts are positive, divine law, unchangeable by man because authored by God.[51]

The New Law also secondarily consists in moral precepts. But these moral precepts are identical with the Decalogue of the Old Law,[52] and the Decalogue and its corollaries are identical with the precepts of the natural law.[53] In the Decalogue and the New Law God has only made evident by revelation truths that fallible man, because of passion or ignorance, might have mistaken, but truths which any rightly reasoning intellect should be able to discover for itself.[54] The Decalogue contains the essence of natural law, ordering man to the final good, which is God, and regulating man in his relations with other men according to justice.[55] The New Law simply renews the precepts of the Old, and both the Old and New simply renew the law of reason. Thus for all moral matters outside the sacraments, the natural law of reason and the Christian law are identified. Such an identification, it is clear, could work in one of two directions. On the one hand, any act prohibited by the Christian tradition could be treated as if it were evil by nature, not by positive law. On the other hand, any act not naturally demonstrable as evil could be considered as not prohibited by Christian teaching. The early scholastics tend to emphasize the first approach; the postmedieval scholastics — not without exceptions — incline to measure moral demands by what is demonstrably rational.

This difference in emphasis was to have important secondary effects on the evolution of the usury prohibition. From the beginning of its development by the scholastics, however, the whole handling of the prohibition hung on their most general assumptions, derived from the Gospel and the Roman law, and summed up by St. Thomas: the moral law is rational, natural, and founded on the intrinsic rationality and naturalness of certain acts; the moral law is universal, nondispensable, unalterable, and distinct from purely human ordinances.[56] These assumptions supply passion to the scholastics' quest for a

[49] *S.T.*, I–II:106:1.
[50] *S.T.*, I–II:108:2.
[51] *S.T.*, I–II:106:4.
[52] *S.T.*, I–II:107:3 ad 2.
[53] *S.T.*, I–II:100:11.
[54] *S.T.*, I–II:99:2 ad 2.

[55] *S.T.*, I–II:100:8.
[56] A number of scholastics are voluntarists in their views on the origin of natural law; that is, they teach that the will of God has constituted the moral law by determining certain acts to be right or wrong by His

a rationale for the usury rule. Where they faltered, as in the case of John Gerson, the rule itself was in danger. They created conflict when the rule was challenged by positive law and custom. Without them the scholastic analysis would have lacked a broad structure and a fundamental stimulus.

2. The Right of Private Property

To know that the scholastics believed in natural law is not, however, to know that they believed private property was naturally inviolable. Yet the usury question is essentially a matter of the natural right of a debtor to be protected from the expropriation of his property by a creditor. If the scholastics had believed private property to be only a human institution, they might have argued that human laws by their own authority could justify the transfer of property from one person to another regardless of existing property rights.

The curious truth is that in the canon law itself Gratian had incorporated a passage from St. Augustine which denied the divine or natural origin of private property and taught that property was a purely human convention. To bolster this assertion Gratian added the teaching of Plato and the Acts of the Apostles.[57] Thus the official code of the Church appeared committed to the naturalness of communism.

The early canonists devoted themselves to minimizing this declaration. Rufinus and Simon of Bisiamo said that the natural law neither proscribed nor prescribed private property, though it indicated that common ownership was good. Huguccio declared that nature approved common ownership, as it did the personal freedom of men, but that as mere *"demonstrationes,"* not precepts, these natural indications were not binding. The real meaning of

---

arbitrary decree. Thus, acts are good or evil because God willed that they should be so; He did not will them because they were good or evil. So Duns Scotus, *In IV libros sententiarum*, IV:46:4:8, *Reportata Parisiensis*, in *Opera omnia*, ed. nova juxta edit. Waddingi (Paris: Vivès, 1891–1895), Vol. XXIV; and John Gerson, *Liber de vita spirituali animae*, col. 26, in *Opera omnia*, ed. L. E. du Pin (Antwerp, 1748), Vol. III.

Logically, it is clear that the fact that all nature originates in God's will does not alter its naturalness; nor does the fact that the origin of the moral law is the will of God affect its naturalness. Both Scotus and Gerson clearly distinguish (1) natural law — the

law which God by His will has instilled in men and by which, consequently, certain acts are intrinsically denominated as good or evil (Scotus, II:22:3; IV:37:5; Gerson, col. 21); (2) positive divine law — the law which God by revelation has added to the law instilled naturally in man; (3) positive human law — local, mutable additions to the natural law.

It cannot be denied that psychologically — although not logically — the notion that God's will is the source of law is a factor sometimes encouraging a narrow and arbitrary interpretation of the law (see the positions of Gerson, *infra*, pp. 70, 158–159).

[57] Gratian, init. D.8. The references are to the *Republic*, III:22, and Acts 4:34.

Gratian's bold phrase, he asserted, was that only in necessity were all things naturally common. This happy explanation was repeated by John Teutonicus in the influential *Glossa ordinaria* on Gratian;[58] and it eventually became the traditional one.

The theologians added to the canonists' explanation a connection between private property and original sin. Before the Fall, says William of Auxerre, nature indicated that property should be held commonly. After the Fall, in the present state of sin, nature permits private ownership. Alexander of Hales subscribes to the same theory, declaring a little more forcefully that nature now dictates private property. St. Albert the Great similarly teaches that private property is natural in the present fallen state. It is not, however, indicated by a first principle of the natural law. But it is prescribed by rational reflection as being for "the convenience and utility of man," just as the election of rulers is also prescribed by rational reflection.[59]

St. Thomas follows in the same tradition. Nature as such is indifferent to private ownership; the rightness of private property is not a primary principle of the natural law, as is the procreation of children.[60] Nonetheless, in this fallen state, rational reflection shows the necessity of private property.[61] Nature does prescribe as a necessary end the preservation of peace, the maintenance of order, the encouragement of human industry; reason shows that the best way of obtaining these ends is the institution of private property.[62] Private property is thus commanded by the *ius gentium* or the secondary principles of natural law.[63] Still, nature itself does not determine who shall own what: the determination of specific property rights is a matter of positive law.[64]

The scholastic defense of private property is a conditional one, expressly championing it only in man's fallen state and as the most rational way of preserving peace. But the individual's right to property in this fallen world is defended absolutely. Every scholastic writer considers theft to be against the natural law.[65] Similarly, then, when the scholastics consider usury, they will find it also against the natural law; like theft, it violates a right to property which natural reason has established as just and necessary in the present order.

[58] Rufinus, p. 6; Simon of Bisiamo, in Lottin, I, 379; Huguccio, in Lottin, I, 385, 386; *Glossa ordinaria*, D.I, c.7.

[59] William of Auxerre, III:7:1; Alexander of Hales, III:2:2:4:3:2; St. Albert, MS. cited in Lottin, II, 49.

[60] St. Thomas, *In IV lib. sent.*, IV:33:2:2:1; *S.T.*, I–II:94:5 ad 3.
[61] *S.T.*, I:98:1 ad 3.
[62] *S.T.*, II–II:66:2.
[63] *S.T.*, II–II:57:3.
[64] *S.T.*, II–II:66:2 ad 1.
[65] *S.T.*, I–II:100:1; and see *supra*, n. 14.

3. The Idea of Justice

Classified by the early Middle Ages as the invasion of a property right, usury fell within relations governed by the requirements of justice; usury analysis took form from the generic understanding of the nature of this virtue. The classification had serious consequences; usury was not to be condemned merely as avaricious or uncharitable. The early Middle Ages had made this far-reaching decision to treat usury as a sin not of uncharitableness or avarice, but as a sin against justice. To those unfamiliar with scholastic theology the distinction may seem a quibble: "A sin is, after all, a sin." Nonetheless, there are two important practical differences between a sin of injustice and a sin of uncharitableness. A sin against justice entailed the obligation of reparation of the damage or restitution of the loss, as a condition for absolution; a sin against charity required simply internal sorrow for forgiveness.[66] Thus, as a practical matter, repentance for injustice involved both more hardship and more complication for the penitent, particularly if many financial transactions were concerned, than did penitence for uncharitableness. Secondly, the command to help one's neighbor corporeally, out of charity, was binding, under pain of mortal sin, only in certain cases, that is, when he was in great need and you had the means to help him. But the precept to do justice was binding in every case, however rich or poor the parties involved. There were thus far more occasions offered in business for sins against justice than sins against charity. Clearly then, it was enormously important that after a three hundred years' development it became axiomatic that usury should be considered a sin against justice, rather than against charity.

Similarly, it was highly important that usury was not considered merely *turpe lucrum*, "shameful gain" — gain acquired out of avarice, or by disreputable means. The taking of such gain was not considered to constitute a positive invasion of another's right, and although the common doctrine was that it should be given to the poor, it entailed no obligation of strict restitution.[67]

As to what was meant by justice, the early writers, treating usury under theft, have the general notion set forth in the Roman law that it is wrong to deprive a man of his property, if he is unwilling.[68] Such a seizure of an-

---

[66] For the common doctrine, see *S.T.*, II–II:62:2.

[67] St. Raymond of Pennaforte, *Summa casuum conscientiae* (Verona, 1744), 2:7:5. See St. Antoninus, *Summa*, Part 2, Title 1, c.16, for a clear and traditional distinction between unjust profit and *turpe lucrum*.

[68] *Justiniani Institutiones*, II:1:1:2; see Peter Lombard, *Sententiarum*, III:37:3; Alexander of Hales, III:2:3:2:1:2:7:1.

other's good is clearly enough distinguished from a sin of uncharitableness or avarice. The words of the *Institutes* of Justinian are doubtless in the minds of the canonists who begin the first rational analysis of usury: "Justice is the constant and perpetual desire to give to each one that to which he is entitled. . . . The following are the precepts of the law: to live honestly, to injure no one, and to give to each that which belongs to him." [69] The essence of natural justice is here set forth; the scholastics will not improve upon it. The definition of an early theological writer upon usury, William of Auxerre, who may be taken as representative, is entirely similar: "If it is strictly used, justice is the virtue by which to each one is rendered what is his own, because it is his own." [70]

The notion of commutative justice proper, which consists precisely in the equality of objects given in exchange, becomes general only with the revival of Aristotle, and the repetition of his doctrine in the commentaries of St. Albert the Great and St. Thomas. Equality of exchange was a sharp and clear concept applicable especially to contracts, but the Aristotelian criterion really only made explicit what the earlier writers had said more loosely. The earlier writers as well as the later ones had seen that justice was no respecter of persons, and that it was as wrong to steal or to take usury from a rich man as from a poor one; and, since they did not make the status of the parties to a contract a test of justice, it is clear that they, too, had implicitly considered the equality of objects exchanged as the test of honesty. The conception of justice underlying the usury theory is a constant.

4. *The Character of Profit*

The just is not necessarily the unprofitable. The usual definition of usury is "whatever is added to the principal" [71] on a loan, or simply "profit from a loan." [72] The scholastics make no attempt to analyze "profit" as modern economics does, but the term is used in its common-sense meaning of the gain that is normally sought by every businessman as the reward of his industry and investment. For example, if a seller of wool sells wool worth 25 ducats for 30 ducats, the scholastics will commonly call the 5-ducat increase in his capital "profit," although 5 ducats may be only a fair return for his labor

---

[69] *Institutiones*, I:1:3.

[70] William of Auxerre, III:7, *De justitia in generali*, f.176r:b.

[71] Gratian, C.14, Q.4, dictum post c.x.; Hostiensis, *Summa aurea* (Venice, 1579), *De usuris*, n.1.

[72] Bernard of Pavia, *Summa decretalium*, ed. E. Laspeyres (Ratisbon, 1860), V:15:1; Joannes Andreae, *Decretalium libros novella commentaria* (Venice, 1581), VI, *De regulis iuris*, "Peccatum," 7.

and investment. Laurentius de Ridolfis' definition would be accepted by all: "Profit is properly said to be the superabundance or increment which one has from a voluntary exchange beyond those goods which were one's own at the beginning of it." [73]

It must be clearly understood that there is no scholastic opposition to profit as such. It is only profit on a loan that is condemned. Every early writer speaks of profit gained in other contracts by laymen as a perfectly normal acquisition. All authors would subscribe to St. Bernardine's dictum, "All usury is profit, but not all profit is usury." [74] St. Antoninus expresses the unanimous opinion when he says, "Nor is hope of profit prohibited in contracts; rather it is commonly present." [75] It must not be supposed, then, that the scholastics held that businessmen must always act out of principally charitable motives, nor that principal hope of profit in all contracts was considered sinful. Only in a loan and in fictitious disguises of a loan was the seeking of profit considered immoral.

5. The Criterion of Intention

It is axiomatic in scholastic theology that the intention to perform a sinful act, even though not executed, is a sin in itself. That mental usury was a sin, and that "hope makes the usurer" were common doctrines taught by everyone.[76] The intention to profit from a loan was as sinful as profiting in fact; no contractual disguise of the loan and no absence of an express contractual provision for the payment of usury freed from guilt the man who desired the usury in his heart. In particular, a special emphasis was placed on intention by the text, "Lend freely, hoping for nothing thereby," and its interpretation given by Urban III in Consuluit. There was also reason for supposing that if a man preferred to lend rather than to invest his money in other businesses, he did so because lending gave him more than other businesses would, and it could be inferred from his preference that he sought profit on a loan, or usury. But starting from an axiomatic principle on intention, a Gospel text emphasizing it, and a reasonable presumption, the early scholastics — as later theologians were to recognize — employed the criterion of intention in a far wider sense than the doctrine itself demanded. In the less critical, early period, "intention to gain from a loan" was so

---

[73] Laurentius de Ridolfis, De usuris, in Tractatus universi juris (Venice, 1584–1586), VII, c.1:1 (n.4).

[74] St. Bernardine, De contractibus et usuris, in Opera omnia (Venice, 1745), Vol. II, Sermon 36, art. 1, c.2.

[75] St. Antoninus, Summa, 2:1:8 (n.14).

[76] Glossa, C.14, Q.3, c.2, at "Expectus." Monaldus, Summa perutilis atque aurea (Lyons, 1500), "Usura," f.289. Astesanus, Summa Astesana (Rome, 1728), Bk. III:11:5.

used that the only loans recognized as licit were those made from charity or under compulsion. The presence of objectively valid titles to compensation beyond the principal was held not to justify a man taking the compensation if he had loaned principally to get it. The hope of even this lawful compensation was consistently construed as a sinful intention to profit. The intention to gain vitiated the objective titles to interest. In case after case, and author after author down to 1500, we shall find this principle dominant.[77] St. Raymond expresses what is common to all: "One ought to lend to one's needy neighbor only for God and principally from charity."[78]

This emphasis on intention was deepened yet further by two favorite comparisons of the scholastics. As early as 1210 William of Auxerre, saying "that a usurious will makes the usurer," compared the sin of usury to the sin of lust which might be committed by unlawful desire alone. St. Antoninus stated another popular comparison as follows: "Just as the principal hope and intention of temporal benefits leads to spiritual simony . . . so also in a loan the principal intention of profit leads to usury. . . ."[79] These analogies were dangerous in that they compared sins which depended largely on subjective factors with a matter where the determination of lawfulness consisted peculiarly in a consideration of the objective components of an act. Simony, for example, is committed by a man who intends gain from a spiritual office, and the sin is committed whether or not some other objective title to gain exists, if the man seeks gain by virtue of his office. In contrast, the sin of injustice in contracts is committed only by one party effecting an objective inequality in an exchange or intending to effect this inequality. It would not, according to the natural law, be a sin if a man sought profit from a loan, if there was an objective title to the profit other than the loan itself, and if he did not specifically intend to commit an injustice.[80] The early scholastics, however, argued that as it is always sinful to intend to gain from a spiritual office, so also it is always sinful to intend to gain from a loan. The criterion of intention was thus reaffirmed as the great guide for the practical application of the usury prohibition. The definition of usury as "whatever is added to the principal," combined with the use of the criterion of intention, led directly to the doctrine that no loan might ever be made in the same spirit as other business transactions. A loan had to be made with the hope of getting nothing back beyond the sum loaned.

[77] St. Raymond, 2:7:3; Hostiensis, *Summa,* V, *De usuris,* n.1; Giles of Lessines, *De usuris,* c.6, in St. Thomas Aquinas, *Opera* (Parma ed., 1864), Vol. XVII; Henry of Hesse, *De contractibus,* c. 16, f.193. See also *infra,* pp. 105, 108, 115, 124.
[78] St. Raymond, 2:7:2.
[79] William of Auxerre, III:21, f.224r:b; St. Antoninus, 2:1:7.
[80] See *infra,* pp. 257, 259–260.

6. *The Distinction between Personal Responsibility and Social Accountability*

The Third Lateran Council had excommunicated manifest usurers — commonly understood to mean men who had been convicted in a court of taking usury, or who were "notorious by fact" by publicly setting themselves up to lend money at a profit.[81] Since judicial prosecutions, whether ecclesiastical or lay, were almost never directed except at declared moneylenders,[82] the canon had the practical effect of excommunicating only the professional lenders who made usury their business. These professional moneylenders were regularly pawnbrokers who made loans for consumption purposes to the poor at high rates: their usual charge was 43½ per cent per annum.[83] According to the scholastic authorities, they might be tolerated by the State as a necessary evil, but not approved or encouraged.[84] Some states seem to have gone beyond giving simple permission and positively licensed these moneylenders and participated in their profits through heavy license-fees.[85] After the Council of Vienne in 1317, such compensation of the rulers of the State brought excommunication upon them, too; but this penalty does not seem to have been an effective deterrent.[86] In the Low Countries, which may be taken as typical, the public usurers were under the special protection of the prince, and the State directed its chief efforts in this field toward eliminating the competition of unlicensed usurers.[87] Occasionally, in waves of reform, the public usurers might be raided or suppressed, much like licensed gamblers today; but they were always found necessary and they always reappeared.[88]

The men who were public usurers were usually either Jews or lombards.[89]

---

[81] Innocent IV, *Apparatus super quinque libros decretalium* (Strassburg, 1478), V:19:3; Hostiensis, *Summa*, V, *De usuris*, 10; St. Antoninus, *Summa*, 3:24:49.

[82] George Bigwood, *Le régime juridique et économique du commerce de l'argent*, (Brussels, 1921), I, 568–585.

[83] Bigwood, I, 453: Raymond de Roover, *Money, Banking and Credit in Medieval Bruges* (Cambridge, Mass., 1948), p. 125. Armand Sapori, *Studi di storia economica medievale* (Florence, 1947), p. 108, reports that fourteenth-century Florentine usurers charged 30 per cent. Forty-three-and-a-half per cent is not a remarkably high rate for the small-loan business. Most modern American companies in the 1930's charged between 30 and 42 per cent — see L. N. Robinson and R. Nugent, *Regulation of the Small Loan Business* (New York, 1935), pp. 248–265.

[84] See Joannes Andreae, VI, *De regulis iuris*, "Peccatum," 17: St. Bernadine, 38:3:3; Alexander de Nevo, *Consilia contra Judaeos foenerantes* (Frankfort, 1478), *Consilium* II.

[85] Bigwood, I, 329, 336.

[86] Cf. de Roover, pp. 100–103; Bigwood, I, 256ff. For the decree of Vienne, see Council of Vienne, Canon 15, in Hefele, VI, Part 2, cols. 694–695.

[87] Bigwood, I, 603.

[88] De Roover, p. 156.

[89] Henri Pirenne, *Economic and Social History of Medieval Europe*, trans. I. E. Clegg (New York, 1937), pp. 133–135. The proper noun "Lombard" seems to have become the common noun "lombard," a term designating

The Jews were, of course, unaffected by excommunication, but according to the Fourth Lateran Council, they were to be boycotted commercially by Christians and were to be held to make up to the Church the taxes on Christian properties which had come into their possession through usury.[90] These provisions do not seem to have been much followed. Yet the traffic of the Jews was never considered permissible, as some modern economic historians seem to think, "because they were damned anyway,"[91] but was universally deplored by the theologians as immoral and unnatural.[92] The Jews, however, not believing themselves bound by the canon law, felt free to enter the business, and did so because few Christians would openly compete with them.[93]

One group of Christians were an exception to the general Christian avoidance of open usury. These were the lombards, men chiefly from the hill towns of northern Italy, such as Asti and Chieri. They spread throughout Europe even more successfully than the Jews, and for some unaccountable reason, showed a strange insensitivity to ecclesiastical and social censure.[94] Both lombards and Jews and other open moneylenders were generally hated by the poor whom they exploited and considered social outcasts by the rest of the community.[95] The social distinction followed the theological one of manifest usurers.

Some historians, imbued with a highly materialistic view, have remarked the absence of external force against many usurious practices and the restriction of the ecclesiastical and social penalties to manifest usurers, and have concluded that the usury prohibition might easily have been evaded.[96] They have pointed out the many contractual disguises by which usury could be cloaked, and one eminent historian has gone so far as to compare the

---

any public Christian usurer. Originally and generally, the lombards were also Lombards, but not all Lombards were lombards. The distinction in spelling insisted on by de Roover seems proper, and although most writers before him have not made the distinction, I have followed him on it in this study. Cf. de Roover, p. 346; Armand Sapori, *Le marchand italien au moyen age* (Paris, 1952), XIV.

[90] Fourth Lateran Council, Canon 67, *Quanta amplius*, in Hefele, V, 1386; *Decretales*, V: 19:18.

[91] E.g., Melvin Knight, Harry Elmer Barnes, and Felix Flügel, *Economic History of Europe* (New York, 1928), p. 113; cf. de Roover, p. 157.

[92] See St. Raymond, 2:7:9; St. Thomas Aquinas, *De regimine Judaeorum*, in *Opera*, Vol. XXVII; Alexander de Nevo, *Consilium* I, ad dubium 142.

[93] Schaub (*Der Kampf gegen den Zinswucher*, p. 167) holds that the Jews voluntarily entered the moneylending business in the eleventh and twelfth centuries, well before there was any restriction on them forcing them into this business.

[94] de Roover, pp. 113ff.

[95] de Roover, p. 108.

[96] E.g., Ferdinand Schevill, *History of Florence* (New York, 1936), pp. 294–295; Endemann, *Studien in der romanisch-kanonistichen Wirthschafts*, I, 30; Thompson, *Economic and Social History of Europe*, I, 438.

usury prohibition to the Volstead Act, which was impossible of literal enforcement and simply existed as a threat over the heads of those engaged
in the prohibited business.[97] Such a view considers only the legal and social
barriers to usury. The usury law was primarily a spiritual matter, and if
the Church hoped that society and the State would endeavor to suppress
public usury, still she relied on spiritual means for its real control. The
theologians knew as well as the economic historians that a thousand disguises for usury existed, yet the Church chose to use the extreme spiritual
penalty only against flagrant violation. But all hidden usury was still a
mortal sin, and the ultimate punishment of damnation still awaited all
hidden usurers. If one considers the genuinely religious attitude of probably
the majority of medieval men, it is not then very realistic to say that the
usury prohibition was meaningless because it was rarely enforced thoroughly
by public authority, and the thousand evasions of it could never be checked.
As medieval men knew well, they could sin in this life without the State
being able to punish them, but they damned themselves for eternity. The
real force of the usury law lay in its hold on men's souls, and there no evasion was possible. The prohibition may have been commonly evaded in
business practice, and economic historians, looking only on the economic results, may conclude that it was therefore economically ineffective. But even
if the prohibition did not have complete economic effectiveness, one should
not infer that it was without practical results. Even when it did not affect
commercial practice, it did affect the spiritual state of businessmen, and
who will say that there is no meaning to the salvation or damnation of a
man? Though businessmen might go on making money by hidden usury,
so that the prohibition remained impotent in business, yet these men were
guilty of sin if they knew they were engaged in illicit work. Though the
number of manifest usurers were few, the number of hidden usurers might
be many; it is in terms of the latter that the full extent of the usury prohibition must be measured. The Church taught that intention to gain from
a loan was mortal sin; as long as this sinful intention was held in a man's
heart, whatever form his contract took, he knew that he was outside the
state of grace.[98]

Conclusion

Distinguishing between a revealed divine law, a rational natural law
which coincided with the divine law in moral matters, and positive human

---

[97] Pirenne, *Economic and Social History,* p. 146.   [98] See, for example, Hostiensis, *Summa,* V, *De usuris,* 8; St. Antoninus, *Summa,* 2:1:6.

law, the scholastics set up a structure in which the usury rule might be studied, explained and limited. Their deep desire to harmonize the types of law, their strong belief in orderly, universal rules, encouraged a rationalistic evaluation of the purpose of the prohibition. The natural law guaranteed the right of private property of which the prohibition was at once a specific protection and limitation. The prohibition was a concrete embodiment of the virtue of justice that required that no one take the property of another against his will. True, this requirement of justice did not prohibit a business- man from making a profit in exchanging property; but, for reasons to be explored, it did prohibit profit on loans. Moreover, as intention to do in- justice is as sinful as the unjust act, intent to profit on a loan was accounted sinful. The criterion of intention shifted the test from the objective equality of the property exchanged to the state of mind of the lender. It provided an effective spiritual control to which public social controls were only a sup- plement in notorious cases. The use made of it was not entirely consistent with the basic conception of the nature of justice. Yet, for the first period, 1150 to 1450, these fundamental notions of law, property, justice, and inten- tion furnished the general shape of the scholastic doctrine on usury.

CHAPTER III

A NATURAL-LAW CASE AGAINST USURY

The positive ecclesiastical rulings set the framework; the common elements of scholastic philosophy provided the terms of the discourse. Within this framework and with these terms, the scholastics undertook a rational development of a case against usury. In this development three stages are discernible: a beginning where the most rudimentary and legalistic arguments suffice; a period of maturity represented by the fundamental formulations of St. Thomas Aquinas; and a third period in which the now traditional arguments are reviewed and used by a host of economic moralists.

EARLY RATIONALIZATIONS

1. *The Palea* Ejiciens

We have said that the early ecclesiastical treatment of usury contains no attempt to attack usury on grounds of natural law alone, but that the *magisterium* simply decides that usury is wrong by its own authority. There is, however, one important exception to this statement. This is the palea *Ejiciens*, a work apparently of fifth-century origin, erroneously attributed to St. John Chrysostom, and incorporated in Gratian about 1180, when it thus became a part of the law of the Church.[1] It is of such immense influence that the portions of it dealing with usury should be considered in full:

Of all merchants, the most cursed is the usurer, for he sells a good given by God, not acquired as a merchant acquires his goods from men; and after the usury he reseeks his own good, taking both his own good and the good of the other. A merchant, however, does not reseek the good he has sold. One will object: Is not he who rents a field to receive the fruits or a house to get an income similar to him who lends his money at usury? Certainly not. First, because money is only meant to be used in purchasing. Secondly, because one having a field by farming receives fruit from it; one having a house has the use of inhabiting it. Therefore, he who rents a field or house is seen to give what is his own use and

[1] It was written by an heretical author of the fifth or sixth century: see Otto Barden-hewer, *Geschichte de altkirchlichen Literatur* (Freiburg in Br., 1923), III, 597.

to receive money, and in a certain manner it seems as if he exchanged gain for gain. But from money which is stored up you take no use. Thirdly, a field or a house deteriorates in use. Money, however, when it is lent, is neither diminished nor deteriorated.[2]

In this crowded and confused statement are contained, at least in potency, many of the arguments to be used by later scholastics: the usurer sells what is God's, by which is presumably meant time; the usurer takes another man's work; money is intended for consumption; money is technically fruitless and useless; money does not deteriorate.[3] These arguments run into each other and are not distinguished or developed, but their significance should not be underestimated. In an investigation that was ruled by authority, every scholastic found here, ready at hand, in the canon law itself, a supply of arguments showing the unnaturalness of usury. This text also establishes officially that rents for profit are in a fundamentally different moral category from loans for profit.

2. *The Roman-Law Concept of the* Mutuum

Outside the official canons and compilations, the commentators upon them were beginning a rational explanation of the usury law. Since the beginning of the twelfth century, the study of Roman law had been pursued at Bologna; and although the civilians made no real exploration of the usury question up to the fourteenth century,[4] the Bolognese school of canonists began to correlate Roman law and the usury problem. Paucapalea, commenting on Gratian's section on usury in about 1165, paraphrased the *Digest's* definition of a loan:

A loan [mutuum] is so-called from this, that mine [meum] becomes yours [tuum]. That is a loan which, consisting in a quantity, is offered by me, while from you I shall receive back only as much of the same kind.[5]

Thus for the first time, there is introduced a technical legal definition of the contract in which usury occurs, and an important etymological pun is mentioned. Paucapalea, however, made no deductions from the concept.

[2] Gratian, *Decretum Gratiani*, D.88, c.11, from *unde super*.

[3] Whether the doctrine that money is sterile, which is asserted here, is to be ascribed to Aristotelian influences, or whether it is independently developed by the anonymous author is a moot question. If Aristotle is considered as the ultimate source, his influence on scholastic thought must be admitted to be considerable, but it is entirely indirect and impersonal. Cf. Schaub, *Der Kampf gegen den Zinswucher*, p. 176.

[4] Terence McLaughlin, "The Canonist Teaching on Usury," *Medieval Studies*, I (1939), 88.

[5] Paucapalea, *Summa*, ed. J. F. von Schulte (Giessen, 1891), C.14, Q.3; cf. *Digesta*, 44:7, f.1, n.2, 4; *Institutiones*, 3:14.

Deductions were drawn by Simon of Bismiano in 1179 [6] and repeated more amply in 1187 by Huguccio, the greatest commentator of the early Bolognese school. The Roman law had known two parallel gratuitous contracts and two parallel onerous contracts: the *commodatum* by which a good was freely transferred as to its use, and the *mutuum* by which a good was freely and temporarily transferred as to its ownership; the *locatio*, in which the *commodatum* was replaced by a charge for the use, and the *foenus*, in which by an added, positive stipulation a premium was charged for the loan.[7] Huguccio's chief point is that to charge for a *commodatum* merely changes the nature of the contract, but does not render it unjust. But to charge for a *mutuum* is usury and wrong. His reasoning is that in a *locatio*, the lessor retains ownership and so charges for the use of his own good; but in a *mutuum*, ownership is transferred, and the lender charges for the use of a good which he no longer possesses. In the loan, mine has become yours, and all I may expect back is what I gave. The Roman-law concession that a positive agreement to pay interest may be added to the loan contract is rejected.[8] Thus, while its definition of *mutuum* forms the basis of the argument, the Roman law is employed selectively: only those of its concepts which support the usury prohibition are used.

Two other basic elements of the Roman *mutuum* are brought forward in the *Glossa ordinaria* upon Gratian. The Roman law said that the matter of loans was goods consisting in number, weight, or measure, that is, goods which were fungibles; since

by giving them we contract a credit; for they can be repaid by being returned in their species rather than individually; and in other goods we cannot contract a credit, because one of these cannot be repaid for another, if the creditor is unwilling.[9]

The law also declared that the peril of the loaned good stood to the borrower, and that he remained obliged to return a similar good, though the loaned object perished by fire or shipwreck.[10] The *Gloss*, which of course is of great importance as the standard commentary upon Gratian, follows the Roman law literally. In the transfer of a fungible good, it says, ownership is transferred and a loan contracted upon which it is illicit to profit; whereas in the temporary transfer of a horse or house, ownership is retained and profit is licit. The reason suggested by the *Gloss* for this moral distinction is that

[6] Schaub, p. 176.
[7] *Codex*, 4:32:3; *Digesta*, 50:16:121; *Institutiones*, 3:14:2.
[8] Huguccio, *Summa*, C.14, Q.3, ante c.1, cited in McLaughlin, p. 101.
[9] *Digesta*, 12:1:2:1.
[10] *Digesta*, 44:7:1:4.

in the loan, the peril of the good is borne by the borrower, "whence it is un-fitting that by the title of that good he should be more oppressed"; whereas the horse or house stand at the peril of the lessor, and so he may charge for them. The notion of risk becomes even more important as a criterion, when the *Gloss* adds that one may licitly "sell the use of money" if he re-tains the peril of the money sold.[11] Although the expression "sell the use of money" will be considered unfortunate in later times, the actual permission granted here will be reaffirmed by every scholastic writer who speaks of money rented *ad pompam*. In such a contract, also derived from the Roman law,[12] money was transferred to a bailee for the specific purpose of display so that he might impress others with his wealth. The money was not consumed, but used, and the charge was for its use. The *Gloss's* treatment here seems to assume that the fundamental distinction between this contract and a loan is the incidence of risk.[13]

3. Pioneer Theologians

Robert of Courçon (d. 1219)

Among the first medieval theologians, as distinct from canonists, to under-take a natural-law discussion of usury is Robert of Courçon, canon of Noyon at Paris in 1195, cardinal and papal legate at the Council of Paris in 1213, director of the Crusade against the Albigensians in 1214, and author of the first constitution of the University of Paris in 1215 — an active, able, and presumably well-informed churchman.[14]

In his *Penitential*, designed for the use of confessors and written about 1202, Courçon discusses usury at length. He finds it universally infecting society, protected and indulged in by princes and ecclesiastics alike, and condemns it for reasons we have seen before. A man "led by cupidity" ob-jects that, since profit is allowed on leases, "why similarly can I not grant my money so that I receive some remuneration, since my money is equally necessary to me as my horse or house?" Courçon answers chiefly with the citation of the Gospel prohibition, but he continues,

and we distinguish between a lease and a loan, because a rented thing does not pass into the ownership of the one receiving it, but remains the thing of him who rents. It is necessary that the whole peril of the thing remain with the lessor, because his thing remains whole. . . . But it is not so in a loan. For a loan is so named because mine becomes yours, or conversely. . . . . It is an inequity, if you,

---

[11] *Glossa ordinaria*, C.14, Q.3, c.1, at *Plus quam*.

[12] *Digesta*, 13:6, f.3, n.6, and f.4.

[13] *Glossa ordinaria*, II:14:3:2.

[14] G. Lefèvre, *Le traité "De usura" de Robert de Courçon*, p. xv.

for a thing which is mine, receive something, because nothing is due you from my thing.[15]

Here the Roman-law arguments on the passage of ownership and peril are decisive, while the reference to a rented good remaining whole hints at an argument which St. Thomas will develop most powerfully.

William of Auxerre (1160–1229)

A theologian of whom little is known except that he was deacon of Beauvais, William of Auxerre wrote between 1210 and 1220 a commentary upon the *Sentences* of Peter Lombard that was to be of considerable popularity throughout the thirteenth century and was known affectionately as a *Summa aurea*.[16] Probably no scholastic writer on usury before St. Thomas is as influential as he is. Usury, William says, is "the will of acquiring something through a loan beyond the principal." Why, he asks, does the Church proceed against it more implacably than against other vices? His first answer, not very clear, states that it is because usury hurts piety, which assimilates one to God. His second answer is that it is because usury is *in se* and *secundum se* a sin, yet men pursue this intrinsically vicious traffic "as if it were a business and a way of living." Hence, there is a particular need to repress such a monstrous vice which is practiced constantly and without cessation. That usury is a sin both in itself and according to its nature is developed by a comparison of the taking of usury to killing. Killing may sometimes be licit, if done under proper authority, because it is sinful only *in se*. Usury can never be licit. Even God cannot order an act which is sinful *secundum se*; for this would be to violate the natural law.[17] William's teaching on the innate, invariable sinfulness of usury becomes common among the theologians. Even more importantly, his argument here is the first influential and direct declaration that usury is against the natural law.

William also states that usury is against justice, because it is against the precept of helping one's neighbor in necessity — an answer seemingly confusing the precepts of justice and charity. With a somewhat similar confusion, he says usury is against the natural law because it is against the precept "Whatever you wish men to do to you, do you to them." But in answering objections, he returns to the Roman-law argument which tries to show the strict injustice of usury. The objection is made that as one can rent horses, houses, vases "for profit," then "much more is it licit to give money

[15] Robert of Courçon, *De usura*, p. 15.
[16] *Dictionnaire de théologie catholique*, ed. E. Amann (Paris, 1930–), VI, col. 1976 (hereafter cited as *D.t.c.*).

[17] William of Auxerre, *Summa aurea*, III:21, Q.1, f.223v:a–b. *See supra*, p. 19, on the non-dispensability of usury.

at usury because it is more useful." William replies that money may be rented as a house is rented, for "it is just," where ownership is not transferred, that the owner profit from his own thing. But "in a loan ownership is transferred; for a *mutuum* is *quasi de meo tuum*." [18] The objection is then made that a borrower is happy to find a usurer who charges "very light usury," and that he gladly pays this small sum; therefore, such usury cannot be theft. William answers that the borrower is conditionally willing to pay this sum in preference to paying a larger sum; but that, absolutely speaking, he is unwilling to pay any sum for a loan. Consequently, his money is taken from him against his absolute will. This distinction between conditional and absolute will in the payment of usury becomes standard among the theologians.[19]

Auxerre also points out that the precise words used do not affect the moral character of the contract. If a man says he sells or rents money, but in fact transfers ownership, he contracts a loan, in which usury may occur. Again, he declares:

> This argument does not hold, "Where there is no loan, there is no usury"; . . . for others are indirectly usurers, to wit, those who in fraud of the precept change the contract and intend to acquire the same thing which they would acquire through a loan.[20]

In discussing the usuriousness of higher prices in credit sales, he develops an argument stated but undeveloped by earlier writers. "It is proper to the usurers," he says, "to sell time." The reason that he finds it necessary to use this argument in the special case of credit sales is clear: the form of these transactions does not give any place for the standard argument based on the Roman-law concept of the *mutuum*. A new argument has to be constructed to defend the usury prohibition rationally in this application; and the objection to the selling of time is produced. William amplifies it as follows, again emphasizing the natural law:

> He [the usurer] also acts against the universal natural law, because he sells time, which is common to all creatures. Augustine says . . . each creature is compelled to give himself; the sun is compelled to give itself to illuminate; similarly the earth is compelled to give whatever it can, and similarly the water. Nothing, however, so *naturally* gives itself as time: willy-nilly things have time. Because, therefore, the usurer sells what necessarily belongs to all creatures gen-

[18] *Ibid.*, III:21, Q.1, f.223v:b.
[19] See St. Thomas Aquinas, *Quaestiones disputatae de malo*, Q.13, art. 4 ad 8, in *Opera*, Vol. XIII (hereafter cited as *De malo*);

St. Bonaventure, *In IV libros sententiarum*, III:37:7 ad 2; Henry of Hesse, *De contractibus*, I:23, f.196.
[20] William of Auxerre, III:21, f.225v:a.

erally he injures all creatures, even the stones; whence if men were silent against the usurers, the stones would cry out, if they could; and this is one reason why the Church so pursues the usurers. Whence especially against them God says, "When I shall take up the time, that is, when time will be so in My hand that a usurer cannot sell it, then I will judge justly." [21]

Although few authors will so stress the metaphysical tendency of all creatures to give of their being, the argument based on the sale of time will henceforth be the standard objection to higher prices for credit sales.

William of Auxerre, then, makes five major contributions to the discussion of usury: he declares that usury is against the natural law; teaches that it is intrinsically evil; makes an important distinction between the absolute and conditional voluntariness of the debtor; gives a general rule for detecting frauds on the usury laws; and produces a new argument on the sinfulness of selling time. Each proposition will become incorporated in the general medieval teaching on usury.

4. The Theologians of the New Orders

As the thirteenth century develops, the intellectual life of the Church develops too, fostered particularly by the intensive study of theology encouraged by the two great new orders, the Dominicans and the Franciscans. The new ferment in theology, however, at first adds surprisingly little to the analysis of usury; and, except for the advent of Aristotle on the scholastic scene, the arguments concerning usury are stale repetitions. Yet that threadbare arguments found acceptance has significance; the effect of Aristotle is important; and the distinguished theologians of the new orders, as will be seen in later chapters, have views on other aspects of the theory of credit which are influential.

St. Raymond of Pennaforte (1180–1278)

Closely associated with the administration of the Church, St. Raymond was the secretary of Gregory IX from 1230 to 1237 and was then elected general of the Dominican order. At Gregory's direction he made the monumental compilation of the decretals, which, with Gratian, formed the basis of the canon law.[22] Thus he acquired his chief fame as a canonist, and he is the patron saint of canonists. His principal original work, however, the *Summa casuum conscientiae*, written about 1236, is intended as a theological

[21] *Ibid.*, III:21, f.225v:a.
[22] Johann Frederich von Schulte, *Die Geschichte der Quellen und Literatur des canonischen Rechts* (Stuttgart, 1875–1880), II, 408.

guide for confessors. St. Raymond's position at the center of the Church at a time when the usury rule was facing a developing Italian commerce makes him an authority from whom much might be expected. But his contribution to the argumentation against usury is disappointing. He makes no attempt to demonstrate its wrongness on natural-law grounds; at best one can infer his thoughts from his citation of *Ejiciens* as offering the controlling distinctions between a loan and a lease.[23]

Alexander of Hales (1168–1245)

One of the few English writers on usury, Alexander of Hales came from Gloucester, studied and taught theology at Paris, and, already a celebrated professor, entered the Franciscan order in 1231.[24] His great work, the *Summa theologica*, has nothing original to say on the nature of usury. Alexander is heavily influenced by William of Auxerre, and most of what he does not take from him he takes from a less well-known brother of his order, John of Rupella.[25] He relies principally on the argument based on the Roman-law concept of the *mutuum* and the lender's transfer of ownership and risk, stating that it is "against the natural law" to take a benefit from what is not one's own, and he cites the other arguments of *Ejiciens*.[26]

St. Albert the Great (1206–1280)

The great Dominican teacher of Cologne and Paris, master of St. Thomas Aquinas, preacher of the Crusade in Germany, lecturer at the papal court, Bishop of Ratisbon, St. Albert was among the most influential authorities on philosophy and science throughout the Middle Ages.[27] He is particularly distinguished for laying the foundations for a revival of Aristotelianism and in being the first scholastic theologian to work to make Aristotle's teachings generally known; his introduction of Aristotelianism into the argumentation against usury is his chief distinction in the history of usury theory.

St. Albert makes a case of his own against usury, which we should consider, in *In Lucam* and in his *Commentarius super libros sententiarum*. In commenting on Luke 6:35, he teaches that usury is a sin of avarice, against charity, because the usurer without labor, suffering, or fear gathers riches to himself from the labor, suffering, and vicissitudes of his neighbor. Here both the acquisition of riskless profit and the exploitation of a neighbor's

---

[23] St. Raymond, *Summa casuum conscientiae*, 2:7:5.

[24] *D.t.c.*, I, cols. 773–775.

[25] See Alexander of Hales, *Summa theologica*, III:2:3:2:1:2:7. The editors have in-

dicated what is taken from William and what from John of Rupella.

[26] *Ibid.*, c.4, art. 2c and ad 6 and 8.

[27] *D.t.c.*, I, cols. 666–670. All of Albert's works are written before 1259.

need seem to offer grounds for condemnation. It is worth noting, though, that St. Albert supposes the money loaned to such a needy neighbor will not be consumed by him, but "converted to licit profit through business." His objection is that the neighbor will have to work for his profit and may not make it, while the usurer is theoretically certain of his.[28] In commenting upon the *Sentences*, St. Albert gives the traditional opinion that usury is against justice, because ownership passes in the *mutuum*. A lease, which is "a certain sale of a utility for a time," is distinct from a loan in that the same object must be restored. But the argument of *Ejiciens*, that a lease or bailment is distinguished by its object deteriorating in use, is criticized: St. Albert sensibly objects that this distinction is not found in all leases or bailments, for example, in a bailment of money *ad pompam*.[29] This slight correction of *Ejiciens* is his one personal contribution to usury theory.

Much more important is the fact that through St. Albert's commentaries on the *Ethics* and the *Politics*, Aristotle first formally enters scholastic thought on usury. It is difficult to know how completely the saint agrees with the Aristotelian doctrines, since he warns against accepting the views set out in the commentary, which aims merely to elucidate Aristotle, as his own.[30] In any event, Aristotle's ideas now beat upon the intellectual world, and their significance for scholastic thought must be appreciated.

In the *Ethics*, Aristotle explains that money has been instituted as the measure by which the values of diverse real goods may be equated with each other. Money is also, he says, a "guarantor of future necessities," but he does not emphasize this function. Further, he teaches, money is instituted by positive law. It has no natural value, but its value is what it is legally determined to be. Nothing is said on usury.[31]

In the *Politics*, Aristotle discusses two kinds of wealth-getting: "the economic" and "the acquisitive." "The economic is part of the management of a household." It is the obtaining of the natural goods necessary to live well and has a natural limit in the natural needs of man. Natural needs led to natural barter and then to the introduction by law of money as the measure of such exchanges. But once money had been introduced, "the other art of wealth-getting, retail trade, arose." Exchanges are now made not to satisfy simple natural needs, but to make money. There is no natural limit to the desire for money, but as man's desires are unlimited, so he seeks infinite

[28] St. Albert, *In evangelium Lucae*, 6:35, in *Opera*, Vol. XXII.

[29] St. Albert, *Commentarius in IV libros sententiarum*, Bk. III, D.37, art. 13 ad 9, in *Opera*, Vol. XXVIII.

[30] G. Meersseman, *Introductio in Opera omnia B. Alberti Magni* (Bruges, 1931), pp. 72-73. Albert's commentary merely restates the Aristotelian observations.

[31] Aristotle, *Ethica Nicomachea*, 1133a.

wealth. Accumulation of money becomes his end, and he unnaturally subordinates other faculties and arts to the attainment of wealth. Even in itself
retail trade for money is unnatural; for its end, the acquirement of money,
is unnatural; and moreover, in it men seek to gain at the expense of each
other. But of all kinds of trade, the most unnatural and most justly hated
is usury. Usury not only seeks an unnatural end, but misuses money itself;
"for money was intended to be used in exchange, not to increase at usury."
Usury is the unnatural breeding of money from money [32] Aristotle's objections to usury are thus finalistic, based on the alleged purpose of money
and more broadly on the alleged purpose of retail trade. It is clear that the
objection to usury is only a particular objection based on a larger opposition
to all pecuniary gain from commercial transactions.

By a happy, or unhappy, fault, however, William of Moerbeke in the
translation of the *Politics* available to St. Albert and St. Thomas, rendered
καπηλικῆς the term for retail trade, as "campsoria," a term with the specific
meaning of money-changing.[33] Thus instead of being presented with a condemnation of all retail trade, which medieval Christian theologians would
not have accepted, the early scholastics found in Aristotle only a condemnation of traffic in money; and themselves already suspicious of the *campsores*,
they found this highly natural. Aristotle's case against usury, which rests
largely on his case against all trade, is accepted by St. Albert and St. Thomas
as simply a case against those who make money from money, a specialized
and suspect group.

St. Bonaventure (1221–1274)

Yet another authority on usury, apparently qualified both by theological
preëminence and administrative experience, is St. Bonaventure.[34] He had
been the pupil of Alexander of Hales at Paris and the contemporary and
friend of St. Thomas Aquinas when he taught theology at Paris from 1237
to 1257. He was general of the Franciscan order for over twenty-five years,
the advisor of several popes, and a cardinal in 1273. He treats of usury in
his commentary on the *Sentences*, his commentary on Luke, and his commentary on the precepts of the New Law.

St. Bonaventure says that some believe that usury is evil because prohibited,
whereas in fact it is prohibited because evil. In one breathless statement he

---

[32] Aristotle, *Politica*, 1256b–1258b, trans. B. Jowett, in *Works*, Vol. X.

[33] See Aristotle, *Liber I Politicorum*, c.7, trans. William of Moerbeke, in St. Albert,

Opera, Vol. VIII. Compare Jowett's translation, *Politica*, 1257b.

[34] *D.t.c.*, II, 964–965.

then runs together the three arguments that in a loan mine became yours; that the borrower's industry is his own; and that time cannot be sold. Usury is accordingly a "perversion of order." He adds that money does not deteriorate in use.[35] Elsewhere, he gives a paraphrase of *Ejiciens*. He also says the usurer sells what he is held to do by a divine precept, to wit, the helping of his needy neighbor. That the neighbor makes a profit with the use of the loaned money he considers immaterial to the justice of the contract.[36]

Like the other theologians of the new orders, St. Bonaventure clearly has added nothing new to the discussion of usury. The introduction of Aristotle is the one substantial addition made to the usury theory by this company of distinguished authors. The Roman-law argument remains dominant.

5. *Two Classical Canonists*

The distinction between a scholastic canonist and a scholastic theologian may seem trifling. Each was a servant of the Church; each was guided by the teaching of the Gospel, the natural law, and the canons. Yet the observer will note differences in their approach to usury that seem best accounted for in terms of their different roles. The canonists were concerned mainly with solutions valid for the external forum of the Church; they were concentrating on the administration of the law. The theologians were focusing mainly on the confessional. Moreover, the canonists, fitting their commentaries to specific canons, made no comprehensive effort to reconcile the canons or to produce a synthesis. The theologians are at once more systematic, more logical, and often more severe.

At the very time that the theologians were repeating the old arguments to prove the injustice of usury, while Aristotle offered new support to their proofs, two eminent canonists, whose opinions were to carry much weight in canon law, attempted a revolutionary departure from the tradition of the past two hundred years. These canonists were Pope Innocent IV and his friend, Cardinal Hostiensis.

Sinibaldus Fliscus was a native of the great port of Genoa. A student of both the canon and the civil laws, he was made cardinal in 1227 and was elected pope as Innocent IV in 1243. His *Apparatus super libros decretalium* was completed only after his election to the papacy, but was intended to be simply the commentary of a private doctor.[37] A famous statesman, Pope Innocent seems admirably suited to discuss usury through his administrative

---

[35] St. Bonaventure, *De decem praeceptis collatio*, 6:19, in *Opera omnia*, Vol. V.

[36] St. Bonaventure, *In IV libros sententiarum*, III:37:7 ad 3; obj. 3 and ad 3.

[37] Schulte, II, 91.

and judicial experience. His qualifications are equalled by Henry of Susa, Cardinal Hostiensis. Hostiensis had taken his doctorate in Roman law at Bologna and studied canon law at Paris. He visited England and in 1244 was sent back as ambassador from Henry III of England to Pope Innocent IV. In the same year he was made a bishop. In 1261 he became a cardinal and archbishop of Ostia. His *Summa* was written between 1250 and 1261, and he worked on his *Commentaria super libros decretalium* until his death in 1270. He is falsely accused by Matthew of Paris of embezzling money from Henry III; the accusation at least testifies to his reputation for financial acumen.[38] He was an exceptionally well-traveled and well-educated prelate, and his and Innocent's opinions on usury reflect an understanding of the issues much more acute than that of the famous theologians of the new orders.

Innocent offers no comment on the old arguments, but ignoring them completely in his formal proof of the wrongness of usury, develops entirely new arguments of his own that show usury to be a social evil, but in no way suggest its injustice. He says frankly that usury is prohibited because of the evil consequences that follow from its practice. If usury were permitted, all rich persons would rather put their money safely in a usurious loan than invest in agriculture. Only the poor would be left to do the farming and then they would not possess the animals and tools with which to farm. Famine would result.[39] Innocent's argument, it might be added, may seem naïve or exaggerated at first, but the experiences of agricultural communities, such as ancient Greece or China throughout most of its history, offer considerable corroboration.[40]

Two lesser arguments are also given. Usury results in poverty for the debtor, if it is taken over a long period, and poverty is dangerous to the soul. Also the taking of usury stimulates a spirit of avarice, for, Innocent quotes, "where your treasure is there will be your heart also." None of the arguments seem to prove that usury is always and inherently a sin, and Innocent even says there perhaps could be found a case in which the

---

[38] Schulte, II, 124–125. As far as the financial accusation against Hostiensis is concerned, Matthew of Paris took a jaundiced view of the papal court, and his accusations are not proof by themselves. Moreover, Henry III employed Hostiensis in an honorable capacity after the date of the alleged embezzlement.

[39] Innocent IV, *Apparatus*, V, *De usura*, ante c.1.

[40] Pirenne remarks, "The scourge of debts which in Greek and Roman antiquity so sorely afflicted the people was spared the social order of the Middle Ages, and it may be that the Church contributed to that happy result" (*Medieval Cities*, p. 126). On the extremely high interest rates that have existed in China, see Lien-sheng Yang, *Money and Credit in China* (Cambridge, Mass., 1952), pp. 93–98. Yang remarks that there has been a vicious circle of high rates of interest and small accumulations of liquid capital (p. 9).

natural law would not prohibit usury; yet, unwilling to relax the universal force of the law, he adds that the general danger of the evils that would usually follow would bar the admission of the exceptional case. Moreover, he declares that some say, "and perhaps not badly," that usury is in every case prohibited "by natural instinct," because usury is always against the charity by which we are bound to help our neighbors.[41]

Elsewhere, and as incidental observations, Innocent mentions that money bears no fruit and that the usurer sells time which is common to all.[42] But he does not use these old arguments as part of his formal case against usury, and it is difficult to believe that he attaches great weight to them. His main effort has been to show the uncharitableness, not the injustice of usury; not once does he even say that usury is unjust. His whole attitude is a startling departure from the tradition of the hundred years behind him.

The influence of Innocent on the interesting evolution of Hostiensis is clear. In his *Summa*, Hostiensis' chief reason against usury is the old one that ownership of a loan has passed to the debtor. He adds to this, however, a new argument, that "there is no use of a loaned good without its consumption."[43] But he does not develop this thought, and its decisive presentation must await St. Thomas Aquinas. At the same time, he boldly attacks an argument which ever since Huguccio had been a favorite of the commentators, namely, that a lease was licit and a loan illicit, because in one the peril was borne by the owner, in the other by the borrower. Risk, he asserts, is not a factor. His reason is that by the criterion of risk the *foenus nauticum* condemned by the decretal *Naviganti* would be licit. We shall discuss this case in detail later.[44] Here it is sufficient to note that Hostiensis has strong grounds for his interpretation and on these grounds strikes vigorously at an essential argument of the early tradition.

By the time of the *Commentaria super libros decretalium*, Hostiensis has been completely converted to the arguments of Innocent. He mentions some of his own old reasons, but goes on to cite the Pope verbatim,[45] and in so doing seems implicitly to agree that usury is a sin of uncharitableness or avarice, or is a social evil, but is not against justice. This mature abandonment of the old grounds is especially significant. When two such highly placed authorities as the Pope and this favored cardinal tacitly abandon the contention that usury was against natural justice, one is certainly tempted to

---

[41] Innocent IV, *Apparatus*, V, *De usura*, n.1. ante c. 1.

[42] *Apparatus*, V:39:48; V:19:6.

[43] Hostiensis, *Summa aurea*, V, *De usuris*,

[44] See *infra*, pp. 137–138.

[45] Hostiensis, *Commentaria super quinque libros decretalium* (Venice, 1581), V:19:2ff.

speculate that the Roman *curia* and its canonists might have considered a general revision of the usury theory. But if this were contemplated, no more was heard of it, and while the canonists hesitated, the theologians continued to maintain steadfastly that usury was *in se* and *secundum se* a sin.

ST. THOMAS AQUINAS (1225?–1274): THE CONTROLLING FORMULATIONS

The life of the greatest scholastic theologian may be summed up in a line; he was a Dominican, a teacher at the University of Paris and various Italian universities, and a saint.[46] A strong influence on his contemporaries, consulted during his lifetime by popes and kings, St. Thomas Aquinas was to be an even stronger influence on the intellectual life of medieval Europe after his death. As far as his work on usury in particular is concerned, he wrote no general treatise, nor did he ever analyze the contracts, other than a loan, in which usury might occur. Nevertheless, treatments of usury are scattered throughout his works, and a subject of such interest in the Italy and France of his day could not help but draw his perspicacious attention. His acceptance and development of certain arguments on usury had a decisive influence on subsequent scholastic theory, and at the very moment that Cardinal Hostiensis and Pope Innocent wavered, he established the theory on formidable ground. Partly because of his general theological preeminence, partly because of the intrinsic weight of his arguments, St. Thomas holds a special place in the development of usury theory; and the importance of his opinions cannot easily be exaggerated.[47]

1. *Commentary on the* Sentences [48]

St. Thomas Aquinas first had occasion to treat of usury as a youthful commentator upon the *Sentences* of Peter Lombard. Here as his first and principal argument, he reproduces the hoary Roman-law point that in a *mutuum* ownership is transferred.[49] But already he is seeking in the natural

---

[46] *D.s.c.*, XIII, col. 254.

[47] Endemann (*Studien in der romanisch-kanonistischen Wirthschafts*, I, 17) well remarks that St. Thomas is the dominating figure in the scholastic treatment of usury.

[48] I follow here the chronology of St. Thomas' writings given by Grabmann, who places his works touching on usury in the following order: *Commentum in quatuor libros sententiarum*, 1254–1256; *De regimine Judaeorum*, 1261; *De emptione et venditione*, 1262–

1263; *In X libros ethicorum*, 1266–1269; *In III primos libros politicorum*, 1266–1268; *Summa theologica*, II–II, 1268–1272; *Quaestiones disputatae de malo*, 1268–1269; *In Psalmos Davidis*, 1270–1272; *III Quodlibetales*, 1270. Martin Grabmann, *Die Werke des Hl. Thomas v. Aquin, Beitrage zur Geschichte der Philosophie des Mittelalters*, Band 22, Heft 1–2 (1931), pp. 241–361.

[49] *In IV lib. sent.*, III:37:1:6.

law for other grounds against usury. Thus he introduces a second argument, which he takes from Aristotle:

> All other things from themselves have some utility; not so, however, money. But it is the measure of utility of other things, as is clear according to the Philosopher in the *Ethics* V:9. And therefore the use of money does not have the measure of its utility from this money itself, but from the things which are measured by money according to the different persons who exchange money for goods. Whence to receive more money for less seems nothing other than to diversify the measure in giving and receiving, which manifestly contains iniquity.[50]

There are two highly interesting divergences from Aristotle here. One is this: while the Philosopher's text cited by St. Thomas declares that the value of money is determined by the goods for which it is exchanged, St. Thomas ignores this and fastens upon the statement that money is a measure. This will be for St. Thomas the essential definition of money; and as it is his custom to treat the essences of things, he will always consider money, formally, as a measure. Two consequences are thereby implied. One is that the goods for which money is exchanged are not considered in his analysis of money itself. In particular, changes in the supply of natural goods affecting the purchasing power of money are not considered; for such changes in relation to money are *per accidens*. They arise fortuitously and do not concern the formal character of the measure itself. The second consequence is that money, thus formally considered, is conceived as having one constant, fixed value — its legal face value. Like other measures, money is considered independently from the things it measures, and as fixed and stable in its measurement. Because it is formally a stable measure, money cannot be sold. This consequence leads to the second striking divergence from Aristotle. Aristotle had objected to usury because it was a distortion of the purpose of money; his objection was based on the contention that money had a fixed natural end. St. Thomas is entirely original in basing his objection, not on the final cause, but on the formal nature of money. If money is a measure, with a fixed value, deliberately to value it differently at different times is to distort unnaturally its formal character. The purchasing power of money may change due to fortuitous causes, such as the increase in natural goods, and since this is not due to the holder of money, there is no moral fault. But the holder of money who himself sets out to produce variations in the value of money is guilty of diversifying the measure. This argument is St. Thomas' own, not Aristotle's.

[50] *In IV lib. sent.*, III:37:1:6.

The concept of money set forth here is central to later usury theory. Money is formally nonvendible. Every later scholastic will use some form of this axiom.[51] Money is a mean between the two terms of a sale; but it can never itself be the term of a sale. To sell money would be to give simultaneously two different evaluations to the same measure. It was indispensable to the usury prohibition that the legal sameness of money at any time be taken to mean formally that its value was the same at any time. Moreover, the thesis that only the formal character of money should be considered in determining the justice of a contract involving money was the necessary assumption for what St. Thomas and the schools in general were to make the principal argument against usury.

2. *Commentaries on Aristotle*

In his commentaries on Aristotle proper, St. Thomas offers little that is original. In the *Ethics*, he repeats the analysis of money as a measure, and following Aristotle, emphasizes its positive legal character.[52] His commentary on the *Politics* is a strictly literal one, differing only slightly from that of St. Albert. He follows the same error in translation, which confuses trade with money-exchange, and here he repeats verbatim Aristotle's finalistic objection to the use of money for purposes other than exchange.[53] This argument apparently pleases him personally, for he uses it again in an answer to an objection in the *Summa theologica*.[54]

3. *The Major Argument*

St. Thomas' chief argument against usury, however, has not yet been given. This is the argument on which he principally rests his case in the *Summa theologica*, in *De malo*, in *III Quodlibetales*, in *In Psalmos Davidis* — in short, in all his later work.[55] The argument, substantially his own, runs as follows:

In those things whose use is their consumption, the use is not other than the thing itself; whence to whomever is conceded the use of such things, is conceded the ownership of those things, and conversely. When therefore, someone

[51] E.g., Giles of Lessines, *De usuris*, c.13; Ptolemy of Lucca, *De regimine pr ncipis*, c.14, in St. Thomas Aquinas, *Opera*, Vol. XXVII; Laurentius de Ridolfis, *De usuris*, 2:53; St. Bernardine, 34:2:3; St. Antoninus, *Summa*, 2:1:7.

[52] *In X lib. ethic.*, Bk. V, Lect. 9.

[53] *In III primos libros politicorum*, Bk. I:6,7,8, in *Opera*, Vol. XXVI.

[54] *S.T.*, II–II:78, 1 ad 3. In the *Summa theologica*, St. Thomas corrects Moerbeke's error and notes that Aristotle treats of "tradesmen" in general (II–II:77:4c). But he does not extend the revision of Aristotle introduced here to cover moneylenders.

[55] *S.T.*, II–II:78:1c; *In Psalmos Davidis*, 14:5, in *Opera*, Vol. XVIII; *III Quodlibetales*, Q.3, art. 19, in *Opera*, Vol. XV.

lends money under this agreement that the money be integrally restored to him, and further for the use of the money wishes to have a definite price, it is manifest that he sells separately the use of the money and the very substance of money. The use of money, however, as it is said, is not other than its substance: whence either he sells that which is not, or he sells the same thing twice, to wit, the money itself, whose use is its consumption; and this is manifestly against the nature of natural justice.[56]

The basic concept on which this reasoning turns is that of a good "consumptible in use." A concept implied by *Ejiciens*, touched on by Hostiensis, and mentioned in the *Speculum conscientiae*,[57] it is elaborated and applied here for the first time with force and clarity. In part, to be sure, St. Thomas owes the argument to the sources just mentioned. More important, however, is his debt to Roman law. It is Roman law that most clearly sets forth the conception of goods consumptible in use, in treating of bequests of money and goods such as wine, oil, and grain. Such goods, the *Institutes* and the *Digest* declare, have no natural usufruct; their value consists in their consumption; and the State by positive authority alone determines that a usufruct be calculated on them when they are bequeathed.[58] The notions that money does not naturally bear fruit and that its value is its use, are thus firmly implanted in the Roman law; St. Thomas can refer directly to the *Institutes* in answering objections to his argument.[59] At the same time, the Roman law is used selectively by him, only to establish the agreement on the natural estimation of consumptibles. St. Thomas does not follow it in admitting the right of a positive law or a positive contract to add a quasi-usufruct which would not naturally exist. He is thus entirely original in his use of the Roman law to show the injustice of usury.

Moreover, though the predominantly legal background of the concept is clear, it is important to remark that the concept is not purely a legal one.

[56] *De malo*, Q.13, art. 4c.

[57] The *Speculum conscientiae* is published among St. Bonaventure's works, but it is probably not written by him, so that its date in relation to St. Thomas' work cannot be established. On the topic of consumptible goods, it runs as follows: "There are certain goods, whose use is their consumption, and whose ownership is transferred to the one receiving them; for example, money, grain, and wine, whence who sells the use of such things is called a usurer, and it has the character of mortal sin, insofar as it is against a mortal precept of justice, because he sells to another what is not his own, since ownership has now passed" (*Speculum conscientiae*, c.2:14, in

St. Bonaventure, *Opera*, VIII).

[58] In the *Institutes* the Senate declares it cannot constitute a natural usufruct on goods "which are consumed by their very use," such as wine, oil, grain, and clothing, "quibus proxima est pecunia numerata; numque in ipso usu adsidua permutatione quodammodo extinguitur." But the Senate adds a civil usufruct to such goods in legacies (*Institutiones*, 2:4:2). In the *Digest* there is a title, "De Usu Fructu Earum Rerum Quas Usu Consummuntur vel Minuentur," where it is said that money has no natural fruit and where money's use is said to be in its consumption. See *Digesta*, 7:5:2,5,6,7, and 10.

[59] *S.T.*, II–II:78:1 ad 3.

The old argument, based simply on the *mutuum*, which St. Thomas employed in his youth but now discards, rests on the technical fact that ownership is legally transferred in a loan; beyond citing this fact it makes no attempt to show why the use and ownership of the loaned good cannot both be charged for. It may have implied or intended to say what St. Thomas says, but it stops short at a citation of the law on loans. It remains a juristic quibble. The present argument appeals beyond the law to nature, and shows that the law is simply a formulation of the nature of things. Some goods, St. Thomas points out, are naturally destroyed in their use; their use and value are thus essentially identical with their substance. Other goods, such as a house, a horse, a book, a garment, are not essentially consumed by their use.[60] A house may deteriorate through use, St. Thomas admits, but this is strictly *per accidens*. "It is not from the nature of inhabitation that a house is destroyed." [61] On the other hand, it is essential to wine-drinking that the wine drunk be destroyed. Thus, St. Thomas reverses the old argument of *Ejiciens* that no price might be charged for money, because it did not deteriorate in use, while a price might be charged for the rent of a house, because it did. On the contrary, says St. Thomas, the deterioration of a house is *per accidens*, but money deteriorates so completely that it disappears altogether; hence its use and substance are identical, and therefore no charge for its use can be made. The old argument is paradoxically inverted. St. Thomas' case rests finally, then, on metaphysical rather than legal grounds. It is the real distinction between accidental and essential change which forms the foundation of his reasoning. It is the structure of concrete beings themselves which, prior to any legal classification, diversifies them into consumptibles and nonconsumptibles.

The character of St. Thomas' reasoning is particularly brought out by his acceptance of the lawfulness of the bailment of money at a profit for display purposes. The *Gloss* and William of Auxerre had simply noted that in this contract ownership is retained by the bailor. St. Thomas more informatively remarks that here money is not used in its primary use; that is, he implies, it is not considered a consumptible. Therefore, the value of its use may here be distinguished from the value of its substance.[62] Every other scholastic writer accepts such a bailment of money in its secondary use as licit,[63] and so establishes beyond dispute one highly important point: it is

[60] *III Quodlibetales*, 3:19.
[61] *De malo*, 13:4c.
[62] *Glossa ordinaria*, 14:3:2; William of Auxerre, III:21:1, f.223v:b; St. Thomas, *De malo*, Q.13 ad 15.

[63] Robert of Courçon, p. 15; St. Raymond, *Summa*, 2:7; Hostiensis, *Commentaria*, V:19: 16; Scotus, *In IV libros sententiarum* (*Opus Oxoniensis*), IV:15:2:26, *in Opera omnia*, XVIII; Aegidius Romanus, *Quodlibetales*

not because money is in general economically sterile, but because it is juridically sterile in a loan, that usury is opposed by the scholastics. In the bailment contract, money is absolutely dead and unproductive. If the scholastics' opposition was simply to the making of a profit from a nonfruitful good, they could far less admit the bailment of money *ad pompam* at a profit, than they could admit usury on a loan. But their opposition is only to profit on a transaction where money is formally and legally sterile, that is, where it is consumed in the sense of being alienated from its possessor by being spent. In other words, sterility is really the same as consumptibility. At times, undeniably, the Aristotelian opposition to any unfruitful good breeding a profit seems uppermost in their minds; and it would be rash to say that they did not at times think of sterility as economic, not legal. But they certainly did not maintain this position with consistency; and if we are to understand the complete and tranquil acceptance of the bailment *ad pompam*, we can only say that following St. Thomas they took sterility as the equivalent of consumptibility.

At the same time, however, that we remark the metaphysical foundation of St. Thomas' general reasoning, a doubt may occur to us about the nature of money. Is money naturally a consumptible in first use, or is such a description of it purely arbitrary and artificial? To answer the question, we must return to St. Thomas' conception of money. Money, as we have seen, is formally a measure for him; its value is to be determined by its face value as a measure. Now, as long as money is considered in a purely formal way and without reference to the goods it can buy, it is certainly a consumptible in its first use. A good is consumed, in St. Thomas' sense, if its essential form is altered. Money is, therefore, a consumptible because its substance must be changed or alienated in order to use it; and when money is alienated by the buyer, he no longer retains the same essential form, though he does have a good of equal worth. In the same way, when one uses wood for fuel its form is alienated, though one receives from its use a good of equivalent worth. Money, formally considered, is thus consumed, whether it is spent for food or factories, whether the ultimate objects purchased by it are consumption goods or production goods. St. Thomas' argument covers both so-called consumption-loans to the poor and production-loans to businessmen; for however the money is spent, it will be consumed in the Thomistic sense.[64] The appropriateness of applying the use—consumption argument

---

(Bologna, 1481), IV:24; Astesanus, *Summa Astesana*, III:11:4; St. Bernardine, 38:1:1; St. Antoninus, *Summa*, 2:1:7.

[64] Cardinal Ernest Joseph Van Roey has made an excellent modern commentary on St. Thomas' fundamental concept here, in *De*

to money rests on the assumption that the justice of pecuniary contracts should be determined by considering money formally, in its narrow legal character and as separate from the goods it buys.

4. A Peculiarity of St. Thomas' Treatments

One important general characteristic of all St. Thomas' treatments of usury is that he invariably considers money as the only subject-matter of usury. If one notes the habitual language of his contemporaries, who speak of all things "in number, weight, and measure," as the matter of loans and usury, it cannot but cause surprise when we see St. Thomas so sedulously speak only of money. In fact his natural-law arguments against usury do not cover the case of all fungible goods.

Both consumptibility in use and fungibility depend initially on human agreement. Consumptibility in use depends on agreement as to the primary purpose of a commodity; fungibility requires assent to a certain standard of quality. The usual scholastic examples of fungibility, grain and oil, are not fungible unless a certain origin and certain age are first assumed. Once agreement has been reached as to use, a consumptible in first use does become a "natural" category, if one accepts the scholastic view that accident and form may be distinguished, or even if one merely distinguishes between rates of durability. Fungibility remains much more a matter of convention than of nature. It is not simply a juristic way of saying consumptibility. The stock scholastic examples of fungibles were also consumptibles. But one can think of many goods which are as fungible as grain and which are not consumptibles in first use: paper clips are an easy example today. Even in an age of little manufacturing, there were many such examples: swatches of cloth, lead for ballast, young pigs, wool for packing. The scholastics' imagination did not extend to them; or at least the scholastics failed to consider the difficulty of applying the usury rule to loans of such nonconsumptible fungibles. May one not infer that St. Thomas, more careful than his contemporaries in distinguishing the limits of the natural law, believed that the natural law taught the sinfulness of usury only in the case of goods consumptible in use? If this is so, a large area of lending would be left outside the natural prohibition as he conceives it.

---

justo auctario ex contractu crediti (Louvain, 1903), pp. 282ff. The central character of the Thomistic conception of money in the argument against usury is well developed by Her-bert L. Johnston in his "Medieval Teachings on the Morality of Usury" (unpublished doctoral dissertation, University of Toronto, 1938), p. 99.

WINNOWING AND CONSOLIDATION FROM
ST. THOMAS TO ST. ANTONINUS

Only one important new argument is introduced in the next two hundred years of reasoning against usury. But it is necessary not only to consider this, but to show how the old arguments were used, evaluated, and criticized. What may fairly be described as the general scholastic theory of usury can only be reached inductively by considering the views of the prominent authors upon usury over this next period of scholastic thought.

1. Typical Treatments

Among the standard authorities of the later thirteenth and early four-teenth centuries, some variety of approach may be observed. At the level of popular presentation to the faithful, Stephen of Bourbon (d. 1261), one of the most energetic of Dominican preachers, left unmentioned the intri-cate Thomistic argument and concentrated on the complaint that usurers sell time. The appeal to fancy of this image must have been considerable, and it gave a preacher an opportunity to draw a severe inference as to the future fate of such sinners:

since they sell nothing but the expectation of money, which is time, they sell the day and night. But the day is the time of light and the night of rest, and so consequently they sell light and rest. Therefore, it is not right that they should have eternal light and rest.[65]

At a more learned level, the Dominicans clung to St. Thomas. The Franciscans may still have hesitated. Durandus of St. Pourçain (d. 1332), a Dominican teacher at Paris, later Master of the Sacred Palace and then Bishop of Meaux, in his commentary on the *Sentences* followed the chief Thomistic argument literally and also cited Aristotle's *Ethics and Politics* against usury.[66] Monaldus (d. 1228?), the Franciscan author of a summa influential throughout the Middle Ages, surprisingly condemned usury only on the basis of the divine law without reference to the natural law.[67]

A more extended discussion of the usury law's rationale is made by Aegi-dius Romanus (1247–1316), a theologian at Paris and later general of the Augustinians and an archbishop.[68] He adopts the strict Thomistic argu-

---

[65] Stephen of Bourbon, *La tabula exem-plorum*, ed. J. T. Welter (Paris, 1926), p. 139.

[66] Durandus of St. Pourçain, *Commen-tariorum in P. Lombardi Sententias Theo-logicas* (Venice, 1586), Bk. III, Dist. 37, Q.2.

On Durandus, see *D.t.c.*, IV, col. 1964.

[67] *D.t.c.*, X, col. 2193.

[68] Maurice De Wulf, *History of Medieval Philosophy*, trans. E. C. Messenger (New York, 1926), II, 64.

ment that the use and substance of money cannot be separated. He adds, however, that one can commit usury by "lending one's house," that is, not by leasing it but by transferring ownership of it for a certain space of time and receiving it back with a profit.[69] This sort of contract is not covered by the Thomistic argument, and consequently it is difficult to determine whether Aegidius believes that such an arrangement is only forbidden by positive law; or whether he takes the true natural-law objection to usury to lie in the lender's profit on a transfer of ownership accompanied by a transfer of risk. More important than his own arguments are his criticisms of other old arguments. He rejects the argument that time cannot be sold, by showing that you could licitly give someone ten horses with an agreement to receive twelve in a year. Such a distinction between goods which bore fruit in time and those which did not was, perhaps, not always observed by popular preachers denouncing "time-sales."

Secondly, and substantially agreeing with St. Albert, Aegidius rejects the ancient argument that money does not deteriorate in use. He points out that one can licitly rent silver for display, yet there will be no deterioration. Finally, and most importantly, he maintains that the absence of risk on a loan is not what makes a creditor's profit sinful; "for someone can licitly receive an income from something rented, even if it is insured by a guaranty."[70] Here is the first mention of insurance in direct connection with the usury theory; and at once the effects of the acceptance of this new contract upon the old doctrine are insinuated. If one recalls how often the presence of risk is taken by scholastic writers as a key to the usury theory, one will see how serious for the theory is a contract which legitimately removes risk. Aegidius barely mentions insurance, and no one really develops its implications for another century, but they are at least suggested here.

In his *De regimine principis*, Aegidius repeats the Aristotelian arguments, that it is unnatural for money to bear money, and that the use of money cannot be sold. The more general argument of Aristotle against retail trade, Aegidius, like St. Albert, takes to refer to exchange dealers alone.[71]

Aegidius' opinions probably received a wider popular circulation than the economic works of more celebrated men through the translation into the vernacular of his *De regimine principis* by Juan Garcia de Castrojeriz, who added to it his own commentary. The *Glosa Castellana*, completed in 1320, had much influence in fourteenth- and fifteenth-century Spain and offers a good example of the more popular thinking upon usury. It rests its main

[69] Aegidius Romanus, *Quodlibetales*, IV:24.
[70] *Quodlibetales*, IV:24.
[71] Aegidius Romanus, *De regimine principis*, in Juan Garcia de Castrojeriz, *Glosa*

Castellana al "Regimento de principes" de Egidio Romano (Madrid, 1947), Bk. II, Part 3, ch. 11.

case on a repetition of Aegidius' purely Aristotelian arguments and adds a poetic reason of its own against usury, considerably like William of Auxerre's, which is worth repeating:

> Usury is much to be reprehended and condemned, because it is against the natural goodness of every creature; for every creature naturally lends, as do light and fire and air and water and earth, which lend and give all their goodness to men and to all beasts and to all creatures.[72]

2. *Criticism of the Thomistic Argument*

John Duns Scotus (d. 1308), professor of theology at Oxford, Paris, and Cologne and the great Franciscan critic of St. Thomas' metaphysics,[73] will not let St. Thomas go unquestioned on the basis for the usury rule. Appropriately enough, in a rivalry sharpened by the difference between Franciscans and Dominicans, he finds his most devastating material in a papal bull especially addressed to the Franciscans. Against the Thomistic analysis, he declares, stands the bull of Nicholas III, *Exiit, qui seminat*, a bull incorporated into the *Liber Sextus* as part of the canon law.[74] The bull itself had nothing to do with usury, but had been principally intended to settle the quarrel raging between the Franciscan Conventuals and Spirituals over the poverty enjoined by the rule of St. Francis. Did the Franciscans having property become its owners in violation of their founder's injunction? The Pope met the controversy with a distinction between *usus facti* and *usus juris*. The friars had indeed the factual use of money when they actually bought a good with it. But until the money was actually spent it was always subject to recall by its donor. Thus, the right of use before actual use did not pertain to the Franciscans. The Pope added that it was a mere determination of the civil law that use and ownership of property could not be separated — a determination made from concern for the temporal welfare of society; but if there was a pious purpose served, there was no objection to the ownership of goods being vested in an authority distinct from their actual users.[75]

An objection of considerable ecclesiastical weight was thus placed against the Thomistic contention that use and ownership cannot be separated in consumptibles; and Scotus, with such authoritative backing, seems well warranted in rejecting St. Thomas. The bull, however, was not used again as an objection to the Thomistic argument for three hundred years, although

---

[72] Juan Garcia de Castrojeriz, II:3:11.

[73] On Scotus, see *D.t.c.*, IV, cols. 1865–1866.

[74] Duns Scotus, *In IV libros sententiarum* (*Op. Oxon.*), IV:15:2:17.

[75] *Liber Sextus Decretalium, Corpus juris canonici*, V:11:3, *Exiit qui seminat*.

shortly after Scotus' death, Clement V in another bull on Franciscan affairs, *Exivi de paradiso*, reaffirmed the teaching of Nicholas.[76] The reason for the nonadoption of Scotus' argument seems clear. In 1322 John XXII, faced with the anarchistic Fraticelli who asserted the absolute poverty of the Franciscans, met them with a return to Thomistic doctrine. The Franciscans, he declared in *Ad conditorem*, necessarily own the things they consume.[77] This bull, following and contradicting the early ones, resulted in Scotus' argument being ignored until Soto and Lessius considered it in the sixteenth century.

Scotus, of course, is not without some natural-law argument of his own against usury. He returns to the old Roman-law, etymological argument that in a *mutuum* ownership is transferred; but he does not seem to be entirely certain that this transfer of ownership really takes place, and he finds his strongest reason to be the other old contention that money does not fructify. When a lender takes fruit from a loan, he takes value that could only come from the labor of the borrower to which he has no title. Other rationales for the usury prohibition are indicated in two rules by which usury may always be determined. The first is that any sale of time is usury. On this ground, credit sales at a premium are forbidden. The second is that usury occurs in any contract concerning a future payment, where one party places himself in a position in which he would normally and safely profit, while the other party runs the risk of loss. This rather cumbersome rule seems intended to prohibit all credit sales in which a definite interest rate was not expressed, but where the price to be paid would generally be greater than the cash price.[78] It emphasizes the policy against riskless profit which motivates some theorists on usury. Both rules have considerable currency among later medieval writers.

3. The Specialists: Giles of Lessines and Alexander Lombard

Usury was an important subject to any thirteenth-century moralist. But it is hard to believe that any of the great speculative theologians, such as Scotus or St. Thomas, regarded it as presenting problems of prime signifi-

---

[76] *Clementis Papae V Constitutiones, Corpus juris canonici,* V:11:1, *Exivi de paradiso.*

[77] *Extravagantes Joannis Papae XXII, Corpus juris canonici,* XIV:3, *Ad conditorem.* Lessius says bluntly that the bulls are contradictory. The point, of course, is not one of faith or morals, or one on which the plenitude of papal authority was exercised. See Leonard Lessius, *De justitia et jure* (Lyons,

1630), II:3:8:37.

John XXII was engaged in a quarrel with the Franciscans which doubtless had a strong influence on his formulation of the abstract propositions on property rights; see Léon Baudry, *Guillaume d'Occam,* Études de philosophie médiévale, XXXIX (Paris, 1953), 108.

[78] Scotus, *In IV libros sententiarum (Op. Oxon.),* IV:15:2:17.

cance. A new stage of interest is reached when theologians devote special treatises to the topic. In 1278, there appeared the first of these — De usuris by Giles of Lessines, a Dominican disciple of St. Thomas teaching theology at the University of Paris.[79] Though the work reflects little of the formal analysis of St. Thomas, it was attributed to him by the Roman editors of his works, although not by earlier authorities. It has, on its own, merits that command respect: balance, considerable perspicacity, and a range of the credit situations involved.

Giles begins his treatise by declaring that anything "determinable in number, weight, and measure is properly and per se matter of usury." Only where a fixed quantity is lent can a usurious surplus be determined. The value of a house, on the contrary, is not fixed, so that rent from it cannot be shown to be usurious. Usury, then, is any superabundance or increment coming from the use of fungible goods.[80] Its proper seat is the loan: "Only in the act of lending, in the exchange of goods therein, primarily and per se inheres the nature of usury."[81]

Giles offers several natural-law arguments against usury. The first is the pure Aristotelian one, unchanged by St. Thomas, that usury is unnatural because it tends to infinity by seeking only the multiplication of money.[82] What is remarkable about Giles' use of this argument is that he presents it after introducing its proper Aristotelian context. Apparently correcting William of Moerbeke's error from his own knowledge of Greek, Giles changes "campsoria" to "commutativa"; so that he has a text in which he can clearly see that Aristotle's attack on usury is only the climax of an attack on all retail trade. Nonetheless, although he cannot accept Aristotle's premises, which meant a condemnation of most of urban life, Giles, without adverting to these premises, or to the fact that Aristotle's argument makes sense only if they are accepted, still feels free to use Aristotle's criticism of usury. This is a striking example of how Aristotle did not dominate the usury theory, of how instead the usury theory used him selectively.

Giles' second argument is that a loan should naturally be gratuitous.[83] Apparently this assertion is based simply on the point that in the Roman law a mutuum is a gratuitous contract, unless changed by a stipulatio into a foenus. Thirdly, Giles says usury is "against justice." He does not use the Thomistic argument to prove this, but seems to think that the only basis

[79] E. Hocedez, "La date du 'De usuris' de Gilles de Lessines," Ephemerides Theologicae Lovaniensis, III (1926), 509; James Quétif and James Eckard, Scriptores Ordinis Predicatorum (Paris, 1719), I, 371.

[80] Giles of Lessines, De usuris, c.2.
[81] c.3.
[82] c.4.
[83] c.4.

on which a usurer could claim a title to compensation is for his concession of time to the borrower. That the usurer tries to sell time is clear, he says, from the fact that his charge varies with the time. "But time is common, nor is it the proper possession of anyone, but is given by God equally." Fourthly, the usurer does not have a claim to gain from labor. His profit comes without labor: "he gains sleeping as working, on feast-days as on feriae."

Such is Giles' stereotyped argumentation against usury. Later, however, he makes an analysis of time, which is considerably more original and rewarding. "Fruits and the uses of goods," he says, "can increase or decrease in worth according to the diversity of time" in three ways, although in no case is time the cause per se of the variation. One way is through natural changes in the supply of goods: wheat is more abundant, and so worth less, in autumn than in spring. A second source of variation is the natural increment which comes to fruitful things such as wheat, woods, and animals. The third source is "the nature of a good relative to a place"; by which Giles presumably means that at some times, in some places, a good will be needed more than at other times and places.[84] Because of any of these natural differences in value in time, a seller on credit may charge more for his good in money, if he believes the good will be worth more at the time he is finally paid. However, in all contracts where time plays a role, and where nothing in the nature of the goods increases or diminishes their value over a period, time is simply "an extrinsic measure of duration . . . conferring nothing and taking away nothing by its nature."[85] In such contracts to charge a higher price because of the time is usury. This rule holds particularly for money, whose intrinsic value is changed by neither demand, supply, nor natural increment. The point will be more fully discussed in Chapter IV under *venditio sub dubio.* It is enough to say here that the Thomistic teaching on money is accepted and perfectly excludes the thought of money changing in value in time.

The Franciscan counterpart of Giles of Lessines is Alexander Bonini, better known as Alexander of Alexandria or Alexander Lombard. He had an academic career at Paris, enjoyed some familiarity with the papal court as a lecturer in theology, and served as provincial of Lombardy, which was the seat of the most notorious usurers of the day.[86] His *Tractatus de usuris*

[84] c.8.
[85] c.9.
[86] Alonzo M. Hamelin, "Le 'Tractatus de Usuris' de Maitre Alexandre d'Alexandrie," *Culture,* XVI (1955), 131–136; cf. *Enciclopedia cattolica* (Vatican City, 1949), II, col. 882.

was apparently composed as an oral discourse at Genoa in 1307.[87] Possibly because of its spoken origin, his work lacks the intellectual distinction of Giles of Lessines'; it would never be mistaken for St. Thomas'. But it covers a variety of credit situations with a firm grasp on the fundamental principles; it had a marked influence on the Franciscan writers of the thirteenth, fourteenth, and fifteenth centuries, and some effect on writers of the other orders.[88] As to the natural-law case against usury, Alexander is narrow and conventional. Like all the other writers he relies heavily on the divine-law argument based on Luke 6:35,[89] and he seems to think that a strong natural-law argument, running parallel, so to speak, is this: in the Roman law a *mutuum* is naturally gratuitous. This question-begging legalism recurs frequently.[90] The Thomistic argument is noted only in passing as a way of distinguishing a loan from a lease: the familiar contention is made that risk is not transferred in a lease, but is in a loan.[91] Some weight is also given to Aristotle's definition of usury and the Aristotelian theme that it is an unnatural use of money.[92] Yet like some of the other specialists on usury, Alexander achieves distinction in the acuteness of his discussion of particular credit contracts, not in his presentation of the natural-law case against usury.

Alexander's work, in addition, must be considered with that of Astesanus, his disciple and successor as minister of the Lombard province of the Franciscans. Astesanus (d. 1330) is not a specialist; he is known chiefly for the influence of his *Summa*, written in 1317.[93] Yet he is so closely associated with Alexander that the work of both should be taken together. Like Alexander, Astesanus came from Lombardy, indeed, from Asti, one of the principal homes of the international usurers, the lombards. A writer on usury from Asti at that time would have been much like a writer on gambling from Monte Carlo today. Astesanus' treatment of the subject, in fact, contains the most liberal theological treatment yet given of several debated topics. But it may be unfair to relate this liberality directly to his background; certainly on the unnaturalness of usury he is as unrelenting as anyone. His heterogeneous and conventional list of arguments against usury runs as follows: (1) usury is a contract of cupidity, not of necessity; (2) it is against the nature of money, which is consumed in use; (3) it is against charity; (4) it is the taking of a neighbor's labors; (5) it is profit

[87] Hamelin, pp. 266–272; cf. Alexander Lombard, *Tractatus de usuris* (Bibl. Vat. Folio, lat. ms. 1237f.), f.153a, ante c.1.
[88] Hamelin, pp. 281–284.
[89] Alexander Lombard, c.2, f.153b, f.154v:a.
[90] c.2, f.153b, f.154v:b; c.3, f.155a.
[91] c.2, f.154v:a.
[92] c.1, f.153b; c.2, f.153b.
[93] Hamelin, p. 266; *D.t.c.*, I, col. 2142.

taken from a thing which bears no fruit; (6) it is the taking of another's good.[94]

4. A Canonist's Critique: Joannes Andreae and the Fixed Value of Fungibles

One of the greatest of medieval canonists, whose commentary on the later decretals became the standard gloss, Joannes Andreae (1270–1348) was a lay professor of canon law at Bologna.[95] His several commentaries on the canon law contain much scattered discussion of usury. That he was a layman as well as a canonist may be not without influence in his attempt to explore the usury teaching. The emphasis in his writing, as in that of a later lay canonist, Laurentius de Ridolfis, has a different shading from the work of the great systematic theologians. And, of course, there is a world of difference between his explorations and the popular preaching of a Stephen of Bourbon.

As befits a man whose knowledge of past legal literature was un-rivaled,[96] Andreae provides the best fourteenth-century review and criticism of the arguments against usury. When he first treats it, he offers verbatim the arguments of Innocent IV based on the evil effects and the uncharitable-ness of usury.[97] The significance of this revival of arguments so foreign to the general scholastic tradition becomes explicit later, when Andreae again addresses himself to the sinfulness of usury. Here he declares that usury is in itself, and from its nature, vicious: so Aristotle has taught; so the canon law describes usury as a kind of rapine; so the Gospel prohibits it, because the Gospel only repeats a Mosaic prohibition where an act is intrinsically evil. But he says frankly, "To assign a reason by which it is evidently demonstrated that the said contract has from the nature of the matter viciousness and convolute malice, I do not think entirely easy. . . ."

Andreae then puts forward the oldest argument of all, which he aptly names "the jurists' argument," that in a loan ownership passes. But for the first time the argument is criticized:

Although the money which is lent passes into the ownership of the debtor as to identity of substance — since the debtor is not held to restore the same money according to its substance — yet this money remains in the ownership of the usurer as to identity and equality of value; . . . . and he demands profit from it according to the mode in which it pertains to him, inasmuch as it is of such value. . . .

---

[94] Astesanus, III:11:3.
[95] Schulte, II, 205–215.

[96] Schulte, II, 227.
[97] Joannes Andreae, V, De usuris, ante c.1.

This criticism, which is to trouble St. Bernardine of Siena and is to be revived by later critics of the scholastics, is at first rejected by Andreae. He replies that the creditor retains not ownership of the money, but the right to it at the end of a period, which is clearly different. Moreover, the money is at the debtor's peril, and incidence of risk is clear indication of where the ownership lies. Nevertheless, although he offers what would seem to be a satisfactory refutation of the objection, Andreae is not content with his answer, and later we find him simply granting that ownership does not pass in a loan.[98]

Andreae next examines "the theologians' argument," the Thomistic contention that the use and the thing are not separable in loaned goods. The objection made is that although the use and substance cannot be separated, yet if they are sold together, each may be charged for. Andreae replies shortly that to charge for such nonseparable goods separately is to sell the same thing twice.

Thirdly, he puts forward "the argument of Aristotle," that usury is unlawful because it is unnatural for an artificial thing to bear fruit. Andreae objects (1) that this argument does not cover every case, for usury may be committed in loans of nonartificial goods such as wheat; (2) that it would at the same time tell against transactions which are perfectly legitimate, such as the rent of a house, which is an artificial good. No reply is given to these objections.

Andreae also dismisses the argument that money does not deteriorate with the example of a house that is improved by habitation and for which rent yet may be charged. The argument that time should not be sold is sharply characterized as "frivolous," "since many licit contracts occur in which is interposed a delay of time, and yet it is not said on this account that time is sold."

Thus of five traditional reasons, Andreae defends only two, and even these he does not rely on, for he goes on to give a new one of his own and a reformulation of the ones that he does accept. His new argument is reminiscent of Giles of Lessines, but makes explicit what Giles only suggests. It is this: Things fixed in number, weight, or measure have an intrinsic value set upon them by their determined quantity; when the lender of such goods expects to receive a greater quantity than he gave, he attempts to make his goods "worth more than their nature"; consequently, he acts unjustly and unnaturally.[99] The argument affirms that the value of,

---

[98] Andreae, VI, *De regulis iuris*, "Pec-   [99] "Peccatum," 12.
catum," 12.

A NATURAL-LAW CASE AGAINST USURY 67

say, 100 measures of wheat is determined by this number, so that only if 100 measures of wheat are returned six months later is equality kept in the loan. It is a lawyer's effort to frame a case against usury, not only in loans of consumptibles but also in loans of nonconsumptible fungibles.

Andreae then slightly reformulates the Thomistic argument so that it accords with this approach, and rephrases the fruitless-good argument to meet his original objection. The reason that money does not bear fruit is not that it is artificial, but that it has a determined value; in contrast a house is artificial but has no fixed value. The argument thus becomes a simple variant of his own position. To this he adds the Aristotelian contention that it is unnatural to devote goods to a purpose for which they were not primarily intended.[100] But what we may call the Andrean argument, the fixed value of fungibles, is his real contribution to the usury theory.

5. Monetary Experts: John Buridan and Nicholas of Oresme

The specialists on usury had not purported to be students of money. Now in the mid-fourteenth century two writers make reputations by studies of the effects of devaluation. One is John Buridan, in 1327 rector of the University of Paris and a noted Occamist dialectician.[101] He is followed by his disciple Nicholas of Oresme (d. 1384), a theologian at the University of Paris and later Bishop of Lisieux.[102] Oresme has established himself in economic history by his *Tractatus de origine, natura, jure, et mutationibus monetarum*, a work which directly influenced the monetary policy of Charles V of France; and perhaps more than any other medieval author he has, on account of this work, enjoyed a reputation as an economist. Did the expertise acquired in a study of money enrich the theory of usury? The answer must be largely negative.

In his commentary on the *Politics*, Buridan analyzes money's nature formally in terms of its four causes. The material cause of money, he says, is some rare material; its efficient cause is the State; its final cause is the needs of men, who must exchange goods; its formal cause is the sign of value upon it. This succinct statement will not be improved by the later scholastics. Upon these assumptions, Buridan discusses the morality of the prince altering the legal value, and holds that such alteration may be made if the community as a whole will be benefited by it, but not otherwise. Sig-

[100] "Peccatum," 13.
[101] Buridan was a disciple of Occam and a professional philosopher rather than a theologian (Hugo Hurter, *Nomenclator literarius theologiae catholicae*, 1906, II, col. 630).

[102] See Nicholas of Oresme, *Tractatus de origine, natura, jure, et mutationibus monetarum*, ed. M. L. Wolowski (Paris, 1864), p. L.

nificantly for the usury analysis, Buridan seems to recognize that the value of money may change even without an official devaluation. He writes, "It is to be known that an alteration in money can happen because sometimes money is called strong, i.e., when its price is increased, and sometimes weak, i.e., when its price is diminished." [103] This observation would seem to strike at the assumption of medieval usury theorists that money could regularly be considered a motionless measure, changeable only by law. But Buridan does not link this analysis to the treatment of usury; instead, he gives the strict Thomistic argument and adds that the usurer sells what is not his own, that is, time. Unlike a gold vase, which may be rented, money in an *instrumentum* whose use is its consumption. Usury, he teaches, is also evil because it is unsocial, unmerciful, and illiberal, and because the usurer seeks avariciously what has no finite limit.[104] These arguments are familiar ones.

Oresme's work, following the path of Buridan, is devoted to the nature of money and to the morality of alterations in its value by the prince. Money, Oresme teaches again and again, was invented for the good of the community and belongs to those who have given up natural riches in exchange for it.[105] It should be "as a certain law and certain firm ordinance," and should never be altered in value unless the community's necessity authorizes it.[106] Oresme makes no reference to a change in value occurring apart from an official devaluation, nor does he even attempt to settle the value of money in loans if an official devaluation occurs. Like Buridan's, his analysis of changes in the value of money remains significantly unrelated to the usury analysis. In passing, he notes that the Scripture shows usury as evil and detestable, and that Aristotle has shown how unnatural it is for infecund good to multiply.[107] He is not primarily interested in developing a case against usury, but a devoted Aristotelian, he takes for granted the usual Aristotelian argument against it.[108]

6. More Specialists: Henry of Hesse, John Gerson, Laurentius de Ridolfis

The most informed and exact writing on usury from the middle of the fourteenth into the fifteenth century is found in special treatises devoted to the subject. One of the first scholastics to write with an eye to economic

---

[103] John Buridan, *Quaestiones super VIII libros politicorum Aristotelis* (Paris, 1513), Bk. I, Q.11, art. 2.
[104] *Ibid.*, I:12.
[105] Nicholas of Oresme, c.6.
[106] c.8.

[107] c.17.
[108] At the beginning of the work (Prologus), Oresme declares that his analysis will proceed "according to the philosophy of Aristotle."

conditions in Germany is Henry of Hesse (1325–1397). A theologian who taught both at the center of scholasticism, Paris, and at the new University of Vienna,[109] Henry is the author of a treatise on justice in contracts. The criterion of justice he uses is chiefly the usury prohibition.

Henry teaches that the only objects of a loan are goods consumptible in use. The unnaturalness of usury is shown by a number of familiar arguments: (1) the Thomistic argument on the identity of use and ownership; (2) the argument that the borrower owns the money loaned and that the usurer seeks to profit by his labor; (3) the argument that time should not be sold. Henry also says that justice "consists in an equality of loss and gain," and that this is violated by the borrower being made to run an unequal risk. Again, he urges the testimony of Aristotle as evidence for the natural odiousness of usury. Furthermore, he says that one should not bring grief to others, that usury violates the Golden Rule. It would be difficult to say that any one of these arguments dominates his approach. Against an objector, he declares that the profits of the borrower from a loan are irrelevant to the justice of the contract concluded with the lender.[110]

The geographical origin of the writer does not appear to be of great importance in the formal case against usury, although it has some effect on the writer's judgment of particular types of credit. At this period the best treatise on usury produced by financial Florence is the *Tractatus de usuris* of Laurentius de Ridolfis, written in 1403. Laurentius, although a layman, was a teacher of canon law; he was also a man of affairs and served as an ambassador of the Florentine Republic.[111] He is characterized by Vespasiano as a man of Roman integrity and deep Christian piety;[112] and his thought on usury is an interesting blend of economic perspicacity tempered by moral scruples. If it were said that he was the first economic man to write theology, the quality of this blend might be suggested. In his formal case against usury, it is significant that he recurs to the pragmatic appeals of Innocent IV: usury has evil social consequences and is uncharitable.[113] At the same time he is conservative enough to use as well the Thomistic argument and the argument that money cannot bear fruit, reformulated in Andrean terms: all fungible goods "have a determined value instituted by nature, and therefore they cannot bear fruit beyond this." [114] The firmness with which the traditional arguments are now established is plain when

[109] De Wulf, II, 194.
[110] Henry of Hesse, *De contractibus*, f.192, 195, 205.
[111] Schulte, II, 393.
[112] Vespasiano da Bisticci, *Vite di uomini*

illustri del secolo XV (Milan, 1951), pp. 380–383.
[113] Laurentius de Ridolfis, 1:7 (n.13).
[114] 1:7 (n.14–15), citing John Calderinus.

they are so staunchly adhered to by an author so sensitive to the commercial temper of his city.

But if even a layman interested in economics would not challenge the natural-law case, John Gerson might. Gerson (1363–1429) was a French priest with a European reputation. Beginning his career as a teacher at the University of Paris, he became its chancellor at the age of thirty-four. From Paris he entered the international field as a leading proponent of the conciliar system and a heroic fighter in the struggle to end the Great Schism.[115] A leading figure in the contemporary Church, an eminent preacher, a master of mystical theology, this many-sided man was seriously concerned with the confusion caused among the bourgeoisie by the usury doctrine. At the Council of Constance he called attention to the great danger of the moralists declaring usurious contracts licit or licit contracts usurious.[116] In 1420 appeared his own treatise, *De contractibus*, in which he presented the familiar Thomistic argument and the worn objection to money bearing money. To these juristic arguments he added that man was bound to labor, and that to live idly on usuries is unnatural; and he made the curious suggestion that the availability of money at usury encourages the idleness of the borrower. But he appeals to the divine law alone, when the objection is made that often the advantages of a loan are such that the borrower would gladly contract to pay for them. Gerson answers that God, the principal owner of all created goods, is unwilling that payment should be made, "whatever the will of the recipient at usury." [117] In short, forced to the wall, he abandons the natural-law defense of the usury prohibition. His belief in a positivist explanation of the law is the key to the evasion of the law, which, as will be seen later, he advocated.[118]

7. The Challenge of Custom: The Traditionalist Answer

John Gerson had gone to an extreme in tacitly abandoning the natural-law objections. But he was not typical, nor did the fifteenth century follow him. The normative attitude is well represented by Nicholas de'Tudeschi, called Panormitanus (d. 1453?), in his standard commentary on the canon law.[119] Without any hesitation, he adopts the Thomistic argument, which, he says, holds true of all fungibles and only of fungibles — an extension of the class of goods covered by the argument which St. Thomas

---

[115] *D.t.c.*, VI, cols. 1314–1323.

[116] John Gerson, *De contractibus, Consideratio* 13; *Consideratio* 15.

[117] *Consideratio* 13.

[118] See *infra*, pp. 158–159.

[119] Schulte, II, 312. Panormitanus was a successful ecclesiastical politician and archbishop of Palermo.

himself had not attempted. He also uses Innocent's reasons and refers to *Ejiciens*. But his favorite argument is that money is a measure and so "not fit to bear fruit." [120]

Panormitanus, the typical compiler and unoriginal uncommentator, never feels the pressures of his times. Yet the fifteenth century was an age of quickening commerce; capitalistic Tuscany was alive with commercial and financial problems; and two Tuscan saints who threw themselves into the life of their times were acutely aware of the pressures. They responded by giving the fullest treatments of usury so far. One is St. Antoninus of Florence (1389–1459); the other St. Bernardine of Siena (1380–1444).

The public life of St. Bernardine of Siena, a Franciscan friar, principally lay in his preaching, a vocation to which he gave himself with apostolic zeal. A close observer of the practices of the people among whom he moved, and a constant traveler in his missionary activity throughout the towns of northern Italy, he was in an excellent position to be informed on the capitalistic activity which characterized the economic life of the northern Italian cities. He confronted an expanding economic world with a firm grasp of the usury doctrine so important to its financial mechanisms, nor did he bend the letter of the medieval rule to accommodate this world's increasing pressure. In 1425 he made a kind of general indictment of his city in a series of Lenten sermons devoted to the various forms of usury.[121] Some of these "sermons" are theological treatises intended only for confessors; some are meant as models for other preachers; and some probably are actual talks given by St. Bernardine himself.[122] We can see here both the scientific and the popular exposition of the usury theory.

St. Bernardine is considerably influenced by Joannes Andreae. He adopts as his first argument against usury Andreae's own chief argument, that fungibles should not increase beyond their determined value. Natural fungibles, like wheat, have their value fixed naturally by their quantity. Artificial fungibles, like money, have their value fixed by law. With either class of goods, it is unnatural to take more than their measure.[123]

St. Bernardine repeats Andreae's reasoning upon the argument that ownership passes in a loan. He first gives the argument, then Andreae's

[120] Panormitanus, *Commentaria in libros decretalium* (Venice, 1558), V, *De usuris*, ante c.1.

[121] A. G. Ferrers Howell, *S. Bernardine of Siena* (London, 1913), pp. 83–217; Alberto E. Trugenberger, *San Bernardino da Siena: Considerazioni sullo svillippo dell'etica eco-* nomici cristiana nel primo Rinascimento (Bern, 1951), pp. 74, 140.

[122] Howell, p. 256.

[123] St. Bernardine, *De contractibus*, Sermon 38, art. 1, c.1. The sermons cited here all belong to the series *De evangelio aeterno*.

objection that the ownership of the value is not really transferred in a loan, and finally Andreae's reply to the objection, distinguishing between right and ownership. But even more than Andreae, he is doubtful about the validity of the argument, and undoubtedly, the earlier hesitations of his fellow Franciscan, Scotus, influence him. Andreae had supported his reply to the objection by noting that the borrower now ran the risk of the good and that the incidence of risk proclaimed the owner. But St. Bernardine says, quite surprisingly, that in the case approved by all the canonists where money is rented *ad pompam*, the money stands at the risk of the bailee; and he infers from this that incidence of risk is not always a proof of ownership. Thus, Andreae's corroboration falls; and although his main reply is not refuted, yet St. Bernardine is so suspicious of the ownership argument that he must be interpreted as disapproving it.[124]

Later, however, in deciding particular cases, St. Bernardine seems covertly to return to the ancient argument. He declares that hidden usury occurs whenever the risk of a rented good is borne by its bailee. This is in direct contradiction to his earlier view on the rent of money *ad pompam;* it means that he considers the temporary transfer of ownership indicated by the transfer of risk and implies that he considers it immoral to profit after ownership has been transferred. The old legal argument is accepted after all, and moreover, in such a way that not only the loan of consumptibles or fungibles, but the "loan" of fruitful goods is considered offering opportunity for usury. According to his formulation of the argument, any bailment at a profit of a horse or any lease of a house, where the bailee or lessee bears the risk of the property, is usury.[125]

St. Bernardine also accepts the argument based on the unfruitfulness of money; the Aristotelian argument based on the purpose of money; and the Thomistic argument in its reformulation by Andreae.[126] He adds a series of variations on the principal arguments: (1) usury is the selling of money, which is naturally non-vendible; (2) it is the unjust getting of a certain gain in returning for giving an uncertain one; (3) it is the selling of his own industry to the borrower; (4) it is against charity.[127] In developing the fourth contention, St. Bernardine is led to extend far beyond the limits customarily set by the scholastics the positive charitable obligation. Commonly it was held that you were bound to lend only to men in extreme distress who personally asked you for a loan. St. Bernardine believes that the

[121] 38:1:2. It cannot easily be supposed that the contract *ad pompam* was always as St. Bernardine describes it.

[125] 39:2:2; see also Sermon 40.
[126] 38:1:2,4, and 3.
[127] 38:1:5,6,7, and 8.

community should function like the human organism, in which the stomach keeps what food it needs and distributes the rest to the other members of the body: "Thus, as we are all one body in Christ Jesus, a Christian having money useless to himself is held from necessity to communicate it to his neighbor who can make it useful for himself." This is, of course, not a natural-law objection to usury; but it does offer an explanation of how he believed the community could prosper without a financial inducement to lending.[128]

A little later, St. Bernardine addresses directly the criticism that usury cannot be unnatural because the State cannot exist without it. Many scholastic writers had affirmed that usury might be civilly tolerated by the State as a lesser evil than eliminating the benefits of loans.[129] But none had considered the obvious implication: If usury had to be tolerated to preserve the economic life of society, could it be entirely vicious? Now, for the first time, a scholastic writer considers the murmur of the people, who affirm that without manifest usury the city could not exist. St. Bernardine begins by saying that those holding this belief — and he implies that it is common — commit a sin of blasphemy, for they say, in effect, that God has placed them under an impossible precept. He recognizes, however, that what has led people into this error is that rarely is there found anyone who will lend gratuitously, yet always, apparently, there is a great need for credit. These appearances lead St. Bernardine to analyze the available sources of money and the causes of the demand for it.

On the one hand, he declares, the real reason why few will lend gratuitously is the general custom of taking usury. But a vicious habit does not excuse itself. Abolish the custom, and you will find lenders ready to charge nothing. Further, there is no need for cash to be always supplied by a loan. People in need could sell their property, and, if usurious pledges were not the custom, many buyers for cash would be found. The rich would take this opportunity to buy at reasonable prices; business would be stimulated by the trade. Thus, on the supply side, there really might be far more cash available in nonusurious ways than the people think.

On the demand side, St. Bernardine finds that there are five classes of borrowers: (1) the really needy poor; (2) gamblers or men of ill character seeking money for vice; (3) avaricious tradesmen and merchants, who seek "to accumulate riches" and borrow usuriously, particularly from widows;

---

[128] 38:1:10. Alexander Lombard, c.7, f.162 r:b, and Giles of Lessines, c.9, speak of a rich man's duty to lend to a poor man, presumably only in extreme need. For a standard treatment of the duty of charity to the poor, see St. Thomas, *S.T.*, II–II:32:5.

[129] E.g., St. Albert, *Commentarius in IV libros sententiarum*, III:37:13; St. Thomas, *S.T.*, II–II:1 ad 3; Andreae, VI, *De regulis iuris*, "Peccatum," 17.

(4) usurers, who borrow to lend at higher rates; (5) those who need money for a short time, because of a temporary emergency. Classes (2), (3), and (4) have no rational excuse for borrowing; indeed they commit mortal sin themselves by leading their creditors to sin through taking usury without just need on their own part forcing them to borrow. Class (1) is only made poorer by borrowing; it needs alms, not loans. Class (5) has the most justification for seeking credit, but it is gradually and insensibly impoverished by the payment of usuries; and such borrowers would save themselves much real misery if they sacrificed their property when they first needed money and avoided entanglement with the usurers. Often the pledges lost by such borrowers in default far exceed the value of the loan they received. Thus, the demand for money at usury is far greater than it should be. Only a small group reasonably and justly needs cash, and even they could find money in ways more beneficial to them than loans. St. Bernardine concludes that there is no rational basis for the belief that usury is essential either to obtain a supply of credit or to meet the lawful demands for cash. Usury is really necessary and of benefit to no group of persons; and if all lived virtuously there would be no need of it.[130] Not only is usury unnecessary, but it is a positive and terrible evil. It has a disastrous effect on the city and on the social organism. The public usurers are usually foreigners, often Jews, and they drain the wealth of the city into other lands.[131] Again, usury concentrates the money of the community in the hands of a few, just as if all the blood in a man's body ran to his heart and left his other organs depleted. Finally, the practice of public usury brings the just chastisement of God upon the city, and invites the Four Horsemen of the Apocalypse.[132]

All this is in the way of temporal evils. Even if usury gave a few temporal advantages, the spiritual disasters it entails would outweigh them. Usury enervates charity; it is a fount of self-love, the mother of deception, a worse evil than robbery, for more cunning and constant;[133] it is "the murder of the poor"; it makes men cruel to their kinsmen;[134] it is a contagious disease, for now all men are usurers, and usurers are honored by the city, take their places in the councils of the great, and are even buried by the Church.[135] Moreover, usury entangles the souls of many who are not themselves formal usurers: "In innumerable ways they are trapped and fall by this usurious stain." Such persons are (1) those borrowing at usury unnecessarily; (2) notaries of usurious contracts; (3) witnesses to these contracts;

[130] St. Bernardine, 43:3:1.
[131] 43:3:3.
[132] 43:3:3.
[133] 44:1:1,2,3, and 4.
[134] 44:2:1,2, and 3.
[135] 44:3:3.

(4) lawyers trying to enforce them; (5) judges ordering their enforcement; (6) the servants of usurers; (7) the wives of usurers, living on stolen property; (8) relatives and friends of usurers receiving gifts from them and not making restitution; (9) heirs of usurers not making restitution; (10) rectors of hospitals and spiritual houses receiving gifts from usurers; (11) executors of the wills of usurers; (12) legislators authorizing a minimum rate of usury; (13) officials enforcing these laws; (14) guardians depositing their wards' funds at usury with merchants; (15) widows doing the same with their dowries; (16) princes protecting usurers; (17) landlords renting to foreign usurers; (18) prelates guaranteeing usurious contracts; (19) confessors absolving unrepentant usurers.[136] The moral precepts determining the sin of these coöperators in usury had long been clear; certain classes of them were excommunicated. But this is the first time such a list has been drawn up to show the manifold evil consequences of usury. In particular, as St. Bernardine notes, the obligation of restitution of goods gained by usury, an obligation which extended to later recipients of the goods, often effected a complex and perplexing multiplication of the initial sin. In a capitalistic town like Siena, St. Bernardine moralistically finds usury and its consequences infecting all of life.

Of course, most of the arguments urged under the spiritual evil of usury are predicated on the assumption that usury is evil; they do not by themselves establish the assumption. It is evident that St. Bernardine, in refuting those who see usury as a benefit, partly appeals to the divine law that has already condemned it. The appeal of the arguments is popular. At the same time the need to use them reflects a certain sense of inadequacy in the undiluted natural-law case against usury.

St. Bernardine also offers an important analysis of time. The Augustinian friar, Gerard of Siena,[137] he says, distinguishes between the "duration which follows the *primum mobile*," which is common time and nonvendible, and the duration "applicable to something, which duration and use are conceded to someone for him to use." The latter time, Gerard says, "is the property of someone, just as the year for which a horse is lent to me is said to be mine: and this kind of time can licitly be sold." This, it is clear, is a radical break with the tradition. Now, says St. Bernardine, why cannot the lender sell the duration of the loan? His answer is a subtle one: the time

---

[136] 44:3:4. *Decretales*, V:19:9, commanded restitution of heirs. *Clementis, De usuris, Ex gravi*, excommunicated classes (12), (13), and (16). *Decretales*, VI, *De usuris*, c.1, excommunicated class (17) and c.2 excommunicated class (19).

[137] A disciple of Aegidius Romanus, who taught at Bologna and wrote *De restitutionibus et usuris*. He died in 1336 (Hurter, *Nomenclator*, II, col. 562).

connected with the loan, like the loaned good itself, is in the power of the borrower, once the loan has been made; therefore, the duration of the loan is not the lender's property to sell. At the same time, however, he admits that he who has time as his own may sell it, and he gives an example. If a man owes a debt of 100 ducats to be paid at the end of three years, he may licitly contract with his creditor to pay at once if the debt is reduced to 85; he will thus charge 15 ducats for the sale of the three years' time; but as these three years were his property, he sells justly. Against two objections, St. Bernardine defends this admission of the selling of time with answers which modify somewhat its original nakedness. He says, first, that what the debtor paying in advance sells is the opportunity of using money. This answer, of course, is a shift from the claim that time can be sold, and will be considered later in treating of *lucrum cessans*. But his answer to the second objection returns to the notion that time is here involved in a sale; he repeats that the ordinary lender is not in the same position as the anticipating debtor, because the time of the loan belongs only to the recipient of the loan. Thus the anticipating debtor is selling time that is his; a lender in charging for his loan is not selling what is his. He finds a final argument in the statement that anticipated repayment of a debt is not a loan; and, of course, usury inheres only in loans.[138]

Incredibly enough, St. Bernardine does not see that his fundamental admission here damages the whole usury doctrine. Any usurer might say that the next ten years were his own as far as his money was concerned, and lend only to borrowers who would pay for the right to use these ten years; and St. Bernardine's argument that the time was not his to sell is readily seen as an equivocation, once he allows the sale of time in debt-purchase. There is, perhaps, nothing like Bernardine's blunder in the whole scholastic tradition of usury. Certainly, no one else will ever be found who will say that "one's own time" can be sold.

Moreover, in his concluding sermons, where he abandons scientific analysis to paint the most lively possible image of the usurer's depravity, St. Bernardine himself insists on the usurer's wickedness in selling time. Jesus Christ, he declares, has declared that "He alone knows the time and the hour. If therefore it is not ours to know the time, much less it is ours to sell it." [139] To this sensational application of Christ's teaching on the time of the Last Judgment he adds the vehement declaration that the usurer has sold time common to all creatures and therefore has offended all creatures:

[138] St. Bernardine, 34:1:1.   [139] *Ibid.*, 43:2:3.

Accordingly, all the saints and all the angels of paradise cry then against him, saying, "To hell, to hell, to hell." Also the heavens with their stars cry out, saying, "To the fire, to the fire, to the fire." The planets also clamor, "To the depths, to the depths, to the depths." [140]

From careful reasoning to sharp denunciation, St. Bernardine wages a war against usury. He will not surrender to Sienese custom; he will not take the word of the merchants that all is necessary and all is well in the world of finance. With vivid imagery he will drive home the character of their vice; with patient constructiveness he will set forth his ideal of the community organism in which all members help each other. The usury rule as an expression of the fundamental charity of Christian brotherhood knows no warmer apostle.

The fervor of his championship of a moral ideal against the pressures of convention is equalled by St. Antoninus, the Archbishop of Florence, the banking capital of Europe. Apostolic Commissary for the repression of usury in Tuscany, and a distinguished ecclesiastical administrator and judge, who daily had to make a multitude of economic decisions, Antoninus was in a position peculiarly advantageous for observing the economic machinery of his day. At the same time, the author of the first *Summa* of moral theology, treated as a separate subject, a faithful Thomist and a compiler respectful of tradition, and yet a man wonderfully aware of contemporary problems, above all, a saint, he is an observer on whose theological science, skill, and prudence one might rely with confidence.[141] Moreover, his work will be popular and frequently consulted in practice in the next 150 years. His *Confessionale* underwent thirty-one printings before 1600, his *Summa theologiae* twenty-four.[142] We have, then, in the short treatment of usury in the *Confessionale* of 1440 and in the much more developed treatment in the *Summa theologiae* of 1449, works that had a practical usefulness well after their author's death. At the same time, his thought marks the summation and end of the first period in usury analysis. Yet by being more systematic, Antoninus is more severe than many of his predecessors. As the late seventeenth century is to draw all the departures from the usury prohibition together in a final, all-inclusive departure, so Antoninus draws together all the strict rules of the early usury teaching into a tight set of rules. No later writer of note will be as severe, as uncompromising, as true to the logic of the earlier conceptions, as he. It is fitting that we should

---

[140] 45:3:3.

[141] R. Morçay. *St. Antonin* (Paris, 1914), pp. 126–148, 389.

[142] Morçay, pp. 404, 415. The *Summa theologiae* is also known as *Summa moralis*.

close our examination of early scholastic teaching with the examination of this man, whose works close the era.

St. Antoninus declares that usury is against the natural law because the use and ownership of consumptibles is indistinguishable; because the usurer tries to appropriate the borrower's industry; because money cannot bear fruit. The multiplication of money by usury "seems miraculous, but in truth it is diabolical." The objection, as old as St. Jerome, is that if the borrower makes 15 per cent, is it not reasonable for the lender to get 8 or 10 per cent of it; the answer, as old as the twelfth century, is that "money insofar as it is the price of purchasables confers no gain, except through the industry of the user." [143] The distinction between common and proper time also appears as an indirect objection, but St. Antoninus, without referring to St. Bernardine's sponsorship of the idea simply dismisses it as a singular opinion.[144] In general, St. Antoninus' reasons represent the solid core of the scholastic argumentation against usury.

The enormity and viciousness of usury are particularly impressed on St. Antoninus, as they were on St. Bernardine, by his daily contact with it in a highly commercial society. Usury, according to St. Antoninus, is the great harlot of Apocalypse 17, "Who sitteth upon many waters, With whom the kings of the earth have committed fornication." [145] He continually emphasizes how not only open usurers, but all coöperators in usury, are "worthy of eternal death." [146] Moreover, in addition to its gravity as mortal sin, usury is a vice whose special aspects render it particularly odious. Other sins only last for a certain time: the sinner does not remain continually in the act of adultery or murder. But, "usury ever breaks and consumes the bones of the poor, night or day, on feasts and feriae, sleeping or waking it works and never ceases." [147] The man with his money loaned usuriously, whether he adverts explicitly to his loan or not, is in a perpetual state of sin. Again, usury, unlike many other sins, is a vice that lasts into old age and entangles the sinner up to the hour of his death. It is a peculiarly difficult sin to repent; for its forgiveness demands restitution of the profits, and indeed unless the man is dying, absolution is not to be given, until the restitution is made. But restitution seems too hard to a prosperous usurer. "And commonly such die as brute animals, or some terrible judgment happens to them, and they are sometimes seized by demons." Antoninus adds a vivid *exemplum* of a

---

[143] St. Antoninus, *Summa theologiae,* 2:1:6.

[144] 2:1:8.

[145] 2:1:6.

[146] 2:1:9.

[147] The phrase is almost identical with one of Giles of Lessines; see *supra,* p. 63.

usurer who was carried off by a whole boat-load of devils. Usury not only damns the original sinner, but also his heirs, who are obliged to restitution and commonly do not fulfill their duty. Antoninus has known one family damned for four generations by its failure to return the goods of a usurious ancestor. He adds another impressive story of a usurer with two sons, whose entire fortune came from usury. The story, as Antoninus recounts it in his terse and vigorous style, pictures the man at his deathbed, urged by his confessor and the two sons to make restitution. The usurer replies to the sons,

"Nothing would remain for you, for all is made up of usuries." "Don't care about us," they said, "Provide for your salvation." "Be silent," he said, "I prefer to go to the mercy of God than to the mercy of men, for they are inhuman and unmerciful; but God is most clement." In his obstinacy, he departed.

The story continues that of the two brothers, one decided to cling to his inheritance, the other to give it to the poor and enter a religious order. The first brother soon afterwards died; and the second brother in the religious order was rewarded by a vision of hell, in which he saw both father and brother each blaming the other for his misfortune, the former because he had not made restitution in order to help the latter, the latter because he was damned by his father's bequest.[148] Such sharp tales illustrate an abhorrence of usury not reflected in the thin natural-law reasonings against the vice.

St. Antoninus is particularly concerned with the many frauds and evasions by which the capitalistic class has endeavored to avoid the stigma of committing open usury. Usury is entrenched, St. Antoninus believes, in the two principal businesses of Florence, exchange-banking and the textile industry; and in addition to the men actually in these businesses, the whole *rentier* class, especially widows, wards, and nobles, have invested in them in usurious fashion.[149] Nor is the city alone accustomed to the practice of usury. In the country, the breeding of animals and the rents of farms, themselves legitimate transactions, are frequently financed by usurious measures.[150] At the same time, the sale of shares in the public debt makes usury open to everyone.[151] In addition, of course, the numerous coöperators with usurers, described by St. Bernardine, are noted by St. Antoninus; so that usury to him appears as a vice whose ubiquity and pervasiveness are hardly matched by any other sin.[152] All this, to be sure, is no proof of the natural law against usury; and lest we digress from this topic now, we shall

[148] St. Antoninus, *Summa theologiae*, 2:1:6.

[149] 2:1:6; cf. 2:1:7.

[150] 2:1:7; cf. 3:3.

[151] 2:1:11.

[152] 2:1:9.

postpone the consideration of the different types of contracts St. Antoninus condemns. It is, however, relevant to our immediate consideration of the natural law and usury to note how many persons are tainted with usury in a capitalistic society, according to the early scholastic analysis. St. Antoninus, as emphatically as St. Bernardine, shows in detail the meaning of the early analysis for an active commercial community.

It is also important to note how the zeal to prevent the use of contracts, which have the same effect, although not the same as for a usurious loan, leads inevitably to other principles beyond the fundamental ones that money does not fructify and that use and ownership are the same in consumptibles. Where able business minds were constantly seeking ways of investing their capital safely, the usury doctrine had to become either an empty form, or had to be extended to cover the new contracts the businessmen invented. Henry of Hesse had expounded on the danger but had made no suggestions for meeting it. St. Bernardine had come to a radical solution in practice, and St. Antoninus follows him, insisting on the principle that where an investment of any kind is made whose risk is not borne by the investor, there is usury. He states as an axiom "the thing perishes to the owner," and applies the converse of this, that the owner is the man who bears the loss of a good. With this axiom in hand, he determines that any lease, even of a fruitful good, is usury if the risk of the leased good is borne by the lessee.[153] In his eyes, usury occurs not only in the temporary transfer at a profit of the ownership of a fungible good, but in the temporary transfer of the ownership — as indicated by the incidence of risk — of any good. The tendency to use risk as the criterion of ownership and its transference as the mark of a loan has been seen as early as the *Gloss* on Gratian. But no author extends the usury doctrine to control all temporary transfers of ownership and risk, without exception, with the rigorous logic of St. Antoninus.

Conclusion

A survey of the rational analysis of usury over three hundred years leads to the following conclusions:

1. The scholastics are unanimous only upon the beliefs that usury is profit upon a loan, that it can occur in other contracts, reducible upon analysis to loans, that it is a sin against justice, and that the person of the borrower and his profit from the loan are irrelevant to the rectitude of the lender's act. These common bases of agreement are all taken from the canon law.

[153] 2:1:7.

2. There is no agreement on the natural-law reasons why usury is a sin. Every juristic reason offered has been criticized by at least one prominent writer. Three arguments, however, are favored by most authors: the Thomistic argument that the use and ownership of consumptibles are one; the Andrean argument that fungibles have a fixed value; the argument of *Ejiciens* that money bears no fruit. One of these arguments serves only for money loans; one only for loans of consumptibles; and only one holds in all loans of fungibles. The social case against usury is not absent from scholastic thought. The evil effects on agriculture, the exploitation of the poor, the encouragement of an idle *rentier* class are dominant considerations with a few authors. But, on the whole, this kind of argument is subordinated to the juristic formulae.

3. Since canon law condemns credit sales, the scholastics condemn them too. None of the principal arguments, however, cover the case of credit sales, since in a credit sale a real good is exchanged for future money. Consequently, in connection with credit sales, there is a marked emphasis on the unnaturalness of selling time. Thus the usury prohibition is extended beyond the bases provided by the principal natural arguments. The unnaturalness of selling time is also the chief popular argument against usury.

4. There is a general tendency to consider as usury all riskless investment. Nearly every author who specifically considers such a case pronounces it to be usury, and St. Bernardine and St. Antoninus treat every temporary transfer of risk and ownership as a loan, and all profit on the transaction as usury. By this analysis, usury can occur not only in the transfer of consumptibles or fungibles, but in the transfer of fruitful, nonconsumptible property.

5. An essential part of the theory, insofar as money is the principal object of loans, is that money is nonvendible and so exempt from the laws of supply and demand.

6. By a strict application of the early theory in capitalistic cities, such as Siena and Florence, nearly the whole community is involved in usury. Whether the more liberal canonists, like Joannes Andreae and Laurentius de Ridolfis, would have concurred in the estimates of St. Bernardine and St. Antoninus is not clear.

CHAPTER IV

THE CONCEPT OF THE JUST PRICE

A great many later historians of scholastic economic thought, anxious to find a single key which will explain all scholastic economics, have declared that the scholastic theory of usury was part of a larger scholastic theory of value and the just price. With this hypothesis have often gone as corollaries the assertions that the scholastics believed that value was completely objective or that the scholastics believed that value was equal to labor cost. These corollaries result largely from taking usury analysis as the typical instance of the just-price theory.[1]

All these hypotheses, so widely accepted as history, are in fact so fallacious and so destructive of any understanding of the usury theory itself that it seems desirable to devote a special chapter to showing what the just price meant to the scholastics. There is, it will be seen, one thin, tenuous link between the concept of the just price and the analysis of usury, a link which alone prevents a formal contradiction from splitting scholastic economics. But, on the whole, one of the most striking features of scholastic economic thinking is that the problem of the just price is treated from an entirely different viewpoint than that from which usury is considered. Even when formally consistent, the just-price theory and usury theory frequently lead to different practical results; and no more bizarre confusion could be made than to derive one theory from the other.

1. *The Origin and Character of the Concept*

The just price is a formula first employed by the Roman law. The Code declares that a seller is entitled to recovery of the "justum pretium" from a buyer who has taken advantage of him, unless what was given him was at least half the just price. The *Digest* declares that "the price of things is not from the affection or utility of single persons, but from their com-

---

[1] See Selma Hagenauer, *Das "Justum Pretium" bei Thomas von Aquin*, Vierteljahrschrift für sozial und wirthgeschaftgeschichte, Vol. XXIV (Stuttgart, 1931), pp. 41, 53, and the authors listed *infra*, p. 397.

mon estimation." It adds that the price is not to be estimated from temporary circumstances or rare necessities, such as occur in a time of bad harvests. Another *Digest* text identifies the value of a good with the price at which it can be sold. These three texts, one from the Code, two from the *Digest*, contain the essentials of the scholastic theory of the just price.[2]

As the *Digest* indicates, price or value is determined by estimation, a subjective human act. What determines estimation? To this question, Aristotle had already answered, need. "Human need," he had declared, "is the single universal standard of human measurement."[3] Taken broadly, with need including all human wants serious or trivial, this answer of Aristotle will be the answer of the scholastic tradition; and estimation, itself a subjective act, will be said to rest, subjectively, on the will and wants of man. The origin of value will be said to lie in human demand.

St. Albert and St. Thomas in their commentaries on Aristotle repeat his words verbatim, though this fact by itself is no evidence of the acceptance of his doctrine, but simply marks the advent into the schools of formal Aristotelian teaching on the matter. St. Thomas himself declares that the value of goods "depends on their usefulness to man." In form this is a definition apparently stressing the objective character of usefulness, but it maintains the radically subjective nature of value because "usefulness" is basically dependent on man's purposes: to value a good because it fills a need or to value it because it is useful are identical acts. Scotus' definition of value is virtually identical with that of St. Thomas.[4]

Similarly, Giles of Lessines teaches that value increases or decreases with changes in the use of the good; that is, with variations in the demand for it. He writes, "According to justice, each thing ought to be of greater worth and price at the time and for the time of its use, than at another time when its use is not so necessary and convenient." John Buridan says explicitly, "A good is worth as much as human need needs it." Henry of Hesse, citing Aristotle by name, declares that the just price consists "in a near equality of goods in proportion to the measure of their market or usual or customary value. This measure, however, which is to be roughly considered, is a value as great as the quantity of human need." In a slightly different formula, but again emphasizing the role of human desire, St. Bernardine teaches that value is determined by a good's utility, scarcity,

---

[2] *Codex*, 4:44:2; *Digesta*, 35:2:63 and 36:1:16. Another text, *Digesta*, 14:2:4, has roughly the same idea.

[3] Aristotle, *Ethics*, V:5.

[4] St. Albert, *In libros ethicorum*, V:2:10:34; St. Thomas, *In X lib. ethic.*, V:9; *S.T.*, II–II: 77:2 ad 3; Scotus, *In IV libros sententiarum* (*Op. Oxon.*), IV:15:2.

and *complacibilitas*, that is, its quality of pleasing the will of a buyer. St. Antoninus incorporates St. Bernardine's doctrine verbatim.[5]

Thus the scholastic teaching puts the source of value in man. It does not entirely neglect the objective qualities of the good. St. Thomas and Scotus, as has been seen, do emphasize the part in determining value played by the good's objective capability of being useful. St. Bernardine and St. Antoninus give, as a second constituent of value, a good's properties, by which it is more efficient or powerful in meeting human needs.[6] But these objective qualities are secondary; they are of interest, they become of value, only if they are properties which do meet a human need.

2. *The Role of Supply*

Yet, it may be asked, have not the scholastics, in their insistence on the influence of need, stated a theory of value which is true enough of value philosophically considered, but not of value economically taken as price? Have they not forgotten the cardinal role of supply in setting economic value? Does not the Aristotelian thesis mean that bread is worth more than diamonds? The answer to the last question is affirmative, if the question is confined to Aristotle's philosophy alone. The answer to all the questions, however, is negative, if they are asked of scholastic economics. The scholastics grant supply its full status as a determinant of value. Either formally, or implicitly and in passing, they recognize that in economics need and demand are relative words, understandable only in terms of their correlative, supply; and they realize that a great need met by a greater supply will lead to a lesser value or price than a small need met by a smaller supply.

St. Thomas discusses the case of a wheat-seller selling at a high price when he knows, but the buyers do not, that more sellers will come later and the price will fall. Without question, St. Thomas assumes as the basis for the discussion that the supply alone will here determine the price. Similarly, Giles of Lessines teaches explicitly that the value of a good varies as its supply varies: so, he says, wheat is worth more in early summer, when it is scarce, than in autumn, when it is plentiful. Henry of Hesse expressly declares that prices are determined by the joint influence of supply and demand. St. Bernardine teaches that scarcity is an essential element in deter-

---

[5] Giles of Lessines, *De usuris*, c.10; John Buridan, *Quaestiones*, Q.12; Henry of Hesse, *De contractibus*, Part I, c.5, f.187; St. Bernar-dine, *De contractibus*, 35:1:1; St. Antoninus, *Summa*, 2:1:16.

[6] St. Bernardine, 35:1:1; St. Antoninus, 2:1:16.

mining value. The elements, fire, earth, air, and water, are vitally necessary for human life, he points out, but they are common and so are valued less than gold or balsam. Thus, too, he says, wheat is worth more in a famine than in a time of plenty. St. Antoninus repeats his teaching and illustrations.[7]

Supply, accordingly, is given its full weight in determining economic value in the scholastic schema. Demand is conceded the primacy, for without the existence of human needs there would be no interest in value; but it is readily granted that supply will limit and channel the force of demand in constituting the price. The just price is seen to be the price where demand and supply meet: in short, the market price.

3. *The Imprecision and Mutability of Price*

A corollary of the fact that the just price is the market price is that it is thoroughly variable, neither precise nor fixed. The early canonists, Hostiensis and Innocent, and the *Glossa ordinaria*, who take their notion of the just price as they find it, in the Roman law, hold that the buyer and seller may lawfully, even in the moral order, take advantage of each other up to one-half of the just price. Their implicit reasoning seems to be that the just price admits of that much imprecision without justice itself being violated. The theologians, such as William of Auxerre and St. Thomas, prefer to take the term "just price" literally and moralistically: they argue that if the price is the "just" one, it is always unjust to depart from it. Eventually their usage is accepted by the canonists.[8] But the theologians no more than the canonists believe that the just price is either exact or invariable.

As to its exact determination, St. Thomas teaches that a small deviation from the theoretically absolute just price is never sinful. Scotus is more openly liberal. He declares that there is "a great latitude" in fixing the just price, and he adds that if both parties knowingly and uncoercedly agree to a price different from the "just price," the contract is still just; for "it is sufficiently probable that when they are mutually content, they mutually wish to remit to each other whatever is lacking from the requisite justice." St. Bernardine repeats Scotus' remarks and adds that the exact value can "scarcely or never be determined by us." St. Antoninus repeats the whole teaching of St. Bernardine.[9]

---

[7] St. Thomas, *S.T.*, II–II:77:3 ad 4; Giles of Lessines, c.8; Henry of Hesse, I:5, f.187v; St. Bernardine, 35:1:1; St. Antoninus, 2:1:16.

[8] Hostiensis, *Commentaria*, V:19:6; Innocent IV, *Apparatus*, V, *De usuris*, 6; *Glossa ordinaria*, V:19:6; William of Auxerre, *Summa*, III:21, Q.3, f.225v:b; St. Thomas, *S.T.*, II–II:77:1 ad 1; see Panormitanus, V:19:6.

[9] St. Thomas, *S.T.*, II–II:77:1 ad 1; Scotus,

The just price is not only inexact at any one time; it also varies with different times and places. In the case of the wheat-seller mentioned above, St. Thomas holds that the early high price and the later low price are equally just and lawful, each expressing the right value at the time at which they are offered. Elsewhere, St. Thomas faces the objection that one who buys low and sells high must violate the just price, for he "must either have bought it for less than its value or sell it for less than its worth"; St. Thomas vigorously rejects the objection. The price of a good, he declares, may increase because of the buyer's labor and risk or simply because of a change of time or place. Similarly, as we have seen, Giles of Lessines teaches that value changes constantly with changes in supply or demand, place or time. Again, Henry of Hesse says that all prices change and that it is irrational to impose prices fixed for all places or all times. Similarly, St. Bernardine and St. Antoninus assume that it is entirely normal and not at all unjust that wheat in a famine fetch a high price.[10]

4. The Influence of Cost

The just price is the market price. Is there, it may be wondered, any effort to approach the problem from the viewpoint of the seller, and to relate cost and market value? In the *Ethics* (V:7), Aristotle had given as an example of commutative justice the exchange of a house for a quantity of shoes, the builder's work in building the house equalling the shoemaker's work in making the shoes. The example is not pressed, and it seems clear that Aristotle intended it as only an illustration, not an absolute affirmation that equality of exchange demanded an equality of labor being matched; a little after this passage, he explicitly says that value is determined by need. St. Albert and St. Thomas, commenting on the *Ethics*, repeat Aristotle's statement verbatim, and so some historians have supposed that they believed that labor alone determined value.[11] But they say nothing similar in their own works, and a repetition of Aristotle in a commentary on him cannot be taken as an expression of the commentators' view.

In Scotus, however, there is a fairly definite linking of the just price and the seller's labor. A seller, he says, sells at a just price if he charges enough to pay for his labor and his risks, and to support himself and his family. Here value seems to equal the cost of labor and labor maintenance as it does in the

IV:15:2; St. Bernardine, 35:1:1; St. Antoninus, 2:1:16. In the same sense, see also Henry of Hesse, I:5, f.188.

[10] St. Thomas, *S.T.*, II–II:77:3 ad 4, and

77:4 ad 2; Giles of Lessines, c.8; Henry of Hesse, II:12, f.210v; St. Bernardine, 35:1:1; St. Antoninus, 2:1:16.

[11] Cf. Hagenauer, pp. 12–30; John A. Ryan,

classical Ricardian formulation. Somewhat similarly, Gerson teaches that it is normally illicit for a merchant to sell at a price which not only repays his labor, expenses, and risks, but also yields him a notable profit. But both Scotus and Gerson are treating of traders, who have bought goods at one price to resell at a higher price. The addition to the original price, they say, should not be greater than the trader's labor; they do not say that the original price was determined by the labor cost of the good. Given the broadest possible interpretation of their views, Scotus and Gerson are still only subscribing to a partial labor-value theory. Moreover, as we have seen, Scotus admits that that price is always just with which the parties themselves are content; Gerson condemns only a *notable* surplus over the labor cost. There is therefore nothing very inflexible in the view of the relation of cost and value of even these writers who approach value from the standpoint of cost.[12]

As for the other scholastics, they assume that any man engaged in an honest trade may and will charge enough to support himself and his family.[13] But they do not believe that the just price on the seller's part will be determined by the cost of his labor alone. St. Thomas teaches explicitly that value may increase by a change in place or time alone without labor or risk by a good's owner; and the other writers we have explored, who teach that value changes with changes in demand or supply, show no disposition to assert that such changes must reflect the cost of labor. Labor will influence cost and so the supply; but no scholastic teaches that it is the sole determinant of value.[14]

5. *The Objective Factors*

If the value of a good is what it sells for, if the just price is the market price, how can injustice ever be committed in sales? The answer lies in the objective aspect of the just price. Any market price is to an individual seller or buyer an objective price independent of his peculiar wishes and wants. This paradox, by which a price determined subjectively by all becomes objective to each, is true of any market. The scholastics give this elementary economic fact a moral meaning. The common estimate, the

---

Distributive Justice (New York, 1916), p. 333; L. Polier, *L'idée du juste salaire* (Paris, 1903), pp. 44, 63; L. Haney, *The History of Economic Thought* (New York, 1948), p. 99.

[12] Scotus, IV:15:2 (*Op. Oxon.*); John Gerson, *Regulae morales*, n.79, in *Opera*, Vol. III.

[13] E.g., St. Thomas, *S.T.*, II–II:77:4; St. Antoninus, 2:1:16.

[14] St. Thomas, *S.T.*, II–II:77:4 ad 2. The supposition that the opposition to usury is founded on a labor theory of value has also influenced authors ascribing this theory to the scholastics. But as will be made particularly clear later, in Chapter VI on partnership, most scholastics do not condemn usury simply because it is laborless gain.

market price, they teach should not be altered because of the need of a particular seller or the advantage of a particular buyer. If a man driven by a desperate need to feed his family wants to sell wheat and the market price of wheat is 100, he is entitled to sell at 100; his need is not to be exploited by a buyer seeking a bargain. If a man needs a common medicine to save his life and its usual price is 10, then 10,000 cannot be asked of him on the ground that it is worth that much to him.[15] Common, not individual, need is the measure of value. "The value of a good ought to be considered not according to the necessity of the buyer or seller, but according to the necessity of the whole community."[16] If the whole community seeks a rare life-saving drug, its price will naturally be high, but the need of a single individual does not by itself create value. Value is social. In the language of St. Thomas, a seller who charges a high price because of the special need of a buyer or because the commodity will be peculiarly profitable to him, "sells what is not his";[17] for the buyer's need or advantage is not the seller's to sell. In the language of any modern economic textbook, in a market where information is perfect and equilibrium has been reached, no buyer or seller will trade at a different price: the equilibrium price, the result of all individual demands and all individual supplies, will be the price at which anyone who trades will trade.

Curiously, the scholastics do admit a departure from the market price, when a seller sells a good or peculiar advantage or sentimental value to him. If he charges more for suffering this extra loss, they argue, he acts justly, because he sells what is his to sell.[18] They do not say, of course, whether any buyer will wish to pay this premium, and presumably in a free market no one would; so that this exception to the norm of the common estimation is not of overriding significance. Similarly, Scotus' admission that an uncoerced buyer and seller may lawfully decide to trade at a price different from the market's is an exception of no great consequence.

The scholastics also condemn attempts to manipulate the market price artificially by monopolistic restriction of the supply or by purely speculative purchases.[19] The just price is the price established by genuine consumer or commercial demand and available supply. But this repugnance to monopoly and sheer speculation does not alter the fact that the just price is normally the market's.

[15] St. Thomas, S.T., II–II:77:1.
[16] Buridan, I:11, art. 3.
[17] St. Thomas, S.T., II–II:77:1; St. Bernardine, 35:1:1; St. Antoninus, 2:1:16.
[18] St. Thomas, S.T., II–II:77:1; St. Bernardine, 35:1:1; St. Antoninus, 2:1:16.
[19] Scotus, IV:15:2 (Op. Oxon.); Gerson, Sermo contra avaritiam, Dominica I post octavas Epiphaniae, col. 1011, in Opera, vol. III; St. Bernardine, 35:1:1; St. Antoninus, 2:1:16.

6. Legal Price-Fixing

The market price is established by the whole community of buyers and sellers, a community the same in fact as the political community. Cannot, therefore, the representative of the community, the prince, determine publicly what the just price of a good is? Is not such determination particularly necessary in the absence of perfect information and perfect competition, inasmuch as the true market price is, in these conditions, difficult to know? The medieval scholastics' analysis suggests an affirmative answer to these questions, but stops short of anything like a full development. St. Thomas speaks of the public authorities setting the measures to be used by sellers in determining weights and lengths, and he says the sellers may not alter these measures; but he does not extend this analogy to the setting of price itself. Scotus suggests that the seller may charge what the State would have to pay to obtain similar goods. Gerson declares that the just price may be determined by a "lord or prelate."[20] As will be seen in the discussion of the price of money, this belief that value may be determined by law may constitute the one formal link between the just price and the prohibition of usury.[21]

7. The Just Price and Usury Analysis

The mutable, imprecise, radically subjective character of the just price has been made clear. The scholastics, it is evident, do not believe in a completely objective determination of price nor in a labor theory of value. Buying and selling, in their eyes, need conform to no absolute, invariable price standard.[22] The just price is the market price; but the just price is a technical concept applying only to commodity sales. It is not applied to loans. Usury is in no way a problem of the just price in the usual scholastic sense. This will be demonstrated by four cases, each involving sales on credit, the one area in which the two theories overlap.

The Distinction by Intention

Perhaps the sharpest, as it is the simplest, distinction between usury and the unjust price is made by the *Gloss*, which distinguishes them purely by a seller's intention. If a seller on credit sells at a higher price because of

---

[20] St. Thomas, *S.T.*, II–II:77:2 ad 2; Scotus, IV:15:2 (*Op. Oxon.*); Gerson, *Sermo contra avaritiam*, col. 1011; compare St. Bernardine, 35:1:1; St. Antoninus, 2:1:16; Henry of Hesse, II:12, f.210v.

[21] See *infra*, pp. 93–95.
[22] See N. Gras, "Economic Rationalism in the Late Middle Ages," *Speculum* (July 1933), p. 305.

the credit involved, he commits usury; if, however, he charges the higher price not for the credit but because the buyer is ignorant of the just price, he commits an injustice but no usury.[23] The distinction is not a verbal quibble without practical effect. To be guilty of public usury is to be *ipso facto* excommunicated, while simple injustice involves no such penalty. The practical consequences involved are thus of the highest moment and depend solely on the distinction between usury and injustice. The *Gloss's* teaching is a classic proof that usury and unjust evaluation were regarded as essentially different matters.

Credit Charges and the Maximum Just Price

Another case involving a distinction between usury and the just price is this: A price differential exists between the cash price and the credit price throughout an industry. It is argued that this is *prima facie* evidence of usury; the higher credit price must be a charge for time. But, replies St. Thomas, the credit price could be the common estimation of the good, that is, the true just price, and the cash price could be a discount gratuitously given by the seller. Or as St. Bernardine and St. Antoninus put it, the just price admits of imprecision: the cash price may be only the mean just price and the credit price be the maximum just price.[24] In this way, St. Antoninus believes he can justify a good part of the Florentine wool trade, largely financed by credit furnished at a premium above the cash price. Here the just-price theory leads to a far more liberal result than the strict application of the usury prohibition.

Credit Sales of Speculative Commodities

According to the usury theory, the present value of the good loaned determines absolutely, exactly, and without margin the value to be returned. Whatever is added to the principal is usury. But, it is objected, the analysis of the just price recognizes that value changes. May not a good bought on credit today be worth more at the time of payment? Should not the debtor pay this higher price? These questions lead to a recognition of a creditor's rights in the case known as *venditio sub dubio*. *Venditio sub dubio* is sponsored as an exception to the usury law by two papal decretals, and all discussion of the case follows these two decisions and a third decretal limiting them.[25] In *In civitate*, the first papal condemnation of higher prices

[23] *Glossa ordinaria*, V:19:6.
[24] St. Thomas, *De emptione et venditione*, in *Opera*, Vol. XXVIII; St. Bernardine, 34:3:1; St. Antoninus, 2:1:8.
[25] *Decretales*, V:19:6, *In civitate*; V:19:10, *Consuluit*; V:19:19, *Naviganti*.

on credit sales, Alexander III admitted an exception: such payments should not be considered usurious if there was a real doubt at the time of the sale as to the future value of the merchandise. At the same time, the Pope counseled against charging more even in such a case. Urban III shortly afterwards declared flatly that a sale on credit at a *much* higher price than the current cash one was usury. Forty years later the celebrated decretal of Gregory IX, *Naviganti*, considered the converse of the case of *In civitate* — payment in advance for goods to be delivered later. The Pope, in a ruling analogous to Alexander's, decided that a discount for the anticipated payment was not usurious if there was real doubt at the time of payment as to what the value of the merchandise would be at the time of delivery. At the same time recurring to the case of *In civitate*, he reaffirmed the licitness of a higher charge in credit sales where there was doubt as to the future value, but added a new condition: the seller must have not intended to sell the goods on credit, but originally must have planned to sell later at the later cash price.

These three canons supplement each other with fair consistency. Alexander III and Gregory IX both believe that the value of a good at the time the contract concerning it will be completed may be considered by the parties to a sale, and that a fair price will be one which allows for a probable increase or decrease in this value. The determination of such a price they take to be entirely different from the usurious sale of time. Urban III condemns only the setting of a price which, beyond reasonable doubt, the merchandise will never be worth. Gregory adds a condition to Alexander's permission. It is a simple application of the doctrine that the intention to gain from a loan is always usurious, and merely points out that a seller intending to gain by a transaction involving credit would certainly be in sin. All the decretals agree that where it is believed or hoped that the future value of the merchandise bought on credit will be less than the price paid, usury is committed; and they similarly agree that usury occurs in the second case, if the buyer thinks that the future value of the merchandise bought in advance will be greater than the price paid; that is, according to the canons, all speculation in commodity futures is illicit. But all the decretals equally assume that where no profit on the credit involved is intended, but the preservation of equality of values is aimed at, the just-price theory and not the usury prohibition applies.

Innocent IV, in his commentary on *Naviganti*, argues that by a parity of reasoning, a seller who intended to sell at a different place, where his goods would be worth more, but who is prevailed upon to sell on credit in the place where he is, can lawfully charge the higher price of the other place, provided he deducts for the labor and risk he has been spared. Hostiensis criticizes Innocent's admission, saying that it opens the way to exploitation of needy buyers and frauds by usurers. "I fear," he declares, "that these words drag to hell many thousands of souls." Yet, he adds, showing a curious mildness towards a teaching with such results, "sometimes good Homer nods; therefore I accuse no one in litigious judgment; but in the penitential forum, it is fitting for each one's own conscience to accuse himself." [26]

The *Glossa ordinaria*, William of Auxerre, Alexander of Hales, and Hostiensis all stress that there must be no intention to gain on the part of the creditor. Hostiensis is particularly disturbed that the condition placed by Gregory, that one must not have originally intended to sell on credit, is rarely observed in practice. He warns solemnly that the written form of the contract is no justification unless one really intended to sell for cash later; for "God questions the heart and not the hand." [27]

All these authors, following the decretals, also insist that there must be a real possibility of a change in the future value of the goods. William of Auxerre says that "a good and wise man" is always to be asked if such a possibility exists. [28] The nature of this possibility that the value will increase is perhaps best explained by Giles of Lessines. His analysis here is closely tied to his analysis of time which we have already examined. He says:

Time can be related to some exchanges of goods as conferring or taking away something of their just value. And in this way, if, on account of time, one sells for more or less, a contract of such a kind will not be usurious; for a measure of wheat is estimated to be worth more — and justly so — in summer than in autumn, other things being equal: this is, to this extent, from the nature of time, and therefore if one accepts more for grain sold for the summer than he would have given in autumn when he buys grain, he is not judged a usurer, provided at that time alone [summer] he had wished to sell the grain, and not at another time. [29]

If the passage of time will give rise to an increase in demand or a decrease in supply or give opportunity for fruits to mature, time has a real influence on the value, [30] and *venditio sub dubio* applies. If time has no effect on the value, a higher credit price will be a charge purely for the credit and so be usurious.

The intention to profit on a sale is lawful, the intention to profit on a

---

[26] Innocent IV, *Apparatus*, V:19:19; Hostiensis, *Commentaria*, V:19:6.

[27] *Glossa ordinaria*, V:19:6; William of Auxerre, III:21, Q.3, f.225r:b; Hostiensis,

Commentaria, V:19:6.

[28] William of Auxerre, III:21, Q.3, f.225r:b.

[29] Giles of Lessines, c.9.

[30] Cf. *supra*, p. 63.

loan illicit. In the case of the credit sale, involving both a sale and a loan, profit on the loan is usury, but the normal profit on the sale is just. There is no formal contradiction here between the usury theory and the just-price theory. One considers only the charge for credit, and prohibits it. The other takes the transaction as a sale and, considering the variable value of goods, allows the parties to make as much profit as they would if both delivery and payment were made at the later date, without credit being involved. The higher credit price is not, in these circumstances, for the credit; it is simply compensation to a seller, who could have sold later at the same price for cash. Yet the case, without showing a contradiction, does demonstrate clearly the difference between usury theory and the just price.

A significant aspect of *venditio sub dubio* not yet mentioned is that it is a plea confined to commodity sales. The decretals pointedly speak only of commodities, and William of Auxerre, Innocent, and Giles of Lessines specifically exclude money from being treated as an object of a *venditio sub dubio*.[31] Similarly, no one ever says that a moneylender may appeal to the theory of value suggested by the just-price analysis. According to this theory, since value is determined by the common estimation and since it varies, every usurer might plead, I sell money at a time when it is commonly in demand and I contract to receive payment at a time when it will be less in demand; therefore, I give money when its value is high for money when its value is low, and I should be able to ask a premium. But it is not even suggested that the usurer can make this defense. Why is *venditio sub dubio* confined to commodities and why is the just-price theory not applied to money? Is there in these divergencies a direct contradiction between the usury prohibition and the concept of the just price?

Verbally, the distinction between the areas covered by the two theories is accomplished by declaring that "money is nonvendible"[32] and that the norm of the just price applies only to sales of commodities. But why, it may be argued, should this verbal distinction make any real difference? Is not all economic value constituted in the same way? Why should not the value of money be determined like the value of other commodities by the common estimation? To these questions the answer implicit in the scholastic analysis is that the just price of money is determined by law; the legal face value of money is its just value. As it has been assumed that the prince acting for the community can establish a just price for commodities, so it is affirmed that he can and has for money. The value of money is therefore determined

---

[31] William of Auxerre, III:21, Q.3, f.- 225v:a; Innocent, *Apparatus*, V:19:19; Giles of Lessines, c.8.

[32] See *supra*, p. 53.

like other values by the common estimation; only here, as with the price of certain other commodities, the common estimation is fixed and proclaimed by the State. Moreover, the face value of money is set for all times. The law does not recognize that 100 florins a year from now are inferior to 100 florins today; and as the legal price binds in conscience, money must be evaluated now and a year later at the same price. Time, therefore, can not change the value of money, as it can the value of other goods; for whether or not the supply and demand for money increase or decrease, the legal face value will hold. Money remains a pure measure fixed by the state and is considered as immune from all fluctuations in worth.

The foregoing analysis, it must be stressed, is only implicitly present in the medieval approach; the later scholastics develop and clarify it. Yet to see the result of this analysis present as an underlying assumption of the medieval scholastics does not seem unwarranted. No other view gives meaning to the standard formula "money is nonvendible." Only by making this assumption could a formal contradiction between the just price theory and the usury theory have been avoided. Moreover, the assumption is contained, in a formulation using different words, in the statement of St. Thomas that money is a fixed measure. As the measures for determining length and quantity which have been set by public authority may not be changed by private persons, so money, which is the measure of price, may not be changed by private persons.

In only two cases is it admitted that the value of money may change. One is the case where the State itself changes the legal value. In such a case an alteration in the measure itself occurs and a real difference in value is effected. In such a case, the principle of *venditio sub dubio* applies: if a lender fears a devaluation by positive law, he can stipulate that his principal be returned to him calculated at the silver-gold ratio prevailing at the start of the loan.[33] But this exception points up all the more the basic scholastic assumptions: the legal price is the just price, and the value of money is its face value. The other case, dealt with by a minority of medieval authors, involved the sale of foreign exchange. This will be considered in Chapter VIII, Banking.

As far as formal theory is concerned, this insistence on the legal value of money reconciles the usury theory and the just-price theory: the one teaches that increment on a money loan is unjust, the other that the value of money fixed by law is to be observed, and according to each theory, to loan or sell 100 florins for 110 is unjust. Indeed, if money alone is considered, it is easy to infer that the scholastics believed that value was always fixed

[33] Giles of Lessines, c.14.

and objective; and a number of modern historians have made this mistaken inference. In fact, however, the scholastics do not think of the legally determined price as the normal case. According to their analysis, the variable market estimation is the usual determinant of value, and value is only accidentally stabilized by law. Consequently, if money could be considered in some way other than as a pure legal measure, the scholastics would not insist on its face value being observed but would leave the determination of its value to the market. If money could be treated as a commodity, without a legal price, its value would be free to fluctuate, and the seller of present money for future money could lawfully make a profit on its sale. The strict usury theory, prohibiting any increment on a loan, would not apply if the transaction were a sale; and if the legal price of money did not have to be observed, the sale could be made a profitable one. Thus, a transfer of jurisdiction from the usury prohibition to the just-price theory could open the way to immensely different practical results, once the legal price of money ceases to hold. In the sixteenth century the theorists effected this transfer of jurisdiction on a large scale; in the Middle Ages the possibility was not exploited and the just-price approach and the usury approach led, in general, to the same conclusions where money and not a commodity was the object of the transaction.

Contracts of Sale and Resale

One type of sales contract exhibited a peculiarly urgent practical problem because of its use by customary or public usurers. This was a contract of sale, with an agreement by the purchaser to resell to the original seller. Although not technically described as mortgages, these contracts were substantially in the form of mortgages as known in Anglo-American law today. Were they to be treated under the rubric of the just price or under the rubric of usury?

As early as Robert of Courçon, we find complaints of wealthy men who buy the vineyards, mills, and chateaux of would-be borrowers and having enjoyed the fruits of these goods for a time, resell them at the same price to the borrower, who has meanwhile had the use of their money. By such sale and resale agreements, the law against the acceptance of the fruits of pledges was easily evaded. Courçon denounces the practice as pernicious usury.[34]

Shortly after this, two letters of Innocent III, later inserted in the *Decretals*, deal with the same problem. In the first case judged by the Pope, the creditor agrees to resell to the original seller between the seventh and ninth

---

[34] Robert of Courçon, *De usura*, pp. 61–63.

years from the date of sale the lands and fields which he has bought, and to charge only about half-price in the resale. The Pope judges this contract to be in fraud of usury on a realistic ground: the low resale price. A true buyer, he seems to reason, would never resell at such a figure.[35] Similarly, in the second case, Innocent declares that two clauses suggest that the resale contract is in fraud: (1) the fruits are to be counted against the resale price, a procedure that would be inexplicable if a true sale had been effected; (2) the original seller is at the same time charged a higher price to redeem his property, again an inexplicable condition, if a real purchase was being made. Moreover, the buyer was accustomed to exercising usury.[36] In neither case, it should be noted, is the simple addition of a resale clause, whether in favor of seller or buyer, sufficient in the Pope's eyes to prove the contract usurious. He appeals to other circumstances suggesting a deliberate evasion in order to establish guilt.

St. Raymond allows a resale agreement in favor of the seller, unless it is done in fraud, as, for example, when the resale price is higher than the original. Innocent IV has substantially the same teaching. Hostiensis also allows the resale agreement and cites the Roman *lex commissoriae* to show that the contract is a valid one.[37] He warns, however, that in the external forum usury will be presumed, if a man seeking a loan is compelled to sell his property and enter such an agreement instead. He believes that many contemporary usurers buy the possessions of the poor, who are then allowed to recover at the same price between the seventh and ninth years. The usurers, he says, "make *baratos* [frauds], and they are truly *baratae*, leading to *barathum* [hell]."[38] "*Baratae*" will be the standard term by which such fraudulent sale agreements will be described. Astesanus, who is the first theologian to mention the contract, follows Hostiensis and allows the resale agreement, unless the price paid is unfair.[39] A general maxim found in the *Gloss*, in Hostiensis, and in other early canonists, which rules their treatment of the sale and resale agreements, is this: "Against usurers it is easily to be presumed."[40] Hence an intrinsically lawful conditional sale would be considered usurious if employed by a public or notorious lender.

The contracts considered by the early writers have all been transactions in

[35] *Decretales*, III:17:5, *Ad nostram noveris.*

[36] *Decretales*, III:21:4, *Illo vos credimus.*

[37] St. Raymond of Pennaforte, *Summa*, 2:7; Innocent, *Apparatus*, III:21:4; Hostiensis, *Summa*, V, *De usuris*, n.8. The Roman law allows a resale in favor of the seller, if the contract specified that he could re-

deem by refunding the purchase price within a certain time. *Codex*, 4:54:4.

[38] Hostiensis, *Commentaria*, III:11:5.

[39] Astesanus, *Summa*, III:11:4.

[40] Astesanus, III:21:4; *Glossa*, 3:17:5; St. Raymond, 2:7:4.

which the disguised lender bought, and the would-be borrower repurchased. Joannes Andreae now considers the converse of this procedure. A man, asked to lend, instead sells a good on credit to the one seeking a loan; he then immediately repurchases the good at a lower cash price. This leaves the borrower with ready cash, and a debt for the larger amount of credit. Despite the use of the sales device, Andreae concludes that this is usury.[41]

Henry of Hesse discusses at some length the resale practice of the kind described by the early writers. For example, instead of lending, an investor buys for one year a house that ordinarily rents for 10 per year. He pays 10 for it and rents it for 10. At the end of the year he resells the house to its former owner at 10. His profit is 100 per cent. This kind of business, Hesse reports, is favored by many rich men. Some of them will not loan at usury because it is clearly a sin; others will not because of the social opprobrium it brings. But both kinds of people like this alternative way of obtaining as much money and more. "It is," says Hesse, "a kind of buying by which the rich get richer and the poor poorer."[42]

But Hesse does more than denounce the practice as a fraud. Unlike the early writers who content themselves with denunciation, he attempts to show why it is unjust. The transaction, he says, does not have the full nature of a sale, for ownership has not passed in it absolutely. The temporary purchaser cannot alienate the good, and alienation is a power possessed by any true owner. Also the original seller, when he repurchases, is allowed to charge the temporary buyer for any damage he caused the good, and this again shows that the buyer was not the full owner. Moreover, he says, the practice is against the natural end of commerce, which is to relieve need, not make someone wealthy. Again, he declares, the fair price of a true sale is generally not paid; the good sold is usually undervalued for the sale. If one replies that the price is less the shorter the time the good is sold for, Henry answers that this reasoning can be reduced to a logical absurdity: according to it, one could become the true owner of all Bohemia for at least an instant by paying an obol. In fact, Henry implies, no true sale's price varies with time alone. On all these grounds, he concludes that the object of the sale and resale contracts is a pledge, not purchased property, and the transaction is a loan at usury.[43] Henry's arguments, it is clear, tell excellently against sale and resale arguments made at unfair prices with conditions showing manifest bad faith. But they do not tell against resale agreements as such.

[41] Joannes Andreae, *Decretalium libros*, VI, *De usuris*, c.1.

[42] Henry of Hesse, II:8, f.208v:b.
[43] Henry of Hesse, II:8, f.209.

The pure resale clause continues to be unassailed in itself, as is particularly evident in the treatment of redeemability clauses on the *census*, a use approved by the papal bulls. At the same time, the abuse of the resale clause by usurers continues. Laurentius de Ridolfis sums up the opinion of everyone: "Experience has taught that when contracts of loan are put aside, the usurers have begun to make contracts of conditional sale, with an agreement to resell the good afterwards." [44]

Scholastic testimony from the twelfth to the fifteenth century supports the truth of Laurentius' observation. It is also clear that such resale agreements may be condemned as naturally unjust, if the price is grossly unfair, or if conditions are attached which show that the so-called buyer does not intend to become the true owner. But, as the scholastics are also unanimous in admitting a resale agreement as licit in itself, no natural-law objection was raised to contracts where a fair price was paid, the purchaser became the true, if temporary, owner, and a resale clause was added.[45] Although such contracts made a portion of the usury prohibition inoperative in practice, it appeared that they could be condemned only by positive law. In short, the theory of the just price worked to a different result than did the strict usury theory. Only by taking the usury rule as a standard and finding the sales contracts "in fraud of it" could the usury rule itself be maintained. The divergence between the two theories was a serious weakness in the natural-law case against usury. At the same time, the fact that the scholastic authors were willing to insist that such contracts be treated as frauds, while no such insistence was made in relation to annuity contracts, suggests very strongly the practical considerations underlying some of the scholastic formalism. The fact that the sale and resale contracts were considered far more suspect than the annuity contracts suggests some practical discrimination by the scholastics as to the type of credit whose interest rate they wished to control.

Conclusion

To recapitulate: the just-price theory supports the usury prohibition in agreeing that the legal value of money is invariable, but it invites avoidance of the prohibition when the legal value is not formally involved. In general, the medieval scholastics refused to permit the evasion which this transfer of jurisdiction to the just-price theory offered; so that the radical difference in

---

[44] Laurentius de Ridolfis, 2:60. On the redeemability of the *census*, see *infra*, Chapter VII, section 1.

[45] The problem of when a sale with a repurchase agreement attached is not to be treated as a sale recurs in a modern context under the federal income-tax laws; see James A. Moore and David H. W. Dohan, "Sales, Churches and Monkeyshines," *Tax Law Review*, XI (1956), 87.

approach underlying the theory did not become obvious in the Middle Ages. In three cases, however, the just-price theory supplanted the usury analysis with markedly differing results: *venditio sub dubio*; credit sales at the maximum just price; and credit sales where the seller's intention was unjust but not usurious. In these situations involving the sale of commodities there was, perhaps, less need to fear the outright exploitation of the debtor against which the usury theory guarded. Only where the whole purpose of the prohibition was threatened with frustration was the usury rule invoked to the exclusion of the just-price rule in sales; this was when the most common type of security device for a lender was cast in the form of a sale. Then, with a disregard for theory that was at once instinctive and unjustified in theoretical terms, the scholastics insisted that the usury rule must measure the justice of the transaction.[46]

[46] The main theses of this chapter, that the just price is normally the market price and that just-price analysis is distinct from usury analysis, have recently received detailed confirmation in a study by John W. Baldwin, "The Medieval Theories of the Just Price: The Twelfth and Thirteenth Centuries," unpublished doctoral dissertation, Johns Hopkins University (Baltimore, 1956). This study also has a much greater appreciation of the distinctions and nuances in development in the two centuries it covers than it has been possible to show in one chapter here, telescoping the development over four centuries.

CHAPTER V

TITLES TO PAYMENT BEYOND THE PRINCIPAL

The canon law, the canonists, and the theologians recognized from the beginning that the usury law, like most laws, permitted exceptions. From the recognition of individual exceptions, there arose a theory, and from the theory of exceptions there eventually developed a theory of interest. This development, however, is far from reaching its maturity in the Middle Ages; only the first halting steps are taken here. From a theoretical viewpoint, development was retarded by the concept of the normally gratuitous loan, which led to a belief cherished by the theorists that ever to admit interest as due from the beginning of a loan would be to destroy the usury prohibition itself. Growth was also checked by the notion of the sterility of money. At the same time, from a practical standpoint, the doctrine on intention prevented any widespread appeal to interest titles. Loans, it will be recalled, were considered licit only if made from charity; compensation on them, even if justified, was thought vitiated if it were sought chiefly for its own sake. Insistence on intention did prevent any evasion of the usury laws, at least in the spiritual order, but it had also the effect of barring the use of legitimate interest titles by many honest lenders. This tight restriction on the interest titles must never be forgotten in considering medieval interest theory. The theoretical barriers of the gratuitous loan and the sterility of money were partially overcome in the Middle Ages, but the doctrine on intention remained an unmovable obstacle.

The interest theory, then, in the Middle Ages was in an embryonic state, but it was an embryo which would in later times become a giant. There is no need to dwell on its subsequent importance. In the end, as everyone knows, interest on loans came to be considered the norm, and usury the exception; and the scholastic analysis of usury came to center on the distinction between usury and interest. What is important now is to understand the early concept of interest, to see how it was first distinguished from usury, and to appreciate its growth. An understanding of its later role must begin with an understanding of its early life.

Before we turn to interest theory proper, however, we must concern our-selves with certain other exceptions to the rule that usury is any payment beyond the principal.[1]

CASES INVOLVING A SPECIAL RELATION BETWEEN LENDER AND BORROWER

The first class of exceptions to the usury law consists in cases where a relation beyond the simple one of lender and borrower exists between the contracting parties. These cases are readily understandable, although they present little theoretic interest, since in each the grounds for payment beyond the principal are entirely accidental and alien to the loan itself. The grounds for payment lie in the special relation of the parties, which has nothing to do with the loan in any way. The cases tell us nothing of the scholastic principles on lending, but they unquestionably had some effect in stimulating the ad-mission of more important exceptions, and they furnished matter for further precisions of the doctrine itself.

1. *The Borrower An Enemy*

From an enemy you may demand usury. This exception is the oldest one recognized by the canon law and is based on a text from St. Ambrose em-bodied in Gratian, which declares, *ubi jus belli, ibi etiam jus usurae*.[2] The relations of justice are suspended between belligerents: if you have the right to kill a man, you have the lesser right to deprive him of his property.[3] This is the foundation of the exception. Interpretation of it varies slightly with different commentators, but none differ greatly as to principle. By "enemy" some writers understand heretics and infidels, particularly the Saracens.[4] Here a secondary consideration of charity enters in, since the main motive in weakening such enemies is the desire to bring them into the Church.[5] Giles of Lessines goes to the extreme of saying that *dispars cultus* is excuse enough for usury, because God, as the owner of all goods,

---

[1] One set of exceptions appears in a mne-monic given by Hostiensis (*Summa*, V, *De usuris*, n.8):

"Feuda, fidejussor, pro dote, stipendia cleri,
Venditio fructus, cui velle jure nocere,
Vendens sub dubio, pretium post tempora solvens,
Poena nec in fraudem, lex commissoria, gratis
Dans, socii pompa: plus forte modis datur istis."

Venditio fructus, lex commissoria, and *socii pompa* we do not consider here, since they do not involve a credit contract.

[2] Gratian, *Decretum Gratiani*, C.14, Q.4, c.12. This exception appears to contradict the teaching that usury, unlike killing, can be licit; see *supra*, p. 42.

[3] *Glossa ordinaria*, C.14, Q.4, c.12; Alex-ander of Hales, *Summa*, III:2:4:2:3:3:1.

[4] Roland Bandinelli, *Summa*, C.14, Q.4; Bernard of Pavia, *Summa decretalium*, V:15, c.5.

[5] Roland Bandinelli, *Summa*, C.14, Q.4. For a later authority, see St. Bernardine, *De contractibus*, 42:3:1.

may be supposed to have given them to the faithful.[6] This interpretation, however, is unusual. Other writers include under "enemy" the enemies of the State and, in particular, of the Roman Empire.[7] Most writers agree that Christians and Jews are not to consider each other enemies, and that the text authorizes neither group to take usury from the other.[8] This is affirmed particularly against Jewish appeals to the text as authorization to take usury of Christians.[9] The *Gloss* points out that the canon may also be understood as saying, Ask usury of whom you wish to harm; but you should not desire to injure anyone, and therefore should not demand usury of anyone.[10] This opinion is repeated as a possible one by most of the later commentators,[11] and it is, of course, abstractly speaking, an unimpeachable sentiment. Nonetheless, since all the commentators recognized the right of just war, they all, at least implicitly, recognized that at times you could wish to take usuries of someone.[12]

The practical importance of this canon was perhaps greater than might at first be supposed, since considerable commerce took place between the Near East and the Italian city-states, and opportunity for lending to an enemy Saracen may not have been rare.[13] Other applications of it do not readily suggest themselves.

2. *The Borrower a Vassal*

Two texts in the decretals allow ecclesiastical creditors to retain the revenues of lands pledged to them in a loan, not counting the revenues towards the payment of the principal, if the pledged land is already a fief of the creditor and if, at the same time, the vassal is freed for the length of the pledge from his normal service.[14] The *Gloss*, St. Raymond of Pennafort, and Alexander of Hales handle this exception very awkwardly, declaring that it is a special privilege in favor of the Church and does not apply to lay fiefs.[15] Their opinion amounted to saying that the Church could commit

---

[6] Giles of Lessines, *De usuris*, c.7.

[7] Hostiensis, *Commentaria*, V:19:16:2.

[8] St. Raymond of Pennaforte, *Summa*, 2:7:9; Hostiensis, *Commentaria*, V:19:16:2.

[9] Hostiensis, *Commentaria*, V:19:6:3; Alexander de Nevo, *Consilium* I, ad dubium 1.

[10] *Glossa ordinaria*, C.14, Q.4, c.12.

[11] E.g., St. Albert, *In IV libros sententiarum*, III:37:13; St. Raymond, *Summa*, 2:7:9.

[12] Benjamin Nelson has attempted to show a varying "range of attitude and scale of values" among the scholastic writers interpreting this exception. But he has given it an importance unknown to the scholastics, and I do not find any difference in their fundamental approach to it. See Nelson, *The Idea of Usury* (Princeton, 1949), pp. 6, 23.

[13] Robert of Courçon, for example, in treating of usury, approves the appropriation of goods in the Holy Land, because it is the patrimony of Christians, recovered in a just war (Robert of Courçon, *De usura*, p. 11).

[14] *Decretales*, V:19:8; cf. III:20:1.

[15] *Glossa ordinaria*, C.14, Q.3; St. Raymond,

usury while no one else could, and this bizarre notion is not supported by more thoughtful authorities. Pope Innocent IV says the rule holds only where the service from which the vassal is freed equals the fruits of the pledge, or where the fief is illegally held by the debtor, from whom recovery is thus sought by peaceful means.[16] Hostiensis, who is personally familiar with the case with which the second canon deals, rejects these explanations as not in accord with the facts. The ground for the exception, he declares, is the legal one that the ownership of a fief is always retained by the seigneur; when the fief is returned to him in pledge, he receives back his own property and is entitled to collect the full revenues of it. At the same time the vassal is freed from the services which he had to render as the condition of his use of the fief, so that no injury is done him. This ground holds for both ecclesiastical and secular fiefs.[17] Hostiensis' opinion becomes the common one.[18]

3. *The Borrower an Unjust Possessor*

A somewhat related case is the permission given to clerics by the Council of Tours under Alexander III to retain the fruits of pledges, not counting them on the principal, if the pledge is an ecclesiastical benefice being redeemed by a layman.[19] The sense of this canon, all the commentators agree, is that the clergy are here given a way of recovering benefices for the Church which are illegally retained by laymen.[20] In effect it is a form of occult compensation. The English canonist Alanus (fl. 1200) and Hostiensis extend this right to laymen as well, when no other means exists of recovering property unjustly held.[21] This opinion becomes general.[22]

4. *The Creditor a Son-in-law*

The canon *Salubriter*, a text from a letter of Innocent III, again deals with a special type of pledge. Here a father-in-law, unable to pay the agreed dowry to his son-in-law, has offered property as a pledge. May the son-in-law keep the fruits of the pledge without counting them as payment on the dowry? The Pope says that he may, because the fruits of dowry itself are often not sufficient to meet the *onera matrimonii*.[23] On the face of it, the

Summa, 2:7:2; Alexander of Hales, III:-2:4:2:3:1:1.

[16] Innocent IV, *Apparatus*, III, *De feudis*, 20:1.

[17] Hostiensis, *Commentaria*, III, *De feudis*, 20:1.

[18] Panormitanus, *Commentaria*, III, *De feudis*, 20:1, testifies that in 1400 the opinion is "more common."

[19] *Decretales*, V:19:1.

[20] Bernard of Pavia, *Summa decretalium*, V:15:5; St. Raymond, *Summa*, 2:7:2.

[21] Hostiensis, *Commentaria*, V:19:1:9.

[22] Panormitanus, *Commentaria*, V:19:8:5.

[23] *Decretales*, V:19:6.

Pope would seem to be saying that since dowries were ordinarily not sufficient, he was allowing a usurious way of supplementing them. The *Gloss*
merely says that, since the burdens of marriage would regularly be met by
the fruits of the dowry, now, when the dowry itself is not given, the fruits
of the substitute should be used for the same purpose.[24] Hostiensis gives
alternative explanations: either no loan takes place, and the usury prohibition does not apply; or, in fact, the son-in-law becomes the owner, not
simply the holder, of the pledge, and so can appropriate the revenues as
his own. Hostiensis emphasizes what the other writers suppose, that the
public good demands that dowries be kept intact.[25] This necessity of public
welfare does not, of course, itself create the right to the fruits, but it is the
only real reason why a search is made for an excuse to assign them to the
son-in-law. The most generally adopted explanation is that of St. Raymond
and Innocent IV; it is that the fruits are given as *interesse*;[26] the *Gloss*, in
effect, has given the same opinion. This explanation is the most consistent,
but a consideration of its precise significance we postpone to a treatment of
interesse itself.

Of the four cases put, payment beyond the principal is allowed because
the normal rules of justice are suspended by a state of belligerency, because
there may be occult compensation for stolen property, because a pledge is
juridically conceived as distinct from a fief, and last, either because a pledge
in lieu of a dowry is not considered to be a pledge on a virtual loan, or
because the fruits are *interesse*. Only in the analysis of the last case is a general or normal title to payment beyond the principal suggested; and even
in this case the normal title is accepted solely because of the special circumstances characterizing a dowry. Each case is one in which relations between
the parties other than the lender-borrower relation are dominant, and these
special relations lead to permission of increment to the principal.

GIFT

As Roman law familiar to the canonists suggests,[27] and as anyone might
think for himself, the debtor is under a natural obligation of gratitude to
return his creditor's favor of the loan. This obligation is entirely distinct
from an obligation of justice, and it can never be made binding in a contract or become a right enforceable by the creditor. But it is entirely proper
if the debtor spontaneously offers a gift to his creditor as an indication

[24] *Glossa ordinaria*, V:19:6.
[25] Hostiensis, *Summa*, V, *De usuris*, n.8.
[26] St. Raymond, *Summa*, 2:7:2; Innocent,
V:19:16.
[27] *Digesta*, 5:3:25:11.

of appreciation for his kindness. The gift, to be licitly accepted, must be wholly gratuitous — for example, not made to obtain a new loan or the prolongation of an old one. Moreover, not only must the lender believe that the debtor makes the gift under no compulsion, but he cannot even have principally hoped for the gift. Here again the early scholastics' doctrine of intention dominates. As it is mental usury to hope for gain from a loan, so it is sinful to lend with the principal intention of receiving profit by a gift. Only a secondary hope of a gift is permissible. This severe and curiously abstract doctrine is stated by William of Auxerre, St. Raymond, Hostiensis, St. Bonaventure, Scotus, St. Bernardine, and St. Antoninus.[28] St. Thomas appears to allow a principal hope of a gift, if it is a token of service or praise not estimable in money.[29] No authority allows as licit the principal hope of a pecuniary gift.

The question of intention in receiving gifts is of more importance than might be suspected in our commercial age, when gifts are not a regular source of profit. In the Middle Ages, many payments for loans were made as gifts, and, in particular, the compensation by kings and states on their loans was often declared formally to be a gift.[30] This formula would free the recipient from public odium or prosecution for usury; but if he had loaned to the king with his eye principally on this expected gift, he would certainly have sinned mortally, according to the common doctrine.

INTEREST DUE TO FAULT

By interest is meant compensation due in justice to a creditor because of loss which he has incurred through lending. Interest in the strict sense is thus distinct from both the payments in the special cases set forth above and the voluntary payment of a gift. The concept and the term "interest" are derived from the Roman law, and it is important to note the sense in which they are used there. The Roman jurists never refer to interest when they treat of the *mutuum* or *foenus*, where *usura* is the standard term to describe payment beyond the principal.[31] It is in discussing actions for damages because of the nonfulfillment of a contractual obligation that they

---

[28] William of Auxerre, III:21, *De super-abundantia in qua non intervenit pactum*, f.226r:a; St. Raymond, *Summa*, 2:7:1; Hostiensis, *Summa*, V:19:8; St. Bonaventure, *De decem praeceptis*, 6:19; Scotus, *In IV libros sententiarum*, (*Op. Oxon.*), IV:15:2:19; St. Bernardine, 37:3:3; St. Antoninus, *Summa*, 2:1:7.

[29] St. Thomas, *De malo*, Q.13, art. 14

ad 13.

[30] See G. Yver, *Le commerce et les marchands dans l'Italie méridionale au 13ᵉ et au 14ᵉ siècles.* (Paris, 1903), p. 379; Bigwood, *Le régime juridique*, II, 266; Y. Renouard, *Les relations des papes d'Avignon et des companies commerciales et bancaires de 1316 à 1378* (Paris, 1941), p. 547.

[31] *Digesta*, 50:16:121.

speak of *quod interest*, of "that which is the difference," between the injured party's present position and the position he would be in if he had not been injured.[32] *Quod interest*, the difference, is what the delinquent party is held to pay the damaged party. It is to be calculated by considering both the actual damage caused and the lost profit the injured person might have made, although the *Code* adds that the total can never be double the sum of the original default.[33] The distinction between *usura* and *quod interest* is made explicit in a law on partnership, which says that if a partner keeps back part of the partnership's profit and uses it for his own benefit before restoring it to the common fund, he is held to pay his partner for the damages caused by this delay *non quasi usuras, sed quod socii intersit*.[34] In the Roman law, then, *quod interest* is far from being considered a special payment on a loan. It is damages due on any contract because of a party's default.

The Roman-law formula was taken up by the twelfth-century Bolognese school. Azzo concentrated the phrase into a single substantive, *interesse*. Among the canonists, Huguccio and Bernard of Pavia are the first to refer to the concept, and they still use verb forms, such as *interesset*. Laurentius Hispanus is the first canonist to employ the new term, *interesse*;[35] his text, incorporated into the *Gloss*, makes the term standard from about 1220 on.[36] It is important to remark how early the term appears. The idea of *interesse* is as old as the rational analysis of usury itself. The sense in which the term is used by the early canonists and theologians, however, is substantially the same as that of the Roman law. Interest is never thought of as payment on a loan; it is the "difference" to be made up to a party injured by the failure of another to execute his obligations. The common distinction is between *usura* and *interesse, id est non lucrum, sed vitatio damni*.[37] Interest is purely compensatory. It is accidentally and extrinsically associated with a loan. Moreover, at no time in the first century of analysis is a general theory of interest developed. The canon law deals with particular cases; the canonists comment on these individually; the theologians mention the same individual cases or treat the problem of interest in their answers to objections to the usury prohibition. General principles are noted only as they arise in particular situations. The early recognition of interest is thus strictly limited to individual cases where the writers have seen that the lender has actually

[32] *Digesta*, 13:4:2:8.
[33] *Codex*, 7:47:1.
[34] *Digesta*, 17:2:60.

[35] McLaughlin, "The Canonist Teaching on Usury," p. 141.
[36] *Glossa ordinaria*, C.14, Q.4, c.7.
[37] St. Raymond, *Summa*, 2:7:2.

suffered damage. Let us now consider these particular cases in which *interesse* is allowed.

1. *Loss by a Guarantor*

The earliest admission of interest on a loan occurred in a case in which the guarantors of a loan had been forced to borrow money at usury to fulfill their guarantee when the principal debtors defaulted. Pope Lucius III ordered that the principal debtors pay back to the guarantors the usuries they had to pay and any other losses they had suffered.[38] The Pope's letters, inserted in the *Decretals*, are the first official recognition of the right to damages by a lender. Of course it is to be remarked that the case is not one of a simple loan, but of a payment forced from the guarantor, who may be supposed to have been entirely unwilling to become a creditor of the principal by discharging his debt. Following these canons, the commentators and theologians generally admit the guarantor's right to *interesse* if he is forced to borrow at usury.[39]

2. *Penalties*

The need to have a check upon a contumacious debtor was recognized by the canonists, though the canon law was silent on the question. Such early writers as Huguccio and Bernard of Pavia explicitly allow the parties to agree to a financial penalty to be paid if the debtor fails to return the loan at the time agreed.[40] But the doctrine of intention is dominant. Bernard of Pavia states the fundamental rule that the penalty must be set "for this, that for fear of the penalty the debtor will pay on the agreed day." [41] If the penalty is set, however, not as an incentive to the debtor to pay, but as a means of evading the usury laws, then it also is usury. A hundred years later, Scotus states the same opinion in slightly different terms: "A manifest sign that a penalty is not in fraud of usury is this: the merchant prefers to have his money returned to him on the agreed day, than to have it tomorrow with the penalty added." [42] The commentators also teach that it creates a presumption of usury if the penalty runs at a rate determined purely by the amount of time of delay, instead of consisting in a fixed lump sum. The penalty is also presumed to be fixed in fraud, if the lender is known to be a customary usurer.[43]

---

[38] *Decretales*, III:22: c.2 and 3.

[39] *Glossa ordinaria*, III:22:2; Innocent IV, *Apparatus*, V, *De usuris*, 19:1; Alexander Lombard, *Tractatus*, c.7, f.159r:b.

[40] McLaughlin, p. 140; Bernard of Pavia, *Summa*, V:15:9.

[41] Bernard of Pavia, V:15:9.

[42] Scotus, *In IV libros sententiarum* (*Op. Oxon.*), IV:15:2:18.

[43] St. Raymond, *Summa*, 2:7:4; Huguccio, cited in McLaughlin, p. 141.

This teaching on intention and fraud is of considerable importance. The payment of penalties, like the giving of gifts, was a frequent source of income on a loan in the Middle Ages, though we might be tempted to think it negligible today. The examples of contracts of loan given by Rolandino de Passagiero, in his standard work for fourteenth-century notaries, all show clauses attached to the loan which stipulate penalties of double the sum lent if the contract is not met.[44] Loans were customarily short-term — a fact which undoubtedly made penalties more lucrative. The records of the Belgian lombards, the public usurers, show much of their profit collected from their debtors as "penalty." [45] Yet if we refer to the standards set by the theorists, those lenders who preferred double their money to getting it back on time were guilty of mental usury; and the lombards, who deliberately set penalties as a means to gain, were innocent neither in the sight of heaven nor of the law.

Poena in itself is really not a case of interest in the strict sense; for it is intended vindictively, rather than as compensation. In itself it is permitted because "it is just to punish negligent or fraudulent deferment of due payment." It is with such a disciplinary penalty that, according to William of Auxerre, thirteenth-century popes and cardinals put out "their pounds" in loans.[46] But there is a marked tendency from the beginning to regulate the amount of the penalty by the damages actually suffered by the creditor due to the debtor's delay. Bernard of Pavia says *poena* is licit, *"maxime si intererat creditoris si solvi"*; William of Auxerre says that the penalty should be proportionate to the expenses the creditor will be put to in recovering a defaulted debt; Hostiensis insists that the Roman-law presumption that a money penalty attached to a loan is usurious should hold if the penalty exceeds the actual damages.[47] Scotus deliberately speaks of penalty being charged only by a merchant who will clearly be hurt by not having his money at a certain time. Although, then, *poena* retains its right as a title theoretically valid in itself, in practice, as far as affording real moral justification, it tends to become identical with the title of delay. The strict difference in theory between the two titles is that *poena* is agreed upon in advance by the parties, whereas delay exists as a title independent of con-

[44] Rolandino de Passagiero, *Summa totius artis notariae* (Venice, 1588), Part I, c.3, *De debitis et creditis*, 1–7. Rolandino (1217?–1301?), the founder of a school for notaries at Bologna, was probably the most influential writer and teacher on the notarial art in the Middle Ages. He himself was a notary of the exchange dealers' guild at Bologna. See Rafael Nuñez Lagos, *El documento medieval y Rolandino* (Madrid, 1951), pp. 5, 18, 36, 41.

[45] Bigwood, II, 4–41; I, 447–449.

[46] William of Auxerre, III:21, f.225r:a.

[47] Bernard of Pavia, V:15:9; Hostiensis, *Summa*, V, *De usuris*, n.9.

tract. The development of penalty into a practical identity with delay simply means that the parties determine in advance the damages delay will cause. The general acceptance of *poena* as a valid title is one step leading to the general acceptance of delay, the interest title proper.

3. *Delay*

Delay by the debtor in repaying a loan is specifically recognized as a title to interest by St. Raymond.[48] He supposes as a condition for appeal to it that the delay will have caused positive damage to the creditor; the example he gives is a creditor forced to borrow under usury to conduct his business when his money was not returned on time. In short, he extends the rights of guarantors recognized by Lucius III to all lenders hurt by a delinquent debtor. John of Rupella and Alexander of Hales proceed in the same way, going from the case of the guarantors to the case of all lenders, and giving as an example of damage the creditor's forced recourse to a loan at usury.[49]

A more general defense of interest in delay is undertaken by Hostiensis. He says flatly that delay is a title to interest, and such interest is licit "because it is sought for the sake of avoiding loss not taking gain." St. Thomas approves the title in the same broad way for the same reason. Giles of Lessines and Monaldus say the same. Scotus is even more positive: the debtor has an obligation in strict justice to pay the creditor *interesse* in delay.[50] By now the concept of *poena* proportional to the expenses caused by default has been accepted and practically merged with *mora*. While delay by itself gave no title to payment unless actual damage had followed it, *poena* allowed an estimation in advance of probable damage, and this sum was then collectable by the creditor, whatever loss he actually suffered. The merger of *poena* and *mora* means, then, that any delay in repayment created a title to interest, whether actual loss was suffered or not. The right to compensation in delay was now firmly established.

One question remains: does *interesse* mean only the positive damage, or does it also include the lost probable profits, as the Roman law declares? The early writers up to 1250 seem to suppose that only the positive injury is to be compensated. St. Thomas Aquinas in his early commentary on the *Sentences*, however, declares that a debtor in delay is held also to repay the

[48] St. Raymond, *Summa*, 2:7:2.

[49] Alexander of Hales, *Summa*, III:2:4:2:-3:3:2:1.

[50] Hostiensis, *Summa*, V, *De usuris*, n.8. He does say that the creditor must be a merchant, lending out of charity and not accustomed to lend at usury: *Commentaria*, V, *De usuris*, n.16. St. Thomas, *De malo*, Q.13, art. 4 ad 14; Giles of Lessines, c.7; Monaldus, *Summa perutilis*, at "Usura," f.286; Scotus, *In IV libros sententiarum* (*Op. Oxon.*), IV:15:2:18.

probable lost profits.[51] In treating of restitution in the *Summa theologica*, he reaches a similar conclusion. There he puts forward the thesis that a thief must restore only what he actually takes. He faces two objections: if a man steals seeds, he occasions the loss of a harvest; and if a man retains his creditor's money, he "occasions the loss of all possible profits." Very significantly, St. Thomas answers these two objections together, although one deals with a naturally productive good, the other with money. He declares,

> One is held, however, to give some compensation according to the condition of the persons and businesses . . . The sower of the seed in the field has the harvest not actually but virtually. In like manner, he that has money has the profit not actually, but only virtually; and both may be hindered in many ways.[52]

What is remarkable in both the *Sentences* and the *Summa* is that St. Thomas here appears to attribute a causal power to money. Money is considered not as a sterile coin: in the *Sentences* it is said that money is "not the only cause of gain" — a statement which certainly assumes that it is a cause of some gain; in the *Summa*, money is conceived as containing profits, as a seed contains harvest. Whereas in St. Thomas's former treatment money is only a measure and all gain is attributed to labor, the creditor here is not compensated for his lost opportunity to work, but for the lost profits which the money would have brought. As in the case of partnership investments, which presently will be examined, a theory of money seems to be used that is different from that employed in the usury theory. Three hundred years later Cajetan will attempt to explain this difficulty.[53] St. Thomas himself attempts no reconciliation. The owner is compensated for the lost profits as if they were the true fruits of money.

As the admission of probable profit as a type of interest thus seemed to involve the admission of a power in money to produce value beyond itself, it is readily understandable why the title was not at once received. St. Thomas is not generally followed in his explicit approval of it. Scotus seems to imply its acceptance, and writers such as Astesanus, who accept it even in the absence of delay, may be presumed to accept it in delay. Yet, after St. Thomas, it is difficult to find any definite statement in the next century in favor of it. At the end of the fourteenth century, the canonist Peter of Ancharano says distinctly that damages for delay should include *lucrum cessans*.[54] He is one of the first scholastic authors to use in connection with interest this precise expression which will become the classical formula for

---

[51] St. Thomas, *In IV lib. sent.*, IV:15:1:5.
[52] St. Thomas, *S.T.*, II–II:62:4:1 and 2.
[53] See *infra*, pp. 252–254.

[54] Peter of Ancharano, *Super Clementina commentaria* (Bologna, 1580), *Ex gravi, De usuris*.

profit lost. After his time the doctrine becomes common. Panormitanus sums it up, saying: "Hold this perpetually in mind, that even according to canon law, something beyond the capital may be sought by reason of interest, not only because of the loss that may occur but because of *lucrum cessans*." [55]

A parallel case of compensation in delay was presented by the problem of what a usurer should restore in making restitution. Should he be compelled to restore gains made with the employment of the money he had exacted usuriously? The approach taken in regard to compensation on loans had emphasized only the lender's loss. But in the early days of the scholastic analysis, the influential William of Auxerre looked at restitution from the viewpoint of the use made of the money and declared that, as the money taken was the root of the profits made, the usurer should restore the profits.[56] This viewpoint was partially supported by Laurentius de Ridolfis two hundred years later on the practical ground that a usurer might otherwise be tempted to take a usurious profit, invest it successfully, repent and restore the original sum, and remain with a net profit. Although not bound to strict restitution, the usurer should give his profits to the poor. As to the theoretical basis for this requirement, he writes:

And if it is said that this [money] is not the principal cause, but the industry of the man, say that rather it is sufficiently the principal cause in fact, or at any rate, the equally principal cause: since without it there occurs no place for gain.[57]

This approach, revealing a belief in the causal power of money and logically leading to measurement of return on a loan itself by the profit made by the borrower, is rejected by the majority. St. Thomas Aquinas, when he treats of restitution, goes directly to William's "root" argument. He says:

The money of the usuries is not related as a root to the profit which is made from it, but only as matter. For a root has to some degree the power of an active cause, inasmuch as it ministers food to the whole plant; whence, in human acts, the will and intention are compared to a root, so that if it is perverse, the work will be perverse; this, however, is not necessary in that which is matter; for someone can sometimes use evil well.[58]

Since money contributes no active power to a business, gain from its use cannot be considered to be due the true owner of the money, but is instead to be attributed to the active power of the industry of the user, and it be-

---

[55] Panormitanus, V:19:8:7. The context makes it clear that he allows the title only in delay.

[56] William of Auxerre, III:21, f.226r:a.

[57] Laurentius, 2:44. Another exception to the rule is Monaldus, *Summa, De restitutione*, f.224v:b, who clearly follows William.

[58] St. Thomas, *III Quodlibetales*, Q.3, art. 19.

longs to him. Therefore the usurer need not restore profit subsequently made
with his usuries. This becomes the common opinion, taught generally by
the scholastics.[59] It reflects a consistent determination to measure interest
only from the standpoint of the person deprived of the money.

INTEREST FROM THE BEGINNING OF A LOAN

The cases of interest we have discussed so far have all involved fault on
the part of the debtor and actual delay in his repayment of the loan. Was
interest ever admitted as a right of the creditor, as something due him from
the debtor because of loss or labor suffered during the agreed-on duration
of the loan? Did the concept of a naturally gratuitous loan exclude all right
to compensation during its normal term? Did the original Roman-law
concept of *interesse*, as "the difference" due to failure to fulfill an obligation, prohibit the admission of such payment without any failure on the
part of the debtor? These questions have not yet been treated, and in answering them we undertake the most critical part of our investigation. The right
to interest would have been of little consequence if it had been restricted to
cases where the debtor was at fault after a loan had been given him. Yet
such was the original conception of interest. The scholastics had to take a
great leap to admit that interest might be due from the start of a loan. To
do this seemed to many of them to abandon the foundation for the usury
prohibition, the normal gratuitousness of a loan, and it was certainly to go
well beyond the Roman notion of *interesse*. But the leap was finally taken.
Let us now examine two cases in which interest from the start of a loan
was allowed without any real change in principle being at issue, and one
case in which the new and daring principle itself was hotly debated.

1. *Labor*

The canon law, in discussing the restitution of church property illegally
detained, admitted that the illegal holder might retain the cost of his care
of the property.[60] Reasoning from this permission, St. Raymond, Hostiensis,
and Monaldus admit that a lender holding a pledge may deduct from its
revenues his expenses in caring for it.[61] This is what is meant by the original
title of "labor." It is a title clearly restricted to the special case of onerous
pledges, and in no way is it meant to authorize generally the taking of any

[59] Giles of Lessines, c.20; Astesanus, III:-11:7; St. Antoninus, II:2:1.

[60] *Decretales*, III:13:11; cf. I:41:1.

[61] St. Raymond, *Summa*, 2:7:5; Hostiensis, *Summa*, V, *De usuris*, n.8. Monaldus, as usual, follows Hostiensis: *Summa*, "Usura," f.292v:a.

compensation for the trouble of engaging in a loan business. It is a title not even mentioned in most authorities, and, one may infer, not widely claimed.

One writer, however, takes up the title of labor and applies it with a boldness which, if it had become contagious, would have substantially changed usury doctrine and lending practice one hundred and fifty years before the developments he suggests did in fact take place. This writer is Durandus of St. Pourçain who, in a prosaic commentary on the *Sentences*, comes forth suddenly with this radical idea: why should not the State appoint certain men as public lenders and let them be paid a salary for their services? There will always be a need for money both by the poor and by the State itself. Is not the sensible course to provide for this constant need by a regular and legitimate service? Usury is "the price of a loan," but his lenders would be paid "a wage for their labor" and "for exposing their own goods," and such a wage would not be usury. The wages would be paid by the borrowers, but "by the authority of the State"; the compensation would not be illicit but just and due.[62] The scheme is unimpeachable, but Durandus adds wistfully, "I have, however, never read or heard of this procedure being decreed or ordered anywhere." His suggestion, indeed, remained without criticism or response, till a century and a half later the whole matter came up afresh in connection with the *montes pietatis*.[63]

If the title of labor as it is understood by Durandus had been generally admitted, one could say that the principle was accepted that interest was due from the beginning of the loan. But the limited labor title recognized by St. Raymond and Hostiensis, although it gave the lender a right to charge during the normal course of the loan, was too specialized to lead to any further developments, and though it suggested a change in principle, it was never widely enough discussed to be of importance to the scholastic theory.

2. *Credit Sales Where Value May Vary*

We now come to a title to interest which seems at first to be a clear and general recognition of the lender's right to compensation from the beginning of a loan, when he has lost by lending. It seems, indeed, to be an early

[62] Durandus of St. Pourçain, *Commentariorum*, III, D.37, Q.2.

[63] One other writer independently recommended a similar idea without result. This was the French lawyer, Philip of Mazières, who made his proposal in 1389 in a work entitled "Dream of the Old Pilgrim." See V. Brants, *Esquisse des théories économiques* (Louvain, 1895), pp. 159ff.

and widely accepted form of what will be the great later title to interest, *lucrum cessans*. It is the case we have earlier examined of *venditio sub dubio*. This highly special case, however, is decided on principles not available for the normal money loan. It is a fatal confusion to assimilate it to *lucrum cessans*. *Venditio sub dubio* is ruled not by the scholastic theory of interest, but by the scholastic theory of the just price.

St. Raymond is the only early author to see in *venditio sub dubio* anything like *lucrum cessans*. In a discussion of *Naviganti* he offers what he apparently believes to be a case analogous to that approved by Gregory IX. Since he was Gregory's secretary, his opinion is of special weight. He writes:

> There can be here supposed a case in which it would not be usury to receive beyond the principal: say, when I had wished to buy or had been ready to buy certain merchandise with money, and you, because of your great insistence, have made me cease from such purchase; then, that I should loan to you there, I say that I wish you to return to me there as much as I would have there had from this merchandise, if I had carried it thither; I, however, take upon myself the risk, as said above.[64]

At first, St. Raymond seems to be arguing boldly that in any case where the lender loses a profit because he is moved to help a needy neighbor, he is entitled to charge the profit lost as interest; his argument about money loans might seem to be a strict parallel to what the decretal itself says about commodity credit sales. The two assumptions, however — that the decretal itself means to authorize interest from the beginning of any true loan, and that money loans in particular may be treated exactly like commodity sales — are, perhaps, hasty. St. Raymond, on closer examination, is really saying little on the decretal itself, for he has added the clause, "I take on myself the risk." If we interpret this clause, as his reference indicates we should, in terms of the first section of *Naviganti*, it means that the creditor takes the risk of any fortuitous disaster and will not hold his debtor if, as the result of some natural misfortune, he defaults.[65] St. Raymond is teaching that the creditor can demand his lost profit back as interest only if he runs the equivalent of some of the risks he might have run in his own business. St. Raymond thus tells us nothing about the meaning of the decretal itself, for his new condition alters its case substantially. It cannot be denied, however, that he himself seems to have felt an analogy between the decretal's case and the case of what will be known as *lucrum cessans*.

[64] St. Raymond, *Summa*, 2:7:5.   [65] For a statement of the first part of *Naviganti*, see *infra*, pp. 137–138.

Later, too, authors such as St. Bernardine will cite *venditio sub dubio* as a precedent authorizing *lucrum cessans*.[66] But in itself, narrowly considered and as it is understood in the twelfth, thirteenth, and fourteenth centuries, *venditio sub dubio* is not the recognition of a general right to interest on a loan. It is an admission made in the name of the rules governing the just price. Carefully excluded as a title on normal money loans, it is a special title available only in commodity sales. Except for the abortive and confused analogy suggested by St. Raymond, the early history of the title demonstrates that it was never considered as anything else.[67]

3. Loss by the Lender

Loss occurring (*damnum emergens*) and profit ceasing (*lucrum cessans*) are the two great titles to interest, as interest is understood today, a return owed without fault of the debtor. We shall henceforth use the terms, unless otherwise qualified, to signify interest due *from the beginning* of a loan, because of damage incurred or profit lost as a result of lending. In all the cases we have examined so far, we have found none of a pure money loan, where no special relation existed between creditor and debtor, in which such interest from the start of a loan was permitted. In the first hundred years of canonist and scholastic teaching, 1150–1250, no interest of this kind is admitted as licit by the leading scholastic authorities.

When eventually such interest begins to be recognized, *damnum emergens* and *lucrum cessans* advance at first into acceptance more or less together, or with equal slowness. It is true that the recognition of *lucrum cessans* seemed to involve another principle also foreign to the scholastic theory beyond the principle involved in admitting *damnum emergens*, the principle that money is a source of gain; in the fifteenth century this added difficulty was to check its acceptance. But the recognition of either title involved abandonment of what seemed the fundamental principle to the early scholastics — namely, that a loan was essentially gratuitous. In practice, moreover, few lenders ever loaned at such a time that they actually hurt themselves immediately. Thus, most cases where interest could be claimed without the debtor's default involved only cases of *lucrum cessans*; and consequently nearly all discussion centers on this case.

[66] St. Bernardine, 42:2:2; Panormitanus, V:19:19:13.

[67] Ashley misunderstands Innocent's admission of the simple case of *venditio sub dubio* and takes it to be an admission of pure *lucrum cessans* (W. Ashley, *Introduction to English Economic History*, I, 401). In fact, Innocent directly rejects pure *lucrum cessans* (*Apparatus*, V:19:19). My own only major disagreement with McLaughlin's excellent article is that he, too, treats *venditio sub dubio* as a case of *lucrum cessans* (see McLaughlin, p. 146).

Early Opposition

The first hundred years, we have said, contain no recognition of *damnum emergens* or *lucrum cessans*. The evidence for this conclusion is mainly negative; the early concept of interest simply does not include the payment of a surplus by a debtor unless he is at fault. In any early list of exceptions *damnum emergens* and *lucrum cessans* are never to be found, and the main reason why our evidence must be negative is probably that it was so unthinkable to allow interest from the beginning of a loan that even the possibility of such an exception was not discussed. There is one text which apparently disputes our conclusion. As early as 1215 the *Gloss* declares that a lender has a right to keep himself indemnified.[68] But its illustration of this right is a case where a debtor is in delay, and since to have declared for a right to interest without delay would have been an astonishing break from contemporary opinion, it is only fair to infer that it means to restrict the right of indemnification to delay. The only early author who even discusses interest due from the beginning of a loan is Cardinal Courçon. The case in favor of it is vigorously and simply presented, and his rejection of it shows the force of the positive law's prohibition:

He [the lender] would have afterwards acquired with his money 100 above the principal, and I give him back nothing above the principal. Therefore, I injure him to the extent of 100. Does he not justly complain of me? I would not wish this to be done me. Therefore, I ought not to do it to him, according to the natural law . . . But I prove that he can seek nothing from me, according to that word of the Gospel, "Lend freely, hoping nothing thereby." For if he hoped to receive something above the principal, he has mentally committed usury.[69]

Courçon says the lender may only hope that the borrower will sometime lend to him in need; no other compensation for "the 100" is allowed.

Approaches to Recognition by the Classical Canonists

In the mid-thirteenth century, Innocent IV implicitly recognized *lucrum cessans* in his discussion of the purchase of a *census*. This contract will be discussed later. What should be noted here is that the *census*, which bears great resemblance to a loan, is declared to be nonusurious only if the gain from it is no greater than the gain would have been from investing the same money in an outright purchase of land.[70] Nonetheless, since this is not a pure loan contract, it is not fair to cite it as an example of pure *lucrum cessans*.

---

[68] *Glossa ordinaria,* C.14, Q.3, dictum ante c.1.

[69] Robert of Courçon, p. 13.

[70] Innocent, *Apparatus,* V, *De usuris,* 19:9, *Consuluit.*

Like St. Raymond's treatment of *venditio sub dubio*, Innocent's handling of this case moves toward recognition of *lucrum cessans* proper, but does not reach it.

St. Thomas Aquinas

St. Thomas Aquinas is the first major authority, either theological or canonical, to express himself in such a way as to seem to favor interest from the beginning of a loan, and even this apparent support is contradicted by his final and definitive verdict on the subject. In the *Summa theologica*, in response to an objection made to the justice of the usury prohibition on the grounds that "each one may licitly keep himself indemnified," St. Thomas replies: "A lender may without sin enter into agreement with the borrower for compensation for the loss he incurs of something he ought to have, for this is not to sell the use of money, but to avoid a loss.' [71] Like the early *Gloss*, St. Thomas seems to be positing a principle that should legitimize at least *damnum emergens* in all cases. But unlike the *Gloss*, he gives no examples of what he means, and it would be rash to conclude from this single statement that St. Thomas is taking a position shared by none of his contemporaries.

In fact, in an earlier letter on usury to James of Viterbo, a Dominican confessor at Florence, the textile center of Europe, St. Thomas, treating of credit sales in the wool trade, seems to think that to admit any right to compensation from the beginning of a loan would be to admit usury itself. He declares of one who claims a discount because he pays in advance, "Nor is he excused through this, that he is hurt by paying in advance, or that he is induced to this by the other, for by the same reason all usurers could be excused." [72]

Then in *De malo*, in his fullest discussion of interest, treating it almost *ex professo* after writing the ambiguous sentence in the *Summa theologica*, St. Thomas expressly declares interest is due only in delay. He is defending the usury prohibition against all objections, and he faces an objection which pleads the lender's right to compensation for actual loss. St. Thomas treats this as a direct threat to the usury prohibition itself; that is, he believes to accept the objection would be to abandon the concept of a normally gratuitous loan. He replies by distinguishing — a debtor is held to indemnify the lender in delay, but is by no means held to give compensation if he pays on time: "For he who lent the money ought to beware lest he incur damage for himself. Nor ought he who receives the loan incur loss from the stupidity

[71] *S.T.*, II–II:78:2:1 and ad 1.   [72] *De emptione et venditione.*

of the lender." [73] This is a frank, if severe, answer: a lender is stupid who lends so as to damage himself, and his folly does not give rise to an exception which would threaten the usury rule. The weightiness and deliberation of St. Thomas' answer seem to make evident that his ultimate opinion on interest is entirely in accord with the hundred years' tradition behind him.

At the same time, it is clear beyond all doubt that St. Thomas rejects completely the claim of compensation for profit lost; for he teaches, "One ought not to sell what one does not yet have and may be prevented from having in many ways." [74] This is so clear to him that in the lengthy list of objections in *De malo*, the objection is assumed to be answered already.[75]

The First Recognition

Hostiensis does not mention interest due from the beginning in his *Summa aurea*, but in his much later work, the *Commentaria super libros decretalium* he is the first author to give unmistakable and full approval to a case of *lucrum cessans*. Just after he has treated all the different rights to compensation beyond the principal, he continues:

For, in what is added to the principal, the seeking of interest is not prohibited, but only the seeking of shameful gain or of other illicit increment, as appears in Causa 14, Q.4, *Si oblitus*. Therefore, I think from the intention of the above laws, that if some merchant, who is accustomed to pursue trade and the commerce of the fairs and there profit much, has, out of charity to me, who needs it badly, lent money with which he would have done business, I remain obliged from this to his *interesse*, provided that nothing is done in fraud of usury, as appears in what is noted in *Supra eo tuas, in fine*, and provided that said merchant will not have been accustomed to give his money in such a way to usury.[76]

It is important to note how Hostiensis insists that the merchant's principal motive must be a charitable one, and how he will not allow the merchant to lend habitually. Nonetheless, this authoritative canonist's recognition of pure *lucrum cessans*, however restricted as to practical conditions, is of the highest moment. For the very first time the honest businessman is given a lawful reason for charging beyond the principal even though his debtor is in no way at fault. It is, of course, impossible to know how many businessmen acted in good faith upon the opinion of a single author, and what the practical consequences of this single recognition were. But the opinions of Hostiensis carried much authority.

[73] *De malo*, Q.13, art. 4 ad 14.   [76] Hostiensis, *Commentaria*, V, *De usuris*,
[74] *S.T.*, II-II:78:2 ad 1.   16; cf. *De usuris*, 19.
[75] *De malo*, Q.13, art. 4, obj. 14.

Continued Theological Opposition

The theologians are unmoved by Hostiensis' opinion and continue in the tradition of Courçon and St. Thomas. Giles of Lessines allows interest only in delay, and in his long discussion of usury he never even mentions the possibility of interest due from the beginning of a loan.

Monaldus recites verbatim the case given by St. Raymond under *venditio sub dubio*, which has already been discussed. He emphasizes that it is not the gain lost, but "the reception of risk which excuses in this case most powerfully." Even more clearly than Innocent, however, Monaldus does apply a notion similar to *lucrum cessans* in allowing the licitness of a *census* contract if the gain there is no greater than would have been made from a purchase of land.[77] A *census*, however, as has been said, is not a pure loan.

Scotus is as adamant against interest of any kind from the beginning of a loan as is St. Thomas in *De malo*. A hypothetical objector, similar to St. Thomas', declares that it is licit for a lender to keep himself unharmed, "but this cannot be done in any other way except by receiving beyond the principal." Scotus, like St. Thomas, sees the objection as telling against the usury prohibition itself. He replies:

If he [the lender] does not wish to be injured, let him keep back the money he needs, because no one forces him to do a merciful deed for his neighbor; but if he prefers to show mercy to the other, he is compelled by the divine law not to vitiate the divine law.[78]

Aegidius and the Spanish *Gloss* upon him do not even discuss interest, and Durandus of St. Pourçain follows St. Thomas literally.[79]

Theological Recognition

The first theologian, as distinct from a canonist, to admit interest without fault by the debtor seems to be Astesanus. He gives a case similar to that of Hostiensis involving *lucrum cessans*, and without discussion, simply citing Hostiensis as his authority, he approves the interest charge.[80] Similarly, he says later, extending the rule to agricultural investors, a man intending to

[77] Monaldus, f.288v:a–b.

[78] Scotus, *In IV libros sententiarum (Op. Oxon.)*, IV:15:2, n.26.

[79] Following St. Thomas' teaching in the *Summa* literally, Durandus gives us the one example of interest, interest due in delay, and so confirms our interpretation of the original meaning of St. Thomas (Durandus of St. Pourçain, III, D.37, Q.2).

[80] Astesanus, III:11:4. He notes that St. Raymond should have reached the same result, but confused his analysis by insisting that the lender also share the risk of the enterprise. For the earlier opinion of Henry of Ghent allowing *interesse* in a special situation where the debtor is in effect in perpetual default, see *infra*, Chapter VIII, n.24.

buy a farm, who is beseeched for a loan and grants it, may charge as much for the loan as he would have obtained from the land.[81]

At the same time that he admits *lucrum cessans*, Astesanus allows the equivalent of *damnum emergens*. The cities of northern Italy, faced with great financial needs, had been forced to expedients unknown to the rest of Europe and had instituted a new method of financing themselves. They sold shares in the public debt to their citizens under compulsion and on them paid a moderate interest. Such sales were more in the nature of a capital levy than a loan, but nonetheless, since their form was that of a loan, the morality of receiving the interest on them was an open question. Facing this new problem, Astesanus holds, in direct contradiction to his teacher, Alexander Lombard, that the interest is licit compensation for damages experienced. He stresses the fact that the loans are compulsory. He insists that the receipt of the interest is licit only as long as the bondholder would rather have his principal back than receive the interest.[82]

Fourteenth-Century Disapproval

The battle for interest is by no means won by the support of a few theologians and the authority of Hostiensis. Throughout the fourteenth century the interest titles are frequently disapproved.

Joannes Andreae directly addresses himself to Hostiensis' case and rejects interest except in delay. Otherwise, he declares, "The way is open to usury."[83] His reasoning, although expressed a little differently, seems to be substantially the same as St. Thomas' — to permit interest from the beginning is to destroy the usury prohibition.

Buridan rejects both *damnum emergens* and *lucrum cessans*, and only makes the concession that they are condemned by positive, not natural law. He writes: "It is a probable proposition that in the case in which the creditor would receive money given only in relief of loss, there is not evil usury, although it be evil because prohibited." If there is any suspicion that the money

---

[81] Astesanus, III:11:5.

[82] III:11:5. Astesanus cites John of Saxony as favoring this view. Alexander Lombard had taken a firm stand against compensation for the lenders. He held that the creditors could not claim profit they might have made elsewhere as *interesse;* for it was not certain that they would have gained. This is the standard objection to claims of *lucrum cessans*. He also faced the plea that the creditors were really paid from their own property, because the interest payments came from the tax receipts. He replied that this was a clear confusion between the property of the community and property of the individual citizens. The general advantage of the forced loans to the city was no argument either, in his eyes, because it was not lawful to take usury even to save a life (see Alexander Lombard, c.7, f.165v:a).

[83] Joannes Andreae, *Decretalium libros,* V, *De usuris,* 19:19:5.

was sought "for the sake of acquiring profit," he adds, it is evil per se.[84]

Henry of Hesse takes the majority view that the plea of *lucrum cessans* is an objection to the usury theory itself. A "defender of the impiety of usury" objects that a lender should be able to charge for "the relief of loss or of the hindrance to gaining which he incurs through the lack of money through such a great time." Henry's answer is simply that if this is true, merchants and exchange dealers could licitly lend money at usury, provided they only took what they would have made in their own licit occupations. But "it is apparent that this does not stand." [85] Therefore, without any real reason being given, the objection is rejected. Later, like Innocent, Henry allows *lucrum cessans*, if the lender assumes the business risks of his debtor.[86] But this is more a partnership than a loan.

Early Fifteenth-Century Opinion and the Effects of the Controversy over the *Montes*

By 1400 the opinion of the theologians and canonists would still seem to be against *lucrum cessans*. But now an increasing number of prominent authorities come to its defense, although the majority may still be said to be against it as late as 1500. Moreover, in the fifteenth century, *damnum emergens* does become commonly accepted, its admission involving only one departure from the old position instead of two. The chief cause leading to the new general attitude is the need to justify the financial practices of the Italian city states.

By 1400 the controversy over the licitness of interest on the forced government loans had become hot. The forced loan had now been employed for a century by the governments of Venice, Genoa, and Florence, the leading capitalistic communities of Europe, because, as St. Bernardine suggests, it brought in "millions" beyond the total value of the State's own resources,[87] while the older *census* contract employed by less prosperous states was often tied to specific tax revenues. The Florentine handling of the loan, which was substantially the same as the financial management of the other two cities, was usually taken as the model for theological discussion, and will be described here as the typical case. The loan was organized in the form of a government fund called a *mons*; every lender was given a share in the *mons*; and these shares were the object of trade. No date was set for the redemption of the shares, although the Florentine statute declared the city might redeem them at will at 28 per cent of par. It is not clear that this

[84] Buridan, I:12, art. 3.
[85] Henry of Hesse, I:23, f.195v:b.
[86] I:46, f.204v:b.
[87] St. Bernardine, 41:3:2.

privilege was much exercised. Annual payments were made "as gift and interest" to the bondholders. In Florence the payments were reduced from 15 per cent in the thirteenth century, to 10 per cent and finally to 5 per cent in the creation of the *novissimus mons* in 1390. The statutes specifically declared that neither in law nor in conscience were the recipients of these payments, spontaneously given by the State, to be obliged to restitution — a provision that looked to both conscience and form.[88]

Since the time of Astesanus' simple acceptance of the *mons* the discussion over it had waxed heavy. The Franciscans, led by Francis of Empoli (fl. 1347), defended this important civic institution; and they were joined by the jurists Frederick Petrucci of Siena (fl. 1343) and Lapus de Castilione (d. 1381). The Augustinians, led by Gerard of Siena, Gregory of Rimini (d. 1375), and Guido of Bellarequardo (fl. 1371), attacked it. They were at first supported by the Dominicans, notably Peter Strozzi (d. 1362) and Dominic Pantaleoni (d. 1376). In Laurentius de Ridolfis' account in 1403 we may follow the arguments of both sides and see how the way to the general acceptance of interest from the beginning of a loan was prepared by the victory of the Franciscan viewpoint. The arguments of Laurentius are substantially the same as those of his Franciscan predecessors and successors; the views he opposes are the typical Augustinian ones.

The heart of the position of the opponents of the *mons* is that interest is due only in default; any interest paid as due from the beginning of a loan is usury. The State is thus guilty of promoting usury, and its creditors are guilty of taking usurious profits. Laurentius replies to this chief argument by centering his analysis upon two facts — the compulsory character of the loans, and the meagerness of the interest paid. Usury, he says, is the voluntary seeking of profit from a loan. But where the loan is forced, there appears no will to profit, and where the interest is a mere 5 per cent, the possibility of realizing a true profit is absent.[89] A great hardship is worked on many people by these conscriptions of capital; in justice their sufferings should be compensated. Not only should there be compensation for losses directly incurred by the loans, but also compensation for *lucrum cessans*, the gain foregone by the merchants, who are the principal bondholders.[90] The higher

---

[88] See Laurentius de Ridolfis, 3:5 (n.12). Cf. St. Antoninus, who follows Laurentius almost literally on the whole subject: *Summa*, 2:1:11, *De materia montis Florentiae*. A good modern summary is provided by de Roover, "Il trattato da fra Sancti Rucellai sul cambio, il monte commune e il monte delle doti," *Archivo Storico Italiano* (1953), pp. 14–17. St. Antoninus speaks of the bonds being redeemable at 25 per cent of par; see *infra*, Chapter VII, Section 2.

[89] De Ridolfis, III:5 ad 1 (n.15).

[90] III:5 ad 1 (n.17ff).

rates of profit elsewhere make it evident that no one would willingly choose the city's bonds as a good investment.[91] The payment of *lucrum cessans* will not be the payment of profit to a usurer, but simply some measure of indemnification to men seriously hurt by lending.

At the same time Laurentius willingly concedes to the opponents that if the lender, though forced, prefers lending and receiving interest to keeping his money without interest, he commits a sin.[92] Similarly, if after the loan has been made by a coerced lender, the lender changes his mind and prefers the interest to getting his loan back, he commits usury.[93] The great difficulty that interest is paid as due from the start of the loan is met by the reply that the city is like a debtor in perpetual delay; for it sets no date for the redemption of its bonds. If interest in delay is licit, so is interest here where the delay is without limit.[94]

Laurentius has made an effective presentation of the case for *damnum emergens* and *lucrum cessans*. But three secondary objections of his opponents, not touching this main case directly have yet to be met. The first is that if the interest were truly donative and compensatory, as the statute declares, it would be paid on a varying scale according to the individual creditor's merits or losses, but here the indiscriminate payment of the same amount to everyone is *prima facie* evidence that the interest titles were fictitious.[95] Moreover, it is urged that the State does not really pay the interest freely, but under compulsion to placate its creditors. Finally, it is noted with some malice that the chief creditors of the State are also members of the governing body which decreed the interest.

De Ridolfis replies to the first argument that it is morally impossible for the State to determine everyone's loss and everyone's merit individually; but, as it is certain that loss is suffered by all the lenders and that a benefit is conferred to the State by them, the State can strike an average which will reward each lender as fairly as possible.[96] To the second objection, he answers that it is difficult to see how a sovereign State can be under any fear of its own citizens, and further that it is presumptuous to suppose that the State perjures itself in its own declaration that the interest is a gift.[97] To the third objection he replies simply that men may licitly function in different capacities, and in one capacity pay, and in another receive interest.[98]

---

[91] III:5 ad 1 (n.28).
[92] III:5 ad 2 (n.31).
[93] III:5 ad 2 (n.21–22).
[94] III:5 ad 2 (n.28–33).

[95] III:5 ad 2 (n.26).
[96] III:5 ad 2 (n.33).
[97] III:5 ad 2 (n.28).
[98] III:5 ad 2 (n.35).

With each individual objection refuted, the intransigent opponents declare that the policy of the *mons* is itself harmful to the true welfare of the State. A few creditors, they contend, are benefited by it at the expense of everyone else. It would be saner to conscript the capital outright and make these wealthy lenders contribute without reward to the cost of the government.[99] Laurentius admits that this approach would be possible; but, "*non omne possibile debet esse volibile.*" Forced collections have had ruinous results. It is better "to provide for everyone's needs, with the peace of all," than to resort to violence, cause scandal, destroy estates, and reduce citizens to extreme poverty. Unless compensation is provided to the citizens financing the government,

they would, perchance, be driven to desperation and would plot against the republic to the serious loss of body and soul and danger to the republic. And if it be said that in such a case, and not otherwise, if the law benefits, it is well, I reply that the law ought to be common for the utility of the republic, lest some be moved by a scrupulous heart, . . . as it would be too hard and difficult to distinguish one case from the other.[100]

This reasoning, it may be argued, is not entirely an appeal to a *raison d'état* to justify usurious measures. But having demonstrated that the means need not necessarily be considered usurious, Laurentius believes that such practical political considerations have weight in determining the morality of the loans.

Indirectly by his arguments supporting the licitness of the *mons* as a policy, as well as directly by his arguments for the licitness of interest compensation, Laurentius is defending the cause of *damnum emergens* and *lucrum cessans*: for his arguments carry the day, and after his exposition of the case, interest on the *mons* is generally admitted. This means that, in one large area of lending, recognition of the right to interest from the beginning of a loan has been won.

In Laurentius' own work the principle of *lucrum cessans* is developed. Although his main stress has been on the compulsory nature of the loans, he is moved to extend his defense of compensation due without delay to all cases where a lender lends chiefly from charity. The reasoning is entirely similar. Usury is the seeking of profit from a loan. But a lender who is led principally by charity, just as a lender who is led by the force of the state, is not seeking profit. Therefore, he has a right to compensation for the loss he suffers and the gain he has lost in other enterprises. This right

[99] III:5 ad 1 (n.15).   [100] III:5 ad 1 (n.17).

is present both for those voluntarily lending to the city at 5 per cent, moved principally by a charitable patriotism,[101] and for merchants lending to private individuals. In the latter case, however, the title must not be abused so as "to open the way to usury"; and the title manifestly is not present if a merchant "keeps his money to trade at usury." [102] At any time, of course, the intention to profit invalidates the title, though it is objectively present.

At the same time that he verbally insists on the rule on intention, Laurentius allows one illogical exception to it — an exception which sharply breaks from the prior scholastic treatment of interest and intention. The city sometimes offers a premium if the bonds are bought before a certain date, and it sometimes declares that no interest will be paid at all on bonds purchased after a certain date. Is it licit to buy early to obtain the interest? [103] The importance of the question for Laurentius must have been great, for he describes the attachment of such conditions to the government bonds as "of daily occurrence," and it would have been a hollow victory if he had succeeded in defending the interest payments theoretically, but had found the actual method of making the payments to invalidate his arguments. Faced with this important difficulty, he says boldly that one may seek interest by buying early. The case is similar to seeking a bonus by entering the army ahead of a certain date when after that date one will be conscripted anyway. The objection is at once made that to seek gain from a loan is different from seeking gain through other acts. Laurentius stoutly replies that as the interest is licit itself, it may licitly be sought.[104] This statement is an astonishing departure from earlier writers and from his own teaching everywhere else. It meant that interest might be sought for its own sake, without any immediate compulsion or charitable motive inspiring the loan. If adopted generally, this view would have had a strong impact on the development of scholastic theory. But, given the usual scholastic attitude on intention, it was destined in 1400 to be confined to this one case. Laurentius' advocacy of it may be seen either as a lack of consistent principle, or as a brilliant foreshadowing of the future.

On all of Laurentius' treatment the influence of the government's financial methods is undeniable. The practical pressures these methods created may be imagined. On the level of theory it seems evident that the fact that the government was in the position of a debtor in perpetual default facilitated the reception of the interest titles already generally recognized as valid in delay.

[101] III:5 ad 1 (n.28).
[102] II:9 (n.38), as modified by II:24 (n.6).
[103] III:5 ad 2 (n.38).
[104] III:5 ad 2 (n.40).

Recognition by St. Bernardine and St. Antoninus

The fullest acceptance of *lucrum cessans* and *damnum emergens*, as well as the most detailed analysis of what they mean, is given by the two saints from capitalistic Tuscany, Bernardine and Antoninus.[105] St. Bernardine's Forty-second Lenten Sermon is entitled "Interest, or in What Cases It is Licit to Receive Beyond the Principal." In it he makes three main divisions of interest — penalty, *damnum emergens*, and *lucrum cessans*. Penalty has been discussed. *Damnum emergens*, St. Bernardine declares, is the loss immediately or subsequently occasioned by a loan and the loss it is estimated it will cause. Under this title, he gives a systematic theological treatment to the cases in the *Decretals* treated by the canonists as they occur in individual papal responses.[106] None of his cases here directly involves compensation from the start of a pure money loan. Elsewhere, treating of forced government loans, he admits *damnum emergens* on them from the beginning, because they are forced deprivations of the property of the lender.[107]

Interest due from the beginning of a normal loan is discussed only in connection with *lucrum cessans*. This title is proposed in the concrete and familiar case of the merchant asked to loan *ex pietate*. St. Bernardine declares that under the circumstances the merchant may demand compensation; for he "gives not money in its simple character, but he also gives his capital." The case is similar to the case of delay where the debtor is also compelled to repay *lucrum cessans*; here, too, "money is treated as capital." [108] The loss of gain from the capital is "a certain damnification of the lender." [109] He cites in support of his opinion the second part of *Naviganti*, which admits compensation to the seller on credit where there is a *venditio sub dubio*.[110]

If money is worth only its face value, to recognize *lucrum cessans* is to attribute to money the ability of producing a surplus value. This objection, which might seem to strike at the heart of the scholastic theory of money, had curiously enough not been reasoned out before by the theorists defending *lucrum cessans*. St. Bernardine's answer to it is exceedingly astute:

---

[105] Panormitanus allows *lucrum cessans* in the case presented by Hostiensis with a doubtful "perhaps" (Panormitanus, *Commentaria*, V 19:19:13).

[106] St. Bernardine, 42:1:1.

[107] 41:1:2.

[108] "Quia non tradidit solam simplicis pecuniae rationem, sed etiam tradit sibi capitale suum" (42:2:2). The word "capitale" has been used by the scholastics before, but this is the first time it is used by a prominent scholastic with the precise sense of "money accumulated for business enterprise."

[109] This is said in defense of *lucrum cessans* paid on the government *montes*, who, St. Bernardine says, are like debtors in perpetual delay (41:1:3).

[110] St. Bernardine, 42:2:2.

it is to be said that that money was truly worth more to its owner than itself because of the industry with which he would have used it. . . And therefore that money has value not from itself, but from its owner's industry, and therefore the receiver of the money not only deprives the owner of his money, but also of all the use and fruit of exercising his industry in it and through it.[111]

The skill of this response is clear: it preserves the scholastic theory of money while narrowly restricting the use of the interest title; it is the only logical reply, if the fruitlessness of money is to be maintained. The answer frankly assigns the cause of gain not to money itself, but to money as providing an opportunity for a merchant's labor. The merchant's enforced idleness is given as reason for compensation. Consequently, the plea of profit lost is limited to those cases where a lender is forced to curtail his business by his loan. If he were simply intending to use the money for consumption goods, or "keep it in a chest," he obviously has no right to interest.[112] In particular, *lucrum cessans*, thus understood, cannot be computed or claimed by a general consideration of what the common rate of profit on money is. The case is given of a man with 100 ducats soon to be expended on domestic needs, who, however, lends them, demanding as interest the profit they would have brought at "John's, a merchant." St. Bernardine denounces this as usury: the money given was not true capital; the money of itself would have borne no fruit; and its owner's labor was not dependent upon it.[113]

Moreover, like Laurentius and his predecessors, St. Bernardine sharply limits the title of *lucrum cessans* to loans made principally out of charity:

For, if except in a case of necessity and piety and at the instance of a plea, he does this, then by the very act he is convicted; because he wishes more to use his money in a usurious loan than in commerce or in profitable purchases as true capital.[114]

The case is similar, says St. Bernardine, to a man who lends for a fixed time, with a "penalty for default," hoping that the debtor will not be able to pay on time. In both cases the intention to profit annuls the legitimacy of the interest. These restrictions on *lucrum cessans* are at least consistent with early scholastic theory. But quite illogically, St. Bernardine denies that merchants can charge *lucrum cessans* in sales on credit; here he forgets his own arguments and simply cites St. Thomas' objection that one cannot sell what one does not yet possess and may be prevented from having.[115] Finally, he lays a severe check on the usefulness of the title by teaching that

[111] 41:1:3 — again, in defense of the montes.
[112] 42:2:2.
[113] 42:2:1.
[114] 42:2:2.
[115] 34:3:2.

the cases in which *lucrum cessans* is a just cause of interest are not to be preached publicly, "because of the peril to the people." [116]

In short, St. Bernardine has granted *lucrum cessans* recognition and given the best theoretical defense of it yet attempted, but he has restricted its application both by severe theoretical limitations and by inconsistent practical restraints. Despite the defects of his treatment, the great unalterable fact is that here a prominent theologian fully commits himself to the thesis that interest from the beginning of a loan may itself be intrinsically lawful. Henceforth, there can be no hesitations on this central point. [117]

The treatment given the title to interest from the beginning of a loan is very similar in St. Antoninus. *Damnum emergens* is admitted readily. [118] *Lucrum cessans* is unhesitatingly allowed in delay and on forced government loans. [119] A businessman's money has "the nature of capital," so he has from the beginning of a loan a right to *lucrum cessans* up to the probable amount of profit lost, allowing for its uncertainty and deducting for expenses. [120] He cannot claim the title, however, if he intends by lending to make a profit greater or more certain than he could in ordinary trade. Nor can *lucrum cessans* be demanded simply because the lender foregoes the opportunity of lending and charging interest to someone else. [121] Again, if a lender lends "beyond the case of necessity and the prayers of his friend," he is "by that very act convicted as rather wishing to use his money for a usurious loan than in business as true capital." Moreover, though *lucrum cessans* is theoretically a valid title, it is practically a temptation to usury, and its use is never to be counseled. [122] With the same lack of consistency as St. Bernardine and using the same Thomistic argument, St. Antoninus rejects the plea of *lucrum cessans* by merchants on credit sales. He has no discussion of the objections to the scholastic theory of money implicit in the notion of "capital"; on this account his theory of *lucrum cessans* must be considered inferior to St. Bernardine's. Nonetheless, he is a powerful authority in favor of the intrinsic soundness of the title.

A REJECTED TITLE OF INTEREST

A ground for interest that would occur to most people today as a plausible title to compensation is the risk that a lender assumes that his debtor may not repay him. By lending the lender places certain of his possessions in

[116] 42:2:2.

[117] Cf. Trugenberger, *San Bernardino da Siena*, p. 113.

[118] St. Antoninus, *Summa*, 2:1:2.

[119] 2:1:7; cf. 2:1:11.

[120] 2:1:7.

[121] 3:8:3.

[122] 2:1:7. Herbert L. Johnston, "Medieval

jeopardy they would not otherwise incur. Cannot he charge for so exposing his goods to danger? Yet we have found no mention of the title of risk in the scholastic list of titles to compensation on a loan.

The kind of risk considered here must be sharply discriminated from the risk assumed by a lender when he agrees not to hold his debtor for the capital if through misfortune he fails. This latter is the kind of risk dealt with by *Naviganti* and is described as *periculum sortis*.[123] It is the risk borne by a partner or an insurer. The risk we now deal with may be called, to distinguish it, *periculum mutui*. It is the simple risk of nonrepayment of the loan. While *periculum sortis* is matter for great debate and is often favored as a title to compensation, *periculum mutui* is never discussed in the twelfth, thirteenth, or fourteenth centuries. One reason why this apparently obvious title receives no attention might be supposed to be the high security demanded by public usurers. Such records as are available show them generally taking pledges worth much more than the loan.[124] Yet such security was not always offered; great debtors often ruined their creditors.[125] The early observation of Ptolemy of Lucca marks a universal truth: "In loans a lender often suffers outrage, because it is the nature of a borrower for it to be difficult for him to return a loan." [126] Moreover, even the practice of high security would not theoretically justify the failure to take account of the lender's risk of his original capital, for theoretically always, and often practically, it is a real loss to a lender to lose his money and get in return some valuable but unsellable pawn.[127]

The real reasons why *periculum mutui* are not even discussed must be supposed to be these: (1) the a fortiori force of *Naviganti*, which denied the licitness of interest even when the creditor took a far greater risk; [128]

Teachings on the Morality of Usury," p. 387, makes an interesting case for the proposition that St. Antoninus did not admit *lucrum cessans* from the beginning of a loan. However, the general context, the earlier tradition, and the example given in St. Antoninus, 3:8:3, all seem to tell against this interpretation.

[123] See, e.g., the unmistakable sense of the term in Giles of Lessines, c.6. The meaning of the expression has changed in modern times.

[124] According to de Roover, the lombards probably lent only about 50 per cent of the value of a pawn (*Money, Banking*, p. 133). Henry of Hesse testifies that "loans are usually made with insurance on their re-

turn," by which he means either pledges or guarantors are regularly given (*De contractibus*, f.192).

[125] Y. Renouard, *Les hommes d'affaires italiens du moyen age* (Paris, 1949), pp. 140, 225; R. de Roover, "Decline of the Medici Bank," *Journal of Economic History*, VII (1947), 82.

[126] Ptolemy of Lucca, *De regimine principis*, II, c.7.

[127] The difficulties the Belgian lombards experienced with the Countess Yolande's jewels (Bigwood, I, 376, 157), are an interesting example of the risks pawnbrokers have always run in taking valuable but not very marketable pledges.

[128] See *infra*, Chapter VI, section 3.

(2) the feeling that risk is implicit in every loan and that to admit it as a title to interest would be to deny the divine law which seemed to demand that loans be normally gratuitous. But these reasons were never stated explicitly; they are only inferred from later discussions. In these early centuries the very idea of charging for *periculum mutui* seems to have been unthinkable.

Yet while *periculum mutui* is never even spoken of as a title to interest on a pure loan, something like it is illogically recognized by an individual writer. Giles of Lessines says that a seller on credit may charge more dearly "on account of the loss he sees threaten him from delay in recovering payment or on account of the trouble which he fears will probably happen to him in seeking recovery of the debt, because of the malice or impotence of the debtor." [129] Yet in his long discussion of the stronger title *periculum sortis*, Giles denies that risk can excuse from usury, [130] and carefully avoids touching on the right to interest arising from the dangers of not recovering a pure money loan. His view on credit sales is peculiar to him. Even Alexander Lombard, who, as will be seen, is more tolerant on some aspects of the risk of nonrepayment, specifically repudiates Giles' position simply on the grounds that it is not lawful for a seller thus to raise his prices. [131]

Later, Laurentius de Ridolfis mentions risk as a reason for interest on the government *montes*. [132] But here the risk arises from the fact that the government is under no obligation to repay at all; so that the case is scarcely comparable to that of an ordinary loan.

Before St. Bernardine, then, there is not even a discussion of the normal *periculum mutui*. His opinions make explicit the thought of the earlier tradition. After discussing various contracts involving risk, partnership, and insurance, principally in connection with *Naviganti*, St. Bernardine reaches a case which he classifies as "execrable."

If someone lending 100 ducats wishes to have thence something beyond the principal because they are not so secure to him as if he had them in a chest, because, indeed, by lending he exposes himself to many chances of losing them, he is not excused because of such risk from usury. In truth, the risk of this case is nothing different from the character and act of lending, or at any rate it is inseparably connected with it, because it has no more vendible a character than a loan *qua* loan. Therefore to profit from this risk is to profit from the act of lending alone.

[129] Giles of Lessines, c.10.
[130] c.10. See the discussion of Conrad Summenhart's similar position, *infra*, Chapter XIV, section 1.
[131] Alexander Lombard, c.7, f.163v:a. As to Alexander's more lenient position on the resale of a right to money at a discount because of the risk involved, see *infra*, Chapter VII, section 2.
[132] De Ridolfis, III:14.

Since St. Bernardine is governed by the concept that the loan itself must always be per se free, to show that risk is of the essence of a loan is to deny it as a title. St. Bernardine adds that since the debtor always remains obliged to indemnify if he defaults, the peril of the creditor is not real.[133]

St. Antoninus gives the same reason as St. Bernardine, differing only in the citation of *Naviganti* as his authority. He says tersely, "By reason of doubt in a loan, which is implicit in it, one may not licitly hope profit."[134] Again, on credit sales, he says that merchants may penalize debtors who default, but that it is illicit to penalize honest and dishonest customers alike by charging all an average interest for risk.[135] Finally, he doubts the sincerity of those who say they ask compensation for the risk, and not for the profit:

> Nor does it excuse them, that they expose themselves to danger in that the merchants with whom they deposit sometimes fail, and from these faring badly and retrenching they sometimes may not have back their capital; for they do not hope for profit by reason of the risk, since, if they doubted about the danger, they would not deposit. But they hope for profit from the loan by reason of the loan.[136]

Conclusion

The following conclusions on the right to payment beyond the principal suggest themselves:

1. The canon law and the scholastics at a very early date recognized the right to an increment on a loan in a number of exceptional cases in which the lender-debtor relation of the parties was superseded by other relations.

2. At an equally early date the right to *interesse*, understood in the strict Roman-law sense of damages due because of default on a contract, was granted to the lender in certain specific cases.

3. More significantly, the seller on credit's right to compensation for profit lost in a *venditio sub dubio* was recognized as early as 1170. But later commentary made it clear that it was admitted under the laws ruling the just price in sales, and that it did not automatically mean the recognition of *lucrum cessans*.

4. However, the influence exerted by the early exceptions, together with the effect of recognizing *lucrum cessans* in cases which were not pure loans, led to an acknowledgment of *lucrum cessans* in 1270 by the canonist Hostiensis and in 1312 by the theologian Astesanus. The majority of authorities, nonetheless, continued to oppose it on the grounds that a loan must be naturally and normally gratuitous.

[133] St. Bernardine, 39:1:3.
[134] St. Antoninus, 2:1:7.
[135] 2:1:8.
[136] 2:1:7.

5. Only the thorough discussion of interest in the controversy over the *montes* led to a general admission of the right to compensation from the beginning of a loan. The acceptance of this right was made easier for the theologians, because the lenders to the *montes* were in the position of creditors confronted with a debtor in perpetual delay.

6. In the fifteenth century, interest developed from being considered compensation due the lender for a fault of the borrower to being considered compensation due the lender from loss suffered by his making the original loan. *Damnum emergens* was generally accepted.

7. *Lucrum cessans* was also accepted by several of the leading fifteenth-century writers. Even by these writers, however, *lucrum cessans* was admitted only on a loan made from charity to a distressed neighbor, by a businessman ordinarily engaged in lawful commerce and not motivated by hope of profit from the loan.

8. The risk inherent in lending was not recognized as a title to interest.

CHAPTER VI

RISK-SHARING INVESTMENT: THE PARTNERSHIP

As important to the understanding of the usury theory as a comprehension of the objections raised to usury and the distinction made between usury and interest is an understanding of the contracts allowed as licit by the theory, for these contracts complement and complete the theory proper. A grossly distorted view of the scholastic judgment on economic operations is obtained if the usury prohibition and the loan contract are considered out of context. By itself the prohibition applied to the loan contract seems to bar effectively any profit from pecuniary investment, any practical development of commercial credit, any capitalistic management of finance. But this isolated view is seriously misleading. Only when the other investment opportunities recognized as lawful by the scholastics have been considered, can we form any sound opinion on the general significance of the theory of usury. It is with this in mind that we turn to a discussion of the *societas*, which was to be one great and universal form of licit investment in commerce throughout medieval Europe.[1]

The scholastic discussion of *societas* is important not only in showing the wide avenue open to investment capital; it is even more significant in its use of the fundamental concepts of the usury prohibition — ownership, risk, and the sterility of money. These basic notions are only partially touched upon in the analysis of a loan proper; yet to understand them completely is a necessary condition for understanding the usury theory at all. In the theoretical treatment of the *societas*, is the usury theory's identification of the use and ownership of money maintained? Is money consistently considered as sterile? Is risk successfully used as a criterion of ownership? The answers to these questions reflect the theoretical weakness and practical focus of the usury rule.

1. Roman-Law Origins

The *societas*, or partnership, was a normal form of commercial organization throughout the Roman world; and it enters scholastic thought largely

[1] See *The Cambridge Economic History* (Cambridge, 1952), II, 173, 323.
of Medieval Europe, ed. Postan and Rich

in the form given it by Roman law. A *societas*, according to the *Digest*, is the union by two or more persons of their money or skill for a common purpose, usually profit. Often one partner will invest money alone, the other labor alone; this is the kind of arrangement which interests us most, because its similarity to a loan is obvious. The partners become joint owners of the goods contributed. Normally, the loss of the property of the partnership through any fortuitous cause, such as fire, robbery, or shipwreck, will be borne by both equally. It is an inflexible rule of the *societas* that one partner cannot have the opportunity of having all the profit while his partner bears only the responsibility for loss. Such a contract is called leonine, from the fable of the lion who devoured the tamer beasts who were his hunting companions; it is null in law. It is possible, however, if one partner contributes a great deal more to the union than the other, that he be freed from responsibility for loss, while his partner bears all this responsibility and gets only a part of the profit. Variations of this are possible, such as one partner bearing one-third of the risk and getting two-thirds of the gain, etc. Although a partnership in which one partner is entirely freed from risk of his capital is indistinguishable in effect from a loan, the Roman law treats a loan as formally distinct from this contract. The great change in the early scholastic notion of partnership is that such a riskless partnership will be treated as a usurious loan. Finally, the Roman law says that all partners may be assessed on all their property for damages caused by a member acting for the partnership; "since a partnership has a certain kind of right of brotherhood in it."[2] This *ius fraternitatis*, in particular, will influence the medieval concept of the partnership.

Another Roman contract with certain effects similar to those of the partnership is the *foenus nauticum* or *pecunia traiectia*. In this contract money or goods are loaned to a shipowner, the creditor assuming the risks of his debtor while the money or goods are actually at sea. If a shipwreck occurs and the property is lost, the debtor will not be liable in any way to return the loan. Once the voyage is completed, however, the borrower trades at his own risk, and if he loses the loan through commercial misfortune, he must still repay the lender.[3] The Roman law permits the creditor to charge double the legal rate of interest for the time he actually runs the risk of the sea. This extra charge is described as "the price of peril." The *Digest* compares the sea loan to a loan to a fisherman or athlete who agree to give you part of their earnings if they are lucky, but will return nothing,

[2] *Digesta*, 17:2:5:1; 17:2:29:1 and 2; 17:2:52:3 and 4; 17:2:58; 17:2:63; *Institu-*   *tiones*, 3:25:2.
[3] *Digesta*, 22:2:3 and 6; *Codex*, 4:33:1.

if they fail.[4] It is clear that in these circumstances, for the duration of the danger, the creditor is really the partner of the debtor, since the creditor bears the risk of the enterprise and the profit is common. The *foenus nauticum* is, in fact, half a loan, half a partnership. The Roman law, however, does not assimilate the case with partnership, but treats it strictly as a kind of licit usury; and the canonists and scholastics follow the sharp discrimination between it as a loan, and the normal partnership.

2. Early Theological References and Contemporary Practice

The *societas* is mentioned in a theological context in the eleventh century by Ivo of Chartres as a contract distinct from a usurious loan,[5] and the *Glossa ordinaria* repeats the distinction. The *Gloss* says simply that if one invests money with a businessman, contracting thereby a partnership so that the risk is shared by both, the contract is licit.[6] Thus, without analysis or debate, this contract so enormously important to commerce is recognized; and what is to be the fundamental principle for the next three hundred years is laid down — assumption of risk distinguishes the capitalistic investment in a partnership from a loan.

At about the same time Robert of Courçon discusses what is plainly the *societas*, although he does not use the exact term. He writes, "Any merchant making a contract with another for trading must, if he wishes to be a participant of the profit, show himself a participant of the danger and expenses which attend all buying and selling." [7] Even if the merchant is sick, Courçon adds, he must still run the risk of the business; the implication is clear that an inactive investor can still be considered a partner if he has risk capital in an enterprise.[8] Similarly, Courçon defends sales on credit if the merchant granting the credit "commits his capital to chance danger" — that is, if he becomes, in effect, a partner of his debtor and agrees to run his risks with him.[9] In each case, the basic element of partnership is considered to be the risk of the investor's capital. Only if the investor runs the risk of the enterprise is he conceded to have a title to gain; although in Courçon's treatment, as in that of the *Gloss*, it is not clear whether the gain is the reward of the risk, or whether retention of the risk shows a retention of ownership, which is the title to gain. But it is clear that any business loan is not neces-

[4] *Digesta*, 22:21:5.
[5] See *supra*, Chapter I, n.23.
[6] *Glossa ordinaria*, C.14, Q.3, c.3, at *Negotiatoribus*.

[7] Robert of Courçon, *De usura*, p. 73.
[8] p. 71.
[9] p. 59.

sarily a partnership; where his capital is safe, the lender is a usurer in intention, although the borrower makes much more than he is charged.[10] William Cade, a celebrated English financier of the twelfth century, is mentioned as a notorious example of someone who became a millionaire by such safe partnerships.[11]

Aside from the *Gloss* and Courçon's indirect reference, the early theological literature has little on the *societas*. Nonetheless, it had been used in commercial Italy since the earliest revival of trade,[12] and the *societas* or variations of it such as the *collegantia* or *accomendatio*, were common in eleventh-century Venice and twelfth-century Genoa.[13] The almost complete lack of theological comment upon these arrangements, and the casual reference of the *Gloss*, would seem to indicate that the conscience of the day readily accepted the capitalistic *societas* as a different matter from usury, and easily saw the distinction. This contract had become essential to the life of business. At the same time a contract in many ways similar to a partnership was being used by Italian commerce in defiance of the rule that it was sinful to gain from a loan. The enterprising financiers of the active Mediterranean ports such as Venice, Marseilles, Barcelona, and Genoa had not been content with the simple *societas*. The *foenus nauticum* had been revived.[14] Contracts of it were recorded usually as *mutua* to sea-going merchants.[15] The high interest payments were sometimes concealed in the form of a return to be made in a foreign currency.[16] Against the background of this practice the two papal decretals which appear on the subject must now be understood.

3. *Two Celebrated Canons*

The first of these documents, the canon *Per vestras*, is a letter of Innocent III to the Archbishop of Genoa on the disposition of a dowry. Not formally treating either usury or partnership, the Pope, at the end of a dis-

[10] p. 61.

[11] p. 71. William of Cade's case is complicated by the fact that he entered "safe" partnerships not with ordinary merchants, but with "lesser usurers." But Courçon seems to mean to condemn both the coöperation in usury and the safe partnership. Cf. H. Jenkinson, "William Cade, a Financier of the Twelfth Century," *English Historical Review* (April 1913), p. 217.

[12] Schaub (*Der Kampf*, p. 160), cites an instance of the *societas* in ninth-century Venice.

[13] A. E. Sayous, "Le capitalisme commercial et financier dans les pays chrétiens de la Méditerranée occidentale," *Vierteljahrschrift für sozial und Wirthschaftegeschichte* (1936), p. 272; cf. Eugene H. Byrne, "Commercial Contracts of the Genoese in the Syrian Trade of the Twelfth Century," *Quarterly Journal of Economics*, XXXI (1916–1917), 136.

[14] Eugene H. Byrne, *Genoese Shipping in the Twelfth and Thirteenth Centuries* (Cambridge, Mass., 1930), p. 14; Pirenne, *Medieval Cities*, p. 113.

[15] Byrne, *Genoese Shipping*, p. 18.

[16] A. E. Sayous, "L'origine de la lettre de change," *Revue historique de droit français et étranger* (1933), p. 88; cf. Calvin

cussion about the rights of a thriftless husband to a dowry, gives orders to execute a contract the significance of which was long to trouble the commentators. He writes:

> We command that you have the dowry assigned to the same man [the husband] under what security he can furnish, or at any rate commit it to some merchant, so that from honest gain the said man can sustain the burdens of matrimony.[17]

It is evident that the phrase "commit to a merchant" means "invest in a partnership," an act the Pope assumes to be licit. At the same time, many writers were to wonder if the insistence on the husband's furnishing security also applied if the partnership investment were made. Was the Pope recommending investment in a riskless partnership? It seems plain that the decretal makes a distinction between the case of the husband and the case of the merchant, and that the Pope meant to ask security only from the former; it would be extraordinary if he had gone against all the traditions of his age to recommend a riskless partnership here. Even so, the slight ambiguity furnished material for later hesitations.

The second decretal, *Naviganti*, is an excerpt from a letter of Gregory IX to Frater R. By any standard it is the most important single papal decree on the usury question with the exception of those containing the basic prohibition itself. It has the paradoxical distinction of containing in two sentences the seemingly most severe and the seemingly most liberal interpretations of the usury law ever put out by papal authority. Its most difficult clause has been variously interpreted as a *lapsus calami* and as a hasty, last-minute change by a papal secretary.[18] But it has been of great value to the analysis of usury. Because of its double difficulty, more than any other text it stimulated theorists to probe the usury doctrine to the fullest.

Having examined the lenient and more explicable second portion of it under *venditio sub dubio* in Chapter IV, we consider here only the first part. This reads, "One lending a certain quantity of money to one sailing or going to a fair, in order to receive something beyond the capital for this that he takes upon himself the peril, is to be thought a usurer."[19] Thus

---

Hoover, "The Sea-Loan in Genoa in the Twelfth Century," *Quarterly Journal of Economics*, XL (1925), 499–518; see also Guido Astuti, *Origini e svolgimiento storico della commenda fino al secolo XIII* (Turin, 1933).

[17] *Decretales*, IV:20:7, *Per vestras*.

[18] See G. C. Coulton, "An Episode in Canon Law," *History*, n.s., VI (July 1921), 72ff. The article is sound enough on the point at issue, although marred by an unscrupulous use of *Ejiciens* to show that the Church was against retail trade.

[19] The difficult text runs as follows in the Latin: "Naviganti vel eunti ad nundinas

was created a great problem for the analysts of usury. The decretal appears to reject incidence of risk as the criterion of ownership, for, though the investor here takes the risk of his capital on himself, he is still considered by the Pope to be a lender, that is, one who has transferred ownership of his good to a borrower. But to deny that incidence of risk was the index of ownership was to leave no way of discriminating between the licit *societas* and any illicit loan: in each, money was given by a capitalist to a trader or worker and returned to him with a profit. If the difference between the two cases did not consist in the different risks run by a partner and a lender, there was no other difference between them. If the implication of the apparent meaning of *Naviganti* were worked out, one would be forced to conclude that every investment of money at a profit with another person would be usury, whatever form the investment took. *Navganti* would seem to strangle commerce at its roots.

Against the commercial usage of the time, we can see that such a wholesale condemnation of all money investments was not intended by the decretal. By its use of the term "loan" and its reference to the salient feature of the *foenus nauticum*, the creditor's assumption of the risk, *Naviganti* is presumably striking at the revival of the sea-loan contract current at cities such as Genoa. If one considers the length of time the *societas* proper had been placidly accepted by everyone, it is incredible that any condemnation of it should have been meant. Furthermore, the qualified statement that the lender is "to be thought" a usurer may mean that the Pope does not consider such a contract in itself illicit, but only that its use creates a presumption of fraud — an observation which would well accord with the facts known about the use of the sea-loan contract. Nevertheless, the qualification "to be thought" is not a strong one to rely on, and, in the precise terms it uses, the decretal offers no distinction between the *foenus nauticum* and the *societas*. The task of the usury analysts will be to note the distinction, to observe the canon, and yet to allow the legitimate partnership.

4. The Canonists' Commentary
St. Raymond

St. Raymond, Gregory's secretary, who knew more about the origin and reasoning behind the canon than anyone else save the Pope himself, begins the scholastic discussion of it by declaring that "some held that there was no usury here, because compensation might be demanded for risk run." How-

certam mutuans pecuniae quantitatem pro aliquid ultra sortem, usurarius est censen-
eo, quod suscipit in se periculum, recepturus dus." *Decretales*, V:19:19.

ever, against these defenders of the contract, he cites *Ejiciens* and points out that it places three differences between a legitimate rent and a usurious loan. In the loan, the owner does not retain the peril; the good does not deteriorate in use; and the good bears no fruit. In the present case, though the first condition is altered, the other two remain. Therefore, the opinion holding the transaction as usurious is "safer," "especially because such men always make such loans because of the hope of pecuniary profit," and intention to gain from a loan is always usurious. Further, the loans are usually made "in fraud of usury."[20] By this last statement, St. Raymond seems to indicate directly that the decretal refers to the sea-loan contracts brazenly evading the usury laws. Nonetheless, in his analysis, as in the decretal itself, nothing is given which would distinguish a licit capitalistic investment in a partnership from a usurious loan. In the partnership, too, a sterile good which does not deteriorate in use is given to another, who returns it with profit. If the sea loan is usury, why, then, is not the *societas*?

Goffredus of Trani

Cardinal Goffredus of Trani (fl. 1245) has the honor of being the first to note an important difference between a partnership and the contract condemned by *Naviganti*. He begins by boldly identifying the case of *Naviganti* with the *foenus nauticum*; then he distinguishes the *foenus nauticum* and the *societas*. In the *foenus nauticum* if the ship is safe the creditor will get a profit on his loan "whatever outcome the business has, whether the debtor gains or loses with his wares." A true partnership, however, demands that all risk of loss be borne in common. *Naviganti* condemns only the first case; there a loan occurs because the lender transfers his good and most of his responsibility for it.[21] That this was the true explanation of *Naviganti*,

---

[20] St. Raymond, *Summa*, 2:7:7.

[21] Goffredus, *Summa, De usuris*, cited in Hostiensis, *Summa*, V, *De usuris*, n.8. In the absence of an available edition of Goffredus of Trani, I have relied, with some hesitation, on the statements of his position found in Hostiensis. The hesitation stems from the frequent unreliability of the scholastics in stating the positions of their predecessors. The method of citing authority by the scholastics should be understood. It is very similar to the method of a modern appellate court citing precedents. Sometimes the authority is cited as controlling, sometimes as analogous; but the scholastic author, like the modern judge, generally writes not as an historian trying to get the exact meaning of a text, but as a man with a thesis to establish, for which he is marshalling support. Not by deliberate distortion, but by the need to interpret the text to meet his problem, he sometimes will not catch the original intention with its original limitations and in its original context. Consequently, it is generally unsafe to rely very heavily on a later scholastic's statements as to what an earlier scholastic wrote. Endemann, for example, suffers considerably from his reliance on Raphael de Turri and Sigmund Scaccia for the statement of opinions of authors centuries earlier. Cf. a similar criticism of Endemann in Hagenauer, *Das "Justum Pretium*," p. 35.

and the distinction it really intended, seems undeniable. Nonetheless, despite Goffredus' early and succinct clarification, the text remained to puzzle other commentators. Even Goffredus leaves unexplained why the creditor cannot profit during the period he actually does bear the risk of disaster.

Hostiensis

Hostiensis' analysis of the *foenus nauticum* and the *societas* is extraordinarily inconsistent, and he seems to approve under one name what he condemns under another. Yet inconsistencies can be instructive as to the state of a theory; and Hostiensis' extended inconsistent treatment shows the immense difficulty of reconciling the application of the scholastic concepts of risk, ownership, and profit to loans with their application to partnerships.

Like Goffredus, Hostiensis identifies the case of *Naviganti* with the *foenus nauticum*, but he does not avail himself of Goffredus' explanation of the difference between it and a *societas*. He says simply that in the *foenus nauticum* a loan is involved; therefore, no profit may be expected. His presentation of the position of the creditor is brusque: "For he wishes to take the peril upon himself, and he can; and so the contract holds: he wishes to demand beyond the principal, but he cannot, and so the contract does not hold." Or, as he presents the case alternatively, if the debtor is aided by the money lent, he is aided by his own property, for the loan has transferred ownership to him; therefore, the creditor cannot demand part of the profit. If the debtor does not prosper, it is equally unjust for the creditor to demand gain he has not made.[22] This analysis makes it evident that incidence of risk is no criterion of ownership: the debtor is specifically considered to own the loaned good during the time of the loan, although the creditor, for part of the time, bears the risk of loss. As we have seen earlier, Hostiensis even uses his interpretation of *Naviganti* to show that incidence of risk is irrelevant to the question of the justice of profit on an investment.[23] But by making clear the irrelevance of risk, Hostiensis leaves unexplained the difference between "lending" and "investing in a partnership."

Nonetheless — showing the strong position *societas* held in the conscience of the age — Hostiensis goes on to accept this contract as licit as a matter of course.[24] Without any explanation at all, he admits under this different name what seems substantially condemned by the standards he uses when discussing *Naviganti*. But even more startlingly, he discusses a partnership in which the capitalistic partner will in no event suffer loss; in which, in

[22] Hostiensis, *Summa*, V, *De usuris*, n.8.
[23] See *supra*, p. 50.
[24] Hostiensis, *Summa*, V, *De usuris*, n.8, at *Quid ergo*.

the technical phrase, his capital will be "safe." This case is prima facie much more an instance of usury than even the *foenus nauticum*, for in the *foenus nauticum* the lender at least bears the risks of disaster at sea, while here he bears no risks at all; yet Hostiensis treats it with surprising gentleness.

On the one hand, he reports, Goffredus does attack the contract as a usurious loan. On the other hand, the Roman law, always of great weight with the canonists, admits the contract. Furthermore, the canonist Albercius defends the contract, first because as the working partner usually prospers, no harm is done him; second because such a positive agreement, freely entered into by the contracting parties, creates a valid obligation, although one beyond the nature of the *societas* in itself. Hostiensis then adds certain arguments of his own on the side of Albercius. A merchant sells you a horse and trades with the money he receives from you; you agree to share the profits with him which you make by the use of the horse; he agrees to share with you the profits from his trading with the money. Though each of you are exposed to a different risk, the contract is valid, according to Hostiensis; he makes no distinction between the profit from the use of money and the profit from the use of nonconsumptibles. Moreover, he adds, following the Roman law, the contract would be valid, though only one of the parties agreed to share his profits, while each ran a risk. The position of the riskless investor here appears similar to that of the investor in the riskless partnership, and there is thus analogous evidence in favor of the latter. Again, in other contracts, such as leases, the risk pertains only to the owner, the full profit to the user. Finally, *Per vestras* appears to be in favor of a riskless partnership, for it permits a dowry to be invested with a merchant, *salvo capitali*.

Yet, though he disavows none of these arguments, Hostiensis does reject the riskless partnership in itself. His appeal is to another piece of Roman law, taken out of context, which, as has been noted, was to become a favorite scholastic axiom: a partnership creates a certain right of fraternity. Then, Hostiensis reasons, this fraternal *ius* is destroyed if one partner secures himself against all loss. The intrinsic nature of the contract is violated, if risk is not borne fraternally, in common. The Roman law and Albercius cannot really mean that a partnership is licit if one partner is freed from every risk to his capital. What they mean is that a partner can be guaranteed against ordinary risks of business; but that if the capital is lost by some disaster, both partners should be liable.

Hostiensis has rejected the completely riskless partnership, but, in reinterpreting the Roman law and Albercius, he has reached a result almost as surprising as if he had accepted the riskless partnership outright; he has accepted as licit the precise case which *Naviganti* condemns. A contract by which the investing partner is held only for the risk of major disasters is no different from the *foenus nauticum;* and now under the name of *societas* Hostiensis allows this. Moreover, even the completely riskless partnership is not rejected by him with much force. In the case where the working partner loses the money by a chance disaster, Hostiensis teaches, the capitalistic partner is *advised* not to press a claim for reimbursement.[25] But he is only advised, not commanded, and from this deliberate choice of language, one must conclude that Hostiensis did not consider a riskless partnership to be contrary to a binding moral precept. Thus under the name of *societas*, he accepts, at least as not clearly illicit, what he condemns as unnatural under the name of *mutuum.*

Pope Innocent IV

Pope Innocent IV has nothing to say on the *societas*, nor does he mention the *foenus nauticum.* He avoids Hostiensis' confusions by holding to the text of *Naviganti.* His analysis of it is succinct:

Where he [the debtor] received money not merely to transport it, but was trading with it, as a means of commerce, here is usury; because in money there is no use or utility of using, nor does it deteriorate in use.[26]

In other words, unlike Goffredus and Hostiensis, Innocent makes no distinction between the *societas* and *foenus nauticum.* All profits on money investments seem to be condemned. *Naviganti* is interpreted literally and absolutely. With St. Raymond, Innocent appears to deny the licitness of financing any business. Yet it may be unwise to extend his meaning so absolutely. Perhaps it were better said of both of him and St. Raymond that they posit principles which seem to lead to the complete condemnation of the *societas*, but which are never extended personally by them to this extreme, and which, it may be supposed, were never intended by their authors to lead there, however logically they should.

Thus the canonists have done little to elucidate *Naviganti* or to justify the *societas.* Goffredus has offered the most sensible explanation of the canon, by making a distinction between partial and full acceptance of risk, but even he has not explained why the lender cannot profit during the time he does

---

[25] *Ibid.*, at *Quid periculum.*   [26] Innocent IV, *Apparatus*, V, *De usuris*, c.19.

run the risk. Hostiensis has taken two entirely contradictory positions, according to one of which no *societas* of any kind should be licit, and according to the other all business loans at usury are just. St. Raymond and Innocent, like the face of the canon itself, make no distinction between the *foenus nauticum* and *societas*, but apparently condemn all money investments. Chaos is perhaps the only accurate word for this situation.

5. *The Traditional Analysis: St. Thomas*

St. Thomas Aquinas affirms the tradition of the general conscience upon the *societas*. He makes no reference to *Naviganti* or the *foenus nauticum*, as a theologian leaving the canonists to disentangle the canonical difficulty by themselves, but he accepts as a common well-known principle the lawfulness of the *societas*.

Why is investment in a partnership licit, and usury illicit? An objector to the usury prohibition declares that a lender gives up more than does one who "commits his money to a merchant or craftsman." Why is the latter allowed to profit, the other not allowed to make a gain? St. Thomas replies with the answer of the *Gloss*, to which he now gives the weight of his immense authority:

He who commits his money to a merchant or craftsman by means of some kind of partnership does not transfer the ownership of his money to him but it remains his; so that at his risk the merchant trades, or the craftsman works, with it; and therefore he can licitly seek part of the profit thence coming as from his own property [27]

There are three important aspects of this concise statement, and all will have a decisive influence on the history of usury analysis. The first is this: St. Thomas here abandons his own principle that the use and the ownership of money are indistinguishable. The capitalist's money is committed to the use of the working partner; according to St. Thomas' earlier analysis, the transference of the use *ipso facto* transfers the ownership, and on the basis of such analysis, a loan and a partnership would not be differentiated. St. Thomas should logically conclude that all pecuniary investments are usury. But the common acceptance of the *societas* and the promptings of natural justice are stronger than his theory. At this critical point he introduces a new principle, the second important thesis in his statement — ownership does not go with the use of a consumptible, but is determined by the incidence of risk. The owner is the man on whom the risk falls; conversely, if a man does not

[27] St. Thomas, *S.T.*, II–II:9:78:2, obj. 5.

run the risk he is not the owner.[28] Thus, St. Thomas accepts completely the suggestion of the *Gloss* and the general conscience that incidence of risk is an effective test of a loan. Yet he does this, as it were instinctively without attempt at analysis or defense. If one considers his formal treatment of ownership, one finds nothing there which would justify this view on risk. Private property, St. Thomas teaches, is established by the *ius gentium* to insure tranquillity, to prevent confusion in the distribution of reward for work, and to stimulate each man's care by making him responsible for his own thing.[29] The first two grounds say nothing as to risk. The last reason might be taken as implicitly indicating a natural responsibility for risk: one might argue that a man would not care for his own, unless he ran the danger of any evil that might befall it. It is difficult, however, to see how responsibility for natural, unavoidable disasters increases an owner's solicitude, nor is it a necessary inference that, where risk is not borne directly by an owner, but is indirectly reflected by an insurance contract, he will become willfully negligent about his property. It is true that risk normally accompanies ownership, but not necessarily or essentially. There is nothing in St. Thomas' presentation of the rational foundations of property that requires the owner and the risk-taker to be one. Faced with an objection, and well aware of the popular tradition on risk, St. Thomas has produced the risk criterion *ad hoc* to distinguish loans from capitalistic partnership. It is against his own theory of the ownership of consumptibles, and it is not indicated by his formal analysis of property. As a practical criterion, it will serve well for two centuries at least. But when finally it comes itself to be questioned by scholastic theologians, no rational basis for it will be found.

The third aspect of St. Thomas' significant declaration on partnership is this: St. Thomas formally refers to risk only as the criterion of ownership, not as the source of profit. The capitalist is not paid the price of peril. But the incidence of risk establishes the owner, and the owner then takes the fruits

---

[28] Schreiber has attempted to show that St. Thomas considers a partner's assumption of risk as equivalent to work and that work is here the ultimate title to reward. He asserts that St. Thomas always ascribes any production of surplus value to labor (*Die volkswirtschaftlich Anschauungen*, p. 109). This may have been what St. Thomas should have taught to be consistent with his doctrine on money; it is not what he did teach. There is no suggestion that the reward on investment in a partnership is in any way proportionate to the risk run. Schreiber (p. 111) admits that St. Thomas' teaching seems in a certain sense opposed to a labor theory of value, but argues that the Thomistic teaching here should be taken as an incomplete exposition, rather than as inconsistent with a labor theory. It seems to me, however, that the teaching on the right to reward depending on ownership is fundamental to St. Thomas and that an attempt to explain it away is an unhistorical attempt to produce a harmony and union the author himself did not achieve.

[29] *S.T.*, II–II:66:2c.

of his property, as the owner of an orchard would take the apples on his trees. The difficulty here, of course, is that the owner's property consists not in apple trees but in money, which is supposed to be sterile. If one believes that all surplus value gained by the use of money is due to the energy of the man using it, why should not all the profit go to the working partner? Whence comes the profit which is assigned to the capitalist? Yet St. Thomas is precise upon this: the capitalist receives "the gain coming thence," i.e., from the partnership's use of money, "as from his own property." In fact, St. Thomas has here changed his mind as to the productive power of money, and assigns it a real function and independent reward. This inconsistency on the nature of money will characterize nearly every scholastic attempt to legitimate the *societas* while denying the right of money to bring a return in a loan.

St. Thomas, then, defends the *societas* on the grounds that in it, the investor, remaining the owner of his investment because he still runs the risk of total loss, licitly profits from the use of his own money. This doctrine, the explication of the teachings of the *Gloss* and Courçon, makes the incidence of risk the key, ignores *Naviganti*, and implicitly denies the sterility of money. It will be the standard defense of the *societas* for the next two hundred years.

6. *Confusion and Acceptance, 1270–1450*

The discussions of *societas* in the following century and a half are meager and confused. They testify to a general willingness to allow the *societas*, a general unwillingness to recognize the fact that money fructifies in a *societas*, a general dependence on the risk criterion, and a general inability to reconcile *Naviganti* and the risk criterion. The meagerness of the treatments may reflect either an ignorance of business or a belief that it was superfluous to say much on a licit and common business practice. The confusion of the treatments comes from the difficulty of reconciling the usury theory and the partnership theory.

Giles of Lessines and Monaldus

Giles of Lessines' inconsistencies are as radical as Hostiensis'. Like him, Giles is at first very firm on the fact that risk does not excuse one from usury. To lend with hope of gain is vicious, although one takes upon oneself the debtor's perils, and indeed loses everything. Such, he says, is the doctrine of *Naviganti*.[30] At the same time, he maintains that one may licitly commit money to a merchant, "if one retains the ownership and common dangers."

[30] Giles of Lessines, *De usuris*, c.11.

What the mystical phrase "retaining the ownership" effects is not explained. A concrete case that Giles adds makes his confusion even more apparent. Although it is often done in fraud of the usury rule, it is in itself licit, Giles teaches, to give animals to a farmer in a partnership for profit, with the agreement that the farmer bear all the risks.[31] Here it is clear that Giles is not using risk as the criterion of ownership, and its transfer as the index of a loan: he allows the investor to profit on a completely riskless partnership. Why does he not extend his reasoning to riskless partnerships in money or to money loans? The answer is that presumably he distinguishes income in fruitful goods from income in sterile goods. But this is no answer at all, for in allowing a profit to the investor in the simple, nonsecured, money partnership, he has already tacitly admitted that money does fructify in a partnership. If he were logical, he would admit profit on a riskless money partnership, as he does on a partnership in animals. The contradiction is unresolved, and Giles leaves equally unreconciled his conflicting views on the nature of money in a *societas* and a loan.

His contemporary, Monaldus, also simply condemns the *foenus nauticum* and allows the *societas*, without explaining the distinction.[32] He offers no comment on the function and reward assigned to money in the *societas*. It is clear to him only that the essential condition for its licitness is that risk of every chance must be run by the capitalistic partner.

Five Early Fourteenth-Century Writers

Durandus of St. Pourçain, Aegidius, and Scotus do not even discuss the *foenus nauticum* or the *societas*. But Alexander Lombard considers the *societas* at some length. If either the *capitale* or the profit is safe, the investor commits usury; this is the case, like *Naviganti*, where the risk of the capital is run by the investor unless it is lost through the negligence or fault of the borrower.[33] An arrangement which guarantees a return of part of the capital and risks the rest of the capital and profit is equally to be treated as a partial loan, and profit on it is usurious.[34] Speaking in Genoa, the seat of the maritime contracts, however, Alexander specifically defends the *commenda* where the merchant is merely an agent of the investor and the investor runs the full risk. More clearly than most writers, he sees the objection that profit is apparently being attributed to money alone in this contract, and again more clearly than most, he answers this objection with

---

[31] c.6.
[32] Monaldus, *Summa*, at "Usura," f.294r:a-b; cf. f.288v:b.
[33] Alexander Lombard, *Tractatus*, c.3, f.156r:a.
[34] c.4, f.156r:b.

the reply that it is not money which is producing fruits, but the goods the money has bought. He even goes so far, apparently, as to contradict his earlier teaching that a contract where any of the capital is safe is entirely usurious; he appears at least to except a *commenda* where only part of the capital is risked.[35]

Astesanus continues in the path marked out by Alexander. The *societas* is licit if both partners share the loss and gain in proportion to their contributions, and the risk is not placed on the working partner alone. This means, says Astesanus, that if there be no profit and no loss, something must be deducted from the capital to compensate the working partner's labor. The possibility that the capitalist may have lost as much as the laborer by having his money tied up in an unsuccessful enterprise is ignored, in conformity with the usury theory's postulate of the sterility of money. At the same time the admission that the capitalist can partake in the profit, if the partnership makes any, denies the postulate.

A case is presented in which A gives C 20 sheep estimated at 10 pounds and demands that C guarantee to return to him at least 5 pounds, whatever happens to the sheep; in other words, A is "safe" as to half of his capital, and will demand a profit, if there is one, upon the whole amount. Astesanus' expansion of the usury-risk theory to cover the case is instructive:

I declare that this is the same as if A, the creditor, had given to C a loan of 5 pounds from which were bought 10 sheep, and they then contracted a partnership and had all in common. Behold, in this case, if A had hurt C by reason of the loan, there would be usury.[36]

The implication is that there is usury here, too, if C has to pay A for the virtual loan; the tacit assumption is that one must run a risk upon all on which one profits. The criterion of risk, then, may be said to distinguish loans from licit partnerships in Astesanus. He makes no attempt, however, to explain *Naviganti*.

Rolandino de Passagiero

In his *Summa totius artis notariae*, Rolandino, who is careful about not setting out usurious contracts,[37] describes, under the general heading of debits and credits, a contract similar to the *societas*, but not specifically named as such. In it a merchant receives capital, binds himself to use it in

[35] c.7, f.166r:a–b.
[36] Astesanus, *Summa*, III:12.
[37] See Rolandino's plea to notaries to avoid frauds on the usury law. He says those co-operating in usurious contracts "gain 11 pennies or so, binding themselves to eternal death" (*De debitis et creditis*, I:3, f.74).

the wool trade only, and agrees to pay in a year the sum plus one-quarter of the gain, or minus one-quarter of the loss. If the whole capital is lost by "divine judgment and fortuitous accident," the merchant will not be held. Because the investor bears the risk, says Rolandino cautiously, the contract, according to the "better opinions and more probable opinions," is not usurious. Many, however, he says, who use this contract desiring not to commit usury, fall into Scylla, avoiding Charybdis.[38] He does not amplify this hint of the opportunity for usury in the contract, but contents himself with the suggestion that many, intending to act uprightly, cross the narrow line separating a partnership and a loan at usury. In Rolandino, it is evident that the criterion of risk marks the line. His opinion is testimony to the common practice.

Buridan

Buridan, surprisingly enough, appears to hold all types of *societas* usurious. He enumerates the types of partnerships and declares, "The first mode is if one rich merchant gives 10 francs with an agreement that he wishes to participate in the profit and the loss; there is usury." The other modes enumerated are a fortiori usurious, since in them the investor only shares part or none of the loss. Later, however, discussing *Naviganti*, Buridan holds that the sea loan is lawful, if the lender truly shares the perils of the sea.[39] To reconcile this opinion with his opinion on the first mode of usury seems impossible, and one cannot make head nor tail of his approach, which, contrary to the general tradition, seems to accept the sea loan, while condemning the *societas*.

Joannes Andreae

Joannes Andreae specifically agrees with Hostiensis that *Naviganti* rules only the case of the *foenus nauticum;* his argument is identical with Hostiensis'. At the same time, he assumes without discussion that the *societas* is licit.[40] In defending the usury prohibition, however, he meets for the first time the objection that if money fructifies in a partnership, why not in a loan as well? Andreae replies shortly that only the work really fructifies in the partnership — an answer sufficient to stop the objector to the usury theory, but remarkable in leaving undefended the capitalistic partner's claim to gain from his money in the partnership.[41]

[38] I:3, f.86.
[39] Buridan, *Quaestiones,* I:13, art. 3.
[40] Andreae, *Decretalium libros,* V, De usuris, 19.
[41] VI, *De regula iuris,* "Peccatum," 34.

In commenting on *Per vestras*, Andreae seems to approve the investment of a dowry with its return guaranteed, on the extrinsic grounds that the special good of marriage justifies this provision for the wife's finances.[42] This defense is of little theoretical interest in the development of a concept of partnership. But Andreae's somewhat vague statement here will lead theologians of a much later age to cite him in favor of the riskless partnership.

Panormitanus

Panormitanus, commenting on *Naviganti*, is frankly confused:

> I seek a clarification of the first part of the canon. Here it is not licit to lend and to receive beyond the principal, even if the creditor takes upon himself the peril; what then of those who daily contract a partnership, where one places his labor, the other his money?

Having tersely exposed the difficulty, Panormitanus simply declares that the *Gloss* and Goffredus say a *societas* is still licit. Presumably he himself, then accepts Goffredus' distinction between the partial risk borne in the *foenus nauticum*, and the full risks borne in partnership, even though this does not explain why the lender cannot charge while he runs the risk of the sea. Treating of partnership proper, he declares that the contract is illicit if the capitalist is insured against losing his capital, while the worker may lose his labor; for a "partnership is in the pattern of a certain brotherhood."[43] He criticizes Joannes Andreae's singular opinion on *Per vestras* as an attempt to justify an intrinsically evil deed because of its good effects: *Per vestras* specifically speaks only of "honest profit" and clearly excludes profit made from the usurious arrangement in which the capital would be always safe.[44] Hostiensis is also reprimanded for the example he gives where only one partner runs a risk. It is not beyond, but against, the nature of a partnership to exempt one partner from loss. The partnership by such a clause is destroyed.[45] Panormitanus' general opinion here, insisting on the risk criterion, yet not explaining *Naviganti* or the divergence between the usury theory's and the partnership theory's concepts of money, is a good example of the normal canonist treatment of the subject.

St. Bernardine and St. Antoninus

The most probing medieval discussions of *periculum sortis* and *societas*, like many of the best discussions of the other contracts and titles, are in the

[43] IV, *De donatione inter virum et uxorem*, *De usuris*, 19:19.
Per vestras.   [44] IV, *De donationibus inter virum*, 20:7:8.
[45] Panormitanus, *In libros decretalium*, V,   [45] V:19:19.

works of the two Tuscan saints. St. Bernardine asks, "When does doubt or peril excuse from usury?" and gives three rules as an answer: Rule 1 says, Never, in a loan, if it is made with hope of gain; a lender's assumption of risk does not suffice to excuse an act vicious in itself. Rule 2 says, Only when one has the ownership and use of the good which is risked, for it is proper that an owner should gain from his own property. Rule 3 in effect repeats Rule 1 and says, never, when something is hoped "because of time." Several cases are then presented exemplifying the rules. The first case is similar to that of *Naviganti*, a *foenus nauticum*. It is usury, because it is against Rules 1 and 2: a loan is made with the hope of gain; the capital becomes the borrower-merchant's own property. The second case is more complex. A man lends 100 at Venice to receive 120 at Cyprus, with the condition that if the money loaned or merchandise bought with it is lost, the debtor need repay only one-half. This again is usury; both Rules 1 and 2 are broken, a loan is made, and ownership passed. In the third case a capitalist gives a man a sum of money to trade with, and demands a fixed return, but agrees to run the risk of loss from any cause. This is licit, because Rule 2 is observed: the capitalist, retaining responsibility for risk, retains ownership. A fourth case is this: an investor gives money to a partner, who is to pay him part of the profits if he succeeds, but nothing if he fails; in either case, however, the partner is held to return the capital. This is manifest usury, for Rule 2 is broken, ownership has passed, and the nature of a partnership, the *ius fraternitatis*, which demands common risk, is violated. In a fifth case, a widow gives a merchant a deposit, the capital is to be safe, and she is to receive half the profit. This is mortal usury, against Rule 2: the widow profits from money no longer hers; in a true partnership, loss and gain must be shared equally, and the working partner's expenses deducted.[46] These cases make it clear that St. Bernardine, like St. Thomas, uses the incidence of risk as the test of ownership and true partnership, and that he believes a true partner has the right to gain on his capital, while *Naviganti* governs only the *foenus nauticum*. There is no attempt to reconcile *Naviganti* and the general risk doctrine.

Elsewhere St. Bernardine discusses the case where there is no profit but at the end of the partnership only the capital remains. He first says that this must then be shared with the working partner to compensate him partially for his labor; otherwise he will have lost all his work, and the capitalist will have lost nothing. It is objected that the common custom is against this. Moreover, it is declared that the capital was never common, but "only

[46] St. Bernardine, *De contractibus*, 39:1:1.

the commodity of the capital," and so against this alone does the worker have a claim. But the benefit given by capital has been lost, just as the working partner's labor has been lost. Therefore, St. Bernardine concludes, the capitalist may withdraw his investment whole.[47] The reasoning here which admits "a commodity to capital," apart from labor, is unreconcilable with St. Bernardine's usual insistence that money is sterile. The claim that the use and ownership of money are indistinguishable is also completely abandoned.

St. Antoninus in a considered analysis of the *societas* affirms the ancient principle that "a partnership is a certain fraternity" and therefore, "loss and gain are to be common." Any addition to the contract removing risk from one of the partners is against the nature of the contract. The most the capitalistic partner may ask is a sterile security, or the observance of certain conditions by his partner in order to protect his investment. Whenever his capital is safe, the investment is usurious. Thus even in a partnership in animals, if the capital invested is guaranteed by the herdsman, while the investor takes a profit, there is usury, for, says St. Antoninus exactly like Astesanus, the effect is the same as if money were loaned the herdsman to buy a flock and profit taken on that.[48] Risk is used as the criterion of ownership, not as the specific measure of what profit may be received. But in St. Antoninus' hands, the doctrine of the incidence of risk is so extended that any temporary transfer of property to another, where risk is also transferred, is called a loan, and profit upon it usury. At the same time he fails to consider *Naviganti*, which so seriously threatens his use of risk as the infallible test of ownership.

Unlike St. Bernardine, St. Antoninus does not allow the capitalist to withdraw his money entire if there is no profit; first the labor of the working partner must be compensated out of his investment.[49] This is an opinion certainly more consistent with the scholastic view of money's sterility. Like Astesanus, St. Antoninus, however, attempts no explanation of how the capitalist receives any reward at all, even when the partnership is successful, upon his supposedly sterile investment.

Conclusion

At the end of two hundred and fifty years' discussion of the *societas* it is still held, as it was in 1200, that where an investor runs all the risks of his partner, he has not loaned to him at usury, but has retained ownership and is entitled to a profit. But all the great problems posed by the acceptance

[47] *Ibid.*, 39:2:3.
[48] St. Antoninus, *Summa*, 2:1:7.
[49] 2:1:7.

of the *societas* for the usury theory have remained unanswered, largely un-considered. These questions are: Why is risk used as the criterion of owner-ship? If it is the criterion, how is *Naviganti* completely valid? If it is the criterion, must not one follow St. Antoninus in treating every transfer of property and risk as a loan? Above all, why is money considered to fructify in a partnership, and not in a loan? Why are the use and ownership of money distinguished in a *societas* and not in a loan? The failure to find any consistent answers to these questions in the first three centuries of analysis presages the disintegration of one part of the usury theory in the next three centuries. In fact, the early scholastics were working with two different theories on money, risk, and ownership, one of which they applied to loans, the other to partnerships. According to one theory, money was sterile, risk was no title to profit, ownership was the same as use in con-sumptible goods. In the other theory, money produced a surplus value, risk became the grounds for a reward, and ownership was determined not by the identity of use and ownership, but by the assumption of risk.[50] Proba-bly the greatest single difference in the two theories was in the treatment accorded to money, and this difference arose from money in loans being considered formally as a measure, while in partnerships money was tacitly identified with the goods it buys and not considered in its formal character at all.

There was practical justification for the different approaches taken. In the partnership the rate of return was normally closely related to what the capital earned. In a loan there was no assurance that a lender's profit bore a fair relation to the productive power of his capital. No business would knowingly borrow at more than it would earn; but, unlike a partnership, a borrowing business would be held to pay the fixed interest it promised. This economic difference, obscurely perceived and never formulated, may have mutely guided the choice of the different legal formulae by the scholas-tics. Their attitude on the sea loan may be explained, with less resort to unexpressed motivations, by supposing that they perceived on a practical level how effective in circumventing the usury rule would be this contract which mixed a partner's and a lender's profit.

In any event, the distinctions as drawn, even by the medieval rigorists, left a wide field open for investment in business. The attempted control

[50] The whole scholastic attitude towards the *societas* is refutation of Tawney's rash assertion, "The true descendant of the doc-trines of Aquinas is the labor theory of value. The last of the Schoolmen was Karl Marx" (R. H. Tawney, *Religion and the Rise of Cap-italism*, New York, 1937, p. 36).

of the high interest rates of the *foenus nauticum* is dramatic evidence that the policy of the prohibition went beyond the control of consumption credit; here commercial credit was regulated. Yet the willingness to accommodate .the *societas* reflects a general belief that the usury prohibition should not eliminate commercial profit, and this belief was ultimately the basis for confining the usury rule to a narrow set of situations. In the Middle Ages, the *societas* made risk-sharing investment a substantial form of capital-rewarding enterprise.

CHAPTER VII

INVESTMENT IN CREDIT: *CENSUS* AND DEBT

As the *societas* was the most usual contract for capital investment in commerce or animal husbandry, so the *census* was the normal form of investment in land and the regular instrument of State credit. Landed nobles and peasants in need found the selling of a *census* on their possessions the most expedient way of raising money;[1] the State financed itself largely by the sale of *census* on its own lands, on its monopolies, and, finally, on its tax receipts.[2] The *census* was also used by some workingmen as a means of obtaining personal credit.[3] In an age where commerce was not highly developed, the type of credit represented by the *census* may have been quantitatively greater than the type of credit represented by the *societas*. In any event, the *census* was clearly of immense importance in providing a licit opportunity for investment in credit; and like the *societas*, it must be carefully considered, if one is not to obtain a fantastic picture of the restrictions the scholastic usury theory placed upon finance. What made investment in a *census* licit? What distinguished it from usury? In answering these questions, the basic concepts, ownership, risk, and the sterility of money do not play the part they had in the discussion of the *societas*. The important concepts here are those of sale, time, and right. These are not so closely involved in the usury theory proper as were the other set, but the development of them in the *census* theory tends to the adoption of an analysis, which, if not contradictory to the usury theory, at least offers an alternative to it which would make the usury theory dead in practice. This alternative is not adopted formally by the medieval scholastics, but

[1] Pirenne, *Medieval Cities*, p. 137: M. Postan, "Credit in Medieval Trade," *Economic History Review*, I (1928), 248-249; R. Génestal, *Le rôle des monastères*, p. 183; Josef Kulisher, *Allgemeine Wirtschaftsgeschichte des Mittelalters und des Neuzeit* (Munich and Berlin, 1928), I, 336; Henri Sée, *Histoire économique de la France* (Paris, 1939), p. 53.

[2] C. Espinas, *Les finances de la Commune de Douai* (Paris, 1902), pp. 314ff.; A. Kostanechi, *Der offentliche Kredit im Mittelalter* (Leipzig, 1889), p. 15; Abbott Payson Usher, *Early Deposit Banking in Mediterranean Europe* (Cambridge, Mass., 1943), p. 136.

[3] Ashley, *Introduction to English Economic History*, I, Part 2, 411. See also the authors who discuss the personal *census*, infra, n. 37.

the elements of it are assembled by them and are made ready for use by their sixteenth-century successors.

1. *The Sale of a Right to Money*

A *census* is an obligation to pay an annual return from fruitful property. No English word renders it precisely, for "annuity," whose meaning would seem to approximate it, does not necessarily imply that the annual return is based on a fruitful good, and so we shall use *census* as the most exact and pregnant term. The buyer of a *census* is in a lender's role: he furnishes the cash. The seller is a debtor: he binds himself to the annual payments.

The contract is unknown to the Roman law. It doubtless was shaped in part by feudal analogies. But its growth may be surmised to have been aided by the ban on profitable loans. When it was first used, the return on the *census* was generally paid in real fruits; and in this case it was obvious, so it seemed, that a sale was effected whereby for so many pounds down a certain quantity of grain or produce was sold for so many years to come. No moralist quarrelled with this kind of exchange, where the only question was the just price.[4]

Gradually, as the money economy developed, payments of fruits were converted into annual installments of cash.[5] And when a new *census* was set up, it would be set directly in terms of cash payments. Was such a transaction any different from a loan? The standard answer was that it was a sale; but it if were a sale, what was sold? Three different answers were possible to this question: the money paid as a return; or the right to the money paid as a return; or an interest in the property producing the return. Each description had its defenders. Henry of Ghent (d.1293), the first prominent theologian to treat the subject, says that money constitutes the consideration offered by each party to the contract. He concludes that the pecuniary *census* is unlawful: money, which is formally nonvendible, is sold, and the sale is in fact a usurious loan.[6] His opinion was singular and apparently startling to his thirteenth-century contemporaries, who had placidly accepted the contract as lawful.[7] At the other extreme stood Henry of Hesse, a fourteenth-century theologian from central Europe, a largely agricultural

---

[4] Génestal, p. 156, notes its development particularly after the Church had condemned the straight agricultural mortgage.

[5] Génestal, p. 172.

[6] Henry of Ghent, *Quodlibetales* (Paris, 1518), Q.8:24.

[7] Note the reaction of Giles of Lessines, *De usuris*, c.9. Henry himself admits he has

been much criticized for his teaching, but he insists that some "great men" feel as he does. At the same time, doubtful of opposing a practice so widespread among ecclesiastical institutions, he hastens to say he will retract his opinion if the Church decides otherwise (Q.2:15).

region where the *census* seems to have been the most popular of all investment contracts. He argued that the purchaser of a *census* in effect became
a part owner of the property on which the return was based. Consequently,
the buyer was entitled to a profit on the *census* arising from his own property.[8]

Each of these extremes was foreign to the common opinion. This is best
expounded by Henry of Eutin, a contemporary of Henry of Hesse and
like him familiar with the economic practice of central Europe.[9] Like him,
too, he is apparently stirred to treat of the *census* by a decree of Count
Rudolph IV of Vienna providing that any *census* might be capitalized at
eight times the annual return and redeemed by the seller at that price — a
decree sorely harmful to numerous ecclesiastical foundations.[10] The practical
desire to avoid further government edicts of this character leads to a learned
and comprehensive study of the nature of the *census* and its natural lawfulness. The *census*, says Henry of Eutin, is the purchase of a right to
money. It is essential, he adds, to distinguish between corporeal goods and
the rights to them. A man has the right to a certain hereditary succession,
but he does not yet possess it. A man has the right to collect a certain
sum of money; he does not yet own the money. Similarly, in the *census*
the right and the money to which a right has been created must be distinguished.[11] The right is bought, as Hesse had maintained, only for the
sake of the money to which it entitles one; nonetheless it is the right and not
the money which is bought.[12]

Eutin's formal analysis of the *census* stands. It is indeed implicit in the
earlier defenders of the *census*, such as Pope Innocent IV and Giles of Lessines, who say that a *census* is distinguished from a loan by being a sale,
although they do not say what is purchased.[13] It is explicitly the position
taken by Alexander Lombard, Panormitanus, Joannes Andreae, St. Bernardine, and St. Antoninus.[14]

The acceptance of the *census* as the sale of a right to money meant that
the contract could be ruled by the laws relating to the just price, not by the

---

[8] Henry of Hesse, *De contractibus*, Part II,
c.33 and 34, f.219.
[9] *Lexicon für Theologie und Kirche* (Freiburg in Br., 1932), IV, col. 932.
[10] Schreiber, *Die volkswirtschaftlich Anschauungen*, p. 196; Henry of Hesse, II:38,
f.223; Henry of Eutin, *Tractatus de contractibus*, Dub. 12, f.245v and Dub. 13, f.246r,
in Gerson, *Opera omnia* (Cologne, 1484–
1485), Vol. IV.

[11] Henry of Eutin, Dub. 2, f.229v:b.
[12] f.230 r:a.
[13] Innocent IV, *Apparatus*, V, *De usuris, In
civitate*; Giles of Lessines, c.9.
[14] Alexander Lombard, *Tractatus*, c.7,
f.164r:a; Joannes Andreae, *Decretalium libros*,
VI, *De usuris*, c.6; Panormitanus, *Commentaria*, V:19:6; St. Bernardine, *De contractibus*,
34:1:2; St. Antoninus, *Summa*, 2:1:8.

usury prohibition. It was, the analysts said, not an exchange of money for money to be returned in time, but an exchange of two present goods, cash and the right to cash. Thus, some of the early commentators appeal to the Roman law on sales, permitting deception up to 50 per cent of the just price, as a defense for this contract in which the returns would eventually exceed the purchase price.[15] More logically, Pope Innocent IV says there is no need to rest on this principle of civil law. If one objects that the price is less than the returns are ultimately supposed to total, the Pope replies that in any kind of sale the purchaser will probably get more ultimately from the property he buys than the price he paid. This natural probability does not invalidate all buying and selling, nor can it invalidate this contract.[16] Or as Eutin puts it, if one gets double or triple his original investment in twenty years, the profit is as legitimate as the profit on any other purchased good.[17] It is objected that it is unjust for 100 now to bring 110 over a period. But Henry replies that the exchange is not of 100 now for all the future payments, but rather is of one good, money, for another good, a *ius* to money, both considered as to their present utility.[18] Therefore, "there may also be considered the circumstances of the seller as to industry and other things of this sort according to which, it may be weighed how much the money he receives is worth to him."[19] Thus, Henry frankly admits that the seller's need for, and evaluation of, present money may play a part in determining the *census* price. Moreover, he says that it does not matter whether the returns are paid successively over a number of years, or paid at once at the end of a certain period; in either case, the buyer gets a profit on his own property, and the seller has received in present value the equivalent of what he gives. Again, Eutin says, one can give money to a church and expect it to pay an annual return on it, as if it had bought fruitful land with the money, whether it actually has done so or not.[20] Similarly, Giles of Lessines, treating of the *census*, declares that the just price in a sale is what the parties estimate it to be, and clearly "future things over a period are not estimated to be of such value as the same things collected in an instant nor do they bear such a great possible utility."[21]

The question at once presses: What does this kind of analysis do to the usury theory? Cannot every usurer justify himself by the same distinction between present and future value? Alexander Lombard, Joannes Andreae,

[15] Hostiensis, *Commentaria*, V:19:6; *Glossa* on V:19:6.
[16] Innocent IV, *Apparatus*, V, *De usuris, In civitate*.
[17] Henry of Eutin, Dub. 4, f.236r.
[18] Dub. 4 ad 11, unnumbered folio before f.237, v:a.
[19] *Ibid.*, v:b.
[20] Dub. 4 ad 11, f.237v.
[21] Giles of Lessines, c.9, part 2.

and Panormitanus make explicit what is probably the common assumption: the purchaser of the *census* runs the risk of sterility of the *census* base.[22] But this assumption does not answer the objection that every agreement to re-pay money could be analyzed as a sale of a right. The coolest answer is given by John Gerson. The objection is made to Gerson by an opponent that "where there is the same *ratio*, there ought to be the same decision of law." A *census* oppresses the poor and is the sale of money; therefore, it ought to be condemned like usury on a loan.[23] But Gerson denies the principle. He declares boldly that the good intention of the buyer of the *census*, who in-tends to act licitly, alters the case, although the effect and the act itself are similar to usury.[24] He introduces a parallel with simony. One priest takes money as the price of a mass; the other for his sustenance. One is simoniacal; the other is not.[25]

Gerson's comparison with simony may be misleading; for simony is a sin against religion, not justice, so that a pure intention could alter the char-acter of the act; while usury is against justice, and no intention could rectify an objective inequality of exchange. But, despite the introduction of this confusing example, Gerson presumably does not mean to defend any propo-sition as unorthodox as that a good intention suffices in matters of justice. His real point is that a good intention suffices, if the act is not prohibited by law. Now with contracts, he reasons, one can be prohibited by law, another unmentioned. A good intention then in making a permitted contract is enough. As he expounds his views on contracts even more decisively:

It stands that two contracts may seem similar and leading to similar good or bad effects, and yet one will be prohibited by law and the other conceded and permitted. An example in contracts: it is clear that to the sellers of perpetual returns can come more losses and impoverishment through the abuse of the sellers or buyers than often come through a loan with the exaction of a light amount above the principal, and yet the first is conceded by the laws, the other pro-hibited.[26]

Or, as he puts it in most positivistic fashion: "When something is prohibited to be done in one way, one does not conclude that it is prohibited in another way, unless the deed itself is prohibited and not merely the way."[27] In short,

---

[22] Alexander Lombard, c.7, f.162v:a and f.164v:b; Joannes Andreae, *Gloss* on *Specu-lum* of *William Durand* (Lyons, 1547), IV:4, *De usuris*; Panormitanus, V:19:6. It should be pointed out that Panormitanus speaks as though the risk run was that of the seller's poverty and consequent insolvency, rather than a risk of the *census* base.

[23] Gerson, *De contractibus*, Part 3.

[24] *Ibid.*

[25] Part 2, Prop. 15.

[26] Part 2, Prop. 14.

[27] Part 2, Prop. 15.

the usury rule is a formal rule, which can be substantially evaded. Is this to say that it is meaningless? I do not think we are forced to conclude that this is Gerson's contention, for form has its uses: for example, the seal on a contract functions as consideration in Anglo-American law; it is not an empty device but serves to distinguish serious undertakings from idle promises. Similarly, the *census* form for Gerson might have performed a channeling function, distinguishing commercial credit from exorbitant consumption loans. Yet, it must be recognized that Gerson seems to admit that the *census* will oppress the poor as much as a loan, and he scarcely develops any theory on form. It merely may have been easier for him to make fundamental admissions about the usury law, with his convictions as to the small natural-law foundation that it had,[28] than for the other scholastic authors.

The majority did not wish to make such a drastic concession, and shying away from the clash of *census* theory and loan theory, they merely asked if in practice, a loan and a *census* could be distinguished. There were degrees of distance, depending on the terms of the *census:* A "newly created" *census* was one formed as a result of the immediate credit transaction; it was distinguished from the purchase of a *census* already in existence. A real *census*, founded on a real-estate base, was tied to specific property. It resembled a loan secured by a mortgage with the important difference that the rate of return was set directly by the estimated productivity of the base. A personal *census* was founded on the returns of the labor of a serf or of the debtor himself. The latter case was hard to distinguish from a loan, except that the debtor had to be an income-producer. Somewhere in between these forms was a *census* founded not on any particular good, but on all the goods of the seller. Similarly a community could found a *census* on specific tax revenues, or alternatively, "upon its person." In terms of definiteness of return, an uncertain *census*, where the returns varied from year to year with the yield of the *census* base, was clearly less like a loan at interest than a certain *census*, where the annual charge was fixed. In terms of time there was also a difference: a life *census* ran for the life of either the buyer or the seller and had an element of chance not present in a loan; a perpetual *census* ran indefinitely and forever at a low annual charge; a temporary *census* was exactly like a loan in that annual charges ran for a fixed number of years. Finally in terms of redemption important differences existed: the *census* might be nonredeemable, or redeemable only at the option of the buyer or only at the option of the seller, or it might be redeemable by either. Redeemability by the buyer made a *census* similar to a demand note. Re-

[28] See *supra*, p. 70.

deemability by the seller might be optional in form, but made obligatory by an understanding that he would redeem. By varying combinations of these various terms, one could approximate a loan in different degrees. An uncertain, real, perpetual *census* which was nonredeemable would be least like a loan; a certain, personal, temporary *census*, which was redeemable at the buyer's option, would be most like one.

The theologians and canonists divided in accepting the different forms. The real, perpetual *census* was accepted almost unanimously.[29] Innocent IV and Joannes Andreae counsel against a "newly created" *census*, and Laurentius de Ridolfis says it is presumed to be in fraud of the usury law.[30] But many authors make no such distinction, and even those criticizing such a contract implicitly concede its intrinsic lawfulness. Two papal bulls in the fifteenth century specifically approved the real *census*, redeemable by the seller, and threatened ecclesiastical penalties for debtors of ecclesiastical endowments who refused to meet their *census* obligations on the grounds that they were usurious.[31] In 1452, Nicholas V issued a bull of even wider significance. The king of Aragon represented to the Pope that in his dominions voracious usury consumed the goods of many forced to borrow, but that individuals, corporations, and churches had found a "less incommodious" way of obtaining funds by selling annuities redeemable by the seller, founded on "their houses, possessions, and properties specially or

---

[29] Innocent IV, *Apparatus*, V, *De usuris, In civitate;* Panormitanus, V:19:6. Even Henry of Ghent points out a way by which the effect of a pecuniary *census* may be licitly achieved: A, needing money, sells his farm to B. B then rents the farm to A for an annual payment. The effect is that of a perpetual *census* (Q.8:24).

Aegidius of Rome, like Henry of Ghent, is puzzled by the difficulty that in a *census* money seems to be purchased, and that in it money becomes "the beginning and the end," instead of serving only as a means, for, according to Aristotle, this seems unnatural. On the other hand, he acknowledges that Giles and the *Gloss* approve the contract, and he seeks to find a compromise. He declares, then, that the *census* is never licit "if only for money money is received." But it is licit, if a right to fruits is bought; and then, the bought fruits are exchanged for a sum of money. Whether this exchange is to be made by the purchaser or the seller of the *census*, Aegidius does not say. In any event, he regards this as a real purchase of fruits, not

money; "and in buying with money, goods, or the fruits of goods over a great period of time, one can licitly make not only 12 per cent but even 100 per cent and more" (Aegidius, *Quodlibetales*, III:24). His solution, insisting on the mediation of real goods, is in principle like Henry's; and it shows the difficulty the scholastics experienced in reconciling themselves to a purely monetary *census.*

There is some ironic commentary as old as the twelfth century on the possibility of perpetual *census* erected on livestock, jocosely referred to as "iron" or "immortal" cows (see Robert of Flamesbury, *Summa de matrimonio et de usuris, Ex Roberti Poenitentiali,* ed. J. F. von Schulte, Gissiae, 1868). Henry of Hesse shows how such a perpetual *census* can be constituted by substituting one cow for another, so that there is no barrier to a perpetual *census* on mobile goods (II:7, f.207v:a).

[30] Innocent IV, *Apparatus,* V, *De usuris, In civitate;* Joannes Andreae, V, *De usuris,* c.6; Laurentius de Ridolfis, *De usuris,* 2:11.

[31] Bull of Martin V, *Extravagantes com-*

even generally on all their goods, returns, emoluments, rights, and things." This custom had been approved by the State, and no one could recall a contrary practice. Now, however, rich men hesitated to invest in this way for fear of committing usury, and the result was that real usurers were turned to, and poor borrowers were oppressed. In answer to this plea, Nicholas V determined that in Aragon and Sicily such *census* as described were licit, provided that they pay not over 10 per cent.[32] The restriction of the amount paid, like the restriction to certain particular countries, must be assumed to have been positive law. But the Pope's approval implicitly established the fundamental principle that a *census* founded on all the goods, indiscriminately considered, of a seller is authorized by natural law.

The real, life and the real, temporary *census* were opposed by both Ghent and Hesse, each from his contrary theory of the nature of the contract: Ghent because he took the position that money could never be sold, Hesse because he found a true sale of the underlying property only in a perpetual *census*.[33] But the majority who took the position that a right to money was purchased in a *census* had no reason for objecting to either. The real-life *census* was accepted by almost everyone: Innocent IV, Hostiensis, the *Gloss*, Giles of Lessines, Alexander Lombard, Astesanus, Eutin, Gerson, Panormitanus, de Ridolfis, St. Bernardine, and St. Antoninus.[34] There is more doubt, however, about the real, temporary *census*, where the definiteness of time makes the result more like a loan. Innocent IV apparently accepts it as intrinsically lawful. Joannes Andreae appears to waiver on it, leaving in doubt whether he approves it if it is newly created.[35] De Ridolfis and St. Antoninus say that it is presumably usurious if newly created. Alexander Lombard and Eutin are clearly in its favor.[36] The state of opinion, on the whole,

---

munes, Corpus juris canonici, III:5:1; Bull of Calixtus III, *ibid.*, III:5:2.

[32] *Sollicitudo*, in *Summa bullarii* (Lyons, 1621).

[33] Henry of Ghent, Q.2:15; he was preceded in this conclusion by Cardinal Goffredus of Trani, who found in life annuities a usurious intention to gain from time (see the citation of Goffredus in Giles of Lessines, c.9). Henry of Hesse, II:33, f.219r:b.

[34] Innocent IV, *Apparatus*, V, *De usuris, In civitate*; Hostiensis, *Summa*, V, *De usuris, In civitate*, n.8, and *Commentaria*, V:19:6; Giles of Lessines, c.9, part 2; Alexander Lombard, c.7, f.162v:b; Astesanus, *Summa*, III:11:5; Henry of Eutin, Dub. 2, f.230r:b; Gerson, *De contractibus*, Part 3; Panormitanus,

V:19:6; Laurentius de Ridolfis, 2:15; St. Bernardine, 34:1,2, and 3; St. Antoninus, 2:1:8.

[35] In commenting on *In civitate*, Joannes Andreae, *Decretalium libros*, V:19:6, clearly accepts this kind of *census* only if not newly created. In his later commentary on the *Speculum* of Durandus, IV:4, *De usuris*, however, he puts a case of what seems to be a new, temporary *census* and approves it. Laurentius de Ridolfis (2:11) argues that a cross-reference to *In civitate* incorporates Andreae's former qualifications, but even he admits that many persons took Andreae's second opinion as overriding his first.

[36] Laurentius de Ridolfis, 2:11; St. Antoninus, 2:1:11; Alexander Lombard, c.7, f.162v:a; Eutin, Dub. 4, f.236.

suggests that the scholastics were troubled by approving a contract so similar to a loan, yet could marshal no arguments to condemn it on intrinsic grounds, and enough authorities supported it in practice to satisfy the conscience of a creditor choosing this form of finance.

If a temporary, real *census* caused hesitations, it would seem that acceptance of the personal *census* would have been unthinkable. In fact, most of the authorities — Henry of Ghent, Joannes Andreae, Panormitanus, de Ridolfis, Gerson, St. Antoninus — follow Innocent IV in condemning such a *census* founded on the debtor's own labor. They admit only that a *census* founded on the labor of a third party, say a serf, would be permissible. Henry of Hesse after much debate joins this majority position, simply saying that such contracts are not beneficial to the community. Astesanus is curiously ambiguous. Henry of Eutin is the outstanding exponent of the minority urging that a free man can sell the rights of his labor just as much as the returns of his fields.[37] No one had a good theoretical reply to this argument, but most authors using the usury rule as a measure were unwilling to permit its circumvention in this easy fashion.

Yet while the personal *census* met general opposition in the form most approximating a loan, a different attitude is observable toward government contracts of credit coming close to bonds. The sale of a state *census* on taxes is approved by Alexander Lombard, Astesanus, Hesse, Panormitanus, and Gerson. It is apparently disapproved by St. Antoninus and by de Ridolfis. But even de Ridolfis admits a government *census* if founded on "the goods of the community" and presumably St. Antoninus' approval of a *census* on a private seller's goods in general could equally be applied in favor of the state *census*.[38] The difference seems to lie in technique of analysis, rather than in substance. Thus, Panormitanus treats the Florentine and Genoese *montes* as justified as the sale of rights to "the returns" of the cities' revenues, whereas de Ridolfis and St. Antoninus approve them in terms of interest on a loan.[39]

Redeemability in favor of the buyer is allowed by Gerson on a perpetual

[37] Henry of Ghent, Q.2:15; Laurentius de Ridolfis, 2:11 (n.45); St. Bernardine, 41:3:2; Henry of Hesse, II:7, f.208 and II:32, f.219; Astesanus, III:1:5; Henry of Eutin, Dub. 2, f.230r:b, and see Dub. 1, f.228r:a–228v:b; John Gerson, *De contractibus*, Part 3; Panormitanus, V:19:6. St. Antoninus (2:1:8) does admit a *census* founded on all the goods of the seller.

[38] Alexander Lombard, c.7, f.164v:a; Astesanus, III:11:5; Panormitanus, V:19:6; Gerson, Part 2, Prop. 12; Laurentius de Ridolfis, 2:18, citing John of Lignano. St. Antoninus (2:1:8) disapproves a *census* "founded on the community's person." A position similar to de Ridolfis is taken by a somewhat later writer, who usually takes a traditionalist position and presumably is following a common method of analysis: Angelus Carletus de Clavasio, *Summa Angelica de casibus conscientiae* (Lyons, 1512), at *Usura*, n.78.

[39] See *supra*, pp. 122, 128.

census, but is not discussed by most authorities and was probably not much used. Redeemability in favor of the seller is disapproved by de Ridolfis, but is allowed by Alexander Lombard, Eutin, Hesse, the papal bulls, and doubtfully by St. Antoninus.[40] It was probably common in practice. A curious note is struck by St. Antoninus' treatment of a case where the buyer is certain that the seller will redeem. The contract, the archbishop remarks with careful ambiguity, "has the nature of usury." But he goes on to cite a remarkable exception urged by a certain William:

This rule ceases for ecclesiastical persons: because upon such returns are churches founded and endowed as if in hope of perpetuating them forever. And if such contracts were prohibited and the returns redeemed, the churches would be destroyed, for they would have no income, except money easily consumed; but, these contracts standing as licit, they may buy again from these monies other returns.[41]

Either this is the strange permission of an illicit means to a good end, or else the proponent does not believe that the knowledge that the *census* will be redeemed, and that the effect will be substantially that of a loan at a profit, constitutes usury. St. Antoninus finds the matter doubtful, but he does not condemn the proposition absolutely. In other words, when he comes to consider the financial dependence of the Church upon such contracts, he hesitates to extend the usury prohibition beyond the case of loans. But that he does not then also release the laity from the burden of sin in such contracts is incomprehensible, until it is realized that throughout the treatment of the *census* the prudential lines of prohibition are often drawn much more sharply than theory warrants, in order to keep some body to the usury rule.

An unusual note for scholastic treatment of a contract, which usually focuses on the objective equality of exchange, is the attention given by some writers to the status of the contracting parties. Both Hesse and Eutin are troubled by the spectacle of a *rentier* class, evading the biblical injunction to labor in the sweat of one's brow, by living off their *census* returns. Only the sick, the old, and ministers of Church and State, who are not able or have not the time to support themselves, Hesse concludes, are morally entitled

---

[40] Gerson, *De contractibus*, Part 2, Prop. 19; Laurentius de Ridolfis, 2:18, citing with approval a reported opinion of John of Lignano and Laurentius de Pinu given to a certain monastery; Alexander Lombard, c.7., f.164v:b; Henry of Eutin, Dub. 5, f.238r:a; Henry of Hesse, II:11, f.210 r; St. Antoninus, 2:1:8. Gerson, Q.83, states that Rolandinus, the prior of a Carthusian monastery in Germany, had asked the Council of Constance as to the licitness of such a *census*, by which the monastery was supported. The Council did not discuss the matter, but four theologians and eight canonists gave their private opinion that the contract was lawful.

[41] St. Antoninus, 2:1:8.

to live off a *census* without doing a day's work.[42] The same conclusion is reached on social grounds: if everyone was indiscriminately permitted to live off the *census*, the cities would be filled with "lazy and delicate — nay, vicious — men." Agriculture would be deserted. Immobile goods forming the base of the *census* would have an intolerable burden placed upon them. The patrimony of the poor would be hurt, since the sellers of the *census* are usually poor men driven by need, and their heirs are usually unable to keep up the payments and so have to sell for a song the goods on which the *census* is based.[43]

The over-all impression from the survey of the authorities is one of considerable confusion. Some authors — Alexander of Hales, St. Albert, St. Bonaventure, St. Thomas, Scotus, Monaldus, Durandus of St. Pourçain — fail to treat the subject at all. Possibly because of the lack of authoritative handling by one of the great thirteenth-century theologians, no clear development of *census* theory occurs. Chronology is not a safe index. De Ridolfis opposes what Hostiensis permitted. Geography offers more of a clue, yet the north is not always more liberal than the Italians: let the rigorist views of Henry of Ghent be compared to the restrained approval of St. Antoninus. None of the authors is distinguished by his theoretical justifications for the limits he puts on the use of the *census* form. Prudential judgments alone provide a reason for limiting its universal use as an alternative to loan credit.

Even within the limits set by the more conservative authors, it is apparent that there existed wide opportunities for long-term or life investments in credit with a real estate foundation. State finance, not very different from municipal bonds, was held to be legitimate by many authors. A body of opinion even supports the personal and the temporary *census*. The existence of this large area of credit, where profit in finance was normal and expected, must be kept in mind if the usury theory is to be correctly appreciated, and its eventual revision understood.

2. The Sale of Debt

A contract closely related to the *census* in that it involved the sale of a right to money instead of the sale of money itself was the sale of debts by a creditor to a third party at a discount. The early writers treat the resale of *census* rights, and they find such a transaction to be a licit sale, not a loan.[44]

[42] Henry of Hesse. II:2, f.206v:b; Henry of Eutin, Dub. 4 ad 3 and 4, Dub. 2, f.229r:b.
[43] See Henry of Hesse, II:2:6 and 7.
[44] Panormitanus, V:19:6; St. Bernardine, 41:3:2; St. Antoninus, 2:1:8. Even Henry of

Ghent (Q.12:21) admits the resale of *census* rights, lamely admitting here that only a right to money is sold. The question of repurchase of one's own debt is a different matter; see *supra*, p. 117.

But most of them do not discuss debt purchases aside from this special case. Alexander Lombard, however, puts the case of a merchant selling to the city of Genoa for payment at a later date; preferring cash, he sells his right at a discount. Many, says Alexander, defend the discount because a right to money and not money itself is sold; and such a right is not as secure as money in hand. This opinion, seemingly so ominous for the usury theory, is accepted by Alexander without objection.[45] It is hard to make his opinion consistent with the trend of authoritative thought unless it be supposed that the fact that the government is the debtor is a relevant point.

In the fifteenth century, Panormitanus teaches that a debt involving a lawsuit may be licitly purchased at a discount.[46] Similarly, St. Bernardine holds that a debt — apparently a bad debt, to whose amount a penalty had been added — can be sold.[47] St. Antoninus also declares that "an aggravated debt," a debt subject to litigation or endangered by a borrower's malice, can be bought below its face value.[48] Thus, as far as ordinary personal debts are concerned, the majority of authoritative opinion on the matter allows a purchase of debt at a discount only when the debtor has in some positive way made the payment of the debt doubtful.

If all there was to report were this opinion on personal debts, it would hardly be worth treating the sale of debts at all. But personal debts were not the only ones for sale. There were also the debts of the government. There was no controversy over the sale of rights to a State *census*, for a *census* was not a loan; nor, on the other hand, was there any doubt about the illicitness of repurchasing a government debt which had arisen from a pure loan at usury. Still, a great middle ground existed to perplex the moralists — a middle ground which was created by the existence of the Italian *montes*. The forced loans to the Italian city states were not loans at usury, but conscription of capital with interest paid as compensation. Was purchase from a holder of a share in a *mons*, then, to be condemned as usury? Undeniably, it was the purchase of a debt and not only of a debt, but of the right to continued interest on the debt. If the simple rule on the purchase of personal debts had applied, there could have been no hesitation. But, like the development of the interest titles, the development of a theory of the discounting of debt was probably affected by the fact that it was the State *montes* which were involved. From a practical viewpoint, the resale of the shares was a highly necessary part of the economy of the great Italian communities; from a more theoretical view-

---

[45] Alexander Lombard, c.7, f.166v:a. For his opinion on the discount of a bank credit, however, see *infra*, Chapter VIII, Section 1.

[46] Panormitanus, V:19:6, c.5.

[47] St. Bernardine, 41:3:2. Again, the repurchase of one's own debt is another problem; see *supra*, p. 76.

[48] St. Antoninus, 2:1:8.

point, the peculiar character of the forced loan may have offered ground for hesitation. In any event, the debts of the *montes* were not immediately treated like other debts, but over them arose a great controversy, which taxed the science of every moralist, brought the whole usury theory and its refinements into play, and ultimately centered on the distinction between money and the *ius* to money.

As early as 1310, Astesanus, following, he said, John of Saxony, had declared briefly and simply that the resale of a government bond was licit, because it was the sale — not of money, but of a *ius*.[49] His short reference came too early to be part of the main discussion. The real debate begins only in the middle of the fourteenth century with the attack on the purchases by Gregory of Rimini. His sally is followed by the replies of Frederick of Siena and Laurentius de Ridolfis, a counterattack by St. Bernardine of Siena,[50] and a summation of the argument a hundred years after it began by St. Antoninus. We shall follow the latter's judicious presentation of the case made out by each side.

It will be well first for us to have an exact account of the practice at issue, and for that no better description could be offered than what is given by the contemporary statutes governing the sales of shares by holders. The statutes are those of Florence, but they are essentially similar to those of Genoa and Venice. By statute, then, the government decrees that

such credits, with the right of receiving increments of this kind, can be alienated to others; with, however, this provision that the community itself may redeem the said debt by paying the creditor for the redemption of the said right at the rate of 28 per 100, so that such a creditor is held to resell to the said community at its pleasure, there remaining to the said creditor the gain made up to the time of the said sale.[51]

In such a resale of the bond:

The purchaser is registered by the public notaries in the book of the said creditors in the place and name of such a one who first was the creditor of the community, and there is added what the aforesaid creditors, etc., can do: they may sell, exchange, alienate these rights, and under any title or cause transfer them to another to be registered in the said books. And those to whom the said rights pass, may enjoy the benefits and rights of the said creditors, or what they ought to receive.[52]

Such was the legal and customary method of resale of the bonds; and in

[49] Astesanus, III:11:5.
[50] Laurentius de Ridolfis, 3:5 ad 4 (n.44ff);
St. Bernardine, 41:3:1 and 2.

[51] St. Antoninus, 2:1:11 (at beginning).
[52] *Ibid.*

Florence they usually sold at a three-fourths discount. Were such resales lawful?

On the one hand, it was argued that here was a simple sales contract. The original owner, if he received interest licitly, might lawfully sell the right to this interest. A true contract followed in which neither money nor time were sold, but a real *merx*, the *ius* to interest, was present and sold. Further,

although the buyer here seeks effectively the same advantage that he would seek if he had lent from the beginning to the community, it does not, however, follow that he contracts a loan with the latter; for it is not by way of a loan, but by a purchase truly without fraud or trick that he seeks such an advantage, and he does not substitute as lender for the lender, but as one buying that right from the seller.

An identity of effect does not necessarily imply an identity of contract.

It is further urged that the registering of the purchase with the city does not constitute a new contract of loan with the city, but is a simple notarization of the transfer. Again, the purchaser assumes a real risk both of receiving back his capital and his interest; and if risk is the criterion of ownership, he is the owner of a purchased good, and not a lender who has temporarily alienated his ownership. Moreover, experience teaches that there is a "great doubt" as to the eventual recovery of the capital; the city may abolish the gratuitously given interest at will. If it is objected that the purchaser will probably receive a profit beyond the capital advanced, it is replied that he received nothing which is not his:

Because the whole *ius* of the seller, both as to capital and to interest, is the capital, and accrues to the capital, of the buyer; for he buys that whole *ius*; therefore nothing accrues to him beyond his capital.

Finally, if it is objected that the purchaser buys the bond at a great discount (75 per cent) and that this discount represents a payment for time, it is retorted that 25 per 100 is all the risky bond is really worth:

A thing ought not to be estimated in a sale except as what it is worth at the time of the contract; otherwise you could not licitly buy land according to equality. Since, then, the right of demanding 100 is not worth now more than 25 florins, because of the doubt which assuredly concerns not only the interest but the capital, and also because it is plain that you in selling do not hold such a right with interest dearer, it follows that it is bought at a just price. . . . It is not the price of time, but the price of peril in time.

On the other hand, it is objected that the new purchaser is inscribed in the book of the notary of the *montes* as the new creditor. Here a new contract of *mutuum* is effected between the city and the purchaser: the city binds itself to repay the capital to this new party, and an "obligation by mutual consent to restore surrendered capital is a contract of *mutuum*." The buyer loans to the community, "since by his will and consent the capital to which he has a right by purchase remains with its use with the community." Nor in the supposed sales contract, is mention made of the right to interest, which is the alleged merchandise sold, but the contract concerns simply the purchase of the city's debt. Moreover, the right to interest would, in any case, be nonvendible, for the payment of the interest is gratuitous, and a gift cannot be sold. The case is similar to that of many other nontransferable rights, such as a vassal's right to a feud, or a husband's right over his wife.

Both the intention and the effect here are those of *mutuum*: for here one "by buying the right to capital seeks gains assuredly in relation to the credited capital to which he buys a right." The new lender takes the place of the old and unlike the old does so, neither through compulsion or charity, but through love of gain. There is little real risk, for, though communities defer payment often, they rarely default. Any fluctuation in the price of the bonds comes not from doubts as to repayment, but from the tightness or plentitude of money in the city. The low price of the bonds arises from the bondholders' need of money. Moreover, the gain is not made from the risk assumed, as in an insurance contract. Here the risk assumed is that of the original bondholder, but the gain is made from the city. Yet again, an unjust and usurious price is paid by the purchaser: "The whole right of the first [bondholder], both as to capital and as to interest, is capital and passes as capital to the second, because he buys that whole; therefore, he buys 100 florins, and he has with the community 100 florins." But he pays only 25, which is manifestly unjust.

To sum up, the defenders of the contract claim it is a true sale, in which all loss and gain legitimately accrue to the new owner of the *ius* to interest. The attackers deny that the *ius* here is, or can be, sold, and assert that the new bondholder, under the cloak of a purchase, becomes the real creditor of the city, loaning to it, and receiving for this loan the interest which has principally led him to the purchase. Moreover, he has defrauded the original bondholder by paying an unjust price for the bond.

St. Antoninus himself, after citing both sides at length, is unable to make up his mind between the conflicting claims. "It is," he says, "a great controversy, and the opinions of the learned both in theology and law differ." He quotes the prudent advice of St. Thomas as to the caution with which a moral theologian is to declare an act a mortal sin, where there is no express declaration of Scripture, Council, or canon law to support him. Accordingly, here he will only counsel, not impose the safer way. Purchasers of bonds are to be advised to give their profits to the poor; but if they refuse this counsel, preferring another opinion, they are not to be denied absolution. He who doubts sins in buying, but he acts within his rights who, following the opinions of many learned men, thinks it licit. However, ordinary usurers buying the bonds are presumed to act usuriously here, too. In preaching, the opinion that the contract is mortal is not to be rashly urged, yet neither is the contract to be publicly approved. It would be best to avoid the topic altogether. Clerics, whose lives should be particularly blameless, should always refrain from such purchases.[53]

We cannot improve on St. Antoninus' summation of the state of opinion on the bond sales in 1450. We may add to his account, however, that the source of all the difficulty was the distinction between the sale of money and the sale of a right to money. This distinction had already been made in the *census*, but there the presence of a real property basis at least preserved some difference in reality between the sale of the *ius* and the sale of money. In the case of a pure money right, however, it became immensely difficult to find any difference. If the licitness of the sale of a *ius* to money had been thoroughly admitted, every usurer would have "bought" a right to a future income, and the price of such a right would have responded to the demand for money. This would have, in effect, meant the abandonment of the usury theory. On the other hand, the licitness of the sale of a *ius* to money could not be denied outright, without denying the theory by which a majority of authors defended the *census*. Hence, in an impossible dilemma, only the conflict and indecision which St. Antoninus so strikingly reveals could result.

Conclusion

If the scholastic treatment of *census* and the sale of debt are considered only in terms of formal theory, the divergency from the usury rule is apparent. If one looks beneath the form—as the scholastics themselves failed to do in explicit terms—more sense appears in the results achieved. The *census* was a type of credit where some regulation of the interest rate might be achieved by the condition that the return be measured by a fruitful base. Moreover, to the extent that risk of the base was run by the *census* buyer, an element of partner-like sharing was introduced. In the sale of government debt, an extraordinary factor of risk of repudiation was present. If it be

[53] St. Antoninus, 2:1:11 (at beginning).

supposed that the most powerful policies supporting the usury prohibition were the desires to prevent exploitation of the poor and to discourage riskless profit, the prohibition was not substantially impaired by the doctrine on *census* and debt. But the medieval scholastics did not think enough in pragmatic terms to formulate the substantial distinctions as differences in consequences. They stuck, instead, to the abstract theory of the sale of rights and reached conclusions theoretically destructive of their own position. This theoretical possibility did not entirely nullify the crude practical check of the usury rule in lessening some kinds of exploitation by lenders, while the acceptance of *census* and the sale of debt provided large avenues for lawful investment in credit.

CHAPTER VIII

BANKING

1. Deposit Banking

Observing the accommodation the scholastic analysis gave to certain types of commercial, agricultural, and governmental credit, one may be led to inquire if any special theory was worked out to cover the banking operations which are the central mechanisms of modern credit.

That banking operations were important, if not central, in the medieval economy has been established by the economic historians. The acceptance of goods or money for safekeeping, the simple *depositum* contract, was familiar to the Roman law and to early medieval practice.[1] But going beyond the Roman law, the *depositum*, as early as the thirteenth century, is more significantly known as a means of investment. In addition to the straight *foenus nauticum* and *societas* we find in Genoa and Venice "deposits" made with the seagoing merchants, which are described as "*fuori del corpo di compagnia*," and so exempt from the risks of the invested capital of the partners. No fixed interest is to be paid on these deposits, but if the venture is successful, a profit will be returned according to the good judgment of the merchant.[2] The transaction which was, of course, a simple loan with optional interest, was still, in legal form, distinct from a *mutuum*.

In the late thirteenth century deposits with commercial companies appear to be considerably increased. Thus, in Genoa deposit banking was well established.[3] In Florence the great merchant bankers, the Peruzzi, the Bardi, the Cerchi, and the Scali — all engaged in the exploitation of the economically backward areas of Europe, such as England and Sicily — had a

---

[1] A. E. Sayous, "Les opérations des banquiers italiens et aux foires de Champagne pendant le 13ᵉ siècle," *Revue historique*, CLXX (1932), 32. In the early Middle Ages the great depositary was the Order of the Knights Templar. The Templars are said to have loaned money, but it is interesting to note that usury was not one of the crimes charged against the order (see L. Delisle, *Mémoire sur les opérations financières des templiers*, Paris, 1888, pp. 2, 5, 14).

[2] Sayous, "Les opérations de banquiers italiens," pp. 10–11, 262–264.

[3] Raymond de Roover, *L'évolution de la lettre de change* (Paris, 1953), p. 24.

pressing need for funds and were willing to pay well for deposits. The Peruzzi would pay 20 per cent for a deposit of four months, and all the companies paid 10 per cent per year on demand deposits.[4] In the fourteenth century the practice was continued at a more modest rate. The Florentine banks paid a fixed interest of from 5 per cent to 10 per cent upon demand deposits.[5] The Peruzzi, making a net profit of from 14 per cent to 20 per cent in the first quarter of the fourteenth century, were happy to pay a fixed 8 per cent on the *sopracorpo*.[6] Like the loans of modern banks, the banks' loans far exceeded their capital, and it seems legitimate to suppose that the larger part of the difference was supplied by their deposits.[7] Their depositors were "all Christendom." But in particular they were Italian nobles, businessmen, and clergy eager to make a profit from these highly successful enterprises.[8]

In the fifteenth century the Medici Bank was organized in the same way. A large portion of its funds was derived from deposits, the bulk of which were made by the owners and managers of the company itself. Like modern income bonds, deposits drew interest only when earned, and there were instances of suspension of the payment of interest, but usually they paid a steady 10 per cent.[9]

The Florence banks were the wealthiest, and the evidence for them is greatest. But the practice of depositing at interest with exchange banks or merchants was clearly not confined to Florence.[10] In particular, two classes of depositors seem to be universal — wards and widows. Both these groups had an urgent need not to consume their capital. In the case of the former, the State usually invested for them or else held their guardians responsible for a flat 5 per cent minimum return.[11] The widows managed for themselves.[12]

At the same time that the trading companies accepted deposits, they also engaged in the most characteristic of commercial banking operations, the

---

[4] *Ibid.*, p. 22.

[5] Renouard, *Les hommes d'affaires*, p. 123.

[6] de Roover, *Money, Banking*, pp. 41–42. Some fourteenth-century companies paid from 5 to 10 per cent; Sapori, *Studi*, p. 108.

[7] For example, the Peruzzi, with a capital of 100,000 florins, were owed 600,000 florins by the English crown and 100,000 by Sicily in 1343 (Renouard, *Les hommes d'affaires*, p. 123).

[8] *Ibid.*, p. 123; de Roover, *Money, Banking*, p. 42.

[9] Raymond de Roover, *The Medici Bank* (New York, 1948), pp. 52–56.

[10] Cf. Sayous, "Les opérations de banquiers italiens," pp. 12, 23; Usher, *Early Deposit Banking*, p. 17; C. Dunbar, "The Bank of Venice," *Quarterly Journal of Economics*, VI (April 1892), 310.

[11] Postan, "Credit in Medieval Trade," p. 253.

[12] St. Antoninus, *Summa*, 2:1:6; Postan, "Credit in Medieval Trade," p. 254. See also Navarrus, *Commentarius de usuris*, n.33, in *Opera omnia*, (Venice, 1618), Vol. I.

creation of deposits. In fourteenth-century Barcelona, for example, it has been estimated that the rate of credit expansion of the banking system of the city was 3.5 times the specie reserve; this creation of credit was accomplished mainly through overdrafts.[13] Similarly, in fourteenth-century Bruges a specie reserve of 29 per cent was maintained by a typical exchange banker.[14] In Venice overdrafts for merchants and government loans were found to take up a large amount of the credit created by deposit banks.[15] Wherever the phenomena occurred, a considerable amount of this credit creation was probably devoted to partnership investments by the banks, rather than to pure loans.[16] Of the loans made, some undoubtedly were forced levies by the government.[17]

The scholastics' reaction to these various banking operations is not as sharp as might be expected. Indeed, their lack of reaction suggests that either the amount of banking activity was less than the economic historians describe, or that the scholastic authors were less perceptive in observing the mechanisms of commercial credit than they were in treating of variations in partnership and *census* contracts. Deposit creation as an economic phenomenon is unmentioned by them. Their moral evaluation of it can be understood only in terms of the standard categories. To the extent that credit creation was used for partnership investment, it was undoubtedly considered licit; indeed, it is probable that the scholastic theory may have encouraged bankers to participate as risk-sharers in commercial ventures, while the prudent banking standards of a different age would never have allowed a bank to act as partner. To the extent that the credit was created to meet a forced government draft, it would similarly have been considered licit by the moralists, as the discussion of the *montes* has shown. But to the extent that deposit creation consisted in pure loans at a profit, no moral extenuation was offered for them by the scholastic authors.

Beginning with the fifteenth century, there is some discussion of deposits made with the commercial companies acting as bankers. Panormitanus suggests that the interest taken by widows on their deposits might be justified as *lucrum cessans* in delay — a highly curious suggestion, given the usual contemporary requirement that one claiming *lucrum cessans* must have been able to apply his money himself to a business purpose.[18] St. Bernardine is

[13] Usher, p. 181.
[14] de Roover, *Money, Banking*, p. 306.
[15] F. C. Lane, "Venetian Banks, 1496–1533, A Study in the Early Stages of Deposit Banking," *Journal of Political Economy*,

XLV (1937), 190, 196; Dunbar, "The Bank of Venice," p. 316.
[16] de Roover, *Money, Banking*, pp. 306–308: Dunbar, "The Bank of Venice," p. 314.
[17] Lane, pp. 187, 197.
[18] Panormitanus, *Commentaria*, V:19:8.

stricter. A deposit with an exchange banker or merchant at a fixed rate is usury. In particular, if a widow deposits with a merchant with the agreement that her capital be safe and that she get half the profit, she sins mortally, although she says she does it not to gain from a loan but to avoid the merchant cheating her in a partnership.[19] If, however, a deposit is made with an exchange dealer without the corrupt principal hope of profit, one may receive a gift from the dealer for the deposit.[20]

As usual, St. Antoninus gives us the fullest information on the current practice. The *depositum*, he maintains, is a widely used fraud of the leisured classes with surplus funds to invest. He declares:

> The nobles, who do not wish to labor, lest money be lacking to them as they gradually consume it, give it to a merchant or a money-changer, principally intending to receive something annually at their [the depositories'] discretion, the capital, however, being kept safe. And although they call this a deposit, yet it is clearly usury [21]

The other great class of offenders here, besides the nobles, are also a non-business class, the widows, who "lest they consume their dowries deposit them with merchants at their discretion and for usuries, according to the above." [22] It is astonishing that such a flimsy disguise could have been so widely accepted. Antoninus has no trouble in showing that

> a true deposit stands to the peril of the depositor, not to that of the depositary, unless he loses it by his own fault, nor does the depositor intend to have gain from the depositary. . . .
>
> But in our case, the money stands, as it is said, to the peril of the recipient in every eventuality, and thence the depositor receives profit . . .
>
> Nor is it an objection that the depositaries are much enriched with this. For the profit was of industry, not of money, and he who received the loan stood the peril of loss, in which peril the depositor did not wish to be a participant.

Even if an explicit agreement for interest is not made, but the deposit is made principally with the hope of profit, usury is committed.[23] Antoninus admits that wards may collect 5 per cent from their guardians — a kind of deposit agreement — but under the title of penalty for negligence on the part of the guardians, and not as profit on the deposit.[24]

---

[19] St. Bernardine, *De contractibus*, 39:1:2, 39:1:3.

[21] St. Antoninus, *Summa*, 2:1:6 ad 2.

[22] 2:1:6. Earlier, in his *Confessionale* (*De septimo praecepto, circa usuram*), St. Antoninus had attacked deposits as peculiarly the sin of women.

[23] St. Antoninus, *Summa*, 2:1:7.

[24] 2:1:9. Henry of Ghent allows the payment of *interesse* to wards as compensation for an injurious detention of their money if they wanted to do business with it and their guardians deposited it, instead, with the city (Henry of Ghent, *Quodlibetales*, Q:14:13).

Deposit banking is also condemned in the form of discounting of payments not yet due from a bank. References to this practice are not many. In the early fourteenth century, however, Alexander Lombard condemns it on the grounds that the bank credits are as good as money in hand; his realistic reason is that otherwise the merchants would not accept payment made through a bank. Almost two hundred years later, the more rigid and conventional Angelus de Clavasio, reporting that this operation is called "a purchase of bank balances," similarly finds it nothing but a usurious loan.[25]

Thus, from every side and without any defense, deposit banking was condemned by the moralists. Did the depositors feel the same way? Were they consciously guilty of transgressing a moral law? These questions will be considered after examining the status of the exchange bankers.

2. *Exchange Operations*

Practice

At least as important in quantitative terms as the deposit business, and far more important in terms of international finance, were the banking operations conducted in foreign exchange. The simplest, and from the usury-theory viewpoint least interesting, type of exchange was the immediate, on-the-spot conversion of foreign coinage. Known as manual or petty exchange, it flourished in an age of many coinages and was the prototype of the more complex transactions.[26] As early as the twelfth century, however, exchange was combined with credit, in the operation known as the *cambium nauticum* or sea exchange. This contract was merely a variant of the sea loan with the added condition that repayment be in a foreign currency.[27] At the same time, there developed in the twelfth century the straight sale of foreign exchange on credit, where, unlike the sea exchange, there was no theoretical assumption of risk by the buyer. Delivery of the exchange bought might be contracted for in the place purchased; but more commonly delivery was to be another place.[28] In Genoa, for example, exchange was thus, as the expression went, "bought on" the Champagne fairs. The purchases of exchange seem to have been the normal Italian way of financing trade to the great fairs.[29] The exchange dealer, buying exchange, would

---

This opinion is clearly an attempt not to condemn completely what was a common practice even in the thirteenth century.

[25] Alexander Lombard, *Tractatus*, c.7, f.-166v:a; Angelus de Clavasio, *Summa*, at *Usura*, n.65.

[26] Endemann, *Studien in der romanisch-kanonistischen*, II, 103; Sayous, "L'origine de

la lettre de change," p. 70; Robert Lopez, "An Aristocracy of Money in the Middle Ages," *Speculum*, XXVIII (1933), 43.

[27] Sayous, "L'origine de la lettre de change," p. 85.

[28] *Ibid.*, p. 91; cf. Usher, p. 67.

[29] Sayous, "L'origine de la lettre de change," p. 91; Sayous, "L'histoire universelle

finance a merchant customer who would deliver the exchange when he sold his commodity at the fair. Such a purchase of foreign exchange is also encountered as an early form of government finance; St. Louis financed the crusade in Syria by exchange purchases from Genoese merchants.[30] Into the thirteenth century the notaries still occasionally use "*mutuum*" to describe these contracts, but the more usual description is "*emptio-venditio*," and the money is said to be paid not on account of a loan, but "on account of an exchange." [31] By mid-thirteenth century this form becomes universal, and the dangerous word "*mutuum*" disappears in these transactions.[32]

The growth of exchange banking is marked by the development of the standard bill of exchange, replacing the more cumbersome notarial contract.[33] As the large Italian companies establish agencies abroad it becomes customary for the home office to issue an informal letter of payment directing its branch to pay a bill; or the branch may draw on the main office. The *cambium per litteras*, as it was called, used the bill of exchange in two ways. The exchange bank was in the position of debtor to its customer if it sold foreign exchange, making the delivery some months later in another city. In this case the customer or lender paid a fee and there was no profit on the credit extended. It is obvious, however, that when the process was reversed and the *campsor* bought exchange, paid first and made a profit, an extension of credit at a gain for the lender was involved with the sale of the foreign exchange. In form, however, the bill of exchange was never a loan, but always a simple sale; and the bills were never discounted.[34]

The bill of exchange became a standard instrument of credit in the fourteenth and fifteenth centuries. It was frequently used as a means of extending credit to a government by the large Italian houses. It was the normal mechanism for effecting sales on credit in international commerce. It was the chief method of financing the wool trade, which rested on a chain of credit from the grazers of sheep to the sellers of the finished cloth. It was the usual means of adjusting international specie balances.[35] Finally, it was a means

---

de droit commercial de Levin Goldschmidt et les méthodes commerciales en les pays chrétiens de la Méditerranée aux 12ᵉ et 13ᵉ siècles," *Annales de droit commercial*, XL (1931), 112.

[30] Sayous, "Les mandats de St. Louis sur son trésor," *Revue historique*, CLXVII (1931), 277. The treasury documents describe the financial transactions interchangeably as "loans" or "exchanges" (*ibid.*, p. 278).

[31] Rolandino, *Summa totius artis notariae*, I:3, f.82.

[32] Usher, p. 68.
[33] de Roover, *L'évolution de la lettre de change*, p. 41.
[34] *Ibid.*, pp. 119ff.
[35] Renouard, *Les hommes d'affaires*, pp. 89, 206; Yver, *Le commerce et les marchands*, p. 37; Postan, "Credit in Medieval Trade," pp. 239 and 246; E. Power and Postan, *Studies in English Trade in the Fifteenth Century* (London, 1933), p. 54; Usher, p. 179; de Roover, *Money, Banking*, p. 66.

for the Italian exchange dealers to speculate on the exchange differentials.[36]

Together with the genuine traffic in exchange there flourished to an undetermined degree *cambium siccum* or dry exchange. The name *"cambium"* was here deliberately used as a cover for a pure loan involving no real exchange sale in any way. It had two common forms. In the first, known as *cambium sine litteris,* or *cambium ad Venetos,* or *cambium grossorum librorum,* the *campsor* lent money, which was to be repaid to him in six months in the same place at the rate such money was worth in Venice or some other foreign city at a date ten days from the beginning of the loan.[37] There was no transfer of exchange letters, nor any real purchase of foreign exchanges. But the exchange rate on the foreign city was simply used as a means by which the rate of repayment was determined. The dealer could lose if the rates suddenly changed; but it was highly unlikely.

The second form of dry exchange involved the actual sending of the bill of exchange to another city where it was known that the seller of the exchange had no money. When the bill was presented for payment, the branch of the exchange bank which had purchased the note took up the bill itself and credited it as paid. In return for this service, the branch drew up a new bill on the original seller in favor of the parent bank. When this bill became due, the seller paid it himself to the home bank. Thus, for a space of four to six months, varying with the time it took the bills to travel out and back, the original seller enjoyed the credit given him by the parent

[36] In a typical case, the main exchange bank would buy foreign exchange in another city. When the bill arrived, the exchange would be paid to its foreign branch by the foreign correspondent of the seller, and the branch would credit the home firm with this amount upon its books. Usually the *cambium* was followed by a *recambium.* The main exchange bank, if it had bought, now possessed its money in a foreign currency in another city. It was essential, in order to determine the ultimate profit, for the branch to use this money to buy exchange in the home city. When this *recambium* was completed, and the money thus bought was delivered to the main firm, the profit was apparent. An actual example from the Medici account books of the mid-fifteenth century may suffice to illustrate the practice followed by the banks from the beginning of the fourteenth century.

"Early in April 1441, the Medici of Venice bought a bill on Bruges at the rate of 52 groats per Venetian ducat. Two months later, when the bill matured, they received in Bruges 52 groats for each ducat. With the proceeds of this bill the Bruges branch, acting as agent for the Venice branch, bought a bill on Venice, payable at the end of two months, at the rate of 51½ groats per ducat. The Medici of Venice thus made a profit of one-half groat on each ducat, over a period of four months, since they received 52 groats and paid only 51½ groats per ducat" (de Roover, *The Medici Bank,* pp. 36–37). In an equilibrium condition, the rate of exchange was always higher in that one of the two places which gave its currency to the other. Factors disturbing equilibrium were (1) changes in the monetary standard; (2) other government regulations; (3) disturbances in the balance of payments between the exchange centers due to commercial causes; (4) speculation of monopolists. Because of the unexpected intrusion of such factors, the bankers could lose, but generally equilibrium prevailed, and they profited (*ibid.,* p. 162).

[37] St. Antoninus, *Summa,* 2:1:8.

bank. At the end of this time he repaid the loan plus the cost of the *cambium* and *recambium*. Again, the bank could lose, but it was improbable. Once more, no real purchase or delivery of exchange was intended.[38]

In their use of genuine bills of exchange, the exchange dealers performed a notable banking service in developing the use of a surrogate currency. In an age when specie was scarce, the perils both of legal devaluation and false coinage considerable, and transportation dangerous, the bill of exchange was a welcome instrument of commerce. Inasmuch as the bankers made the bill of exchange a ready and easy way of securing credit, they contributed to the creation of a purchasing power which would not have existed in a simple specie system. Moreover, many bills of exchange were met by transfers of credit, and a reëxchange might be effected which again would be met by a credit transfer. The effect would be entirely similar to transfers of credit between different banks by check today.[39] There was, in short, true credit creation as in a banking system. The extent of such operations among the main banks is not certain, and possibly the economic historians may have exaggerated their importance in the Middle Ages. But some credit creation certainly took place by these means.

The central financial function of the exchange dealers is particularly evident in their use by the papacy, the largest international organization engaged in financial transactions in the Middle Ages. The exchange dealers who had the papal business, *campsores Apostolicae Sedis*, fulfilled an indispensable function in the administration of the Church: they made possible the centralized financial system necessary to support a centralized authority. By the use of drafts upon their branches or home office, they obviated the need to transport much specie.[40] Moreover, the movement of their own trading funds was usually the converse of the movement of the papal funds — that is, they were buying and paying in the countries from which the popes were collecting revenue. Hence, they could use the immediately available papal monies on the spot for their own expenses, while transmitting a similar amount to the credit of the papacy in Avignon or Rome, without the neces-

[38] de Roover, "What is Dry Exchange?" *Journal of Political Economy*, LII (1944), 262–264. It should be noted that the term "dry exchange" is not always used with a fixed meaning among scholastic writers. For example, Silvester da Prierio uses it to encompass all sales of bills of exchange, including those where the customer is paying first and receiving no credit (Silvester da Prierio, *Summa summarum que Silvestrina dicitur*, Bologna, 1515, *Usura*, IV:9:2).

[39] de Roover, *Money, Banking*, pp. 52, 57, 58; Sayous, "Les opérations des banquiers italiens," p. 32; Sayous, "Les opérations des banquiers de Genès à la fin du 12ᵉ siècle," *Annales de droit commercial*, XLIV (1934), 294–295; Pirenne, *Economic and Social History of the Middle Ages*, p. 326.

[40] Sayous, "Les opérations des banquiers italiens," p. 24.

sity of great withdrawals in specie which might have occasioned far more objection from the countries taxed by the pope.[41] Further, they were able to furnish the papacy with funds quickly, and they were able to effect payments in distant places for the papacy readily.[42] In supplying credit at the place needed, they may be considered to have performed a true banking service.

Data from the fourteenth-century record show that the exchange houses' fees for their important services were very moderate. Sometimes nothing was charged for a transfer of funds and never was more than 5 per cent asked. On actual loans to the papacy the great companies made no interest charge whatsoever. It need not be supposed, however, that these active businessmen performed their work simply out of Christian love. Their noncontractual remuneration was high. First, they often received direct pecuniary gifts from the Holy See and their families enjoyed a considerable advantage in the obtaining of benefices and other favors. Secondly, they had behind them in all their trading the immense prestige attached to the papacy. Occasionally, the papacy would support them directly with ecclesiastical censures against their recalcitrant debtors.[43] More important was papal recommendation to other ecclesiastical employers, such as bishops and abbots. In particular the cameral firms had the opportunity to lend to newly appointed holders of benefices and bishoprics who were unable to pay at once the substantial sum set as a tax upon such appointments. The exchange firms advanced the cash in the form of a purchase of bills of exchange to be met in the bishop's own territory, when he had the time to collect his diocesan revenues.[44] As early as 1200, loans extended to those "approaching the Roman court" in the form of exchange bills payable at the fairs are noted as characteristic transactions of the cameral banking firms;[45] and similar contracts continued to be employed throughout the Middle Ages.[46] Thirdly, and perhaps above all, the exchange houses had the opportunity of using the idle papal funds which were deposited with them. This was a privilege expressly guaranteed to them. At a time when reservoirs of liquid capital were not many, the opportunity was a great one.[47] Certainly some of the early prosperity of Siena must be attributed to its papal banking business;

[41] Renouard, *Les hommes d'affairs*, p. 153.

[42] Renouard, *Les relations des papes d'Avignon*, pp. 552–554.

[43] *Ibid.*, pp. 537, 542, 547, 558. Cf. W. E. Lunt, *Financial Relations of the Papacy with England to 1327* (Cambridge, 1939), pp. 289, 602.

[44] Lunt, pp. 472–473; Renouard, *Les relations des papes d'Avignon*, p. 539.

[45] Robert of Courçon, *De usura*, p. 65.

[46] Lunt, pp. 471–472, 602; cf. St. Antoninus, *Summa*, 3:11:3.

[47] Sayous, "Les opérations des banquiers italiens," p. 24; Bigwood, *Le régime juridique*, I, 645; Yver, p. 391; Lunt, p. 602; cf.

and when Siena's obstinate Ghibelline sympathies alienated the papacy from it, the papal business, transferred to Florence, unquestionably contributed to the success of her banks.[48] As long as Florence was the financial center of Europe — that is, until the end of the fifteenth century — her firms handled the pope's account.

The Moral Evaluation

What was the reaction of the scholastic moralists to this activity in the business of credit, so often useful to the papacy and so standard a part of international commerce?

As upon *census* and *societas*, the early canon law is silent upon *cambium* proper; and there was no Roman law upon the subject to inspire the canonists. The papal legislation on credit sales and the *foenus nauticum*, however, may be considered as indirectly concerning it. *Naviganti*, condemning the sea loans and fair loans, which in practice usually involved exchange sales, may be presumed to mean that the inclusion of an exchange sale does not extenuate a loan from usury.[49] Similarly, the canons condemning sales on credit offer no exceptions for the international trade, where exchange also played a part.[50] Yet although all these canons seem to condemn exchange loans, they do not mention *cambium* specifically, and so they offered at least no insuperable barrier to the admission of bills of exchange as licit at a later date.

The interpretation that the canons at the time were meant to condemn all loan transactions at a profit, even in the form of sales of exchange, is confirmed by what theological commentary upon such transactions is available. Cardinal Courçon discusses the papal exchange bankers' loans to abbots, bishops, and others, which are repaid in a different currency at "the fairs" and which the bankers persuade the pope himself to notarize. Courçon, who believes these exchange sales to be usurious, says bluntly that if the pope does sign such documents, he does not know what he is doing.[51] Even canonists closely associated with the curia are hostile, so one cannot infer that the papacy had drawn some distinction between traffic in exchange

---

Pirenne, *Economic and Social History*, p. 132. It is noteworthy that the Medici bank in Rome apparently needed no capital investment, because of the large sums on deposit by the curia; see de Roover, "I libri segreti del Banco de Medici," *Archivio Storico Italiano*, CVII (1949), Disp. 2, f.284. For example, the sums on private deposit in the bank included large sums for Pope Martin V and numerous car-dinals; *Archivo de Storico di Firenze*, Contato 1427, No. 51, f.117h.

[48] Sayous, "Les opérations des banquiers italiens," p. 27; Séc, *Modern Capitalism*, pp. 8-9; Thompson, *Economic and Social History*, I, 415.

[49] See *supra*, pp. 19, 90–92.

[50] See *supra*, p. 91.

[51] Robert of Courçon, p. 65.

and in loans to protect its bankers. Cardinal Goffredus of Trani, Cardinal Hostiensis, St. Raymond of Pennaforte all condemn the buyers of exchange upon the fairs.[52] These men, Hostiensis declares, charge 100 per cent a year and exercise an execrable usury.

At this period the contention — apparently made by the merchants themselves — that an exchange is not a loan, but "a simple purchase or sale," is contemptuously rejected. William of Auxerre treats this as a mere verbal defense not in the least excusing the usury of the fair bankers.[53] Both Goffredus and Hostiensis say that usurious lending in fact occurs "under the name of exchange."[54] St. Albert treats the exchange dealers as lenders.[55] St. Thomas Aquinas, commenting on Psalm 5:5, "Who has not given his money to usury," finds the verse applicable to "the *campsores* who commit many frauds, and against the sellers of cloth and other goods."[56] Without even mentioning the defense of a sale, Monaldus simply treats as a usurious loan the giving of money in one city to receive more in another.[57] This tendency to ignore the exchange form and focus on the credit transaction involved is equally evident at this period in the treatment of sales on credit paid for by foreign exchange. Like the canons, no writer makes an exception for a credit sale involving an exchange transaction. St. Thomas, for example, condemns all credit advances for a profit in the international wool trade, without reference to the exchange sale in which credit in this business was so often extended.[58]

Reinforcing the general objection to exchange transactions as loans came the specifically Aristotelian objection based on the purpose of money. This first occurs in the mistranslation of Aristotle to which we have already referred.[59] That William of Moerbeke should have found it natural for the *campsores* to be condemned by the Philosopher for their unnatural acquisitiveness is itself a suggestive fact. Both St. Albert and St. Thomas, commenting on the *Ethics*, expatiate on the topic by describing the success the exchange dealers have in multiplying their money by transferring it "where they can make the maximum profit."[60] As both St. Albert and St. Thomas are purporting to interpret Aristotle, their own opinion is not entirely certain from these commentaries. But the Aristotelian view that the exchange

[52] Hostiensis, *Summa*, V:8 *in fine*; St. Raymond, *Summa*, 2:7:5.

[53] William of Auxerre, *Summa aurea*, III:21, f.225v:a–b.

[54] See *supra*, n.52.

[55] St. Albert, *Liber I politicorum*, c.7.

[56] St. Thomas, *In duo praeceptos caritatis et decem legis praeceptos*, c.24, in *Opera*, Vol. XXVII.

[57] Monaldus, *Summa perutilis*, at "Usura," f.288r:b.

[58] St. Thomas, *De emptione et venditione*.

[59] See *supra*, p. 47.

[60] St. Albert, *Liber I politicorum*, c.7; St. Thomas, *Liber I politicorum*, c.6.

dealer's art "is justly vituperated" at least accords with St. Thomas's own statement on Psalm 5:5. A few of the later thirteenth-century writers — for example, Aegidius of Rome and the Spanish Gloss on Aegidius — consider the Aristotelian objection decisive: it is not natural to deal in money, to make money the beginning and the end of a transaction.[61]

Thus from the late twelfth century almost to the end of the thirteenth century objection to the exchange dealers is universal.

Surprisingly, two immediate disciples of St. Thomas appear as the most lenient thirteenth-century authorities on exchange. In completing St. Thomas' *De regimine principis*, Ptolemy of Lucca says that money is not necessarily a fixed measure. Money can also be considered as appropriate for other purposes: for example, when it is *"pecunia campsoria,"* "money used in the exchanges." [62] This reasoning, if developed, would have permitted a traffic in *pecunia campsoria*. But Ptolemy fails to develop his own suggestion. It is the merest hint of an idea, which remains to be exploited by the later scholastics.

Giles of Lessines is somewhat more helpful to the exchange dealers. Stating the premise that money itself is "nonvendible," he defends the dealers who receive payment "because of the risk and as interest" to pay the expenses of their servants. Moreover, he adds that the dealer gives what has "more utility" to his customer than what his customer gives to him.[63] Are these statements made in defense of the exchange bankers, or are they merely meant as justification of the petty exchange dealers? The reference to "risk" suggests the presence of a credit transaction, and the reference to servants might be taken as one to the bankers' correspondents. On the other hand, the statement as to what the customer gives the dealer seems to imply an exchange of present monies. This interpretation seems confirmed in the next chapter where Giles deals explicitly with what he calls "loans" on the fairs, and these transactions were the typical operations of the bankers.[64] In his treatment Giles reveals an almost total absence of comprehension of the common exchanges. He speaks of a lender loaning 100 pounds to be repaid the value of 100 pounds at the fair. He finds this contract unlawful if the lender has entered it fearing a legal devaluation of the pound; it is lawful if pounds at the time of repayment are "worth more" than the sum repaid. But

[61] Aegidius Romanus, *De regimine principis*, Bk. II, art. 3, c.10; cf. 2:3:16; *Glosa Castellana*, 2:3:16.

[62] Ptolemy of Lucca, *De regimine principis*, II:13.

[63] Giles of Lessines, c.13. It must be noted that "risk" may mean "risk of transportation" of an exchange dealer selling a bill of exchange and actually exporting cash to meet the bill. This usage is clear in Antonio de Rosellis, *De usuris*, in *Tractatus universi juris*, VII.

[64] Giles of Lessines, c.14. The limited defense of only manual exchange by the appeal to *interesse* and expenses is even clearer in Henry of Ghent, Q.6:22.

he conspicuously fails to deal with the usual case in which the sum repaid will be worth more than the pounds lent, not because of a legal devaluation, but because of a change in the market for money. It thus seems probable, although the evidence is not conclusive, that his first defense of the exchange dealers applies only to petty exchange, not exchange involving an extension of credit.

Although equally confused, the plea in favor of the exchange dealers becomes stronger in the writings of Alexander Lombard, who is peculiarly sympathetic to the cause of the financiers. He focuses on a fact which his predecessors had not found of theoretical significance: "The Church always condemns and pursues usurers, but it does not condemn and pursue the exchange dealers, but, rather, fosters them, as is apparent in the Roman Church."[65]

This fact is the starting point of a theoretical justification for the dealers. To begin with, the dealers in petty exchange are clearly engaged in lawful and useful activity. The strict Aristotelians are wrong, says Alexander, adopting Ptolemy of Lucca's position without citing him, in thinking that money has only one function; if coinages are various, money must necessarily be exchanged. Moreover, the value of the money given by the dealer is not determined by law, but by its weight and matter. Finally, in Giles of Lessines' phrase, "more utility" for the customer exists in the money he receives than he had in the money he pays.[66]

The hard case is the transaction in which the dealer extends credit to be repaid later at the fair. Alexander's approach to it is patterned on the *Decretals'* treatment of *venditio sub dubio*. If the dealer would have kept his money had he not engaged in the exchange, and if the money would have appreciated due to an increasing demand for cash at the fairs, the dealer can receive in payment a value equal to the value of money at this later date.[67] To give an example implicit in this analysis: If 100 pounds now equal 100 ducats, and three months later at the fair will be worth 120 ducats, the dealer can stipulate that he be paid 120 ducats, provided he would otherwise have kept his pounds and provided also that the debtor before maturity is free to repay the 100 pounds. In other words, as with *venditio sub dubio*, a qualified *lucrum cessans* is permitted, and in permitting it a limited market in money is permitted. This is an admission of high theoretical significance, for it shows a perception that once money is not treated as a legal measure a market in it is conceivable. But it is also a very limited admission. It does

[65] Alexander Lombard, f.167r:a.   [67] f. 168r:b.
[66] *Ibid.*

not permit the dealer to profit on the credit transaction, but allows only an equality of exchange. The 120 ducats the dealer gets for his 100 pounds are worth no more than those he gave; the dealer can be no richer than if he had made the whole exchange at the later date, giving 100 pounds for 120 ducats. Literally applied, this doctrine would not have helped the bankers at all. Yet was this confused analysis without significance? Perhaps the very existence of such a defense in a scholarly work lent itself to a popular interpretation justifying at least some transactions of the fair bankers.

The attempted defense of Alexander Lombard was repeated verbatim by Astesanus, who is also struck by the fact that "the Roman Church fosters the exchange dealers." [68] But he also tries to defend the fair bankers from a different viewpoint. It is on their behalf that, as we have seen, he enters the first theological defense of *lucrum cessans*.[69] This was a defense not readily available to the bankers, if all the early medieval conditions were insisted on. Nonetheless, its appropriateness for the exchange bankers who were also merchants should be appreciated. Astesanus anticipates a development that must await the seventeenth century to reach its height.

A reasoned defense of the exchange bankers, or even an understanding of the issues they presented, is strikingly missing among the more prominent writers of the later fourteenth century. Great canonists such as Joannes Andreae and daring innovators such as Gerson fail to deal with the problem at all. A strong hostility continues to predominate. This takes two forms. Some writers such as Henry of Hesse continue the early medieval tradition of seeing the exchange dealers simply as lenders engaged in usury and in no position to meet the requirements for asking *lucrum cessans*.[70] Other writers such as Nicholas of Oresme reflect the blind Aristotelian tradition that the trade of money for money is unnatural. Not condemning exchange transactions as usurious per se, Nicholas characterizes exchange as vile, an occupation which necessarily stains the soul as sewer cleaning necessarily stains the body.[71]

Only one writer of any prominence undertakes the defense of exchange,

[68] Astesanus, III:11:4.

[69] See *supra*, p. 119.

[70] Henry of Hesse, I:23, f.196–197.

[71] Nicholas of Oresme, *Tractatus*, c. 17. He notes that St. Matthew was a *campsor*, but unlike St. Peter, did not return to his profession after the Resurrection. Yet, that the legal profession at this time drew some line between usury and exchange is indicated on a practical level by the open use of exchange contracts in contrast to the avoidance of loans at usury (see Rolandino, *Summa totius artis notariae*, L:3). At a theoretical level the civilian Baldus distinguishes "exchanges" from usury by saying that a *permutatio*, not a *mutuum*, is involved, and, moreover, the dealer is not certain of profit (Baldus, *Ad libros VII codicis commentaria*, *De usuris rei judicatae*, II:2). It will be noted these arguments are paraphrases of the theological ones already put forward.

and then it is done in a way as ambiguous and inexact as that of Giles of Lessines. The new defender is John Buridan, who argues that *cambium* is necessary for human life, because the merchants need it, but who does not say whether he is defending the simple *cambium manuale* or the *cambium per litteras* as well. Buridan merely distinguishes two kinds of exchange: (1) where the dealer "takes more than he gives"; and (2) where the dealer "gets only as much as he gives." The second is certainly just. The first is just, if the dealer's surplus is due his labor. It may also be justified, even if there is no equivalence, if the exchange is useful to the "common good." [72] With this surprising thought, Buridan makes a radical departure from the scholastic tradition whose normative rule was that objective inequality and injustice could not be rectified by the end served. The argument suggests the tension between theory and practice. But there is no suggestion by Buridan that *raison d'état* can legitimate usury in ordinary business; the argument, significantly, is advanced only in favor of the respectable exchange bankers.

In the fifteenth century the pressures of commercial life against theory increased; and the theological concern became better informed and more fully expressed. For the first time exchange is treated with some thoroughness. The way is opened by Laurentius de Ridolfis. Teaching in the banking capital of Europe, Laurentius had excellent opportunity to be informed upon exchange and excellent reason to give a theological account of it. He begins by saying that if *cambium per litteras* is not licit, many will be damned; and it seems implied that he is not reconciled to a wholesale damnation of the Florentine business class. Curiously enough, however, he does not then consider the purchase of exchange by the exchange dealer, the contract which involved a loan, and which the economic historians tell us was the common one. But he centers his discussion entirely on the exchange sale by the banker, when the banker is in the role of debtor, delivering the money he sells in another city. The dealer delivers less money than he has received, but this, says Laurentius, is licit, because he is entitled to a charge of *interesse*, for his work and expenses, and the wages of his factors and apprentices.[73] Moreover, there is a real difference in the value of money "through diversity of place." A florin plus a denarius in one town are equal to a florin alone in another. The dealer delivering money in the other city

---

[72] Buridan, *Quaestiones*, I:11, art. 3. It must be admitted that Buridan's text, read literally, speaks as though the money made by the exchange dealer had to be devoted to the common good. But the context and sense favor the interpretation that the exchange is justified if it is made for the common good. [73] Laurentius de Ridolfis, 2:21. Note the similarity of the argument to Giles of Lessines'.

has the right to charge the difference to his customer: "Not, therefore, is money sold which is nonvendible, but here is paid as much as it is worth in cash there."

Are we to infer from Laurentius' silence on the exchange sales where the dealer is the buyer and makes a profit on the extension of credit that he considers the case already judged by the usury prohibition? Or are we to suppose the reference to the dealer's *interesse*, and the expenses of his banking establishment are tacitly intended to justify the exchange purchases, too? The answer is not easy. If we go by later theological opinion in Florence and suppose it accurately reflects earlier opinion, we will conclude that Laurentius felt the exchange already condemned. If we are guided by Laurentius' frequent tendency to defend the practices of his fellow citizens, we may conclude that he held the exchange licit. But nothing can be said decisively.[74]

It seems all the more mysterious that Laurentius does not mention the exchange sale contract, when we find him weighing the justice of the far more dubious contract of dry exchange. He describes it by the pejorative phrase *cambium siccum*, but is clearly hesitant about condemning it outright. He first offers a possible analogy. The value of the florin varies "from time to time, from diverse causes"; and it is no sin to profit from this in a loan. At the moment a borrower uses the money, he gets a florin's worth of goods; if he pays it back to the creditor at a time when the florin is worth more, the creditor will still get only "a florin's worth of goods." Laurentius, sticking closely to the concept of money as a measure, contends that equality is kept if the same formal amount is maintained, though the content of the measure changes.[75] This change in the value of money during the period of a loan offers a parallel to the instant case. Money is given in one currency and returned in another currency which may be of a greater *value*, but is technically equal to the *quantity* originally given.

Secondly, he names the factors effecting variation in the value of money. The most obvious are the intrinsic quality and the intrinsic weight of the metal of the coin. There is also a variation due to changes in the price of gold over a period. But most importantly there is one nonmetallic factor.

---

[74] A plausible suggestion is made by Trovamala that Laurentius is defending transactions where the seller of the bill of exchange is selling only as the best way of transferring funds already on hand, say, in London to his home office in Florence; see Trovamala (Joannes Baptista de Salis), *Summa rosella* (Venice, 1495), *Usura*, VI:21. In other words, though there is no economic distinction, a line would be drawn between sales of bills of exchange as a way of raising new funds and sales to transfer funds at hand.

[75] Laurentius de Ridolfis, 3:1.

This is the demand for money. Following the suggestion of Alexander Lombard, Laurentius candidly admits that the value of money depends, like that of every other good, upon supply and demand.[76] This is an admission, not developed or applied to the usury theory proper. But it stands here, a foreshadowing of future theory, and a present support for the international exchange bankers.

Dry exchange could, then, be defended on the grounds that the increase coming to the exchange dealer is simply an increase due to a change in value of money a year later as a result of fluctuation in the demand; the dealer could be said to get back only the value he lent. But following Alexander Lombard's approach to exchanges, Laurentius concludes that the case is ruled by the same principles as those governing *venditio sub dubio*. There must be a real doubt as to what the value of money will be at the time of repayment; the stipulated repayment price must be understood as equivalent only to the value the dealer would have had in hand if he had kept his money instead of lending it. As normally the dealer does better than this, it must be concluded that he has made a loan with the intention to profit. He would not so contract unless gain was usual, and he commits at least mental usury. Yet Laurentius reaches this result with reluctance; there is a note of hesitancy in his final condemnation.[77] He may be tempted by the perception that if money can be considered a commodity a market in money is possible. Clearly the commercial life of Florence called for this result. But he turns his back on the temptation and reaches a rigorist conclusion that St. Antoninus can cite with approval.

The possibilities that the commodity approach to money might open up are also suggested in the *De contractibus mercatorum* written about 1430 by John Nider. Nider, a German Dominican of no great influence, must at least be taken as reflecting a sentiment with some general currency. He says flatly that "For whatever cause or operation a merchant may lawfully receive profit . . . so can an exchange dealer." The reason is clear: "Because just as merchandise varies in the estimation of men, so do moneys, although not so commonly and to such a great extent." Therefore, an exchange dealer can charge for his care, labor, risk, and interest in the sense of compensation for loss. This would appear to be a sweeping defense of the bankers. It is limited, however, and probably reduced to Alexander Lom-

[76] 3:1.
[77] 3:1. His last words on the subject are a "counsel" to avoid dry exchange, and these are open to the interpretation that he does not believe the contract definitely sinful. Yet I believe St. Antoninus is correct in taking the teaching of Laurentius in its entirety to be that the contract is inherently unlawful (see St. Antoninus, 3:8:4).

bard's position by Nider's rules on time sales, as these rules would be equally binding in sales of bills of exchange. His rules are (1) time should not be sold; (2) a higher price may be charged only if there is doubt as to what the value will be at the time of payment; if the seller generally gains it is clear that he is selling time and committing usury.[78]

In any case, Nider did not speak with the authority of a St. Bernardine of Siena. It might be expected that if Laurentius de Ridolfis hesitates, St. Bernardine would be even less sympathetic to the exchanges. In fact, he is harshly critical. The dealer can charge for custody of his customer's money; for the difficulty of handling foreign coins; for the difference in the weight and goodness of the coin. It is also licit to lend money that one believes will be devaluated by law and it stipulates that one receive the old value in return. This is not to profit, but to avoid loss, and the borrower has the use of the money at the old rate. But it is always usury to lend in one currency with the hope of receiving more in another, and this holds for *cambia*, too. Thus, the fair merchants, who are also exchange dealers, customarily commit usury, St. Bernardine declares; and it would seem that all exchanges by bills of exchange in which the buyer of the bill profits were usury by St. Bernardine's standard. A fortiori, the *cambium per Venetos* is a loan made with the hope of gain; even when the dealer actually loses by a sudden change in the rates, "doubt and peril do not excuse in usury." The saint's judgment on these widespread banking phenomena is sombre: "Such exchanges are in modern times the ruin and destruction of the citizens."[79]

The unfavorable judgment of exchange banking is given definitive and comprehensive form by St. Antoninus. In the fullest discussion yet attempted of exchange, he distinguishes four principal types of exchange. The first is *minutum cambium*. The profit is due the dealer's labor and is licit. The second type is *cambium per litteras*, by which St. Antoninus means the contract in which the exchanger sells exchange and delivers it in another city. The contract is neither a *mutuum* nor an *emptio pecuniae*, but a *contractus innominatus*, where the labor, expenses, and risk of delivery justify the exchanger's profit. The third type of exchange is the *cambium siccum* or *per Venetos*. He agrees with Laurentius in condemning the contract. There is an advance of money in the fictitious guise of an exchange contract; there is hope of profit from this advance. Therefore there is usury.[80]

[78] John Nider, *De contractibus mercatorum*, Part I, in *Tractatus universi juris*, VI. On Nider, see Hurter, *Nomenclator*, II, col. 863.
[79] St. Bernardine, 39:3:1.

[80] St. Antoninus, 3:8:3; cf. 2:1:7. The exchange is said by him to be a common Florentine practice, *Confessionale, De septimo praecepto, De cambiis*.

The fourth type of exchange St. Antoninus describes as "mixing" the second and third. It is, in fact, the exchange purchased in a foreign city by the dealer — the bill of exchange involving an extension of credit, which we have seen as the common form. Those who defend the contract, St. Antoninus says, do so on five grounds. The first is that the transaction is similar to the simple transfer of coins from one city to another, because in the second city they are worth more. Thus an exchange dealer could transport florins from Lyons to Florence and licitly realize the profit on the increase in value. St. Antoninus denies the analogy. Here a true loan is involved and there is desire of profit from the loan. Secondly, the defense of *lucrum cessans* is advanced. It is rejected because the dealer has never intended his money for purposes other than such a lending trade; he gains more than he would in business; he does not act out of charity. Thirdly, the risk of nonrepayment is urged; and it also is rejected because risk is no defense from usury. The advocates of the contract then urge extrinsic reasons for it. Such exchange, they say, in Buridan's language, is necessary for "the utility of the State." St. Antoninus does not dispute this contention; the banking system was entrenched. But he denies the conclusion that such exchanges are licit. Prostitution and public moneylending are also necessary to the utility of the state, to avoid worse evils, but no one, he says, suggests that their necessity makes them lawful. Finally, the advocates plead that similar exchange purchases are tolerated at the Roman Curia. St. Antoninus' answer to this is sharp: the Roman Curia tolerates other abuses which it cannot eradicate. Yet unless an official decree of approval of a practice is issued, mere toleration of an evil proves nothing.

St. Antoninus then describes in detail the benefice contract which was a variation of the exchange purchase:

Those receiving benefices or dignities there [at Rome] have to pay a tax or the first fruits of the benefice, as it is said, for the help of the Apostolic treasury, within a brief time according to the tax which is customary there. The prelates or beneficed dignitaries receive under the name of exchange from the exchangers the sum to be paid the Apostolic treasury, obliging themselves to restore it in those parts where they are beneficed and in the money there current, and beyond the profit which they seek by the difference in the money there to be restored, they [the exchangers] wish themselves to be given so much per hundred, say 5, or 7, or more or less, according to the greater or less length of time which they have to wait for the return of their money. And they have drawn up an instrument of the obligation owed, not only of the money loaned, but also of the added usury, as if the whole were of capital; so that if the exchangers loan 1000, and they want to have at the place of return 1050 by reason of the loan, the instrument speaks of 1050 as loaned and to be restored at such a time; whence for delay they seek more, say 50.

This contract has a special viciousness as it encourages simony; for the exchange bankers, being prosperous and influential men, seek benefices for prelates who will be their customers. In any case, every form of credit extension in an exchange sale, St. Antoninus concludes, is usury, or at least mental usury; for every such sale involves a loan and the sinful hope of profit upon it.[81]

Rejecting the benefice contract, St. Antoninus acts in a tradition as old as Robert of Courçon: the administration of the Church is condemned, but the usury theory is maintained. So the theoreticians speak to Alexander Lombard and Astesanus who start from the fact that "the Church fosters the exchange dealers." Rejecting the purchase of bills of exchange generally, St. Antoninus gives the answer of the theoreticians to the businessmen and bankers. With St. Antoninus' thoroughgoing and well-informed condemnation of the credit side of the exchange business, the old opposition to the bankers reaches its climax. Antoninus sums up the medieval antagonism to them.[82]

Conclusion

The teaching of the scholastic upon exchange from 1200 to 1450 may be summarized in two broad conclusions:

1. After some initial hesitations due to Aristotelian views on money, the scholastics admitted that manual exchange and bills of exchange, where the exchange dealer profiting was the debtor and transporter, were licit.

2. Opinion is generally against the licitness of profit obtained through the extension of credit by exchange bills. The majority condemn exchange banking. Astesanus, however, supports the exchange dealers where *lucrum cessans* can be found to justify their profit. Buridan defends them by *raison d'état*. Giles of Lessines, Alexander Lombard, Laurentius de Ridolfis, and John Nider provide a small loophole for the bankers under the tight conditions governing *venditio sub dubio*.

[81] St. Antoninus, 3:8:3; cf. 2:1:7.
[82] One writer of little authority who supports the dealers with some firmness is the Bolognese canonist and ecclesiastical politician, Antonio de Rosellis (1400?-1466. See Hurter, II, col. 955). He defends the *cambium ad Venetos* if the lender would otherwise have kept his money and the debtor were free to repay at any time. He defends the purchase of a bill of exchange as a means of extending credit on the grounds that it is not a loan, but a contract *do ut des* where the dealer is entitled to charge for his expenses; de Rosellis, *De usuris*, in *Tractatus universi juris*, VII. But such a relatively obscure writer would carry little weight against a tradition ranging from Hostiensis to St. Antoninus.

The question presses: why were such pains taken to put loans in the form of *deposita* or *cambia*, if they were considered usurious in any event? Two replies, each partially answering the question, may be suggested. The first is that manifest usury, entailing excommunciation and social disgrace, was charged only against those publicly setting themselves up to lend money at profit, who made moneylending their trade. The merchant bankers were engaged in lawful commerce, and such lending as they did was never in the bare form of the *mutuum* at a profit, which publicly proclaimed the contract to be usurious. However much they might commit sin by mental acts, they did not use such contracts as declared externally that their intention was to profit from a loan. To this extent the theological and the popular views concurred, for the theologians taught that no one was a manifest usurer, *ipso facto* excommunicated, unless he was notoriously in the business of moneylending or was proved in court to have taken usury — and judicial measures were taken only against the lombards and Jews. The people agreed in respecting the bankers. There was thus ample reason for the bankers not to lose their external standing by simply saying that they, too, lent money at a profit.

The distinction between them and public usurers was not, to be sure, as absolute as de Roover suggests.[83] In economic backwaters like England there was a dark suspicion of all finance and a patriotic prejudice against Italians, and the Italians bankers there were the principal targets of accusations of usury.[84] In more civilized France, the Italian bankers, too, might fall under public displeasure, and the measures of Phillip the Fair against public usurers told severely against the Florentine bankers.[85] Even in Italy, the home of commerce and credit, Dante could accuse both the petty money-lenders of Cahors and the great merchant bankers of his own city of usury.[86] Joannes Andreae relates that the decree of Vienne against usury was leveled chiefly at the men from Florence, Siena, Pistoia, Lucca, and Asti, and he makes no distinction between the banking towns and pawnbroking towns.[87]

Nonetheless, in Italy always, and usually in the rest of Europe, the mer-

[83] de Roover, *Money, Banking*, p. 17.
[84] E. Lipson, *Economic History of England* (London, 1937), I, 618; Lunt, p. 600; Postan, "Credit in Medieval Trade," p. 260.
[85] Robert Davidsohn, *Geschichte von Florenz* (Berlin, 1925), IV, Part 2, 212.
[86] Dante, *La divina commedia* (Florence, 1928), *Inferno*, Canto 11:49 and Canto 17:72. Sapori, *Studi*, p. 553, has identified Catullus Gianfigliazzi as the usurer meant by Dante. He was a lender to Charles II, King of

Naples and Lord of Provence, who also described him as a usurer.
[87] Joannes Andreae, VI, *De usuris*, c.1. Sayous remarks that men from cities such as Asti and Chieri, the principal homes of the pawnbrokers, were considered socially inferior to men from banking cities like Florence, Siena, Genoa, and Lucca ("Les opérations des banquiers italiens," p. 4). In a list of public usurers in thirteenth-century Pistoia no names of merchant bankers appear (Sapori, *Studi*, p.

chant bankers mingled on an equal social footing with the other bourgeois of the town. They were not condemned like the public moneylenders, nor were they at once established as disreputable, unnatural, godless men. Their business was not considered to disqualify them from civic honor or social preferment. They were distinguished leaders of commerce, important figures in the city government, patrons of churches, art, and learning; and the community did not condemn the source of their wealth. Indeed, a banker's social standing in thirteenth-century Florence was probably at least as good as in twentieth-century New York.

A second reply, supplementing the first, is this: there may have been a real divergence on the morality of exchange between the leading theologians and the merchants. It seems exceedingly difficult to believe that virtually the whole capitalistic class of every medieval city would have habitually committed sins of usury by participating in either exchange or deposit banking, if they had truly believed the contracts to have been usurious. There may have been a kind of inculpable ignorance on the part of many which led them to regard the change in the form of the contract, and the fact that the profit was taken not from the poor but from successful businessmen or from States, as sufficient grounds for thinking that banking was not usury. There may have been many sincere bourgeois who really believed that usury was committed only in public moneylending to the poor. In the eyes of theologians, like St. Bernardine, of course, they were wrong, and St. Antoninus would even hold that their ignorance was culpable.[88] But in a matter where so much depended on legal forms, it would seem harsh to judge too sharply. Finally, and most practically, there was a substantial difference in the interest rates of the merchant bankers and those of the public usurers.[89] The popular practice was supported by at least some contemporary authority. And in the long run, as we shall see, it was to be vindicated by the common theological opinion.

---

122). But a theologian, a moralist, a satirist, or a northern European would still probably have called all the Italian financiers usurers. Suspicion of usury could even tarnish the reputation of a merchant banker among his fellows: see Iris Origo, *The Merchant of Prato* (1957), pp. 153–154.

[88] See St. Antoninus, 2:1:6. One realistic test suggested is whether the merchant bankers on the point of death felt obliged to attempt to make restitution by their wills of the profits from finance. It is urged that there is some evidence that as a class they felt no such obligation (Robert S. Lopez, "Italian Leadership in the Medieval Business World," *Journal of Economic History*, VIII [1948], 65). Sapori gives an example of the will of an unhappy banker, who, on the failure of his company, sank to public usury. Unlike testators of his former status, he left his gains from his later business to his victims (Sapori, *Studi*, p. 97).

[89] See *supra*, Chapter II, section 6, on the rates of the public usurers.

CHAPTER IX

THE SCHOLASTIC THEORY OF USURY,
1150–1450

Having now surveyed the natural-law arguments against usury and the natural-law reasoning by which the principal contracts of economic life were judged to be or not to be usurious, we are ready for some general conclusions on the usury theory itself.

1. Usury, the act or intention of taking a profit on a loan, was universally considered to be a sin against justice. Although the primary reason for considering it sinful was its condemnation by authority, nevertheless, beginning with the study of Roman law, arguments based on law and nature were advanced to show its injustice. The two principal arguments were the indistinguishability of the use and ownership of money and the fixed value of fungibles. Two essential assumptions of all arguments dealing with usury on money loans were the exemption of the value of money from the laws of supply and demand, and the refusal to identify money and the goods it bought. The socially undesirable consequences of usury were urged as the rationale of the prohibition by some authors. Stress was frequently laid on risk-participation as a test of usury.

2. Interest was allowed on loans, but its licitness was rigorously governed by the intention of the lender. Interest was licit only as compensation on a loan made from charity. Interest might never be sought for its own sake. Only towards the end of our period, after 300 years of discussion, did it become at all common to allow even compensatory interest from the start of a loan. The lender's risk of nonrecovery was never admitted as a title to interest.

3. The contracts generally approved as forms of investment were the *societas* and the *census*. These contracts provided considerable scope for commercial enterprise. The financing of the State was also allowed for by the licit *census* contracts or by the forced loans resulting in the government *montes*. *Cambium per litteras* was permitted in the form of profitable exchange sales; but only a minority of scholastics allowed profit on purchases

of bills of exchange. Traffic in government bonds was permitted. It would be a serious error to describe these licit contracts as "evasions" of the usury prohibition, if by "evasion" one means a deliberate attempt to circumvent the intention of a law. All these contracts had grown up naturally in the course of business and had received theological approval as contracts distinct from loans at a profit. At the same time it is true that such contracts would never have been as popular as they were, if lending at interest had been licit. The *census* in particular was a substitute for moneylending which came very close to being identical with it.

4. No evaluation will be made now of the soundness of the principal natural arguments against usury, of the correctness of the emphasis on intention, or of the use of risk as a criterion — for it is preferable to let the later scholastics pass judgment themselves on these matters. But it is proper at this point to observe the serious internal difficulties caused the scholastic theory in the condemnation of profit on a loan, and the simultaneous admission of profit on a *census* and in a *societas*. The admission of the licitness of pecuniary *census* involved the admissions that the right to money might be sold and that its price varied with supply and demand factors; and the more common *census* theory involved a hardly tenable distinction between a right to a good and the good itself, and a threat to the fundamental axiom that money could not be sold. A similar result followed in tolerating the sale of debt and the sale of shares in the government *montes*. The admission of profit on capital invested in a partnership involved the admission that money might be fruitful; and this admission was generally unreconciled with the treatment of money by the usury theory. A similar difficulty was involved in admitting *lucrum cessans*.

5. These inconsistent approaches prevented a rigorous ban on profit in credit, in the way that more consistent later writers attribute to the early authorities. After three hundred years of debate and limited exploration there was no single scholastic theory. Parts of a theory were assembled for later development. Pending this development, it was, perhaps, fortunate that the lack of a unified theory led to control of some types of credit while leaving open other channels for investment. The test of a theory need not be consistency. Form counted for nothing when the scholastics condemned time sales, or contracts of sale and repurchase; these were evasions of the usury prohibition in the field of consumption credit. Form meant much in the justification of the *census* as the sale of a right to money. If the key to these differences is sought in the abstract world of legal concepts, it will not be found. There are unformulated practical concerns here which led the

theorists to stress form in one place, ignore it in another. In the face of gaps in theory and contrary postulates, the usury rule — to a limited degree — worked. It worked in providing some moral guide to conscientious investors prepared to extend credit to the poor, to businessmen, or to landholders. On a straight consumption loan to a needy person the rule made it difficult for a scrupulous man to seek anything but the most limited compensatory interest; here evasion through the *census* was not easy. On credit extensions to business the rule stimulated sharing of the risk through a partnership with a moderate return to the investor. In agricultural credit the rule encouraged sharing of the risk of the *census* base. On credit extended to the state it provided little guidance, ungracefully accommodating itself to the exigencies of public debt. The rule, as applied, did not choke commerce. It regulated, in some measure, the course of credit.

6. Whether they were culpably or inculpably ignorant, medieval businessmen did not observe the prohibition in its entirety; and secular rulers made no attempts to enforce it completely. Particularly in sales on credit, in purchases of bills of exchange, and in deposit banking, the theories of the leading moralists were ignored. This popular rejection of the strict rules may itself be considered a factor conditioning the meaning of the early analysis. The practical morality of the times may have been more in accord with later liberal developments than a mere reading of the old theological texts would suggest. Probably the chief economic result of the prohibition was to restrain conscientious Christians from entering the small-loan market and to stimulate a greater use of risk-sharing investments than might otherwise have occurred.

Part Two

CRITICISM AND REVISION OF THE USURY THEORY,
1450–1750

INTRODUCTION

In Part Two, we shall examine the modifications and revisions which the later scholastic writers made in the medieval theory of usury. The modifications result from (1) changed economic circumstances; (2) different analyses of the facts; and (3) a different attitude towards finance. These factors may not be isolated from each other, nor on the other hand resolved into each other. If economic circumstances had not altered, doubtless analysis and attitude would not have, either; but different analyses and attitudes were also necessary if the economic changes were to be given full weight in moral judgments.

Unquestionably the changed economic circumstances were the greatest factor in producing the general later modification. No code of economic morality can operate in a vacuum. In one age the opportunities for productive employment of capital may be few; in another age they may be extensive. Moralists will probably judge differently of the strength of certain justifications of profit, according to the objective differences in the use and value of money at the different times. In the sixteenth century Europe was undergoing a commercial revolution in many ways no less far-reaching in economic consequences than the Industrial Revolution of the late eighteenth and nineteenth centuries. Vastly increased commercial prosperity led naturally to modifications in theory on the nature of credit extended to commerce and on the strength and availability of the title *lucrum cessans* and the wider title *carentia pecuniae*.

By "different analyses of the facts" are meant a recognition of the legitimacy of new interest titles, such as risk; an altered view of the character of money; and a new evaluation of certain types of credit transaction. In general it may be said that each new step is the development of some principle implicit or even expressed in the medieval tradition, but never developed or applied to usury analysis proper.

By "a different attitude towards finance" is meant a far greater willingness to recognize the good intentions, honesty, and social utility of the financiers and to find moral justification for practices which are accepted without complaint by the persons most directly affected by them. If practices flourish and bring prosperity and are accepted by the common conscience, it is generally reasoned that there must be some objective foundation for the profits gained from them.

A large part of the development in theory, involving all three factors listed above, consists in the development of alternative analyses of operations which are often in practice indistinguishable from loans. Instead of treating a credit operation as an illicit loan, the majority of scholastics resolve the transaction into another, lawful contract. It may seem at first sight to the modern reader, as to the rigorist theologians of the later period, that this alternative analysis is simply a verbal trick, designed to cloak usury under another name. Such a judgment, however, can only result from a misunderstanding of the common position. The scholastics began from a positive, legal prohibition of profit on a loan; and they developed certain arguments from the natural law to show that such profit was unjust. But these natural-law arguments covered only certain cases, analyzed in a certain way. On the level of the natural law there was nothing to prevent the scholastics from developing other analyses which avoided the objections possible in theory if the cases were considered as loans. Then, as far as the Church's legislation was concerned, it was the Church's choice to let the legislation entrusted to her keeping be interpreted narrowly and strictly, so that by "usury" was meant only profit on a formal loan contract. If the legislator allows a legalistic and close interpretation of his law, it is scarcely the part of others to challenge his liberality; and in such a case, it is not discreditable for an interpreter of the law to insist that it not be extended beyond the cases it formally proscribes. The teaching of St. Antoninus was that every act which had in practice the substantial effect of a loan at a profit was to be considered condemned by the usury prohibition. The doctrine of Gerson was that every act, which could analytically be reduced to a form other than a loan, and which was not intended with the positive will of doing injustice, was not to be ruled by the prohibition. The Church, guardian and interpreter of the divine law, did not reject the Gersonian doctrine as applied to the usury rule. Hence, neither from the natural law nor from the Church was there objection to the new approaches to credit operations; and the scholastics favoring them did so without hypocrisy.

The terms of the dialogue on usury have to be kept in mind. The scholastics wrote within a formal framework. Within it certain transactions, formally analyzed, were condemned; other transactions, having the same effects, were accepted. A modern reader wonders why the bonds of formalism were not broken. But the wonder is anachronistic; the mind of the age liked this formalism. In secular law the same preference for change through the medium of devices, the same preference for preservation of the shell while the substance is replaced, may be observed. Even today, how many "legal fictions" are necessary to effect orderly change within any legal tradition that purports to be merely the unfolding of precedent? Moreover, the degree of scholastic formalism should not be exaggerated. The scholastics' analysis, it is true, is highly formal. But their attitude toward practice is increasingly plastic. As the chapter on implicit contracts and implicit intention will make clear, it was not necessary for a creditor to use a prescribed formula to escape the usury prohibition. The later scholastics became more and more inclined to justify his act of credit extension if it could be analytically reduced to a nonloan transaction whatever the form actually employed. This highly pragmatic tendency does not prevail in the scholastic approach to every business situation, but it becomes common in regard to some of the most typical forms of credit.

The development and revision of theory by the later scholastics occur at the point where the pressure for consistency in the usury theory is becoming acute. A rigorously logical development of the postulates of St. Antoninus would have meant general condemnation of credit extensions. Yet the later writers cannot bear the piecemeal theory and illogical exceptions that made the early teaching tolerable. In moving towards a unified but practicable theory, they work towards one in which some postulates of the past must be rejected, and in which usury will be treated as the exception to a general rule of the lawfulness of profit in credit transactions. It would be a mistake to see this development as a surrender to expediency. It would be rash to suppose that the moral fervor of a Cardinal Lugo is less than that of a Cardinal Courçon, that the saintly zeal of St. Alphonsus is inferior to that of St. Raymond.

CHAPTER X

THE TRIPLE CONTRACT

From the viewpoint of pure theory, perhaps the most momentous of all modifications of the scholastic position occurred through the later scholastics' acceptance of the application of insurance to the contract of *societas*. This application struck at the one practical test of usury — the criterion of the incidence of risk. At the same time it led indirectly to a clear abandonment of the thesis of the sterility of money. Thus toppled two great pillars of the usury theory, the doctrines that an investor must run a risk to make a profit and that money must be considered as unfruitful. To be sure, neither doctrine had been upheld consistently in judging all economic areas in the Middle Ages, but each had been maintained strenuously in connection with the usury rule. In the triple contract each was rejected in relation to usury analysis proper, and the usury theory was seriously altered.

Nor was the change momentous from the viewpoint of theory alone. The practical importance of the admission of the triple contract was immense. It opened the way for legitimizing nearly all transactions involving the extension of commercial credit. It made licit the financing of business by bonds as well as by stocks. It removed one important field of credit from the stern surveillance of the usury prohibition. The acceptance of the contract may be taken as evidence of the force of practice upon theory; for the part that business usage had in compelling its acceptance cannot be overlooked.

A necessary introduction to this matter, which turns so largely on the morality of insurance, must be a brief survey of doctrinal opinion in the Middle Ages on property insurance.

1. *Early Opinion on Insurance and Guarantee*

Property insurance was not a contract used by the Roman law, and the early Middle Ages were similarly unfamiliar with it. Insurance first developed in the fourteenth century in Mediterranean ports as the best means of securing risks in maritime commerce; by the end of the century the idea of property insurance, in which an owner for a fee transferred the risks of his property to an insurer, had become familiar to all the commercial cities of Italy.[1] In the early fourteenth century, the great civilian Baldus defends the contract. Only in 1403, however, is judgment ventured upon its lawfulness by a leading moralist. Then, Laurentius de Ridolfis, citing Baldus, says that it is licit to sell risk. *Naviganti*, he declares, is no objection, for that deals with a sale of risk associated with profit on a loan. In the normal insurance contract no loan exists, but in the contractual formula of the Roman law — "I give that you may give" — a burden is assumed and a compensation is given for its assumption.[2]

St. Bernardine similarly rejects the possible objection based on *Naviganti*, for no loan exists. Maritime insurance is the hire of the insurer's services. The contract is beneficial to the community. St. Antoninus also defends insurance as the rendering of service for a price.[3]

Thus, without any important opposition whatsoever, the insurance of property was accepted by the theologians. Only one obscure late fifteenth-century writer seems to have sensed the peril the acceptance of insurance held for the usury theory. This is John Consobrinus, who, in the short treatise, *De justitia commutativa*, published in 1494, forthrightly attacked marine insurance as usurious. He says:

This contract is usurious on both sides, because each one intends to place himself in gain and the other in loss. . . . [Also] he [the insurer] sells for 50 pounds, what is not his own, nor can be, because it is of God alone to preserve the ship. Therefore, he does a great injustice to God. . . . Whence briefly I say that every lucrative contract which does not depend on a man's industry or diligence or on his own property is illicit and usurious. . . . It is indeed licit to a man to expose his things at his own peril, but not at the peril of another: because never does the risk pass to some other person, except in those things in which passes the ownership.[4]

Here is a very explicit statement of the theory of the identity of risk and ownership, which the scholastics had made essential to the application of the usury prohibition; and, despite the naïve confusion of Consobrinus' other arguments, which patently mistake the insurer's function, it must be confessed that Consobrinus, better than any famous authority, grasped what the theological approval of insurance would do to the usury theory. But he was not an influential writer; his words had no echoes; and the common

[1] Sayous, "L'histoire universelle de droit," p. 315.
[2] Laurentius de Ridolfis, *De usuris*, 3:8.
[3] St. Bernardine, *De contractibus*, 39:1:3;
St. Antoninus, *Summa*, 2:1:7.
[4] John Consobrinus, *De justitia commutativa* (Paris, 1494), Part II, c.6.

opinion at the end of the fifteenth century stood clearly for the licitness of property insurance. Indeed, the only real reason for rejecting it would have been to save a portion of the speculative reasoning behind the usury theory, to condemn a just contract for the sake of a debatable theory. Consobrinus alone proposed to treat matters from this viewpoint.

If a charge for insurance was lawful, what about a charge for the guaranteeing of a loan? Guarantors, of course, were frequently used on loans, and their right to damages had long been recognized. In 1400 Laurentius de Ridolfis had proposed for the first time the right of a guarantor to charge a flat 2 per cent for his services. He granted that the guarantor made a virtual loan to the debtor in paying the debt for him and that the debtor remained obliged to repay him. But he claimed that the charge was not for the loan proper, but for "the sale of the guarantor's credit"; and he added that to conserve one's credit is a costly business. At the same time, defending the contract in principle, he advised all to abstain from it.[5]

St. Bernardine indignantly repudiated the contract of guarantee at 2 per cent. It was to him a clear attempt to profit from a loan. St. Antoninus said the contract was commonly a simple fiction, in which the guarantor and the original lender were identical, so that the lender collected usury in the form of the fee for the guarantee. Moreover, even if the lender and the guarantor were distinct, a fee was usurious, for it was the price of credit, which is the same as the price of a loan.[6]

It is against this background of acceptance of insurance and rejection of guarantee that the controversy over the triple contract occurs. Possibly for this reason the terms *assecurare* or *assecuratio*, the words for insurance, are the standard ones used in a situation where modern business usage would speak of "guaranteeing."

2. *The First Application of Insurance to the* Societas

No one up to 1485 had related insurance to investment contracts in such a way that the effect upon the usury theory was evident. In that year appeared the *Summa angelica de casibus conscientiae*, a work destined to be of great popularity, written by Angelus Carletus de Clavasio, vicar-general of the Franciscans of the Observance. Angelus discusses the investment in a partnership, in which St. Thomas and every scholastic writer after him had used the incidence of risk to distinguish a usurious loan from a true partnership. Angelus, too, says that it is usury if you put your money in a

---

[5] Laurentius de Ridolfis, 3:3 (n.9).
[6] St. Bernardine, 39:1:3; St. Antoninus, 2:1:7, citing Laurentius and Francis of Empoli.

partnership, your capital is guaranteed by your partner, and he pays you an additional reward at his discretion. But Angelus adds that you could insure your capital with a third party and still licitly take your profit from the partnership. Then, he continues quietly,

And the same may be said, when the partner receiving that capital agrees freely with the partner giving the capital about returning him a small part of the profit which reasonably some other one would thus make; so that, if the one giving the capital foregoes the whole profit which otherwise he ought to have from such a partnership, the other insures him on the principal, and even if there is no profit, will pay the insurance. For example, a businessman is of such a reputation that he finds insurance by paying 3 per cent or 4 per cent, and as commonly for profit of the partnership he would have received 6 per cent or 8 per cent and sometimes more, so he agrees with his partner that his partner give him only 3 per cent or 4 per cent as profit and insure him on the capital.

Money normally stands in a partnership at the peril of the investor, Angelus concludes, but the risk may be transferred at a just price.[7]

Of course, Angelus' assumption that the case was already decided was not to remain undisturbed. Since the insured partnership at 4 per cent was virtually indistinguishable in practice from a loan at usury of 4 per cent, a great debate was to take place over the admission of the contract. But the debate was chiefly between the authority of the dead medieval writers who condemned a riskless partnership and the ingenuity of the living later writers who defended it; and in this debate two theses, questioned by neither the dead opponents nor the modern defenders, decided the outcome in advance. The first of these theses was that the insurance contract was licit in itself and might be made without an owner losing title to his property. The second was that profit on investment in a partnership was not purely a reward for risk. By the first thesis it was admitted that ownership and risk were not necessarily identical and that normally an owner could transfer his risk and still benefit from his property. At the same time, in the second thesis, the early scholastic inconsistencies on the reward due to money suddenly constituted a practical danger for the usury theory by the collapse of the risk criterion. As we have seen, the early scholastics had unanimously maintained that the capitalist's reward in a partnership came as fruit from the use of his money, and that responsibility for risk was not his title to payment, but simply evidence of his ownership. When the risk criterion disappeared, it became evident that in the partnership money was treated as fruitful, and the old theory was unable to deny that this might be done.

[7] Angelus Carletus de Clavasio, *Summa angelica*, *Societas*, n.7.

In short, the medieval tradition against which the defenders of the triple contract had most to contend had already conceded, though not in relation to the particular contract they fought for, the main premises of the defense. There were, to be sure, new attacks on the contract on new grounds, some of which were serious. But most of the prominent scholastics after 1485 were in favor of the contract, and their great opponent was the medieval theory, which had in fact delivered itself into their hands.

With the premises of the defense understood, and with the great theoretical and practical importance of the acceptance of the contract in mind, we may now review systematically the writings of the more prominent later scholastics upon it.

3. Adoption by the Tübingen School and Popularization

Strong support for the new approach came from the newly founded University of Tübingen. The university at the time must have been almost as much a center of liberal economics as centuries later it was to be a center of liberal theology. In 1484 it had as professor of philosophy Gabriel Biel, who established a reputation in economics by a treatise on currency devaluation in the tradition of Oresme and an extended discussion of credit contracts in his commentary on the *Sentences*.[8] The tradition he began was continued by his pupil, Conrad Summenhart, the author in 1499 of a landmark in usury theory, the *Tractatus de contractibus licitis atque illicitis*. This work is one of the most learned, certainly the most extensive, and in many ways the most acute treatment of the usury question up to this time. Friendly to economic enterprise, its opposition to what had been considered usury is hardly more than verbal. In the skilled hands of Biel and Conrad, powerful support was to be furnished for an analysis as helpful to business as the triple contract.

Biel in the *Sentences* commits himself to Angelus de Clavasio's teaching without discussion.[9] Conrad develops these embryonic ideas to their full measure. The great objection to the insured partnership is the objection of all the old scholastics to partnerships where the capital is "safe": a guarantee of the capital breaks the *ius fraternitatis* and destroys the nature of the partnership, making it a loan. Conrad answers this objection by a highly abstract analysis of what is meant by "the nature" of a contract. "Nature," he says, can mean either substance itself, or simply what is concomitant to

---

[8] Gabriel Biel, *Tractatus de potestate et utilitate monetarum*, trans. R. B. Burke (Philadelphia, 1930); Biel, *Collectorium super IV*   [9] Biel, *Collectorium*, IV:15KK:Q.11KK. *libros sententiarum* (s.d.).

substance. In the first sense it is man's nature to be rational. In the second sense, part of man's nature is the capacity to laugh. If we take "nature" in the first sense, then the objection means that insurance destroys the essence of a partnership contract. But this contention is not valid, because the original assumption of risk by the capitalist does not constitute the essence of the partnership. The partnership is essentially constituted by the association of funds and skill for a common purpose. Similarly, the assumption of risk by a borrower is not the essence of a loan; a loan consists essentially in the borrower's acquisition of the loaned property. Nor is the essence of a sale the assumption of the risk of the merchandise by the buyer; a sale consists essentially in the buyer's acquisition of the goods sold. In short, Summenhart rejects entirely the old premise that the assumption of risk is part of the essence of ownership. It is only in the second sense of nature, he says, that risk is natural to ownership and that it is natural for a partner to run the risk of his investment. If the objector to the secured partnership contends that insurance is against the nature of the partnership in the second sense, he will not deny it. But although a normal concomitant of partnership is taken away by insurance, the substance of the partnership remains intact. For the fraternity required by a partnership, he continues, returning to the Roman law, a sharing in the profit suffices. Further, he argues, if a true sharing in the capital were a necessary condition for partnership, at the end of every partnership the capital would be divided equally among the partners; but no one claims that this is necessary.

The objection is then made that the guaranteed partnership is indistinguishable from a loan. Conrad grants that the act by which the capitalist invests money with his partner is similar in both cases. But, following in the Gersonian tradition, he appeals to the capitalist's intention. In a loan the lender intends to transfer his money abdicatively, conferring its ownership on the borrower. In the partnership, the capitalist transfers his money "communicatively, making B [the partner] his co-owner." Like Gerson, Conrad holds that a good intention and a contractual formula different from that of a *mutuum* is a sufficient defense from usury. He concludes that a substantial and essential partnership exists in the contract under examination; there is no loan because a loan was not intended; and the addition of insurance does not destroy the essence of the partnership which was intended. The capitalist might insure his money elsewhere. It does not destroy the justice of the contract, if he insures his money with his partner. The guaranteed partnership is not unjust.[10]

[10] Conrad Summenhart, Tractatus de contractibus, Q.97.

While he defends so vigorously the justice of the contract and so may be considered a believer in its essential lawfulness, Conrad holds that at the present time its use is sinful. Such use is against charity. Although the intention of the investor is not to make a usurious loan, his intention is not clear to other men, who only observe "that in all things the form is that in which a loan is made." This scandalizes the investor's neighbors, who are also tempted to commit usury, and it defames the investor himself. Thus, it is against the duties of both love of neighbor and love of self. Secondly, prudence dictates that the contract be not allowed; for if it were allowed, "the door would be open to all usurers." Everyone, instead of lending at usury, would say, "I will not lend it to you, but I will give to you in a partnership, so, however, that the peril of the whole of this money be yours, and you will give me a part of the profit if it comes."[11]

It is plain that Conrad's objections would be of weight only as long as the public conscience believed profit on riskless business investments was usury; and perhaps even in his own day, not many merchants entertained this suspicion. A prudent innovator, he does not personally declare the contract at the moment lawful, but makes its legitimacy only await a popular acceptance which probably already existed.

What he did not attempt personally, his pupil, John Eck, did. Eck had become lecturer in theology at the University of Ingolstadt outside of Augsburg, a city with a particularly intense interest in finding licit means for safe investment.[12] Augsburg at the time was the leading financial city of Germany, and stimulated by the prosperity of a boom in minerals, was threatening Florence for the financial leadership of Europe. Of her many commercial and banking houses the most prominent was that of the Fuggers, who had already captured the papal banking business from Florence.[13]

In 1514, the twenty-eight-year-old Eck, criticizing the theologians for keeping back the truth on the partnership contract from the people, boldly taught at the university that the guaranteed contract was licit. The merchants were jubilant. The learned were dismayed at the publicity. The bishop forbade any further public discussion. Eck was insulted by many as a scandalmonger. The theological faculty of Mainz, consulted on the matter, replied, however, that the question was an open one.[14]

In July 1515, blessed by the papal nuncio and partially financed by his

[11] *Ibid.*, Q.97, *contra primum modum*, p. 538.

[12] J. Schneid, "Dr. Johann Eck und das Kirchliche Zinsverbot," *Historisch-politische Blätter für das Katholische Deutschland,* CVIII (1891), 574.

[13] See J. Strieder, *Jacob Fugger: The Rich Banker and Merchant of Augsburg,* trans. M. Hartsough (New York, 1931), pp. 31, 50.

[14] Schneid, pp. 660, 662.

friends the Fuggers, Eck set out to defend his thesis at the center of canonist learning, Bologna. He disputed for five hours before the full university and was generally favored by the jurists. The humanists at Nurenberg, avowed enemies of Augsburg and scholasticism, at once spread the rumor that Eck had defended usury at Bologna.[15] In 1520 with the outbreak of the Reformation, Eck found a different task and his greatest claim to eminence in his disputations with Luther. Nonetheless, despite his short connection with the triple contract and the lack of any definitive outcome to his efforts in its behalf, Eck is of great importance to the history of usury, for he made the triple contract known both to all the learned world of Europe and to the merchant bankers of his time.

Eck's theses, which excited such interest and which were the first public defense of the guaranteed partnership not in a work intended simply for confessors or the learned, are contained in an unpublished *Tractatus de contractu quinque de centum*, which he must have written in 1515, shortly before his expedition to Bologna. He defends the contract under the name of the "5 per cent contract" — the popular term for it in Germany taken from the fact that the net return to the capitalist partner was currently 5 per cent. At the same time he is the first author to describe the transaction as involving three contracts instead of two: the original contract of partnership; a second contract of insurance of the principal, in which insurance is given in return for an assignment of the future probable gain from the partnership; and a third contract by which an uncertain future gain is sold for a lesser certain gain.[16] The third contract, which is essentially a guarantee of a fixed interest return, had not been specifically considered in the discussions of de Clavasio and Summenhart, and there is a clear step forward here in making the contracts even closed to a stable loan. The triple contract becomes the standard form of the operation, and *"contractus trinus"* becomes its standard theological description.

In his defense of the contract Eck uses all the arguments of Summenhart in its favor, explicitly denying the old scholastic axiom "the good perishes to the owner." The 5 per cent is justly paid for "the advantage of the money," always understood, of course, that such a profit can only be made on money in the form of a partnership and not in the form of a loan. If money is

---

[15] Schneid, pp. 670, 676, 789. Eck was reported to have been bribed by the Fuggers. Schneid dismisses this rumor, circulated by enemies, as unsubstantiated and as inconsistent with Eck's known character. It is certain, however, that the Fuggers helped him with material aid on his trip to Bologna. See Schneid, p. 668.

[16] John Eck, *Tractatus de contractu quinque de centum* (1515, University Library of Munich, Codex, ms. No. 125), Arg. 1–4, f.241–f.250.

unfruitful, how does the capitalist profit in a regular partnership without labor and out of proportion to his risk? Industry associated with money is productive, Eck answers, and the capitalist who gives "the commodity of his capital" is entitled to his share.[17] This is an argument, it should be noted, not directly used by de Clavasio and Summenhart, although both assume it as a prerequisite for their case.

Eck also asserts that while a loan is regularly unproductive in further wealth to the borrower, the transaction he defends is highly profitable to the working partner. In fact, he declares, it is the merchants who have invented the contract in order to be free from the interference and suspicions of investors, not the investors who have desired this as a way of exploiting their merchant partners. There can be no question of usurious intention on the part of the capitalist where the merchant-partner himself solicits the arrangement.[18] The objection is brought forward that the riches gained by the merchants are not sufficient to justify the return, that, in truth, they are hurt by their obligation to make the return. Eck replies confidently that this is not true of the prosperous merchants of Augsburg, whose riches are celebrated.[19]

Against Conrad's prudential restrictions, Eck declares that, while a simple man may not be able to distinguish the 5 per cent from usury, the merchants and investors who customarily make such contracts are well able to do so. As for the neighbors, they should presume the contract licit until the opposite is proved; any scandal would be pharisaical. There is no danger of defaming one's own character, for the contract is generally in use. Moreover, Eck adds the interesting information that it has been in use for forty years, and no one has ever been refused the sacraments for using it. There is no danger of open usury resulting from its acceptance, if it is confined to the merchants, as it is in Augsburg. There is more danger of usury, Eck adds sharply, in the *census* than in the 5 per cent contract.[20]

As to qualifications with which he would safeguard its use, he insists that (1) it be done only with a merchant, for an actual business purpose; (2) the investor have the intention not of lending or of profiting on a loan, but of entering a lawful and true partnership; (3) the merchant agree to the insurance clauses perfectly freely; (4) a just price be paid for the insurance. If the last provision is violated, he adds, it will be a case of injustice, but not of usury. At the present, 5 per cent seems a reasonable return to the

[17] Arg. 6, f.253v.
[18] Arg. 7, f.256r.
[19] Arg. 11, f.261v.
[20] Arg. 11, f.262v, 263v. The recurrent de-

fense of capitalistic investors is raised: widows and orphans are the chief beneficiaries of the contract; Arg. 10, f.261r.

investor, leaving enough in the way of compensation to the merchant for his insurance services.[21]

There was an immediate reaction to Eck's theses in theological circles. The faculty of theology at Paris, asked for its opinion, was, for unspecified reasons, silent. But its dean, the Scottish theologian John Major, offered an unhesitating assent to the arguments of Eck and Summenhart. He added only that it was not advisable to preach on the contract to merchants.[22]

Even more important, however, was the opinion sought from Thomas de Vio, Cardinal Cajetan. Cajetan was a man of enormous ability, prestige, and power. Elected general of the Dominican order in 1508 and created a cardinal in 1517, he was one of the chief champions of the papacy in the troubled years of the beginning of Lutheranism.[23] Considered by many to have been the ablest Thomistic philosopher since St. Thomas, he treats of economic morals with the astuteness, care, and subtlety that distinguished him in metaphysics. Not infected by Conrad's basic skepticism towards the usury rule, he is a loyal Thomist here as elsewhere. But as St. Thomas adapted Aristotle, so he adapts St. Thomas, and his own views, large and liberal for his age, use the original Thomistic teaching only as a starting point.

His opinion on the triple contract in particular was solicited in 1514 by an abbot of Ulmer, Conrad Koellin, who was disturbed by Eck's preaching.[24] Answering the request, Cajetan concentrated chiefly on the price of the insurance contracts. He seriously doubted that any ordinary insurer would undertake to insure capital and a 5 per cent gain simply for an assignment of future probable profits beyond the 5 per cent; and he said that "the most wealthy merchants themselves" confirmed this suspicion that no one normally would offer insurance and be content with the assignment of a mere hope as payment for their risk and obligations. Furthermore, Cajetan said, any explicit contract taking away the equality of risk in a partnership made it, in the scholastic jargon, leonine, or so inequitable as to be unlawful.[25]

Nonetheless, as is clear even from his concentration on the insurance price, Cajetan's opposition to the contract is not intransigent. The contract is not to be introduced, he continues, because it would open the way to the cloaking of usury. But where the custom of using it prevails, he will tolerate

[21] Arg. 9, f.260r; Schneid, pp. 482, 483, 487.

[22] John Major, In quatuor sententiarum quaestiones (Paris, 1514), Dist. 15, Q.49.

[23] D.t.c., II, cols. 1313–1320.

[24] Schneid, p. 660.

[25] Cajetan, De societate negotiatoria, in Scripta philosophica, ed. P. Zammit (Rome, 1934), n.425, n.428, n.430.

it. It is preferable to loans at manifest usury.[26] Moreover, if the second and third contracts are entered into separately and independently from the partnership contract, and with the aim only of freeing the investor from care and fear of fraud, they are entirely licit. The real danger is that the contracts be entered into with every person promiscuously, and in every case 5 per cent be said to be the proper return. The proper return and the just price of the insurance should vary with the situation, the business, and the person. Experience shows many sins arise from indifference to the due circumstances of this contract.[27]

In this last revision of his opinion at the close of his letter, Cajetan seems close to saying that the triple contract is licit in itself and is vitiated only by particular abuses. Certainly in saying that it can be tolerated he indicates that he does not think it unmistakably usurious. His opposition is of a very weak and hesitant character. It is particularly noteworthy that he challenges neither the notion of riskless ownership of an investment, nor the fertility imputed to money in the partnership. With prudential reservations he is on the side of the contract.

Thus with no real opposition by the leading theologians of the early sixteenth century, the triple contract was proposed and popularized. But its conflict with some of the earlier scholastic assumptions led to doubts and scruples among men inclined to a strict adhesion to early theory. The practical character of these doubts is well illustrated by the history of the 5 per cent controversy.

4. *The Jesuits and the 5 Per Cent Contract* [28]

In 1560, forty years after Eck's bold defense of the triple contract, the Society of Jesus, a new, vigorous, and reforming order, arrived in Augsburg under the leadership of St. Peter Canisius. The Jesuits were at once appalled by the corruption of the other clergy, secular and religious, and by the im-

---

[26] n.432.

[27] n.433, n.434.

[28] The material on which the following account is based is contained almost entirely in St. Peter Canisius, *Epistolae et acta*, ed. O. Braunsberger (Freiburg in Br., 1896–1922). The material has been used by B. Duhr, "Die Deutschen Jesuiten in 5% Streit des 16 Jahrhunderts," *Zeitschrift für Katholische Theologie* (1900), and by Cardinal Van Roey, "Le Contractus Germanicus," *Revue d'histoire ecclésiastique*, III (1903).

Unfortunately, "the 5 per cent contract"
is not, strictly speaking, identical with the triple contract. The triple contract is only one contract into which it was suggested the 5 per cent contract could be resolved, or by which it could be replaced. Later we will have to discuss other contracts also debated in connection with the 5 per cent contract. Here we shall give the main steps in the dispute over the 5 per cent in general, and in particular all matters in connection with it which throw light on the triple contract and the latter's ethical and practical significance.

morality and ignorance of the townsfolk.[29] In particular, they were struck by the general and open practice of usury in the form of loans at 5 per cent. Canisius preached zealously against those taking the 5 per cent and refused to absolve them in confession.[30] The Secretary-General of the Jesuits wrote to Canisius in 1561 that since many citizens of Augsburg were alienated from the Jesuits by their teaching on usury, it would be better to treat no contract in particular, until a firm general basis of morality had been reëstablished among the people.[31] In 1564 the chapter of Augsburg cathedral protested Peter Canisius' refusal to absolve those taking the 5 per cent, and he replied, "Real usury is here openly committed . . . whatever objections are made by certain men skilled in law, who think many things of this kind are to be dissimulated according to the prudence of this world but against the common and received opinion of the old and new theologians and canonists." [32]

In April 1565, Ursula Fugger, wife of the richest banker in Europe and a recent convert to the Church, wrote Francis Borgia, Secretary-General of the Jesuits, asking his counsel "about the usurious contracts in which our family is not a little entangled." Borgia replied that some of the contracts probably could be deservedly excused, and that Canisius would explain in detail.[33] Two years later, on June 7, 1567, Borgia wrote Canisius that Pope Pius V had been consulted by the Jesuits on the triple contract bringing a 5 per cent return, and that the Pope, speaking as a private theologian, had declared this licit. The Pope's approval was not to be publicized, lest it encourage avarice.[34] This is the first official mention of the triple contract as a way of solving the difficulties caused by the 5 per cent contract, currently referred to as "the German contract."

In 1568, after reports of new scruples and difficulties, Borgia again declared that the Jesuits might recommend the triple contract, but only after attempting to persuade their penitents not to take the 5 per cent.[35] In October 1568, Octavian Fugger, a Jesuit novice at Rome, wrote that the Jesuits again were taking up the 5 per cent contract with the Pope.[36] In late 1568 and early 1569 a commission of Roman Jesuits reëxamined the 5 per cent question.[37] Canisius twice wrote to Rome to get their decision, but apparently received no answer.[38] In May 1569, Borgia wrote to Hoffaeus, the new Jesuit provincial in Augsburg, that the long delay in any conclusion

[29] James Broderick, *St. Peter Canisius* (London, 1935), p. 585.

[30] St. Peter Canisius, *Epistolae*, II, 855; III, 646; IV, 543, 849.

[31] II, 763.

[32] IV, 563.

[33] V, 533–534.

[34] V, 486–487.

[35] V, 529–530.

[36] VI, 205.

[37] VI, 235.

[38] VI, 287.

by this commission reflected the great uncertainty at Rome on the matter.[39] In October 1569, John Fugger set out for Rome to propose his doubts upon his business.[40] On March 18, 1570, Borgia wrote to Hoffaeus that the commission approved the 5 per cent contract with the merchants.[41] But a little later, in April, Canisius complained to Hoffaeus, "What about the contracts and commerce of the Fuggers? I wonder that nothing is proposed, nothing is decided at Rome, and this seems to me to happen by a singular fraud of Satan."[42] In the same month Borgia wrote that a new investigation was intended. On June 17, 1570, he advised Hoffaeus that the Pope allowed the 5 per cent if it were made by widows and wards who had no other means of support. The logic behind this permission is not given.[43]

In June 1571, Hoffaeus forwarded to Borgia the arguments of the Fuggers' lawyer for the licitness of the 5 per cent and hoped for a good answer. Borgia replied that the Pope had assigned the matter to the Jesuit Toletus, who knew the German Jesuits' feelings. In July 1571, Menginus, another Jesuit in Germany, wrote the Jesuit procurator, pleading for advice on the 5 per cent contract and declaring that "other religious concede it, turning the whole populace from us."[44] Canisius, writing the vicar-general of the Society in 1572, hoped for some certain decision and declared that other confessors absolve all who use the contract.[45] In November 1572, the University of Ingolstadt was reported to hold the contract usurious.[46]

On June 22, 1573, the second Roman commission, of which Toletus was the most active member, and which for three years had been said to be studying the matter, gave its report; and on receiving it, a congregation of Roman Jesuits adopted an important series of resolutions. A simple loan at 5 per cent was illicit. A number of alternative contracts and titles to interest were licit. Among these was the triple contract.[47] This approval is the first decisive evidence of crystallization of official Jesuit thought in favor of the contract.

The decision did not decide matters in Germany. In September, Theodoric Canisius, Rector of Dillingen, wrote Edward Mercurian, the new General, saying that the Roman decisions presented great danger in practice. In January 1574, he complained that Hoffaeus was forcing the Jesuit confessors to excuse all their penitents from the restitution of usury.[48] In May, Hoffaeus

[39] VI, 369.
[40] VI, 391.
[41] VI, 403.
[42] VI, 416.
[43] VI, 410.
[44] IV, 416.
[45] VII, 10.
[46] VII, 91.
[47] VII, 672. Here the text of the Congregation's decisions is given.
[48] VII, 157.

reported that his theologians still hesitated about "what was resolved at Rome with such great labor and so many witnesses about the 5 per cent." [49]

In 1575, Egolphus, Bishop of Augsburg, encouraged by the rigorist Jesuits, decreed that no one taking the 5 per cent should receive absolution. This edict was an egregious error. He was deluged by protests that the contract was everywhere in use, and that his decree could not be enforced. Faced with revolt, he was compelled to say that he had not meant to condemn the common contracts, and the anti-usury forces suffered a severe loss of prestige. [50]

In January 1576, Maynard, the new Bishop of Augsburg, imprisoned two priests, former pupils of the Jesuits, who would not absolve those taking the 5 per cent. Theodoric Canisius, who reported this incident to Mercurian, declared that the Bishop is "too ignorant to know that the contract is openly usurious." The Bishop gave as his reason only that if it is forbidden a great disturbance would follow in the State. Theodoric noted that the 5 per cent contract was not so old that Catholics could not remember more virtuous times. As for the triple contract, Theodoric said, "It is so subtle, that by our Germans, even the more prudent ones, it is ridiculed; and they say in this way we wish to open a door to all usuries, not 5 per cent but much more." [51]

In February 1576, Rosephius, S.J., reported to Mercurian that the Bishop now said:

If the Pope sent me his *Motu proprio* and ordered this contract to be abolished, I would not in the least do it, but first I would send my information to Rome, which I know His Holiness would sufficiently approve.

The Bishop also mentioned that the Germans

do not wish to hear about an implicit contract of partnership and similar things, for they are easily suspicious, so that they always fear for themselves where there are so many clauses, etc. [52]

After these complaints from his subordinates in Augsburg, Mercurian consulted the Pope, who ordered the Jesuits not to absolve the 5 per cent takers, but left the Bishop unchecked, except for a warning not to discriminate against the Jesuits because of their views. [53]

[49] VII, 158.
[50] F. Zech, *Dissertationes tres in quibus rigor moderatus . . . D. N. Benedicti XIV . . . exhibetur*, III:2:8, 253–255, in H. Leotardo, *Liber singularis de usuris* (Venice, 1762). Cf. Migne, *Theologiae cursus completus* (Paris, 1841), XVI, cols. 995 and 1007,

where the writings of Barth and Biner, Zech's two collaborators, are distinguished. All references are to the Venice edition.
[51] St. Peter Canisius, VII, 342.
[52] VII, 342.
[53] VII, 343.

In May, Theobald Stoz, S.J., reported to Mercurian a conversation with "a powerful noble" in Germany, who said that 5 per cent was no sin and advised the Jesuits not to mix in politics. When Stoz suggested the triple contract to him, he replied: "It is not necessary to use tricks by which we seem to wish to deceive God." [54] Hoffaeus in April again reported that everybody else was absolving the takers of the 5 per cent, and that the Jesuits by their stubbornness were in danger of losing all their penitents.

In 1580 the theological faculty of Ingolstadt advised Duke William of Bavaria that the 5 per cent contract was illicit, but later in the same year it said that the German contract could probably be resolved into the triple contract, which was probably licit. In October, however, Hoffaeus reported to Rome that Peter Canisius and Caspar Heywood, S.J., were attempting to persuade Duke William to issue an edict against the 5 per cent; he asked for their removal.[55] Hoffaeus then enjoined silence on the subject on Heywood, who appealed to Rome.[56] The Duke also wrote to Rome asking for a decision. The Pope transmitted his and Heywood's questions to the General Congregation of the Jesuits then meeting in Rome,[57] and in April 1581, this Congregation gave its reply. Its decisions are a milestone in the history of usury theory, for, though in most cases identical with those of the 1573 Congregation, they obtained an acceptance which the earlier decisions had not obtained. We shall refer to it often for its opinion on other contracts. On the points under discussion now, it substantially affirmed the teaching of the 1573 Congregation: a simple 5 per cent loan was usury, but the triple contract was permissible.[58]

On the basis of this decision, the Pope advised Duke William that the straight 5 per cent contract, indiscriminately used, was illicit, but he strongly hinted that other contracts would be found to justify the taking of 5 per cent in practice.[59] The Duke eventually, on the advice of the Jesuit, Gregory of Valentia, allowed the triple contract in his domain.[60]

The subsequent history of the dispute over the 5 per cent belongs to the history of the *census* contract and will be discussed later. As far as the triple contract is concerned, the affirmation of the 1581 Congregation was decisive. From then on a majority of moralists were on its side. After almost thirty years of experiment and uncertainty in a principal banking city of Europe, the Jesuits had become wholly committed to the defense of the contract, and henceforth, were its advocates.

[54] VII, 574.
[55] VII, 574–575.
[56] VII, 578, 584.
[57] VII, 590.

[58] Zech, III:2:8:258–263.
[59] Canisius, VII, 590.
[60] Zech, III:2:8:270.

The history of the controversy well indicates the difficulty in accepting the triple contract experienced by men committed to the medieval scholastics' traditional theory on money and ownership, and the powerful forces of practical life urging the acceptance of the contract as a means of avoiding a condemnation of all business activity. Still, the known integrity and religious zeal of such defenders of the contract as St. Francis Borgia and St. Pius V are sufficient evidence that the final acceptance was based on the mature conviction that the contract was not unjust, and that theory had best accommodate itself to moral and economic realities.[61]

5. *The Spanish Theologians*

The history of the triple contract is now enlivened by the personal clash of two great theologians, each of them an expert on usury theory. In the late sixteenth century, the age of Spanish power, it is scarcely coincidental that both were Spanish. One was Dominic Soto (1495–1560), a Dominican professor at Salamanca, Spain's leading university. The other was Martin Azplicueta, called Navarrus (1493–1586), a canonist and sometime professor at Toulouse, Cahors, Salamanca, and the Portuguese University of Coimbra. Each was the friend and consultant of the rulers of Catholic Europe. Soto was consultor and imperial representative at the Council of Trent, confessor and counselor of the Emperor Charles V.[62] Navarrus was counselor to the King of Portugal, then to Philip II of Spain. He concluded his career

---

[61] The Jansenists later accused the Jesuits of laxity in their economic morals; Pascal has made their charges famous (B. Pascal, *Les lettres provinciales*, ed. H. F. Stewart, Manchester, 1920, Letter 8); and a modern historian has seen fit to repeat them (H. M. Robertson, *Aspects of the Rise of Economic Individualism*, Cambridge, 1933, pp. 137–159). J. Broderick has demonstrated the unreliability of the Jansenist diatribes on which a good part of Robertson's work is based. Cf. J. Broderick, *The Economic Morals of the Jesuits* (London, 1934). The history related here may seem to confirm these charges. In fairness, therefore, it should be recalled that the triple contract had already been theoretically defended by Franciscan, Dominican, and secular theologians; it is not a Jesuit invention. Also, every other contract or title approved by the Jesuit Congregations had been approved by distinguished moral theologians of other orders. Further, although all Jesuit theologians will henceforth defend the con-

tracts approved by the Congregations, they will do so on grounds which seem reasonable to them and which are not always the grounds suggested by the Congregations, but far sounder interest titles. Moreover, in pure theory on the *census*, the great Jesuit theologians are far more conservative than the leading Dominican, Dominic Soto; so that it is not exact to suppose that the Jesuits were always more liberal than any other order. In general, it is true, the Jesuits incline to a liberal view of economic contracts, and possessing some of the most eminent moral theologians of modern times, the Jesuits' adherenece to the liberal view is generally decisive in leading to the theological acceptance of the contracts. But they were not innovators; they followed paths marked out by pious predecessors; and there is no evidence that they did not sincerely believe in the justice of the contracts they defended.

[62] *D.t.c.*, XIV, 2423–2427.

in Rome as the advisor of three succeeding Popes, Pius V, Gregory XIII and Sixtus V.[63] Soto's great treatise, *De justitia et jure*, appeared in 1553. It is the work of a man with a peculiarly personal independence of mind, boldness of judgment, and acuteness of perception. It combines a fondness for rigorous logic, leading to conservatism, with a real freshness of view. Navarrus, on the other hand, is comprehensive, moderate, and liberal. His writings on usury, most of which appeared in Spanish first and then in Latin, began in 1544; his early works were revised and new treatises appeared almost up to the end of his long life. His special opponent is Soto, for whom he seems to have had a personal dislike. His characterization of the latter's work on usury is telling: it is, he says with courteous irony, "more erudite than suited for use and practice." Apparently suspected by Soto of being too lenient on many points, he tells with wry candor how his own efforts at reform in the financial practices of the University of Salamanca were laughed to scorn by the academic council. No less than Soto, he suggests, is he against exploitation of the poor, but he approaches the matter more benignly and less doctrinairely than his rival.[64]

Treating of the triple contract, Soto asserts categorically the old scholastic principle, "he is truly the owner to whom the good perishes if it is lost." [65] Consequently, although an insurance contract and a partnership are licit separately, together they constitute a loan; for then money is temporarily transferred together with responsibility for its risk, and this necessarily constitutes a temporary transfer of ownership or, in other words, a loan. Hence, the triple contract is usurious. Soto does not explain why ownership is not transferred to an insurer in other insurance contracts, if the doctrine, "a good perishes to its owner," is axiomatic.

In his discussion of partnership proper, Soto gives himself a much more solid basis for opposing the triple contract by teaching that in the simple partnership the capitalist's return is to be calculated not in proportion to his investment, but in proportion to the risk of his money.[66] This is, of course, what the medieval scholastics should have taught, too, if they had been consistent in maintaining that money bore no fruit. Yet no authority had ever applied this axiom on money explicitly to the *societas*. Soto, in being logical, is far more rigorous than any predecessor. His opinion that the investor's reward can be due only to risk automatically disqualifies the triple contract, which presumes that the licit return on the full investment is

[63] Schulte, *Die Geschichte der Quellen*, III, 715.

[64] Navarrus, *Commentarius de usuris*, 2, n.2; 12, n.28–31.

[65] Dominic Soto, *De justitia et iure libri decem* (Lyons, 1569), Bk. VI, Q.6, art. 2.

[66] *Ibid.*, VI:6:1.

greater than the price of the risk. Yet in treating the triple contract itself, Soto does not urge this opinion as an objection. Possibly he assumes that it is unnecessary to repeat it. But it is clear that he places his chief reliance, not on his new theory on partnership returns, but on the standard medieval teaching that a partnership plus transfer of risk equals a loan. Here he is an uncompromising upholder of an anachronistic position.

Navarrus had already advised the King of Portugal that the triple contract was licit when Soto produced his work attacking it, and in his written work he is much concerned to refute his rival's objections. Soto's doctrine that only the risk, and not the quantity of the money invested, is compensated in a partnership is stigmatized as a "new invention," contrary to Roman law and to "the judgment of the learned." [67] As for Soto's other contention that the incidence of risk indicates the owner, this is not true in a contract of *commodatio* or *depositum*, where the keepers of the good are liable for damage to it and yet are not the owners. Again, if a third person insured the money invested in the partnership, the working partner would not be freed from his obligation to return the money to the investor, so that it is clear that here insurance does not transfer ownership; why should it, when the partner is himself the insurer? The way is not open to usury, for no loan takes place. Even if the ownership of the money invested does pass to the working partner, as its use is still restricted, the investor may profit on it.[68] In other words, Navarrus suggests, as long as a kind of control is retained, the investor has some claim to profit.

Navarrus continues his defense with some observations based on practice. In actual use, the contract usually brings 4 per cent to the investor. A partner would normally gain 12 per cent. To pay 4 per cent for the insurance of the capital, 4 per cent for the certain gain, and be left with 4 per cent seems equitable.[69] Further, Navarrus adds, the "immemorial custom" and the common practice of Europe stand for the licitness of the contract. Wards, widows, and the Church are all supported by such investments. It is unthinkable that this common custom should have arisen and continued for so long if it is truly damnable usury. Finally, he declares, he argues for the contract not to encourage avarice, but because the force of truth impels him to recognize it, "and because we greatly desire to entice men avid to make great profits in illicit ways to seek these small profits in a licit way." [70]

---

[67] Navarrus, *Manuale*, 17, *De usura in societate*, n.252, in *Opera*, Vol. I.
[68] Navarrus, *De usuris*, 14 (n.36, 37, 35).
[69] *Ibid.*, 14 (n.34).
[70] *Ibid.*, 14 (n. 33, 39).

6. *The Bull* Detestabilis avaritia

Before 1586, there had been no positive papal intervention on the triple contract. One might have supposed that *Naviganti*, which condemned a loan even where the lender ran the risk, would have proved an insuperable obstacle to it; but since *Naviganti* spoke only of a loan, not a *societas*, it was generally ignored on this question and had little effect. On the other hand, *Per vestras*, which spoke of committing a dowry to a husband "with security," might have been construed to favor the triple contract. Some of the defenders of the contract did, in fact, cite it.[71] But the majority, even of the defenders, had not felt the decretal clear enough to be decisive.

In 1586, then, papal authority appeared to enter the dispute for the first time with the issuance by Sixtus V of a bull beginning with the ominous words, "Detestable avarice." "Many seeking gain too avidly," the Pope says, "have fallen miserably into snares and deceits" so that "by various tricks" they have led themselves "into the whirlpool of usury." These men have used "the specious and honest name of *societas*, as a pretext for their usurious contracts," by giving money or animals to a merchant, businessman, or agricultural worker, in the name of a partnership, but actually with the provision that their capital be always safe and that the so-called partner run all the risk of loss. To stem "this contagious disease" before it spreads further, the Pope, "by the plenitude of Apostolic power" given him,

damns and proscribes all and any contracts, agreements and pacts afterwards to be made, by which it is guaranteed to persons giving money, animals, or any other things in the name of a *societas* that, even if in some fortuitous case, disaster, loss, or lack happens to occur, the principal or capital will be always safe and restored entire by the partner receiving it . . . . We decree that contracts, agreements, and pacts of this kind are after this to be thought illicit and usurious.

Further, if any one use these contracts, or if persons

on the pretext of similar contracts, agreements, and pacts begun in the name of a partnership, which have lasted up till now, dare to proceed in the future to the exaction of the said principal or capital or its price and value, after it in whole or in part has perished or been lost by a fortuitous event, or to the exaction of a fixed annual or monthly sum or quantity promised, they incur, together and singly, *eo ipso* the penalties decreed and promulgated by the sacred canons and general councils, against manifest usurers and moneylenders.[72]

This solemn condemnation, enforced by such severe penalties, and ap-

[71] For example, Navarrus, *De usuris*, n. 35, and Eck, *Tractatus*, in Schneid, p. 477.
[72] Sixtus V, *Detestabilis avaritia, Bullarum* *diplomatum et privilegiorum sanctorum Romanorum Pontificum Tauriensis Editio* (Turin, 1863), VIII, 783–785.

parently directed at the increasing popularity of the triple contract, might seem to the superficial observer a decisive blow. At first, it was reported that it had decided the controversy between Navarrus and Soto.[73] In fact, however, it remained without effect upon the great debate. Two theories to explain it were generally put forward. One was that the bull was purely positive legislation, not a declaration of the divine or natural law; in particular, it was noted that the bull seemed to be only prospective in its condemnations. Purely positive legislation lapses, according to the usual principles of canon law, if not renewed by the legislator, when it is not received by the subjects of the law; and when unreceived by a State, it has no binding force. If the bull was considered positive law, this usual rule applied automatically. Since the bull was received nowhere, it had, insofar as it was positive law, no force whatsoever.[74]

The second theory, advocated by those who thought the bull insisted too much on its basis in divine law to be taken as purely positive, was that it merely prohibited contracts of partnership which were "naturally usurious," where no compensation was paid for the insurance of the capital. Since only such "naturally usurious" contracts were condemned, and since the triple contract was not "naturally usurious," it was argued that the bull left the latter untouched.[75]

Sixtus V himself was reported to have declared in a private response to a question on the bull that he "only condemned what the doctors condemned," and this was widely interpreted to mean that he did not condemn the triple contract. A close advisor of the Pope, Cardinal Toletus, continued to publish a work in which the triple contract was defended. In 1602 the Sacred Rota declared that insurance contracts made separately from the partnership contract were not affected by the bull.[76] In the eighteenth century, Pope Benedict XIV declared that the use of the triple contract was only "less congruous" to the intention of the bull.[77] Thus, neither by the common opinion of the theologians, nor by authority itself was the interpretation supported that the bull definitely outlawed the triple contract.

7. *Three Famous Jesuits and Full Approval of Commercial Credit*

The most representative authorities on economic morals and the triple contract in the late sixteenth and early seventeenth centuries are the Jesuits

[73] P. Ballerini, *Opusculum*, II:3:45, in *De jure divino et naturali circa usuram* (Verona, 1747).

[74] See St. Alphonsus Liguori, *Theologia moralis*, II, Bk. III:5, c.3, Dub. 14, n.908.

[75] *Ibid.*

[76] Zech, III:2:2:175.

[77] Benedict XIV, *De synoda diocesano*, 7:50.

—a fact reflecting the intellectual preëminence the new order had attained. On the Iberian peninsula the dominant figure was Louis Molina (1536–1600). In theological circles he is chiefly known as the author of Molinism, a subtle metaphysics of the relation of grace and free will. But though a man with rare skill in abstract theory, Molina had a remarkable knowledge of contemporary economic life. Consulted by judges, lawmakers and merchants in his own lifetime, Molina in his treatment of usury produced a work that was to be relied on by men of law and business throughout Catholic Europe.[78] The treatise, *De justitia et jure*, appeared in 1593–1597, and reflects the matter of his courses at Coimbra and Evora of an earlier period.

The tradition of intelligent comprehension of business problems is continued by Leonard Lessius (1554–1623), a Belgian Jesuit of the next generation. Lessius taught theology at Louvain and became familiar with the economic life of Antwerp, perhaps the leading financial city of his age.[79] He is the theologian whose views on usury most decidedly mark the arrival of a new era. More than any predecessor he would probably have felt completely at ease in the modern financial world. Careful, perceptive, boldly logical, modest, and sure of himself, Lessius is a master of scholastic economic analysis.

The third of these Jesuits, who are the authorities at the height of the development of the usury theory, is John de Lugo (1593–1660). A Spaniard who spent twenty-two years teaching theology in Rome, he was made a cardinal in 1643 and for almost seventeen years thereafter was an influential member of various Roman commissions. St. Alphonsus has described him as the greatest moral theologian after St. Thomas.[80] As an economic moralist he is subtle, comprehensive, and exhaustive in analysis; more theoretical than Lessius, he engages in subtleties which may be exasperating to a modern reader. But reading him, one cannot but be impressed by his brilliant grasp of theory.

To turn from eulogy to the texts, what did these acute moralists have to say on the triple contract device?

Molina accepts the standard arguments and notes the prevalence of the contract in Portugal. Widows find it advantageous; merchants like it because they are freed from the trouble of satisfying a suspicious regular partner that he is getting his full profit. There is no danger that the contract will cause scandal, for it is used by everyone.[81] At the same time, he is not

---

[78] *D.t.c.*, X, 2090–2091.
[79] *D.t.c.*, IX, 453.
[80] *D.t.c.*, IX, 1071; St. Alphonsus, III:5, c.3,

n.552.
[81] Louis Molina, *Opera omnia de justitia et jure* (Cologne, 1745), II, *Disputatio* 417:1, 16,

sure enough of his arguments to rest his case on the partnership contract alone; and he adds that, even supposing a true loan is effected, the investor can take a profit under the title of *lucrum cessans*.[82] If a man has the opportunity to invest in a partnership as a full partner and receive 10 per cent, when he foregoes this opportunity in order to lend, he clearly has the right to compensation of, say, 5 per cent. This argument is thoroughly modern in placing more reliance on a direct interest title than on the device of the triple contract. At the same time, it sacrifices the advantage the triple contract offered of removing the entire transaction from the strict rules governing loans; and to use it together with the standard defense of the triple contract leads to the weakness produced by every attempt to defend a position on two mutually exclusive bases. This attempt in connection with the triple contract is not common. Molina's advocacy of *lucrum cessans* as a justification for the transaction may be considered either as a tacit repudiation of the defense of the contract in itself, and a regression in liberality, or as a brilliant suggestion of the proper way of legitimizing all business loans without the cumbersome and curious procedure of the triple contract, and thus a step forward in the practical tolerance of business finance. In any case, his suggestion was not generally adopted until two hundred and fifty years after his day.

Like Molina, Lessius found the triple contract a popular and necessary device. The common theological teaching is in its favor.[83] Some troublemakers in Belgium, however, oppose it to the great spiritual harm and confusion of the people and to the temporal loss of the community. Yet the contract is for the good of souls, because it leads men from usury, and is for the temporal good, because it benefits wards and widows and simultaneously furnishes capital to the merchants at a low cost. If the merchants could not get money in this way, they would be driven to raise it through selling bills of exchange at a cost of 12 to 18 per cent.[84]

The contract is not only expedient; it is licit in itself. The capitalist partner originally is due a reward both for his risk and for the commodity of his capital.[85] The insurance offered on the risk by the merchant is not worth a

---

and 11. Molina (417:11) adds an apposite legal argument: the insurance agreement does not transfer ownership from the investor because, on termination of the partnership by the merchant's death, the investor has a right to recover his property in the partnership, and it is not subject to claims of nonpartnership creditors of the merchant.

[82] 417:12. Broderick (pp. 125, 135) com-

mits a serious anachronism in writing that the triple contract was defended as a case of *lucrum cessans* during the 5 per cent controversy.

[83] Lessius, *De justitia et jure*, II, c.25, d.3:23.

[84] 25:3:32.

[85] 25:2:14.

great deal — say 4 to 6 per cent. The merchant customarily makes 10 to 12 per cent. After he pays the insurance charge, the capitalist makes a fair profit, if he takes the current rate of 6¼ per cent.[86] Lessius will not, however, condemn a capitalist who wants 10 or 12 per cent from an exchange dealer or a trader in the Indies, who customarily makes huge profits. Thus there is a steady growth in the amount of profit on riskless capital considered licit by the theologians.

Lessius repeats the old qualification that the merchant must enter the insurance contract freely; but he renders it practically meaningless by saying that the investor may properly refuse to invest unless the merchant enter both insurance and partnership contracts at once.[87] The merchant is simply "free" to decline the whole transaction; but the earlier sense of "freedom," by which it seemed to be implied that the investor could not impose the insurance contract as a condition of investing, is gone. Probably the practice had long been conformable to Lessius' theory; but he is the first theologian to recognize the practice explicitly. Thus, by this stated recognition of the investor's right to insist on the insurance, by his acceptance of a high rate of return to the capitalist, by his firm insistence on the contract's spiritual and temporal benefits, rather than by any specific advance in theory, Lessius is the most liberal writer to this date upon the contract. It is a way of reaching a sound commercial result with which he sympathizes.

Lugo, like Lessius, says the common opinion is for the contract, and uses all Lessius' arguments in its favor.[88] He adds one theoretic refinement in answer to the objection that ownership is transferred and a loan made, because the investor is secure against any injuries to his investment. This result, the objector contends, proves that the investor has surrendered his title to the money, because there can be no right where no injury can be suffered. Lugo replies that although no physical loss results, there can be injury against one's right, when one's property is used and when one is unwilling that it be used. For example, if another occupies a vacant house of yours, for which you had no use, he nevertheless commits a trespass and injures your right. Similarly, in the guaranteed partnership, the investor retains a right, which can be injured, although no physical loss follows: he

---

[86] 25:3:26, 31. Lessius (25:3:28) appears to misstate Molina's legal argument by taking the position that the investor is the owner because he will be preferred to creditors on the termination of the partnership; he fails to distinguish between creditors of the merchant and creditors of the partnership. More explicitly than Navarrus, he states the argument that ownership is not completely transferred in the partnership, for the money must be used for a fixed purpose.

[87] 25:3:28.

[88] John de Lugo, *Disputationes scholasticae et morales*, Vivès edition (Paris, 1893), VII, *Disputatio* 30:4:38–43.

retains the right to the licit gain of the partnership, and corresponding to this right is the merchant partner's obligation to use his money in the business agreed on, and to carry out the business in the name of the partnership. It is true that whether the merchant carries out the agreement or not, he will be bound to pay the investor, so that the investor will suffer no direct harm by the neglect of his right. But this does not destroy the fact that he has a right and consequently remains owner, and not lender, of the property.[89]

The leading scholastic moralists of the golden age of usury analysis thus support the triple contract. Lugo's refinements are the nice speculations of a theorist; Molina is shrewder and on stronger ground; Lessius shows the contract's easy application to business practice. All three are witnesses to the need for this intricate analysis as a way of justifying commerial credit.

8. *Eighteenth-Century Controversy*

In the eighteenth century a rigorist reaction against the liberalness of seventeenth-century moral theology gained force in all ethical fields, and as part of the general tendency a movement developed among one group of moralists against the concessions made in the doctrine upon usury. The two most famous defenders of what they asserted to be the threatened dogma on usury were Daniel Concina and Peter Ballerini. With unrestrained zeal they condemned almost every modern contract which the moralists of the past two hundred years had admitted as an alternative to lending at usury. The viewpoints of both men are substantially the same,[90] and we obtain the essence of the arguments of both in outlining the exposition of Ballerini.

Peter Ballerini was a secular priest of Verona, rector of the Veronese Academy, a distinguished scholar, and an editor of the works of St. Leo the Great.[91] In 1740 he brought out a new edition of the *Summa theologiae* of St. Antoninus, and upon the subject of usury he was himself like a St. Antoninus *redivivus*. St. Antoninus was the most consistent and so the most rigorous of medieval moralists on usury; by his standards most of the population of capitalistic Florence were committing mortal sin. Ballerini is St.

---

[89] 30:4:44. To the objection that all kinds of usury could be cloaked by the triple contract, Lugo replies simply that the same might be said of the redeemable *census* (30:4:45). With Lessius, he admits that the investor can insist that all contracts be entered into at once, while the merchant is free only to reject them together (30:4:45).

[90] See Van Roey, *De justo auctario*, p. 43.

[91] *D.t.c.*, II, 131. Ballerini's great work on usury is the monumental *De jure divino et naturali circa usuram*, a well-documented historical review of Christian teaching on the subject, to which work was added a *Vindicatio* against the laxist Jansenist, Nicolas Broedersen, and three *opuscula* on particular aspects of the usury problem. One of these last works treats specially of the triple contract.

Antoninus come to life three hundred years later, when not only Florence but all Europe is thoroughly capitalistic, and in the same spirit as St. Antoninus, logically, consistently, and perhaps even more severely, he judges and condemns current practice in the light of an explication of the implicit assumptions of the formal usury theory. The very eccentricity of Ballerini's position, as it appeared in relation to both business and confessional practice, shows strikingly how far the scholastic theory had gone from the period of St. Antoninus and the medieval assumptions. We could not ask for a better way of measuring the developments in theology upon the usury question than to compare Ballerini's assertion of anachronistic theses with the common theological teaching of his day.

Like Soto, Ballerini takes the fundamental position that only the risk of the capitalist constitutes his title to profit in the simple partnership, but unlike Soto, he applies this theory explicitly to the case of the triple contract. On the basis of it he argues that when the risk is removed in the insured partnership, the investor loses all title to compensation. In his view, the triple contract is obviously unjust; for the capitalist first claims a profit of 7 per cent in the simple partnership by reason of his risk; and then makes the merchant assume the same risk for only 3 per cent. It is a clear case, Ballerini says, of forcing the merchant to buy high and sell low simultaneously under the pressure of need.[92]

Apart from this argument essentially based on the doctrine of money's sterility, Ballerini, like Cajetan, questions the justice of the price paid for the guarantee, hypothetically supposing a guarantee to be separately paid for. But he is more forceful than Cajetan by being specific. The profit paid the guaranteed capitalist is usually 4 per cent. A normal business makes a profit of about 10 per cent, of which at least 4 per cent is due the merchant. If the merchant then gives a fixed 4 per cent to the capitalist he must be considered to be taking the remaining 2 per cent as payment for the double obligation of guaranteeing the investor's capital and an interest of 4 per cent.[93] It should also be noted that he is insuring the capital against all risks, while in maritime insurance, where the insurance is against only one specific risk, 2 to 5 per cent is usually charged.[94] Would any sane person, who was truly free, contract in this fashion? Ballerini asks. Would any independent insurer undertake the risk of capital against all perils and pay a fixed income, for a charge of 2 per cent? Is it not clear that the transaction is really a loan, and that the investor exacts profit only by virtue of the loan?

[92] Ballerini, *Opus.* II:3:37.   [94] II:3:22.
[93] II:3:21.

Besides this principal and telling argument, Ballerini maintains the old position that a partnership demands a sharing of loss and gain by its nature. If the working partner was assured a fixed return, whether the venture succeeded or not, the contract would be changed from a partnership to a hiring of labor by the capitalist. When the capitalist gets fixed or riskless return, the contract becomes a loan.[95] Finally, Ballerini even denies that the capitalist may insure his capital and profit with individuals distinct from his so-called partner. He does not deny the licitness of insurance in itself, but he does deny the licitness of any riskless profit.[96]

The great objection that Ballerini fears is that if the triple contract is condemned, business itself will be condemned[97] — an objection that strikingly illustrates the pervasive use of the contract to justify eighteenth-century commerce. To answer this anticipated difficulty Ballerini can only suggest that merchants obtain cash by selling exchange, by selling their goods for cash and repurchasing them at once on credit, by borrowing from those who have true titles to *lucrum cessans*, and by selling a *census*. These methods, he declares, will assure business and government of sufficient capital without the use of the usurious triple contract.[98]

Ballerini has made a powerful attack on the contract; it is not without significance that it was only two hundred and fifty years after the first exposition of the transaction that such a complete, sustained, and consistent criticism of it was launched. Of his objections the most serious is that the insurance price theoretically paid by the investor is unjustly small, an objection telling more against the practice than the form of the contract. His more basic objection that a low and a high price are simultaneously set on the risk assumes that the investor should get no reward for the use of his money considered by itself; this assumption had never been fully accepted in relation to partnership by most scholastics of any period. His other basic objections, that riskless investments are usury and that a partnership naturally demands a sharing of loss and gain, are also asserted with a certain arbitrariness, although these objections had been the basis of the medieval stand against the guaranteed partnership. They had been abandoned by modern authors when they had been found indefensible by the natural law.

The Jesuits at the University of Ingolstadt, a focus of liberal thought on usury since the time of Eck, had been particularly attacked by Concina; and to defend their own reputation, the current practice in Germany, and in general, the more lenient theses on usury against the two Italian rigorists,

[95] II:3:25.
[96] II:3:33.
[97] II:4:52–53.
[98] II:4:81.

Concina and Ballerini, Francis Zech, a leading Jesuit canonist at Ingolstadt, produced a work pointedly entitled *Moderate Rigor of the Pontifical Doctrine on Usury.*

On the triple contract, Zech argues that the joint sharing of risk is natural, but not essential to a partnership, and that for a just compensation risk can be removed from an investment without destroying the partnership contract or hurting justice. He replies to Ballerini's capital objection on the smallness of the insurance price that the justice of a price is established by the common estimation; as a theologian he only considers the nature of the contract, and the nature of the contract is unimpeachable.[99] He finds it unnecessary even to notice Ballerini's argument that reward is due the investor only for his risk. In general, his presentation of the case for the contract adds nothing new. But it is an eloquent demonstration of how the defenders of the contract were unaffected by the new and vigorous assaults of Ballerini and Concina.

The final word of the eighteenth century and the final word on the controversy is given by Alphonsus Liguori (1696–1787). A lawyer before he became a priest, bishop, and founder of the Redemptorist order, St. Alphonsus is the great master of moral theology.[100] According to an unusual decree of the Church, it is safe for confessors to follow his opinions without weighing the reasons on which they are based.[101] Free from any taint of laxism, and equally averse to the harsh rigorism of some eighteenth-century reactionaries, St. Alphonsus in a balanced and moderate way presents the common conclusions of the sixteenth and seventeenth centuries' investigations in moral science. We may rely on him to present fairly the common contemporary teaching on usury; his work sums up the developments that the main tradition of scholasticism had taken on the usury theory from 1450; and in concise form, reflecting the settled conclusions on the matter, St. Alphonsus contains the essence of the developed theory.

Despite the objections of Soto, Concina, and Ballerini, St. Alphonsus says, "the more common opinion is for the triple contract." He himself states concisely the familiar arguments in its favor and declares for it. He adds that there has existed "an immemorable custom of contracting in such a way in Spain, France, Italy and in almost the whole Church."[102] Thus approved by practice and by the greatest moral theologians, the triple contract now stands established.

[99] Zech, III:2:6:178–179.

[100] *D.t.c.*, I, 906–914.

[101] Berthe, *St. Alphonse de Liguori* (Paris, 1900), II, 672–673.

[102] St. Alphonsus Liguori, *Theologia moralis*, III:5:3:14:908 (his *Theologia moralis*, published in 1748, then revised and greatly augmented, was republished in 1753–1755).

Conclusion

Our survey of the principal later scholastic authorities on usury shows clearly that the triple contract was accepted by the majority of leading theologians. Begining in 1485 with its proposal by Angelus de Clavasio, its licitness had clearly become the common teaching by 1581, when the second Jesuit Congregation approved it. It was never free from sharp individual attacks, but in practice all businessmen must have used it, and few confessors can have troubled them. Since its effects were distinguished from those of a loan only by the designation for a business purpose of the funds it conveyed, there were no practical differences between it and a loan for business. In 1823 when Cardinal Luzerne defended the *prêt-de-commerce* or business loan, he said with simple accuracy that what he defended was only the triple contract under another name.[103] The moralists' acceptance of the contract meant the practical exclusion of the old usury theory from business finance.

As the triple contract smacks so much of sophistry, what it achieves should be precisely noted: as Molina implied, it is merely a roundabout way of legitimating *lucrum cessans*. It is a legal fiction reaching a sound practical result. One may object to the clumsy analytical device; one might even object, on substantive grounds, to *lucrum cessans* as an interest title. But once *lucrum cessans* is seen as sound in principle, there can be no substantive objection to using the triple contract formula as a cumbersome means of defining the class of business contracts where *lucrum cessans* is always present.

The implications for the scholastic theory of usury proper were as profound as the practical consequences were widespread. Acceptance of the contract meant the definitive rejection of the theses that any temporary, riskless transfer of property was usury; that the incidence of risk was the criterion of ownership; that money was sterile and could not bring a reward to itself. The first thesis had been tacitly assumed by a number of medieval authorities, although no rational defense of it had ever been attempted. The second thesis had already been rejected by the scholastic acceptance of insurance, and the third had always been rejected by the scholastic theory of *societas*. The triple contract established definitively that a riskless transfer need not be usury; it destroyed the use of risk as the index of ownership by the usury theorists; and it made dominant for usury theory the concept of capital which partnership analysis had always implied.

[103] William César, Cardinal de la Luzerne,   1823), p. 141. *Dissertations sur le prêt-de-commerce* (Dijon,

CHAPTER XI

THE PERSONAL, GUARANTEED, AND MUTUALLY REDEEMABLE *CENSUS*

At the same time that the acceptance of the triple contract was so greatly expanding the possibilities of business finance, modifications in the conditions of the *census* contract opened up a wide range of licit opportunities for more general credit extension. At the beginning of the period we examine there was a strong attempt made by two prominent authors to develop the medieval theory which held that the *census* was simply the purchase of a right to money, and to analyze a vast number of credit transactions, in the light of this theory, as purchases of a right to money. This extension had been suggested, at least, by the works of Henry of Eutin; it is difficult to believe that there was not already a strong bias in its favor in Germany. From Biel to Zech we find German theologians defending it. The extended theory really removed all matter from the usury prohibition.

Against this theory a conservative tendency consequently developed, encouraged not by the rigorists, but by usually liberal Jesuit theologians. These authors insisted that the *census* should be analyzed as the purchase of some property other than a right and were obviously apprehensive that any other analysis would destroy the usury prohibition altogether. This conservative tendency led, not logically but practically, to a defense of the personal *census* by interest titles, as if it were a loan, rather than a consideration of it as a sale: logically, even the conservatives might have accepted a personal *census* as a true purchase of labor; practically, they thought that a personal *census* in common usage was treated only as a purchase of a right. The interest titles, however, were allowed more liberally on the *census* purchase than they were on a true loan. This is a continuation of a tendency to consider the *census* as a loan and yet be more liberal about it than about a loan—a tendency as old as Innocent IV and Monaldus. In pure *census* theory there is, then, no real advance over the Middle Ages; conservative and liberal nearly balances each other, and considerable confusion still exists as to what exactly is sold in a *census*.

Far more important are two qualifications allowed on the *census*, which do not involve its formal character. One of these qualifications is the admission of contracts of guaranty. By the addition of a guaranty to a *census*, payment is assured even though the *census* base perishes; in effect, it transforms even the most rigid real *census* into a personal obligation to pay. Formal guaranteeing of the *census* had not been mentioned by any prominent scholastic in the Middle Ages, although much the same effect had been obtained when a *census* payment was based upon all the seller's goods. The other qualification allowed is mutual redeemability. The similarity of a buyer redeeming to a lender reclaiming his principal after he has received his profit in installments is too obvious to need comment. Redeemability by a buyer had been allowed only by a minority of medieval authorities. Yet strikingly enough, the Jesuits who attacked the right-sale theory of the *census*, were completely in favor of the two additions of guaranty and mutual redeemability; unopposed by any but the most intransigent medievalists, both these conditions were generally accepted as licit. By their admission the controversy over the *census* concept itself was substantially diminished in importance, for any guaranteed, mutually redeemable *census* was in practice so close to a loan that most investors would have been entirely content with it.

Thus, in the early bold development of the old *census* theory, in the continued lack of valid objection to at least a true personal *census* based on a purchase of labor, in the acceptance of mutual redeemability and guaranty, we shall see a large area of credit transactions removed from the rule of the usury prohibition.

1. *Radical Development of the* Census *Concept: Germany, Spain, Italy*

As might be expected, the Tübingen school is the center of early liberalization of *census* theory. Gabriel Biel himself adds nothing to the prevailing analysis of the *census* as a right to money from a fruitful base,[1] but he accepts and defends so many varieties of the basic contract that he must be counted a powerful supporter for the position that most credit transactions can be analyzed as lawful *census*.

A *census* on either immobile or mobile goods is licit, Biel says, and a *census* may be constituted on a *census*.[2] More important, a personal *census* is also lawful, provided the seller is able to work and will not lack the necessities of life. A personal *census* may be either on specified or unspecified

---

[1] Biel, *Collectorium*, IV:15:12, 1st and 3rd dub. 1; also IV:15:12, 2nd and 3rd dub. 1.   [2] 15:12:2, coroll. 3.

persons; consequently, a *census* can be founded on the citizens of a city.[3] Temporary, life, and perpetual annuities are all equally justified. But on the temporary *census* the annual payment times the number of years it is to run should equal the price of the *census*, unless there is danger that the *census* base would perish. On the perpetual annuity "the price is equal to the merchandise, when the seller according to the common course can obtain as much utility from the price as the buyer from the merchandise." Often the seller of a *census* will be willing to pay a high annuity in order to get ready cash to invest in something he considers more profitable. Of course, both sides hope to gain, and both may gain in fact:

> For a buyer desiring merchandise, unless he hoped for more advantage from the merchandise than from the money he gave, would not buy; nor would a seller sell, unless he hoped for profit from the price.

But this is no sin: "The Lord said, 'Lend, hoping nothing thereby'; He did not say, Sell, etc." The buyer of the annuity, if he makes a profit, receives the profit from his own property. In general, Biel adds, the price will vary with time and place, the fertility of farms, and the scarcity of money. The proportion between the price paid and the annuity received is moral, not mathematical. It is proper to consider the value of present cash to the seller in estimating what is a fair price to pay him.[4] From all of these remarks, it is abundantly obvious how the value of money was allowed to be estimated above its face value in the *census*, if not in the loan, and how profitable an extension of credit through the *census* might be.

Against Henry of Hesse Biel holds that if the *census* is redeemable at the seller's will, the price should be less, because an obligation is imposed on the buyer, preventing him from reselling the *census* to others. He adds, in passing, that often the sellers are rich men raising funds by the *census*, and declares that at any rate rarely are the sellers of a *census* in "extreme necessity."[5]

As to mutual redeemability and redeemability at the buyer's will, Biel is the first influential authority since Gerson to defend these clauses, and he declares that he sets forth the opinion "only recitatively and probably." Yet he adds in defense of his position that redeemability alters neither the merchandise nor the price nor does it change the character of the contracts. He admits that in such a contract only a reserved ownership is sold, and notes that if the buyer avoids all risk usury is to be presumed. But he

---

[3] 15:12:2, corroll. 2.
[4] 15:12:2, corroll. 3.
[5] 15:12:2, corroll. 4.

asserts that the practice of redeemability by the buyer is frequent, and he himself finds nothing wrong with it.[6]

Like Henry of Hesse and Henry of Eutin Biel does offer some restrictions as to the kind of person who may lawfully buy a *census*. Someone acts unlawfully who buys "to avoid labors, or to be able to live at ease, or to give free rein to pleasures and pomps . . . or to gather treasures superfluous to his person and state." But ecclesiastics may live on the returns, as may others with duties to the State. Also a worker who provides for his old age or sickness may enjoy the annuities, as may one who wants an income so that he may have more time for spiritual labors.[7] These restrictions were scarcely rigid or far-reaching.

Conrad Summenhart developed Biel's position with a radical and startling logic. His sweeping use of the *census*, coupled with an attack on the medieval concept of the value of money, results in the emptying of the usury prohibition of all practical significance.

Summenhart begins his defense of the personal *census* by showing that the constitution of such an obligation upon a person is not itself unnatural. One may sell oneself into slavery; one may oblige oneself to do some work; therefore, one can oblige oneself to provide the fruits of one's work annually. Or an alternative defense exists in the common thesis that a *census* is a licit purchase of a right to fruits. It is true, he concedes, that in this way money itself is bought, but it is bought only mediately. Moreover, he adds with great boldness, although money as the measure of prices is nonvendible, it may also be used in other ways — for example, as a commodity trafficked in for profit.[8] Summenhart goes on to declare what he thinks to be the essential difference between a *census* and a loan; and here his logic carries him to a revolutionary stand. A loan, he says, occurs only when a good of the same genus is to be returned. A *census* is not a loan, but a sale, because in it money is exchanged for a good of another genus, that is, a *right* to payment. Then it is objected, why cannot every usurer say:

I do not give this money, obliging you to give me a good of the same *genus*, to wit, money; but I give it to you for a good of another genus, to wit, the *right* of demanding such an amount from you in money, even beyond the principal given you by me.[9]

Answering, Summenhart says that intention determines in usury, as in simony, and that in this case, then, if a man truly intends to buy the right

[6] 15:12:2, corroll. 4.
[7] 15:12:3, ad dub. 4 and 5.
[8] Summenhart, *De contractibus*, Q.79.

concl. 3, p. 352.
[9] Q.80, concl. 2, p. 363.

to money, and not money itself, the transaction must be considered a sale. In other words, he admits the objection. Every lender can, instead of lending, buy the right to money from his would-be borrower.

Treating of the purchase of debts, the leader of the Tübingen school is even more explicit. The purchase of a debt is like the purchase of a *census*, he declares, for it is the purchase of a *right* to money. The same principles rule both. Hence,

it does not matter whether that action belonged to the seller [of the debt] before the sale, or whether he newly constituted it. . . . Similarly it is not necessary to distinguish, nor does it matter, whether that action newly constituted be constituted on the seller himself or some other person.[10]

In this astonishing statement, Summenhart is saying very concisely that it is not usury if a lender purchases a discounted debt from a borrower, although the debt is, in fact, created by his very purchase of the debt from that borrower.

As the price of merchandise, unlike money itself, was always regulated by supply and demand, Summenhart can urge that this market price prevails in the usual difference between the price paid for a temporary *census* and the return expected: "The usual value of merchandise to be evaluated is determined by taking the adequation of merchandise and price according to the aptness of the merchandise for human convenience." Here the right to 100 at some future date is clearly not so advantageous to a man as 100 in hand; raising the amount repayable to 110 makes the estimation equal. "The price and the merchandise are equal in fact and in the estimation of the buyer." [11]

Yet the purchase of the newly constituted debt may be characterized as an implicit loan. Summenhart is disinclined to admit this, but he says, even admitting it, he finds no usury. The buyer hopes no profit from the loan, because he values the future 110 as worth 100. With this statement it is clear that Summenhart abandons completely the assumption of the old theory that money cannot be evaluated other than at its legal price. He does not have here the defense that money is considered as a merchandise, but he accepts fully a fluctuating evaluation of money *qua* money. Obviously, if his thesis, that the lender may licitly get back what he thought his money was worth to him, had been accepted, there would have been few loans which could have been considered usurious.

[10] Q.80, concl. 5, p. 367.   [11] Q.80, concl. 4, p. 366.

Having gone this far, however, Summenhart then offers some illogical but prudential qualifications. If the buyer prefers to buy because he thinks the 110 is more desirable than the 100 at hand, one may consider a plea of *lucrum cessans*, but there is danger of usury, and he counsels restitution. In fact, he says, a *census* in which the buyer will certainly get more than he paid is licit only "*in rigore scholastico*." If there is danger of scandal, it should not be employed. On the other hand, he hints, if its use is the general custom and it is used by respectable men who are not thought to be usurers, the contract may be approved.[12] In short, as in his treatment of the triple contract, he hesitates about admitting a credit contract in practice because of the dangers of abuse and scandal, but offers no substantial reason against its licitness, so that according to his theory, the contract simply awaits establishment by custom to make it wholly legitimate. In his hands, the personal *census*, the purchase of a right to money, legitimately evaluated at less than present money, becomes an easy and moral means of extending credit at a profit. In Germany his theory of the *census* was realized in fact.[13]

That Summenhart should have reached his radical position on the *census* can be explained as a result of both his own skepticism toward the usury theory and the economic pressures in Germany. But how explain the stand of Dominic Soto, an ultra-conservative on all other aspects of the usury question? Spanish practice is undoubtedly a factor, but Soto is not an author to be daunted by custom he finds mischievous. Yet he is almost as liberal upon the *census* contract as Summenhart. Here the rigor of his logic is put on the side favoring profit in credit transactions. The large loophole he creates must be borne in mind when his restrictive judgments on other contracts are considered.

Soto focuses on the central concept: a *census* is a purchase not of the fruits of the base, but of the simple right to seek payment of the fruits. He makes the narrowly logical deduction: every kind of purchase of a right to seek payment is justified. The personal *census* is then completely licit; and Soto adds that the usual real *census* is in fact a personal *census*, in that the common practice is for the seller of the *census* to be obliged personally to provide the payments, though the fruitful base of the *census* perish. Naturally, variations of the personal *census*, such as a real *census* where the fruits of the property will not equal the return paid, are also licit. Most important of all, since Soto does not include the purchase of fruits as an essential part of a *census* contract,

---

[12] Q.80, concl. 4, p. 366.
[13] See *infra*, pp. 247, 279. Summenhart also approves a contract redeemable by the buyer and the mutually redeemable *census* (Q.83, Q.84, concl. 5).

he does not even ask that the personal *census* be founded on someone's labor. In his analysis, a personal *census* can be contracted with anyone by giving him money, and constituting a *census* "on the use of it." [14]

How does such a personal *census* differ from a loan at usury? Instead of distinguishing between the return of a good of the same genus and the purchase of a good of a different genus, as Summenhart had, Soto answers by positing one essential difference between a loan and a *census*. In a *census* the money given is irrevocable by the buyer; in a loan the lender's right to reclaim is essential. A *census* redeemable by the buyer is then a loan, and:

whenever money or some other good consumptible in use is given with an agreement to receive back the same thing, or its value, and something beyond the principal, there usury is manifest or hidden. [15]

By the same token, however, whenever a loan is not redeemable, it may, according to Soto's analysis, be treated as the purchase of an annual income or a licit *census*. It is certainly of high significance that Soto thus distinguishes loans and sales by nothing the scholastics would have called "intrinsic" in the transactions but by a "secondary" characteristic of redeemability or non-redeemability. The effect of his answer is to rule out the mutually redeemable *census*, but otherwise there is little practical difference between his position and Summenhart's.

Like Summenhart, Soto does confess some embarrassment about the temporary, personal *census*, in which it is certain that the returns in a fixed period will exceed the purchase price. This contract, he says, is suspect of usury, unless there is a substantial doubt about the payments being made or a real fear of expenses in collecting the payments. Yet he does not call the contract a loan, nor does he offer any reason why his defense of the personal *census* in general should not apply to it; and he says that if someone wants to use it, he will not condemn him. Moreover, he adds, the contract is not usual. What he defends wholeheartedly, and what he believes is common, is the perpetual personal *census*, where the lack of a fixed date of expiration marks it off more clearly from a loan, although, obviously, the payments on it may ultimately be much more than the purchase price. [16]

In Italy, too, the *census* received broad approval from Silvester da Prierio, O.P. (1460–1523), one of the last of the summists. [17] He defended both real and personal *census*, provided the seller had a right to redeem. There

---

[14] Soto, *De justitia*, VI, Q.5, art. 1.   [17] Schulte, *Die Geschichte der Quellen*, II,
[15] VI:5:3.   455.
[16] VI:5:2.

was no difference between an "old" and a "new" *census*: each was the sale
of a right to money. Similarly, a community could finance itself by sales of the
right to tax returns.[18]

2. *The Bull* Cum onus: *Failure to Curb the Contract*

In 1569, the exuberant tendency to approve all kinds of *census* contracts
received what might have seemed at first a severe blow in the issuance of a
stern papal decree upon the matter. Earlier papal bulls had explicitly approved the real *census* only, even though Nicholas V had gone as far as
allowing a real *census* based on all one's property in general; a tacit disapproval of the personal *census* and the mutually redeemable *census* might
have been seen in the failure to mention them among the legitimate forms
of the *census*. Yet nothing had been expressly said upon the subject by the
Popes before this date.

In 1568, however, St. Charles Borromeo had become archbishop of Milan,
and horrified to find usury practiced as a matter of course by the merchants
of his diocese, he had requested Pope Pius V to speak out strongly on
modern evasions of the usury prohibition. This request had led to the creation
of a theological commission to study dry exchange and the *census*; its report,
in turn, resulted in the issuance of two bulls by Pius V, the first of which,
Cum onus, issued January 19, 1569, concerns the *census*.[19]

The Pope begins by saying that the *census* contracts daily celebrated not
only do not keep the limits set by his predecessors, but show a manifest contempt for the divine law. He then declares that no *census* may be constituted
except on a fruitful, immobile good, specifically designated to pay the *census*
returns. He invalidates all guarantees of *census* by the seller. He orders that
every *census* be redeemable by the seller, and that, on the other hand, no
buyer force an unwilling seller to redeem them. In a word, the personal, the
guaranteed, and the mutually redeemable *census* all are outlawed. All contracts not observing these rules, the Pope says, are "to be considered
usurious." [20]

The thinking behind *Cum onus* is probably clearest in the works of
Navarrus, who had a strong influence on its composition.[21] Consulted by the
Jesuits as to its exact significance, Navarrus advises them that the clause re-
quiring the *census* to be on a fruitful, immobile good is a matter of natural

---

[18] Silvester da Prierio, *Summa summarum
quae Silvestrina dicitur, Usura*, II:12:31 and
V:1.

[19] This account of the origin of the bull
is furnished by Ballerini in *Vindiciae juris*

divini, c.4:2.

[20] Pius V, *Cum onus, Bullarium Romanum*,
VII, Part 2, pp. 737ff. "To be considered"
is clearly not the same as "are."

[21] Navarrus, *De usuris*, 22, n.81.

law. In other words, the personal *census* is a violation of natural law. Soto is soundly criticized for favoring it; almost all theologians, says Navarrus, agree in rejecting it. But the grounds of Navarrus' stand against it are revealing: the personal *census* is attacked not as a loan but as a cause for scandal and a way of "hiding usury." He adds, the pledge of one's person for a debt is generally held to be illicit; the personal *census* is even more onerous than such a pledge.[22] The arguments, in short, fail to touch the theory relied on by the proponents of the personal *census*. Indeed, Navarrus himself, treating of the sale of debts at a discount, concedes that such sales are lawful, "both because a claim on something is worth less than the thing itself, and because it is plain that that which is not usable for a year is less valuable than something of the same quality which is usable at once."[23]

The opposition by custom and the failure to develop a theory in terms of the natural-law requirements of justice presage the failure of *Cum onus* to control the *census*. The majority of theologians rejected Navarrus and held that the principal requirements set forth by the Pope were matters of positive, not natural, law. A positive promulgation by the Pope had to be received by either the governments or the common practice of a country in order for it to retain the force of law. No country received *Cum onus*. St. Alphonsus Ligouri states that the bull had no force in southern Italy, Spain, France, Belgium, Germany, and even Rome itself.[24] The bull remained an empty form, used by rigorist theologians to defend their positions, but powerless over the common conscience of Europe. It is of interest simply as a useless testimony to the failure to establish the conservative theory of the *census* by fiat. The almost immediate reduction of the bull to an ineffective velleity is clear in the history of the 5 per cent controversy, to which we again turn.

At the time that the triple contract was being urged as justification for the 5 per cent contract made with merchants, it was necessary to find a justification for the people in the country and for those in the city who did not make

---

[22] *Ibid.*, n.81–85.

[23] Navarrus, *Consilia*, V, *De usuris*, 18. The same failure to articulate a different theory, coupled with a keen awareness of the practical consequences to the usury rule if the *census* is unrestricted, guides Navarrus in peremptory rejections of the guaranteed *census* and the *census* redeemable at the buyer's option. The guaranteed *census* he describes as merely a usurious loan in which the *census* base serves as a pledge; it is a common way of exploiting the poor (Navarrus, *De usuris*, 22, n.74–78).

In accordance with modern commercial usuage I have usually referred to the assurance of a fixed return on the *census* as "guaranteeing" of the return, even though, as in the case of the triple contract, the scholastic writers usually speak of "insurance" of the return.

[24] St. Alphonsus, *Theologia moralis*, III:5:3:9, 849; similarly Lessius noted that the bull contains "many conditions not the least required by the natural law" and denied that it was binding where the custom of the people contradicted it (*De justitia*, II:22:-12:98).

the contract with businessmen; for the 5 per cent contract was celebrated "not in the larger cities only, but in almost all provinces, and in those of all Germany." [25] The attempt to analyze the contract, or rather, particular cases of it, as a *census*, then develops simultaneously with the controversy over the triple contract; having given the main outlines of the history of the latter, we shall fill in here only what concerns the *census* in particular. Again the history of the dispute is of great importance to the history of usury theory in that it led the Jesuits ultimately to take almost as firm a stand for the personal and mutually redeemable *census* as for the triple contract.

At first it might not have seemed that the 5 per cent contract could be regarded as a redeemable *census*, since as recently as 1542, Charles V had declared that a *census* redeemable by the buyer was to be held usurious by the courts.[26] Yet in 1562 John de Polanco in the name of James Laynez, the Jesuit General, wrote Peter Canisius that the German contract could be justified if it were a true sale of returns.[27] He seems to have received a discouraging response to this suggestion, for nothing more is heard of the *census* for ten years. The Jesuit General Congregation of 1573, however, acting on the report of the theological commission which had conducted the long examination of the problem, implies that the mutually redeemable *census* is licit by saying that the seller cannot be obliged to redeem except in those regions where *Cum onus* is accepted.[28] This decision is remarkable in two ways. First, it is clear evidence that only four years after the issue of *Cum onus* the most eminent authorities of the Jesuit order were treating it as pure positive law. Secondly, the acceptance of the mutually redeemable *census* is itself noteworthy, since it had so few theological defenders before the decision. The Congregation's acceptance of it must be considered as a great step towards its general acceptance. The Congregation says nothing on the guaranteed or on the personal *census*, but only declares vaguely that the *census* must be on a fruitful good or the returns of a city.

Apparently the Jesuits in Augsburg felt the same doubts about acting on the Congregation's advice about the *census* as they had on its advice about the triple contract. The letter of Theodoric Canisius, Rector of the University of Dillingen, to Mercurian of February 12, 1576, says:

To pacify the souls of many, some amongst us wish and urge that there be conceded and advocated the German mutually redeemable *census*, but since neither the Supreme Pontiff nor the imperial laws up to now have approved it, but

[25] Bishop Egolphus of Augsburg, quoted in St. Peter Canisius, *Epistolae*, VII, 342.
[26] Zech, *Dissertationes tres*, III:2:7:203.
[27] St. Peter Canisius, *Epistolae*, III, 543.
[28] *Ibid.*, VII, 672–673.

rather condemned it, and as the just price of this *census* is unknown, and as it has a great appearance of palliated usury, and as it is *ex professo* rejected by the most learned jurists, the more learned theologians of this province do not see how such a *census* can be permitted or advocated by us.[29]

The really decisive step in the acceptance of the new modifications of the *census* was taken by the Jesuit Congregation of 1581. The Congregation makes three important declarations on the contract. The mutually redeemable *census* is allowed. For the first time, guaranteeing of the *census* is also officially allowed, so that the buyer may licitly be assured a return whatever happens to the base. Finally, the personal *census* on a working person is admitted to be licit in form although "most dangerous" and "not commonly to be tolerated." [30] The only advance later theologians will make on this decision will be to admit the personal *census* as generally licit in practice. The effect of the Congregation's decision, as we shall see even more clearly when we discuss implicit contracts, was to legitimize virtually every 5 per cent contract made with a working person.

As mentioned above,[31] Gregory XII acted on the advice of this Congregation when he wrote Duke William of Bavaria that a simple loan at 5 per cent was illicit, yet hinted strongly that many 5 per cent contracts could be held to be other than loans. Nonetheless, since the papal brief formally condemned the 5 per cent loan, William thought it his duty to ban the 5 per cent contract in his county and to order courts not to enforce it. This measure caused widespread complaint, and in 1583 the legislators of Bavaria petitioned the Duke to revoke it, saying that it was destroying not only commerce, but churches and monasteries dependent on the 5 per cent for their income.[32] Duke William replied that he could not allow usury, but would allow the mutually redeemable *census*. The legislators replied that this was all that they ever sought. The Duke answered that this had not been clear from their original petition; he added that formal *census* contracts were not much used in the region, but, acting on the advice of Gregory de Valentia, S.J., he allowed the *census*.[33]

From this point on, "the German contract" or 5 per cent contract seems clearly to be identified with the personal, mutually redeemable *census*, whereas when it first appeared it tended to be identified with the triple contract.[34] The imperial laws against a buyer's redeeming a *census* were not repealed, but they were abrogated in Bavaria, and a century later were not

[29] *Ibid.*, VII, 342.
[30] Zech, III:2:8:263.
[31] See *supra*, Chapter X, section 4.
[32] Zech, III:2:8:265.
[33] *Ibid.*, III:2:8:265–276.
[34] Cf. Van Roey, "Le contractus germanicus," p. 945.

effective even in other parts of the empire.[35] Thus throughout one large
section of Europe the habit of taking a moderate reward for the extension of
credit became general with the approval of the theologians. How many contracts were actually expressed as *census* and how many were only interpreta-
tively reduced to the *census* is difficult to tell. It is certainly of great significance that the ordinary German term for interest on a loan is *zins*, a word
derived from *census*.[36]

As far as the Jesuits are concerned, the controversy over the *census* continued for a few more years after the Congregation's decision and Duke
William's edict. In 1586 it was found necessary for the Jesuit faculty at
Dillingen to declare again, in a decision ratified at Rome, that the mutually
redeemable *census*, although not counseled, was licit and was to be explained
to those refusing to leave the practice of usury. Another German Jesuit in
Germany, Jerome Torres, however, again questioned this *census* in 1588. In
reply to his questions and objections, Claude Aquaviva, General of the order,
ordered in 1589 that the licitness of the contract be held without dissent by
the German Jesuits. In May of the same year, another commission of Jesuit
theologians, set up by Aquaviva, approved the redeemable and also the
guaranteed *census*.[37] The dissention in Germany ends with Aquaviva's order.

3. *The Shift to Interest Titles*

Authority had decided the case in Germany. It had not decided the
theoretical approaches of the leading moralists. Molina, Lessius, and Lugo
still had problems of theory to resolve.

Molina takes the position that the conventional *census* theory justifies all
usury. In a personal *census*, "Nothing else is bartered but the personal obligation of paying something successively and the personal right of demanding
and receiving it." Now, "A right to receive 100 in a year or in two years in
truth not worth less in itself than 100 when it is morally certain that it will
then be paid entire and without labor and expense." This must be so, says
Molina, reasoning backwards from the usury prohibition, otherwise usury
would be licit.[38]

Ignoring the decision of the Jesuit Congregation of 1583, Molina adopts
Navarrus' explanation of *Cum onus* and finds the personal *census* naturally
usurious. It is justified only by the ordinary interest titles on loans, which are
not common. But if the personal *census* is usurious, Molina feels some compulsion to contrive an analysis of the *census* that will exclude the personal

[35] Zech, III:2:8:274; III:2:7:205.
[36] Funk, *Zins und Wucher*, p. 115.
[37] Canisius, *Epistolae*, VIII, 282.
[38] Molina, *De justitia*, II:386:7; 361:9.

census and yet admit the real *census* which the pontiffs have formally approved. Accordingly, he declares that in the real *census*, what is bought "is not a right in, and a personal obligation for, the payments materially considered," but "part of the right in the property or part of the plenary ownership of the property." The payments themselves are not purchased, except as they are in the potentiality of the property.[39] This theory allows the real *census*, because there is no objection to profit on the sale of real estate, and it presumably excludes the personal *census*, because one could not well say that the purchaser of that actually acquired part ownership of the seller's person. It avoids the inconsistency that comes of admitting the lawfulness of buying the right to money at a profit while condemning usury on loans. It is a clear return to Henry of Hesse, although Molina does not mention him by name.[40]

As a way out of the difficulties of the *census* theory the solution was far from ideal. Molina does not explain how it applied to a kind of *census* which he admits was very common and which he seems to think licit: the purchase of annuities from the king. It is not easy to see how one could be said to acquire part ownership in the persons paying the taxes, which were, at least in part, the fruits purchased in these contracts. Moreover, as Lugo was to point out, repeating the objection that Henry of Eutin had made to Henry of Hesse, the seller does not intend to give up ownership, nor does the buyer intend to acquire it.[41]

The teasing problem of a *census* theory reconcilable with the usury rule remained. Lugo agrees with Molina that the medieval *census* approach legitimizes most usury.[42] With his usual ingenuity he has a new solution. The correct concept of the *census* is that in it

part of the usufruct of the field on which the *census* is constituted is bought. Then, . . . by another contract, which is implicitly contained in the very constitution of a real *census*, it is agreed by the parties that, for the hope of the fruit which the buyer has from that usufruct, the seller binds himself to pay such an annual payment of money; — and in this way the prior contract is reduced to the obligation of paying only an annual sum, by which the seller redeems the partial usufruct of the field which he had sold; the field itself, however, remaining really obliged in the manner of a pledge for the payment of the promised money. . . .

Lugo adds that his theory will not only distinguish the *census* from a loan, but will also show the irrelevance of the argument that from the *census* "arises all the evils of usury," namely, men living without sweat on the labor

[39] II:386:5.
[40] See *supra*, pp. 155–156.
[41] Lugo, *Disputationes*, 27:2:17.
[42] 27:2:19.

of others, charity impeded by the rich who buy a *census* instead of lending freely, the poor becoming further impoverished by the pledging of their goods on the *census*. These arguments, says Lugo, tell equally against the purchases of immobile goods, which the rich buy from the poor. Because of such purchases, too, the rich fail to lend, and instead of working, rent the farms and fields back to the poor and live in leisure on the returns. These phenomena do not prove the purchase of immobile goods to be usurious; neither should they prove the *census* usurious or unjust.[43]

But like Molina's *census* theory, Lugo's leads to the flat rejection of the personal *census* as a contract distinct from a loan. He declares frankly that "in the personal *census*, strictly speaking, nothing else is sold or given, except the payments themselves which are to be made." Unlike a commodity, money payments cannot vary in price; "for a payment of money, like a liquid debt in money, has in itself a determined and invariable value; for 100 goldpieces are always worth 100 goldpieces, whether the buyers are few or many."[44] He considers the contention that it is the sale of the fruits of one's labors and characterizes this as

a mere excogitation against the mind and intention of the parties, who intend nothing less than to buy or sell personal work, nor does the seller of the *census* wish in any way to constitute himself slave or servant of the buyer.

Moreover, in practice, the seller of a personal *census* often does no work at all. Again, a higher price is not paid for a personal *census* on the work of eminent men. Again, if a real sale of services were meant, the seller could not sell several *census* on his labors, but such sales are frequent. Again, how could heirs be obliged to carry out the personal work of the seller, as in the so-called perpetual personal *census*? Lugo concludes that the personal *census* may be defended only as a loan on the basis of the usual interest titles.[45]

This sensible, practical, and realistic conclusion had already been reached by Lessius. He wastes no time on subtle attempts to refine *census* theory; the conventional analysis suffices.[46] But profit on the purchase of the *census* right is justified only in cases where interest would be justified.

Lessius can take this approach without encountering practical objections because he inclines to the belief that interest is commonly justified: "A personal right is almost always joined with dangers and difficulties, and with money in hand fruitful goods can be bought or business executed with great profit."[47] Similarly, he notes that the sale of debt at a discount is licit

---

[43] 27:2:20, 21.

[44] 27:2:25, 27.

[45] 27:2:28. The sale of a debt at a dis-

count is similarly treated, 26:7:93–95.

[46] Lessius, *De justitia*, II:22:12:97.

[47] II:22:4:31.

if there is risk of the deprivation of "some power which present money gives, which a note of debt does not have." [48]

Yet even in the practical hands of Lessius the importance of the *census* form is not entirely lost. In admitting the prevalence of interest titles, he is clearly bolder in regard to *census* sales than he is in regard to loans. He even considers it necessary to emphasize the form. To an objector contending that the personal *census* is palliated usury, Lessius replies with a firm assertion of the Gersonian principle: "One and the same thing is differently estimated according to the different contracts employed." [49] A more concise statement of the analytical serviceableness of the *census* contract could not be made.

As might be expected from writers justifying the *census* by interest titles, Molina, Lessius, and Lugo all permit the guaranteeing of repayment whatever happens to the *census* base. [50] Molina, however, objects to giving the buyer an option to force redemption unless the price paid for the *census* is increased. Failure to make this allowance for the heavy onus imposed on the seller is common in Spain and makes the contract unjust, although not usurious. [51] Lessius treats the mutual redeemability of the *census* as common and licit. [52] Lugo comes to the same conclusion, adding only the somewhat meaningless formula "provided one's soul is not usurious." [53]

At this stage of development of *census* theory, the remark of Lugo on the ways of justifying purchases of debt at a discount is appropriate: "I think that this controversy is more speculative than practical." [54] Once it was established that the purchase of a right to money should be justified by interest titles, the only practical question was: Was a right to interest present?

4. Eighteenth-Century Epilogue

As upon the triple contract, Ballerini, Zech, and Liguori are representative authorities of the eighteenth-century view of the *census*: Ballerini as an example of a minority effort to construct an ideal past age where *census* theory was pure; Zech as an example of the loose use of *census* for all credit transactions; Liguori as an example of the matter-of-fact acceptance of the contract by the main line of moralists.

Ballerini's position is more rigid than any writer, modern or ancient, and reveals what medieval theory would have been if it had been consistent. He approves only a real, perpetual *census*. [55] The perpetual *census* may be sold

[48] II:21:8:73.
[49] II:22:4:33.
[50] Molina, *De justitia*, II:387:10; cf. 385:17 on the price of the guarantee. Lessius, II:22:-11:65–67; Lugo, 27:8:102.
[51] Molina, II:391:19; cf. 378:15.
[52] Lessius, II:22:10:57.
[53] Lugo, 26:13; see also 27:8:121.
[54] 26:7:93.
[55] Ballerini, *De montibus pietatis*, Opus. I in *De jure divino*, c.4:87.

at a price less than the fruits will ultimately bring because it is like the outright sale of a field, whose fruits must ultimately exceed the price paid; the basis of the calculation of the price is the field itself and not the fruits. But he will not allow even a real, temporary *census* giving the buyer a profit, because here there would be a profit by the sale of time.[56] According to his system, as he admits himself, a *census* for three years at 4 per cent should cost 112, while a perpetual *census* at 4 per cent, which might in practice run for 50 years, would cost only 100. To a charge of absurdity about this, his reply is only that the basis of calculation is different and that a similar extraordinary difference is often seen when the rents from a house in a few years exceed the price of the purchase of the same house for perpetuity.[57]

On the personal *census*, Ballerini is even more severe. A temporary personal *census* is illicit, like a temporary real one, because it is a profit made out of time.[58] A perpetual personal *census* cannot even exist, because no person exists perpetually.[59] Nor can he justify the personal *census* in practice in some other way, as Lugo does by the interest titles. Ballerini admits the *census* buyer may claim interest, but according to his standards, interest titles are not usually available.[60]

As for the mutually redeemable *census*, Ballerini describes this as a scandalous invention of modern theologians. If theoretically it cannot be shown to be entirely wrong, yet in practice in the past and present it has always been used as a loan. According to Ballerini, who ignores its history in Germany, it was first appealed to in late sixteenth-century Belgium, where the money of wards was put out at interest to the poor. Theoretically, the wards were supposed to claim only *lucrum cessans*, and their money was to be considered like a *mons pietatis*. But soon interest was always asked on the money, whether *lucrum cessans* was present or not, and the money was loaned to merchants and not to the poor. This practice was then justified as a mutually redeemable *census*. Several Belgian synods condemned it, and in 1607 and in 1688 the theologians of Louvain described such a *census* as a true loan. Nevertheless, in practice, Ballerini reports, nothing was done about the custom of using it for profit, because it was so thoroughly rooted in the economic life of the country. In 1727 French Jansenists, fleeing to Belgium, objected to the contract as usurious, and a general controversy broke out over the *census*, but since the contracts were in fact loans, the discussion became a more general one over whether usury itself was licit, and

[56] 4:94.
[57] 4:95.
[58] 4:91.
[59] 4:89.
[60] See *infra*, pp. 266–267.

the Jansenists, who had begun by attacking the *census*, ended by reversing their position and defending usury. This history, Ballerini holds, shows well that the mutually redeemable *census* was always only another name for a loan.[61] He notes that in current practice the parties to a mutually redeemable *census* think of it as a loan; moralists should judge about what happens in practice. Many theological writers on usury, he adds, live in an abstract world, not thinking of the practical application of, and the practical dangers in, the theories they allow.[62]

The combination of redeemability with a temporary *census* is especially shocking, for nothing really remains to be redeemed. In the perpetual *census*, at least, the seller redeems his obligation to keep on paying the annual installments indefinitely. But in the temporary *census*, when the period of the *census* has expired, and the seller still has to redeem, he redeems no further obligation to pay but simply returns the money he was given. Thus, a man sells a twenty-year *census* for 100, pays 5 a year for 20 years, and then has to "redeem" the *census* for 100, although what he redeems is nonexistent. The case, Ballerini declares, is clearly one of a loan and usury.[63] Guaranteeing of the *census* is similarly illicit. It transforms the contract from a genuine sale to a loan, with the good, which is the supposed *census* base, serving in fact only as a pledge for the loan.[64]

By being more logical than the medieval writers, Ballerini arrives at extremes that they arbitrarily avoided. He is, in fact, faithful to the majority position in an earlier age of usury analysis only by his objection to the mutually redeemable and the guaranteed *census*. Like his views on the triple contract, his opinion here was without influence. But it does offer an illuminating comparison between the logic of the past and the practices of his day.

In direct contrast, Zech readily approves every kind of *census*, personal, guaranteed, and redeemable, and, unlike the seventeenth-century Jesuits, does so without appeal to interest titles.[65] His one restriction is that a personal *census* may not be purchased from a man whose work produces just enough to support himself.[66] As for the redeemability of the *census*, this may be provided for in a special contract, in which compensation is given for redeemability, so that a redeemable *census* is different from a loan, in which there is an automatic obligation to restore.[67] In Bavaria, the common practice

[61] Ballerini, *Vindiciae juris divini*, c.1:1–2. It is true that Lessius defends the contract precisely in relation to the money of wards on deposit (22:10:62).

[62] Ballerini, *Opus*. I, 4:54.

[63] 4:91.

[64] 4:67.

[65] Zech, III:2:7:234, 230.

[66] III:2:7:216.

[67] III:2:7:241.

is to exclude the seller's right to redeem, so that it is entirely within the buyer's option when he will terminate the seller's payments and demand back his principal. But even this is licit, if a just price is paid.[68] It is objected that the imperial laws fixed 5 per cent as the just price for a *census* redeemable only by the seller, so that it does not seem fair that a *census* which is a much heavier burden on him should have the same price. Zech replies that times and circumstances have changed since the imperial laws were given on this and also that the just price knows three degrees, so that the price of the latter *census* could be the lowest just price and the price of the other the highest just price without any injustice. The common estimation, after all, determines the just price. The mutually redeemable *census*, he says, once disapproved by the ancients, timidly put forward by the moderns, is now commonly held as licit.[69]

Zech also defends as a *census* a contract which he calls "the German contract," in which the term *census* is not itself employed. We shall consider this in our discussion of implicit contracts. It is abundantly evident here that the admission of this contract, like Summenhart's admission of the purchase of a simple right to money, is the practical legitimation of every credit transaction. The legitimation follows logically from the old theory which distinguishes the *census* from a loan, and defends it, as the purchase of a right to money.

St. Alphonsus gives a somewhat less extreme statement of the common teaching. He says that either theory of the *census*, the medieval one which sees it as the purchase of a right to money, or Lugo's theory that it is a usufruct, is acceptable, but he prefers the latter.[70] He sees no natural-law objection to a personal *census*, and he thinks the bull *Sollicitudo* of Nicolas V can be construed in its favor. The difference between a personal *census* and a loan is that the former may be terminated at the seller's pleasure, while a loan runs until the end of the time agreed. The only naturally illicit *census* is one founded on an unfruitful thing or person, for there no real good or usufruct is purchased.[71] The risk of the *census* base is intrinsically the buyer's, but an added contract of guaranty is licit. A mutually redeemable *census*, even if personal, is probably licit, although there is a danger of usury.[72] Thus, the personal, guaranteed, and redeemable *census*, or any variation of this, is, in the eyes of St. Alphonsus, formally in accordance with the standards of natural justice.

[68] III:2:7:230–232.
[69] III:2:8:287, 289.
[70] St. Alphonsus, III:5:3:9, 839.

[71] III:5:3:9, 840.
[72] III:5:3:9, 842, 843.

Conclusion

We have seen the medieval theory of the *census* developed by authors of authority to a point where any purchase of money, even without a *census* base, has been defended as licit. This logical extreme has been rejected, at least tacitly, by most authors; and the theory on which it was based, that a *census* is the purchase of a right, has been vigorously repudiated by some. But the more conservative *census* concept has by no means won general approval either, and doubt still remains as to what a *census* really is. Leaving aside all questions of the pure *census* concept, no really successful criticism has been made of the true personal *census*, and guaranty and redeemability have been generally accepted. The guaranteed personal *census*, redeemable by either party, is distinguished from a loan only by the highly theoretical requirement that the seller of the *census* should have labor to sell. The tendency to justify the contract by interest titles becomes prevalent as interest is more generally admitted. Acceptance of the contract is not unanimous, but there is certainly enough scholastic opinion in its favor to justify any one using it in practice; and the use of the contract seems to be universal. Here again an operation which in practice is indistinguishable from a loan has been analyzed from another standpoint and found licit.

CHAPTER XII

PROFIT AS THE MEASURE OF INTEREST

It may well strike us today as strange that a development of interest titles recognized by the medieval scholastics did not appear to the later writers as the easiest and most obvious way of showing the moral licitness of the vast amount of credit business accepted by the common conscience. In particular, it may seem surprising that *lucrum cessans* was not at once and commonly invoked. But it should be recalled that the majority of medieval scholastics had allowed interest only when the debtor was at fault or the lender had been put to some direct expense by the loan. Although a minority, increasing in number throughout the fifteenth century, had defended *lucrum cessans*, even they had defended it with one oppressive restriction: *lucrum cessans* might be licitly sought only if the loan had originally been made out of charity. Moreover, despite a certain exaggeration in the medieval insistence on charity, the insistence did have this basis: if someone, not led by charity, preferred to loan rather than to do business, there was a presumption that he loaned because he intended to make a greater amount by lending than he lost by not doing business, and this was to seek profit from a loan, or to commit usury by everyone's standards. Faced with the unanimous tradition on the necessity for a charitable intention, the later scholastics found it easier to defend what may seem today the more dubious devices of the triple contract and the personal, redeemable *census*, where no charitable motive was required, than to defend compensation directly sought on a loan. Throughout the sixteenth century, the triple contract and the personal *census* are more important than the interest titles.

Two causes, however, combine to promote the case for *lucrum cessans*. One is the immense increase in business activity following the discovery of the American and Asiatic worlds and the commercial revolution of the sixteenth century.[1] This increase in commerce rendered it objectively more probable that a lender underwent a true loss of profit when he loaned his money instead of using it in business, and made it more likely that what he

[1] Sée, *Modern Capitalism*, p. 41.

received as interest was no more than he would have earned in trade. The other factor leading to a new respect for *lucrum cessans* is the sharp criticism made by the later scholastics of the medieval scholastics' use of the criterion of intention, and the consequent elimination of the insistence on a charitable motive in lending. A philosophical clarification thus leads to a highly practical result.

Throughout much of this period *lucrum cessans* was not used as it is today, because its presence was not generally presumed, nor was it admitted that there could be a common estimation of *lucrum cessans* which might be claimable by everyone, whether he personally suffered loss or not. In this approach, we see a traditional characteristic of the treatment of usury: problems involving the just price were always resolved by the standard of the common estimation, but problems involving loans were regularly judged by the particular, private loss involved in individual cases.

Yet, despite its restriction to individual cases, where loss could be proved, *lucrum cessans* becomes increasingly recognized as the justification for taking something beyond the principal on a loan. The period we survey begins when *lucrum cessans* is still tightly restricted by its medieval bonds. At the opening of this period occur the unprecedentedly comprehensive analyses of the title by Summenhart and Cajetan. There follow the self-destructive reaction of Soto, the conservative approval given by the Popes, and then the more liberal defenses of Molina and Navarrus. By the beginning of the seventeenth century, *lucrum cessans* has become the usual plea on loans. Its triumph and dominance as the regular title to licit gain in finance are assured. We shall trace the major steps in the development of this great and common claim to payment on a loan.

1. *Limited Expansion: Summenhart and Cajetan*

For a radical writer on usury, Summenhart is surprisingly conservative upon *lucrum cessans*; his conservatism is eloquent testimony to the great suspicion with which the title in any form was still viewed. What he does in hostile circumstances is to offer the most extended defense of it yet given by any scholastic, and then severely restrict the title's use by eight limiting requisites, which faithfully continue the medieval attitude toward it.

In defense of the title he begins by taking *interesse* to mean "the losing of some temporal good now held, or the not seeking of some temporal good obtainable." One is entitled to compensation for *interesse*, and *lucrum cessans*, a special case of it, is consequently a claim to compensation, because the profit contained in the goods of the one hindered is already in some way his own. Therefore, if one impedes him from seeking it, one not only impedes him from seeking it, but one even takes away from him what is already as if held by him.

The crucial objection is made that money does not fructify; therefore, it contains no profit in potency. But this objection carries little weight with Summenhart, who, as we shall see later, is in general disagreement with the scholastic tradition on the sterility of money.[2] Here he answers that a house does not fructify, yet one must compensate its owner if one prevents him from renting it; again, he says, with a bolder comparison of money to naturally fertile goods, a field only bears fruit through human labor, as does money, and everyone admits that one must compensate an owner of a field for lost potential fruits if one deprives him of the field itself. Further, he offers a third analogy, more in keeping with the earlier traditions on money and suggestive of St. Bernardine's position that *lucrum cessans* is paid only for the lost opportunity to work, not for the money itself. You must, he says, compensate a worker for his lost profit if you take away the tools by which he earns his living. Money is the merchant's tool, and, like the mechanic, he can make his personal labor fructify only by the use of his tools. Consequently, he should be paid when he is deprived of the use of it.

A second critical objection is made that the lender lends voluntarily, "but to one acting voluntarily, no injury is done"; therefore, the lender is not entitled to compensation. This is basically the argument of St. Thomas and Scotus, that no one is entitled to compensation for a harm they stupidly but wilfully bring on themselves. To this Summenhart replies that if one induces a merchant or a mechanic to cease voluntarily from work, one is held to compensate him for his lost profit if that is the condition under which he agrees to cease work. So here, the merchant foregoes his profit in business only on condition that he will be compensated. It would be an injury to him if the condition upon which he acts were not executed.

Having thus made a defense of the essential justness of the title, Summenhart then sets the harsh conditions which must be observed so that taking *lucrum cessans* is not usury. They are in substance: only the loss actually incurred through making the loan, minus the expenses that would have been made in business and allowing for the doubtfulness of the profit, may be charged; the title may not be used on loans where one is bound by a precept of charity to lend; it must not be used if it will scandalize one's neighbor or hurt one's own reputation; most important of all, "the lender, if he had to consider temporal advantage only, would prefer to retain

---

[2] See *infra*, Chapter XVII, section 1.

the principal and so avoid the loss occurring, than lend and so receive beyond the principal." By the last clause, *lucrum cessans* is still confined to loans made out of charity. If the lender seeks the interest in itself, if he prefers the interest to keeping his money, "then it is a sign that he hopes some temporal advantage will follow beyond the restitution of the loss suffered, and so he intends to seek usury." [3] Summenhart thus remains a medievalist as to practice, but he has made two bold advances in theory: he has compared money directly to fruitful goods, and he has decisively answered the objection that one should not be compensated for a loss voluntarily incurred.

A more detailed and closely reasoned examination of the title is undertaken by Cajetan in an effort to reconcile the inconsistent positions of Thomas Aquinas. In the end he rejects *lucrum cessans* considered absolutely, on the grounds that St. Thomas gives: its admission would destroy the usury prohibition proper. At the same time he surrounds his formal rejection by so many qualifications that the net effect of his treatment is a liberal advance in acceptance of the title considered in practice.

Cajetan begins by citing St. Thomas' condemnation of *lucrum cessans* and then urges against the Thomistic thesis four strong objections. First, St. Thomas himself allowed *lucrum cessans* to be calculated in the repayment of overdue loans and in the restitution of stolen money. Now,

one having money either has something more than the quantity of money or not. If he has something more, it follows that he can sell it and lead it into a contract; if not, it follows that after delay more is not owed to him.

In the development of this objection, the standard medieval criterion of intention is, for the first time in the history of the interest titles, dismissed. It should not matter, says the objector, that in one case the lender seeks the compensation, in the other it is paid him for what he lost involuntarily: "Commutative justice is the adequation of thing with thing, whether voluntarily or involuntarily one sustains a loss."

Secondly, it is objected, money is the instrument of a businessman; he should be compensated for the loss of the profits it would have brought him, as he would be compensated for the loss entailed by the loss of other instruments. Thirdly, it is contended:

the lender has two things, to wit, money and potentiality of profit or fruit; and, because he lends he deprives himself of both, to wit, the money and the opportunity of gain; therefore he can bring the restitution of both into the contract.

Fourthly, it is maintained that in a sale it is licit to add to the common

[3] Summenhart, *De contractibus*, Q.30.

price if the object sold has a peculiar value to the seller; similarly here, the money has a peculiar value to the businessman that makes it worth more to him than its absolute value. Therefore, he should be allowed to charge for this. The objector concludes that *lucrum cessans* is licit because it is received not "by reason of the use of money, which would be usury, but by reason of the recognized potency of gain," which is a title distinct from the loan. He adds that St. Thomas contradicts himself.[4]

Cajetan then says, "But if some one says that he has something more and that it is licit for him to sell it, the way is open so that in any loan of money he can demand something beyond the principal by virtue of the contract, which all deny." Faced with what seems a threat to the usury law itself, Cajetan proceeds to a closer examination, a refutation of the objections, and a defense of St. Thomas.

The power of money to produce profit, Cajetan declares, is to be distinguished. On the one hand, there is its absolute power insofar as it is simply an exchange medium by which other profitable goods may be acquired. This absolute power is common to all money and cannot be distinguished from the substance of money. The absolute power of money may be compared to the absolute power of a grain of wheat to produce more wheat; this power is identical with the grain itself, and the grain taken abstractly is not valued more because of it. The grain may be used for sowing, in which case its power will become valuable, or it may be eaten at once, in which case its power of providing fruit has no value. Similarly, money may be used either to make a profit or consumed in common exchanges. Absolutely speaking, the value of money is simply its exchange or face value.

On the other hand, there is a power in money "not absolutely, but insofar as it is subject to the industry of such a businessman or buyer at such a time, in such a place, in such a commodity, etc., and this is called the power of money as it is subject to industry." This power is not common to all money. It exists "in relation to some person"; and "it is susceptible of being greater or less, according to its proximity to profit and the quantity of the business, of labor, etc." Money about to be used to gain a profit is like seed about to be sown. The more prepared the seed is for actual fruition, the more valuable it is. Similarly, money about to be used to make a profit is more valuable, the more ready it is to be used in this way and the closer is the realization of the profit. This secondary, relative power of money, is not considered by theologians when they speak of money, absolutely: "And about this power

---

[4] Cajetan, *Commentarium in summam theologicam S. Thomae Aquinatis*, Leon. edi- tion (Rome, 1882), II–II, Q.78, art. 2, III.

are not to be understood the sayings of the doctors. Rather, to sell this beyond the principal, or, to put it better, to redeem this, is licit. . . ." [5]

By this distinction between the potentialities of money Cajetan confirms one part of St. Thomas' teaching. If the writer is a businessman, it is licit for him to demand *lucrum cessans* in delay or in the restitution of stolen money, for this is to receive compensation for the special power of his money of which he was deprived.[6] Nevertheless, the distinction seemingly makes St. Thomas' stand against *lucrum cessans* apart from delay even less defensible. Cajetan has reached a point where apparently the evidence in favor of *lucrum cessans*, due the lender from the beginning of a loan, is overwhelming. But his analysis is not finished. At this critical juncture, he declares again that if *lucrum cessans* on a loan not in delay is admitted, "each one, after he had once exposed his money to business, could transfer it to lending, with a moderate profit, such as a thief would be held to restore; and so everywhere experience would teach that usury would not be reputed to be a sin." [7]

As the postulated conclusion is untenable, Cajetan presses his analysis. He first notes that the extra value of money in a particular advantageous condition is not retained by it after it is reduced to the common condition of money. He then says that a distinction is to be made between the unwilling and willing transfer of money from a more valuable to a less valuable condition. If the owner suffers a transfer, as in delay and theft, he is to be compensated; but if the owner willingly transfers the money to a less valuable condition, he himself is responsible for the change in value and so is not entitled to compensation. The voluntariness or involuntariness of a contract, as the hypothetical objector said, is irrelevant to the justice of the contract, if the objective values involved are the same in both voluntary and involuntary contracts. But here, Cajetan implies, the voluntary act itself alters an objective value, so that the wilfullness of the contract is crucial in determining its justice. Consequently, although a merchant places a special value on money he has ready for business, he has no title to *lucrum cessans* if he voluntarily lends it for a nonbusiness purpose. Thus, as a general rule, *lucrum cessans* may not be claimed on a loan, and St. Thomas is vindicated.[8]

Cajetan, however, adds two qualifications which considerably soften this formal adhesion to St. Thomas. The first is that a lender can charge *lucrum cessans* when forced to loan — a concession, not very generous in itself, except that Cajetan declares that the need of a neighbor is a kind of compulsion to loan. Here Cajetan joins the medieval theologians, who allowed *lucrum*

[5] *Ibid.*, 78:2:IV.
[6] 78:2:VI; cf. 62:4.
[7] 78:2:VI.
[8] 78:2:VI, VII.

cessans provided that charity was the chief motive of the loan. The second, much more important qualification, is that if a loan is made for a business purpose with money previously intended for the business, full *lucrum cessans* may be charged even if there is no compulsion nor charitable motive present. Cajetan's theory is that the money in a business loan is kept in the specially valuable condition it was in when owned by the businessman lender. Consequently, the value of the money remains at the high value it possessed in the hands of the lender. The lender has not, as in the consumption loan, voluntarily transferred his money to a less valuable state; it is just as valuable to the borrower as it was to him. Hence, the lender is entitled to demand back, not only the money itself, but the surplus value it represented in his hands and still represented when first delivered to his borrower's business uses.[9] In this bold analysis, Cajetan goes farther than any writer before him has ever gone, because he eliminates the need for a charitable intention on the part of the lender. In a loan by a businessman to a businessman, interest is licit, even though primarily sought in itself. The defense from the charge of usury is that what is sought is not pure profit on a loan, but only the extra, relative value inhering to money in certain concrete circumstances.

Although Cajetan's first insistence that a voluntary loan will by itself alter the value of the money loaned may not seem defensible, his fault must not be held a great one. This insistence, which leads to a rejection of *lucrum cessans* as a universal rule, is clearly motivated by an unnecessary fear that if he is less strict, the usury law itself will be empty. But, both in his initial defense of the title and in his final admission of it on business loans, Cajetan has been the title's strong and subtle advocate. His analysis of *lucrum cessans* and his acceptance of it in commercial credit open a new epoch.[10]

2. *Soto: No Compensation for Voluntary Loss*

This new epoch is not, however, entirely recognized by Soto, who, despite the growing popularity of Cajetan's arguments and the general prestige of his fellow Dominican, makes a sharp critique of his position. As we have already seen in discussing the triple contract, Soto is strictly committed to

[9] 78:2:VI.
[10] Cajetan's careful study of money should be contrasted with the perfunctory treatment of theory, but broad practical approval of *lucrum cessans* by Silvester da Prierio. Silvester, like Cajetan, reduces the insistence on "a charitable intention" to desire to help a friend. Then he gives as an example a case where "the friend" could double his money if given a loan; in other words, the loan need not be to help the poor, but to help a businessman. *Lucrum cessans* may be claimed if ultimate gain by the lender were at least probable (Silvester, *Summa*, at *Usura*, I:23, 19).

the theory that money by itself can never be a title to gain and that labor alone can justify profit on an investment — a severe theory, which perhaps should have been held by the medieval authors and best explains some of their argumentation on the usury prohibition, but which, in fact, had never been consistently supported by them. Soto's rigorism here, as on the triple contract, arises from his desire to be consistent to an extent that no scholastic author had ever been on all aspects of money investments. He consequently elects a more logical, less liberal theory of *lucrum cessans* than had Cajetan. Then carrying his attack farther, he is led to make an assault on the doctrine of intention, and so doing he paradoxically undermines the rigorist position; his conclusion does not have the consistency on which he prides himself.

He begins by attacking vigorously the comparison of money to a tool or to a seed, on which Cajetan had rested much of his case for *lucrum cessans*. You can, Soto says, pay a worker not to use his tool, for the tool has a use that is rentable. But you cannot pay someone not to use money, for the use of the money is the same as the money itself. Similarly, you can sell a seed at the value of its potential fruit; but you cannot sell money in the same way, for there is no potential fruit there to be distinguished from the money itself. "You have nothing which you may sell." The Thomistic doctrine of the identity of the use and substance of money is reasserted against Cajetan, who seems to Soto to have confused the consumptible, money, with non-consumptible goods. The extra value that Cajetan says money has is not a power resident in the money yet distinct from it, like the utility of a tool or the potentiality of a seed; it is a value, as Cajetan himself says, which money possesses only in relation to labor, and, in fact, the profit that will come from the use of the money is due to its user's industry alone. Therefore, Soto concludes, *lucrum cessans* may not be claimed because money itself is worth more in a particular situation. But it may be claimed as compensation for the impediment offered to one's labor by the deprivation of one's money.

If Soto admits *lucrum cessans* may be paid as compensation for a lost opportunity to work, if not for money itself, what is the practical difference between his opinion and Cajetan's? The answer is that he adds to his analysis of the basis of *lucrum cessans* an independent thesis: no one can be compensated for damage he willingly brings on himself. This, of course, had been Cajetan's position, too, as it had been that of St. Thomas and Scotus; but Cajetan had modified it by arguing that money intended for business, which was then voluntarily put into a business loan, remained in the same valuable state. This modification is impossible for Soto, who concludes simply that all *lucrum cessans* voluntarily sought is illicit, because no one is genuinely impeded from working by his own voluntary action, and no one can claim damage if he voluntarily hinders himself. At the same time, saving St. Thomas' other opinion, Soto allows that *lucrum cessans* can be asked in delay, theft, or compulsory loans; in all these cases an external force prevents the victim from the opportunity of laboring with his money. It is remarkable that in none of these arguments does Soto attempt to answer Summenhart's contention that one is held to compensate a man voluntarily ceasing from work if the paying of such compensation is the condition under which he foregoes his work. This sensible position is completely ignored.

Soto notes that the defenders of *lucrum cessans* say that a charitable motive in making the loan is necessary to legitimate the taking of interest. Suddenly and strongly he attacks this insistence on intention which had been the standard medieval way of controlling interest: "But how imbecilic this condition is is openly demonstrated: that which in its own nature is licit, it is no sin to desire; nor does such a desire vitiate a contract." However, instead of concluding from this that *lucrum cessans* may be claimed more extensively, he sees the use made of the intention criterion by the title's defenders as a reason for suspecting its validity. If the title is a good one, everyone can claim it — not only charitable lenders. But if everyone can claim it, "the way to usury is laid wide open." Consequently, he reasons from the existence of the usury prohibition, the title cannot be a good one. His opponents have tried to make a charitable intention rectify an objectively unnatural act.

If Soto is so clear that intention is irrelevant to the justice of the act here, and that *lucrum cessans* cannot be sought even on a loan made from charity, why, one may ask, does he think interest may be paid on compulsory loans? The difference would seem to be that in the cases where he allows *lucrum cessans*, the lender has been physically prevented from exercising his labor; in the cases, including that of a lender moved by charity, he voluntarily hinders himself. Now according to his analysis, it is never illicit to desire a licit thing, but it is illicit to bring about damage to oneself and then ask compensation for one's own wilful act. Hence the voluntariness of the lender can vitiate the legitimacy of interest, and his involuntariness make it proper; although, if a right to interest existed objectively by itself, as Soto's opponents believe, preference for such interest would not make it immoral to take it.[11]

After all his arguments against it, however, Soto admits *lucrum cessans* apart from compulsion as being favored "by a less probable opinion" — a qualification that is by no means a pure condemnation. More significantly, when treating of *damnum emergens* he allows it precisely under the con-

[11] Soto, *De justitia*, VI:1:3.

ditions he criticizes the defenders of *lucrum cessans* for stipulating: the lender must be asked, and he must lend out of charity.

Despite this last inconsistency, his fierce criticism of the use of intention as a criterion is a step towards its complete rejection. A rigorist on interest titles, Soto becomes an important influence towards the liberalization of their use in practice. His stubborn denial of the right to compensation for damage voluntarily incurred, after Summenhart's demonstration of the fallaciousness of this position, must be ascribed to a fear that to admit *lucrum cessans* was to abandon the usury prohibition. As he believes, "this ghost of *lucrum cessans* not many years ago opened that chasm and whirlpool of usury."

3. Papal Approval and Ecclesiastical Attitude

The first direct papal approval of *lucrum cessans* occurred in connection with the financing of the *mons pietatis*. These charitable institutions, of which more will be said later, were seriously restricted in their efforts to help the poor by their lack of capital. In order to supplement the charitable donations which had formed their original supply, it was proposed that they accept deposits from wealthy men and pay 4 to 6 per cent interest on them. In 1542 Paul III, in a brief to the *mons* at Modena, said this interest might be licitly received by the depositors if it were paid for true *lucrum cessans*. Similarly, a brief by Julius III in 1555 to Vicenzia and a brief by Pius IV in 1563 to Verona approved the payment of *lucrum cessans* by their *montes* and its acceptance by the depositors. Each brief says that the compensation must be taken only on money which the depositors had ready for an immediate business investment, that the compensation must be less than the business profit would have been, and that the depositors must be moved principally by charity.[12]

The Fathers of Trent also gave an unofficial opinion on *lucrum cessans* when Pius IV consulted them on the practice of the Veronese of depositing money at interest with their local *mons*. The Tridentine theologians replied that only the depositor was freed from usury,

who had money ready to buy at once fields or merchandise or something similar of this kind, and, moved by charity to the poor, or even invited by the governors of the *mons* or some other upright man, changing their plan, prefer to help the needs of the poor and to deposit at the *mons* with less certain profit.[13]

It will be observed that both the Tridentine Fathers' and the Popes' approval of *lucrum cessans* is highly conservative, insisting on the principal

[12] Ballerini, *Opus. I, De montibus pietatis*, 3:11, 13.　　[13] *Ibid.*, 3:12.

charitable intention and showing no awareness of Cajetan's modern liberalization of this principle. The late date of the papal recognition, one hundred and fifty years after Laurentius de Ridolfis began making the title popular, is also noteworthy.

The limitations still surrounding *lucrum cessans* and the prevalent ecclesiastical conservatism are further reflected in the history of the Jesuits and the 5 per cent contract. Unlike the triple contract and the redeemable *census*, this title is not urged as the solution for the difficulties over the legitimation of the German contract. If *lucrum cessans* had been accepted as fully and as unqualifiedly as it was to be later, it would have been the obvious way out of the trouble. Instead, it was rarely suggested as a possible justification for the exaction of the 5 per cent.[14] The 1573 decision of the General Congregation of the Jesuits does mention it as a licit title, and the decision adds that it may be claimed by merchants who lend with money they would otherwise have used in exchange purchases.[15] Yet the title is not referred to in the more important decisions of 1581, and it is not clear that any of the theologians consulted believe that it would justify very many cases of interest.

4. Elimination of the Criterion of Intention and Full Expansion of the Title

Navarrus takes the greatest step forward in making *lucrum cessans* a generally practicable title by banishing the insistence on a charitable intention. How different his approach is from the medieval scholastics, who always looked on *lucrum cessans* as an infrequent, special case, is clear from the very beginning of his discussion of usury. Here, in his first presentation of the doctrine, he puts forward *lucrum cessans* as an integral part of the usury doctrine proper, so important a matter that it is at once to be carefully distinguished from usury. Usury is gain sought by virtue of the loan itself. *Lucrum cessans* is gain sought under a just title as compensation. It is never to be confused with usury. Hence, to seek it wilfully is not to seek usury, but to seek something licit in itself.[16] As he explains more fully later, Cajetan and the medieval defenders of the title are wrong in thinking that at any time the lender's intention to gain would vitiate the contract, and similarly Soto is wrong in thinking that *lucrum cessans* would be licit on a compulsory loan if it were not always licit. The willingness with which the lender lends in order to receive *lucrum cessans* is irrelevant. Navarrus declares bluntly:

---

[14] E.g., St. Peter Canisius, *Epistolae*, III, 585.

[15] *Ibid.*, VII, 673.

[16] Navarrus, *De usuris*, 5, n.6.

"By no law or reason is it proved that an intrinsically just way of gaining becomes unjust by will alone and by pleasure in using it." Justice in contracts lies not in intention, but in the equality of things. *Lucrum cessans*, if it is licit at all, may be sought principally for itself.[17] The scruple which had paralyzed medieval thought on this point, that to seek *lucrum cessans* wilfully would be to violate the command to hope "nothing" from a loan, does not even occur to Navarrus. If it occurred to him, he would doubtless have answered that by "nothing" was only meant "nothing without a just title," "nothing by force of the loan alone." His consistent refusal to admit that a mere intention makes an objective equality unequal is a great gain in clarity of ethical analysis.

The objective basis for *lucrum cessans* is, in Navarrus' analysis, as in Cajetan's, the fact that money in a concrete situation is worth more than its face value because it is related to some user's ability and knowledge. When an able user foregoes use of his money in order to loan it, he foregoes the profit he would have made with it. His claim for compensation is not based, as Soto thinks, on his lost opportunity to work. It is based on the lost profit which would have come from the use of the money. The case is entirely similar to one in which compensation is due a man for voluntarily foregoing other advantages he might have obtained if he did not sacrifice them for a price.[18] Navarrus makes no attempt to defend the fruitfulness here attributed to money in particular circumstances. It is obvious that he thinks Soto's labor theory of value is so generally disregarded that it needs no explicit refutation.

Navarrus still sets forth as a requirement of justice in claiming *lucrum cessans* that it be a loss truly suffered. Accordingly, only those who were really going to use their money for business or other licit investment can claim compensation for business profit lost. He will not stretch the title even to defend "the infinite number of honest Christians" making money by dealing in exchange; to the extent that these are men "having cash and not willing or not able to use it in trade or in buying fields," they may not claim *lucrum cessans*. After money has been withdrawn from business to be devoted wholly to exchange, its owner has no right to compensation, "for after he has taken his money from business and does not wish to do business there is no true or probable *lucrum cessans*."[19] A customary usurer, or a merchant who reserves a specific sum from business in order to be ready to loan with it, cannot be justified by the interest title, nor can those who

[17] 15, n.42 and 52; 16, n.53.
[18] 15, n.52.
[19] Navarrus, *De cambiis*, 34, 35; *Manuale*, 17, n.296, 301.

collect money from others in order to loan it at a higher rate.[20] These are familiar qualifications insisted on by every defender of *lucrum cessans*, but Navarrus also makes one new admission. It is licit to claim *lucrum cessans* if one lends money intended for business, although one has in reserve another sum of money for one's necessities, with which one could conceivably replace the money loaned. As long as the money loaned was meant for business, a loss is suffered by lending it, and there is no obligation for a lender to draw on his private reserve to keep on in business. This is an important clarification, which had perhaps been assumed by other writers, but which had never been made explicit.[21]

At no time in his treatment of *lucrum cessans* does Navarrus consider the frequent objection of earlier authors that to admit the title without restriction was to destroy the usury prohibition itself. This confident ignoring of the old bugbear shows how firmly Navarrus had grasped the essential principle that to seek gain by a licit title was never usury and was condemned by no law, even though such a title might often coincide with a loan. More surprisingly, he even says that the lawfulness of *lucrum cessans*, as he understands it, is favored by the common opinion. In fact, as we have seen, no important writer before him had been so logical, so sensible, and so bold in proclaiming the right to *lucrum cessans* or to compensation which might be principally sought for its own sake, without charitable motive and apart from compulsion. Navarrus adds little to the essential analyses of Summenhart and Cajetan. But he carries their analyses through to their natural conclusion, that *lucrum cessans* is a common title available without other requirements than that the lender charging it have truly suffered the loss of the profit for which he asks compensation.

This approach is solidly supported by Molina. In presenting the usury prohibition proper, he says plainly that the prohibition does not apply to the lending of money otherwise destined for business or other licit investment.[22] In other words, like Navarrus, but even more strikingly, he introduces *lucrum cessans* not as an exception to the rule, but as a principle itself fully as important as the usury law. Also, while his contemporaries still prefer to use the plea of different contracts rather than rely on the interest titles for justification, the notion of *lucrum cessans* is so acceptable to Molina that he urges it as the proper justification of the triple contract and personal *census*.

All writers agree, Molina says, that *lucrum cessans* may be claimed if it is involuntarily suffered. The only question is whether it may be claimed if it

---

[20] *De usuris*, 19, n.58.
[21] *Manuale*, c.17, *De septimo praecepto*, n. 212.
[22] Molina, *De justitia*, II:304:6–7.

is spontaneously incurred. The common opinion, to which he subscribes, favors it even in the latter case. Voluntariness is irrelevant to the determination of the just value. Four separate and mutually supporting arguments are then given in favor of the title. First, money is worth more when it is subject to a merchant's industry; therefore, the merchant can charge according to its higher value. Second, what is of special value to the seller can be sold at a higher price by him, and money is of special value to businessmen. Third, money is a tool, and the lender, depriving himself of his instrument, can ask compensation for it. Finally, the hope of gain has a pecuniary estimation and can be sold; therefore, a lender can sell the hope of the gain he would have made.[23]

Molina restricts the title in two ways only. The title may not be urged if there has been only a possibility that the loaned money will be used for business and there was no definite intention to use it there. Nor may the title be claimed if one's business actually suffers no decline because of the loan. In particular, merchants selling on credit, who often increase their business by their virtual loans to customers, cannot charge more for the credit price on the strength of *lucrum cessans*. This is a new, important, and not mild reservation.[24]

On the whole, however, Molina is a warm and convinced supporter of the title. The easy way with which he dismisses the old insistence that the loan must be involuntary or charitable shows how at last this rule had ceased to be of particular importance. In Molina's hands, the title *lucrum cessans* is not completely unrestrained, but it is securely entrenched and firmly believed in.[25]

Lessius goes even farther in admitting *lucrum cessans* without restrictions. The most acute of economic moralists, he finds the title a congenial one; and he does not stop at compromises in allowing its place in economic life. His great innovation is to extend the title to money taken from business in order to have it ready for lending. The loan the lender eventually intends to make, says Lessius, is the mediate cause of the loss of business profit to him. Therefore the lender "can charge for having reduced money from a fecund to a sterile state." Thus the merchants are excused who withdraw their money from business in order to be ready to loan to the king. It is also licit to charge *lucrum cessans* if the money you lend had not even actually been taken from business, but had only been conditionally intended for business; that is,

---

[23] II:315:11.
[24] II:316:2, 4.
[25] See his use of the title in defense of

the triple contract and personal *census*, *supra*, pp. 222–223 and p. 241.

lucrum cessans can be claimed if you had the intention of using your money in business unless many would-be borrowers sought loans from you. To this admission the objection is raised that it is here illicit to collect *lucrum cessans* from any particular borrower because you have not foregone business profit on his behalf, but, as you intended to loan to many, rather than to devote your money immediately to business, you simply forego a loan to someone else in lending to another, and it is never licit to charge *lucrum cessans* simply for foregoing an opportunity to make profit on another loan. Lessius replies:

> Although no particular loan, separately considered, be the cause, all, however, collectively considered, are the cause of the whole *lucrum cessans*; for, in order to lend indiscriminately to those coming by, you abstain from business and you undergo the loss of the profit which would come from this. Therefore, since all collectively are the cause, the burden of compensation for this profit can be distributed to single loans, according to the proportion of each.[26]

The distribution of the debt of interest among the collectivity who caused it, according to the proportion of the benefit received, is, Lessius declares, exactly similar to the process by which the *mons pietatis* collects interest. The only qualification necessary is that the lender "always retain the intention to do business, if a loan is not sought." This could not have been a very formidable requirement to lenders constantly asked for loans.

It needs no commentary to point out how far Lessius' general argument goes to justify all professional lenders. No major authority before had ever allowed *lucrum cessans* to any but businessmen or investors actively planning to use their money in commerce or agriculture. Here, for the first time, the title is granted to men whose main business would be moneylending. It is a momentous, if logical, step. Lessius only restrains the full force of the title by adding that it is "not easily" admitted into practice, though theoretically sound. But "not easily" is not much of a restraint.

On two other smaller points, Lessius also brings forward a new view. Following Navarrus, he says that *lucrum cessans* may be charged on the loan of sums meant for business even though one has at the time a reserve of cash for other purposes; more comprehensively than Navarrus, he adds that interest can be charged, though this reserve is kept out of "empty fear." He also denies that the lender need subtract the value of the labor he would have expended in business from his estimation of *lucrum cessans* if he would have preferred to work than to have lost profit through not working.[27] This position is entirely new, every preceding theologian of importance having said that the expenses and labor of doing business must be deducted from

---

[26] Lessius, *De justitia*, II:20:11, n.91.　　[27] *Ibid.*, n.87, n.98.

the gross profit in determining *lucrum cessans*. Lessius, by adopting his stand, makes it explicit that *lucrum cessans* itself is not paid for giving up the opportunity to work, but for the profit coming from the money itself. The extra amount added on here to *lucrum cessans* is the compensation for the work which the lender would have preferred to undergo if he were not paid to sacrifice it.

With Lessius, *lucrum cessans* is thus a title available to almost all lenders, not only businessmen and investors, but potential businessmen and investors; it is chargeable though the lenders have cash reserves for irrational reasons; and the value of the lender's labor need not be taken from the value of his capital in calculating the interest. This is a broad, inclusive, and unprecedented position.[28]

It is entirely supported by Lugo. *Lucrum cessans* is "the general title for purging usury." [29] He defends it by the now standard arguments and says the common opinion is for it. With Lessius he argues that the title is present on money deliberately withdrawn from business to have it ready to loan. The loan is the final cause of the businessman's loss, although he has not yet been asked to lend. The foreseen will of the borrower petitioning for a loan is the efficient cause of his ceasing business. In the grand language of speculative theology, the needs of borrowers in general cause the *lucrum cessans*, just as all sinners in general were the final cause of Christ's Passion. This argument, Lugo adds, will justify both those who "foreseeing the king will seek a loan, withdraw their money from business, so they may have such a sum on hand," and also those who withdraw their money to meet the needs of borrowers in general. Merchants need not deduct their labor in estimating *lucrum cessans*, for, with almost the same amount of work, they would have earned more profit if they had kept the money they loaned.[30]

Thus supporting Lessius, Lugo goes beyond him in allowing that even remote gain, as well as probable lost gain, may be calculated in determining *lucrum cessans*, provided the profit is evaluated with deduction for its doubtfulness. Similarly, the profit a lender would have made by reinvesting the lost profit may be added in calculating the total interest due.[31] Later, in treating of the obligation of restitution on a usurious contract, Lugo says more sharply,

For interest of *lucrum cessans* it does not suffice that the lender could have gained

---

[28] Lessius notes that, surprisingly, only "the almost common opinion" is for the licitness of spontaneously sought *lucrum cessans* (II:20:11, n.79).

[29] Lugo, 25:5:51; 25:2.
[30] 25:6:91–99.
[31] 25:6:95.

in some other way, but it is required that *de facto* he would have gained if he had not loaned.

But he adds, again leniently, that a confused knowledge of how he would have gained suffices to justify the lender.[32]

At the same time, Lugo is far more conservative than Lessius in insisting that the borrower has the right to choose how the *lucrum cessans* he pays will be calculated. There are two alternatives. By one method the *lucrum cessans* will be determined by the success of other businesses similar to that in which the lender is engaged in during the period of the loan, and the borrower will be held to keep the lender only in the same condition as these other businesses. If they lose, the borrower may deduct the amount of the loss from the loan and return even less than he borrowed. It is unjust, Lugo says, for the lender to be certain both of his capital and his full profit by force of a loan, when he would not have this certainty if he did not lend. By the second method, the probable *lucrum cessans* is estimated in advance, according to past experience, but a deduction is made for the possibility of loss. Under this alternative the lender gets security of capital and profit, but not the full profit he might have made.[33] Presumably, this second way was the common way of computing interest, for it is difficult to believe that the cumbersome first procedure was practicable. Nevertheless, Lugo teaches theoretically that the borrower must be given his choice, for if one or the other method is imposed on him, an extra obligation beyond that of compensating the lender is usuriously imposed on the borrower by force of the loan.

Lugo's teaching is also restrictive in following Molina's doctrine that merchants cannot charge *lucrum cessans* on credit sales which actually increase their business. Lugo states here what may be taken as a general principle governing the determination of interest: "It [*lucrum cessans*] is not only to be considered in relation to a single borrower, but in relation to the whole operation."[34] Although merchants may lose money on individual loans, by the whole operation of credit sales they increase their profit and hence have no claim to interest.

Finally, and most importantly, Lugo is conservative in pointing out the value of the medieval criterion of intention and in restoring it in a modified form to a place of importance. Intention alone, he teaches, cannot make an act unjust. But if one prefers lending and receiving *lucrum cessans* to doing business and making a profit in that, there is a clear indication that one

[32] 25:9:181.
[33] 25:6:105.

[34] 25:6:89.

hopes to receive more through the loan than one would actually have made through the business, or that one hopes to avoid some difficulties of work, and, as even the avoidance of work has a pecuniary value, there is evidence of an intention to gain from the loan. The lender preferring lending to other work is probably asking more for his loan than he actually has a title to by *lucrum cessans*. There is no objection, however, to preferring lending to other work if a lender chooses it not as a way of getting greater profit or avoiding difficulties estimable in money, but because "that way of making money is more according to his talents and character, and he avoids some inconvenience, which, however, he would not redeem at a price." [35] These precisions on the place of preference in regard to interest titles had not been so moderately and so exactly stated by the medieval writers, who made intention the supreme criterion, and they had been overlooked by the modern writers who swept the intention criterion aside completely. Lugo deserves some recognition for making such necessary clarifications, though their effect is conservative and restrictive. His basic acceptance of *lucrum cessans* as "the general title for purging usury" shows that his reservations were not thought by him to press too heavily on lenders in practice, and his estimate that *lucrum cessans* was the "general title" reflects his age's complete approval of it.

5. *The Eighteenth Century*

Ballerini here, as usual, takes a stand of great rigor, and his views, which are a strong return to the opinions of the fifteenth century, offer a striking contrast to the trend of theory and practice. He insists that a loan must be charitably intended, that interest can never be sought for itself, and that it would be entirely wrong to make a business of lending by seeking *lucrum cessans* on money conditionally intended for other investments. One can never licitly prefer to lend, and the mere hope of gain will vitiate any title present. The loan must be the immediate, not the remote, occasion of the loss of profit. If one has a cash reserve he cannot claim *lucrum cessans*. The general rule is that true interest is a pure indemnity; it can never be lucrative. He agrees that his standards will seem "wonderful" to those who judge by daily practice. In general his contemporaries, even those who have a just title, primarily seek profit, not indemnification from a loan, and so by the ancient definition are usurers.[36]

To this anachronistic voice, Zech replied with the standard later scholastic

---

[35] 25:6:108.   3:1:14–19.
[36] Ballerini, *Opus.* I, *De montibus pietatis,*

arguments and with one of the first explicit theological recognitions that there had been a change in theological opinion on the title:

This is a memorable example, in that an opinion, either openly condemned by the older writers, or at any rate never set out in plain words, still in the time of Soto recognized as less probable, defended by its later patrons, as Soto says, with fear and trembling, is now everywhere common.[37]

The truth of Zech's last observation, that the opinion for it is "everywhere common," is confirmed by St. Alphonsus, who defends *lucrum cessans* in almost the same terms as Lugo.[38] The language in which he defends the lender charging interest on money that he had "conditionally devoted" to business and then lent is significant:

Although he has an inefficacious will of doing business, yet he wills efficaciously to gain justly; and because he can gain, he can now gain justly from the loan, since the loan is the true and efficacious cause that gain from businesses ceases for him.[39]

This language is not precisely a declaration that profit can be sought on a loan by force of the loan alone. But it is a recognition that interest, which objectively considered is only compensation, will normally be looked on by the lender as profit. Here the most respected interpreter of the late scholastic tradition approves the common custom of speaking of interest as gain on a loan. In this recognition and approbation the title of *lucrum cessans* receives its fullest and freest acceptance.

Conclusion

Lucrum cessans, an object of suspicion up to the end of the fifteenth century, has become accepted as the normal source of profit on a loan. The medieval period had laid the basis for the title in allowing it when the debtor was in delay; for even this limited admission involved recognizing a causal power in money independent of labor, or, to put it more accurately, it involved recognizing that money need not always be considered by moralists formally as an empty measure, but could be considered as interchangeable with the productive goods it could buy; and as in the case of the triple contract, one inconsistent medieval admission was sufficient ground for a great development in later times. The productive power of money in concrete situations is clearly shown by Cajetan, and after him, except for the reaction of Soto to a pure labor theory of value, it becomes generally acknowledged

---

[37] Zech, *Dissertationes tres*, II:1:2:26:17; cf. II, ante sec. 1.

[38] St. Alphonsus, III:5:3:7:768, 769, 772.
[39] III:5:3:7:772.

by the scholastics that money destined for business should not be treated simply as a sterile measure. At the same time that Cajetan pursues the analysis of the nature of money to its logical conclusion, Summenhart strikes at the notion that one cannot be paid for voluntarily damaging oneself and shows that compensation is perfectly proper if one foregoes an advantage or suffers a loss on condition that compensation be made for it. But it takes another fifty years for Cajetan's and Summenhart's analyses to be given full weight. Then Navarrus strikes off the fetter of the charitable intention, and the title becomes a generally practicable one. With Molina it is finally established, though not used without certain reservations. Lessius takes the next great step of allowing it even when the loan is only mediately the cause of the lost profit, and even when the money loaned was only tenuously and conditionally destined for business; and he makes the important addition that it can be asked, even though one foolishly has other money in reserve. Lugo, generally supporting Lessius, makes necessary clarifications on the nature of preference. The title is now accepted without limitation or real reservation, except for the useless and lost protests of Concina and Ballerini. With St. Alphonsus, we find *lucrum cessans* acknowledged as profit which a lender may, under a just title, legitimately seek upon a loan.

CHAPTER XIII

IMPLICIT INTENTION AND IMPLICIT CONTRACTS

As important as the developing general acceptance of any contract or interest title was the increasing recognition given the good faith of the average investor and the rectitude of customary business practices. In the Middle Ages any intention in making a loan, other than that of charity, was condemned, and any contract effecting approximately the same results as a loan was suspect of being done in fraud; from the beginning of the sixteenth century the increasing tendency was to presume the intention and the contract of the investor justified, unless the contrary was clearly demonstrated. Increasingly it was postulated that a lender or investor had an implicit intention to gain by an honest title or contract; and simultaneously, the objective counterpart of an implicit intention, an implicit title or contract, was found to exist in contracts that on their face might have been considered loans at usury.

The development of the idea of implicit contracts and intentions was, indeed, absolutely necessary if the triple contract, the personal, insured, or redeemable *census*, and *lucrum cessans* were to be of great practical usefulness; and it is safe to say that the two new contracts and the great interest title would not have been of much importance to the mass of businessmen, bankers, and investors unless these contracts and titles had been found to exist in common economic life by the aid of the doctrine on implicit intention. A somewhat artificial impression is given by treating this teaching apart from the contracts to which it was intimately linked. Nonetheless, since the same basic idea is involved in a variety of applications, it is most instructive to consider the idea by itself, immediately after the contracts and interest title it most concerned, to relate it to them in particular, and at the same time to look ahead to other applications in relation to contracts of exchange.

1. *Application to the Triple Contract*

The first use of the idea of "implicit contracts" is found without very much elaboration in the discussion of the triple contract. Giving the history of the formal defense of the contract, we have expounded it as three separate contracts, into which it was formally analyzed. In fact, as its name itself implies, it was normally a single contract with a triple effect. The very existence of the triple contract regularly depended on the acceptance of the doctrine of implicit intention. This is perfectly clear in Cajetan, who states the form of the contract as it is commonly used in Germany, as it is defended by Eck, and as it is reported by Abbot Koellin. According to Cajetan's report, the form of the contract simply states that Peter gives Paul, a merchant, 100 florins, on condition that Paul assign him for his share of the profit 5 florins annually; the rest of the profit is left to Paul, and Peter's capital is kept safe.[1] The words "loan" and "at usury" are, of course, not used, and the formula employed of "consigning money" might have been the customary form for investing in partnerships. There is, however, no formal mention of partnership or insurance, nor any explicit statement that three separate exchanges of value take place. The bare facts are set forth. The theologian is allowed to analyze their substance. The defenders find there the triple contract. Yet the three contracts, as Abbot Koellin reports, are claimed to exist only virtually; or, as the defenders also say, they are "presupposed."[2] The actual form of the contract does not differ except by its judicious wording from the form of a loan.

Since the form Cajetan gives is, according to his authorities, the standard one in use in Germany, and as the German triple contract is the center of most sixteenth-century discussion, it is a fair inference that the triple contract was a case where implicit contracts had to be assumed — at least if the triple contract was to be used to justify common practice. This inference is confirmed by Summenhart's statement that "the form" of the guaranteed partnership is not different from "the form" of a loan.[3] Also, both Eck and Major speak of the triple contract as favored by wards and widows;[4] and since these persons were accustomed to deposit with merchants at a fixed rate, it may well be that Eck and Major understood such simple deposits, too, as implicit triple contracts.

Of the early writers defending the triple contract, however, only Major finds it necessary to engage in a defense of the existence of the implicit contracts. He offers the pious conjecture that in some earlier age, when the contracts first arose, the three must have been made separately, but now, he says, "they are presumed to exist by the common custom."[5] The hypothesis of the

[1] Cajetan, De societate negotiatoria, n.422.
[2] n.423, 434.
[3] Summenhart, De contractibus, Q.97.
[4] Major, In quatuor sententiarum quaestiones, IV:15:49; see supra, Chapter X, n.20.
[5] Major, IV:15:49.

past practice, which Major apparently requires in order that there be some basis for the actual, if implicit, existence of the three contracts, is, of course, a myth. But despite this, in Major's understanding of the contemporary practice, any investment with a businessman at a fixed rate, the investment being insured, is presumed to be a triple contract because this is the common way of contracting with businessmen. There apparently needs to be no explicit differentiation from a loan, if the three contracts can be discovered implicitly upon analysis, and if the custom is to understand such investments in such a way.

Navarrus extends this simple defense at length in the *Commentarius de usuris*.[6] Citing the Roman law, he declares that "regularly there is the same power in what is tacit as in what is expressed"; therefore if three explicit contracts are licit, so are three implicit ones. But how is one to know that these implicit contracts exist or were intended? Navarrus's first answer to this delicate question is to give an example. A merchant publicly announces that he will receive money from anyone wishing to give it to him in partnership with agreements guaranteeing the return of the principal and a fair reward, the merchant keeping the rest of the profit in exchange for the insurance he gives. Afterwards, anyone acting on this offer presumably intends to contract partnership with, and to receive insurance from, the merchant, if he declares it to be his intention to follow the terms of the offer. But this is only a textbook illustration. What Navarrus finds in practice, as we have seen above, is "an immemorial custom" of putting out the money of widows, wards, and the Church with merchants at 4 per cent; and apparently in such investments the three contracts are not explicitly expressed. Now Navarrus admits that the contracts cannot always be presumed where money is given to a merchant by a deserving person such as an orphan. The contracts "cannot be subunderstood from the nature of an [investment] contract by itself." Nor has there been any public announcement by the merchants that they will take money in such a way. Yet the 4 per cent investment contracts are made by pious men, and the custom is old and general. Are the investments to be condemned because the triple contract is not explicitly made by the investors? Is there any way of supposing it to exist implicitly?

Faced with the *de facto* situation, Navarrus, like Major, first supposes that at some earlier period the contracts were made explicitly. The custom of making them explicitly would have been like the public announcement of

---

[6] Navarrus, *Commentarius de usuris, Si foeneraveris*, 14, n.33. In the *Manuale* (17, *De usura in societate*, n.257), he merely says that the triple contract may be made "formally or equivalently."

his hypothetical merchant; persons investing their money with businessmen accustomed to contract in this way would intend to enter the three customary contracts. In time it would have been taken for granted that the three contracts were made whether they were expressed or not; and so a habit of using implicit contracts in this matter would have arisen, and the fact that the present contracts were simply a continuation of past practice would show that the three contracts were still implicitly intended, although they were now not necessarily expressed. A person acting on the usual custom would intend the three contracts, just as much as a person acting on the public offer of the hypothetical merchant.[7]

As for the assumption that such a custom of making the three contracts explicitly did in fact once prevail, Navarrus thinks its correctness may be proved easily. Certainly in an earlier age guaranteed investments at 4 per cent were made. But since this earlier age was a more pious and scrupulous one than our own, it is inconceivable that such a custom would have become widespread unless the three contracts had been explicitly made. This purely theoretical reasoning is reinforced by only one document, the decretal *Per vestras*, which, Navarrus claims, approved an investment in the form of a secured partnership in the thirteenth century.[8] By this hypothetical historical reconstruction, for which no single bit of evidence exists except his distorted reading of *Per vestras*, Navarrus defends the old contracts of deposits with merchants and bankers considered as usurious throughout the Middle Ages.

In truth, despite his first insistence on the custom of explicit contracts as a prerequisite for the legality of implicit contracts, Navarrus places no real weight on this; for we soon find him saying that the original users of the contract could have expressed their intention "tacitly and implicitly"; so although he says the contracts cannot be always "subunderstood," we find him doing precisely that in the past as well as in the present, and now he insists on the observation of only one new essential condition. This essential condition, on which Navarrus really rests his acceptance of the existence of implicit contracts in a simple investment contract, is that the return guaranteed on the investment be a low one. He argues that the merchants usually make 12 to 15 per cent with the money invested with them; therefore, if the investors receive only 4 per cent, the difference between the two returns can be explained only by supposing that 8 per cent of the investor's return has been allocated by implicit contracts to pay for the guarantee of his capital and the steady 4 per cent.[9] Again, in his *Consilia*, when he is asked

---

[7] Navarrus, *De usuris*, 14, n.32, 33. 34.   [9] *De usuris*, 14, n.34.
[8] *De usuris*, 14, n.34.

if a guaranteed partnership at 5 per cent is licit, he urges that three explicit contracts be made; yet he does not condemn the contract absolutely as it stands without the explicit clauses, but says only that, as he is not a merchant, he will not judge the justice of the price; nor does he here plead an antecedent custom of explicit contracts. On the other hand, if the investor's profit is a sure 8 per cent, as is customary in Rome, there is no evidence that a proper sum has been paid for the guarantee, and so Navarrus finds that the investor commits usury, although it is the Roman custom to contract in this way and at this rate.[10] In short, Navarrus finds the existence of implicit contracts wherever the rate of return on a deposit or similar investment is substantially less than the profit the recipient of the deposit gets from his use of it. He is forced to this position if he is not to condemn "the immemorial custom" of France and Italy, which he is at such pains to justify by the triple contract.

Molina, although he is far briefer, takes substantially the same position. He writes,

Never are the simple, who do not know how to distinguish these matters, to be condemned, if they give their money with agreements of this kind to one who they do not doubt wants to do business with it and profit by it.[11]

Lessius similarly approves a formula virtually identical with the one described by Koellin to Cajetan.[12] Lugo says simply and comprehensively that the necessary three contracts may be conceded to exist implicitly if the investor gives his money in good faith to a merchant.[13]

2. *Generalization of the Approach*

Although the appeal to implicit contracts was peculiarly apt in treating of the triple contract, it was not confined to this. As early as 1498 Cajetan discussed the subjective counterpart, implicit intention. He presents the case in this way:

when some confusedly intend to profit licitly, not from the use of money which they give the exchanger, but from an exchange from which they believe others to profit, it does not seem that they are condemnable — rather their contracts should be interpreted to the better part. For from this, that they say they wish to profit from exchange, they seem to insinuate that they wish to enter such a contract although they do not know how; especially if they claim that they wish this profit, because if those exchangers conversely made such a contract with them, they would demand greater profit. For, from this, it now appears manifest that they intend to enter the above-mentioned exchange contracts, and so much the more justly as more mildly than the exchangers.

---

[10] *Consilia*, V:19:16; and V:19:8.
[11] Molina, *De justitia*, II:417:14.
[12] Lessius, *De justitia*, II:25:3:27.
[13] Lugo, *Disputationes*, 30:4:47.

This may be admitted, because it does not seem true that commonly in practice those wishing to transfer their money with profit say they wish this for the use of the money; but perchance there are some evil persons saying this, or, as I think truer, those words are said ignorantly by some, believing they assign a rational cause. And if some, ignorantly assigning a reason of this kind, intend to enter a contract of exchange and by this to bring back a profit, although they err in assigning the reason, they do not commit an injustice; just as if one believed himself to gain licitly in a contract of buying and selling because of the time in which he kept his money tied up, and yet he neither bought nor sold, except at the just price.[14]

Cajetan thus takes the position that if objective justice is observed and the parties intend to act justly, it is morally irrelevant if they say and even believe that they gain on the loan itself.

The radical postulation of good faith in the investor is carried further by Summenhart. He has said, it will be remembered, than an ordinary *census* is not usury because it is the sale of a right.[15] He maintains further that the use of "loan" instead of "*census*" says nothing as to the true nature of the transaction. Although the word "loan" is retained, the contract becomes a sale when the grant of money becomes irrevocable. It is objected that if a man intends to loan at a profit, he is a usurer; and here the alleged buyer believes that he loans at a profit. Conrad replies that he "virtually consents to a loan clothed with such circumstances that it has been made a purchase and sale." But, the objector presses, if a man commits adultery with a woman whom he believes not to be his wife, although in fact she is, he sins. Similarly, a man believing himself to loan at a profit, although in fact he does not, sins. Conrad replies with an answer, which like Cajetan's on exchange, indicates a great willingness not to condemn popular usage which simply fails to use theologically acceptable formulas:

It is to be said that it [the alleged analogy] is not similar: because the man knowing his own wife, while believing her to be another's, acts against conscience — which leads to hell: because he wishes to perform an act illicit in itself; because he believes her to be another's and yet performs the act. Therefore, God imputes it to him, as if in fact she were another's, for he would not know her less if she were another's: . . . but it is not thus in the case of our conclusion: because A, performing a contract licit in itself, although he believes it to be a loan, yet, nevertheless believes that loan not to be of the number of those of which Luke 6:35 is spoken. But he believes that loan to be another case and in the number of those cases in which it is licit to receive beyond the principal, of which cases, one is that in which there does not remain the nature of a loan; and he acts in good faith.

[14] Cajetan, *De cambiis*, n.305–306, in *Scripta philosophica*.   [15] See *supra*, p. 233.

Technically any loan is covered by Luke 6:35. But Conrad argues that a man may have a just title entitling him to compensation on a loan, or his transaction may not be a formal loan at all. The man acts in good faith to collect his objectively licit gain. He simply is ignorant of the technical formulae to justify his action. His good faith is his protection. The would-be adulterer acts not only out of ignorance of his true rights, but with the consciousness that he performs an evil act — a consciousness entirely unlike the mental state of innocence of the lender.[16] Conrad thus joins Cajetan in maintaining that if the party's intention is good and his contract can be objectively analyzed into a contract other than a loan, no sin of injustice is committed, though the investor believes he profits on a loan.

Cajetan had dealt with good faith only in regard to the exchanges; Summenhart had formally considered only the rather special case of an "irrevocable loan," not extending his analysis to the temporary *census*. But by far the most extensive, as well as the most official, approval of the use of implicit contracts, into which *prima facie* loans might be analyzed, was given by the Jesuit theologians in the course of the 5 per cent controversy. At first it seems clear that the Jesuit confessors regularly tended to persuade their penitents to make their contracts explicitly different from loans;[17] but, as we have seen, their efforts met with the stubborn popular suspicion of complexities added to a simple contract.[18] The 1573 Congregation decided that the triple contract might be understood to exist virtually if money was given to a merchant for a partnership, with the capital safe and the profit fixed. At the same time it said that custom of itself would not legitimize the straight 5 per cent contract.[19] The 1581 Congregation was far more liberal. The cases in which the 5 per cent was a loan were treated as an exception, not the rule. The 5 per cent contract was approved "unless it had the character of a loan"; and the Congregation added that the contract "has not necessarily such a character, unless it is made without respect of persons." The 5 per cent was to be considered usury, if it was sought by force of a loan alone; or if in a loan it was sought without pretext of title, or with false title, or with the deliberate exclusion of all titles, or in a contract not called a loan where no pretext existed. But if the person of the borrower was considered by the parties — that is, if the borrower were a merchant, or the owner of fruitful lands, or a working person, and the contract was made with him principally in consideration of his status — the 5 per cent contract

[16] Summenhart, *De contractibus*, Q.33, 4th arg., p. 156.
[17] See Canisius, *Epistolae*, V, 530; VII, 342.
[18] See *supra*, p. 215.
[19] Canisius, *Epistolae*, VII, 672, 673.

could be interpreted as either a triple contract or a real or personal *census.*
It would then have "the character of a licit partnership or some tolerable
census." The Congregation states specifically that the implicit intention of
gaining in a licit way suffices to justify the contract, and that

> although they [the parties] do not know of a type [of contract] expressed in
> such a way, yet if the circumstances are such on the part of the thing itself, so
> that they contract with a merchant or person not having fruitful goods, yet
> having the ability to work, there is no doubt that this 5 per cent is licit.[20]

In other words, wherever the ownership of money is temporarily transferred
to a merchant or worker, if the parties intend to act licitly, the contract may
be analyzed as a triple contract or *census* and the profit on the contract may
be legitimized. The far-reaching implications of this decision are evident,
and the influence of the decision was as widespread. In practice, it meant that
only loans to aged or infirm persons without property or loans bearing a
rate of interest beyond that obtainable in a triple contract or *census* need be
considered as true loans falling within the usury prohibitions.[21] This is an
extreme conclusion to reach as to the meaning of the Congregation, but no
other is indicated by the documents.

In the seventeenth century Lessius adds some new illustrations of the
principle: the contract by which wards' money is given to merchants at
5 per cent is an implicit, mutually redeemable personal *census.*[22] Similarly,
purchases of exchange where there is an increased charge because a longer
time is allowed for meeting the bill may be excused by understanding the
single exchange transaction to contain implicitly several transactions of exchange and reëxchange. If the exchange taker, the borrower, had to pay when
the bill of exchange reached the place it was drawn on, he would have to
meet his obligation by taking a new exchange, which, in turn, he would have
to meet by another reëxchange. These several operations are assumed to have
been carried out by the single exchange contract which gives as much time as
would be allowed for several reëxchanges and charges the borrower the total
he would have to pay in the course of several exchanges where payment
was on demand at the end of each exchange.[23] This is a radical example
offered by no previous writer.

Again, it is sufficient in accepting interest, Lessius says, to have the general
implicit intention of accepting payment for one's loan under any just title.
Those who put out money on the Antwerp Bourse with the general intention

---

[20] Zech, *Dissertationes tres,* III:2:8:263.
[21] Canisius, *Epistolae,* VIII, 65.
[22] Lessius, II:22:10:62.
[23] II:23:6.

of profiting licitly can receive *lucrum cessans*, although they do not actually refer to the title at the time they contract for payment. The general implicit intention to profit by a just title, and not to profit except by such a title, is enough. Lessius says the necessary implicit intention exists, if the lender

is so disposed in act, that if he were asked by what title, or what form of contract, he intends to gain those 6 per 100, he would reply, "By every good means I can" — a clause the notaries are generally accustomed to add to instruments. . . . [24]

One could not ask for a broader or more inclusive admission of intention.[25]

Throughout this two-hundred-and-fifty-year period, the only vocal critic of the implicit contracts was the incorrigible Ballerini, and to him we are indebted for a work entitled, "The Inane System of Implicit Contracts." He asserts that since 1600, "the thing being unchanged, a principle has been introduced by which that very thing which was always held for usury is now contended to be usury no more." This principle is that of the efficiency of the implicit contract. The result is that no one is ever said to commit usury on a loan, "except perchance he who deliberately wills a usurious contract." When one lends to a borrower who owns a farm, an implicit real *census* is supposed to be contracted. When one lends to a laborer, it is an implicit personal *census*. When one lends to a merchant, it is an implicit triple contract. Confessors now never question their penitents about usury:

and so in practice usury dominates in fact, as if a dogmatic error on usury flourished. . . . in setting out their money for profit, the people do not advert to those contracts and almost none understand or will them, but truly wish to profit on a loan of money, not on some other contract.[26]

At least, says Ballerini, the existence of an implicit contract should somehow be made manifest by the parties: their virtual intention should be actual in some way. But there is no evidence at all of any intention, beyond the intention to make a loan. There is no effort by the parties to make specific triple contracts or clauses, but these contracts are supposed only in the idle dreams of those who would later justify the transaction.[27] In fact, the parties, lender and borrower, have never thought about contracts other than the loan. They may wish to gain in a licit manner, but in truth they wish to gain from a loan.[28] They may seek this gain in good faith and may be in invincible error, but, at the same time, this good faith does not create a new contract

[24] II:20:12.
[25] Lugo has nothing to add to Lessius.
[26] Ballerini, *De inani contractuum implicitorum systemate*, *Opus.* III:1:2, in *De*
jure divino.
[27] 2:5;7.
[28] 2:6.

in place of the loan, nor does it alter the fact that they commit what is objectively a sin, nor does it relieve theologians of the responsibility of enlightening them about their error.[29]

It is hard to dispute Ballerini's description of current practice; for clearly the resolution of loan contracts into implicit licit contracts had been generally authorized at least since the general Jesuit Congregation of 1581, and, as he suggests, very few loans would have been found usurious under the system of implicit contracts recommended by the leading theologians of the day, with the important qualification, ignored by Ballerini, that the return would have to be moderate. The wisdom or value of his uncompromising logic, which left no room for economic change or analytical development, may not be evident. But his protest is some measure of the distance the body of scholastic opinion had advanced from the fifteenth century.

Against this attack Zech reasserts the two fundamental principles governing the later scholastic theory of the implicit contracts. The first is

that nothing is more certain than the same effect, the same profit, can be sought through different contracts and interpreted differently. Profit on a loan can be illicit, the same profit on a *census* will be licit.[30]

The second principle is that the contractual formula itself does not need to be explicit, if the parties intend to contract licitly, and if their contract can be reductively analyzed as a licit one.[31] Contractual formulae are concise like algebra, and there is no need for them to express everything in detail, if custom has established that certain formulae mean a particular kind of transaction.[32] Zech grants that implicit contracts within the main contract might not be supposed to exist, if the transactions indicated by them were a novelty; at an earlier age a good intention was not sufficient, because the licit contracts of today were not known. But when the custom exists of transacting in this way, not expressing the contracts explicitly, it is a fair presumption that the ordinary person means to use them, when he contracts in the customary manner.[33] Similarly, the reception of money by a priest for conducting a religious burial might be considered as simony in itself. But if it is customary for a gratuity to be offered for such a service, the priest's implicit intention may be presumed to be an intention to accept a payment as a gift.[34] Moreover, ignorant persons make contracts all the time, guided by the customary approval of the learned, without being explicitly aware of the nature of the

[29] 1:1; 2:6.
[30] Zech, III:2:6:179.
[31] III:2:8:290.
[32] III:2:9:295.
[33] III:2:6:180.
[34] III:2:6:173.

contracts they enter.[35] Few persons who buy the real *census* or the life *census*, which Ballerini allows, are aware in one case that they are buying part of a farm; nor in the other, are they usually aware of the exact price of a man's average life span. Most people act in the ways they find taken for granted as licit and pay the price generally supposed to be just. They need no more than their general intention of acting justly in order to enter particular contracts justly.[36] Every contract that can be analyzed as other than a loan should be so treated even though the words "loan" and "usury" are used in the contract.[37] Moreover, Zech says, with real originality, not all contracts are to be found in Roman law: a new contract is to be judged by the substance of its act, and if the substance is identical with the triple contract or *census*, it is to be judged as such, and not as a loan.[38] With this introduction, he defends "the German contract"; it is, in effect, the same 5 per cent contract over which we have seen such heated discussions in the sixteenth century. It is a splendid example of a contract containing a legitimate contract only implicitly.

St. Alphonsus says nothing specifically on implicit contracts; but he approves the seeking of profit on a loan, where *lucrum cessans* would exist only implicitly, and he approves the triple contract as it is commonly practiced.[39] Hence we may fairly conclude that he too, at least implicitly, approves them.

Conclusion

The notion of implicit contracts was first proposed in an isolated case by Cajetan, then accepted unanimously by all defenders of the triple contract, then, after the Jesuit Congregation of 1581, applied to guaranteed partnerships, the *census*, exchange, and cases of interest. Perhaps more than any other single factor, it transformed the scholastic theory of usury. Not only were the effects of the triple contract and *census* those of a loan, but even their form did not need to be explicitly different from a loan, if the form could be analytically reduced to a licit contract. Interest became lawful, even when the damages compensated by it were not specifically alluded to. By appeal to the implicit intention of acting justly and to the implicit existence of other contracts and titles, most of the credit business of Europe was considered moral. Even the initial requisite of a preëxisting custom of making expressly the contracts now assumed to exist implicitly was never seriously demanded, nor could it have effectively been met. In truth, the general theological practice

[35] III:2:8:290.
[36] III:2:9:295-297.
[37] III:2:8:244.

[38] III:2:33-39; cf. III:2:8:244.
[39] See *supra*, pp. 228, 267.

tended to legitimize any credit operation where the interest rate was not exorbitant and the helpless were not exploited.

In the face of this highly practical tendency to look at the substance, not the form, there may well be astonishment that so much time and thought were lavished on highly formal analyses of *census*, *societas* and the exchange contracts. Could not every credit transaction be analyzed as a sale of a right to money and the rigid usury theory forgotten? The question is not an easy one to answer. In partial response a distinction must be drawn between what the scholastic moralists were willing to permit among the uneducated faithful and what they felt it their duty not to permit in analysis. The tradition of analysis was technical, subtle, and in its way sophisticated. The scholastic analysts no more considered abandoning its niceties than they would have considered abandoning the discussion of free will and grace, although the simple faithful knew as well as they the simple answer. A more fundamental reason for the continuance of the formal analysis is that there was always the danger of a regression to a *simpliste* interpretation of the usury theory which would make prohibition of gain on any credit transaction the rule. Ballerini, in fact, is an example of just such a regression. Consequently, pressure always existed on the more sensitive moralists to show that each contract — the *census*, the exchange, the guaranteed partnership — could be justified on its own merits. Until a general transformation of viewpoint was achieved so that profit on credit transactions was commonly accepted by the moralists, each contract had to be considered a separate battleground. Until the time of St. Alphonsus, then, there is formalism in the scholastic analysis, but a formalism necessary to secure the theoretical advances made by those endeavoring to show the many ways in which the usury rule did not confine the course of credit.

CHAPTER XIV

THE RISK OF LENDING

The triple contract, the personal, redeemable *census, lucrum cessans,* and implicit contracts were gradually accepted. Yet the apparently much clearer case of the risk involved in lending was treated with far greater circumspection. In the Middle Ages, *Naviganti* outlawed as a title to interest even *periculum sortis,* a risk assumed by a lender acting as insurer for his debtor, and except for the doubtful deviation of Giles of Lessines, the medieval tradition was unanimous and adamant against allowing the much lesser risk of the loan itself as a title to compensation. Because the scholastic tradition was so strongly against it, and because risk seemed inherent in lending, so that to admit it as a title appeared to admit usury itself by abandoning the ideal of a gratuitous loan, the new title was admitted only reluctantly and with the greatest qualifications. One traditional factor in its favor was the medieval allowance of the purchase of contested debts at a discount. But, in substance, risk was an entirely new title, and the development of opinion in its favor was a completely postmedieval enterprise. In the course of this development a significant change in the meaning of terms occurs: where *periculum sortis* customarily referred in medieval times only to the risk of capital borne by the borrower or by the lender acting as insurer, it now became the term to describe *periculum mutui,* the lender's risk in letting out his capital. We turn to a survey of the revolution by which risk became a common title.

1. *Risk in Credit Sales*

The exception to the unanimity of medieval opinion against the title of risk was, it will be remembered, Giles of Lessines' singular declaration that risk could justify merchants selling on credit who feared expenses in collection.[1] Conrad Summenhart revived this opinion. A merchant may ask compensation for his fear of expenses in collecting a debt, provided that he

---

[1] See *supra,* p. 130.

would prefer not to sell on credit at all.[2] It is objected that a merchant can secure himself in other ways against nonrepayment — for example, by demanding a pledge — and so never needs to worry about being repaid. But Summenhart realistically replies that asking pledges might cause so much irrational complaint from customers that the merchant would lose business. Therefore, he should be free to lend without security and be able to ask payment for his consequent anxiety. Unlike St. Antoninus, Summenhart believes, too, that a charge for the general risk of having some bad debts, difficult to collect, may licitly be spread over all the customers.

At the same time Summenhart insists that the merchant may charge only for his fear of the expenses of collecting a bad debt, not for his fear of the simple loss of his capital. A merchant cannot charge for risk, for example, because he fears his debtor will default or run away. If a merchant fears losing his principal in this way, he ought to fear equally the loss of any interest he charges; the charge is no protection. Here, reversing his earlier position, Summenhart will not admit that the risk of having some bad debtors can be spread over all borrowers.[3]

The distinction between a fear of the expenses of collection and a fear of a simple default may seem somewhat tenuous. But what Summenhart wants to allow is a charge for the possibility of such clearly extrinsic expenses as the cost of traveling to another city, court charges, and lawyers' fees. These expenses he feels are not inherent in lending, but, since risk of them is assumed by a seller on credit, he can ask his buyers to compensate him for them. On the other hand, the loss of the capital itself is inherent in lending. As he remarks, the merchants equate any loan with "an assumption of risk."[4] He will, then, not allow a charge for this risk where there is no danger of physical expenses beyond the loss of the principal itself; for presumably he feels that the admission of such a charge would be to deny the usury prohibition. Moreover, at no time does he extend even his limited admission of the title of risk of expenses beyond the special case of credit sales to the case of loans proper. Thus, even this bold author, full of so many daring proposals on usury, offers only the most cautious and restricted recognition to risk.

2. The Bull Inter multiplices

In 1516 the Fifth Lateran Council ratified the bull *Inter multiplices* of Leo X, approving the *montes pietatis*. In the introductory section of the bull, usury is said to occur when "from the use of an unfruitful thing, without

---

[2] Summenhart, *De contractibus*, Q.59, coroll. 1, p. 281.

[3] Q.59, coroll. 2, p. 281.
[4] Q.59.

labor, expense, or risk, one seeks to acquire gain and increase." [5] At a much later date some authors urged that the bull, by its declaration that usury was what was taken without risk, meant to imply that if the charge was for risk, no usury occurred.[6] This interpretation is not possible. First, it is by no means clear that the bull means to say or imply anything on the nature of usury itself. The introduction may be only summarizing the position of the opponents of the *mons*, although one might argue, without too strained an exegesis, that the Council does accept this definition of usury as a proper one. Secondly, and much more importantly, it would have been a radical innovation if the Council had meant that *periculum mutui* was a title to interest when not a single scholastic theologian had ever admitted it. That the bull meant to make such an innovation without explanation or discussion is incredible. Clearly, what it means by *"periculum"* is *"periculum sortis"* in the medieval sense, the risk assumed by an investor in a partnership; for this is the only kind of risk that would normally have been understood as a possible excuse by any theologian of the period, and we cannot suppose that the bull meant to use the word in a different sense from the common theological one. Cajetan, one of the leading theologians of the Council, had curtly dismissed the possibility of charging for risk in *De cambiis*. The simple peril of nonrepayment of a debt, he had written, "is reputed for nothing in exchanges; . . . for he who lends or sells on credit does not licitly demand something more for risk of this kind which can happen with delay in time. . . ." [7] Moreover, in enumerating the causes for which the *mons pietatis* itself may charge interest — and this is the doctrinal and definitive portion of the bull — there is no mention of risk, even though the borrowers were to be poor men, who offered great risk, and even though a charge for risk could have been an alternative to asking a pledge. *Inter multiplices*, despite its anachronistic use by later authors, is itself no authority for the risk title.

3. *The First Defense*

John Medina (1419–1516), a Spanish professor of theology, who spent his life teaching at the Collegium Idelphonsinum at Alcala, is the first

[5] Mansi, *Sacrorum conciliorum nova et amplissima collectio* (Venice, 1759–1798), XXXII, col. 905.

[6] E.g., St. Alphonsus, III:5:3:7, 765. Ashley also seems to understand it in an anachronistic sense (*Introduction to English Economic History*, I, Part 2, 449). The later scholastics are particularly unreliable in interpreting the earlier scholastics in regard to risk. For ex-

ample, Lessius interprets a straightforward text of Angelus de Clavasio dealing with *periculum sortis* in regard to *Naviganti* as an opinion supporting the risk title in the modern sense: compare Lessius, *De justitia*, II:20:13, with Angelus de Clavasio, *Summa angelica*, at "Usura," I:38.

[7] Cajetan, *De cambiis*, n.274. Cajetan, however, was not present at the Council session

scholastic author to take the momentous step of allowing a charge for interest because of risk to which the lender may expose himself by lending.[8] He begins his discussion in relation to sales on credit and then extends his reasoning to all loans. A loan itself is always to be made gratuitously, according to the precept of the Lord. But, Medina argues, it is one thing to lend, and another to lend with the risk that the loan will not be returned:

that a man throw away his own property for another, or expose it to the risk of being lost, is sellable, and purchasable at a price, nor is it among those things which are to be done gratuitously.

A lender can ask a pledge from his debtor or refuse to lend. If the debtor cannot provide a pledge, he usually seeks a guarantor and pays him to guarantee his loan. The moralists agree that the guarantor acts lawfully in receiving such a fee for his service. When a borrower offers neither pledge nor guarantor, why cannot the lender charge for assuming a risk which is essentially similar to that for which the guarantor charges his fee? [9] This analogy between a lender and a guarantor is Medina's principal argument. A secondary argument is this: If I rent a house to one whose known rashness or negligence make me fear I will lose the house, I can charge him an extra fee beyond the ordinary rent, for the risk to which my goods are exposed; therefore I can charge when I expose my goods in a loan to a similar risk of loss. A third analogy is the charge an owner licitly makes when a bailee takes his goods on a dangerous journey. The one great objection Medina anticipates is that if the lender's capital is not lost, he will receive beyond the principal in getting back both his capital and the fee for risk. But his steadfast reply is that the lender receives not for the loan, nor does he ask a fee for the actual loss of the capital; he asks compensation for the real risk which his property runs for a time. That his good is eventually returned is irrelevant: "not because of that did it cease to be in peril at the time of the contract." [10] In the three analogies he has given, although no eventual loss came to the guarantor or property-owner, he could charge for the risk he ran; why cannot the lender? Again, Medina argues that a lender can charge for his fears of expense in recovering the loan; by a parity of reasoning, why cannot the lender charge for his equally real fears of losing the loan itself? The objection that the fee for risk is as likely to be lost as the capital itself is irrelevant; this likelihood places only an extra burden on the creditor.[11]

adopting the canon (Lugo, Disputationes, 25:10:189).

[8] On Medina, see Schulte, Die Geschichte der Quellen, III, 713.

[9] John Medina, Codex de restitutione et contractibus (Alcala, 1546), Q.38 ad 3c.

[10] Q.38 ad 3, r.3.

[11] Q.38 ad 3, r.2.

The case of *Naviganti*, which is urged as an irrefutable objection, is different from the one he discusses. There the lender, by force of the loan, insists on making his debtor insure his own business, and this is usury because it is a legal obligation imposed by means of a loan; here the lender asks for compensation for a risk the borrower has imposed on him.[12]

At the same time that Medina so stoutly defends the title in principle, he severely limits its application. A lender or seller on credit cannot charge all his borrowers indiscriminately a fee for risk of nonrepayment. There are some men about whose repaying of a loan there can be no doubt. It is then a sin, and one often committed, to charge all alike a fee for risk. Medina does not even suggest that the risk charge might be averaged out over all borrowers; he assumes that each borrower may be charged only for the probable danger of default that he personally presents. He continues, instead, with a second restriction: the charge can be made only if the borrower fails to furnish a pledge or a guarantor. Above all, Medina insists on the medieval criterion of intention and preference. The lender must be at least indifferent as to whether he sells at the current price or whether he sells on credit with a higher price for risk. If he prefers to lend and get the higher price, he commits usury. He may only charge for risk when he is solicited to take the risk by a borrower and does not assume it voluntarily as a way of seeking profit. Finally, he may not charge for risk if, by so doing, he injures his own reputation by seeming to be a usurer, or if his example will scandalize others and make them think that higher prices for credit sales are always licit.[13]

Medina's restrictions are narrow and medieval and they reduce the practical value of the title. But it must not be forgotten what a startling break from tradition he has made in admitting the title at all. Unsupported by authoriy, except for the opinions of Summenhart on a somewhat analogous case, Medina has defended a title that no one before him had dared to defend.

4. *Rejection by Soto and Navarrus*

Soto at once rushes to the support of the traditional position against Medina's bold innovation. With the authors of the past, he affirms solemnly that to admit the title of risk of nonrepayment would be to destroy the usury prohibition itself; for if one can charge for risk, it would be always licit to take something beyond the principal. All the debtor is held to do, says Soto, in order to relieve the lender of his fear, is to repay the loan. The risk cannot be evaluated apart from the good itself; if the good is returned, since the risk had no value independent of the good, no extra charge can be made for

[12] Q.38 ad 3, r.4. [13] Q.38 ad 3c.

it. As to Medina's first analogy, the guarantor charges not for risk but for his assuming the obligation to lend under certain circumstances; there is no similarity between his position and that of an actual lender asking money for his risk. In both the second and third analogies, the charge for risk is made by the present owner of the exposed property. But a lender has ceased to be the owner of the good loaned; the borrower bears all the responsibility for the real risks which threaten it; the lender's place bears no fundamental resemblance to that of the owners in the alleged parallels.[14]

All that Soto will allow is what Summenhart allows: a seller on credit may charge for expenses that it is feared will be incurred in recovering a debt — for example, if a debtor lives in another city, it will be costly to institute action against him if he defaults.[15] But there may be no charge for the simple risk of the principal. Here the intransigence of the past reasserts itself against the logic of Medina.

Navarrus gives even shorter shrift to the risk title than his usual opponent. The title of risk of nonrepayment, he asserts, is admitted only by Medina. It is opposed by all other theologians, by the canon law, by the natural law, and by divine law.[16] He offers no particular proof of the opposition of these sources of authority; his inclusive citation is apparently justified by assuming that the risk title would destroy the natural gratuitousness of a loan.

5. Support by the Jesuit Moralists

The risk title is unmentioned in any official ecclesiastical document even when the most desperate expedients were suggested during the 5 per cent controversy. But it finds warm defenders among the later Jesuits. What is more surprising than their support of the title is the manner in which Molina initiates it. In his opening presentation of what usury is, where he is making the fundamental definitions and distinctions which will guide hs later treatment, he declares,

Again no one denies that, if what is given is exposed to danger, either of being not repaid, or of being repaid only with labor and annoyance to the lender, it is right to accept a price for that peril and those annoyances to which the lender exposes himself. For a good given in a loan, provided it is exposed to a morally probable peril of this kind, is worth so much the less, the greater or more likely the risk.[17]

It is impossible to explain Molina's complete assurance in stating that the title is accepted by all without citation of authority, nor can we understand how

---

[14] Soto, De justitia, VI:4:1 ad 1 and ad 2.   [16] Navarrus, Consilia, V:32:3.
[15] VI:4:1.   [17] Molina, De justitia, II:304:8.

he feels no need to defend it further. But the fact remains that thus simply and calmly he adopts the new view.

Later, discussing sales on credit, he explains a little more fully that the seller on credit may charge for the fear of losing his capital only if "the fear comes from the nature of the thing, and not from the avarice or pusillanimity of the seller." Also, he says, the buyer must be warned that a charge has been added for risk because he may not wish to pay for the seller's assumption of such risk and may decline to buy at all. In any event, there is great danger of scandal.[18]

Again, discussing the purchase of debts and other personal obligations to pay, Molina says that risk may excuse a purchaser buying at a discount. But he warns that the title of risk is not always available.[19] If we consider this warning together with his remarks on credit sales, we must conclude that despite his easy assumption that the title was good in principle, Molina is almost as reserved as Medina in admitting it in practice. Nevertheless, he does free the title from Medina's chief inhibition that it must not be sought for itself, and his immense prestige is influential in furthering the title's greater acceptance.

As might be expected, the liberal Lessius accepts the title wholeheartedly. His case is essentially that of Medina, improved to meet the attacks of Soto. A guarantor charges not only for his obligation to lend, as Soto claims, but for his assumption of a risk, as is clear by his charge varying with the risk. If a guarantor can charge for his services, as all admit, so can a lender. A bailor who charges for risk when his property is exposed to the hands of a rash or negligent bailee has full right to the return of the good, just as a lender has full right to the return of his property; yet all admit the bailor can charge for the risk, although the bailee is in any case fully responsible for returning the good. Therefore, it is irrelevant that in the case of the loan, ownership has passed and the borrower is fully responsible for the good; the lender can still charge for the risk to which he is exposed. Again, a lender can demand a pledge or a guarantee from a borrower, and this is the imposition of an obligation beyond the return of the principal. If he foregoes this demand, he can, with justice, demand a fee to compensate him for the security he does not seek.[20]

The only conditions by which Lessius limits the title are that the borrower must be given the choice of offering satisfactory security or paying for the risk; the charge must not be greater than that which an independent insurer

[18] II:356:4 and 5.
[19] II:361:9 and 7.
[20] Lessius, II:20:13.

would make; and the lender's fear must be prudent and the peril probable. By probable peril Lessius would at first seem to mean peril which would not be common to most loans. The examples he gives are of lending to a man the lender does not know well, of lending to one whose credit is doubtful, of lending where great difficulty in recovering the principal is foreseen. Yet in treating of the purchase of a debt or of a personal *census* at less than its face value, Lessius asserts that the risk of nonpayment is common: "a personal right is almost always joined with some difficulties and dangers."[21] Perhaps he is a little more lenient in considering these contracts since they are not formally loans, and probably he would not allow that every loan was accompanied by a chargeable risk. Yet he is unquestionably more inclined to see the title as a usual one in practice than are either Medina or Molina; and his arguments for it are the most careful ones yet formulated.

Lugo follows Lessius and confirms and broadens his position. Like Medina, he chiefly fears the objection that "he who returns the principal by that very act takes away all detriment and loss." Just as a borrower satisfies for *damnum emergens* by offering to pay all that actually occurs, so, it is objected, a borrower satisfies for the risk of the loan by actually returning the loan itself. Similarly, a thief, returning a good, is not also held to compensate for the danger that had existed that the good might not be recovered.

To this developed argument Lugo, with Medina, replies that the loss caused by risk may be distinguished from the principal itself and is not compensated for by the simple return of the principal. The loss caused by risk is the mental anguish and fear which the lender suffers while his good is in his borrower's hands. This must be paid for, even after the principal has been safely returned. When there is danger that a bailed good may not be returned the bailor can charge more for his fears; so here the lender may charge for suffering which is distinct from the act of lending. He may even charge for his imaginary fears; the price asked is for mental anguish and should be proportionate to it. Regularly, however, it will be unjust to charge for the risk if one has received a pledge or if one's borrower is a man of good reputation.[22] But treating of the purchase of liquid debts, Lugo makes it plain that, like Lessius, he thinks enough risk is commonly incurred in the purchase of debts, and — it is implied — in loans, to make the title of risk well-nigh universal: "Where today is there to be found a debt so placed in safety that in security it equals ready cash?"[23] Lugo's question is one that might have been asked not only in 1640, but at any time before or after. That

[21] II:22:14.   [23] 26:7:96.
[22] Lugo, 25:6:79–85.

it was at last so bluntly posed shows that the risk in loans had finally been fully recognized by the moralists. With Lugo's acceptance of the right to charge even for imaginary fear of nonrecovery, and with his appreciation of the lack of absolute security in most debts, the title of risk has achieved full power.

6. *Propaganda's Decision on the Chinese Christians*

An exotic oriental strain enters the history of the usury question with the intrusion upon it of the difficulties of the Chinese converts to Christianity — an intrusion which led to the first ecclesiastical approbation of the risk title. The morality of the interest charged by the Chinese had been a subject of controversy between the Jesuits and the other missionaries in the East. In 1645 the Sacred Congregation of the Propaganda was asked by the Jesuit missionaries in China if they might tolerate the practice of Chinese Christians who lent at interest of 30 per cent, sought neither as *damnum emergens* or *lucrum cessans*, but demanded because there was likelihood of flight by the debtor, or because there might be delay in repayment, or because repayment might have to be forced by recourse to the courts. The Congregation, Pope Innocent X approving, replied that of course nothing might be charged "by reason of the loan, immediately and precisely." But, it continued:

If, indeed, they receive something by reason of a probably imminent danger, as in the case proposed, they are not to be disturbed, provided there is considered the equality and probability of the danger, and provided that there is kept a proportion between the danger and what is received.

The specific lawfulness of the 30 per cent is not decided, although the Congregation's response seems to favor it. The Pope, wishing above all to halt the controversy, decrees that the Congregation's decision is to be observed by all missionaries under pain of excommunication *latae sententiae*.[24] This papal act was interpreted as positive papal approval of the grounds for interest set forth by the Congregation. The decree and the papal enforcement are the most important approbation the risk title has yet received.

7. *Echoes in the Eighteenth Century*

It is hardly necessary to say that the redoubtable Ballerini will accept no such novelty as the title of risk. His belief is that most modern theologians who have accepted the title have been ruled by the authority of Propaganda's

[24] St. Alphonsus, III:5:3:7, n.765. Interest rates at the time in China probably ranged from 36 to 60 per cent (Yang, *Money and Credit in China*, p. 98).

decision on the Chinese;[25] but, he says, they have misinterpreted the decision. The Congregation, he declares, allowed a charge for the risk of expenses that might be incurred in collecting a debt, as is evident by the cases they enumerate, in all of which there is a probable danger of having to take costly steps to recover one's capital. But it did not allow a charge for the simple risk of nonrepayment.[26] In other words, Ballerini argues that the Congregation approved Summenhart's position but not Medina's.

Having disposed of the Congregation's decision, Ballerini asserts the fundamental basis for his opposition: no ancient author ever allowed a charge for the risk of the capital, even though in the past there were as many bad debts as there are today; therefore, it is against the authority of tradition to approve the title.[27] To this fundamental objection he adds what he considers arguments from reason. First, the debtor has assumed the whole estimable risk by obliging himself to return the amount loaned. Any other risk is *"periculum facti"* and cannot be given a pecuniary estimation.[28] For example, even the proponents of the triple contract will not admit that an investor in a partnership, once his capital is insured, may charge for the risk that his insurance may not be paid; the risk of nonpayment of the insurance is a case of *periculum facti*.[29] Similarly, therefore, a lender should not be able to charge for the risk that his debtor not pay.

Second, Ballerini revives the old argument that a thief in making restitution is not held to pay for the risk to which he exposed stolen goods.[30] Third, Ballerini uses the preference criterion. It is always usury to seek a profit. But lenders who charge for risk seek a fee not for compensation but for profit. No one lends to a person he really fears will not repay. The real motive in making the risk charge, therefore, is not fear, but hope of gain. Nor is it an answer to say that the lenders charge all borrowers a small sum to compensate themselves for the probable defaults of a few; as St. Antoninus said, it is unfair to charge every debtor for the faults of a few.[31] Fourth, the seeking of interest for risk is not the same as seeking a pledge. A pledge is sought as security against loss; a charge for risk adds no security, but is for gain.[32] Fifth, and finally, says Ballerini, appealing to social consequences, if risk demands pecuniary compensation, the most interest should be taken from

[25] Ballerini, *De jure divino*, VI:3:26.
[26] VI:3:28. Ballerini notes that a decision by Propaganda enumerating interest titles for the Japanese Christians in 1676 did not mention risk as a just title to interest, although risk had been alleged as a title by the petitioners for whom the decision was given (VI:3:32).
[27] Ballerini, VI:3:18.
[28] VI:3:6.
[29] VI:3:7.
[30] VI:3:13.
[31] VI:3:2.
[32] VI:3:3.

the poor, so that great oppression of the neediest will be justified in the name of risk.[33]

This strong attack is met by Zech with a careful reformulation of the arguments for risk. He begins by more tightly restating Lessius' argument: everyone allows that security may be licitly demanded from the borrower by a lender; therefore, it is evident that a loan is not intrinsically accompanied by the peril of irreparable loss, since there are cases of loans well secured by pledge; consequently, to admit interest for risk is no repudiation of the usury prohibition which forbids only that profit be extracted by what is intrinsic to a loan. If a lender does not ask security, he runs a risk which he is not necessarily bound to undergo and, since this risk is extrinsic to the act of lending, he may charge for it.[34] Zech then makes a change in the standard presentation of risk and says that the risk charge is not for the fear of loss, nor for the actual loss, but for the probable loss. The probable loss is calculable as an average of the total loss suffered by a lender over such and such a period or number of borrowers. As an average, based on the probability that a certain number of borrowers will default, although the lender cannot know in advance which ones will be delinquent, it may be charged of all borrowers, whether loss occurs in any particular case or not.[35] This teaching is an important development, for it eliminates the insistence of earlier defenders of risk that interest be charged only where a lender fears a particular borrower may not repay; at the same time it answers Ballerini's objection that no one ever lends to a man that he really fears will not repay. Indeed, it may be said that the force of Ballerini's objection forced Zech to a more reasonable position than taken by his predecessors.

Moreover, Ballerini to the contrary notwithstanding, *periculum facti* is estimable. Wherever risk of any kind exists, it has a pecuniary estimation. In the calculations of the just price in the triple contract, the risk that the insurance itself may not be paid is included in estimating the final just price of insurance. Again, growing plants and immature debts are exposed to the risk that they may not be collected; these are cases of *periculum facti*, where the good is valued at less than its mature value because of this risk. In the case of a loan, *periculum facti* should equally be estimated, for the borrower's obligation to pay is of no benefit to the lender if the borrower cannot or will not pay; and there is a real possibility that this inability or unwillingness will occur.[36] Nor is the analogy between the borrower and the thief valid. You cannot, for example, ask a pledge from a thief. Peril is not

---

[33] VI:3:2.
[34] Zech, *Dissertationes tres*, II:1:3:34.
[35] II:1:3:53.
[36] II:1:3:56.

estimated after the event but before it, so that a borrower may be charged for it, and a thief not. If you rented a horse and the bailee was going to take it on a dangerous trip, you could contract in advance that he pay extra for the risk to which he exposed it; but if you did not contract in advance and he returned it safely, you could not then ask compensation for the peril to which it had been exposed.[37] Finally, if it is objected that no one may charge another for a risk unless he in some way relieves the other of it, it is replied that the rule is not generally true; for merchants include a charge in their prices for the perils of their business, although they relieve no one of the perils. It is added that here the borrowers paying a fee are relieved of the obligation of furnishing pledges. Justice is observed if the borrower is given the choice between offering a pledge and paying for risk.[38]

Zech testifies that the title is still much debated and that he assented to it personally only after long hesitation.[39] But there is no hesitation or doubt in his cogent presentation of the case for the title and his forceful answer to Ballerini. He is the title's ablest defender. His establishment of the calculation of interest for risk on the basis of an average is the final perfection of the risk interest theory.

St. Alphonsus brings the debate to a close with a restatement of seventeenth-century opinion. Although he endorses it, he is neither analytical of, nor enthusiastic about, the title. He begins by citing an author in favor of the title of peril, if there is a "true and extraordinary danger of losing the principal or of not recovering it except with great expense," and if the lender has not refused insurance in the form of a pledge or guarantor. But a little later St. Alphonsus himself remarks that the danger of flight by the debtor, delay in repayment, and expense in recovering, which are the bases for Propaganda's decision, are not extraordinary, and therefore, he modifies the condition of "extraordinary danger" to that of "extrinsic danger."[40] He also seems to suppose such danger may be common, if we may infer his opinion on loans from his opinion that debts may be regularly purchased for less because of the usual difficulty in collecting them.[41]

Conclusion

The flat rejection of the risk title by such liberal theologians as Cajetan and Navarrus, the bitter assaults on it by Soto and Ballerini, the limited approval of Conrad, and even the somewhat ambiguous decision of Propaganda,

[37] II:1:3:59.
[38] II:1:3:57 and 39.
[39] II:1:3:38, 66.
[40] St. Alphonsus, III:5:3:7, 765.
[41] III:5:3:8, 829.

all reflect the reluctance to admit a title to interest absolutely new and unknown in medieval times. Medina makes its first great defense, but its chief
champions are the Jesuit theologians. Even they divide as to the ground
on which it is based. Molina, Lessius, and Lugo consider the interest paid
as compensation for the lender's fears; they believe the charge should vary
with the credit of each borrower. Zech takes the lead in arguing that the interest paid is proportionate to the probability of loss taken as an average,
and that an average risk interest may be charged every borrower. There is
general agreement that the charge cannot be made if security is offered by
the borrower. Although by 1750 a complete rational case has been made out
by the scholastics for risk interest, it is the least warmly accepted of all the
titles to gain from credit extension.

CHAPTER XV

PROFESSIONAL AND INSTITUTIONAL LENDING

The medieval usury doctrine especially discouraged the small-loan business. Public lending to the poor was manifest usury; the *census* and *societas* provided no effective alternatives for achieving the same result. To accept lending as a profession, to admit public dealing in simple consumption loans as desirable, was to make a radical break with the past. This break occurred with the acceptance of the *montes pietatis*. With this came not only a belief that lending could be a livelihood: although the *montes* themselves were pawnshops, their acceptance led to acceptance of much of the structure of institutional banking, and in particular, to the approval of investments in lending institutions and a charge for the institutional obligation of being in a position to lend.

1. *The Early Controversy*

Throughout the Middle Ages, the moral pressure on lenders had generally been unable to bring below 35 per cent the rate of interest charged by the public usurers, who were tolerated by the civil law as a necessary evil.[1] At the same time, the rulers of any city or state who went so far as to give positive permission to the public usurers incurred excommunication according to the legislation of the Council of Vienne.[2] Although there is little indication that in practice any officials were openly treated as excommunicated, no head of a government could have felt entirely at ease with this heavy conciliar sanction on the books. From the viewpoint of the poor and from that of the rulers, there was an urgent need to find a substitute for the Jews and lombards. Moreover, in many places in the fifteenth century there was a strong anti-Semitic tinge to the feeling against operators of the small-loan

---

[1] We have noted already (*supra*, Chapter III, n.40), that the great hold which the usurers had on ancient Greece and Rome was denied them in medieval society by the usury prohibition, but this did not mean, of course, that medieval society had success- fully and completely solved the problem of the supply of consumption credit. See Maurice Weber, *Les origines des Monts de Piété* (Rixheim, 1920), p. 22; de Roover, *Money, Banking*, pp. 100, 125.

[2] See *supra*, Chapter II, section 6.

business.[3] If the demand for credit was licit, was there no licit way of supplying it? If need for it was so great, could not its cost be lowered and could it not be furnished by Christians?

In 1462 the answer to the problem was given by the realization of the early dreams of Durandus of St. Pourçain and Philip of Maizières about a public institution which would lend to the poor at a low rate intended only to compensate it for the cost of the services provided. In 1461 Hermolaus Barbarus had been sent to Perugia as papal governor, and being a scrupulous man, he had found the city's statute authorizing the Jews to take limited usuries in the city a direct infringement of canon law, incurring excommunication for a governor enforcing it. He had accordingly abolished the statute and had been left with the problem of finding some way of meeting the needs of the poor for credit. To fulfill these needs, he instituted the first *mons pietatis*; [4] and the institution spread throughout Italy with amazing rapidity.

A *mons pietatis* was a public pawnshop, regularly financed by charitable donations and run not for profit but for the service of the poor. It charged a small fee for its care of the pawns and for the expenses of administration, including the salaries of its employees, so that the capital would not eventually be exhausted by the costs of the business.[5] In Italy this fee came usually to 6 per cent, as compared with the 32½ to 43½ per cent charged by the public usurers. The directors of the *mons* were usually one or two ecclesiastical representatives and several respected merchants of the town.[6]

From the first, the *mons* met theological opposition on the grounds that it was an institution making a business of lending at usury. But in 1467 Paul II approved the constitution of the original Perugian *mons*, and successive Popes approved the *montes* in other Italian cities.[7] The Franciscans espoused the institution, and Blessed Bernardine of Feltre, a great Franciscan preacher, was its special apostle, traveling throughout Italy attacking Jewish moneylenders and pleading for the *mons* as the remedy for usury. Some *montes* founded by Franciscans originally loaned entirely gratuitously, but in 1493, Bernardine convinced a general council of the order that the only practicable ways of preserving them was to charge interest; accordingly, an interest charge was made mandatory for all Franciscan establishments. At the end of the fifteenth century, there were eighty *montes pietatis* in Italy — a growth which itself is perhaps the best indication of the necessity of their work.[8]

[3] E.g., Alexander de Nevo, Cons. III: St. Bernardine, *De contractibus*, 43:3:3.

[4] Ballerini, *Opus.* I, *De montibus pietatis*, 1:2–3.

[5] Cajetan, *De monte pietatis*, in *Scripta*

philosophica, c.1 (p. 41–42).

[6] Weber, pp. 52, 64.

[7] Ballerini, *De montibus pietatis*, 2:5–7.

[8] Weber, pp. 46–52.

The *montes,* involving such a momentous break from the past, were, however, not accepted without further protest. They became an issue between the orders, and while the Franciscans championed them, the Dominicans almost everywhere attacked them as usurious.[9] The papal briefs approving individual *montes* had left room for argument by approving their constitutions generally, but with the provision, "saving the sacred canons." The Dominicans attacking the *montes'* morality argued that though the popes approved the founding of charitable organizations, this provision specifically reserved any approbation of the interest charges.[10] The controversy waxed hot. The Dominicans used their inquisitorial authority on occasion to investigate the defenders of the *mons* as heretics. At the same time Angelo de Clavasio, the head of the Franciscans of the Observance, called on the secular arm to repress those impious enough to question a practice approved by the popes.[11]

The first written attack on the *mons,* the *De monte impietatis* of Nicholas Bariani, an Augustinian, was launched in 1494. In reply to this, there appeared in 1497 the first written defense, the *Defensorium montis pietatis contra figmenta omnia aemulae falsitatis,* of Bernard of Busti, a Franciscan. In turn, to refute Bernard, Cajetan in 1498 wrote his *De monte pietatis.*

In Cajetan's calm and philosophical work, unaffected by the bitterness of the contemporary conflict, the principal current arguments in favor of the *mons* are stated and then their refutation is undertaken. The author, despite his dispassionate tone, is concerned to prove the *montes* illicit, and he may sometimes seem to overlook the obvious while he pursues a subtlety. But his attack is ingenious, and his distinction between defenses based on collective and distributive justice is an important one, which few later writers will observe so nicely.

Cajetan begins by declaring that the application of the usury prohibition is a matter of natural law, and that he will accordingly judge the *mons,* not by any appeal to authority, but by the certain principles of natural justice.[12] He proceeds to analyze the case of his opponents. He is familiar with two principal lines of defense. The first approach defends the *mons* on the grounds of commutative justice, saying that it is right that the borrowers be held to make up, proportionate to their loans, the expenses incurred by those lending to them. It is substantially a defense which relies on showing this is a particular case of *damnum emergens,* and it would hold for a private lender as well as for a public *mons.*[13]

[9] Zech, *Dissertationes tres,* II:1:6, 296–298.
[10] Cajetan, *De monte pietatis,* c.15 (p. 88).
[11] Zech, II:1:6, 298.
[12] Cajetan, *De monte pietatis,* c.2 (p. 43).
[13] c.1 (p. 41).

Let us, says Cajetan, analyze the expenses for which compensation is claimed: they are the expenses of keeping money to loan, guarding the pledges, the keeping of accounts, and the hiring of men to perform these offices and to stand ready to loan. Now, only the obligation of being ready to loan is one incurred in favor of a particular borrower, who will benefit directly from having someone ready to loan. All the other expenses are incurred directly in favor of the lender. Pledges are taken and conserved, and accounts are kept, in order to render the lender secure. The individual debtor does not care if these things are done or not. It is true that if the debtor offers an especially perishable pledge, requiring special care, he adds an extra burden and should pay the lender for taking the extra care necessary to preserve it. Ordinarily, however, he should not be held to pay for the care of the pledge nor for the keeping of the accounts, because commutative justice demands that one pay only for what is given one, and here the debtor is asked to pay for services undertaken for the benefit of the lender. A lender can ask *damnum emergens* only when his loan is the direct cause of his loss. Here his loan is the remote cause of his loss, but the immediate causes are the measures taken in his own favor to preserve his money. "They are not incurred per se in favor of John, the pauper receiving the loan." Consequently, it is unjust to charge the borrowers from the *mons* at the rate of so much per cent per month. Every borrower should pay something for the lender undertaking the obligation to lend to him; but there is no reason to calculate the fee in proportion to the amount and time of each debtor's borrowings, for the obligation the lender undertakes to be ready to loan is not increased or decreased by the amount and length of borrowings from him. If this fee were made as a flat charge, it would come to only about one-third of what each borrower now pays. Also, borrowers offering perishable pledges should pay for their extra care, but this charge should not be distributed over all the borrowers. Therefore, since the borrowers must by force of the loans they receive pay for services undertaken on behalf of others, Cajetan concludes that the *montes pietatis* by the standards of commutative justice are usurious.[14]

Cajetan does not deny that someone should pay for such expenses as the care of the ordinary pledges of the *mons* and the rent for its buildings. He says only that the one who should pay these expenses is not the borrower, but the owner.[15] Yet who is the owner of the *mons pietatis*? The usual answer given this question leads to the second attempted defense of the *mons*. This defense is based on a claim that distributive justice provides the proper norms here; whereas the first defense would also have applied to any private

14 c.6–8 (pp. 53–65).   15 c.8 (p. 63).

individual setting up money in a *mons* and charging for his services in lending it, the second defense justifies only the *montes pietatis*. It declares that the true owner of the *mons*, a charitable fund instituted to help the poor, is the community of poor or of the borrowers themselves. The money is conserved only in order to be available to help them. Consequently, all expenses undertaken in order to render loans secure and to insure the preservation of the *mons* are undertaken on behalf of the collectivity of borrowers, actual and potential. According to distributive justice, then, it is proper that the individual members of the collectivity of borrowers should be assessed proportionately for the expenses undertaken for the whole community; and the fairest way of distributing the assessment proportionately would be to make those who have the greatest advantage from the *mons* pay the greatest fee. Hence, a charge based on the amount and length of the loan accurately distributes the greatest burdens to the greatest beneficiaries.[16]

Cajetan replies to this formidable argument with a subtle disquisition on the nature of distributive justice. Commutative justice demands a strict equality between person and person. The debt of a community, however, being distributive, is owed by the members of a particular community in geometrical proportion to their place in that community. Now in a community, Cajetan argues, distribution of a good is made according to the members' dignity or position, as that dignity or position is determined by the character and purpose of that community. The persons of greater dignity receive the greater good, and so on. Similarly, he argues, when a burden is distributed, the persons of greater dignity in the community, being entitled to greater good than persons of lesser dignity, should feel less of the burden. The least burden should be imposed on the person of greatest dignity. The case is as if a community were set up in which A had the highest place and was entitled to 5 of the benefits of the community, B to 3, and C to 1. If there were no benefits, but a deficit, the original scheme would be most nearly kept, if A were held for −1, B for −3, and C for −5. The case is not one of commutative justice, where if A is to have the chance to gain 5 and C only 1, A would be expected to run the chance of losing 5 and C of losing only 1. The merits entitling A and C to their shares in the benefits have already been earned before the distribution. A's and C's dignity in the community does not depend on their assumption of a risk. But given that their relative dignity has been determined to exist in this proportion, the rule follows that the greater benefit will always go to A.

[16] c.10 (pp. 72–73).

Now, a community of paupers is constituted by need. Need is the basis on which it is formed, and need is the requisite for admission to it. Accordingly, the needier a person, the greater his dignity or place in the community. Hence, the *less* he should be assessed in the payment of a debt. The proponents of the *mons* favor a straight interest charge which, of course, takes most from him who borrows most. But he who borrows most is the neediest. According to Cajetan, then, he should pay least of all.[17] Therefore, the charge of the *mons*, insofar as it is for expenses incurred on behalf of the community of borrowers, is unjust.

The defenders of the *mons* reply with an insistence on the general principle that it is just for him who partakes of more good also to feel more evil. Cajetan denies this principle to be true, if dignity in a community has already been established. Here the community is based on need, "so that the needier someone is, the more good is owed him." Even if his opponents will not agree that this community is constituted and ruled by need, he adds, they should realize that it is unreasonable for the neediest to have to pay the heaviest burdens.[18]

With this appeal to charity, Cajetan ends an attack in which the surest handling of the scholastic theory of justice is mixed with the most sophistical construction-making. He has assumed that a community organized for charity must be treated as a charitable organization for all purposes. His ingenious argument, based upon this construction, seems singularly forced and unreal. Yet his exposition of the principles at stake is not without value. Moreover, it is important to note that at no time does Cajetan attack the fundamental basis of the *mons*: the right to set up an institution to lend and to have such an institution charge at least for its obligation to provide the service of a loan. Although this is the great innovation, the founding of a professional lending institution, it is unquestioned, because the medieval theory on the pecuniary value of the obligation to lend binds even the strict followers of the medieval tradition. A *mons* charging a fee only for its obligation to lend is licit even according to its rigorous demands.

Cajetan's acute and curious criticism did not, of course, settle the controversy, which raged yet more violently and passionately throughout Italy. Theological disputes over the *montes* became a public scandal. In 1516 a papal bull intended to settle the matter was placed before the Fifth Lateran Council, an ecumenical Council, presided over by Leo X, the first Medici pope. With one dissent, entered by the Archbishop of Trani, who said that experience

[17] c.11–12 (pp. 74–77).   [18] c.12 (pp. 76–77).

had shown the *montes* were impracticable although not intrinsically immoral, the bull *Inter multiplices* was accepted by the Council.[19]

The bull first described the arguments of the opponents of the *mons*, who asserted that the *mons* broke the precept of the Lord, "Lend freely, hoping nothing thereby"; that it was usury to see gain from an unfruitful thing; and that Cajetan's objections were valid. On the other hand, the supporters of the *mons* said that "nothing was sought nor hoped by reason of the loan," but that a moderate fee was charged for the indemnification of the *mons* to pay its expenses and conserve its being, and they asserted that the borrowers rightly were charged the fee according to the rule of law "that he who feels the benefit, ought also to feel the burden." This opinion the Pope held to be true, and, the Council approving, he decreed and defined that the *montes pietatis,* "in which for their expenses and indemnity something moderate is received beyond the principal, not for the profit of the same *montes,* but for the salaries of their employees and other things necessary to their conservation," were not at all evil, but praiseworthy. Excommunication *latae sententiae* was decreed for all those presuming to dispute this decree.

It is important to note that the bull does not explicitly declare whether the charge is exacted in the name of commutative or in the name of distributive justice, so that it would not be possible to tell whether the Council approved in principle lending as a business conducted by private individuals charging *damnum emergens* as a matter of commutative justice. In any case, the Council is definitive on the *mons* itself.[20]

Silvester da Prierio and Soto are the only writers to ignore the decree and to challenge the lawfulness of the *montes.* Unreconciled to the defeat of the Dominicans, Soto follows Cajetan exactly, allowing a very small charge by the *mons* for its undertaking the obligation to lend, but repeating Cajetan's objections to the interest currently charged by it. To the decree of the Council, Soto says it may be answered that either the Council did not have authority to decide purely philosophical issues, or that not all of the decrees of the Council have been received.[21] This attitude towards an ecumenical council passing legislation on a matter of morals was a matter for astonishment and regret among later scholastic authorities.

---

[19] Leo X, *Inter multiplices,* Fifth Lateran Council, Session 10, in Mansi, *Sacrorum . . . collectio,* XXXII. cols. 905–907.

[20] After the Lateran Council, the popes continued to sanction the charters of various Italian *montes,* and in 1539 Paul III approved one in Rome itself (Weber, p. 54). In 1562 the Council of Trent referred to the *mons pietatis* as one of the pious works to be subjected to a regular episcopal visitation (Council of Trent, Session 22, *De reformatione,* 8, in Mansi, XXXIII, col. 135).

[21] Soto, *De justitia,* VI, Q.1, art. 6.

2. *Justification at a Theoretical Level*

Curiously enough, despite the large amount of official approval bestowed on the *montes*, Navarrus is the first important canonist to make a detailed defense of them. He is also the first leading scholastic to discuss their financing; he is the first to extend the principles used in this defense to other lending organizations.

In the *Commentarius de usuris*, Navarrus says that it is just that the officers of the *mons* be paid for their "burden of guarding, lending, and recovering." Payments made on the loan are not "by reason of the loan," but "by reason of the administration of the *mons*." If the payments are licitly received, by whom should they be made? "Nothing more equitable" than that the poor who receive the loans should pay, in proportion to the benefits they receive, at the rate of so much per month. It is objected to this that, by a parity of reasoning, a private person could set up a *mons* and make a living from lending by charging for his salary and labor; yet all agree that this is illicit. Navarrus, significantly enough, does not challenge the assumption that the private *mons* is sinful. But he replies that in the case of the public *mons* the owner is the poor. The borrowers from it then charge themselves.[22] A second defense is expanded in the later *Commentarius de cambiis*. Here he declares plainly that every exchange dealer, who also lends money, and who enjoys his office by royal authority, can charge for his services as a public lender, as do the *montes pietatis*. The charge is not usury, because it is asked, not for the loan, but for the lender's sustenance. Similarly, he says, a priest is not simoniacal if he receives money, not for his mass, but for a journey undertaken in order to say the mass; similarly a judge is paid, not for his decisions as such, but for his support while he devotes himself to judging.[23] Yet Cajetan has objected that such an argument legitimizes all usury and has asserted that, as it is not licit to make a business of lending, so neither is it licit for one to receive support while in the business. Navarrus replies that there is no usury if the charge is not made "by reason of the loan," and here the charge is made for the assumption of the obligation to lend, which has a pecuniary estimation. Therefore, all men, bound by a public office to lend, may charge their borrowers in proportion to their loan for the obligations they, the lenders, assume in their behalf.[24]

But can even a public duty to lend be assigned a cost sufficient to justify the interest fees charged? Since the claim of obligation in *De cambiis* is used

[22] Navarrus, *De usuris*, 20, n.61–62. [24] *De cambiis*, 13, n.16–18.
[23] Navarrus, *De cambiis*, 13, n.15.

as a basis for defending charges which will support a lender, Navarrus presumably believes the charges may be high. He might well argue that the proper charge was whatever the market was willing to pay those who assumed the obligation of lending, even if it were 6 or 8 per cent, since because the fee was the price of an obligation distinct from a loan, it could be set by the common estimation.

In taking this position Navarrus was exploiting an old inconsistency. William of Auxerre had taught that a lender may not contract, as part of the price for a loan, that the debtor be held to loan to him in return at some future time; for usury consists in the taking of anything of pecuniary value beyond the loan, and the obligation to loan is an obligation estimable in money.[25] This teaching was repeated by Hostiensis, St. Raymond, St. Thomas, Monaldus, Astesanus, and the scholastics commonly.[26] None of these authorities, however, discussed the anomaly that the mere obligation to loan should be considered to be estimable in money, while a loan itself, the act entailed by the obligation, was considered to be worth nothing. This strange distinction had had no great practical consequences for the usury prohibition proper, as long as no one was lawfully allowed to be in the business of lending. But once an institution was set up the purpose of which was to lend, the distinction became of high practical value. Part of the charge by such an institution could be defended as a fee for its assuming the obligation of being ready to lend; and no one could challenge this defense without challenging the whole scholastic tradition. Here again, as in so many other instances we have investigated, a theoretical inconsistency in the early presentation was used to justify a practical liberalization in later analogous cases — the common way of development in a case system.

Molina buttresses Navarrus' defense of the *mons* proper on the simple grounds that commutative justice imposes an obligation to compensate another for what he does in one's behalf. Borrowers must compensate a lender for the expenses he undergoes "in order that a loan may be always ready to be given in their behalf, and that it may be given them when they wish it." Replying to Cajetan's objection that many of the expenses of the *mons* are undertaken primarily for the sake of the lender, Molina asserts that the expenses of the *mons*, even insofar as they are incurred in order to preserve the money of the *mons*, are incurred in order to have money ready to lend, and since this is for the sake of the borrowers, the borrowers may be charged

[25] William of Auxerre, *Summa aurea*, III:21.

[26] Hostiensis, *Summa, De usuris*, n.10; St. Raymond, *Summa*, 2:7:3; St. Thomas, *S.T.*, II–II:78:2 ad 4: Astesanus, *Summa*, III:11:5; Monaldus, *Summa*, at "Usura," f.293.

for them.[27] Lessius defends the *montes* on substantially the same ground.[28]

In the later seventeenth century Lugo is even more explicit: he defends the interest charges varying with the time of the loan, on the grounds that the borrower who borrows longest causes the most expenses in connection with his pledge, and that the *mons* could lend the money again and collect interest from someone else, if it were returned sooner. This second reason seems to be tantamount to admitting that *damnum emergens* can be charged when one foregoes one loan in order to make another, and is so foreign to the whole scholastic tradition on usury that it can only be understood as a careless mistake by the author. Lugo is clearly and intentionally more liberal than Lessius only in allowing that the *mons* may charge at an interest rate which in some years leaves it with a net surplus, provided that over a series of years there are an equal number of deficits, so that there is no ultimate profit.[29]

The eighteenth century finds the *mons* an institution accepted placidly by all. Even Ballerini, faced with a conciliar decree, accepts the *mons*; and St. Alphonsus thinks it necessary merely to cite *Inter multiplices.*[30]

3. *Financing of the* Montes

A great step in the development of the *montes* was the permission accorded them to raise money by paying interest. They needed capital, since gifts alone did not provide sufficient funds for them to offer enough competition to the public usurers. Accordingly, as we have already seen in discussing *lucrum cessans*, several sixteenth-century pontiffs authorized particular *montes* to accept deposits and pay interest upon them in compensation for the *lucrum cessans* suffered by the depositors. As we have also seen, the strict rules for *lucrum cessans* set out by the popes were not kept, and by the middle of the sixteenth century it became common practice to accept the deposits of anyone who wished to invest and to pay 5 per cent upon them.[31] From this time on, then, a good number of the Italian *montes* were "mixed" *montes* — that is, institutions not financed purely by charity, but by private investment; gradually they came to lend to businessmen at 8 or 10 per cent, as well as to

[27] Molina, *De justitia*, II:325:3–6.

[28] Lessius' language does seem to indicate that, unlike Molina, he considered the expenses caused the *mons* by the borrowers to be a debt of commutative justice, owed by one collective person, the borrowers, to another person, the *mons;* but that he thought that the debt was assigned for payment according to distributive justice, the borrowers being considered a community in which status

was determined in proportion to the very payment of interest fees, instead of according to need, as Cajetan assumed. He does not, however, make this analysis explicitly (see Lessius, *De justitia*, II:20:23).

[29] Lugo, *Disputationes*, 25:10:195.

[30] Ballerini, *De montibus pietatis*, 2:8; St. Alphonsus, *Theologia moralis*, III:5:3:7, 765.

[31] See *supra*, p. 258; cf. Weber, p. 63.

the poor.[32] The secular mixed *montes* were not like a commercial banking system, for they did not create credit. But their structure was substantially similar to that of savings banks, financed by deposits and lending at interest to all.

Navarrus is the first influential canonist to try to justify this finance. He declares that the state may create a *census* at 5 per cent and then lend money obtained from the *census* sale to the poor, charging 5 per cent interest for the *damnum emergens* suffered by it in paying the *census* returns.[33] Apparently, the *census* itself would not be created on the interest returns, but on some other property; the interest returns would be used only to compensate for the *census* paid, so that the *census* would not be directly based on interest payments. The practical effect, of course, is the same: the purchaser of the *census* gets 5 per cent from loans made to the poor, and since the form of his contract is a *census*, not a loan, he needs no interest title to collect it lawfully.

Lessius takes a more radical position in theory: a *census* may be created directly on interest returns.[34] The advantage of his proposed method over financing by deposits was that depositors, as true lenders, could accept payment only when they had an interest title, and sometimes they might be considered to commit usury because they lacked a title. The holder of a *census* needed no other title to take a return. The advantage over Navarrus' plan was that here the *mons* needed no property. In Lessius' scheme, the investor in the *mons* licitly drew a profit from his investment, because his investment itself was not a loan, but the purchase of a right to an annual payment from the *mons*; at the same time, the *mons* itself was justified in collecting the money it took from the borrowers to pay the *census*, for it sought no profit on a loan, but asked its borrowers for compensation for the burden of *census* payments it undertook on their behalf. Presumably the higher the *census* payments, or the more money the investors demanded, the higher the interest rates would be made in order to meet the *census*. Thus by the interposition of the corporate fiction of the *mons*, an investor might make indirectly what is, in fact, nothing but a profit on a loan. Yet at no time does Lessius consider the moral objections to this. Uttering the magic word *census*, he assumes, without debate, that such an investment system would be lawful.

At the time Lessius wrote *De justitia et jure*, the *montes* were not known in Belgium, and there were only the Italian examples to be guided by. But

[32] Zech. II:1:6, 265. 339.
[33] Navarrus, *Consilia*, V:16 (*De usuris*),
cons. 3.
[34] Lessius, II:20:23.

Lessius does not stop with observations on the theory of the *montes*. After giving his defense of them, and his new suggestion for their financing, he wrote,

From what has been said, it is clear that it is much to be wished and labored for that everywhere through the cities *montes* of this kind should be erected, and that the usurers, who everywhere dominate and exhaust the people, should be expelled.

He then gives four good reasons why the *montes* would be advantageous to Belgium. They would stop the sin of usury. They would keep money in the country that went to foreign usurers. They would offer a good investment to the rich, for the *census* on the *mons* would "be the best and most secure." They would be a place where businessmen could get cash at 6 to 10 per cent.[35] In short, Lessius visualizes not merely a pawnbroking institution, financed by charity and designed to help the poor as in Italy, but an institution startlingly like a modern bank, financed by private capital and providing capital to entrepreneurs.

Lessius' idea did not remain inoperative. In 1600 the government of the southern Netherlands had attempted to reduce the rates of the public usurers from 33 to 22 per cent, and after several years their failure to enforce the reduction was evident. Lessius then came forward with his proposal of the *mons pietatis*. After several more years of debate, his plans were largely adopted. In 1618 the public usurers were outlawed. Then throughout Belgium a system of *montes* was erected. Funds were obtained through *census* sales at 6¼ per cent, and the *montes* themselves charged 15 per cent in order to meet the *census* payments and their own expenses. The Belgian bishops specifically approved their organization. A special effort was made to attract men of piety as employees and managers for each *mons*, whose personnel thus made a sharp contrast to the socially disreputable one of the average usurer's shop. Wencelas Coberger, a man of considerable economic genius, was made the chief administrator of the system. At first, all flourished. The *montes* were not able to fulfill Lessius' hope of providing capital at 6 to 10 per cent, but some *montes* were able to reduce their charges to 12 per cent. The envious, dispossessed lombards, who had been unwilling to take 22 per cent, now offered to reënter the business at 15 per cent.[36]

There was, nevertheless, considerable theological grumbling about the

---

[35] *Ibid.*, II:20:23.
[36] Pierre de Decker, *Études historiques et*   *critiques sur les Monts de Piété en Belgique* (Brussels, 1844), pp. 56–60, 76, 115–116.

montes' charges, and in 1625, Lessius felt compelled to add an appendix to his *De justitia et jure*, in which he undertook an *ex professo* defense of the Belgian *montes*. His chief reliance here is on the Lateran Council's decree. He argues that if it is right, as the bull indicates, for the borrowers to be held to pay the salaries of the *montes'* employees, it is equally right that they be held to pay the *census* returns and the expenses of the buildings.[37] He repeats again and again that usury occurs only when payment is asked "by force of the loan." Payment on a loan by virtue of some other title such as *damnum emergens* is never usury. It is plain that his opponents simply insisted on Luke 6:35, and Lessius comments on this wryly: "Surely, if the words of the Lord should be understood as they insinuate, so that in a loan it is not at all licit to demand beyond the principal by any title whatsoever, it must be confessed a supernatural mystery."[38]

Lessius does not discuss the licitness of the owners of the *census* receiving a return founded on interest payments, but strikingly enough, he compares the *census* on the Belgian *montes* to the pure loans used to finance the Italian *montes*.[39] Yet while the depositors in the Italian *montes* can receive interest only if they have a claim of *lucrum cessans*, the holders of his *census* contracts can profit whether they have interest claims or not.

Lessius says that the *montes* are distinguished from public usurers because the latter seek only to enrich themselves; but he has no real answer when it is objected that if it is licit for the *montes* to charge 15 per cent, then it should be equally licit for the lombards to charge 15 per cent as they now offer to do. He merely says that experience shows that they will raise their price again, whenever they feel secure.[40]

Of the later authorities, Lugo deals only with the Italian *montes* financed by deposits and defends them on the lines of the sixteenth-century papal briefs: the *mons* may charge the borrowers for the interest it pays to attract

---

[37] Lessius, Appendix, *De monte pietatis*, Q.1.

[38] 2:36.

[39] Q.1.

[40] 2:87. The *montes* so brilliantly defended by Lessius and so ably begun by Coberger, did not have the prosperous career their proposers envisioned for them. The first disastrous step occurred as early as 1625 when the Infanta Isabella forced the *montes* to lend to her. Other government levies, a premature reduction of the interest rate to 10 per cent in 1635, mismanagement by Coberger, and concealment of the true state of the associations while new *census* sales were made, all combined to hurt the *montes*. In 1648 they were forced to suspend payments on the *census*. In 1652 *census* payments were resumed at the much reduced figure of 2½ per cent, while the interest charge was restored to 15 per cent. The *montes*, thus revived, continued in existence down to the French Revolution. (See de Decker, pp. 117, 135–147, 153, 166–167, 182, 278.) They remained, however, government pawnshops, affording neither good investments nor providing business capital, and never realized Lessius' dream of great credit institutions providing a service to both investors and business borrowers.

capital; the depositors receive this interest licitly if they have a claim of *lucrum cessans*.[41]

In the eighteenth century, Ballerini is unreservedly shocked at this common way of financing the Italian *montes*. Since, as we have seen, his conditions for licit interest-taking are severely restrictive, he believes that most depositors commit usury.[42] Accordingly, he suggests other alternatives for raising capital. One is for the *mons* to sell a real *census*, based on property it may own or on income other than the interest returns, such as income due it by endowment.[43] But, Ballerini admits, the *montes* do not often have any property or funds to offer as a real *census* base. Another way of financing them is for a city interested in a *mons* to sell its own property with a repurchase clause in its own favor, give the proceeds of the sale to the *mons*, then rent back its property at, say 5 per cent per year, and charge the *mons* for this expense incurred on its account. The idea is in essence like Navarrus' simpler plan. In Ballerini's scheme the ultimate investors are justified because they have truly purchased property and receive a return on a just rent. The city is justified becaues it asks compensation from the *mons* for expenses incurred on its account and yet it suffers no eventual loss on the transaction. The *mons* is justified because it asks the borrowers to pay only what it has to pay the city. This elaborate scheme had actually been put into effect in 1581 by Bishop Valerio of Verona, who had thus hoped to stop the paying of usury to depositors. But soon, Ballerini confesses, the instruments of purchase and rent used by the city came to be treated as simple loans on which the city pledged its property for greater security, "so that what ought to be a remedy, is now a cloak for usury."[44]

Ballerini does not even mention the possibility of erecting a *census* on the *mons'* interest returns themselves, but since in general he allows the licitness of only a real, perpetual *census*, we can be certain he would have rejected Lessius' idea with horror. Now, since his two suggestions were almost completely impractical, one is left with the impression that he had despaired of legitimizing the procedures of the investors in the *mons*. At the end he says that, if necessary, the *mons* may borrow at usury, and charge its borrowers to pay it.[45] In that case the ultimate lenders sin, but not the *mons*. This, according to his standards, must have been the common practice.

In contrast, Zech's position is as broad and liberal as Lessius'. He defends the *montes*, public and private, by *damnum emergens*, and he admits the licit-

[41] Lugo, 25:10:198.
[42] Ballerini, *De montibus pietatis*, 3:19.
[43] 4:30.
[44] 4:31–32–33.
[45] 5:104.

ness of selling a *census* on them as in Belgium.[46] In Italy, however, he believes that the bull *Cum onus*, fixing by positive law certain requisites for a *census*, still binds, so that a *census* could not be sold on interest-returns there; moreover, in fact, the *montes'* depositors there intend to loan, not buy, a *census*.[47] Angered by the rigorist position on the German *census* of Concina and Ballerini, Zech then makes the most of the difficulty to which the Italians should be put to justify the common method of financing the *montes* in Italy. Is it, he asks, that the Italian theologians are simply inured to the making of thousands of usurious contracts, so that they overlook the usury here, in the same way that those living by cataracts become deaf to the sound of rushing water?[48] Although he taunts his opponents with their position before the common practice, however, he really seems not to disapprove the practice himself; his aim is, rather, to force his Italian critics to abandon their own rigorism or condemn completely and explicitly the economic life of their country. It may be inferred, although he does not say so directly, that Zech personally believes that *lucrum cessans* will normally justify the depositors collecting interest on the Italian *montes*.[49]

4. *Justification of a Lending Business*

To approve a public lending institution, even one privately financed, was not to approve a *mons* run for profit by private owners. Such *montes* had appeared in the late sixteenth century in Italy; in Belgium, after the partial failure of Lessius' scheme, the old lombards returned to their business, charging lower rates. Did the late scholastics accept this final stage of open, professional moneylending?

Navarrus, as we have seen, adopted the somewhat artificial position that a "public" exchange dealer could make a sustentative profit, but a private *mons* could not.[50] Molina argued that a private person, as well as a community, could set up a *mons* and charge his borrowers for his expenses in running and preserving the capital.[51] It is not clear whether such expenses included "sustentative profit" of the entrepreneur. The medieval authors who permitted *damnum emergens* in a particular case never allowed that one could support oneself by charging it, so that it is conceivable that Molina would allow a charge for expenses and yet now allow a man to make lending his livelihood. Molina himself is silent on the ambiguous point, and it is impossible to be certain of his opinion. Nonetheless, since the employees of the

[46] Zech, II:1:6:339; II:1:6:360.
[47] II:1:6, 349.
[48] II:1:6, 352.
[49] See *supra*, p. 267.
[50] See *supra*, p. 301.
[51] Molina, II:325:6.

public *montes* were certainly paid salaries sufficient to support them, it would seem a just inference that, according to Molina, a private *mons* could pay its manager, although he was the investor himself, a sufficient salary to support him. If this estimate of Molina's mind is correct, he has gone one step beyond Navarrus to admit that not only publicly-obliged lenders, but even pure private lenders can make their livelihood out of lending. This is a momentous step, although Molina's advocacy of it should not be overemphasized, since he refrains from defending it explicitly.

Even Lessius does not face the issue in express terms. But in approving the private financing of the *montes*, he avoids the need for facing it. Any officer or employee of the *mons* could be paid a salary; any investor could take his return in the form of a *census*. With Lessius private professional lending is so justified that the question of "sustentative profit" by the lender is henceforth academic.

Conclusion

The idea of a lending institution charging interest for its services has been overwhelmingly accepted. Unquestionably, the virtual unanimity of assent to it by theologians after 1516 is to be ascribed to the force of the conciliar decree. Yet the natural-law argument, based on *damnum emergens* and on the right to charge for assuming the obligation to loan played a great part in winning rational consent to the institution. Unfortunately, no theologian after Cajetan makes explicit whether his defense of the *mons* is by commutative or distributive justice. But it seems implicit in the standard arguments that the interest debt is considered one of commutative justice, owed by the collectivity of borrowers to the lenders and distributed by the standards of distributive justice among the debtors, who form a community to which interest payments are precisely the admission and the determinant of rank. This is not a confusion of commutative and distributive justice, as happens in the case Cajetan opposes, where the borrowers are considered owners of the *mons* and then are assessed by commutative standards. Here the collectivity first contracts a debt of commutative justice, just as any collectivity does when it deals with an individual; then like any other collectivity it assigns its debt to its members in proportion to their position. The only difference between this community of debtors and other collectivities is that here one's part in the payment of the community's debt is what determines one's place in the community.

The acceptance of charitable lending institutions leads to the acceptance of noncharitable lending institutions, and, as the first kind are allowed to charge for their services and pay their employees' salaries out of interest, so are the second. Thus, ambiguously with Molina and indirectly with Lessius, there is also an acceptance of the idea of sustentative profit: the lender is allowed to charge enough to support himself, if he makes lending his business. In this way, by the acceptance of the *mons pietatis*, professional lending becomes accepted. By approving the Belgian *montes*, Lessius, the Belgian bishops, and the scholastics writing on these institutions, also approve their financing by *census* sales which are paid by interest returns alone — in other words, investment in lending institutions and profit on such investment paid from interest returns. While formally maintaining the usury prohibition, they seem to have left no limit to the possible gain on a loan licit in practice; the sole proviso is that the gain be realized by the indirect means of putting money into a lending business.

CHAPTER XVI

EXCHANGE BANKING

Beginning with the end of the sixteenth century and continuing through the seventeenth, exchange banking underwent a great expansion, and, already in medieval times the most important source of pure financial profit, it made its influence tenfold more important in these centuries. By the beginning of the eighteenth century, enough other ways of profiting in finance had been opened up to reduce exchange to a secondary role; but for two centuries exchange banking was the heart of the European credit system.

The new importance of exchange was signalized by the rise of two great new money markets, Lyons and Antwerp. Each was a commercial center developed into an international center of finance.[1] These markets were the centers of commercial finance, pure speculation, and extended governmental credit operations. The rise of the new national states led to borrowing on a new scale, both to meet ordinary expenditures and particularly to finance the large demands of war on a national basis. France, the Austrian-Spanish Empire, England, Portugal — all became large customers of the exchanges.[2] Much of the large borrowing by governments at Antwerp and Lyons was in the form of exchange sales; and given its volume, it is explicable only if it is understood as involving much pure credit creation.[3]

Was this tremendous business in credit at Antwerp and Lyons and the lesser exchange centers regarded as usurious? By the standards of St. Raymond and St. Antoninus there was no doubt but that it was usury throughout. But the revisions of the later scholastics extend to this field, too; and

[1] Richard Ehrenburg, *Capitalism and Finance in the Age of the Renaissance*, trans. H. Lucas (New York, 1928), pp. 236, 265, 283ff. De Roover maintains that the works of Endemann, Ehrenburg, and Tawney have led historians to exaggerate the commercial and financial innovations in the exchange market in the sixteenth century (*L'évolution*, p. 64). But he does not deny that in the sixteenth century there is an expansion of the exchange business.

[2] Ehrenburg, pp. 28ff.; cf. de Roover, *L'évolution*, pp. 64–66. On the activity at the Spanish fairs, especially at Medina del Campo, see Ramon Carande, *Carlos V y sus banqueros: La vida economica de espana en una fase de su hegemonia* (Madrid, 1943), pp. 212–214.

[3] Usher, *The Early History of Deposit Banking*, pp. 112, 122–123; M. Vigne, *La Banque à Lyon du 15° à 18° siècle* (Paris, 1903), p. 147.

the verdict is not the majority verdict of an earlier age, although by no means is the whole business of the bourses approved. The later scholastics' judgment on exchange banking is characterized by three fundamental admissions: the banker's purchase of exchange at a profit is licit; supply and demand influence the price of money; the technical characteristics of exchange operations are just. Both Alexander Lombard and Laurentius de Ridolfis had recognized the effect of supply and demand on the money price. But no systematic exploration of the meaning of this admission had been made. The medieval majority, moreover, had drawn a hard and fast line condemning the banker's purchase of exchange and maintaining the formal stability of money as a measure. The new scholastic approach is a revolt from these theories of the past. The result is a revolution in the practical judgment on exchange banking among the theologians. They go forward to meet the views that the medieval merchants had always held. As a by-product they achieved a considerable development of the theory of money and value.

From the extent of their treatises on exchange, as well as from the references to daily practice contained in them, it would be easy to infer from the scholastic writers alone the immense role the exchanges played in furnishing credit for the commerce and for the governments of Europe. These authors were occupied here with the problem which was at the heart of European economic life, and they lavished proportionate attention upon it. For two centuries the best moral analyses of economic operations occur in their discussions of exchange banking.

1. *The Impact of Custom on Theory*

Throughout the scholastic discussion of exchange from the end of the fifteenth century onwards, the most striking aspect is the willingness of most of the authorities to consult the merchants and to be guided by commercial custom. Thus at the beginning of this period, Summenhart believes two important questions which confessors should ask their penitents engaged in finance are these: Did the dealer's customer take the exchange because he was driven to it by necessity? Is the exchange customary in the country? An affirmative answer to the first question and a negative to the second create a suspicion of usury.[4] Here there appears to be a real willingness to abide by business practice, although Summenhart, like other medieval innovators in the usury field, says that the exchange contracts he defends *de rigore scholastico* may be imprudent in practice, and this prudential hesitancy aligns him

[4] Summenhart, *De contractibus*, Q. 99.

more with the medieval writers than with the bolder later scholastics.

With an even stronger concern for practice, Cajetan, before writing *De cambiis*, the most thorough and influential scholastic treatise on exchange of its age, had the dealers explain their business to him; his treatise becomes a careful attempt to offer justification for a business which has become common, and yet, as he remarks, had become so involved in complexities unknown to the ancients that many modern authors preferred to be altogether silent on it.[5] Instructed by the bankers, Cajetan denies that exchange was instituted to evade the usury laws. It is "laudable, as invented for purposes at once just and useful."[6] Merchants are necessary to supply the needs of cities, and they cannot conveniently function without exchange. Exchange is consequently necessary for economic and political life.[7] The old Aristotelian objection that a business which seeks money as an end tends to infinity and has no natural limit is met firmly: "[If exchange business is] ordained to the decent support of one's family and status, it is licit, in the same manner as other businesses, for it can be that what considered in isolation does not seem fitting, can be rendered so from an added end."[8]

Recognizing its usefulness, Cajetan approves the prices charged for exchange and the profit authorized by custom. The just price of an exchange is not a matter of exact science, but it may be presumed licit, if the common custom approves.[9] In any case, it is a fundamental rule that profit on the exchanges is entirely licit and expected. "A notable profit can thence arise . . . for such monies in such exchanges, much declining from the character of money, are exchanged as if they were certain commodities."[10]

Among the major theorists only Dominic Soto fails to show any friendliness to the exchange dealers. He catalogues the facts showing the prevalence of subterfuges obviously violating anyone's theory of the usury prohibition. For example, usance on bills from Spain to Flanders is for three months, but it takes only two weeks to deliver them.[11] The *cambium per Venetos* is an openly used means of borrowing on the market.[12] A fictitious gold to silver ratio is used by many exchange banks.[13] The bankers borrowing in behalf of the king pretend to exact usury only to pay his creditors; in fact, they usuriously take more than they pay and even declare publicly that, if they pay money to others, they may pay it to themselves.[14] With sales on the

---

[5] Cajetan. *De cambiis*, ante c.1.

[6] c.8, n.304; cf. n.295.

[7] c.5, n.250.

[8] c.5, n.248. This is the answer St. Thomas had given to Aristotle's objections against all retail trade, but which he had not used to defend the specific case of the exchanges (see St. Thomas, *S.T.*, II–II:77:4c).

[9] Cajetan, *De cambiis*, c.7, n.294.

[10] c.6, n.255.

[11] Soto, *De justitia*, VI:12:2.

[12] VI:12:4.

[13] VI:12:1.

[14] VI:13:2.

fairs, the price varies with the time to the fairs, and this fluctuation is especially evident in the common drawing of bills to mature nine or twelve months later at the third or fourth fair distant.[15]

In Soto's view, usury infects almost all types of exchange and every practice of it. Is there any explanation for the well-nigh universal corruption? Soto's belief is that it is war which led to this ugly phenomenon. The kings needed money desperately; they sought it particularly at the famous fairs; and because of their need, "a crowd" of hitherto illegal exchanges was permitted.[16]

A war-created evil or the common practice of Christian merchants? Navarrus takes the more charitable view that it is the latter and implies that Soto's position owes more to the rigor of his theories than to the unscrupulousness of the bankers. He does agree that there is a certain amount of usurious dry exchange "carried out daily with kings and dukes, businessmen and others." [17] But he suggests that even some of this business can be justified by *lucrum cessans*.[18] More importantly an "infinite number of decent Christians," merchants, nobles, widows, and even ecclesiastics commonly invest in exchange.[19] The knowledge of answers to problems it presents is highly necessary "to the confessors of all businessmen in the whole Christian world." [20] Navarrus will not "damn the whole world" by too rigorous standards.

Moreover, like Cajetan, he is aware of practical, as well as spiritual, reasons for a reasonably tolerant approach. "To abolish it [exchange] would be to plunge the realm into poverty." [21] Nor does he condemn the exchanges as a source of gain for the bankers. Many, he reports without disapproval, have doubled, quadrupled, and even made ten times their capital in exchanges on Lyons or Antwerp.[22] Sometimes the profit per exchange is 10 per cent per fair, or 30 per cent per year.[23] Many use the exchanges to make their fortunes, and "many I know follow no other way." [24] Navarrus, like Cajetan, is ready to give weight to the reasons these respectable financiers assign in defense of their profits.

A final witness on the new attitude toward exchange banking is Molina. He is less liberal than Navarrus, but far from the austerity of Soto. He finds

[15] VI:12:5.
[16] VI:13:2. On the financial difficulties of the Spanish Crown, see Ramon Carande, *Carlos V y sus banqueros: La hacienda real de castilla* (Madrid, 1949), pp. 96–141.
[17] Navarrus, *De cambiis*, 15, n.25.
[18] *De cambiis*, 17, n.34. But compare the restrained approval of this title for the exchanges in 19, n.47.
[19] *Manuale*, c.17, n.302.
[20] *Manuale*, c.17, n.297.
[21] *De cambiis*, 22, n.72.
[22] *De cambiis*, 9, n.11.
[23] *De usuris*, n.14.
[24] *De cambiis*, 22, n.68.

a good deal of dry exchange prevalent, and, in particular, an exploitation of the nobles by the merchants through its use.[25] He even warns that the exchanges are easily abused and that their use is never to be counseled.[26] But his observations on the just price in exchanges show his kinship of outlook with Cajetan:

> The practice of the merchants makes a better estimation of goods than the scholastic doctors, and the merchants' judgment is rather to be abided by about the value of goods, especially when they use them in the business they exercise with one another, no one of them complaining or objecting.[27]

If the businessmen do not believe they are unjustly treated by the exchange banks, who are the doctors to dispute them?

It is against this background of a willingness to investigate commercial custom, to accept the possibility of large profits in banking, and to legitimize the main functions of the exchanges, even if specific practices are condemned, that the major scholastics of the later period make the innovations in theory that achieve the acceptance of exchange banking.

2. *Virtual Transportation*: *A Service Charge by the Exchange Banker*

The first theoretical break with the past is the admission that the banker can profit on his purchase of a bill of exchange. It is now taught that a transaction where credit is extended and even created can be the source of profit to the exchange dealer; whereas the medieval majority had held that an_exchange bank could profit on an exchange sale only where it held the role of borrower, not lender. This significant step is first made in a qualified way by Biel, and then more thoroughly by Cajetan. It is the establishment

---

[25] Molina, *De justitia*, II:405:5.

[26] II:410:15.

[27] II:407:7. Thus, as Molina observes, large profits will be made "if the exchange dealer has dexterity in conjecturing the place and time, in which money will be worth much more, because of the lack of it and the necessity for it of the merchants and others: for example, when the prince in that place prepares for war and collects everywhere all the money of that region, whence it is believed likely that the merchants of the fairs in that region will have great need of that money, as not rarely happened in Flanders, when Charles V dwelt there" (II:408:3).

One example Lessius gives of an exchange operation on which he was actually consulted by the merchants of Antwerp offers some interesting information on what his judgments on exchange were in practice. The merchants were to give the equivalent of 94,000 ducats in Antwerp to the King of Spain for his military expenses, and were to receive in return 100,000 ducats in Spain in two months. The contract was to be repeated, so that the bankers would make 300,000 ducats, or over 38 per cent per year. Lessius declines to pronounce definitely on the size of the profit, though he thinks the danger run on royal loans makes it seem reasonable. In form the contract is an exchange, and in form Lessius says that it is just. This concrete case gives some indication of how the exchanges could be used to make high, licit profits out of operations that had all the effects of loans (II:23:4).

of an analysis of exchange which made possible, at least in theory, the legitimizing of most exchange banking.

The change is effected in this way. The early scholastics had admitted that a dealer could charge for virtual transportation of a client's money, but they had found such transportation to occur only when the dealer was drawee. Now, Gabriel Biel argued, why not look at the sale of a bill of exchange from the drawer's viewpoint? Is not his money "virtually transported" to the city where he draws? If the drawer is a client, has not the bank, in providing ready cash where the client wants it, performed a service? The answer is self-evident: the banker can charge for the expenses and danger of the transportation of which he relieves the client.[28]

What is meant by this "virtual transportation" charge, to which Biel and the later scholastic writers on exchange recur? Did they mean by it a sum equivalent to the actual cost of transportation? If they did, of course, their analysis was erroneous. The actual cost of importing foreign specie only sets the limits on exchange fluctuation; it is not itself an element entering into the exchange bank's profit. Possibly some writers, among them Soto, took "virtual transportation" charge in this literal and erroneous way. Such incorrect analysis appears to underlie the provision in the bull *In eam*, that charges on an exchange must vary with the distance between cities.[29] But it seems more reasonable to understand most of the writers as using "virtual transportation" charge as a construction, not a literal description. Their approach is legal, not economic, and their term here, in cumbersome legal fashion, describes the reality they obscurely perceive. In a word, their emphasis is on the "virtual." What they are saying is that a transportation company would be morally justified in charging a fee for moving specie. A bank which effects the same result stands in the shoes of the mover, morally. Hence, some profit on this kind of business is moral. The bank is performing a service and can charge for it. The scholastic analysis focuses on the existence of a "title to payment," and it finds a title to payment which is most accurately described in modern terms as a "service charge." So understood, the scholastic analysis is not erroneous. In the fifteenth century, as today, a bank charged something for its professional services. Between banks these charges may cancel out, but a bank dealing with a nonbank client normally will profit by the charges. The scholastic analysis, initiated by Biel, approved this profit.[30]

[28] Biel, *Collectorium*, 4:15:11MM.

[29] *In eam, Bullarium Romanum*, VII:880.

[30] Summenhart, Q.99; Cajetan, *De cambiis*, n.268; Soto, VI:12:2; Navarrus, *De cambiis*, 21, n.62; 22, n.73, 77; Molina, II:404:3; Lessius, II:23:4; Lugo, 28:3:48; St. Alphonsus, III:5:3:10:853.

3. A Market in Money

The "virtual transportation" argument, developed by the Tübingen school, is standard among the later scholastics of major importance. But more significantly, the concept serves as a construct by which the idea of a market in money becomes acceptable. The admission is the most exciting from the viewpoint of both theory and practice: for the notion that the value of money is immune from both supply and demand factors was at once the theoretical postulate and the practical requisite of medieval usury rules. To admit that the value of money is indirectly subject to supply and demand brings up the question of why its value is not directly subject to supply and demand, at least if it is absent in time. The attempts to deal with this question, to analyze the factors determining the price of money, to admit an exchange market and not a loan market, lead to the most probing and the most revealing investigations in the later scholastic treatments of exchange.

The investigations begin with Cajetan.[31] Money, says Cajetan, is to be

[31] The confusion and uncertainty which existed about the morality of exchange banking in Cajetan's time are illustrated by several sources. One specialized treatise has the peculiar distinction of having been written by St. Rucellai, who had been an exchange banker before entering the Dominican order. Asked by Savonarola for his opinion on the exchanges, Rucellai's answer is one of complete indecision. He notes forthrightly that the exchanges produce an almost certain profit to the bankers lending to businessmen needing short-term loans. On the other hand, he says, if the exchanges are not licit, trade is impossible. He condemns explicitly, however, the dealing in exchange bills payable at the Lyons fairs, where the cost clearly varied with the time to the fairs (see Rucellai, *Tractato brieve de cambi*, edited by Raymond de Roover in "Il trattato di fra Santi Rucellai," disp. 1).

The same uncertainty is manifest in the works of the writers of more general competence on morals, the summists. Thus, the Franciscan Trovamala (Joannes Baptista de Salis) in his *Summa baptisiniana* in 1484 simply followed Alexander Lombard (*Summa baptisiniana*, Usura, 6:21, Mantua, 1495). In his second edition in 1495 he showed considerable receptivity to the forces favoring the exchange bankers (*Summa rosella*, Venice, 1495). He still condemned exchanges which were completely "dry" (i.e., those in which no bills of exchange were sent). He con-

demned the Roman benefice contract. He condemned exchanges where a bill was sent, but the seller had no bank credits at the city of destination and the transaction had been effected as a means of giving the seller a loan. He distinguished this case sharply, however, from the case of a seller of a bill of exchange having money or credits actually in another city and selling the bill simply as a means of getting that money to the city he was in. In the latter situation, the exchange dealer might profit on the difference in value between the two cities and might charge for the risk of a value change and the expenses of his business. But what Trovamala found to be the difficult case, the one he explores hesitantly but thoroughly, in this: A customer of a bank of exchange in Venice, needing money in Venice, sells in Venice a bill of exchange to be met in Bruges. It would seem that this transaction could be classified as one of those already discussed. But after an exhaustive review of the authorities, Trovamala says only that the matter "is not clear." He would advise a banker not to engage in the transaction; *post factum* he would not hold one guilty for having engaged in the transaction. The most important arguments — attributed to Francis of Trevi (fl. 1437) — in favor of this exchange are that the risk of the exchange differentials changing makes the transaction different from a loan, where, it is implied, such value changes

distinguished as expendable and nonexpendable. As expendable, it has a fixed legal value as the measure and price of other goods, and this value is unalterable by private persons. As nonexpendable, money loses the character of legal measure and becomes a commodity. When does money become nonexpendable? Clearly, says Cajetan, when it is "absent" from the place where one wants to spend it. Thus, money in another city, sold by the drawer of a bill of exchange, is nonexpendable. As nonexpendable and thus as a commodity, such money is subject to the laws governing the price of commodities. This absent money is, in fact, simultaneously a measure and a commodity. It does not cease to have a legal value, it is not estimated solely by its intrinsic metallic content; at the same time its legal face value is not necessarily governing here, and it may be valued at more or at less, as other commodities are valued at more or at less.[32] "On this foundation," Cajetan observes, "arises the whole doctrine on the exchanges."[33] To give expendable

---

will not occur; that there is a difference in the value of money at different places; that, although the transaction has the effect of a loan, it is nonetheless a sale of money and not a loan.

The uncertainty and hesitancy of Trovamala are avoided in a drastic fashion by Angelus de Clavasio in his *Summa*, through a firm insistence on the criterion of intention Wherever the exchange dealer enters a credit transaction with the intention of profiting he commits usury (*Summa, Usura,* 54). Angelus specifically condemns the Roman benefice contract, and denounces as "the worst" an exchange to London or Bruges where the customer has no credits in London or Bruges and payment of the bill is met by a reëxchange. He will admit as lawful an exchange involving credit only in the case of a genuine traveler, fearing dangers of the road and buying exchange, say, at Genoa to receive payment at London, not with the intention of gaining a profit, but solely with the intention of having cash on hand in London.

Silvester da Prierio is less rigorous but not any better informed. This is surprising, because his work appeared sixteen years after Cajetan's, and as a fellow Dominican, Silvester would have been particularly responsive to Cajetan's work. Silvester appears to hold a position somewhat similar to Alexander Lombard's, that the exchange dealer can ask to be repaid more only if there is a real doubt as to what the value of money will be at

the time of repayment; but he adds that the exchange dealer may also charge because he buys money "at a distance." Such money is worth less because it is subject to risks. Although Silvester denies that the transportation costs have anything to do with the proper charge, this theory is essentially the same as Cajetan's that money subject to transportation has less value. At the same time, Silvester does not go on from this position to admit the market in money envisaged by Cajetan (Silvester, *Summa, Usura,* IV:9:1–3). At least, however, his approach justified some profit by the bankers, whereas all profit had been foreclosed by Angelus' insistence on intention. Moreover, Silvester explicitly contradicts Angelus on an important practical point, holding it irrelevant to the justice of the contract whether the drawee possesses the bank balance he is purporting to sell, or whether he is subsequently to borrow to meet the bill of exchange (IV:9:6). Silvester does maintain a strict view on the *cambium ad Venetos,* concluding that if there has been an intention to profit on the credit transaction, it will be illicit (IV:10:1). He also maintains a strict position in denying that it is lawful to charge more for long-term bills, or that the exchange dealers may charge because their money is tied up in the exchange (IV:9:3).

[32] Cajetan, *De cambiis,* n.260.
[33] *In summam theologicam,* II–II, Q.78:1 ad 6.

money for money considered as a commodity is not to lend, and from such an act there may licitly result "a notable profit." [34]

In the exchanges, the purchased money is nonexpendable; it is in a different place. As with any other commodity which has to be transported to the place where the demand for it exists, the determination of its true value is to be made with account taken of the cost and the dangers of transporting it to the place where it is needed. Money at another place is consequently always worth less than money in hand; just as money physically exposed to a storm is worth less than money absolutely considered. The dealer, providing money on the spot in Milan, can licitly profit because he gives his money for a commodity which is worth less on account of its absence in Lyons. [35] The fact that he may have agents at Lyons who will receive payment of the bill and use the money as well in Lyons as he could in Milan is *per accidens* and irrelevant to the justice of the contract, which per se rests on the fact that money subject to transportation is worth less than money in the same place. [36]

What is meant by "worth more" or "worth less" in this context? The scholastics do not elucidate the meaning of value in reference to money, and it might be supposed that, as the exchange markets made valuations in terms of a gold standard, references to value mean the worth in gold of the currency. But this meaning will not make sense in the context of many scholastic discussions of exchange; and a sound principle of interpretation would seem to be to assume, wherever possible, that an author is trying to make sense. Hence it may be suggested that for the scholastic authors "value" means "purchasing power." This meaning is implicit in Cajetan and explicit in Navarrus. Of course, without price indices, purchasing power is a vague concept. But it was evident at the common-sense level at which the scholastics were proceeding that money sometimes buys more goods, sometimes less. Money at a distant city always bought less goods than the same quantity of the same currency at hand. In this sense, money "at a distance" is always worth less.

This analysis is challenged two hundred years later by Ballerini. He argues that sometimes present money is valued at *less* than absent money. For example, he says, if money is in demand in Venice and not in Rome, one may give 101 in Rome and get 100 in Venice. Then, if the market has changed in Rome, one may give the 100 in Venice and get back only 100 in Rome. It is thus evident that not only does the exchange dealer not make a profit from providing present money for absent, as the usurer does, but that, as the

---

[34] *De cambiis,* n.260.
[35] *De cambiis,* n.267.
[36] *De cambiis,* n.269.

dealer's profit normally depends on the reëxchange, he actually runs the chance of losing on the whole transaction.[37]

This analysis of Ballerini, correct in itself, glosses over the fact that on any single exchange, the banker providing present money always profits by his service charge, just as a usurer always profits on his provision of present money. The present money, for one reason or another, is always valued more, and, if a smaller *quantity* is repaid in another place, it is a quantity yet worth more than the money given by the banker, because it equals the value of the sum he gave, and, in addition, includes his charge. Ballerini, in his anxiety to distinguish profit on the exchange from profit on loans, has confused quantity of money with value.

The same confusion, in more complicated terms, is apparent in Soto's critique of Cajetan. The dealer, he says, cannot charge for the transportation of his customer's money and simultaneously charge for the difference in the value of the money. Cajetan, Soto says, has confused these two charges. If the dealer has chosen to make the exchange by providing money in this city and receiving a greater quantity in another city, this exchange of one money for another has in itself effected the transportation of the money, and, since the dealer has profited on this, he cannot add another charge for the service of transportation. If, on the other hand, the dealer physically or virtually transports money and charges for this, that money must be considered as his customer's, and he can no more profit from increase of its value than any other carrier can, because the object he transports has more value where he brings it.[38] It is apparent that this argument rests on the assumption that the quantity of absent money necessary for equivalence with present money will not necessarily include an interest or service charge. Yet this charge is always present. It will be called "interest" by a modern economist; or it can be called a "virtual transportation" charge as most of the scholastics designate it. It is only nonsense to deny its existence as Ballerini and Soto do.

But why does not this view of absent money destroy the usury theory altogether? To return to Cajetan, he has said that nonexpendable money may be treated as a commodity, and he has even added that money absent in time is nonexpendable.[39] Why, then, cannot money absent in time be sold at a discount like money absent in space? The answer is that distance in time alone, unlike distance in space, gives rise to no physical process affecting the value of money. Money distant in space is theoretically subject to the

[37] Ballerini, *Opus.* II, *De pravitate contractum trium*, 4:74, 4:72.

[38] Soto, *De justitia*, VI:12:2. He adds, inconsistently enough, that the dealer can make only "a very slight" charge for transportation if he chooses to profit on the value change.

[39] Cajetan, *De cambiis*, c.5, n.253.

real expenses and dangers of physical transportation and thus is of diminished value. Money distant in time is theoretically subject to no physical process for delivery, so that, up to this point at least, no reason has been given for believing that absence diminishes its value.[40] In other words, interest in the form of a service charge will be allowed only on money in the exchange, not money in loans.

So far, Cajetan seems to have gone no further than Biel. It would appear that the dealer could profit only by his "virtual transportation" charge. But once Cajetan has established that money absent in space is to be regarded as a commodity, his procedure is radical. He now admits that its price may be determined like that of other commodities by the laws of supply and demand. Presumably if his first statement of the case were accurate, the chief changes in price would occur only with variation in the estimation of the dangers and expenses of transporting money. But, in the common exchanges he next considers, it is at once evident that transportation costs do not govern the price of the exchanges. It is the supply and demand for money in a given locality that cause the price to vary, as Cajetan himself confesses. It is the pure demand and supply of credit which dominate the exchanges and simultaneously make them of importance. Cajetan remarks:

Unless there were need of this kind for money, with an intermediate time in which the quasi-sellers could provide for their businesses with the money received by them, no one would be found as a quasi-seller in these exchanges.[41]

The cost of exchange varies with different times, in that the banks can purchase exchange at a high discount when the fair is a good way off, while they have to pay an increasingly high price as the fair approaches; or, in other words, the longer the credit is extended to the sellers of exchange, the more expensive it is for them. But Cajetan says this variation of price in direct relation to the time of the credit given is no index of usury:

In a certain way, the intermediate time is the occasion where the quasi-sellers are found, so that much intermediate time is the occasion of many sellers, and little intermediate time is the occasion of many buyers.[42]

The higher price for a longer time is not a charge for time; it simply results from a greater market estimation of the merchandise, money, when there is a greater demand for it. But this is an admission that the price of money can rise or fall with the demand and supply. It is an admission with revolutionary implications.

[40] c.6, n.273.
[41] c.7, n 290.
[42] c.7, n.291.

Moreover, not only does Cajetan recognize that the immediate supply and demand for money will play a dominant part in fixing the just exchange price, he allows an estimate of the future market to influence the price. He reasons in this way. The value of any commodity to be delivered later may be estimated according to its probable value at the time of its delivery, and it will be valued at more or less, as it is believed that some event happening in the time intervening between purchase and delivery will affect its value. Now money in the exchanges is considered as a commodity, and its future value may be estimated in the same way. This, Cajetan maintains, is not to say that time alone will confer new value on money, but it is to say that "the events happening in time" may confer new value. For example, if it is believed that war will have broken out at the time when the money is to be delivered, money may well be worth more because of the demand for loans by a belligerent country. But along with events purely extrinsic to the money market, such as wars and famines, Cajetan includes among the events, occurring in time and affecting the price of money, increases or decreases in the supply of money itself.[43] By so doing he admits that if it is estimated that the supply of credit will be greater at some future date than it is at the present, a dealer can value his money higher now and ask to be later paid more money than he gives. This is to consign completely the price of money to the fluctuations of supply and demand, both present and future. It is to admit a full-fledged market in money. It remains a mystery how Cajetan believed his reasoning could be true of the exchanges alone and not of straight loans. His analysis is a momentous event in the scholastic approach to banking. Approving the exchange market in general, he challenged later theorists to justify it without abandoning the usury rule.

Soto, the next important writer on exchanges, also recognizes that the "great foundation" of the exchanges is the demand and supply for the same kind of money.[44] There are "absolute" causes for variation in supply and demand, such as economic disaster or the king's needing money for war; and "relative causes," to wit, the number of buyers and sellers actually in the exchange market.[45] Since both absolute and relative causes bring about a real difference in the value of money, simple justice authorizes the dealer to demand the equivalent value of the money he gave in the place where he will receive it.

Making this concession, Soto then severely limits it; for he treats a de-

[43] c.6, n.276.

[44] With his usual self-assurance, Soto says that hitherto exchange has been little understood by the scholastic authors, and he even unfairly reproaches Cajetan for not seeing that the foundation of exchange is the supply and demand for money (VI:12:2).

[45] VI:12:3.

liberate attempt to raise the price by the bankers' limiting the supply of cash as probably fraudulent or wrongfully monopolistic; and he treats any increase in price for long-term bills due to the increased demand for them as usurious.[46] In practice, as we have seen, he considers almost all exchanges to be infected with usury. Yet, severe as he is in his judgment on actual operations, he has made the foundation of his theoretical analysis an observation which is itself embarrassing to the pure usury theory. If supply and demand due to absolute causes can determine the price of money in exchange, why cannot they do so in loans? Soto poses the problem. He answers it only by saying, "For a loan no price may be demanded."[47]

The problem could not be settled by this appeal to fiat. The probing of value in the money market is continued by Navarrus. Like the other Spanish theologians, struck by the effects of the increases in the money supply so dramatically brought about by the importation of gold from the New World,[48] he states that the price of money depends on the varying supply and demand, and that this is "recognized by the common sense of all good and bad men in Christendom, and so, as it were, by the voice of God and nature."[49] Does this mean that the price of money varies only as it is a merchandise or does it mean that the price of money as it is itself a measure varies? If the

---

[46] VI:12:3 and 5.

[47] VI:12:2. Although Soto was alone among the major theorists in taking an inflexibly rigorous position, he was not without support in the attitude of lesser theologians of his period, who apparently were ignorant of, or uninfluenced by, Cajetan's masterful treatment of the subject. For example, in 1532 the Spanish colony of merchants at Antwerp sent their confessor to the University of Paris to get the judgment of the faculty of theology on the business of the Antwerp Bourse. The merchants strenuously insisted on the economic usefulness of the exchange business, pointed out that both the banker and his customer usually profited, and urged that the risk of loss due to changing exchange rates should be an additional defense of the exchange contracts against a charge of usury. They also urged that, as money was the merchants' tool, they should be allowed to charge for the use of it in the exchanges, and that the exchange dealers should be allowed to charge for their expenses. Fifteen theologians, headed by the rather influential John Major, replied, categorically condemning the typical bill of exchange. The transaction was characterized as illicit and usurious.

The defense of usefulness was rejected on the grounds that usefulness and benefit to both parties was no excuse for public usury, nor was risk an excuse for a charge on a loan, nor was the money of a merchant more capable of being charged for than the money of any usurer. Finally, the theologians said that a charge for the dealer's expenses would be constant, but that here the exchange price varied with the time. The documents are reproduced in J. A. Goris, *Étude sur les colonies marchandes méridionales à Anvers* (Louvain, 1925), pp. 520ff. The general similarity of these views with those that Major had earlier expressed in his own commentary on the Sentences is clear; see Major, IV:15:30, and compare Louis Verecke, "La licéité du 'cambium bursae' chez Jean Mair," *Revue historique de françaises et étrangers*, XXX (1952), 138.

[48] The importance of this phenomenon for Spanish economic thought is well brought out by Margaret Grice-Hutchinson in her valuable study, *The School of Salamanca: Readings in Spanish Monetary Theory, 1544–1605* (Oxford, 1952).

[49] Navarrus, *De cambiis*, 20, n.51.

second alternative is affirmed, then it would seem that the estimation of money should increase with the lack of it, and, with the usury prohibition in mind, such a result constitutes a real objection to the theory. Cajetan has accordingly answered that it is only as merchandise in the exchanges that money has a fluctuating value. But Navarrus says that this answer is contradicted by experience.[50]

Navarrus then offers a new answer of his own: money could be said to be determinately valued only as it is legal tender in sales or debts, in that no one can be compelled to value money at more or less than its face value in settling such transactions. At the same time the valuation of money could be said to be left to each person's discretion in that the possessor of money could value it at more or less according to the private utility it offered him. Yet this answer, Navarrus himself concludes, is not satisfactory, because it would justify a higher valuation being placed on money only by those who derived some particular benefit from retaining it; whereas in daily practice, whether one gets a particular benefit from his money or not, both businessman and nonbusinessman value money more in time of need.[51]

There remains the possibility of admitting frankly that the value of money changes with supply and demand; and Navarrus chooses to make this recognition. Money differs from other goods in that its value is only "more permanent" than that of other goods; but its stability is relative and not absolute. Put in another way, what Navarrus does is to abandon the earliest scholastic distinction between "money as money," that is, as a measure and a price, and money as merchandise, that is, money as non-expendable in some way. He admits that money as a measure may vary and it may be the subject of trading on the exchange market.[52]

This frank recognition of the less than permanent character of money would seem to be a major advance in theory. But the theoretical advance is not completed: Navarrus makes no attempt to relate it to a market in money in loans, as distinguished from exchanges. In the very section of his work in which he makes the admission, he still distinguishes true exchanges from usurious loans.[53] He makes no attempt to explain how a loan can be usurious if it reflects the market price for money. More candid than Cajetan, he is even less satisfactory in attempting to find some way out of the paradoxical admission of a market in the changing value of money when the speculators are exchange dealers, and the denial of such a market when the speculators are lenders not making "true exchanges."

[50] 20, n.57.
[51] 20, n.58.
[52] 20, n.57; 20, n.55.
[53] 20, n.59; cf. 19, n.47.

In contrast to Navarrus, Molina returns to the tradition which attempts to distinguish money in loans and money on the exchanges. He reinforces and clarifies the old assumptions. The State fixes the legal value of money at its face value in its primary use within a country. Hence, "in relation to the place in which it is, money never has the character of merchandise, but always retains the price or value fixed by law." [54] One hundred ducats are always worth one hundred ducats in the same place, as long as their legal value remains unchanged; so, although time passes in a loan, money lent must always be treated as a fixed measure. On the other hand, the State has never determined the value of money in respect to other places. In relation to other places, money loses its character of a price and becomes merchandise, subject to the laws of supply and demand. [55]

This explanation so carefully worked out by Molina to guard the usury theory is exploded a century later in the exhaustive analysis of Lugo. The legal value of money, Lugo says, is fixed, not in relation to one place, but in relation to all places within a State. The legal value of money in Spain and the Spanish Indies is the same. Yet because of extrinsic reasons, because money is more abundant in the Indies than in Spain, money is more valuable in Spain. [56] It is clear that money can vary in value, even though its legal value is supposed to be the same. Therefore, if the dealer may ask more to be returned to him by reason of the extrinsic value of money in another place, a lender may ask more to be returned to him by reason of the extrinsic value at another time. Molina has at least allowed that the lender, foreseeing an increase in the extrinsic evaluation of money, can demand compensation under the title of *lucrum cessans*. But this answer is not adequate. The case is not one in which the lender has lost profit he might have made in business, but it is a case in which, whatever the lender's use of the money would have been, the value of the money that was his is altered. [57] Thus, Lugo seems to reach the place Navarrus' logic led, that every lender, like every exchange dealer, can charge for anticipated extrinsic variation in the value of money.

At this point, however, his reasoning becomes extraordinary. He observes that if the anticipated increase in extrinsic value is by itself admitted as a title to charge in a loan, "a wide gate will be opened to receiving profit from a loan." [58] Every lender in a time of necessity will be able to demand that a larger sum be returned to him, if the loan itself is to be repaid at a time of less necessity. In Lugo's eyes, the usury prohibition itself is threatened. To

[54] Molina, II:410:4.
[55] II:406:3.
[56] Lugo, 28:3:42.
[57] 28:3:46.
[58] 28:3:48.

preserve it, he rejects the claim of extrinsic value for the lender; and to be consistent, since he has said the case is the same for either the lender or the exchange dealer, he rejects it also for the dealer.

If one wishes to appeal to the usury theory as an arbitrary and inexplicable mystery, and from it as a base, condemn all which seems to threaten it, Lugo's procedure up to this point cannot be criticized. But Lugo is not content with appealing to the usury law as an ultimate authority dictating his action. He now attempts to defend his rejection of the title of extrinsic value on rational grounds, with an argument that surely must be ranked as one of the grossest fallacies ever recommended by an eminent moralist. He admits that if wheat were being exchanged or loaned, and a change in its value were foreseen, this change should be considered in calculating the true amount to be returned. But money, he now maintains, never changes either in legal or in extrinsic value. This astonishing statement, contradicting all his own and other scholastics' admissions, is defended in this way:

Although then [at the time of the loan] there can be bought with that money twenty measures of wheat, while later, because of the greater supply of money, there can be bought only sixteen measures of wheat, yet these sixteen are not of less value, but of equal value with the twenty of the preceding time, because the greater supply of money has made the wheat increase in value. . . . The reason of this is that, for a good to be of greater or lesser value, it must be bought at a greater or lesser price: since therefore money is alone the price of other goods, other goods are said to increase in value and in price, when the supply of money increases, but money is not said to decrease in value and price, because it has always the same value and price.[59]

In short, Lugo has identified the value and money price of goods, and he has separated the value and the purchasing power of money. A dinner costing two ducats today and costing ten ducats a year later because of an inflation, is, in his account, five times as valuable because it costs five times as much. Yet, he says, two ducats are worth the same at each time. Money's value remains constant, because all other values are determined by it. His position becomes a kind of *reductio ad absurdum* of the theory that you can intelligently consider money as a pure measure, abstracting from its purchasing power. Lugo is the only scholastic writer to develop the medieval thesis to this fantastic degree, because he is the only scholastic writer to treat money in the same way in loans and exchanges; his acceptance of this extreme shows his accurate perception of what the other scholastics' theory of exchange would, if applied to loans, have done to the usury theory.

Yet, even Lugo cannot long maintain the logical but absurd position to

[59] 28:3:47.

which his perceptions have driven him. In accordance with the common teaching, he admits that a dealer can profit on the virtual transportation charge. He then tries to argue that the fluctuation in transportation prices alone will render exchanges in different directions profitable. But, almost immediately, he tacitly recognizes the impossibility of applying his theory in practice, and we find him simply assuming that there is a difference in the extrinsic value of money in different places — the difference which he had so recently and so emphatically denied. He now allows that the money exchanged may be at least adjusted according to differences in extrinsic value, so that the dealer will not actually lose money on the exchange.[60] All that Lugo retains of his original position is that no profit can be made on the extrinsic difference in any one exchange. But he grants that it is licit for exchange dealers, foreseeing a shortage of funds in a place, to buy bills maturing there; so that he recognizes that dealers will rightly try to make a profit over a period on the extrinsic differences.[61] His position reduces itself to that of Cajetan and Molina, at the cost, of course, of contradicting his earlier position.

The eighteenth century has little interest in the problem so the exploration of value in the money market comes to an inglorious end with Lugo.[62] Yet the effort made from 1500 to 1650 has not been without fruit. The factors affecting the price of money have been recognized. The failure to reconcile these factors with the older theory of usury is a failure to do the impossible.

4. *The Price of the Lack of Money*

Instead of engaging in the prodigious difficulty of distinguishing money on the exchanges from money in loans, the writers of the period might have

[60] 28:3:49.

[61] 28:10:132.

[62] The importance of exchange and the scholastic interest in it decline markedly in the eighteenth century. Zech in a very perfunctory fashion cites nearly all the reasons ever used to justify the exchanges as exchanges or as loans. The dealer may charge for his virtual transportation of money; for variation in the value of money in different places; for expenses of the exchange business; for his undertaking of the obligations of a public office; for the loss of business opportunities for his money; for his risk of nonrepayment (Zech, *Dissertationes tres*, III:2:2:73–75).

Even the intransigent Ballerini looks with a milder eye on the exchanges and actually recommends them as one honest way by which credit may be given. He admits that the exchange dealer can always charge for his virtual transportation service. He even admits that the price of exchange licitly varies with the demand for it (*De pravitate trium contractuum*, 4:65; 4:72).

The common stereotype to which the discussion of exchange has fallen from its seventeenth-century height is indicated by St. Alphonsus' brief treatment. He follows Lugo's theory that the virtual transfer of money and the insurance of the transportation constitute the exchanger's title to profit (III:5:3:10:853). He has no discussion whatsoever of the effect of supply and demand on the market price, although presumably it is expected that the exchange dealer will obtain money of at least as much value as what he gave, and that this quantity will be different on different markets.

taken the simpler approach of defending the exchanges on the same ground as loans. In 1499 Summenhart did suggest that a right to interest was an alternative defense, saying frankly that the purchase of a bill of exchange was a mixture of an exchange and a loan.[63] But Cajetan's objection had seemed decisive: The dealers themselves testified that they sought no interest, but profit:

> For if the exchange dealers sought nothing else from the exchanges than to keep themselves whole, the exchanges would not be multiplied, and they would keep their money, or expend it in other ways, as they themselves admit.[64]

Now it is not licit to seek such profit from a loan, nor is it licit to seek to support oneself by lending or to acquire from it what Cajetan calls "sustentative profit":

> As experience is witness, it is not lawful to make an art of lending, so that by taking account of one's works, labor, and industry, more than the principal is received, whence one is supported with his family, as is licit in other arts and businesses.[65]

For the next century, Cajetan's approach is dominant: treat exchanges not as loans, but as contracts *sui generis* and explore the sources of profit in the exchange market. But with the increasing strength of the interest titles it began to seem more rational to justify profit on the exchanges on the same grounds on which compensation was sought by lenders.

Navarrus, who goes to such elaborate lengths to establish the conditions of a market in exchange bills, admits *lucrum cessans* may sometimes also be a defense for the dealers.[66] Even more significantly, as we have seen, he justifies a charge by an exchange banker for his services as a "public lender," obligated to make exchanges.[67] This is the most radical approval yet given of a lending business operated for sustentative gain. That it should be given in connection with the exchanges is a significant reflection of the tendency to legitimize the activities of the respectable bankers.

A century later, an important elaboration of Navarrus' idea is made by Lugo, linking a banker's compensation directly to the amount of credit he gives. The exchange dealer, he says, can demand reward not only for his labor but "for his dignity of person, for not every person is fit for such an office." In making an exchange or loan the banker can charge for his skill in proportion to the amount involved, because, the greater the amount, the

[63] Summenhart, Q.99.
[64] Cajetan, *De cambiis*, c.2, n.220.
[65] c.2, n.222.

[66] Navarrus, *De cambiis*, 15, n.26; 17, n.34.
[67] See *supra*, p. 301.

more it interests the recipient that a skillful banker should handle the business for him.[68]

In this work of Navarrus and Lugo the "service charge" notion merges into "compensation for lending." But the factors affecting the exchange market are not yet merged with those affecting loans. This is the particular achievement of Lessius. Discussing the exchanges made on the fairs in which the price of the exchange varies with the time to the fair, he proposes his new and favorite title. He does not defend the practice of charging more for the longer credit, as Cajetan does, on the grounds that the price varies with the demand, not the time; nor does he, with Soto, condemn the exchanges as usurious. He says frankly that, since in these exchanges a greater time for payment than that necessary for the passage of the exchange bills to the other place is customarily allowed, it is clear that a loan is intended, and that a loan occurs. But these exchanges, which are truly loans, he says, may be defended, because, the longer the time allowed in them, the longer the exchange dealers suffer the lack of their money; and their charge is to compensate for this lack of money. *Carentia pecuniae*, the title "lack of money," is much broader than the qualified title, *lucrum cessans*; detailed consideration of it must be reserved for Chapter XVII's discussion of the revision of the usury theory itself. Here we need cite only Lessius' testimony that the dealers themselves declare that unless this title is admitted, all the exchanges of the day are unjust.[69]

Lessius also appeals to *carentia pecuniae* when he tries to explain how the exchange rates vary as the exchange bank is payee or drawee. If, for example, an exchange dealer receives 400 at Medina del Campo, he will engage to deliver 350 at Antwerp; but if he first pays 360 at Antwerp, he will ask 430 at Medina del Campo. In the first exchange, 400 at Medina del Campo equals 360 in Flanders, and the dealer deducts 10 for his service. But, in the second exchange, when he gives 360 in Flanders, why does he not expect to receive their equivalent, 400, in Medina del Campo plus 10 for his service, or 410 in all? Where does a claim to the extra 20 arise? It is due neither to transportation charges, which should be approximately the same each way, nor to difference in the value of the ducat, which has already been allowed for. The extra 20, Lessius says, is asked for the dealer's *carentia pecuniae*. A charge of 20 in this case, Lessius adds, is excessive, and, in fact, no one makes such profits today. But he accepts the principle of such a charge as fundamental.[70] Similarly, when he discusses why absent money is less valuable

[68] Lugo, 28:6:73 and 74.   [70] II:23:4.
[69] Lessius, II:23:6.

than present, he gives not only the standard reason that it is subject to transportation, but twice says that present money offers "greater facility and convenience." [71] This is a reason which comes to the same thing as *carentia pecuniae*.

As distinct and different from *carentia pecuniae*, *lucrum cessans* is also noted as a licit title to gain for the exchangers. Moreover, risk of nonpayment is advanced as a particular reason for a charge in the exchanger's loans to kings. Thus Lessius defends the common exchanges by titles authorizing interest on a loan rather than by the principles regulating the just price in sales and commodities. Exchanges are distinguished from loans in this analysis only by the freer way in which the price of "the lack of money" is allowed as a common justification. The economic basis for this distinction is this: the exchange market might be considered to have set a common price on money, while in less well-organized loan markets each case of *lucrum cessans* would have to be individually established.

The theoretical significance of Lessius' position assimilating exchanges to loans may be made clear by comparing what he admits to the conclusions reached by Cajetan and Navarrus. All agree that supply and demand set the price of money on a specific exchange market. The demand for money on a particular market arises either from the need of it for consumption uses, particularly by governments, or from the need of it for production uses, particularly by expanding businesses. The supply of money on the market is determined by the number of persons who prefer providing money to (1) using it in business; (2) holding it in reserve for personal emergencies; (3) holding it in reserve until better business opportunities present themselves; or (4) holding it in reserve until the interest rate on credit extensions has risen. The price of money on the market will, as Lessius observes, be equally the price of the lack of money, the price at which the holders of money are willing to forego other uses of it.

Now if the price of money on exchanges is licitly determined by the operation of the several causes enumerated here, as these writers admit, may the same causes validly affect the value of money in loans? Certainly, (1), (2), and (3) all represent reasons for reserving one's money which are perfectly legitimate, and although the title is far wider than *lucrum cessans*, there seems no reason to deny *carentia pecuniae*, understood as the estimated value of the foregoing of uses (1), (2), and (3). But reason (4) seems to have force purely from a desire to make a profit on a loan, and the scholastics have never admitted the foregoing of profit on one loan as proper grounds

[71] II:23:1; and 23:4.

for asking compensation on another. Moreover, since a large part of the demand for money will probably arise from consumption needs, particularly those of governments, it is clear that there can easily be a great demand for money, and yet no use for it on the part of the possessors of money, except to lend it or hold it until the price has risen. Here is where the difference between money as a commodity and money as money becomes important. On the exchanges, where in the Cajetan–Navarrus analysis money is nonexpendable and hence a commodity, the pure supply and demand can set the price; and, unless the exchange banker is a monopolist or acts uncharitably, he may morally wait to buy exchange at the moment when it will give him the greatest profit. As all the scholastics admit, the skillful banker will hold back his money in order to provide it at the place and time of the greatest demand. In loans, however, in this analysis, money is only money, that is, a legal measure with a fixed face value. The demand for money by itself cannot alter its objective value, and the lender acts unjustly if by waiting he hopes to produce a different value for money by producing an increased demand for it. On this account, speculation in changes in the value of money must be accounted licit in exchanges where no objective value rules, and illicit in loans, where the value of money is governed by the law. This conclusion at least seems implied in the scholastic approach to usury, which assumes that the value of money set by law cannot be altered by its possessors. The position of Lessius, however, approaches the formal abandonment of this rule; for failing to distinguish between loans and exchanges, he tacitly admits that in both the price of the lack of money may be set by the holders of cash.

5. *Technical Conditions of the Exchange*

It would have been a hollow victory for exchange banking if the scholastics had approved it in principle but still found usurious the practices that characterized its operation. Two such practices proved troublesome. One was the sale of a bill of exchange by a person not possessing a credit balance at the time he drew but hoping to have a balance at the time the bill was presented. A related but distinct practice was an agreement between the drawer and the banker that the bill would not be met in cash but by a reëxchange, that is, by a new bill to be paid by the original drawer on its reaching the city where he had sold the first bill of exchange. The objections to both these practices were not on a theoretical level, but on the practical ground that they made exchange transactions even more like simple loans at interest; they were practices emphasizing the element of credit creation in exchange banking. And they were essential to exchange banking as it then operated.[72]

The first practice is condemned by Conrad Summenhart, but he tacitly admits the impracticality of his own standard in defending the Roman benefice exchange contract. In this contract, so vigorously censured by St. Antoninus, the ecclesiastic meeting the bill of exchange always collected the money to meet it after drawing it. Yet Summenhart defends it as a legitimate *cambium per litteras*.[73]

Soto, however, with his rigorist suspicion of the exchanges, simply stigmatizes such practice as usurious lending.[74] It is only with Navarrus that the objection is laid to rest. He points out that if Soto is right, almost no one makes a lawful exchange; even the wealthiest merchants usually do not possess the balances they sell at the time they draw a bill of exchange. He then makes the obvious point that it is irrelevant to the justice of the contract whether the seller actually possesses what he sells, provided he delivers at the time agreed on, and provided there is no charge for time.[75] And, of course, the second proviso has already been met in the standard defense of the exchange market.

The admission of exchange and prearranged reëxchange was complicated by the issue of the bull *In eam*. Throughout the Middle Ages, there had never been any papal, conciliar, or canonical declaration on the subject of the exchanges, nor were exchanges a matter of controversy in the discussions on the 5 per cent contract, although the business of the Fugger banking house

---

[72] See the description of medieval practice, *supra*, Chapter VIII, n.36. It is not clear whether the operation typically discussed by the scholastics was that technically described as the *ricorsa*. The outstanding characteristics of the *ricorsa* was that in an operation such as that described above the rate of exchange on repayment was set in advance. Hence, the slight possibility existing in other reëxchange operations, that market fluctuations might upset the dealer's planned profit, was eliminated (see Mandich, *Le Pacte de la Ricorsa et la marche italien des changes au 17ᵉ siècle*, Paris, 1953, p. 9). Navarrus does not refer to such a fixed rate of interest, and on the whole, it seems probable that he was defending only exchange with an agreement to reëxchange (*Consilia*, V:19:1:1–5).

Lessius refers to the *cambium Besuntium* or "exchange on the Besançon fairs" (II:23:7).

According to Mandich, p. 134, these fairs were the origin of the true *ricorsa* bill where not only the reëxchange but the rate of reëxchange is set in advance. Lessius, however, uses "*cambium Besuntium*" to refer only to the reëxchange agreement, not the determination of rate, which he treats as a separate problem (II:23:9).

Lugo is the only one of these scholastic authors to use the term *ricorsa* (28:7:76). He emphasizes the reëxchange agreement as the characteristic feature of it, not the determination of the rate.

[73] Summenhart, Q.99.

[74] Soto, VI:12:2.

[75] Navarrus, *De cambiis*, 12, n.14 and 21, n.74. Even the wealthiest merchants, he observes, do not possess, at the time of the sale, exchange balances they sell. This position is also taken by Silvester, *Summa, Usura*, IV:9:6.

was a main issue in these discussions. Pius IV, shortly after his election to the papacy, found it necessary to rebuke the bankers "following the Roman court" for their grasping conduct toward prelates seeking exchange. But the situation dealt with was a local one, and, while usurious practices were mentioned, the Pope aimed at abuses and did not attempt to lay down any general rules for the exchange business.[76] The exchanges became a subject for more thoroughgoing official consideration only as a result of the inquiry of St. Charles Borromeo, which has already been noted;[77] and the bull *In eam* issued by Pius V, January 28, 1571, was the result of the work of the same theological commission which had investigated the *census*. The bull declares that the useful and necessary operation of exchange has been abused and made usurious by some avaricious persons. The Pope, therefore, condemns all dry exchange, by which, he says, are meant contracts taking the form of exchange in which either bills of exchange are not sent to another place or, if they are sent, are not paid there, but return empty to be paid by the seller of the bill in the same place, as it was agreed or at least certainly intended by both parties. In addition to these condemnations, the Pope, to take away any opportunity for sin, prohibits exchanges made to any but the next fair, and also the fixing of standard interest rates. The penalties for violating the bull are to be the penalties of the canons against usurers.[78]

The bull had little effect on practice. True, Molina read it as determining the unlawfulness of the exchange in which the dealer's correspondent acted for the customer in seeking the first bill by a reëxchange. Navarrus apparently agreed.[79] But in his later *Consilia*, Navarrus reconciles the bull with the operations of the bankers. Two different exchanges, he says, take place. There is no reason to call them a loan, more than other *cambia per litteras*, and there is no ground for presuming usury. One person can act in two different capacities simultaneously. The Pope damned only dry exchanges where payment is not made in another place, but here two exchanges take place, each paid in a different place.[80] Navarrus' approval of the contract must have carried considerable comfort to scrupulous exchange bankers who used it as a routine practice.

The practice, however, still continued to be a source of difficulty. Among the theologians, Lessius, asserting that it was "speculatively" defensible,

[76] Pius IV, *Moto Proprio*, 1559, *Bullarium Romanum*, VII:1.

[77] See *supra*, p. 237.

[78] *In eam, Bullarium Romanum*, VII:880. Presumably *lucrum cessans* determined by the actual course of the business in which the lender would have invested is untouched by the bull.

[79] Molina, II:404:12. He cites Navarrus in favor of his own position, apparently not aware of his later change of position.

[80] Navarrus, *Consilia*, V:19:1:6-10.

doubted that in practice the dealer's correspondent really acted for the debtor and really made a new contract, so that a dry and usurious exchange usually occurred.[81] Yet on his grounds the whole transaction might have been defended as a loan; and it is significant that he does defend — on grounds purely applicable to loans — an interest rate fixed in advance on the reexchange. This, he says, is licit if the rate is fixed by *lucrum cessans* and *periculum sortis.*[82]

Among those unwilling to take Lessius' approach justifying exchange on the basis of interest titles, debate apparently continued until a series of decisions by a Roman Congregation in 1631. It is clearly dry exchange if a dealer at Rome purchases exchange in Florence from one who is known to have no credit balances there, so that the bill will be returned by reëxchange to Rome, where the borrower will pay both the exchange and reëxchange fees. Here, the object of exchange, money to be delivered in another city, does not exist.[83] But, the Congregation held, if the seller has a correspondent in Florence who will act for him, pay the first exchange, and draw a second draft on him in Rome, in order to recover his money, true and licit exchanges have taken place, in which money is really delivered in places other than those in which it was bought. It is, then, also licit if the seller asks the original exchange banker to find a correspondent for him in Florence who will act in this way, and if the seller guarantees payment if the correspondent defaults.[84]

Building on this decision, Lugo adds that it must also be licit if for a fee the exchange banker acts as a guarantor for his customer, so that a correspondent in Florence will not hesitate to pay for him and make a reëxchange.[85] It is also licit if the exchange banker goes to Florence with money, takes the part of his customer's friend and acting in person for his customer, himself pays the debt owed himself, and draws in his own favor.[86] After these somewhat artificial hypothetical cases have been set up, Lugo approaches the practical problem of the meeting of a bill by a reëxchange agreed upon in advance where the exchange dealer's correspondent acted for the customer in paying the first exchange and drawing the reëxchange note in favor of the dealer. The case is, of course, really resolved by the opinion that the dealer himself may come to Florence and act personally for his customer. There is no reason why his agent cannot perform the same role. If the agent has cash

[81] Lessius, II:23:5.
[82] II:23:4.
[83] Lugo, 28:7:78.
[84] Lugo, 28:7:84.
[85] 28:7:81–82.
[86] 28:7:85.

which he can assign to the customer in order to pay the first debt for him, a real delivery of money takes place, albeit the agent acting in one capacity simply transfers the money to himself acting in another.[87] Even if he does not have cash ready to assign, he may, if he has credits which may be theoretically assigned to the customer, act for him; for credits as well as cash may be accepted as deliverable exchange.[88] Only if the correspondent has no money or credits whatsoever which might be assigned to the customer does a fictitious exchange take place; for here no delivery of money at Florence in any way occurs, but the correspondent simply marks the first note paid and draws a second note on the customer in favor of his principal; and the transaction, begun and ended at Rome, is a loan at usury.[89] Although Lugo does not comment on this, the likelihood of a banker's agent having neither cash nor credits which he could theoretically assign to pay an exchange bill was remote, so that, for practice, the procedure is approved.

Lugo warns, however, that such reëxchange must be executed "seriously and truly," not fictitiously.[90] A customer cannot be compelled to take the reëxchange, because this demand would make the transaction too close to a loan. The two exchange contracts must be considered separate contracts, so that if the customer defaults on paying the second one, the correspondent, not the customer, is held responsible to the exchange banker for the first exchange.[91] The reëxchange contracts are counseled against because of the danger of sin.[92] These qualifications do impose some restraint on practice. Still, the basic operation of exchange and reëxchange with the same banking house remains established. As to the fixing of rates of reëxchange in advance, Lugo raises no objection, if they reflect true *lucrum cessans*.[93]

With the Congregation's decision, reinforced by Lugo's approbation, the techniques of the exchange bankers have now official approval. True, even in the eighteenth century, St. Alphonsus condemns the practice.[94] But this disapproval, surprising as it is, comes too late in the history of exchange banking to be of much significance. By this date there were many other ways to make a profit from credit extensions. St. Alphonsus' position is also anomalous. Even the implacable rigorist Peter Ballerini believes that the exchange and reëxchange practice is lawful.[95]

---

[87] 28:7:88.
[88] 28:7:89.
[89] 28:7:92–97.
[90] 28:7:100.
[91] 28:7:101.
[92] 28:7:98.

[93] 28:9:120–123. The Roman Congregation appears to accept a fixed interest minimum, too (28:7:84).
[94] St. Alphonsus, III:5:3:10:854.
[95] Ballerini, *De pravitate trium contractuum*, 4:79.

6. *Deposit Banking: The Price of the Obligation to Lend*

Related to exchange banking in a rather subordinate way by the scholastics are questions of deposit banking. In this connection an old and undeveloped medieval principle becomes important: the obligation to lend has a price.

The astonishing truth is that Dominic Soto is the first scholastic writer specifically to describe and to evaluate morally the credit creation of the banks, though this had been an economic activity which had prevailed for over three hundred years; and even as he approaches the subject, he confesses the scant knowledge in his own day of the essential characteristics of lending operations: "For, beyond the businessmen, we are rare, even among the scholastics, who understand these facts."

What he discusses are the activities of the exchange dealers who credit their depositors with 20 to 50 per cent more money than they have deposited, and let them draw on this to pay debts at the fairs. This is a restricted kind of credit creation, a development of the old fair-lenders' underwriting of their customers' debts, and the credit is still limited to use at the fairs to settle debts and letters of exchange. It is by no means completely mobile. But, since the banks, as Soto testifies, try to pay as much in bank credit as possible, and since consequently their addition to their depositors' accounts never has to be equalled by any real addition to the monetary medium, we have a real case of credit creation.

Now the banks, as Soto understands their operations, never charge for their credit creation as such. They give the extra credit to their depositors to entice them to deposit with them. They charge only when they cannot settle a depositor's debt by a credit transfer, and are forced to pay cash. Their normal charge, then, of .5 per cent is licit, Soto says, for it is not a charge for a loan, but a charge for assuming the obligations of a guarantor and, in effect, paying a depositor's debt which he is unable to meet at the moment. Surprisingly, justification is also found for the depositors who accept the benefit of the extra credit freely extended to them in return for their cash deposits. The banks give this credit, Soto says, as a reward for the benefit of using their depositors' cash — a defense which would, of course, justify the payment of money on every loan.[96]

Navarrus describes the same banking operation as Soto and as usual takes the opposite view from Soto; where Soto is lenient, Navarrus becomes a rigorist and condemns the transaction here in two ways. The bank gives its depositor extra credit in order to retain his business; therefore, it lends with

[96] Soto, VI:11.

the intention to gain and commits at least mental usury. On the other hand, the depositor takes the extra credit as a reward for his deposit in place of interest; therefore he, too, has sought a premium on a loan, and has committed at least mental usury. There is no attempt by Navarrus to consider the advantages as reciprocal and equal. He looks on each party's act separately and judges each as usurious. Similarly, while the payment of 5 or 6 per cent on deposits as a pure gratuity is licit, he regards as usurers those depositors who expect the banks to give them free services, such as the transmission of their money to another place, in return for their deposits.[97] All that Navarrus will permit in the way of gain for either party to a contract of deposit is a charge by the banks for acting as pure depositories, and a small fee by them for handling the account, when they make a payment in cash on behalf of a depositor, provided the depositor and not the payee is charged.[98] In practice this small fee may have been as much as Soto would have allowed under the title of the right to charge for the obligation of lending. But the difference in theory is important. Navarrus allows a charge for service completely distinct from lending itself, while Soto had allowed the charge for an act relating directly to lending. Navarrus seems to feel that the depositors commit usury more often than the bank, but for both banks and depositors his standards leave little leeway.[99]

Molina's moral analysis of the banks is a blend of Soto and Navarrus. The .5 or .6 per cent charge made by the fair bank obligating itself to pay its customer's debts is licit, because the obligation of lending has a pecuniary estimation. The bank may also charge the payee a small sum for its service in counting the coin. It is usury, however, if the bank charges interest for paying a customer's creditor in advance, before his note is due at the end of the fair.[100] The depositors commit usury if they demand extra credit as a condition of depositing, or if they demand that the bank furnish other services free. The banks may, however, be willing to offer voluntarily many free

---

[97] Navarrus, *De cambiis*, 18, n.27, 40. The somewhat obscure original text reads as follows: "Aliam usuram committunt in hoc eodem permutatores, si scilicet qui mercatori, qui apud se vel in sua capsa mensaria pecuniam numeratam deposuit, expedit illam, et aliquid amplius in alia mensa nummularia in usus suos necessarios ad tempus aequale atque ille illius pecuniam apud se habuit: modo sibi mercedem quam ratione numeratae pecuniae soluturus erat relinquat. Quod saltem in ipsorum animis est usura manifesta: quia mercator lucrum quod suo judicio pro comparato habet, ob depositionem numeratae pecuniae permutatori remittit, ut sibi altero tantam per chirographam aut certam aliquam ad nundinas proximas mutuet; et permutator mutuat, ne solvat illud, quod iuxta suam malam consuetudinem se deponenti debere arbitratur."

[98] *De cambiis*, 18, n.36, n.38.

[99] The same attitude is apparent in the bull *In eam*, which prescribes the canonical penalties against usurers for depositors with the exchange banks.

[100] Molina, II:409:14.

services in order to attract depositors, and it is then licit for the depositors to accept them.[101] Molina thus avoids the narrowness of Navarrus, while not admitting Soto's anomalous position that the depositors have a right to service in return for their money. The fundamental defense of the banks is their right to charge for their obligation to lend, an obligation they assume by granting credit.[102]

One of the first scholastic recognitions of the reserve principle on which banks operate occurs when Molina writes of the exchange bankers: "It never happens that all the depositors need their money, for always many thousands of ducats remain on deposit with which the bankers can do business to their own advantage or disadvantage." [103] But his only comment on this practice is to warn severely against the immorality of banks imprudently investing their deposits and being unable to repay them.[104]

In general, the scholastic writers deal only with banks that charge a small fee for their credit services, and not with organizations which make their principal profit from direct deposit creation. They are more concerned with the usury that may be committed by the depositors than with the possible usury of the banks. Nevertheless, the principle which they believe applicable in regard to the banks as a defense has a wide application. If a bank can charge for acting as guarantor on the fair accounts and upon apparently wider extensions of credit, can we infer that the scholastics would have defined all deposit creation, where cash was not at once paid to a borrower, not as a loan, but as the undertaking of an obligation to lend later? If so, then much banking would have been outside the usury prohibition, and its just remuneration would be determined, like the price of any service, by the market evaluation alone. The scholastics are dealing chiefly with a special class of bankers, where the guaranteeing of the customer's account is the traditional contractual form; but implicit in Molina and Lugo is the extension suggested.

Conclusion

In a variety of ways, exchange banking has operated to undermine medieval views on a market in money. The analysis begun at the end of the fifteenth century by Biel and Cajetan leads to recognition of a full market in money, when money can be considered a commodity, and of a limited market in

---

[101] II:409:6.

[102] Lugo, 28:6:66, concurs with Molina; Lessius, II:23:8, simply says that the banks can charge for "their service" in providing payments in cash, keeping accounts, and taking care of deposits.

[103] Molina, II:408:5.

[104] II:408:7.

money, a market considering anticipated changes in money's purchasing power, when money's value is objectively set by the law. In Lessius' analysis the final step has been taken of letting possessors of money themselves determine a price for its lack, and so a full-fledged money market in loans is itself tacitly acknowledged. Accompanying these theoretical developments has come approval of the technique of exchange operation and the acceptance of the deposit banking that provided the capital for the exchange banks.

Does any substance remain to the usury rule in theory or practice after these admissions? This question we shall consider formally in the following chapter.

CHAPTER XVII

CRITICISM AND REVISION OF THE USURY THEORY

In the development of the triple contract, the personal, mutually re-deemable *census*, and the bill of exchange, great areas of finance were cut away from usury prohibition. In the development of *lucrum cessans* and *periculum mutui*, the scope of just interest on loans proper was immensely enlarged. The discussion on exchange resulted in the abandonment of the idea of money as a fixed measure and the restricted recognition of the effect of market factors on its value. After these modifications and alterations, what arguments were strong enough to support the usury prohibition itself? What revisions were necessary in the statement of the rule?

1. *A Radical Critique: Conrad Summenhart*

The most critical and comprehensive examination of all the arguments showing the unnaturalness of usury is undertaken by Conrad Summenhart, and the result of this unprecedentedly thorough review is a revolutionary conclusion. He offers twenty-three natural-law reasons in favor of the usury prohibition, criticizes, modifies, and rejects most of these reasons, and ends with two tenuous formal arguments against usury left standing. At the same time, he puts forward strong objections against the prohibition, which he leaves unanswered, and if these objections are taken as they stand, without interpretation, they seem to prove that usury itself is licit. His examination ends in a rejection of the past. Usury is left assailed in name alone. The early scholastic theory of usury is abandoned.

As many of the arguments and objections are repetitious, we shall present only his main theses.

The Thomistic Argument

The principal Thomistic argument against usury is stated, and Summenhart first objects merely to its formulation. Use and substance, he says, are distinct in money, for the *usus facti* is successive, while the good itself is immediately possessed; the *usus juris* inheres in a man as its subject, while the good itself exists independently of man. For example, a servant may hold and use money for his master; he will have both the *usus facti* and the *usus juris*, and yet not be the money's owner. Ownership of a consumptible is therefore distinguishable from any kind of right to use the consumptible, and the assumption of the Thomistic argument is refuted. Summenhart replies to this refutation that the objection holds only against the absolute assertion that the use and ownership of a consumptible are inseparable, but that the Thomistic argument still is valid in the case of a loan. In a loan the borrower is given both the ownership and the right of use, and, in fact, these constitute one *value*, although they are theoretically distinguishable.[1] This restatement of the Thomistic argument in terms of value is a clear improvement, making explicit what is latent in the original argument. But there is a major objection to it: it misses the point.[2] The Thomistic argument assumes that the usurer is charging for his borrower's use of his money. In fact, the usurer is always charging for his own lack of use:

And so it is denied that the lender tries to separate the good and its use, as if he demanded one thing for one of them, and another for the other; but for the whole aggregate, to wit, for the good conceded for the use of an intervening time with the renunciation, or lack, of his own use of it, he demands this other whole aggregate, to wit, the principal and increment.

To this difficulty it is answered that when the borrower restores the good loaned, he restores the power of using it, so that he gives back all that was given him. Summenhart replies:

But he does not restore to him [the lender] the use of the intervening time, so that he will be able to use it [the money] for that intervening time, because that passes irrevocably into the past. And so, granted even that the usurer demands the principal itself for the loaned good, and profit for the use of the good, yet the equivalent principal is not restored at the time the loan is made, but only after a time. Therefore, it is not equivalent to the good loaned and the use in the intervening time.[3]

The early scholastics have admitted that the lender may charge for his lack of use of his good under the circumstances in which *damnum emergens* or *lucrum cessans* occur. But Summenhart's claim here is far more sweeping than the interest titles limited to specific cases of loss from the lack of use.

---

[1] Summenhart, *De contractibus*, Q.23 ad 6.
[2] A minor objection is this: Because a man's body and soul are inseparable and a man cannot give his body to work without giving his soul, it does not follow that a man's body and soul constitute a single value; therefore, the factual inseparability of ownership and use in a loan do not make them one in value (Q.23 ad 6). Conrad has no comment on this confused analogy.
[3] Q.23 ad 7; ad 6.

He is arguing that always, in justice, a lender is entitled to an increment on his loan in order to compensate himself for the lack of the loaned object during a certain time. The voluntary sacrifice of any good has, in inself, a pecuniary estimation, regardless of what use would have been made of it. The lack of a consumptible for a period has a value distinct from the value of the substance of the consumptible. One who charges for this lack is not trying to sell the same good twice, nor is he trying to sell time. He charges neither for the good itself, nor for the extrinsic measure of motion, but he charges for the lack of his good during a particular time.

The defenders of the Thomistic position may reply that the transfer of the substance of a good in a loan is inseparably connnected with the lack of the good to the lender, and that unless some specific loss results to the lender, the mere lack cannot be given a value apart from the good itself. Summenhart admits that the transfer of the substance and the consequent lack of use are inseparable, but he insists that the two results do not constitute a single value. It is, he says, as if one should buy white chalk; the whiteness of the chalk is inseparable from the substance of the chalk, but the value of the substance considered alone is not the total value of the chalk, which consists in the combined values of the chalk and the whiteness. Similarly, the value of a loan should equal the substance of the good loaned, plus the value of the lack of the object to the lender. Bolstered by this analogy, Summenhart not only rejects the Thomistic proof of the unnaturalness of usury, but in his rejection appears to have offered a positive proof for the justice of usury.[4]

The Andrean Argument

The second major argument of the early scholastics, the Andrean argument, that fungibles have a fixed value which cannot be increased, is also rejected by Summenhart in a way which leads to a counterproof in favor of usury. He objects that goods have their *value* not from number, weight, or measure, which determine only their *quantity*; their values arise from their estimation by human prudence. A hundred measures of wheat always have the same number of grains of wheat in them, but the value and the price vary with different times or places. Similarly, the value of money varies with circumstances. A lender should be able to estimate his good not as a simple quantity fixed by nature or human law, but "at its usual value."[5] A fungible may have one value at the time of a loan and another at its repayment; Andreae's idea that the value is fixed results from a confusion of

[4] Q.23 ad 6.   [5] Q.23 ad 7, ad 2.

quantity and value. Summenhart does not develop further the implications of this conclusion, but it clearly suggests that a lender at a time of necessity may value his money more highly than at a time of plenty and at such a time may charge for the extra value of his money. Leaving the value of money open to common estimation, the argument opens the way to a market in loans.

The "Barren-Metal" Argument

Thirdly, Summenhart considers the popular cry that it is unnatural to take profit from an unfruitful good. As an argument, this slogan is inadequate in two ways: it does not explain why it should be usurious and unnatural to lend grain, which is a fungible, consumptible good, yet fructifies; it does not explain why it should not be usurious and unnatural to take profit on the rent of a house, which is naturally sterile. In truth, money is as fruitful as a house is — that is, subject to human use, it produces benefits. Moreover, money is a partial cause of the gain of the borrower, and as such a cause, it deserves a reward.[6] Again, Summenhart not only rejects the argument against usury, but concludes positively in its favor.

The "Riskless-Profit" Argument

That the lender profits without risk, while the borrower unfairly runs all the risk, is rejected as an untrue statement of the facts. The lender runs the considerable risk of his borrower's bankruptcy. The borrower also has a good chance of profiting more by his investment of the money loaned than the lender will from the loan.[7]

The Aristotelian Argument

The argument of Aristotelian finalism is characterized as absurd. Does one sin by using wine to extinguish a fire? Does one sin by using a shoe as a storage-place for money? There is nothing in the natural law to show that a material good must always be used for a particular purpose.[8]

Valid Arguments

In defiance of the past, Summenhart has given three positive reasons why a lender can receive an increment beyond his principal, and he has dismissed the other arguments against usury as irrelevant. But there are, he says, valid arguments. Two of them show that usury is wrong on loans to the poor;

[6] Q.23 ad 2, ad 3, ad 13.
[7] Q.23 ad 12.
[8] Q.23 ad 8.

members of a community, like the members of the human body, are obliged to give their superfluity to the members needing strength; you should do unto others as you would have them do unto you.[9] But, in the past, usury has been said to be against justice; it has been declared repugnant to nature to take usury from anyone, whether poor or rich. What argument does Summenhart offer to support this standard thesis? Only one: usury is unnatural because Aristotle, by natural reason alone, was led to declare it unnatural.[10] The answer is so trivial as to suggest that Summenhart is speaking ironically. The arguments by which Aristotle himself was influenced have just been refuted. Summenhart's proof consists in the assertion that because one ancient philosopher, using mistaken reasons, found usury unnatural, it must be unnatural in fact. His only additional comment is that, although his arguments against usury have been refuted, they were "probable," and in moral matters probable reasoning suffices.[11] The simple testimony of Aristotle will stand at least for a "probable showing" of usury's unnaturalness. The proof is purely formal. Wishing to keep from saying outright that he does not believe that usury is unnatural, Summenhart contents himself with offering as his sole unchallenged argument an appeal to a famous name.

Summenhart still believes that the divine law prohibits it [12] and he makes no exception in this law, taken strictly. Since he has no convictions, however, on the unnaturalness of the act of taking profit on a loan, he is willing to construe the divine law very narrowly and to admit in practice profit on any transaction which is not purely and formally a loan. As we have seen, this leads him to concede that the profitable purchase of a newly created right to money is licit. He still has given strong reasons for a natural obligation to lend freely to the poor, so that he does not deny that there is some type of usury which must be avoided. But the old scholastic position on the general injustice of usury has, in effect, disappeared.[13]

[9] Q.23 ad 15, ad 19.

[10] Q.23 ad 20.

[11] Q.23 in fine.

[12] Q.22.

[13] It is a curious irony of history that Conrad, who is the first Christian author ever to make a detailed criticism of the arguments against usury, has become known to posterity only as a particularly obstinate and strangely stupid defender of the usury prohibition. His own writings have attracted no attention among modern historians. But Charles Du Moulin, who is popularly supposed to have been the first author to criticize the arguments against usury, took Conrad's twenty-three tentative arguments against usury as the typical scholastic arguments, and, while in many cases he adopts Conrad's own objections to the arguments, he never once acknowledges that Conrad himself had made these criticisms. Instead, Conrad is derided as an arrant sophist, and as Du Moulin's writings have alone become famous, Conrad has appeared to posterity only as Du Moulin caricatures him. See Charles Du Moulin, Tractatus commerciorum contractuum, n.9, in Opera (Paris, 1624), Vol. II.

2. A Century of Acceptance

For a century Summenhart's criticisms found no authoritative support within the scholastics' ranks. Some leading authors treated the natural-law basis for the usury rule perfunctorily, as though the origin of the rule was a problem without contemporary consequences. They accepted its existence as a datum, and while they developed exceptions to it, saw nothing to be gained by an elaborate investigation of its rationale. Cajetan, for example, agreed with Summenhart that the argument based on Aristotelian finalism was irrational, but found a sufficient basis for the prohibition in the classic Thomistic argument.[14] Navarrus contented himself with a surprising return to the ancient and ineffective "Roman law" argument that in a loan, ownership of the good loaned passes to the borrower so that a lender cannot profit from it.[15]

The only marked interest in the theoretical justification for the prohibition is found in Soto and Molina, and even here there is no attempt to deal with all Summenhart's points. Soto addresses himself to a reconciliation of the Thomistic argument with the three papal bulls on ownership. It will be recalled that Scotus had used the bull of Nicholas III, *Exiit, qui seminat*, declaring the use and ownership of consumptibles were separable, to oppose the Thomistic position; but although *Exivi de paradiso* of Clement V had supported Nicholas, Scotus' argument had not been repeated because *Ad conditorem* of John XXII had contradicted the earlier bulls. Soto is the first scholastic to consider all three bulls together, and to try to preserve both the Thomistic position and the rule that the Franciscans own no property. "The matter is certainly difficult," he confesses frankly, but he proceeds to an analysis. Full ownership, he teaches, consists not only in the right to consume a good, but in the right to alienate, neglect, or defend it. The Franciscans, although they have the right to consume the consumptibles they use, do not have the right to alienate, neglect, or defend them, and they are, therefore, not truly owners. Consequently, ownership of, and the right to use, consumptibles can, in a certain way, be distinguished. St. Thomas is to be understood as saying only that the use of a consumptible cannot have a value separate from the good itself.[16] This is a conclusion substantially identical with Summenhart's revision of the Thomistic argument. Or, as Soto puts it in another way, a consumptible's use, inasmuch as it is a quality, can

---

[14] Cajetan, *In summam theologicam*, II–II:78, art. 1:I.

[15] Navarrus, *De usuris*, 6, n.7.

[16] Soto, *De justitia*, IV:1:1; cf. *supra*, Chapter III, section 3.

be distinguished from the consumptible itself, which is a substance. But its use and the consumptible itself, or its ownership, cannot be valued separately. The usurer places a value on that which has no separate value and so acts unnaturally.[17]

Molina, in a conventional presentation of the Thomistic, the Andrean, and the riskless-profit arguments, also explores one new objection.[18] One might be tempted, he says, to concede that the lender could charge not for the loaned good, but for his *action* of lending, on the grounds that a man may licitly charge for the performance of a good action which he is not bound to do. But, Molina continues, in a sale one cannot charge separately for the good sold and for one's action in selling it; neither, therefore, in a loan can one separate the value of the action from the value of the good given. In a sale, the seller's action, selling, is equalled by the buyer's action, paying cash; in a loan, the lender's action, lending, is equalled by the borrower's action, returning.[19]

Soto and Molina's concern for the refinement of the natural-law case against usury has a probable origin of much significance. Soto is the first scholastic to doubt that Luke 6:35 is a precept. Luke 6:35, he declared, has no relevance to the justice of lending at a profit. The popes who have referred to it have not meant to canonize their own interpretations, but have simply found a certain appositeness in the text. Moreover, he continues, since the Old Testament laws do not bind, unless they are renewed by Christ or are part of the natural law, and since the usury prohibition was not clearly renewed by Christ, there is no biblical authority for the usury law, unless one recognizes that the Old Testament laws on usury are also part of the natural law. Hence, "If you remove the natural law, you leave the most tenuous foundation for the conclusion [that usury is unlawful]." [20]

Molina takes the same position. There is no biblical text sufficient in itself to prove usury a sin; the Church would not have prohibited usury unless it were against the natural law.[21]

This view of the character of the usury rule is not generally accepted. Navarrus' reaction is typical. He makes a sustained attack on Soto for his interpretation of Luke 6:35, relying heavily on papal and conciliar use of the text to show that the traditional interpretation has been approved by the Church.[22] He has several centuries of usage to support his sense of outrage.

[17] Soto, VI:1:1.
[18] Molina, *De justitia*, II:304:2, 3, 4, 12.
[19] 304:9–10.
[20] Soto, VI:1:1.
[21] Molina, II:304:14.
[22] Navarrus, *De usuris*, 6, n.8–10.

3. The Value of the Lack of Money

At the beginning of the seventeenth century, then, the usury law has been questioned both as a command of nature and as a command of God. But the traditionalist positions have not been forsaken by the bulk of the major writers. Two tendencies now become noticeable: one is an attempt to suggest as alternatives to the loan-usury analysis not only the older credit forms such as the *census* but new forms that will displace the usury prohibition entirely. The other tendency is to concede that in given economic or political conditions, loans will normally be nongratuitous.

The first tendency is illustrated by Lessius in his handling of the old problem of the bulls on ownership. Following *Exiit, qui seminat* and *Exivi de paradiso*, Lessius says that the use of a consumptible can be conceded in two ways: (1) irrevocably, and then the right to use is "not much different from ownership"; and (2) revocably, so that the use may be terminated at the pleasure of the owner — and here the right of use is clearly different from ownership, for ownership is a full and absolute right to a good, while a revocable use is a conditional and weak right. The first kind of use, *usus juris*, is of the same value as the ownership of the good, so that if in a loan this use is conceded, St. Thomas' argument holds. The second kind of use, *usus facti*, being distinct from ownership, might be conceded in a loan and charged for separately, and then by a second contract the lender could sell the ownership itself. Lessius is the first scholastic author to note that this transaction could take place and take place with perfect lawfulness. He simply comments on it, "This mode of contracting is not used, for it would easily cloak usuries, although per se it is not illicit." [23] The theories of Clement V, Summenhart, and Soto thus yield for Lessius an important restriction on the standard Thomistic argument.

A similar theoretical toying with a lending system that would evade the usury rule altogether is seen in Lugo. He calls his system "lending on condition." It is licit, he argues, to lend to laborers on condition that they work on your farm; this is to impose an obligation not as "the price of a loan," but as "a condition of lending." It is also licit to loan one commodity to a man in order that at the same time he lend another commodity to you. Again, his loan is asked only as a condition of your loan; and it is proper for you to ask this condition because you do not wish to loan to an ingrate. Molina, the Spanish Jesuit John de Salas (1553–1612), and Antonio Diana, a Theatine from southern Italy (1585–1663), are cited in favor of this.

[23] Lessius, *De justitia*, II:3:8:37.

Again, it is licit to loan to someone with the condition that the loan is to be repaid when he ceases to come to your school or your mill. Molina and Salas approve this, although it is admitted there is peril of usury. Finally, Lugo declares it is licit to loan with the condition that the loan will cease when the borrower ceases to pay .3 or .4 per cent, per month, which he pays, not as the price of the loan, but as evidence of his gratitude for it. Salas is cited in favor of this. It is objected that all usury can then be excused because every lender can say, "I ask no price for the loan; I wish, however, to test your gratitude and that ceasing, I want my loan returned." Lugo replies that there is "a great difference" between this procedure and a loan at usury, because, in a regular loan, there is a specific contractual time for which it will run, and the lender binds himself absolutely not to reseek it before the end of this time and the borrower binds himself absolutely to pay a fixed return; whereas, in the proposed procedure, both parties remain free to cease their mutual offices of beneficence at any time. Lugo agrees that the difference between his plan and usury would be made clear only by a declaration of intention by the parties. The matter, he adds, is "slippery"; there is great danger of palliated usury; the plan is not to be counselled. But he accepts it as in itself moral and lawful.[24]

This kind of playing with the usury rule is perhaps to be taken more as symptomatic of discontent than as serious reasoning. A more substantial effort is made by Lessius to explore the economic basis for a normally nongratuitous loan. Lessius cites the classical Thomistic argument as the one natural-law argument against usury. He then places three objections to the usury prohibition: the lender should be allowed to charge for the time during which his money is used; the lender's labor in lending should be compensated; the lender should be allowed to charge for his obligation not to demand his money during the period of the loan and the consequent lack of his money during this period. Lessius replies to the first objection that time in itself cannot be sold and the value of the use of a consumptible in time is not distinguishable from the value of the consumptible itself. To the second objection, he answers that it is proper for the lender to be compensated for any labor he undergoes in connection with a loan, but he does not believe this admission tells against the usury prohibition proper. To the third objection, however, he has no immediate answer. He merely says that a charge for the obligation not to demand a return for a period and for the lack of one's money would not be per se usury, in that such a

[24] Lugo, *Disputationes*, 25:5:51–54.

charge would not be made for the loan itself, and he says he will consider the matter at length later.[25]

Later, he takes up the subject *ex professo* and identifies John Medina's casual expression *carentia pecuniae*, which is strictly the same as *lucrum cessans* in Medina's usage, with his own broad conception.[26] Medina becomes an authority to show that Lessius is not without respect for the past. But good reasons are even more important. There are two main lines of argument. There is, first, the identity of the title of *carentia pecuniae* with payment for the obligation not to reseek the loaned good during the period of the loan. Compensation for such an obligation should be lawful. A guarantor of a loan can licitly charge for obliging himself to be ready to pay a loan if the principal debtor defaults, but a lender undertakes a greater obligation than this; a fortiori he should be allowed to charge. Similarly, anyone may charge for obliging himself to be ready to loan during a certain length of time; again, the obligation of the actual lender is greater than the obligation of the merely potential lender.

The second main argument emphasizes that the lack of one's money always involves a real sacrifice which should be compensated. For everyone and anyone, experience shows that to lend and not have one's money on hand is a burden, for often unexpected situations arise which could far more readily be met if one's money was not in possession of a borrower. In particular, it is a burden for businessmen:

Since money is their instrument of doing business, and to deprive oneself of the instrument of one's art is estimable in money, why cannot the merchants set some price for the lack of money by common consent, especially if the common good demands it? That the common good demands it, however, is proved, because, since many need present money and there is not easily found anyone who wishes to lend freely — partly on account of the risk of capital or the difficulty in recovering it, partly lest one deprive oneself of the advantage of doing business in various ways, especially through exchanges, which flourish at this time — reason demands that the merchants by common consent constitute fixed prices for the

[25] Lessius, II:20:4.

[26] Medina's principal arguments against usury are the Thomistic argument and the argument that money bears no fruit (*Codex de restitutione, De rebus per usuras acquisitis,* f.130). In treating of the just price in sales, Medina says that a merchant selling on credit can charge a higher price because he suffers "the burden of the lack of his money" (Q.32 at "Inde inferetur," f.130). He immediately explains that by this "burden" he means *damnum emergens* or *lucrum cessans,* and he says that he will discuss these titles in detail later. Subsequently he has a full treatment of *lucrum cessans* and declares that it cannot be claimed by someone with idle cash, that it must not be sought voluntarily, and that merchants selling on credit rarely have a right to the title in practice (f.142). Hence it is clear that by the expression *carentia pecuniae,* "lack of one's money," Medina means nothing new or unusual.

lack of money, after having weighed all those circumstances from which that lack can be estimated at more or less at a particular time.

Is not this second argument the same as the argument for *lucrum cessans* as an interest title? In a sense it is, but *lucrum cessans* was a far narrower title than *carentia pecuniae*. *Lucrum cessans* was compensation for a peculiar, private injury; it could not be claimed by those who suffered no injury; it could be claimed only by those who had at least the intention of doing business. *Carentia pecuniae*, on the contrary, was a title available to all, whether or not they suffered loss and whether or not they intended to do business. It depended on the establishment of a common price for the lack of one's money; like any other commonly established price, this price might then be charged by all. In modern times *carentia pecuniae* and *lucrum cessans* may seem to be the same, but it is a serious anachronism to suppose that the seventeenth century so considered them. Lessius treats them as entirely different titles. The setting of a price on the lack of one's money, Lessius adds, is actually the practice at the busy Antwerp Bourse, where the merchants and exchangers daily determine the price of the lack of money. There the price averages 10 per cent, reaching a maximum of 12 per cent according to Charles V's edict of 1540. Lessius grants that 10 per cent is a reasonable price for the lack of money, when on the exchanges one may make 30 per cent. Further, the arguments advanced seem "probable" and the argument that one should be compensated for the lack of one's money is "most powerful." Yet Lessius' final opinion is this:

Nonetheless, I feel that such lax reins are not to be given the merchants, nor is it to be conceded that they may demand something beyond the principal, if to them from their lack of money, no profit ceases, no danger impends, no inconvenience is feared. First, because that opinion seems to be new, and I do not find it among the authors, and hence, in a moral matter of such moment, it is not easily to be admitted. Then, because the lack of money and obligation of not reseeking before a certain time is intrinsic to the nature of a loan: otherwise a loan would not differ from a *precarium*; whence, if a loan ought to be made freely, as is clear from what was said above, nothing is to be sought for this lack or obligation.[27]

Lessius, then, formally rejects the title *carentia pecuniae* on one basis alone, the argument that a loan must be gratuitous. But this is an assumption, which, at least according to the natural law, must yield to unrefuted arguments challenging it. Moreover, as Lessius himself said earlier, usury

---

[27] Lessius, II:20:14. A *precarium* is a Roman-law contract by which a good is given to another, but is recoverable at the giver's will. See *Digesta*, 43:26:1.

is only profit on a loan taken without just title; if the present title is just, there is no need to reject it. Lessius, not refuting the arguments in its favor and appealing only to the authority of the earlier writers and the alleged necessity that a loan be gratuitous, seems, in fact, to admit tacitly that the title cannot be proved unnatural.

Moreover, he not only offers no cogent theoretical defense for his final formal opinion, but he abandons it in practical application. Discussing exchange banking, he carefully distinguishes *lucrum cessans* and the greater title of "lack of one's money." He continues:

> And this *carentia pecuniae* is what the merchants in exchanges at this time consider the strongest title, as they themselves eloquently confess, adding that all the exchanges of this time are unjust, if this title is not just.[28]

At this point, Lessius offers no comment on the merchants' assertion, but a little later, specifically discussing exchanges which are implicit loans, he urges *carentia pecuniae* as a probable justification of them. He says:

> For ordinarily the exchange bankers value more the lack of their money for five months than the lack of it for four, and the lack of it for four more than three, and this is partly because they lack the opportunity of gaining with that money, partly because their principal is longer in danger; wherefore this evaluation is not irrational, for it is founded on a just reason, and it is made by the common judgment of the merchants and exchangers.

Lessius continues with another pressing consideration:

> From these [above arguments], it is plain that such exchanges are not to be condemned, especially since everyone, everywhere, uses them, among whom are many upright men of religious conscience, and, if they were ordered to abstain, only the laxer men would use them; whence it would result that the prices of these exchanges would catch on fire [*incenderentur*] with great inconvenience to the State; for it can never be obtained that the merchants do not value a long-term concession higher than a short-term one.[29]

In a word, Lessius accepts, at least in some circumstances, the title *carentia pecuniae*, which throughout the Middle Ages had been considered an objection to the usury prohibition itself. Twice again, as we have noted above, he asserts that ready money is valued more highly than money absent in time, because it furnishes a certain "advantage" to its holder;[30] this claim is substantially the same as the title of *carentia pecuniae*. By this bold step he reduces greatly the practical meaning of the usury prohibition. His accept-

[28] Lessius, II:23:4.
[29] II:23:6.
[30] See *supra*, Chapter XVI, section 4.

ance of the fact that "it can never be obtained that the merchants do not value a long-term concession higher than a short-term one" is the acceptance of the inevitability of the regular and customary taking of interest.

The lender's lack of his money is viewed by Lugo as the problem of why a lender cannot charge for his obligation not to demand the return of the principal for the period of the loan. John Medina and Peter Ledesma (d. 1616), Lugo inaccurately relates, have excused from the charge of usury a lender charging for this obligation. Yet, Lugo observes, "If this were true, no contract would in fact be usurious, except *per accidens* because of the ignorance of the contracting parties who would not know how to distinguish their titles to profit." [31]

But, says Lugo, it would be proximate to theological error to deny that usury is against the natural law; the Thomistic argument shows that in fact it is against the natural law. Papal authority, moreover, has interpreted Luke 6:35 as a binding precept of the divine law.[32] Consequently, the prohibition must be defended, and to defend it Lugo feels obliged to attack this variant form of Lessius' argument.

The argument in favor of the objection is this:

He who obliges himself to that [not to reseek the loan for the duration of the period of the loan] by that very act deprives himself of something estimable at a price . . . [if he receives beyond the principal] he receives for his lack of power to reseek and to make a profit during such a great time, which lack of power in itself seems estimable at a price.

The common answer to this argument is that the obligation not to seek one's money back for a period is intrinsic to a loan, and therefore, should be gratuitous like the loan itself. But, Lugo remarks, this assumes what is to be proved. It is also, he continues, no answer to say that a man cannot charge for an obligation which causes him no immediate inconvenience. If you agree not to cultivate a field for a year, you may charge for assuming this obligation, even though you had not intended to till the field in any case.

Lugo then proposes his own solution. The lender is repaid according to equality when he receives his money back, because he receives not only his money, but the power of which he deprived himself. It is objected, as Summenhart had objected, that the lack of this power for the period of the loan has still not been compensated. In this difficulty Lugo appeals to a curious sophism:

[31] Lugo, 25:3:16. It is certain that Lugo is inaccurate about Medina: Ledesma, a Spanish Dominican, speaks of a long-term obligation; see *infra*, p. 356.
[32] 25:2.

It is replied that the money in the following year with the power of using it all the time following is not worth less than the money given this year with a similar power, but each power is reputed among men to be entirely of the same estimation and price.

So, Lugo says, a field is not sold for less a year later, because the buyer did not have the use of it the preceding year; so, too, the glory received by a soul in heaven is not less for its being received later than another soul received his glory.[33] Lugo avoids recognition of the obvious fact that in the parallels he gives there is no voluntary sacrifice of the use of a good to be compensated; in his case, the lender has voluntarily sacrificed his use, and no compensation has been given him. Lugo has made no answer to Summenhart's contention that the loss of the use of money for a specific time is irretrievable to the owner who foregoes the use. The source of his difficulty is this: he has accepted the comparison of the lack of the use of money to the lack of the use of nonconsumptible goods. In so doing, he has given away his case against a lender's charge for the simple and absolute lack of his money.[34]

At the same time that the great seventeenth-century moralists were probing the economic justification for normally nongratuitous loans, the Jesuits at Ingolstadt made a radical appeal to political justification: the State by its own power could achieve a moral legitimation of usury. The doctrine was first proposed in 1620 by Adam Tanner[35] and was vigorously propagated by his pupil Christopher Haunold. As Haunold presented the case, it was tied closely to the custom of taking 5 per cent in Germany. This custom, he said, was morally justified, even though the lender had no title to interest. The State validated the custom by its power of eminent domain, transferring the property of the borrower to the lender. The State, it was generally admitted, had the power of eminent domain to dispose of private property for the common good. Here, for the common good, the State decreed that the borrower's property be used to pay the lender. Normally, the exercise of eminent domain demanded compensation to the private persons affected. But no compensation was necessary when these persons consented and their property did not go directly to the State. Here the borrowers were glad to pay 5 per cent to get a loan, and the property taken was only indirectly used for the benefit of the State.[36]

[33] 25:3:21-25.
[34] Van Roey has made an excellent analysis of Lugo's fallacy here. See Van Roey, De justo auctario, pp. 251ff.
[35] Adam Tanner, Theologia scholastica (Ingolstadt, 1626), III:4:7:79.
[36] Christopher Haunold, Controversiarum de justitia et jure privatorum (Ingolstadt, 1672), IX:3:10:8.

This daring approach never received much support outside of Ingolstadt. There, however, the tradition continued and was given strong support in the eighteenth century by Vitus Pichler (d. 1736) and Francis Barth. These authors made the theory into one of universal application, teaching that moderate usury which was not repugnant to charity was not naturally immoral if permitted by law or custom. The premium paid for a loan in such a situation was not usury in a strict sense, but a reward to a lender which the law allowed on the occasion of a loan. Of course, the State could not arbitrarily give a reward to private persons, but it might benefit private persons when this was a necessary way of benefiting the community as a whole. As in the conferring of property rights by adverse possession, a private person was given the right, which he would otherwise not have, to take the property of someone else, in order that the general welfare be promoted. But how was the general welfare promoted? On the one hand, by happy borrowers: it would be easier to get loans. In fact, Pichler said, more people were hurt by the unavailability of lenders than by the multiplicity of usurers. On the other hand, by deservingly enriched lenders: churches, widows, wards, the sick, and the disabled would be able to enjoy an income from lending; unduly scrupulous lenders, who probably had some interest title anyway, would have their consciences made tranquil. To the strong ecclesiastical objection that the Council of Vienne excommunicated legislators approving usury, so that it would scarcely seem that the law was capable of making usury legitimate, Pichler replied that the decree referred only to those legislators permitting excessive or uncharitable usury.[37]

As Pichler alternatively phrased the argument and as Barth expanded it, there were some principles of the natural law which apply only conditionally. For example, it is wrong to kill a man, but in certain conditions, such as a just war or the execution of a criminal, killing is permitted. The usury prohibition similarly applied only conditionally. Where the State permitted a premium on the occasion of a loan, a condition was set up which made the prohibition inoperative. Or, to put it another way, the thesis is that usury is unnatural; however, in a certain hypothetical situation the equivalent of usury may be justified. This hypothetical condition exists when the State by the exercise of its power of eminent domain gives the borrower's property to the lender.[38]

In an attempt to assimilate its doctrine to other interest titles, the theory

---

[37] Vitus Pichler, *Ius canonicum secundum V decretalium titulos Greg. Papae IX explicatum* (Venice, 1758), V, *De usuris*, 19:1.

[38] Francis Barth, *De statuto principis*, Dissertatio II, sec. 5, c.1, in Zech, *Dissertationes tres*.

of the Ingolstadt school was generally known as the "civil title to interest." But the difference from the other interest titles, which relate to the lender's loss, is substantial. The doctrine is, in fact, much more like the belief of Salmasius that what the civil law allows to be taken is morally legitimate. The strongest scholastic arguments made by Pichler and Barth in its favor were that it was merely a recognition of the general availability of *lucrum cessans,* and that the *census* contract already reached the same result under another name. But its formal structure is novel; it can claim no important scholastic ancestors or antecedents. Yet it is a striking commentary on the weakness of the natural-law case against usury in the seventeenth and eighteenth centuries that even unimportant scholastic writers can urge the political solution to the moral difficulty. The new doctrine was carefully constructed to avoid the answer which appeal to custom had received in the Middle Ages: that *raison d'état* cannot justify moral wrong. The difference was technical and not convincing. The only substantial justification for the new approach was that, in a political form, it was simply a variant of the economic arguments already advanced by Lessius.

4. Ecclesiastical Control of the Discussion

With the usury theory floundering in severe difficulties, the central ecclesiastical authority made two serious efforts to inject new vitality into the rule. The first is part of the general effort under Popes Alexander VII and Innocent XI to check laxist tendencies in moral theology. Two propositions on usury were papally proscribed, and their defense was prohibited under pain of excommunication *latae sententiae.* The first proposition, condemned by Alexander VII on March 18, 1666, ran:

It is lawful for a lender to require something beyond the principal, if he obliges himself not to demand the principal for a certain time.

The minimum censure attached to the proposition is that it is scandalous.

The second proposition, condemned by Innocent XI on March 2, 1679, ran:

As cash is better than money to be delivered later, and as there is no person who does not set greater value on present than on future money, a creditor can demand something more than the principal from a borrower and on that title be excused from usury.[39]

The minimum note of censure is "scandalous, and pernicious in practice."

[39] H. Denzinger, *Enchiridion symbolorum,* n.1142, 1191. ed. J. B. Umberg (Freiburg in Br., 1937),

These condemnations are, according to the usual rules of interpretation of canon law, to be interpreted restrictively. First, it is to be noted that the propositions are not defined as intrinsically erroneous; the note of censure attached does not bear on their theoretical truth or falsity. Secondly, it is to be remarked that the propositions are universals and that the Popes condemn them only as universals. What are rejected are the general assertions that the obligation not to reseek a loan has always a pecuniary estimation demandable by a lender, and that present money, always and universally, is more valuable than future money. The condemnations say nothing as to the number of particular cases in which these titles may be justified by concrete circumstances.

The precise significance of the propositions may be gauged by the position subsequently taken on them by St. Alphonsus. Ledesma, Serra (d. 1645), and Medina, defend an opinion "not lacking in probability," that the obligation to wait a long time for the return of one's money is extrinsic to the nature of a loan and so may be charged for, just as the obligation to be ready to loan over a period may be charged for. The Salamancan school and several fairly obscure theologians defend an opinion slightly different, but substantially similiar to this. They say:

Since it is morally impossible that a lender waiting through a long time not suffer danger, loss, or inconvenience, or at any rate be not impeded from exercising some act of liberality or some other honorable act, he may on this account contract for and receive something beyond the principal.

St. Alphonsus associates himself with the second opinion. The proposition condemned by Alexander VII, he explains, was condemned solely because it was too general. The obligation not to reseek may licitly be given a pecuniary estimation in particular cases; it may be charged for in long-term loans.[40] St. Alphonsus does not add how long a loan must be to qualify as a long-term loan.

The second papal effort was made seventy years after Alexander VII by one of the wisest and ablest of modern popes, Benedict XIV. The occasion for this attempt, appropriately enough, owed its origin to the efforts of Peter Ballerini. In 1740 Ballerini had brought out in Verona his new edition of St. Antoninus. This publication coincided with the sale of a bond issue at 4 per cent by the city of Verona. His edition was prefaced by a sharp attack on modern usury; there broke out a lively public controversy over the morals of the subscribers to the bonds. This controversy merged into a larger

----

[40] St. Alphonsus, *Theologia moralis*, III:5:3:7.

one three years later when Nicholas Broedersen, the Dutch Jansenist, published his *De usuris licitis et illicitis*. This work taught that usury was only profit made uncharitably from loans to the poor and that moderate profit on loans to businessmen or rich men was always licit.[41] In the following year, Scipio Maffei, a layman and close friend of Benedict XIV, undertook the defense of the Veronese bondholders with his *Dell' impiego del danaro libri tre*, a treatise clearly influenced by Broedersen and advocating substantially the same position as his.[42] To settle the mounting conflict, Benedict XIV, on November 1, 1745, issued the encyclical *Vix pervenit* to the bishops of Italy.

Vix pervenit reasserted the scholastic teaching on usury. Usury is "profit beyond the principal taken by reason of the loan itself." It is a sin against commutative justice, and restitution of usuries is necessary to salvation. It would be false and rash to suppose that there are always present titles or contracts excusing from usury; "in many cases" a man is held to help his neighbor by an entirely free loan. It is certainly no excuse to say that the profit on the loan is moderate, or that the loan is to a rich man or to be used for production purposes. At the same time it cannot be denied that there are extrinsic titles by which something beyond the principal may be demanded on a loan, and there are also licit contracts, distinct from a loan, by which money may be profitably employed. The Pope specifically declares that he pronounces no judgment on contracts or titles discussed by the theologians.[43]

This encyclical, the Pope says, is issued in fulfillment of his apostolic duty to refute unsound doctrine, and it was extended to the universal Church by a decree of the Holy Office of July 28, 1835.[44] Although not an *ex cathedra* pronouncement, it carried a weighty dogmatic authority. It is the last *ex professo* treatment of usury by a pope. It is an espousal of the central scholastic position. It leaves a great deal unsaid. By the explicit reservation that contracts or titles discussed by the theologians are not rejected, the field of discussion is left virtually unchanged. Lessius and Lugo could still have accommodated most interest-bearing credit transactions within the confines of the encyclical; and St. Alphonsus does so accommodate them.[45]

[41] Ballerini, *De jure divino*, Preface, n.2, 31, 32.

[42] F. Scipio Maffei, *Dell' impiego del danaro libri tre* (Rome, 1746). Cf. Van Roey, *De justo auctario*, p. 41.

[43] Benedict XIV, *Vix pervenit*. In Migne, *Theologiae cursus completus*, XVI, col. 1059ff.

[44] Van Roey, *De justo auctario*, p. 44.

[45] Cf. *supra*, n.40. St. Alphonsus accepts the Thomistic argument and also asserts the formal sterility of money (III:5:3:7). Zech similarly accepts these arguments (I, n.86, 155, 160). But as has been seen with the *census* and triple contracts, formal acceptance of the old arguments did not restrain these authors from adhering to most of the ways around them. On the small effect that the Encyclical had on Maffei himself, see *infra*, Chapter XVIII, section 4.

Conclusion

We may now attempt to answer the questions proposed at the start of this chapter and evaluate the state of the scholastic theory of usury in 1750, after three hundred years of close reëxamination by the scholastics. The following points are clear:

One argument showing the unnaturalness of usury has been successfully challenged by no one and has in itself been accepted by everyone: this is the Thomistic argument, revised by Summenhart and Soto, that the value of the use of a consumptible cannot be distinguished from the value of its ownership when both ownership and use are transferred to a borrower, and that consequently, a lender charging precisely for the use of his money by a borrower commits an unjust act.

No other argument of the medieval scholastics against usury has survived the test of time and criticism. The second favorite argument of the medieval writers, that the value of fungibles is fixed, is still accepted by Molina. But Summenhart has clearly demonstrated its fallaciousness by showing that it rests on a confusion between a fixed value and a fixed quantity, and no later writer except Molina finds the argument of importance. A corollary of this result is that there is no natural-law argument proving that usury is unjust in loans of fungibles which are not consumptibles. The argument that money is sterile and should not produce a profit has been severely criticized by Summenhart, who has shown that a house is sterile in the same economic sense. This Aristotelian argument against taking a profit from "barren metal" had already been undermined by the medieval permission of the rent of money *ad pompam*, and it is now completely abandoned by the later scholastics. By sterility of money, if they speak of it at all, they mean only the formal, juridical sterility of any good consumptible in first use, so that the argument based on money's sterility is identical with the argument based on money's consumptibility. The popular argument that the usurer sells time is no longer urged by itself, being recognized as simply a vulgar expression of the main Thomistic argument. The "legal argument," based on the simple transfer of ownership in a loan, is used by Navarrus, but in every other author it has merged into the fuller Thomistic account. The argument that riskless profit is wrong, clearly implied in many medieval approaches, has been abandoned wth the admission of the triple contract and the guaranteed *census*. A corollary of this result is that there is no practicable way of distinguishing a loan from a bailment in many concrete cases; in particular, there can be no objection to renting nonconsumptibles at a profit, though their risk is borne by the lessee. The Aristotelian objection that a trade in money is unnatural and tends to infinity has been attacked by Summenhart and Cajetan and subsequently adopted by no one of importance. There thus remains only one argument showing the injustice of usury.

While no direct challenge has been made to this one argument, the Thomistic argument, an evasion of it has been attempted: Summenhart has declared that the use of his good for a particular time is always surrendered by a lender and always may be charged for. This argument would destroy the usury prohibition. Lugo has been unable to answer the argument because he has compared the loss of the use of a consumptible to the loss of the use of a nonconsumptible. The proper reply, implicit in the scholastic analysis, is a denial that a privation has any value distinct from the value of the good of which it is the privation, unless it in some way results in other loss. The value of the use and ownership of a consumptible good have been shown to be identical. The privation of use, therefore, cannot be valued more than the value of the consumptible itself. Accordingly, the lender cannot charge separately for the good itself and the privation *qua* privation. Summenhart's argument is a confused attempt to give a value to a negative being. The scholastics also reject as an attempt to give value to a valueless entity the theory that the pure obligation of not reseeking a loan for a length of time is vendible. The obligation to deliver, as Molina says, has no value apart from the property itself. Similarly, the obligation not to reseek, if it occasions no loss, has no value other than the value of the good loaned.

The scholastic analysis assumes that each contract is to be considered by itself and that justice in it depends on the immediate equality of the objects exchanged, not on the subsequent profit resulting to one of the parties. Hence, the objection of Summenhart that a lender should be recompensed because he is the cause of a businessman-borrower's gain is considered irrelevant. Centered on the object involved in the contract, the scholastic analysis refuses to consider other objects for which the contractual object might be exchanged. A contract about money is considered a contract about money, not a contract about real capital. Money is not identified with the goods it buys. This firm isolation of the object of the contract is essential to the main Thomistic argument, for unless money is considered rigorously as money, its consumptibility in first use cannot be asserted.

The scholastic analysis also assumes that a value fixed by law cannot wilfully be altered by a private person. Summenhart has objected that money, not mathematically but morally and customarily, is always worth less if it is absent in time than if it is present in cash. With this objection is joined the difficulty raised by the admission of a money market on the exchanges. If the price of money on the exchanges is ruled by supply and demand, why cannot the price of money in loans be similarly governed, and if borrowers are willing to pay more for ready money, why cannot lenders charge them what they are willing to pay? To these objections, it is answered that the objective value of money, set by law, cannot be altered by the demand for funds, and that money absent in time cannot be valued for less simply because it is absent. Pure subjective impatience cannot here alter the legal price, any more than subjective evaluation can alter other legal prices. Hence Innocent XI teaches that money cannot always and universally be regarded as more valuable merely because it is present. In the absence of any objective reason for difference in evaluation, the scholastics assume that the law has fixed unalterably the value of money present or future.

Thus, standing on the two assumptions that justice depends on the equality of objects exchanged, with the objects being considered precisely by themselves, and that a legal value cannot be altered by subjective demand, the scholastic theory of usury by means of the Thomistic argument shows clearly and consistently the natural injustice of usury in money loans. The theory is formally perfect. But its formal perfection has been attained only at the cost of a multitude of admissions which render the cases where it is applicable rare, and the prohibition, in general, nugatory. Following the theory, we may now enumerate the conditions under which profit may be taken by one giving credit.

In many concrete circumstances, the privation of a consumptible will mean the loss of more value than the value of the consumptible itself. If the concrete circumstances of economic life are such that the privation of money commonly entails extra loss, there seems no reason why a common price cannot be set for the price of the privation of money — a price which can be charged by everyone whether they suffer loss or not. These circumstances obtain when there are objective factors which increase the value of present money over future money, so that the supposed legal equality between money at different times must give way to the objective pressure creating a difference. The holders of money lawfully value their money higher than its face value because (1) it gives them security against unexpected emergencies; (2) they wish to invest in a profitable business; (3) they wish to hold it until business opportunities are more favorable before investing it.

The price of the privation of money should compensate for the foregoing of these several purposes. Thus, there may be legitimate speculation on the interest rate, based on the lender's estimate of future, as well as present opportunities for business investment, and a lender may justly charge a premium if he fears an inflation.

In a limited way the interest titles *damnum emergens* and *lucrum cessans* recognized these rights of the lender. They have been further developed by the scholastic treatment of the exchanges. Above all, they have been asserted in Lessius' admission of the right, in a given market where opportunities abound, to charge for "the lack of one's money," and in St. Alphonsus' allowance of a charge for the lack of use in at least a long-term loan. In some economic conditions, most scholastics assert, the lack of one's money may entail no loss. But when the lack of use is a source of loss to the lender, he can charge, and economic conditions may be such that a lender always suffers a loss. Then a common price may be set on the lack of the use of money. Prudential scruples still keep most scholastics from recognizing the universal right to such a charge even in the eighteenth century; but the principles are there, only awaiting bolder application. The defenders of the civil title to profit on a loan have made this application, although they have couched their recognition of the common price of money in political, rather than in economic terms.

The risk of lending is also a title to interest. After Zech, it is established that charges may be averaged out over all borrowers.

All other expenses directly and indirectly incurred by lending are a title to interest.

The obligation to be ready to lend is distinct from a loan, and, as the discussions on the *montes pietatis* showed, may be charged for. A man engaged in the lending business may even seek "sustentative profit."

All interest may be sought under the name of "profit," as St. Alphonsus has pointed out. Interest only becomes usury when there is no just title to profit.

At the same time it has become clear that the formal usury rule has no application in a multitude of situations. The triple contract and bill of exchange have nullified the prohibition's effect in commercial finance. The *census* has ended whatever jurisdiction the rule ever had over governmental and agricultural credit and even over credit extensions to laborers. The just-price concept rules these transactions, demanding equity but not forbidding profit. The notion of implicit contracts has made it analytically possible to reduce most transactions to one of these acceptable forms. What is left of the usury rule, merged as it now is in practice with the demand for a just price, is an objection to immoderate interest. It would be perhaps impossible to think of a transaction involving the extension of credit at a moderate profit which could not have been justified in terms of the revised scholastic analysis.

Part Three

THE USURY THEORY FROM THREE PERSPECTIVES

CHAPTER XVIII

A COUNTERTHEORY OF USURY

During the centuries in which the scholastic theory was undergoing extensive modifications at the hands of the scholastics themselves, a powerful movement was developing in European intellectual centers to abandon the scholastic theory altogether. As the fate of the scholastic theory in modern times and modern evaluations of it were to be largely influenced by this new movement, we may here consider its chief leaders. The practical differences between the developed scholastic theory and the new theory of usury are not, perhaps, very great. But the theoretical differences are substantial.

1. John Calvin (1509–1564)

For five hundred years the canon law defining usury as "whatever is added to the principal" had dominated European thinking on usury. The Reformers, no longer bound by the canon law, could make a fresh start. Yet they still were bound by a vigorous tradition of Christian opposition to usury. John Calvin, the Protestant leader to make the most notable contribution to a new theory, abandons completely the detailed analysis of the scholastics in order to urge one general principle: follow the Golden Rule.[1] Contracts made according to this great law will be unimpeachable; contracts which offend it must be condemned. Accordingly usury must be redefined. It is not *lucrum ex mutuo*; it is *lucrum ex damno alieno*.[2] It is sinful only if it hurts one's neighbor;[3] and charity and natural equity alone can decide in what particular cases a charge for a loan does hurt a neighbor.[4] Away with technical rules and an elaborate system of exceptions.

---

[1] John Calvin, *In librum Psalmorum commentarius*, Psalm 15:5, col. 148, in *Opera quae supersunt omnia*, ed. G. Baum, E. Cumitz, and E. Reuss (Brunswick, 1863–1906), Vol. XXXI.

[2] *In viginti Ezechielis prophetae capita*, c.18:8, col. 430, in *Opera*, Vol. XL.

[3] *In librum Psalmorum*, 15:5, col. 148.

[4] *Consilia, De usuris*, cols. 248–249, in *Opera*, Vol. X. This is a letter answering a letter dated November 1545 from Claude de Sachins, a correspondent troubled by the conflict between the old tradition and the views of some recent "preachers of the Gospel." See *Opera*, Vol. XII, col. 211. Calvin in reply professes his great reluctance to discuss

A parson cannot know all the details of business.[5] But let each believer's conscience be his guide. On loans to the poor a profit will be clearly wicked.[6] On loans to the rich and to businessmen a lender's profit may be no worse than a seller's profit on a sale.[7] Biting usury, usury which sucks the substance of another while the usurer runs no risk, usury above the legal limit, are always condemned by God's law.[8] On the other hand, a modest profit on a loan under any and all circumstances is by no means forbidden.[9]

The only arguments against all profit on a loan that Calvin knows are those drawn from Scripture and a maxim of Aristotle's. As for Scripture, Luke 6:35 merely commands generous lending to the poor.[10] Some of the Old Testament passages, indeed, seem to condemn usury without distinction.[11] The passages are to be interpreted as requiring only the observance of charity and equity toward the poor, or, if one wishes to interpret more strictly, they still may be considered only as positive political law appropriate for the Jewish economy, but no longer binding today.[12] As for Aristotle's argument that money is sterile, Calvin has only contempt for it. A child can see that money locked in a box is sterile.[13] But who borrows to keep the money idle? Merchants borrow to increase their goods. Money is as fruitful as a house or as many other kinds of merchandise. When money buys a field, money then bears money.[14]

At the same time that Calvin attacks the general usury prohibition, he is by no means ready to give a general usury permission. Moderate usury is necessary for business, but it would be better if all usury were abolished.[15] The taking of even moderate usury should never be made one's occupation: all habitual usurers are to be expelled from the church of God and the well-ordered state.[16] Usury is never to be taken from the poor; it should never exceed the legal limit and often should not be as great; the word of God, not custom, should guide the lender; the lender should have no greater profit from the loan than the borrower.[17] Ministers of the gospel, if they must make

the subject at all, lest he trouble the scrupulous or inspire too liberal and loose a view on interest-taking.

[5] *Sermons sur le Deuteronome*, Sermon 5 on c.23:18–20, col. 120, in *Opera*, Vol. XXVIII.

[6] *In octavum praeceptum, Ex. Deut.*, 23:19, col. 680, in *Opera*, Vol. XXIV; *In Ezechielis*, 18:8, col. 431.

[7] *In octavum praeceptum*, col. 682.

[8] *Sermons sur le Deuteronome*, 5 on c.23:18–20, col. 117.

[9] *In Ezechielis*, c.18:8, col. 431.

[10] *In octavum praeceptum*, col. 680; Con-

silia, *De usuris*, cols. 245–246.

[11] *In librum Psalmorum*, 15:5, col. 148; *In Ezechielis*, 18:8, col. 430.

[12] *De usuris*, col. 246; *In librum Psalmorum*, 15:5, col. 148.

[13] *De usuris*, col. 247. Calvin refers to the argument not as Aristotle's but as St. Ambrose's and St. John Chrysostom's.

[14] *De usuris*, col. 247.

[15] *Ibid*.

[16] *In Ezechielis*, 18:8, col. 431; cf. *In octavum praeceptum*, col. 682.

[17] *De usuris*, cols. 248–249.

investments, should lend only to merchants and in such a way that their profit is not certain.[18] The general rule is that usury is licit "not everywhere, nor always, nor in all goods, nor from all." Indeed, Calvin exclaims, "scarcely ever can it happen that he who takes usury does not hurt his brother"; [19] and according to his rule such usury would be illicit. But at least on loans to rich men who borrow to increase their profits, usury will be lawful.

Not only is Calvin not enthusiastic about permitting usury, he makes a strong attack on the interest titles allowed by the scholastics. Referring to men who fraudulently pretend not to lend at usury, he says,

they treat usury as if it were compensation of as much loss as the difference caused by the lack of the use of their money. But there is no kind of usury which this specious title may not cloak. For each one has present money, when he loans it, which would have been useful to him if he had bought something, and at each moment matter of profit presents itself. So always will there be a place for compensation, since no creditor gives his money to another without loss.[20]

This claim he declares is a trick and a cavil, and God will not be deceived by it. Again, he declares that the French have invented the term "interest" to evade the laws against usury, and he adds, "Never was there any kind of usury among the ancients which today is not comprehended under that name." [21]

Now, it is true that no scholastic writer contemporary with Calvin interpreted the right to interest in the very broad way he describes. But his description is evidence of how the scholastic titles might have been regularly used in practice, even to take profit from the poor. Thus on this point Calvin is more severe than the scholastics, whereas in allowing profit on loans to wealthy merchants, he permits no more than Angelus, Biel, Summenhart, Cajetan, and Eck had permitted in approving the triple contract. Moreover, much of his criticism of the Aristotelian argument is no different from Andreae's or Conrad's, and he does not even touch the formidable Thomistic argument. Nonetheless, he does mark a new approach in two ways: first in denying an absolute divine prohibition of all usury; secondly, in suggesting that money be identified with the goods it buys. This last point is the essential theoretical one, but it is only suggested, not developed, in Calvin.

2. *Charles Du Moulin* (*Molinaeus*) (*1500–1566*)

A distinguished French lawyer, Charles Du Moulin, is the first Catholic writer to urge the licitness of moderate usury. A Renaissance jurist, full of

[18] "Lettre à Morel," January 10, 1562, cols. 245–246, in *Opera*, Vol. XIX.
[19] *In Ezechielis*, 18:8, cols. 431–432.
[20] *In octavum praeceptum*, col. 681.
[21] *In Ezechielis*, 18:8, col. 431.

knowledge of the Roman law and contempt for scholasticism, he boldly attacks the "ignorance" of the canonists, but he is careful to try not to oppose the Church herself; and his divergence from even the scholastic position should not be overestimated.

As to the divine law, he, like Calvin, holds that both Old and New Testament prohibit usury which is biting, which offends charity, which is taken from the poor.[22] But he finds nothing in the divine law nor in the natural law which prohibits all usury.[23] More acute than Calvin, he assaults directly the principal natural argument against usury based on the consumptibility of money. This argument, he declares, is "puerile": "because the use and fruition of money not only consist in the first momentary expenditure or application, but also in the successive use of the wares or goods bought with it." [24] In this terse statement is the first clear rejection of the Thomistic argument against usury, and this rejection is based on the direct indentification of money and the goods it buys.

Further, Molinaeus says, the scholastics admit that money may be rented *ad pompam*, and this rent could be made at the risk of the bailee. Therefore, he continues, identifying incidence of risk and ownership, "the transfer of ownership of itself does not make the use beyond the principal less able to be sold." [25] He even questions that a loan transfers ownership, as the Thomistic argument assumes. In Roman law, a slave, with power to administer, but not alienate, his master's goods, can make a loan, and though the physical body of money is given forever, the lender retains his rights to the same value.[26]

Moreover, Molinaeus presses, in business loans the creditor is "the near and efficacious cause, that is, as they commonly say, the *sine qua non*" of the profit the borrower makes; therefore, he should be able to share in it.[27] Finally, if usury is defined as "gain by force of the loan," profit taken merely for the act of lending, it is certainly unjust.[28] But no lender, Molinaeus declares, ever charged narrowly and precisely for this act. A lender charges for the utility offered by his money, and this utility has a value which is properly charged for.[29]

At the same time that Molinaeus rejects the usury rule, he makes a strong attack on the use made of the title of *lucrum cessans*. This title he reports is used by the merchants to justify "the most cruel usuries of Lyons," where

[22] Charles Du Moulin (Molinaeus), *Tractatus commerciorum*, n.8–9.

[23] n.9.

[24] n.530.

[25] n.530.

[26] n.449.

[27] n.9.

[28] n.21, 75.

[29] n.440, 499.

the rate is 18 per cent per annum.[30] Men, he says, retain the name of merchant so that they can claim the title, but in truth they make lending their business. "They set up exchange dealers' tables or partnerships which they call *banks* and exercise pure and simple usury, and yet in this they wish to exercise the privilege of just merchants."[31] They use the term "deposit" for loan, thinking a word will cover their "crimes."[32] These hypocrites, he cries, put the name of God on their bills as if they were pious, while in fact, charging even above the legal limit, they commit a shameful sin.[33] The interest they ask, he continues, is never really compensatory, for they would not be lenders if they could make more by doing business, nor do they curtail any profitable business they have in order to lend.[34]

All this criticism is really directed at the abuse of the title *lucrum cessans* carried to an extreme allowed by no scholastic author. But Molinaeus declares, the scholastics are responsible for this abuse, because they said interest should be determined by individual cases, instead of by the common estimation.[35] Their approach opened the way to everyone claiming exorbitant interest. Moreover, their system is no bar to profit on a loan, for, Molinaeus significantly asks, who cannot claim *lucrum cessans*?[36]

If one considers only Molinaeus' attack on the arguments against usury, his identification of money and the goods it buys, and his declared opposition to the current way of estimating *lucrum cessans*, one will think him a bold reformer indeed. On the other hand, he often insists that the Roman jurists defended only compensatory, not lucrative, usury,[37] and his defense of the charge for the use of money can accordingly be considered simply a developed form of *lucrum cessans* itself. No contemporary scholastic would have understood the title so broadly, or admitted the rate to be determined by the common estimation. But the scholastics had granted the principle that compensatory interest is licit, and Molinaeus' position can be interpreted as easily as a development of this thesis as a defiance of it.

Moreover, Molinaeus specifically agrees with Aristotle that unbounded lust for making money by lending is illicit.[38] He also believes that the medieval encouragement of free loans was desirable.[39] Further, he agrees with the scholastics in accepting the triple contract, though he accepts it as a case of moderate usury.[40] He also himself appeals to *lucrum cessans* as a

[30] n.506.
[31] n.504.
[32] n.507.
[33] n.506.
[34] n.509.
[35] n.499, 500, 504.

[36] n.505.
[37] n.26, 75, 81.
[38] n.533.
[39] n.583, 521.
[40] n.668.

reason for a high return in an exceptional case where sure profit was lost by selling on credit.[41] Above all, he argues that the *census* is the modern succedaneum of the old loans at usury; for in it "money immediately bears fruit in money proportionately to the principal and time," and it is at once a means for a rich man to invest funds and a needy man to obtain them.[42] Molinaeus even adds that the *census* redeemable by the seller is a better means of making credit available than the loan, for it gives the creditor an income, while it leaves the seller free to end the obligation when he has the money.[43] Such *census* are indeed the best remedy for exorbitant usury.[44]

Thus as far as practice goes, Molinaeus really differs very little from the scholastics, approving what they approve and condemning only what they would have found an abuse; and even his theory is often put forward by him in scholastic form as a defense of the lender's right to compensation. Nonetheless, on the issue of the determination of *lucrum cessans* by the common estimation he is clearly an opponent of the scholasticism of his day, and on the larger issue of the nature of money in loans he audaciously and completely breaks from the scholastic tradition. His work was far enough removed from the common teaching to be placed on the Index.

3. *Claude Saumaise (Salmasius) (1588–1653)*

The hardiest defense of usury yet undertaken was made in 1630 by a curious champion, the Calvinist classicist, Claude Saumaise (Salmasius). While Calvin had been reluctant to admit usury of any kind, and Molinaeus had at least forbidden it on loans to the poor, Salmasius enters a ringing defense of the most brazen of all usurers, the licensed, public moneylenders who drew their profits from the poor. His works are principally directed against the illogic of the Calvinist communities which would not condemn usury outright, but which persisted in excluding professional usurers from communion. The three works, *De usuris liber*, *De modo usurarum liber* and *Dissertatio de foenore trapezitico*, altogether compose as strong a case for the pawnbrokerage and small-loan shop as these institutions have ever had made out for them by a professedly disinterested observer. Since Salmasius not only represents a complete break from the usury prohibition, but also contains much criticism reflecting on the scholastic theory, we may consider his case at length.

His general position is that selling the use of money is a business like

[41] n.224; but cf. n.493–494.
[42] n.443; cf. n.109.
[43] n.447.
[44] n.447; cf. n.124.

any other business.[45] If it is licit to make money with things bought with money, why is it not licit to make money from money? [46] Everyone makes his living from someone else; why should not the usurer? [47] The seller of bread is not required to ask if he sells it to a poor man or a rich man. Why should the moneylender have to make a distinction? [48]

The moneylender performs a highly useful service, as does anyone who provides a means for meeting a great public need.[49] Moreover, since he is licensed by the State, he has the State's approval; he is in some sort a public official, like a tax collector; and if he is guilty of sin, the State is guilty, too.[50] The rates he charges are those approved by the State, of if there is no maximum legal limit, they are the rates set by supply and demand.[51] There is no fraud or theft in charging the highest market price for other goods; why is it wrong for the usurer to charge the heaviest usuries he can collect? [52]

Descending to the particular case of Amsterdam, Salmasius notes that the public usurers there usually charge 16 per cent on small loans. The usurers then have to bear the cost of obtaining their money at lesser usury, of holding some money idle, of hiring a large house to hold their pledges, of taking losses on some pledges, of paying an auctioneer to auction the pledges, of paying other servants, of paying a yearly license fee and an original permit fee. Deducting expenses, the moneylenders make only about 8 per cent — barely enough to keep them interested in the business.[53] It is granted that the higher rates on short-term small loans hurt the poor most. But the heavy charges are beneficial in stimulating the borrowers to repay more quickly. Negligence, inertia, or prodigality are the real enemies of the poor, not the usurer.[54]

Is there any law against usury? In the Bible, it is true, the Jews were forbidden to take usury from any other Jew, poor or rich. But this prohibition was political and given chiefly because the Jews were united in a blood brotherhood; it no longer held after the destruction of the Jewish state.[55] As for the Gospel, Jesus Christ means to teach nothing about civil polity or economic transactions.[56] The only ecclesiastical law against usury that Salmasius knows of is the papal law; and why should one obey the Pope? [57] Moreover, "what [the canonists] took away with one hand, they restored

[45] Claude Saumaise (Salmasius), *Dissertatio de foenore trapezitico* (Leyden, 1640), Preface.

[46] p. 361.

[47] Preface.

[48] p. 603.

[49] pp. 22–23.

[50] Preface and p. 114.

[51] Claude Saumaise, *De usuris liber* (Leyden, 1638), c.19, p. 583; *De foenore*, p. 119.

[52] *De usuris liber*, Preface.

[53] *De foenore*, pp. 742–749.

[54] *De foenore*, pp. 756–758.

[55] *De usuris*, c.20, p. 605 and 617.

[56] *De usuris*, c.21, pp. 629–630.

[57] *De foenore*, Preface.

with the other." [58] The *census* is but usury made licit by another name.[59] The exchanges to the fairs are also usurious.[60] Above all, *lucrum cessans* is really just another word for usury. All usury, if you like, can be called compensatory. No usury is sheer profit: "All profit indeed, if you calculate it rightly, is always compensation, either of labor, or of work, or of office, or of service, or even of other gain which I could have taken from my good or work, if I had not offered this." [61] No one ever lent money, if it was really going to injure him; that supposition of the canonists is absurd. But if the canonists want to allow "compensatory" interest, a lender can always justly claim usury as some kind of compensation.[62] Thus the natural-law objection to usury is also answered: a lender charges usury for a lack of use and for the risk involved which are always a source of loss to him. Or one can say equally well that usury is the licit rent of the use of a fruitful good.[63]

Secondarily, Salmasius also tries to prove that ownership is not transferred in a loan, but here he falls into contradictions,[64] and it is not essential to his case which rests well enough on the thesis that the lack of the use of money always has a price. The argument that the money is sterile is refuted by the usual comparisons with idle houses and fields.[65] The other Aristotelian argument that usury tends to infinity is met with the melancholy answer that almost all men seek as much money as they can get, and once you permit them to seek what is "sufficient," rather than what is strictly necessary, there is no limit one can rightly set.[66] Innocent's old argument that usury discourages agriculture is met by a denial of fact. Furthermore, Salmasius reasons, if usurers increase and farmers diminish, competition between the usurers will drive down the price of money.[67] Finally, if you consider the natural law and the Golden Rule attentively, you will see that there is a natural obligation on the borrower to pay for the favor of a loan. A contractual obligation is necessary only because all borrowers are not sensitive to their natural duty.[68] In a word, usury is as natural a trade as any, and better than some. "I would rather be called a usurer, than be a tailor," declares Salmasius.[69]

In Salmasius' account the identity of money and that for which it is exchangeable are not the center of attention as they are in Molinaeus. Often

[58] *De foenore*, p. 91.
[59] *De foenore*, pp. 4, 81.
[60] *De usuris*, Preface.
[61] *De foenore*, p. 84.
[62] *De foenore*, pp. 85–87.
[63] *De usuris*, c.7, pp. 161–178.
[64] *De usuris*, c.8, pp. 202–223.
[65] *De usuris*, c.8, pp. 200–201.
[66] *De usuris*, c.14, pp. 410–411.
[67] *De usuris*, c.8, pp. 223–224.
[68] *De usuris*, c.20, p. 599.
[69] *De usuris*, c.18, p. 530.

he defends his theory in terms of a broadened right of *lucrum cessans*. But he is clearly on the side of the innovators in denying any divine prohibition of usury and in assuming that a trade may be driven in money as in other goods. In the end, he is far more radical than either Calvin or Molinaeus, leaving only a legal barrier to usury and sweeping away all objections from justice or charity against lending at a profit to the poor. In Salmasius, all religious scruple against usury is brushed aside, and the secular law alone sets a limit to profits.

4. *Scipio Maffei* (1675–1755)

Up to the middle of the eighteenth century, however, no Catholic author had been able to expound the Calvinist theory of the licitness of moderate usury without his orthodoxy being challenged. Now Scipio Maffei, a Veronese count and a friend of the reigning Pope, Benedict XIV, issued a defense of usury based on the Calvinist position. The occasion, as has been noted earlier, was the controversy over the licitness of 4 per cent interest on a Veronese bond issue, a controversy stirred by the ardent attacks of Ballerini on the usuriousness of the transaction.[70] Maffei, consulted by the troubled bondholders, came as an amateur theologian to their defense.

Maffei's main theses had all been stated before in Calvin, Molinaeus, Salmasius: the Old Testament prohibited usury only from the poor; the New Testament simply required one to be charitable in a general way; the Fathers and Councils condemned only excessive usury; the only usury condemned by any law is usury that hurts one's neighbor; money is not sterile, but the instrument of business, than which "nothing in the world is more fecund"; loans at interest are necessary for commerce; the State not only tolerates but actively enforces loans at usury; usury is already permitted by the personal *census*, the triple contract and *lucrum cessans*, understood broadly to include the loss of all future investment opportunity.[71] The main natural-law argument, Maffei asserts, is that ownership passes in a loan, but he denies that this happens: the lender still is the owner because he can bequeath or donate the value of the loan; he alienates only the physical quantity, not the value of the money.[72] The ownership of the money

---

[70] See *supra*, Chapter XVII, section 4.

[71] Maffei, *Dell' impiego del danaro libri tre*, pp. 25, 48, 75–147, 204, 178, 205, 247, 199, 209–221, 168–169. Whereas St. Bernardine had stigmatized as a blasphemy the argument that the usury prohibition was an impossible precept, because it interfered with commerce, Maffei reverses his position and

declares that it is blasphemous to say that such an impossible precept had been imposed. He adds rhetorically, "Dare we attribute to our divine and lovable Legislator a law which would be impracticable and from which extreme inconvenience would threaten civil society?" (p. 199).

[72] Maffei, p. 188.

could not pass without the consent of the lender, and the lender never consents to such an absolute transfer. The borrower's power of using the money at will is not equivalent to undisputed ownership.[73] Therefore, if the lender is still the owner, he can collect rent, as any owner does on property given to another for use.[74] The consumptibility of money is also directly denied. "Money does not consume itself in use; on the contrary it multiplies." [75] In an awkward anticipation of later theory differentiating production and consumption loans, Maffei tries to distinguish between cases where "the money is gone" and those where something of value remains. He appears to draw the line, without much logic, on the basis of the charitable purpose of the loan. Money used to feed a needy family or free a prisoner, he says, is consumed, and here no interest should be charged on the loan.[76] But where the borrower spends the loaned money for less urgent needs, Maffei finds that the value of the money remains with him. Before use, money can be considered neither a consumptible nor a nonconsumptible, and all argument based on its consumptibility is vain.

Maffei's position, then, is not as extreme as Salmasius'. He will not have usury on loans to the poor or to those in great distress borrowing to recover from some disaster, or even on short-term loans of small sums. But his stand is identical with that of Calvin and Molinaeus. Charity provides the governing standard. Loans to businessmen or the rich may always be a source of profit.[77]

After the appearance of *Vix pervenit*, specifically condemning the general licitness of profit on loans to the rich or to businessmen, it might have been thought that Maffei would have been crushed. On the contrary, he republished his book with the *imprimatur* of the Master of the Sacred Palace and a letter to the Pope, in which he thanked him for confirming his views and gave a politely legalistic reading of the encyclical, stopping a little short of open irony. Like the Pope, he agreed that there were many cases where a loan should be given gratuitously, as to the poor; like the Pope, he condemned all usury in a strict sense, that is, profit taken by force of the loan contract itself; but also like the Pope, he recognized that there were many titles and contracts which were necessary to civil life, whose justice was debated by theologians, and which were uncondemned by the Church. Such contracts, like the rent of money, and such titles as *lucrum cessans*, understood in a broad sense, were all that his book contended for.[78] As he

[73] pp. 182–183.
[74] p. 238.
[75] p. 192.
[76] p. 193.

[77] p. 206.
[78] Maffei, *Opere* (Venice, 1790), Vol. XVIII, pp. 21–27.

remarked, everyone already took interest or moderate usury on their loans, though some called it one thing and some another.[70]

Conclusion

The most striking feature of all these nonscholastic critics of the scholastic position is their agreement that the scholastics already admit what they want. Calvin, Molinaeus, Salmasius, and Maffei all grant that the *census*, triple contract, and *lucrum cessans* authorize all the profit that should be taken by anyone on a contract of credit. The struggle then seems to be largely over words: the scholastics do not wish to admit "profit on a loan"; their critics wish to abandon the other contracts and titles and say directly that profit on the use of money loaned is licit.

There are, it is true, three great theoretical differences between the scholastic and the nonscholastic positions: the scholastics assert that all usury is condemned by the divine law, while their opponents say that only uncharitable or even only illegal usury is condemned; the scholastics analyze the loan contract on the basis of the equality of the objects exchanged, while their opponents consider the person of the parties to the loan, and the benefits they subsequently receive; the scholastics treat the chief object of loans, money, as bare cash, while their opponents identify it with capital.

These theoretical differences are real enough, and under certain economic conditions, they could lead to substantial practical differences. But they do not in fact lead to substantial differences here; for the scholastics teach that the divine and natural prohibition of usury is only of profit taken without just title on a loan contract, and they are able to find a multiplicity of titles and contracts by which profit may be received. To take the most obvious example, compensation for a lender's lack of use of his money in an expanding economy becomes identical with paying him for the use of his money. The developed scholastic theory and its critics agree in approving the same act, and their only real and common opponent is the early scholastic theory with its arbitrary restrictions.

Of course, there is a difference in connotation, in emotional significance, in attitude, between the scholastics and their opponents: the scholastics begin with a general prohibition and find the exceptions; their opponents begin with a general permission and make restrictions. Of course, too, most scholastic authors had not as yet approved the full development of the interest

---

[70] *Dell' impiego*, p. 200. Maffei cites several standard Italian dictionaries where interest is defined as "licit profit on the use of money," and usury is defined as "excessive interest" (p. 2). "Everyone," he remarks, "lends at interest as if the opinion of our adversaries never existed" (p. 230).

titles to the general right to charge for the lack of the use of one's money —
though, indeed, the implicit personal *census* and implicit triple contract came
to the same thing. There are still prudential reservations and hesitations on
the scholastic side. But fundamentally the critics of the scholastic theory
testify to the truth of the conclusion of the previous chapter dealing with
the modifications in the scholastic theory itself since 1500; it would be
perhaps impossible to think of a transaction involving the extension of credit
at a moderate profit which could not have been justified in terms of the
revised scholastic analysis.[80]

[80] One step beyond the extreme recommended by Salmasius had not been taken by
1750, but was taken twenty-five years later.
Since this step had no effect on scholastic theory
in any way, it is here placed in a footnote. But
if you like, it is also a landmark in being
the most complete abandonment of the old
Christian prohibition of usury as well as the
scholastic theory. It is a recommendation
which would have been no less unacceptable
to the major critics of the scholastics than
to the scholastics themselves, and unlike
the other proposals outlined in this chapter,
it would have meant considerable change in
practice. It is a plan for a repeal of even the
legal limit on usury.

This plan was set out in 1787 in a series
of celebrated letters by Jeremy Bentham.
Bentham takes Salmasius' position that moneylending is a trade like any other, and from this
basis argued logically that there is no more
reason to suppose that the legislature should
determine the proper price of money than it
should determine the price of other goods
(Jeremy Bentham, *Defence of Usury*, London,

1818, pp. 9–13). The government, he assumes,
should stay out of business. Let every man
be free to make his contracts as he will,
and if a sane man prefers to pay usury to going
without a loan, let him do so without hindrance of the law (p. 2). The law, as it
is, protects no one, but raises the cost of
money by exposing lenders to an additional
risk and prevents the poor from being
assisted (pp. 47, 53).

The sources of this foolish and ancient
law, Bentham adds, are not hard to discover:
a Christian opposition to temporal prosperity,
an anti-Semitic distrust of Jewish methods,
an ignorant reverence for Aristotle's maxim
that money is barren, and a worldly love of
present pleasure and hatred of the abstemious
lender (pp. 96–106). These four motives
combined to set in motion the whole formidable machinery against usury, vestiges of which
still plague England. As for him, he dismisses all scruples against usury. Usurers are
men as honest as other tradesmen, and he
hopes to be rewarded by their prayers, if
he wins no other benefit.

CHAPTER XIX

THE USURY THEORY AND THE
SCHOLASTICS' SUCCESSORS

By 1750, then, the scholastic theory and the countertheory, approaching the same problem from different theoretical viewpoints, agree in approving the common practice. The scholastic theory, however, is stated in stern negative rules which can still cause doubt and hesitation for the scrupulous lender or spiritual director; and such doubts and hesitations do occur in a number of cases at the beginning of the nineteenth century. Then, in a series of decisions between 1822 and 1836, the Holy Office, the Roman congregation charged with the supervision of Catholic doctrine and morals, ends all doubts and practical difficulties by publicly decreeing that the interest allowed by law may be taken by everyone.

Both before and after the Holy Office decrees there is considerable theoretical controversy. Many, even among the scholastic authors themselves, are inclined to abandon the traditional theory for the new one. The licitness of the rent of money as a fruitful good, at least in production loans, is asserted. The title of the civil law is revived. The biblical and conciliar prohibitions of usury are explained as prohibitions only of excessive usury. Calvin, Molinaeus, and Maffei become the new authorities, while the scholastic defenders of the new theory assert that only in terms of it can the general permission to take interest be understood and modern commerce be justified. The champions of the old theory, on the other hand, reassert the familiar arguments against all usury, while they point out that the general permission to take interest can be understood as an extension of the title of *lucrum cessans* and need involve no abandonment of the old principles. Their contention had particular cogency in view of the enormous quickening of economic life at the beginning of the nineteenth century. The Industrial Revolution, already in full progress in England, now began to affect the continent as well,[1] and the Holy Office decrees coincide with the acceleration of its influence there.

The conflict between describing the common practice in terms of the old

[1] Sée, *Modern Capitalism*, pp. 142–147.

or new theory continued into the twentieth century and eventually was resolved only by statements of the usury prohibition which might be reconcilable with either. The whole quarrel is still, if you like, a quarrel of words. The major modifications in the scholastic theory had been made between Summenhart and St. Alphonsus. All later work, including the Holy Office decrees, are simply clarifications or at most slight developments of the theory of 1750. Practice remains substantially unaffected. But it may yet be of some interest to see how the theoretical quarrel went and how the old scholastic theory fared in modern times. We shall here, then, set out in order the decisions of the Holy Office; the pleas of the scholastic defenders of the new theory; the syncretist tendencies at the end of the century; various additional papal observations and rulings on usury; and the present state of the case.

1. *Responses of Rome, 1822–1836*

The answers of the Roman authorities to questions about usury from perplexed bishops and theologians between the years 1822 and 1838 form a definite series.[2] The first response is a decree given in 1822. "A woman of Lyons" who "gave her capital to certain persons that she might receive from them a profit at the rate prescribed by the civil law" appealed her confessor's refusal of the sacraments and order of restitution of these gains. The Holy Office, judging the appeal, declared that "a response will be given at a suitable time"; that meanwhile, however, restitution was not necessary; and that the woman might receive the sacraments.[3]

A second decree was given in reply to an inquiry in 1830 from the Bishop of Rennes. The confessors of his diocese were divided on the question of "interest taken from money lent to a businessman, who employs it in commercial ventures, where he enriches himself." Some confessors, thinking they had found a *via media*, asked of penitents taking such interest a simple promise to submit to a papal decision which would determine this point. If

[2] The practical uncertainty caused by a literal reading of the usury rule by a man ignorant of the scholastic development is illustrated by the case of the Irish priest, Jeremiah O'Callaghan (see O'Callaghan, *Usury*, New York, 1856). Unable to convince his bishop that sales on credit were usurious, O'Callaghan came to America, found New York "the very focus of usury," and, as a priest in Burlington, Vermont, successfully opposed a proposed savings bank as a scheme to entail his Irish flock in usury while simultaneously defrauding them of their deposits (*ibid.*, pp. 19, 30, 394). O'Callaghan's suspicions of banking were confirmed by the numerous bank failures in nineteenth-century America, as his feelings against banks were intensified by the Jacksonian campaign against the Second Bank of the United States (*ibid.*, pp. 369–375). But his main reliance was on the usury rule without reference to interest titles, *census*, or triple contract. This pious, if simple-minded, application of the rule in Burlington was to be its chief impact on the American banking system.

[3] De Vic, *Litterae monitoriae*, in Migne, *Theologiae cursus completus*, XVI, col. 1065 (hereafter cited as *T.c.c.*).

the promise is given, the confessors, "although convinced of the greater probability of the contrary opinion, do not deny absolution," nor do they question
penitents who do not mention their gains from loans, although the confessors
have heard that they make such profits. The Bishop asked,

Can one approve the practice of these confessors? Can one exhort the more
rigid confessors who proscribe this contract, under pain of refusal of the sacraments, to conform to the milder conduct of the first?

Pius VIII, after consultation with the Holy Office, personally replied:

To the first question, they are not to be disturbed. To the second, it is answered
in the first.[4]

A third decision suggested an even more liberal position. A perplexed
vicar-general asked,

Whether a confessor sins, who sends away in good faith a penitent, who demands from a loan the gain allowed by the civil law, apart from any extrinsic
title of *lucrum cessans* or *damnum emergens* or extraordinary danger?

The Penitentiary, the Roman tribunal for issues of the internal forum,
replied in the classic formula that "*Non esse inquietandum*," provided he is
ready to obey a decision of the Holy See.[5]

A troubled theologian, Denavit, now sought information on precisely the
same subject. He declared:

The undersigned writer, thinking it licit by no contract to withdraw from the
doctrine of Benedict XIV, denies sacramental absolution to priests who contend
that the law of the prince is sufficient title for taking something beyond the sum
lent apart from *lucrum cessans* or *damnum emergens*.

In answer to his question if his conduct was, then, too severe toward these
priests, the Holy Office again replied, "*Non esse inquietandos.*"[6]

In the years following, six more decrees of the Penitentiary repeated and
confirmed the earlier responses.[7] Then the Bishop of Viviers sought to know
(1) if the past decisions authorized interest on loans to businessmen, apart
from the title conferred by the civil law; and (2) if the very existence of civil
law regulating interest, *ipso facto*, without the State's explicit intention of
exercising its prescriptive power, created a just title to interest. The Holy
Office simply referred him to the earlier replies, thus implicitly indicating an
affirmative answer to both questions.[8]

[4] *Ibid.*, col. 1066.
[5] *Ibid.*, col. 1067.
[6] *Ibid.*, col. 1068.
[7] *Ibid.*, cols. 1069–1071.
[8] *Ibid.*, col. 1073.

The twelfth decision raised the question of the justice of interest in the broadest form yet suggested. The collegiate chapter of Locarno had been dispossessed of its ancient prebends by the State and had been compensated by a lump sum of money. It was essential for the chapter to invest this sum and draw an income from it, for the monks would quickly consume the capital amount if it remained idle. They could, however, find no investment that would yield more than 2½ per cent. In this emergency, faced with eventual starvation, "unless it obtained interest from the prebends," the chapter asked the Holy See if it might plead its very necessity "to be a sufficient and valid title just like the other titles approved by the Church" and so be entitled to loan its capital at interest. The chapter also asked if such a title could be pleaded for other churches, monasteries, and indeed all wards in a similar position. Finally, and separately from its need, the chapter asked "whether such contracts are sufficiently justified by the civil laws and forms which now generally ratify them and order them fulfilled, and also by the common and tacit consent of the people which, by now an ancient custom, seems to substitute these contracts as more convenient in place of others more involved and difficult?"

To all these questions, the Holy Office, Gregory XVI approving, had but one reply: "*Non esse inquietandos.*" [9]

Decree XIII dealt with yet another inquiry as to the morality of taking the legal rate of interest on the strength of the civil title alone, and the Penitentiary, as well it might, referred the inquirer to Decrees V, VI, VII, and VIII. Decree XIV similarly only referred the inquiring bishop to the same decrees. Decree XV simply noted the ordinary theological requirement that "good faith was always supposed" in those taking interest on the grounds of the legal title. [10]

Decree XVI is highly important. The Bishop of Viviers asked what attitude he should adopt toward those of his clergy who preached that the legal title was clearly valid, omitting any reference of the possibility of a future decision of the Holy See. Cardinal Gregorio, the Grand Penitentiary, wrote to him explaining the intention of its earlier decisions:

The Sacred Penitentiary wished to define nothing at all about the question, debated by theologians, of the title derived from the law of the prince; but only to provide a norm which confessors might safely follow in regard to penitents who take a moderate profit determined by the law of the prince, *with good faith and ready to accept the commands of the Holy See.*
Those, therefore, who in preaching teach absolutely that it is licit to take profit

from a loan by title of the civil law . . . define by private authority a question which the Holy See did not yet wish to define.[11]

The last decree of this series replied to a question of the Bishop of Nice touching penitents who took "moderate profit on a loan on the sole title of the law, with bad or doubtful faith." Could these penitents, provided they were sorry for their bad faith, be absolved without obligation or restitution? The Holy Office replied affirmatively.[12]

If the authority of these decrees seems clear,[13] their correct interpretation is not as easily determined. Does the Holy Office mean definitively to approve the legal title? De Vie, Bishop of Bellay, in a pastoral to his clergy issued in 1838, answered this question affirmatively. He maintained that the decrees authorize him to conclude that belief in the validity of the legal title "is an opinion, which with a safe conscience, can be held and followed in practice, like many others not defined by the Church." [14]

On the other hand, the Sulpician theologian Boyer held that the Holy Office was not asked if the legal title or the productive character of a loan were justifications in themselves. The petitioners, he contended, were generally convinced that the titles were not good and wished only to know, "Is this principle stamped with a degree of falsity which renders it intolerable and worthy of the refusal of the sacraments?" [15] The Holy Office replied to this question, "*Non sunt inquietandi,*" which Boyer interprets in this way:

"*Non sunt inquietandi.*" Do not disturb them, do not treat them as possessors in bad faith, as public sinners convicted by the notoriety of fact with the crime of heresy, do not refuse them absolution on the sole fact of the conviction they have that these two contracts, supported by the titles of commerce and of law, are legitimate and that they can use them in practice. Their opinion may be false; but it is neither an error, nor heresy, nor a censured doctrine. . . . The affirmative and negative in such a case are, in the eyes of the Holy Office, indifferent opin-

[11] *Ibid.*, col. 1081.

[12] *Ibid.*, col. 1083. "Bad faith" in this context means "believing one is acting against conscience."

[13] The Sulpician theologian Boyer, in a contemporary work specifically written to defend these decrees, declares that the responses have the "greatest authority which can pertain to ecclesiastical authority, which is not of the universal Church." He notes that "these consultations have been made with such great solemnity, and that the replies have been repeated seventeen times over a sufficiently long period; they could not have been ignored by the head of the Church;

they draw from this single fact of his tacit approbation a great weight. But there is more — several of them carry as a heading 'Ex assistentia summi pontificis.' The decisions sent to the bishops of Rennes and of Viviers have been reviewed by the Pope; they have, in some fashion, the stamp and seal of Peter." Boyer, *Apologie du Saint Office en ses décisions sur le prêt à intérêt*, in Migne, *T.c.c.*, XVI, col. 1099.

[14] De Vie, *Litterae monitoriae*, XVI, col. 1086.

[15] Boyer, *Lettre de l'auteur de la défense de l'Église*, in Migne, *T.c.c.*, XVI, col. 1115.

ions, which do not give rise to any characteristic note of bad doctrine. . . . The Holy See decides nothing about the fundamental question; the severe doctrine can be the most probable, the most reasonable; you are not prohibited from attaching to it the degree of certitude you wish, provided that you do not make it a dogma, an article of faith, prior to a final decision by the Church; if you think your opinion judged, defined, passed into dogma, by force of the encyclical of Benedict XIV, your pretention is an error.[16]

Or, as Cardinal Gregorio had put it, the aim was "only to provide a norm which confessors might safely follow." The decisions are practical ones, bearing on the objective rightness or wrongness of taking the legal rate of interest in a modern economy. The practice of taking such interest is approved; the theoretical basis for the approval is deliberately left undecided. The Holy Office cannot be said positively to favor the civil and commercial titles; at the same time, since it does not condemn them, it does appear to invite their theoretical development by the theologians.

2. Defense of the New Theory of Usury

The Holy Office's decisions were made at a period which was the nadir of scholastic theology. Partly because of the disruptive effects of the French Revolution, partly because of a general lack of interest in scholastic philosophy, competent scholastic theologians were rare and great scholastic theologians were nonexistent. Consequently, no commanding figure arose to defend the old theory, although since all the weight of traditional authority was on its side, it still was generally accepted. But facile and persuasive writers were urging its abandonment and the acceptance in greater or less degree of the theory of Calvin and Maffei. Two of these pleas for the new theory occur contemporaneously with the Holy Office's decisions and were probably of considerable influence on the congregation. Two of these pleas come later and are probably influenced by the congregation's practical prescriptions.

William Cardinal de la Luzerne

The first of these works pleading for a substantial change in theory is the *Dissertations sur le prêt-de-commerce*, published in 1822 by William César, Cardinal de la Luzerne. The principal contention of the book is that the *prêt-de-commerce*, or business loan, is in no way a *mutuum* or loan which should naturally be gratuitous. In the business loan, there is no transfer of a consumptible, as there is in a proper *mutuum*. On the contrary, the matter

[16] Boyer, *Apologie*, col. 1098.

of the loan is not money which will be dissipated, but "the value which will increase by the use one makes of it." [17] Consequently, the usury prohibition which applies only to loans of consumptibles does not apply to such a contract.[18] The theory here is substantially the same as Calvin's, identifying money and the goods it buys. But, as Luzerne emphasized, the practical results are the same as the triple contract, so that all authors approving the latter, in effect, approved his proposition.[19]

The work centers about the defense of the business loan. But secondarily, Luzerne, in agreement with the critics of scholasticism, contends that the only usury condemned by natural law is that which oppresses the poor, and that the criterion of justice is the advantage or disadvantage to the borrower, not the equality of goods exchanged.[20] At the same time, the cardinal admits that the *mutuum* proper is usually a source of injury to the poor when coupled with usury, so that ecclesiastical law had acted correctly in prohibiting usury on the pure *mutuum* under any circumstances.[21] Yet, he insists, this prohibition is a purely penal, prudential enactment of positive law: the natural law itself dictates no such general prohibition.[22]

More important, perhaps, than his natural-law defense of the *prêt-de-commerce* is Luzerne's effort to show that no dogma is imperiled by admitting moderate profit on loans to businessmen and the rich. Pointing out that the marks of a dogma of Catholic faith are that it is defined by a pope or council or taught universally and with more unanimity by the theologians, he makes an extensive review of papal, conciliar, patristic, and scholastic teaching on usury.[23] This investigation establishes to his satisfaction that the only dogma that can be said to exist on usury is that excessive or oppressive profit on a loan is evil.[24] As to the business loan in particular, he demonstrates that distinct condemnation of it is confined to the scholastics of the thirteenth, fourteenth, and fifteenth centuries, and by all the tests of dogma, such transient and local opinion cannot be elevated above the rank of positive law.[25] He ascribes the medieval position to the economic conditions of the time, to the tyranny of Aristotle, and to ignorance of the Fathers.[26]

Luzerne's analysis of the origin of the scholastic views is not very adequate, and his analysis of the decrees on usury of the medieval Councils is open to

---

[17] Luzerne, *Dissertations sur le prêt-de-commerce*, Vol. III, Part I, p. 32.

[18] Part I, p. 235.

[19] Part I, p. 141.

[20] Part I, p. 1.

[21] Part 2, p. 730.

[22] Part 2, p. 731.

[23] Part I, pp. 1ff.

[24] Part 2, p. 730.

[25] Part I, p. 36.

[26] Part I, pp. 40–45. According to the ecumenical Council of Vienne, it was heresy pertinaciously to affirm that usury was not sin; *Clementis*, V:5.

dispute, but his is the most successful effort yet to show how part of the old usury prohibition could be treated as positive law without compromising any dogma, and his work thus removed one of the most serious objections to the new theory. Simultaneously, he rallied the whole tradition in favor of the triple contract to the support of the Calvinist thesis. As far as practice goes, his ideas are no more radical than Eck's or Molina's.

Mark Mastrofini

An equally influential and even more enthusiastic advocate of the new theory was the canon, Mark Mastrofini, a member of the papal court. His work, *Discussion sur l'usure*, written in 1828, was graced with an approbatory letter from Thomas Turco, a consultor of the Holy Office, and according to report, it was generally received with admiration in Rome.[27]

The work itself is simply a forceful presentation of the familiar theses sustained by Molinaeus and Maffei. Its most original part is its formulation of their theory in terms of money's "applicability." By "applicability" Mastrofini means both the power of being able to use money and its actual use.[28] This applicability, he declares, is separate from money itself and may always be charged for.[29] Like any potency, it is fecund.[30] It remains in existence, though the money is spent for other goods; the same value of applicability then resides in the goods bought.[31] Whether the lender was or was not using his money fruitfully, and whether the borrower uses the loan productively or for consumption, the applicability of the money as a real value distinct from the money itself is estimable and may licitly be charged for. A worker cannot be asked to work for nothing simply because he is idle; nor can a lender with idle funds be asked to surrender their applicability freely. An employer who fails to use a worker's labor profitably still has to pay him; and a borrower who hires the applicability of money must pay for it whatever use he makes of it.[32]

Secondarily, Mastrofini argues that ownership, the full right of disposal of a good, does not pass in a loan, and a lender is therefore a bailor of money;[33] that if money can be bailed *ad pompam*, it can be bailed for use, because the price of the latter includes the price of the former and is a fortiori just;[34] that the price of money increases or decreases with the quantity available like the price of other goods; that as the State creates money, so it

---

[27] See Migne, *T.c.c.*, XVI, col. 1131.
[28] Mark Mastrofini, *Discussion sur l'usure*, trans. M.–C.– (Lyons, 1834), p. 269.
[29] p. 270.
[30] p. 275.
[31] p. 272.
[32] pp. 276, 282, 321.
[33] p. 199.
[34] p. 217.

simultaneously creates a use of money separate from its face value, as the custom of all civilized nations testifies.[35] The popes and the scholastics condemn only usury taken by force of the loan contract itself, and their condemnation is proper because the loan contract itself simply specifies the return of the object loaned.[36] But extrinsic to the loan contract is commonly understood a contract hiring the use of the object, and to collect profit by this contract is never condemnable usury.[37] As for the Scriptures, they prohibit only frauds, immoderate usury, usury which violates charity.[38]

Rejecting the old theory completely, Mastrofini still admits, indeed argues, that he asks for nothing new in practice. *Census*, he says, is simply the term used in Germany for a loan at a profit.[39] The triple contract, the exchange business, and *lucrum cessans* are dependent for their justice on the licitness of renting the use of money.[40] His opponents concede him everything except the names he fights for.

Francis X. Funk

A little later, in the middle of the century, Francis Funk, a German theologian and distinguished ecclesiastical historian, also put the weight of his scholarship at the service of the new theory. Engaged in debate with the German historians, Maximilian Neumann and William Endemann, who accused the Catholic Church of outright inconsistency in its usury doctrine, Funk took the position that money in one economy might be considered fruitful and in another, sterile.[41] In the Middle Ages, the feudal and guild systems restricted the opportunity for investment: ownership of the land was ruled by feudal agreements, while the labor supply was either in feudal vassalage or controlled by the guilds. At the same time, commerce was hampered by war, brigandage, and both national and municipal trade barriers. In this static world, where land and labor were frozen and capital accumulation difficult, money had no mobility. It could not be freely exchanged for productive goods. It could not be considered the equivalent of fruitful capital.[42] Borrowing was usually for consumption purposes, and the borrower's need gave a lender with idle cash opportunity to exploit him. The general usury prohibition was based on these general conditions.[43]

[35] pp. 220, 264.
[36] pp. 162, 423.
[37] p. 445.
[38] p. 460.
[39] p. 363.
[40] pp. 376, 398, 378.
[41] Funk, *Zins und Wucher*, p. 92.
[42] Funk, pp. 38, 48–55. In the twentieth

century, Funk's general defense of the medieval usury prohibition has been most effectively repeated by Francis Zehentbauer, *Das Zinsproblem nach Moral und Recht*, Theologische Studien der Osterreich Leo-Gesellschaft, LXXIV (Vienna, 1920), 144, 157.
[43] Funk, p. 55.

Undoubtedly, a small capitalistic class would have had a right to profit on their loans, and their right was destroyed by the general prohibition, but law is made for what happens generally, and here the majority were protected.[44]

Further, Funk continues, law, either moral or statutory, which regulates economic activities, is necessarily preceded in time by the activities regulated. Certain general moral principles, to be sure, are changeless, but their application in particular laws depends on the economic pattern of a society.[45] Such a particular law as one concerned with usury does not remain abstractly motionless, but develops with economic changes; yet as the economic changes must occur first before a change in the law is appropriate, there will always be a natural lag between economic development and modification of the law.[46] In fact, as the economic structure of Europe changed, money became capable of widespread fruitful employment, and the Church altered the law to meet the new conditions. The exceptions broadened into a general permission, according to a tendency remarked by the great legal historian Ihering, "The exception is often only the form in which the principle itself is rejuvenated." [47] Today, when loans are generally for production, money is considered fruitful, and the Church allows the general taking of interest. So Funk explains the change in practice by a change in economic circumstances, while he insists that the only dogmatic principle involved is that it is sinful to exploit your neighbor, and that this principle remains unaltered, though differently applied in different conditions.[48]

But while Funk defends medieval practice, he condemns medieval theory. The early scholastics had protected the needy borrower. But they were right for the wrong reasons.[49] They proceeded legalistically, using the abstract forms of the Roman law, without examining either the economic significance of these concepts or the moral essence of the usury law.[50] Providentially, their theoretical deficiencies led to no practical errors. But the proper theoretical approach is set out in the new theory: abandon the legal technicalities of contracts and titles; adopt one general moral principle, that no contract should injure an impoverished neighbor; and consider always the economic purposes of a loan.[51] Where money is lent for productive purposes, it should be considered a productive good and lawfully rented. It is, indeed, a positive injustice to the lender to deny him this right.[52] There is neither

---

[44] p. 62.
[45] pp. 11, 19.
[46] p. 95.
[47] p. 102.
[48] p. 197.

[49] p. 177.
[50] p. 211.
[51] pp. 23, 213.
[52] p. 222.

scriptural nor natural reason for opposing this new approach; and only a Jansenist clinging to formalism would advocate the retention of the old usury and interest title theory in today's circumstances.[53] The right to interest, taken in its old form with the conditions required by the old scholastics, would not justify many of the economic operations of the present which are advantageous to everyone; therefore it should be abandoned.[54] The pillars of the old theory are no longer standing: the transference of ownership in a loan is a determination of positive, not natural law, and if one defines ownership as an incorporeal right, it will not pass in a loan;[55] the sterility of money is no longer true today.[56] The Bible is seen to disapprove only exploitation of the poor.[57]

Still, says Funk more sternly than Mastrofini, when a borrower borrows for consumption purposes, he is in need, and the money lent is not productive; therefore to charge him for the loan is sinful usury.[58] This restriction is a severe one. But, his whole attitude implies, the case of pure consumption credit is rare. Money is normally productive, and the rent of it as a fruitful good is normally licit.

John Gury

The extent to which the new theory of usury made headway may be gauged by the fact that by the middle of the century it was not only defended in special treatises like Funk's and Maffei's, but incorporated in such a standard theological text book as the Jesuit John Gury's *Compendium theologiae moralis.* In such a work, of course, there is no great development of the argument; but it is noted without hostile comment that many believe that the rent of money as a fruitful good is today lawful.[59] Thus in the schools themselves the old scholastic theory began to be abandoned.

3. *Revival of the Civil Title*

The questions submitted to the Holy Office, it will be recalled, had concerned chiefly the validity of the civil title to interest; but the Holy Office had said nothing directly upon it, and, curiously enough, less theoretical support could be rallied for it than for the entirely new theory of usury. The truth is that it was not very much liked by either side. On the one hand, it

[53] p. 117.
[54] pp. 123, 188.
[55] p. 184.
[56] p. 161.
[57] pp. 205, 220.

[55] pp. 267, 168.
[59] J. P. Gury, *Compendium theologiae moralis* (4th ed., Tournai, 1852), *Tractatus de contractibus,* Part 2, c.6, art. 3.

was associated with the old scholastic theory in being a special interest "title" which was pleaded instead of the inherent fruitfulness of money; so that it was disliked by the radicals, who saw in its possible acceptance a barrier to the acceptance of their system.[60] On the other hand, it had been almost unanimously rejected by the old scholastics, while it had some association with the theory of Molinaeus and Salmasius, who argued that the law could determine where interest became usury; so that no defender of the old positions was very willing to espouse it.

John Gury is one of the few writers to defend the civil title. He states that the prosperity of modern society depends on credit; that therefore the State may act to issue a supply of credit by exercising eminent domain and authorizing lenders to collect interest. He adds that no compensation is necessary for those thereby deprived of their property, because the burdens and advantages of the State's action average out, and each one is sometimes benefited, sometimes hurt by the general custom of taking interest.[61] This suggestion that compensation is effected by the economic mechanism itself is the only theoretical advance over the defense of the title as propounded by Pichler.

The 1902 edition of Gury, revised by Anthony Ballerini and Thomas Sabetti, says that there is "today scarcely any doubt" about the validity of the civil title, but that there is some difference in opinion as to its foundation. Some appeal to eminent domain; others, however, "make the far better plea of the right and duty the supreme authority has of decreeing a premium to those who help commerce by supplying money. Indeed, natural equity dictates that this premium be paid by those who get a benefit from it." [62] This would seem to be a defense of the legal title as an exercise of the power to tax, employed in favor of those who perform a service for the community. Those receiving the service are held to pay the tax directly to their benefactors. This is an entirely new argument in favor of the title. It is unchanged in the 1939 American edition of Gury – Ballerini – Sabetti.[63]

The majority of writers, however, showed little enthusiasm for the title even with the new argument; and Augustine Lehmkuhl, the German Jesuit, summed up the general opinion of radicals and conservatives alike in saying that "the law finds, but does not create a title to interest." [64]

---

[60] Cf. Luzerne, III, Part 2, p. 731; Funk, p. 122.

[61] Gury, Part 2, c.6, art. 3.

[62] Gury, 9th ed., revised by A. Ballerini and T. Sabetti (New York, 1902), De contractibus, 2:1:6, n.528.

[63] Gury, 34th ed., revised by A. Ballerini, T. Sabetti, T. Barrett, and D. Creeden (New York, 1939), De contractibus, 2:1:6.

[64] Augustine Lehmkuhl, Theologia moralis (Freiburg in Br., 1910), I, n.1102.

4. *The Encyclical* Rerum novarum

In 1891 Leo XIII issued the encyclical *Rerum novarum,* "On the Condition of the Working Classes." Enumerating the evils of *laissez faire* and the exploitation of the helpless laborer, the Pope declared,

The mischief has been increased by rapacious usury, which, although more than once condemned by the Church, is nevertheless under a different guise, but with like injustice, still practiced by covetous and grasping men.[65]

What the Pope meant by usury "under a different guise" has remained obscure, and this passing reference to the evil had no effect on usury theory. Yet since this was the first papal rebuke to usury since *Vix pervenit* a century and a half before, it is important to remark that the papacy was not unmindful of the possibility of usurious injustice even in modern economic conditions.

5. *Reaffirmation of the Traditional Theory*

In the face of many defections from the scholastic theory even within scholastic ranks, one of the ablest presentations of the old theory ever made was set forth at the beginning of the twentieth century in the *De justo auctario ex contractu crediti* of Joseph Ernest Van Roey. Van Roey, then a young theologian, later cardinal-primate of Belgium, vigorously objected to the confusion of money and real capital made by the sponsors of the licitness of the rent of money. The object of a money loan, he insisted, is money, not real capital; and to treat a loan as the rent of real capital is a fundamental error in theory.[66] The consumptibility of money, not its productivity, is at the heart of the old analysis; and money's consumptibility is unchanged by its subsequent exchange for real goods.[67] Modern practice may be understood not as the rent of money, but as the universal claiming of *lucrum cessans*; for in today's economy every holder of money can employ it profitably, and to forego money's use in a loan gives every lender a right to interest.[68] Practice has changed with economic change, but the scholastic principles, which are part of Catholic doctrine, remain unchangeable and equally good in their new application.[69]

[65] Leo XIII, *Rerum novarum, S. D. N. Leonis Papae XIII Allocutiones Epistolae Constitutiones* (1893), IV, 177. For a rather broad interpretation of Leo, see Joseph Husslein, S.J., ed., *Social Wellsprings* (1949), p. 168.

[66] Van Roey, *De justo auctario ex contractu crediti,* p. 226.
[67] p. 233.
[68] p. 272.
[69] pp. 298-299.

6. Syncretist Tendencies

Elsewhere, however, no such firm declaration for the old theory as Van Roey's is to be found in the standard theological textbooks of the turn of the century. Characteristic, instead, is a statement of doctrine on usury in terms reconcilable with either old or new theory. Thus, Arthur Vermeersch, a Belgian Jesuit and perhaps the best of contemporary moral theologians, taught:

> In order that, in a certain condition of society, money can be justly lent by all at a moderate interest, it is sufficient that money be commonly estimated according to the hope of a fruitful use of it or according to the credit which it gives. For then, from this hope the possession of money draws a *value* of which the creditor is deprived for a time and whose compensation he justly demands through interest.[70]

This statement can be interpreted either as a presentation of the right to interest as *lucrum cessans* or as a variation of the theory which holds that money can be treated as a fruitful good because it is convertible into a fruitful good. Vermeersch inclines to the former theory, as is clear in his later warning that usury is to be presumed when, as in China and India, the rate of interest exceeds the return from investments.[71] But, as Van Roey objected, his approach might be understood as a recognition that money could be treated as a fruitful good itself.[72]

Similarly, the French Sulpician, Adam Tanquerey, author of a popular theological textbook, taught that money was, in today's economy, virtually fecund and could be rented at a profit because the lender always suffered *lucrum cessans*: a statement of the case that in effect combines the two theories.[73] The German Jesuit, Jerome Noldin, declared that money was today readily substitutable for fruitful goods and that therefore anyone surrendering its use deprived himself of an estimable good; and here again the appeal is equally to *lucrum cessans* and to the fecundity of money.[74]

At the same time the new theory of usury won a clear victory when the tendency became general to reject the old claim that Luke 6:35 was a strict precept forbidding all profit on a loan, and to take it as a counsel of perfection only.[75]

[70] Arthur Vermeersch, *Quaestiones de justitia* (Bruges, 1901), n.375:2, p. 483.

[71] Vermeersch, *Theologiae moralis principia-responsa-consilia* (Bruges, 1924), II, n.450.

[72] Van Roey, p. 265.

[73] Adam Tanquerey, *Synopsis theologiae moralis et pastoralis* (New York, 1904), III, n.903.

[74] Jerome Noldin, *Summa theologiae moralis* (New York, 1906), II, n.570–571; Lehmkuhl, I, n.1102.

[75] See Vermeersch, *Quaestiones*, n.358:1:b, p. 443; Tanquerey, III, n.868. Noldin, II, 585:2, and Lehmkuhl, I, n.1097, are less clear.

7. The New Code of Canon Law

A final formal step in the acceptance of general interest-taking occurred with the issue in 1917 of the new *Codex iuris canonici*. This monumental codification replaced all earlier collections of canon law, such as Gratian, the *Decretals* of Gregory IX, and the *Extravagantes*, and became the sole statute book of the universal Church. The many and complicated responses, decrees, and bulls on usury of the old canon law are now summed up in a single rule:

> If a fungible thing is given someone, and later something of the same kind and amount is to be returned, no profit can be taken on the ground of this contract; but in lending a fungible thing it is not itself illicit to contract for payment of the profit allocated by law, unless it is clear that this is excessive, or even for a higher profit, if a just and adequate title be present.[76]

The Code did embolden the defenders of the legal title to interest. The Dominican Dominic Prummer declared for the validity of this title in the absence of all others,[77] and the Jesuit Thomas Iorio said that the new canon, which was the long-awaited answer of the Holy See to the nineteenth-century inquiries about the *lex principis*, clearly and certainly approved the civil title as self-sufficient.[78]

But Vermeersch, a more expert canonist, saw no specific approval of the civil title in the canon,[79] and the American Jesuits T. L. Bouscaren and A. C. Ellis, in a standard commentary on the new Code, declared that the canon "states implicitly that in modern times there is always present in such a loan some just reason for demanding the legal rate of interest. . . . The canon, however, deliberately avoids determining what these just reasons are, leaving that to Catholic moralists and economists to determine."[80] Moreover, the canon itself speaks of legal interest which may be excessive and hence immoral, so that it is clearly implied that the law by itself does not create a right to interest.

Aside from the revival of speculation about the legal title, the Code affected usury theory in no way, and the general state of opinion remained substantially that of the beginning of the century with syncretist presentations of the usury theory dominant.

[76] *Codex iuris canonici* (Rome, 1920), c.1735.
[77] Dominic Prummer, *Manuale theologiae moralis* (Freiburg in Br., 1923), XI:2:1:4.
[78] Thomas Iorio, *Theologia moralis* (Naples, 1946), II:831, 834.
[79] Vermeersch, *Theologiae moralis*, II, n.450.
[80] T. Bouscaren and A. C. Ellis, *Canon Law* (Milwaukee, 1947), p. 780.

8. *Pius XII*

The most recent official ecclesiastical pronouncement on any matter related to the usury theory occurred in an allocution of Pius XII to the employees and directors of the Bank of Rome on June 19, 1950. The Pope's remarks are by no means of dogmatic force, but they have more authority than those of a private individual, and they indicate clearly the modern ecclesiastical position on systematic profit from the creation of credit. Felicitating the group on their piety, the Pope declares that he takes the opportunity "to define clearly" his view on an "unhealthy" and oppressive opinion which held that "the banking system was by its nature stained with guilt," that the banking profession inevitably exposed one to the danger of losing eternal salvation, and that bankers ran a great risk of becoming too attached to material riches. The Pope vigorously repudiates this opinion. Banking can be, and has been, abused, but he finds no inherent iniquity in the system. Bankers "earn their livelihood honestly." His approval, he emphasizes, is intended not only for employees of a bank, but for "the financier in the proper sense of the word." He stresses that it is the banking *system* which he approves. A banking system has always been necessary to society; it is the heart of the economic organism. The banking system has power, utility, and responsibility; it is essentially honest.[81]

Conclusion

This brief survey of the two centuries since St. Alphonsus and Benedict XIV reveals the following developments:

1. A slight development in practice, so that the custom of making a profit on money loans is held to be just without doubt or scruple, and the reigning Pope can publicly praise the banking system. The change is small,

---

[81] Pius XII, Allocution, June 19, 1950. Reported in *L'Osservatore Romano* (Vatican City, June 19–20, 1950), p. 1. The most important section of the text runs as follows:

"Mentre pertanto vi rivolgiamo questa meritata lode, veniamo con cio stesso a definire chiaramente la Nostra posizione di fronte ad una concezione non sana e non rispondente a 'quella liberta a cui Cristo ci ha affrancati' (Gal. 5:1). Come, cioè, se il sistema bancario forse per natura sua macchiato di colpa. Come se l'esercizio della vostra professione e l'oggetto stesso del vostro lavoro vi mettersero inevitabilmente in pericolo di contaminare il

vostro cuore. Come se a voi fosse piu particolarmente difficile di liberare l'animo vostro dall'attacamento ai bene effermi e fallaci, di passare attraverso la fiamma delle richezze temporali in guisa da non perdere i tesori eterni. Voi avanzate nella vostra carriera come gli altri nella loro — e forse spesso la percorrete confatica — guadagnando onestamente la vita per voi e per i vostri curi.

"Tutto cio vale no solo per il modesto subalterno nel suo lavoro di semplice esecuzione e di computiste-meria, ma equalmente per gli alti impiegati della finanza, per il finanziere nel senso proprio della parola."

because probably most lenders in 1750 believed they had some contract or title to justify their profit, though the scrupulous might hesitate.

2. A considerable development in pure theology in the general abandonment of the position that "Lend, hoping nothing thereby" was an absolute prohibition of all gain on a loan.

3. A merging of the defenses of the contracts of the old scholastic theory such as the redeemable, personal *census* and the triple contract in the general plea of *lucrum cessans*, and simultaneously an expansion of this right so that it could be used by everyone in an economically flourishing society.

4. Considerable defection from the old scholastic theory of usury even among Catholic theologians, and finally the creation by the canon law itself of a presumption in favor of the legal rate of interest, while the Code and the leading commentators on it hold that the legal rate may be excessive. The usury rule, sapped of its vitality in modern economic conditions, is not abandoned, but so limited in the likelihood of its applicability that profit on credit transactions is made the norm, and usury the exceptional case of unjust exaction.

CHAPTER XX

THE USURY THEORY AND SOME HISTORIANS

The present chapter reviews some modern accounts of the usury theory with a view to marking where they disagree from the preceding pages. These areas of disagreement sometimes result from a difference in emphasis, sometimes from a difference in motivation. The reader must judge for himself the soundness of the criticisms here offered.

1. The "Barren-Metal" Dogma

Probably the most conventional, as it is the most dramatic, account of the usury theory declares that the theory rested on "the dogma of the unfruitfulness of money." This dogma, usually attributed to Aristotle, is asserted to be the foundation stone of usury analysis, at the same time that it is interpreted to mean that the scholastics denied that money could be used productively. For example, the noted French historian, Henry Hauser, in his *Les débuts du capitalisme*, declares that the economic sterility of money was "the heart of the scholastic theory of usury" and adds the astonishing information that John Calvin "discovered the fertility of money." [1] James Westfall Thompson, in his widely used *Economic and Social History of the Later Middle Ages*, similarly teaches that only at the end of the fifteenth century did "men realize that money might be productive by itself." [2] Ernest Troeltsch, in his influential *The Social Teachings of the Christian Churches*, also asserts that the scholastic theory rested largely on Aristotle. [3] This attribution of the scholastic theory to Aristotelian views on money is made not just in such general surveys or popular textbooks. A more specialized work, such as Francis Funk's *Zins und Wucher*, insists that the usury prohibition rested on the unproductivity of money, [4] and, most authoritatively, William Endemann, in his comprehensive *Studien in der romanisch-kanonistischen Wirthschafts- und Rechtslehre bis gegen Ende des siebenzehnten Jahrhunderts*, says that

[1] Henry Hauser, *Les débuts du capitalisme* (Paris, 1927), pp. 54, 60.
[2] Thompson, *Economic and Social History*, p. 434. See also Will Durant, *The Age of Faith* (New York, 1950), p. 630.
[3] Troeltsch, *The Social Teachings of the Christian Churches*, I, 320.
[4] Funk, *Zins und Wucher*, p. 125.

the prohibition was based on "the dogma of the sterility of money."[5]

There is, of course, a large element of truth in these presentations. The scholastics in supporting the usury rule consistently refused to identify money with the goods it buys; in this sense, for the purposes of the usury discussion, they unanimously considered money to be sterile. In other contexts, discussing *societas, lucrum cessans,* and restitution of the profits of a usurer, they did not choose this viewpoint but looked on money as productive. If the viewpoint adopted on these questions had been taken on money in loans, it would have been difficult to maintain the theoretical justification of the absolute prohibition.

Yet a distinction must be drawn between the meanings of the "sterility of money" in scholastic usage. The key concept of the usury theory was that money was a consumptible in first use. This is a legal determination based on a fact as indisputable now as then. Money cannot be spent without being consumed; the legal determination based on this is that it cannot be transferred in use without being transferred in ownership. Such juridical sterility is formally compatible with the economic fertility of money considered from a different viewpoint. The scholastics subscribed to the viewpoint that insisted on juridical sterility. But real economic sterility in the Aristotelian sense that it is unnatural for money to be a source of income was only a secondary support for the usury theory. Its appeal was chiefly popular. It was criticized by such leading scholastics as Andreae and Summenhart. It became unimportant in the sixteenth and seventeenth centuries. At no time was it consistently applied by the scholastics to all credit transactions. Moreover, its force may be gauged by this: the unanimous tradition asserted that the economically sterile rent of money *ad pompam* was lawful.

Still, all the popular accounts we have mentioned and even Endemann's history assert or imply that scholastics made their doctrine turn on the economic fruitlessness of money. These assertions and implications are misleading. Funk is equally at fault in implying that money was "sterile" in the Middle Ages and "fertile" today. Of course, investment opportunities abounded at one time and not at the other; and if the foundation of the usury theory is taken to be the lack of investment opportunity in the Middle Ages, there is no great inaccuracy in expressing this view in terms of the sterility of money. But there is danger of confusion, for if the terms are used in the scholastic sense, money is always sterile if taken by itself, and it is always fertile if it is identified with what it buys.

Certainly the "barren-metal" concept is a cliché which was a battle cry,

---

[5] Endemann, II, 359; see also his "Die nationalokonomischen Grundsätze der kan- onistichen Lehre," in *Jahrbücher für National- okonomie und Statistik* (1863), I, 720.

a battle cry used by some scholastics and more often attributed to them by their opponents from Calvin to Mastrofini. But it conceals the real issue at stake: is money to be identified with the goods it buys? As Calvin says, no one doubts that money kept in a box is sterile; the scholastics' critics do not deny that. Similarly, no one doubts that money invested in a fruitful enterprise yields a return: the scholastics do not deny that. What the scholastics mean by maintaining the sterility of money is that money should properly be considered by itself without identifying it with the capital or consumer goods for which it may be exchanged. What the scholastics' critics mean by asserting the "fertility of money" is that they have identified money with real capital. The choice between these two ways of considering money is a real one, and modern monetary economists such as Kurt Wicksell and Lord Keynes would say that the scholastic choice is the theoretically correct one: money, not real capital, is what is loaned in a money loan.[6]

2. *A Labor Theory of Value*

Related to the account which founds usury theory on the economic sterility of money is the account which attributes to the scholastics a labor theory of value. Thus the Dominican historian Bede Jarrett, in *Saint Antonio and Medieval Economics*, writes that St. Antoninus insisted on the labor theory of value "which Marx has made so popular."[7] So R. H. Tawney, the English sociologist, declares that St. Thomas Aquinas taught a labor theory of value and that consequently "the last of the Schoolmen was Karl Marx."[8]

The fundamental error of both authors is the belief that theorists are always completely consistent with themselves: since the scholastics denied a reward to capital, these interpreters seem to reason, they must have done so because they considered labor to be the sole source of lawful gain; consequently they anticipated the economics of Marx. Usury was condemned because it was profit without work; the usury theory was only part of a larger opposition to workless gain.

Unlike the socialists, however, the scholastics are dominated by no such single, consistent doctrine. The opposition to laborless profit is a minor argument against usury. But it is by no means fundamental, and the usual medieval treatment of the *census* and the *societas* runs along lines entirely foreign to labor-value theory. In these contracts, reward to the factors of pro-

[6] John Maynard Keynes, *The General Theory of Employment, Interest, and Money* (London, 1936), pp. 167, 352; cf. Bernard Dempsey, *Interest and Usury* (Washington, 1943), pp. 8, 219–220.

[7] Bede Jarrett, *Saint Antonio and Medieval Economics* (St. Louis, 1914), p. 64.

[8] Tawney, *Religion and the Rise of Capitalism*, pp. 36, 40.

duction is assigned on legal, not economic grounds, and there is no attempt
to restrict the capitalist's profit to his share of the risk. In the later scholastic
analysis, the development of these forms of credit into the triple contract
and the guaranteed *census*, and the acceptance of exchange banking, show
conclusively how far from Marxian economics the main scholastic tradition
stood.

3. The Just Price

A third common view of usury theory makes the prohibition of usury a
simple deduction from the rule of the just price and usury theory a part of
the theory of the just price. This view is advanced by Selma Hagenauer,
Edmund Schreiber, George O'Brien, and Patrick Cleary.[9] Cleary is writing
primarily as an apologist, anxious to justify the Church's permission of interest today, while defending its consistency with the earlier theory. Consequently, he declares that the just price of money has changed: at the
time of the Council of Vienne, 100 in hand was worth only 100 a year
later; now 100 in cash is worth 110 or 115 a year later. The Church condemned usury at Vienne because a premium on money violated the just
price; it allows a premium on money today, because the just price is thereby kept. The others writers, presumably acting as simple historians, are
misled not by a moralistic motive, but, like Tawney and Jarrett, by the
belief that the scholastics are entirely consistent in their approach to economics. They suppose that the just-price theory is the general theory under
which all the scholastic investigations of economics may be subsumed because this supposition produces the assumed consistency.

But that an author will be consistent is at best a tentative hypothesis,
and it is dangerous to reject the evidence of clearly divergent approaches
on the simple hope that the writer had one master plan by which he worked.
Nor is apologetics served by a distortion of the facts. In truth, as we have
seen, the theory of the just price and the theory of usury come from different
origins. The idea of the just price was based on a concept of value as something determined by subjective desires and by the available supply, varying as
desires and supply varied. Usury theory was completely committed to the concept of an unvarying value. To be sure, theorists on the just price insisted that
when a price was set by law, it must be maintained, and if the face value
of money is considered to be its legal price, the just-price theory would

---

[9] Hagenauer, p. 90; Schreiber, *Die volks-
wirtschaftlichen Anschauungen*, p. 115; George
O'Brien, *Essay on Medieval Economic Theory*
(London, 1920), pp. 134 and 182; Patrick
Cleary, *The Church and Usury* (Dublin, 1914),
p. 201.

also lead to the conclusion that no premium beyond the face value be asked. But the moment money is considered in any way other than as a legal measure, the just-price theory offers no bar to a profit made from lending it, and as we have seen, the great effort of the later scholastics to legitimize certain types of contracts centered on the transferring of these contracts from the jurisdiction of the usury prohibition to the jurisdiction of the just price. Here the usury theory and the just-price theory clearly lead to contradictory results. Moreover, even in medieval times, as we have emphasized, cases on credit sales involving the just price are sharply differentiated from cases on credit sales involving usury. No account, therefore, could be more confusing than those which make the usury theory not only harmonious with the just-price theory, but actually a deduction from it.

4. Theological Superstition

Yet another view of the usury theory sees it as entirely merged with theology. "'Mutuum date, nihil inde sperantes,'" Endemann has quoted. "In these words are contained the entire source of the usury theory," and he goes on to lament the influence exerted by this theological rule unrelated to the needs of economic life.[10] Even more tendentiously, William Lecky, in his History of the Rise and Influence of the Spirit of Rationalism in Europe, a classic of nineteenth-century liberalism, has argued that the usury prohibition, a creation of dogmatic superstition, was finally routed by the new rationalism in Europe.[11] Such other noted nineteenth-century critics of clericalism as Andrew White and H. C. Lea have vigorously assented to Lecky's view and have joined him in celebrating the disappearance of the usury prohibition as a triumph of the liberal reason over authoritarian dogma.[12]

That the usury theory was born of, and nurtured by, theology is indisputable, although it is clearly a mistake for Endemann to restrict the theological source to a single text which was neither decisive in the formative years of usury speculation, nor of any real influence in the sixteenth and seventeenth centuries which Endemann specially treats. As for Lecky, Lea, and White, their bias is too well known to require demonstration. Yet their charge here is specious. Clearly, simple dogma is dominant in the medieval

[10] Endemann, Studien in der romanisch-kanonistichen, II, 359.

[11] William Lecky, History of the Rise and Influence of the Spirit of Rationalism in Europe (London, 1904), II, 258ff.

[12] Andrew D. White, The History of the Warfare of Science with Theology in Christendom (New York, 1922), II, 264; Henry Charles Lea, "The Ecclesiastical Treatment of Usury," Yale Review, II (February 1894), 375, 384–385.

period, while later the medieval theory is modified by writers appealing frankly to nature and reason against the past. Clearly, there is a development of doctrine in which rational investigation plays a decisive role. Clearly, the resultant usury rule has not the force or sweep that the early law had possessed. But to recite these facts is not to prove that the medieval theory was pure theology, nor that the later theory broke completely from the old, nor that the development was due to the rise of rationalism. Lecky, Lea, and White ignore the large amount of rational construction in the early usury theory and the fact that both interest titles and alternative methods of credit, besides the loan, are integral parts of medieval doctrine. Indeed, more rigorist than the medieval rigorists themselves, they persist in regarding all forms of interest and profit on all kinds of credit extension as usury, and they refuse to admit that interest titles and the other contracts of credit were put forward sincerely and in good faith. They are thus more Catholic than the pope. At the same time they do not remark that the great development of interest titles and alternative methods of credit occurred in response to a great expansion in European commerce and owes as much to a change in economic conditions as to a change in speculative viewpoint. Finally, and above all, they do not see that what modification occurred was essentially effected by the scholastic writers of the sixteenth and seventeenth centuries, not by rationalists in the nineteenth-century sense of the term — that is, men freed from faith and allegiance to authority. The work was done by thorough dogmatists, and it cannot reasonably be ascribed to the emancipated reason celebrated by the later liberals. It is difficult to imagine men less rationalistic in the Victorian sense than such typical scholastics as Molina and Navarrus, yet it was such men who accomplished the real changes in the usury theory. To cite these changes as a triumph for rationalism is as sound history as making communism responsible for the Glorious Revolution of 1688 on the grounds that both Communists and Whigs believe in revolutions. The moderate, disciplined, and cautious appeal to reason by a seventeenth-century theologian is a far cry from the unrestrained rationalism whose victory is proclaimed by Lecky, Lea, and White.

Moreover, as far as dogma in the technical Catholic sense is concerned, there is only one dogma at stake. Dogma is not to be loosely used as synonymous with every papal rule or theological verdict. Dogma is a defined, revealed doctrine taught by the Church at all times and places. Nothing here meets the test of dogma except this assertion, that usury, the act of taking profit on a loan without a just title, is sinful. Even this dogma is not specifically, formally defined by any pope or council. It is, however, taught by the tradition of the Church, as witnessed by papal bulls and briefs, conciliar acts, and theological opinion. This dogmatic teaching remains unchanged. What is a just title, what is technically to be treated as a loan, are matters of debate, positive law, and changing evaluation. The development on these points is great. But the pure and narrow dogma is the same today as in 1200.

5. An "Attenuation in Love"

A sociological approach having certain distant ties with Lecky's is advanced in Benjamin Nelson's *The Idea of Usury*. Nelson's thesis, taken from Henry Sumner Maine and Max Weber, is this: Originally men are united as brothers within the blood relations of a tribe, while they regard the men outside the tribe, "the others," as enemies, in relation to whom no ethical restrictions apply. Gradually, however, the religious sense of brotherhood within the tribe and the warlike exploitation of the stranger are both replaced by an economic calculus governing all relations. "Brotherhood" now becomes competitive, not coöperative, at the same time that it becomes universal and not tribal. To use Nelson's slogan, "all men become brothers" but by becoming equally "others." [13]

This general thesis, Nelson declares, is demonstrated in a particular case by the history of the Judaic-Christian tradition on usury as illustrated by different ages' interpretation of Deuteronomy 23:19-26, "Thou shalt not lend to a brother money at usury, nor corn, nor any other thing. But to the stranger." The text itself, Nelson says, is a striking example of the pure tribal concepts of blood brotherhood and free exploitation of the stranger. The first step in the development of these early notions occurs with the efforts of medieval Christianity to preserve religious brotherhood and simultaneously to extend it to all, by prohibiting the taking of usury from either brothers or strangers. The last step is the complete triumph in the eighteenth century of a capitalistic exegesis, in which both tribal discrimination and religious prohibition totally disappear. Today, Nelson says, the "transvaluation of values" is perfected; the world has become one at the price of an "attenuation in love." [14]

The soundness of Maine's and Weber's general position is not a subject to be investigated here. But Nelson's particular demonstration of it in regard to usury analysis is simply the manipulation of history in the interests of a thesis. Like Lecky, he makes the cardinal error of treating interest and usury as identical. This basic confusion precludes any rational discussion

[13] Nelson, *The Idea of Usury*, pp. vii–viii.   [14] *Ibid.*, pp. xv–xxi, 135–138.

of the growth or change of usury theory, which at all times and in all places assumed that under some conditions interest might be lawful. He also refuses to consider the possibilities for profit on other credit transactions besides the loan. Thus on the one hand, he postulates a certain mystic abhorrence of making a profit from a brother, an abhorrence springing from the particular state of social development of medieval folk, and on the other hand, he leaves unexplained and indeed unmentioned the fact that this abhorrence extended to only one peculiar type of economic operation.

On charity and brotherhood there is no significant development reflected in eight hundred years of scholastic opinion. Cardinal De Lugo is as opposed to economic exploitation as Cardinal Courçon; St. Alphonsus' concept of charity is no whit less zealous than St. Antoninus'. Usury theory is modified, but it is modified in response to changes in economic conditions or as a result of more thorough investigation of the rational demands of justice. Its modification reflects no transvaluation of values and no attenuation in love.[15]

6. A Condemnation of Capitalism

So far we have considered primarily or professedly historical descriptions of the usury theory. Now we shall examine a group of authors who clearly are chiefly interested in influencing current practice, but who are compelled to indulge in certain historical descriptions to support their practical prescriptions. We challenge here only the accuracy of their history.

Let us note first a group of Catholic extremists, who condemn by the usury prohibition all cases of capitalistic finance. These authors' interpretation of the usury prohibition is not much different from that of Lecky or Nelson, but writing as Catholics they come to different practical con-

[15] Lewis Haney, *The History of Economic Thought*, pp. 102–103. A view similar to Nelson's is advanced. Haney writes, "The social organizations with which Biblical writers, Aristotle, and the schoolmen alike were associated were non-capitalistic and largely self-sufficient. They were not exchange economies. The political counterpart of this industrial condition was a predominance of clan or family feeling, a feeling which appears in the guild, and even in the medieval municipality. This explains to a large extent the general condemnation of interest-taking. Loans at interest generally involve a rather abstract or impersonal relation between the parties, such as became common with the establishment of a money economy. Even to-day the purely business relation is apt to become unsatisfactory when existing among relatives or persons belonging to the same social organization, and the condemnation of usury was natural when most of a man's dealings were with such persons."

Again, we must ask, were not the *societas* and the *census* abstract, money relationships? Were curial canonists like Hostiensis and Innocent IV living in a more brotherly organization than Lugo or St. Alphonsus? Did not the entire scholastic theory of usury develop in a money economy?

clusions from their common starting point. They identify all interest sought as profit with usury and hold that most interest taken today is usurious. But they do not condemn the Church for changing her teaching: they excuse her by pleading that she only tolerates an evil she cannot prevent. She tolerates a social order founded on usury, they assert, as she once tolerated a social order founded on slavery, but she maintains the objective sinfulness of the practice. Meanwhile, until a better day comes, the poor and helpless Christian who is entangled by economic forces may lawfully take interest by one title: the title of occult compensation by which the victim recovers covertly in the shape of interest the interest stolen from him by others.[16] These views were first set forth by Karl von Vogelsang, and they were subsequently developed by his disciples, Aloysius Wiesinger and Anton Orel, two Austrian Cistercians.[17] Of an impractical and romantic character, the views have had no reception beyond central Europe.

The theological impossibilities involved in the Viennese school's position have been pointed out by such authors as the German Jesuits Joseph Biederlack and Augustine Lehmkuhl;[18] but leaving theology aside, we may note the historical inaccuracies involved. What the Viennese have done is to take the old medieval theory of usury, strip it of its later modifications and even of the allowances it made for forms of credit other than the loan, and apply the denuded theory to a vastly changed economy. They are unfaithful to the scholastic tradition in its developed form, and they do not accurately or fully present even the medieval theory. The result of their labors is as bizarre as might be expected if a section of any law, ripped from its context, were applied in this truncated form to much changed conditions. Seeking to revive the past, they ignore the history of the past, and their theory is not so much an anachronism as a novelty.

7. A Ban on Consumption Credit

Not so unmeasured in their cries as the Viennese monks, but lamenting not far from them, have been certain English Catholic laymen, of whom the most prominent are J. A. Benvinisti and Hilaire Belloc. Benvinisti, in a work ominously entitled *The Iniquitous Contract*, takes the position that profit on consumption loans is probably unjust and that professional moneylending for profit cannot be justified by interest titles which are supposed to be solely compensatory.[19] Hilaire Belloc holds that interest on production

[16] Anton Orel, *Oeconomia perennis* (Mainz, 1930), pp. 224ff., pp. 301ff.

[17] Cf. August Knoll, *Der Zins in der*

Scholastik (Innsbruck, 1933), p. 168.

[18] *Ibid.*, p. 182.

[19] J. A. Benvinisti, *The Iniquitous Contract:*

loans alone is justified and that profit on loans to states for consumption purposes is particularly usurious; he implies that the present order is dominated by international usurers.[20]

As practical judgments on the present, these views do not properly fall within the scope of this study; but since they also purport to be a faithful continuation of the medieval tradition on usury, it is necessary here to point out how they distort this tradition. Their chief distinction, between consumption and production loans, is totally unfounded; and while Maffei and Funk are untraditional in making the productive character of a loan an excuse for approving a profit on it, Benvinisti and Belloc are equally unhistorical in making the consumption uses of a loan an excuse for rejecting interest on it. Benvinisti ignores the later scholastic developments when he refuses to admit that professional moneylending can be justified by the interest titles. Belloc is even more lacking in historical perspective when he denounces profit on credit extended to states and when he decries international moneylenders: historically the scholastics always approved the annuities which were the earliest form of state deficit finance, and historically, the exchange bankers, international financiers on a grand scale, were encouraged by the Church and approved by the developed scholastic theory. Again, authors professedly appealing to history have remade history to support their preconceived positions.

8. A Prohibition of Credit Creation

Far more scientific and subtle than the rhetoric of the Viennese circle and the indignation of Belloc and Benvinisti is the criticism launched against the present order under the banner of the usury theory by Bernard Dempsey. Dempsey, a contemporary American Jesuit, presents his findings as the results of an historical comparison; however, they are not only history, but a moral judgment on the present. We shall consider them only as they relate to an understanding of the historical usury theory. They center on the morality of the American banking system.

In Dempsey's work, *Interest and Usury*, a study of the interest theories of the modern economists, Kurt Wicksell, John Maynard Keynes, Joseph Schumpeter, Irving Fisher, and Ludwig von Mises, is undertaken, and a comparison then instituted between their views on the price of money and the usury analyses of Molina, Lessius, and Lugo. Dempsey finds that where the modern economists find an important source of economic disequilibrium,

An Analysis of Usury and Maldistribution (London, 1937), p. 10.   [20] Hilaire Belloc, *The Restoration of Property* (New York, 1936), p. 14.

in the credit creation of modern banking,[21] the scholastics would find usury; and he himself finds the modern banking system guilty, by scholastic standards, of "institutional usury." His position is that the scholastics' principles imply that no credit can be created, unless the creating agency foregoes income equal to the credit it has produced. Accordingly, what is in Dempsey's eyes usury, what he formally describes as *lucrum ex mutuo*, is *any* profit arising from credit creation, considered in its total effects, obtained by *any* person who did not acquire a right to the profit by suffering *lucrum cessans.*[22]

[21] The economists studied all agree in rejecting the nineteenth century's confusion of money and real goods, in treating interest as the price paid for money, not productive capital, and in believing that time as such adds no new values to the economy. See Dempsey, pp. 186–187. Their approach is thus in some ways very close to the scholastic one, and certain of their emphases constitute a vindication of the scholastic approach so scorned by the nineteenth-century schools of economics.

[22] Dempsey, pp. 209, 228. A second argument against the banking system which Dempsey's book suggests (pp. 199–201) may be worth examining in some detail, to bring out the character of the scholastic theory as applied to modern banking. The banking system, taken as a whole, loans credit far in excess of its cash reserves. It cannot, however, be said to suffer *lucrum cessans*, for the creation of credit and its lending are simultaneous operations, and, if the banking system did not loan, it would not create deposits which are the basis of its continued expansion: "In a sense the bank is having its cake and eating it, too. It is lending the depositors at interest its own credit, namely the right to draw money on demand, and then keeping part of the credit it has loaned" (E. Kemmerer, *Money*, New York, 1935, p. 41). In fact, the American banking system keeps most of the credit it has loaned and yet draws interest on all of it. The credit created was never intended for business investment: there is no sacrifice of alternative investment opportunity in lending it. The credit is produced *ad hoc* and almost *ex nihilo* to satisfy the demand for money in loans. If *lucrum cessans*, stretched as liberally as possible, is the general title for purging loans of usury today, the banking system is in serious plight. It may be objected, however, that if each individual bank acts justly in charging *lucrum cessans*, the whole system must perforce act justly, as the whole is only the sum of its parts. To this objection, it might be replied that often incorporation in an organic system changes the function of the incorporated units. As a part of the banking system, an individual bank collaborates in building up the credit structure of the system; as a member of the system, when one bank draws on its reserve of claims on other banks in order to lend, it sacrifices a claim to value which it has itself helped to create. As members of a system creating money to lend at a profit, the banks are coöperators in the total result produced; and their actions must be considered jointly. As participants in the system, all individual banks create credit for loans, and they no longer have the right to claim *lucrum cessans* which they had, considered abstractly and in isolation. As the system as a whole, and as the individual banks as part of the sytsem, have no right to charge for *lucrum cessans* or *carentia pecuniae* on their deposit creation, and as these are the most common titles to interest, a *prima facie* case has been made out that the banking system is usurious.

Such is Dempsey's argument in expanded form. Let us, in place of it, use the conventional scholastic tests. First of all, from the strictest standpoint, considering all their transactions as formal loans, the later scholastics would teach that the banks might charge (1) for their assumption of risk; (2) for all expenses necessarily incurred by their loans, including rent, office expenditures, and wages sufficient to support all the employees and to pay executives a salary in proportion to the responsibility of their office; (3) for their undertaking the obligation of being ready to lend, a burden distinct from either the act of lending or any expenses incurred in

Three examples he gives will show more clearly what he means. If a banking system creates funds *ad hoc* to purchase war bonds, it creates credit without suffering *lucrum cessans*. An inflation results, which injures some persons who remain uncompensated for this injury. At the same time, "in the case of all persons who participate in war-time profits, we have a *lucrum ex mutuo*, arising from the fact that the lending operations cause a rise in the price of products of war-time industry." [23]

Again, if a businessman borrows from a bank and is financed by creation of credit, he gains new purchasing power which he has not earned by past productive services. At the same time, the new addition to the general money supply will produce an inflationary effect which will sustain the price of his goods, while consumers suffer a consequent loss in purchasing power. Both the net gain and loss to any particular person from this process may be extremely diffused. The inflationary effect may be so spread out that consumers hardly notice it. The businessman may lose most of his initial gain in paying interest. The bank may receive what to it is only a negligible return. Yet, says Dempsey:

an erratic element has been introduced into the pricing process; someone has entered the market for the common appraisal with a significant handicap; there is

lending; and (4) for the *lucrum cessans* suffered by the investors of the original capital of the bank, which is proportionately and partly consumed by every loan the bank makes, so that the bank has on this ground alone a right to charge an interest rate sufficient to pay a dividend equal to the amount its invested capital would regularly gain in other enterprises. These four titles are available, according to the scholastic theory, to every bank considered as an individual or as part of a system. The system does not affect their validity in the least.

Moreover, according to scholastic standards, much of a bank's business need not be considered as consisting in formal loans at all. Most obviously, the purchases of government bonds, which make up a substantial part of the banking system's credit creation, might be considered as the implicit purchase of insured, redeemable, or nonredeemable *census*, founded on the tax revenues. Credit extensions to business, where the credit is specifically designated for productive or commercial uses, and where the rate of interest is below the probable profits from the business, might be regarded as implicit, secured partnerships. The name *contractus trinus* has disappeared;

but such contracts are substantially the same today as in Augsburg in 1573. Again, as with the *census*, the profit on such a contract would be ruled not by the available interest titles, but by the common estimation of the proper reward of such investments. Finally, one might follow Soto and Molina and consider all creation of credit on the books of a bank as the guaranteeing of future payments by the bank of any debts contracted by its depositors; and the bank might morally charge what is the common price set on the service of such a guarantor.

Thus from half a dozen different angles the business of modern banking could be analyzed and found licit. These alternative analyses, too, would follow not only the general doctrine of the later scholastics, but their spirit: to interpret the maximum of normal commerce leniently, to place the best construction possible on a contract, to give full credit to good intentions, to accept what businessmen and bankers accept in their dealing with each other.

[23] Dempsey, p. 222. Here he specifically states that he is not now considering the morality of the interest payments at all.

some price which is not a common price and somewhere a gain from a loan, to which no adequate title corresponds. No single person, perhaps, would be convicted by a Scholastic author of the sin of usury. But the process has operated usuriously; again we meet systematic or institutional usury.[24]

Dempsey also finds the following transaction usurious: a bank does not lend, but makes an investment, for which it pays by a deposit creation in favor of the seller; an inflation ensues as a result of the credit creation; the asset bought by the bank appreciates, while currency depreciates. The bank pays off its debt to its depositor in the now depreciated currency; then it sells its asset and participates in the consequent contraction of credit, in which the money it now holds from the sale becomes increasingly valuable. The bank's gain is pronounced usurious.[25]

In each case, and in general, it is clear that what Dempsey is interested in is the effect that credit creation has in altering the purchasing power of money, and the consequent loss and gain distributed to persons because of this alteration. Gain from credit creation becomes usury in his sense of the term, which he also asserts is the scholastic sense. Of course, one may define words as one chooses; and even within a settled legal doctrine, expansion of a concept may be fruitful. Dempsey's analysis is suggestive and stimulating. But we may fairly object to his attempt to find historical justification for his position in Molina, Lessius, and Lugo. He considers none of their writing on the credit creation of their time, the exchange contracts; he ignores their explicit commendation of deposit banking. Relying solely on the texts dealing explicitly with usury, he departs even then from the accepted scholastic usage. Usury to the scholastics is not "gain from a loan," taken to mean gain by any and all possible beneficiaries of the loan. Usury is gain from a loan sought directly by lenders without a just title. In the first two cases Dempsey gives, no gain is sought without a title by a bank charging its usual small fee for its services. The gain, as he admits, goes not to the lender, but to "war-time industry" and the entrepreneur with increased purchasing power. In the second case it is the borrower who commits usury, not the lender. In the third case, a loan does not even occur; Dempsey has not distinguished credit creation and lending. In general, he has tried to show "a radical kinship" between the scholastic theory of usury and the modern economists' approach; and he has produced as the scholastic theory what is only a restatement, with serious moral implications, of the economists' theory. The similarity between his view of usury and the scholastic view is largely verbal.

[24] p. 225.   [25] p. 277.

Conclusion

In general, leaving aside the prejudice attributable to religious interest or practical motive, it is clear that almost all the historical errors about the scholastic usury theory arise from a single failure: a failure to consider the theory broadly enough, to take into account either the multiple character of its foundations, theological, economic, and legal, or the multiple aspects it presented in practice, particularly the aspects under which it encouraged the growth of interest titles and above all the use of alternative methods of credit besides the loan. There has been a temptation to restrict the usury theory to some very simple base, be it the unfruitfulness of money, the just price, the labor theory of value, or the arbitrary fiat of ecclesiastical authority; there has been a tendency to consider the usury prohibition as if it forbade absolutely and in all ways the making of profit through the extension of credit. To simplify, to find a neat, consistent, logical pattern, to teach a single lesson or draw a universal prescription — these aims have animated many accounts of the old theory.

The usury analysis, however, is the result of the interaction of many forces, and its history carries with it no ready prescription. The analysis has a religious origin; religious authority controls much of its development. An ideal of justice underlies every statement of it. It is also Western man's first try at an economic theory; the theory's tools are legal concepts. Religiously motivated, the scholastic analysts with these clumsy instruments attempt to regulate the cost of credit. For three centuries some of the best minds of Western Europe participated in this idealistic effort to frame the intellectual and moral conditions under which credit might justly be extended. Robert of Courçon, William of Auxerre, Hostiensis, Giles of Lessines, St. Thomas Aquinas, Joannes Andreae, John Gerson, St. Bernardine, St. Antoninus — Frenchmen, Englishmen, Germans, Italians, Spaniards; theologians, canonists, administrators, saints — all felt that usury was a pressing problem and devoted their thoughts to arguments against it, distinctions between it and lawful profit, and investigations of the nature of money and value. The theoretical structure they erected was not a consistent piece, but it encouraged risk-sharing investment and charity to the poor; its practical success may be measured by a comparison between the conditions of credit in medieval Europe and those in classical Greece or China or India.

From 1450 to 1750 the analysts are engaged in an attempt — again mainly with the use of legal concepts — to adjust the letter of the old law to changed economic circumstances and a new willingness to consider the commercial lender's viewpoint. The leaders of this effort — Conrad Summenhart, Cardinal Cajetan, and Leonard Lessius, to name three masters — understand the new situation and the intellectual reformulations required of them. Aspects of the old theory had always been favorable to capitalism; the revised theory approved all the basic financial mechanisms of a capitalistic society.

The long history of usury theory is filled with controversies in which asperity more than charity has distinguished the disputants; and in criticizing the views of living authors there has been no intention of making this study yet another contribution to controversy. It was begun without prepossessions as to any particular view of the usury theory or of its modern significance; and it has tried only to be guided by all the available evidence as to what the scholastics thought and taught. The presentation of this evidence is essentially itself the evaluation of other views of the scholastic theory; and such evaluation is all that has been attempted here.

BIBLIOGRAPHY

PRIMARY SOURCES FOR THE SCHOLASTIC
TEACHING ON USURY

Abbreviations

P.l.   J. P. Migne, *Patrologiae cursus completus, Series Latina.*
                  Paris, 1844–1861
T.c.c.   J. P. Migne, *Theologiae cursus completus.* Paris, 1841
Trac. univ. juris *Tractatus universi juris.* Venice, 1584–1586

Aegidius Romanus. *De regimine principis.* In Juan Garcia de Castrojeriz, *Glosa castellana al "regimento de principes" de Egidio Romano.* Madrid: Instituto de Estudios Politicos, 1947.
—— *Quodlibetales.* Bologna, 1481.
Albert the Great, St. *Opera omnia.* Edited by A. Borgnet, Paris, 1890–1899.
—— *Commentarius in quatuor libros sententiarum.* Vol. XXVIII, *ed. cit.*
—— *In evangelium Lucae.* Vol. XXII, *ed. cit.*
—— *In libros ethicorum.* Vol. VII, *ed. cit.*
—— *In libros politicorum.* Vol. VIII, *ed. cit.*
—— *Summa theologica.* Vol. XXXIII, *ed. cit.*
Alexander of Hales. *Summa theologica.* Quaracchi, 1924–1948.
Alexander Lombard (Alexander of Alexandria, Alexander Bonini). *Tractatus de usuris,* Bibl. Vat. Folio, lat. ms. 1237, f.153–174.
Alexander de Nevo. *Consilia contra Judaeos foenerantes.* In Nicolaus de Ausmo, *Supplementum summae pisanellae.* Frankfort, 1478.
Alphonsus de' Liguori, St. *Theologia moralis.* Rome, 1947.
Andreae, Joannes. *Decretalium libros novella commentaria.* Venice, 1581.
—— *Gloss* on *Speculum* of William Durand. Lyons, 1547.
Angelus Carletus de Clavasio. *Summa angelica de casibus conscientiae.* Lyons, 1512.
Anselm of Canterbury, St. *Homiliae et exhortationes.* In Migne, *P.l.,* Vol. CLVIII.
Antoninus of Florence, St. *Confessionale.* Venice, 1476.
—— *Summa sacrae theologiae.* Venice, 1581–1582.
Aristotle. *Works.* Edited by W. D. Ross. Oxford, 1928-.
—— *Ethica Nichomachea.* Trans. W. D. Ross, Vol. IX, *ed. cit.*
—— *Politica.* Trans. B. Jowett, Vol. X, *ed. cit.*
Astesanus. *Summa astesana.* Rome, 1728.

Auxerre. See William.

Azpilcueta, Martin. See Navarrus.

Ballerini, Peter. *De jure divino et naturali circa usuram libri sex.* Bologna, 1747.

Bandinelli. See Rolandus.

Barth, Francis X. *De statuto principis.* In Migne, *T.c.c.,* XVI.

Bartholomew of Exeter. *Penitential.* Edited by A. Morey. Cambridge, 1937.

Bernard of Pavia. *Summa decretalium.* Edited by E. Laspeyres. Ratisbon, 1860.

Bernardine of Siena, St. *Opera omnia.* Edited by J. de la Haye. Venice, 1745.
Vol. II.

Biel, Gabriel. *Collectorium super IV libros sententiarum* (s.d.).

—— *Tractatus de potestate et utilitate monetarium.* Trans. R. B. Burke, Philadelphia, 1930.

Bonaventure, St. *Opera omnia.* Quaracchi, 1882–1902.

—— *De decem praeceptis collatio.* Vol. V, *ed. cit.*

—— *In quatuor libros sententiarum.* Vol. IV, *ed. cit.*

Buridan, John. *Quaestiones super VIII libros politicorum Aristotelis.* Paris, 1513.

Cajetan. *Commentarium in summam theologicam S. Thomae Aquinatis.* In St.
Thomas Aquinas, *Summa theologica,* Leon. edition, Rome, 1882.

—— *Scripta philosophica: Opuscula oeconomica-socialia.* Edited by P. Ammit.
Rome, 1934.

Canisius, Peter, St. *Epistolae et acta.* Edited by O. Braunsberger, 8 vols. Freiburg
in Br., 1896–1923.

Cantor, Peter. *Verbum abbreviatum.* In Migne, *P.l.*

Castrojeriz, Juan Garcia de. *Glosa Castellana al "regimento de principes" de
Egidio Romano.* Madrid: Instituto de Estudios Politicos, 1947.

Clavasio. See Angelus.

Concina, Daniel. *Theologia christiana dogmatico-moralis.* Rome, 1749–1751.

Conrad. See Summenhart.

Consobrinus, John. *De justitia commutativa.* Paris, 1494.

Corpus juris canonici. Edited by E. Friedberg. Leipzig, 1879–1881.

Corpus juris civilis. Edited by T. H. Mommsen, W. Kroll, P. Krueger, and R.
Schoell. Berlin, 1928–1929.

Courçon, Robert de. *De usura.* Edited by G. Lefèvre, in *Le traité "De usura"
de Robert de Courçon, Travaux et mémoires de l'université de Lille,* X. Lille,
1902.

Duns Scotus, John. *Opera omnia.* Ed. nova. juxta edit. L. Waddingi. Paris,
1891–1895.

—— *In IV libros sententiarum, Opus Oxoniensis.* Vol. XVIII, *ed. cit.*

—— *In IV libros sententiarum, Reportata Parisiensis.* Vol. XXIV, *ed. cit.*

Durandus of St. Pourçain. *Commentariorum in P. Lombardi Sententias Theologicas.* Venice, 1586.

Eck, John. *Tractatus de contractu quinque de centum*. University Library of Munich, Codex ms. No. 125.

Franciscus de Mayronis. *Scriptum super quatuor libros sententiarum*. Venice, 1520.

Gerson, John. *Opera omnia*. Edited by L. Ellies du Pin. Antwerp, 1748.
—— *De contractibus*. Vol. III, *ed. cit.*
—— *Regulae morales*. Vol. III, *ed. cit.*
—— *Sermo contra avaritium Dominica I post octavas Epiphaniae*. Vol. III, *ed. cit.*
Giles of Lessines. *De usuris*. In St. Thomas Aquinas, *Opera omnia*, Vol. XVII, Parma, 1864.
Glossa ordinaria on *Corpus juris canonici*. Venice, 1605.

Haunold, Christopher. *Controversiarum de justitia et jure privatorum*. Ingolstadt, 1672.
Henry of Eutin. *Tractatus de contractibus*. In Gerson, *Opera omnia* (Cologne, 1484–1485), Vol. IV, ff. 224–254.
Henry of Ghent. *Quodlibetales*. Paris, 1518.
Henry of Hesse (Heinrich Hainbuch von Langenstein). *Tractatus de contractibus*. In Gerson, *Opera omnia* (Cologne, 1484–1485), Vol. IV, ff. 185–224.
Hostiensis (Henry Bartholomew of Susa). *Commentaria super quinque libros decretalium*. Venice, 1581.
—— *Summa aurea*. Venice, 1579.
Hugh of St. Victor. *De sacramentis*. In Migne, *P.l.*, Vol. CLXXVI.
—— *Summa sententiarum*. In Migne, *P.l.*, Vol. CLXXVI.

Innocent IV. *Apparatus super quinque libros decretalium*. Strassburg, 1478.

James of Vitry. *The Exemplars of Jacques de Vitry*. Edited by T. F. Crane. London, 1890.
Joannes Andreae. See Andreae.
Joannes a Capistrano, St. *De usuris seu de cupiditate*. In *Trac. univ. juri*, Vol. VII.

Lainez, James. *Disputatio de usuris variisque negotiis mercatorum*. In H. Grisar, *Jacobi Lainez . . . Disputationes Tridentinae* (Innsbruck, 1886), Vol. II.
Laurentius de Ridolfis. *De usuris*. In *Tract. univ. juris*, Vol. VII.
Lessius, Leonard. *De justitia et jure ceterisque virtutibus cardinalibus libri quatuor ad 2.2.D. Thomae a quaestione 47 usque ad quaestionem 171*. Lyons, 1630.
Lombard, Peter. *Sententiarum libri quatuor*. In Migne, *P.l.*, Vol. CXCII.
Luca, John Baptist. *Theatrum veritatis et justitiae*. Rome, 1669–1681.
Lugo, John de. *Disputationes scholasticae et morales*. Edited by Fournials. Paris, Vivès edition, 1893. Vol. VIII.
Lupo, John Baptist. *De usuris et commerciis illicitis*. Venice, 1577.

Major, John. *In quatuor sententiarum quaestiones.* Paris, 1514.

Mansi, John D. *Sacrorum consiliorum nova et amplissima collectio.* Venice, 1759–1798.

Medina, John. *Codex de restitutione et contractibus.* Alcala, 1546.

Mercado, Thomas. *Summa de tratos y contratos de mercaderes dividida en seis libros.* Salamanca, 1569.

Molina, Louis. *De justitia et jure.* In *Opera omnia,* Geneva, 1733, Vol. II.

Monaldus. *Summa perutilis atque aurea.* Lyons, 1500.

Navarrus. *Opera omnia.* Venice, 1618.

——— *Commentarius de usuris.* Vol. I, *ed. cit.*

——— *Commentarius resoltivus de cambiis.* Vol. I, *ed. cit.*

——— *Consilia.* Vols. IV and V, *ed. cit.*

——— *Enchiridion seu Manuale Confessor.* Vol I, *ed. cit.*

Nicholas of Oresme. *Tractatus de origine, natura, jure, et mutationibus monetarum.* Edited by M. L. Wolowski. Paris, 1864.

Nicolas de'Tudeschi. See Panormitanus.

Nider, John. *De contractibus mercatorum.* In *Tract. univ. juris,* Vol. VII.

Panormitanus. *Commentaria in libros decretalium.* Venice, 1558.

Paucapalea. *Summa.* Edited by J. F. von Schulte. Giessen, 1891.

Peter of Ancharano. *Super Clementina commentaria.* Bologna, 1580.

Pichler, Vitus. *Ius canonicum secundum V decretalium titulos Greg. Papae IX explicatum.* Venice, 1758.

Prierio or Prieras. See Silvester.

Ptolemy of Lucca. *De regimine principis.* In Thomas Aquinas, *Opera omnia,* Vol. XXVII, Paris, Vivès ed.

Raymond of Pennaforte, St. *Summa casuum conscientiae.* Verona, 1744.

Ridolfis. See Laurentius.

Robert of Courçon. See Courçon.

Robert of Flamesbury. *Summa de matrimonio et de usuris, Ex Roberti Poenitentiali.* Edited by J. F. von Schulte. Giessen, 1868.

Rolandino de Passagiero. *Summa totius artis notariae.* Venice, 1588.

Rolandus Bandinelli. *Die Summa magistri Rolandi nachmals papstes Alexander III.* Edited by Friedrich Thaner. Innsbruck, 1874.

Roselli, Antonio de. *De usuris.* In *Tract. univ. juris,* Vol. VII.

Rucellai, Pandolfo, St. *Tractato brieve de cambi a Fra Hieronymo Savonarola da Ferrara.* In Raymond de Roover, "Il trattato da fra Sancti Rucellai sul cambio, il monte commune de il monte delle doti," *Archivo Storico Italiano,* 1953.

Rufinus. *Die Summa Decretorum des Magister Rufinus.* Edited by Heinrich Singer. Paderborn, 1902.

Salis, Joannes Baptista de (Trovamala) *Summa baptiniana.* Mantua, 1495.

——— *Summa rosella.* Venice, 1495.

Silvester da Prierio. *Summa summarum quae Silvestrina dicitur*. Bologna, 1514.

Soto, Dominic. *De justitia et iure libri decem*. Lyons, 1569.

Speculum conscientiae (anon.). In St. Bonaventure, *Opera omnia, ed. cit.*, Vol. VIII.

Stephen of Bourbon. *La tabula exemplorum*. Edited by J. T. Welter. Paris, 1926.

Stephen of Tournai. *Summa des Stephanus Tournacensis über das Decretum Gratiani*. Edited by J. F. von Schulte. Giessen, 1891.

Summenhart, Conrad. *Tractatus de contractibus licitis atque illicitis*. Venice, 1580.

Tanner, Adam. *Theologia scholastica*. Ingolstadt, 1626.

Thomas Aquinas. St. *Opera omnia*. Edited by P. Maré and S. E. Fretté. Paris, Vivès, 1871–1880.

────── *Commentum in quatuor libros sententiarum magistri Petri Lombardi*. Vol. X, *ed cit*.

────── *De emptione et venditione*. Vol. XXVIII, *ed. cit*.

────── *De regimine Judaeorum*. Vol. XXVII, *ed. cit*.

────── *In X libros ethicorum ad Nichomachum*. Vol. XXV, *ed. cit*.

────── *In III primos libros politicorum*. Vol. XXVI, *ed. cit*.

────── *In Psalmos Davidis*. Vol. XVIII, *ed. cit*.

────── *Quaestiones disputatae de malo*. Vol. XIII, *ed. cit*.

────── *Summa theologica*. Vol. III, *ed. cit*.

────── *III Quodlibetales*. Vol. XV, *ed. cit*.

Thomas de Vio. See Cajetan.

Trovamala. See Salis.

Valentia, Gregory de. *Commentarii theologici in summam D. Thomae*. Ingolstadt, 1591–1597.

Vitoria, Francis de. *Commentarios a la Secunda secundae de Santo Tomas*, t. 4. Edited by Vicente Beltran de Heredía, O.P. Salamanca, 1934.

William of Auxerre. *Summa aurea in quatuor libros sententiarum*. Paris, 1500.

Zech, Franz X. *Dissertationes tres, in quibus rigor moderatus doctrinae pontificae circa usuras a sanctissimo D. N. Benedicto XIV per epistolam encyclicam episcopis Italiae traditus exhibetur*. In H. Leotardo, *Liber singularis de usuris*. Venice, 1762.

INDEX

Note

For various religious orders, the following abbreviations have been used:

Augustinians — O.E.S.A.	Jesuits — S.J.
Dominicans — O.P.	Redemptorists — C.SS.R.
Franciscans — O.F.M.	Sulpicians — S.S.

Errata

On p. 122: *for* Bellarequardo, *read* Bellareguardo; *for* fl. 1371, *read* fl. 1371.
On p. 191: *for* Phillip, *read* Philip. On p. 315 n.27: *for* 300,000 ducats, *read* 36,000.

CL Press

A Fraser Institute Project

https://clpress.net/

Professor Daniel Klein (George Mason University, Economics and Mercatus Center) and Dr. Erik Matson (Mercatus Center), directors of the Adam Smith Program at George Mason University, are the editors and directors of CL Press. CL stands at once for classical liberal and conservative liberal.

CL Press is a project of the Fraser Institute (Vancouver, Canada).

CL Press includes a series called CL Reprints. CL Reprints was undertaken to make selected older works-no longer under copyright, chiefly-more available.

People:

Dan Klein and Erik Matson are the co-editors and executives of the imprint.

Jane Shaw Stroup is Editorial Advisor, doing especially copy-editing and text preparation.

Zachary Yost is Production Manager for CL Reprints.

An Advisory Board:

Jordan Ballar, Center for Religion, Culture, and Democracy
Caroline Breashears, St. Lawrence Univ.
Donald Boudreaux, George Mason Univ.
Ross Emmett, Arizona State Univ.
Knud Haakonssen, Univ. of St. Andrews
Bjorn Hasselgren, Timbro, Uppsala Univ.
Karen Horn, Univ. ofErfurt
Jimena Hurtado, Univ. de los Andes
Nelson Lund, George Mason Univ.

Why start CL Press?

CL Press publishes good, low-priced work in intellectual history, political theory, political economy, and moral philosophy. More specifically, CL Press explores and advance discourse in the following areas:

- The intellectual history and meaning ofliberalism.

- The relationship between liberalism and conservatism.

- The role of religion in disseminating liberal understandings and institutions including: humankind's ethical universalism, the moral equality of souls, the rule oflaw, religious liberty, the meaning and virtues of economic life.

- The relationship between religion and economic philosophy.

- The political, social, and economic philosophy of the Scottish Enlightenment, especially Adam Smith.

www.ingramcontent.com/pod-product-compliance
Lightning Source LLC
Chambersburg PA
CBHW010937120626
46554CB00008B/2508

*9 7 8 1 9 5 7 6 9 8 1 7 5 *